Piracy

Piracy

THE INTELLECTUAL PROPERTY WARS

FROM GUTENBERG TO GATES

*

Adrian Johns

THE UNIVERSITY OF CHICAGO PRESS

Chicago and London

ADRIAN JOHNS is professor of history and chair of the Committee on
Conceptual and Historical Studies of Science at the University of
Chicago, and the author of *The Nature of the Book: Print and Knowledge in
the Making* (1998), published by the University of Chicago Press.

The University of Chicago Press, Chicago 60637
The University of Chicago Press, Ltd., London
© 2009 by Adrian Johns
All rights reserved. Published 2009
Printed in the United States of America

18 17 16 15 14 13 12 11 10 09   1 2 3 4 5

ISBN-13: 978-0-226-40118-8 (cloth)
ISBN-10: 0-226-40118-9 (cloth)

Library of Congress Cataloging-in-Publication Data
Johns, Adrian.
    Piracy : the intellectual property wars from Gutenberg to Gates / Adrian
Johns.
        p.   cm.
    Includes bibliographical references and index.
    ISBN-13: 978-0-226-40118-8 (cloth: alk. paper)
    ISBN-10: 0-226-40118-9 (cloth: alk. paper)
        1. Intellectual property infringement—History.   2. Piracy
(Copyright)—History.   3. Copyright infringement—History.
4. Software piracy—History.   5. Printing—History.   I. Title.
    K1401.J645   2009
    346.04'8—dc22   2009017513

♾ The paper used in this publication meets the minimum requirements of
the American National Standard for Information Sciences—Permanence
of Paper for Printed Library Materials, ANSI Z39.48-1992.

For David.

And it is, it is a glorious thing
To be a Pirate King!

Contents

1

A General History of the Pirates

In mid-2004, executives at the Tokyo headquarters of the huge electronics multinational NEC began to hear reports that its products were being counterfeited and sold in Chinese stores. Nobody was at all surprised. Reports of this kind were routine for any corporation of NEC's size and reach, and in this case they initially seemed to concern small stuff—blank DVDs and the like. The company nevertheless moved swiftly to put into action its standard response in such cases, hiring a firm called International Risk to look into the matter. There was no reason to suspect that this would prove to be anything more than yet another incident like all the others—irritating, no doubt, but impossible to suppress entirely. Piracy of this kind was the unavoidable price of doing business on a global scale.

Two years, half a dozen countries, and several continents later, what International Risk had unveiled shocked even the most jaded experts in today's industrial shenanigans. They revealed not just a few streetwise DVD pirates, but an entire parallel NEC organization. As the real company's senior vice president ruefully remarked, the pirates had "attempted to completely assume the NEC brand." Their version, like the original, was multinational and highly professional. Its agents carried business cards. They were even recruited publicly by what looked like legitimate advertising.[1] The piratical firm had not only replicated existing NEC goods, but actively invested in research and development to devise its own. Over time, it had produced an entire range of consumer products, from MP3 players to lavish home theater systems. These goods were of high quality, with warranties emulating NEC's own (in fact, the conspiracy came to light only when users tried to exercise their warranty rights by contacting NEC). To manufacture them the impostor multinational had signed royalty arrangements with more than fifty businesses scattered through China, Hong Kong, and Taiwan, at least some of which seemed to believe they were working for the real NEC. And it had developed its own sophisticated distribution networks, allowing its products to reach a global market extending at least as far as Africa and Europe. If this was indeed, as the international press called it, the "next step in pirating," then it was a very dramatic and impressive step indeed.[2]

When news of the pirate NEC broke in mid-2006, the story quickly winged its way across the Internet. Readers and commentators in the blogosphere reproduced the original press reports many times over. They expressed dismay at the implications. But their dismay was often accompanied by a drop of schadenfreude. Now, they realized, none of them could really be confident that the "NEC" disk drives, chips, screens, or keyboards on which they were doing their blogging were what they claimed to be. Some found this ominous, because of what it implied about knowledge in general in the networked world. Others acknowledged those implications but were only too happy to profess that they found them appealing: here was a gigantic corporation coming a cropper at the hands of unbranded outlaws who had proved themselves faster, nimbler, *smarter.* The Net's echo-chamber amplified the incident into a symbol of every cultural fear, epistemic doubt, and libertarian dream suggested by the digital age. Here, it seemed, was a glimpse of where everyday menaces like phishing and identity theft were inexorably leading.

This case of a doppelgänger multinational does indeed seem to mark some kind of culmination. It is hard to imagine a more spectacular act of piracy, unless perhaps one could conjure up a fake World Intellectual Property Organization. And in fact the venture came to light almost exactly on cue, just as impersonation of this kind had been identified as a growing piratical trend, set to succeed hacking and pharming as the mode of digital banditry du jour. "Brandjacking," it was called. It had even been singled out as a looming problem by the CEO of International Risk— who, not coincidentally, was a longtime veteran of the Hong Kong police experienced in tackling human kidnappings. Such piracy, he had cautioned in public speeches, was fast becoming a fact of life for the electronics and pharmaceuticals industries, with a recognizable modus operandi. An episode generally began when a legitimate company licensed a factory to manufacture its goods; the brandjackers who stood behind the factory would then take the documentation involved in the license, duplicate it, and redeploy it in order to recruit other plants. These other operations often remained blissfully unaware that they were dealing with impostors. After all, the outlaws helped themselves to the very devices—affidavits, bills, forms, contracts—that are supposed to guarantee legitimacy in modern capitalism. Especially hard to fight were brandjackers who operated across national boundaries, particularly the strait separating Taiwan from mainland China. The authorities in the People's Republic might well prove reluctant to prosecute local businesses that could plausibly claim to be acting in innocence. All of these vulnerabilities were exploited to the full by NEC's evil twin.[3]

NEC's discomfiting experience throws into sharp relief the sheer range of phenomena that fall under the term "piracy" as it is nowadays used. They extend far beyond the piecemeal purloining of intellectual property. They reach, in fact, to the defining elements of modern culture itself: to science and technology; to authorship, authenticity, and credibility; to policing and politics; to the premises on which economic activity and social order rest. That is why the topic of piracy causes the anxiety that it so evidently does. Ours is supposed to be an age of information—even of an information revolution. Yet it suddenly seems as though enemies of intellectual property are swarming everywhere, and the ground rules for an information economy are nowhere secure. Universities find themselves havens for countless devotees of file-sharing software, making blithe use of services that the recording industry condemns flatly as piracy. Biotechnology companies, testing genetically modified organisms in Indian cotton fields, accuse local farmers of being "seed pirates" when they use part of one year's crop as seed for the next. And Hollywood executives make front-page headlines when their companies join forces to sell movies online, having been spurred into rare cooperation by their mutual fear of losing control of their intellectual property. So serious has the prospect of piracy become for them that in the United States the Digital Millennium Copyright Act has even outlawed the promulgation of algorithms that *might* be used to disable or circumvent copy-protection devices. A graduate student coming to Nevada to present a technical paper can be arrested, not for pirating anything himself, but for divulging principles that might allow others to do so. In today's global economy, there are not just pirate books, CDs, and videos, but pirate jeans, pirate motorcycles, pirate pharmaceuticals, pirate aircraft parts, and, of course, pirate Pokemon. One recent novel mischievously imagines the ruin of the entire U.S. economy after the source code of major proprietary software is released en masse onto the Net. "The Chinese never liked 'intellectual property,'" explains a Nobel laureate scientist in 2044, and they eventually "called our bluff." "So now, thanks to the Chinese, basic science has lost its economic underpinnings. We have to live on pure prestige now, and that's a very thin way to live."[4]

Implicit in that resigned lament is a recognition that information has indeed become a principal foundation of modern social, economic, and cultural order. As it has become the key commodity in the globalized economy, so control and management of information have vastly increased in overt importance. In the nineteenth century, manufacturing held the key to economic power; for much of the twentieth, energy occupied that position. Now knowledge and imaginative creativity seem to be challenging for primacy. Piracy is the biggest threat *in* this emerging economic order, and it is commonly represented as the biggest threat *to* it. A specter is haunting Europe, as a latter-day Engels might have written. Only it is not just Europe that is spooked, but the entire economic world; and the ghost looming before us is not a communist, but a pirate.[5]

Yet the problem is even thornier than that may imply, because it is not reducible to any kind of informational class war. The pirates, in all too many cases, are not alienated proles. Nor do they represent some comfortingly distinct outsider. They are us. Biotechnology companies certainly complain about seed piracy, for example—but also find themselves confronted by protests at their own alleged "biopiracy." The same charge is liberally hurled at high-tech "pharmers" in the West—the word here referring not to unscrupulous forgers of Web sites but to highly credentialed bioscientists and ethnobotanists traversing the tropics in their search for new medicines. In such cases, the institutions of scientific and medical research on which we depend are being denounced as pirates not for destroying intellectual property, but precisely for introducing it to places where it did not previously exist. It sometimes seems that there is only one charge that all players in the globalization game, from radical environmentalists to officials of the World Trade Organization, level at their respective foes, and that charge is piracy. Marking the repudiation of information capitalism at one extreme and its consummation at the other, it has become the definitive transgression of the information age.

This makes piracy a compelling subject as well as an attractive one. Its consequences extend beyond particular cases, and beyond even the law itself, to impinge on the basic ways in which ideas and technologies are created, distributed, and used. Conflicts over piracy involve strongly held ideals of authorship, creativity, and reception. Society can therefore find itself forced to articulate and defend those ideals, and sometimes to adjust or abandon them. That is the common thread that ties together all our most important piracy debates, whether the specific allegations relate to gene patents, software, proprietary drugs, books, ballet steps, or digital downloading. What is at stake, in the end, is the nature of the relationship we want to uphold between creativity, communication, and commerce. And the history of piracy constitutes a centuries-long series of conflicts— extending back by some criteria to the origins of recorded civilization itself—that have shaped this relationship. Those conflicts challenged assumptions of authenticity and required active measures to secure it. They provoked reappraisals of creative authorship and its prerogatives. They demanded that customs of reception be stipulated and enforced. Above all, they forced contemporaries to articulate the properties and powers of communications technologies themselves—the printing press, the steam press, radio, television, and, now, the Internet.

Yet setting out to rescue the history of piracy from obscurity may still seem a quixotic quest. While its present and future receive daily attention in the mass media, its past remains almost completely veiled. To be sure, a few isolated episodes are cited repeatedly: Charles Dickens haranguing American publishers for reprinting his novels; Hamlet answering his own question, "To be or not to be," with the phrase "Aye, there's the point" in an unauthorized quarto of Shakespeare's play; Alexander Pope assailing the Grub Street bookseller Edmund Curll for helping himself to Pope's letters. But these tend to be offered up as whimsical anticipations of our current predicament, or else as reassuring evidence that there is nothing new under the sun. The big questions—where piracy came from, how it developed and changed over time, what its consequences have been— have never been properly asked, let alone answered.

There are two reasons for this. The first derives from received opinions about the digital and biomedical advances that are taking place all around us. Ours is routinely invoked as a moment of radical transformation—an information revolution that constitutes a clean break from all that has gone before. Therefore, if piracy is the definitive transgression of this moment, it too should be a phenomenon without a past. It could have a prehistory, but not a history. The most that one could expect to find in earlier periods would be episodes resembling modern practices in some charming but in the end inconsequential way. And so this is indeed all that we have found. The second reason bolsters this by supplying a rationale: that piracy is not really a subject at all. To jurists and policymakers in particular—but the impression is widely shared—it has a derivative status. It simply reflects the rise of intellectual property. To look for its history would be, on this assumption, futile in principle. The real subject would be intellectual property itself, and more specifically intellectual property *law*. That alone could have a real history to excavate.

To be blunt, these assumptions are false in fact and iniquitous in their consequences. Piracy is not peculiar to the digital revolution—a revolution that is in any case pervaded by historical inheritances. Nor is it a mere accessory to the development of legal doctrine. Yet neither is it an offense of timeless character, universally definable by a priori criteria. It is far richer and trickier than that. It has its own historical continuities and discontinuities, and its own historical consequences. The relation of piracy to doctrines of intellectual property, in particular, must clearly be a close one; but piracy cannot be adequately described, let alone explained, as a mere byproduct of such doctrines. It is empirically true that the law of what we now call intellectual property has often lagged behind piratical practices, and indeed that virtually all its central principles, such as copyright, were developed in response to piracy. To assume that piracy merely derives from legal doctrine is to get the history—and therefore the politics, and much else besides—back to front.

Granted that the subject exists, a problem of definition still dogs it. What is piracy? It is not entirely clear that we agree on the answer. An official study for the European Union once defined it rather impishly as whatever the knowledge industries said they needed protection from.[6] There is a certain logic to that, as will become clear, and in the end it may even be the most adequate definition we can get; but it will scarcely do as a starting point. Nor, however, will the standard definition of piracy as the commercial violation of legally sanctioned intellectual property. This too falls short, because (unless we embrace a very wide notion of intellectual property indeed) it would exclude many instances in which piracy has been recognized to be going on, but where intellectual property per se is not at issue. The very concept of intellectual property did not really exist until the mid-nineteenth century, by which point there had been over 150 years of denunciations of "piracy."[7] Even after that, there are many cases where too strict a definition in these terms would be prejudicial. One example concerns buses. In London, independent bus operators date back at least to the tourism boom that accompanied the Great Exhibition of 1851. Their vehicles were soon popularly termed "pirate" buses; a music-hall song called *The pirate bus* was popular for a while in the late Victorian era. They remained a presence on the city's streets beyond World War II.[8] Only by stretching the term "intellectual property" to breaking point could a pirate bus fit the orthodox definition. To exclude such usages, however, would rob us of the opportunity to consider what pirate buses had in common with pirate radio, pirate publishing, and pirate listening — three other kinds of piracy that were also popularly recognized in the period, and which we shall encounter later. By the same token, a doctrinaire definition might actually force us to count as piratical certain instances of expropriation that contemporaries did not identify in this way. An obvious example would be America's wholesale redistribution of foreign companies' patents (those of allies as well as the defeated Germans) after World War I. The legality of this hugely important move was unclear, but few in the United States, at least, would have called it piracy.

This is an apparent problem that can be turned to real advantage. It is certainly true that the nature of piracy has changed over time. For that reason, we need to respect its historical meanings rather than imposing its current one on our ancestors. Accordingly, some person, thing, or act has to have been characterized as piratical by contemporaries themselves in order for it to count as such in this book. But at the same time, we cannot simply take such characterizations at face value. Those who were called pirates almost never did: they always repudiated the label as inaccurate and unjust. The point is that when they did so, they often triggered debates that threw light on major structural issues and had major consequences as a result. We can profit by focusing on precisely these contests — and the more prolonged, variegated, and ferocious they were, the better. They strained relations between creativity and commercial life, and at critical moments caused them to be reconstituted. The history of piracy is the history of those transformations. Every time we ourselves buy a book, download a file, or listen to a radio show, our actions rest on it.

PIRACY AND THE PRINTING REVOLUTION

The period of time that we need to traverse is a long one, but it is not indefinitely long. For although appropriators of ideas may always have existed, societies have not always recognized a specific concept of intellectual piracy. Far from being timeless, that concept is in fact not even ancient. It arose in the context of Western Europe in the early modern period—the years of religious and political upheaval surrounding the Reformation and the scientific revolution. In particular, it owed its origin to the cultural transformations set in train by Johann Gutenberg's invention of the printing press. At the origin of the history of piracy thus lies one of the defining events of Western civilization.

Printing posed serious problems of politics and authority for the generations following Gutenberg. It was in the process of grappling with those problems that they came up with the notion of piracy. At their heart was the question of how to conform the new enterprise to their existing societies. For, following Gutenberg's first trials in Mainz in the mid-fifteenth century, printing had spread rapidly to the major European cities. It was a rapidly expanding and potentially revolutionary activity, and it would eventually inaugurate a transformation in practices of authorship, communication, and reading. But in the shorter term, in the fifteenth and sixteenth centuries, contemporaries could and did find ways to apprehend the press in terms relatively familiar to them. At the heart of printing, as they saw it, was a practical activity—a craft. It was a fast-growing and in some ways extraordinary one, to be sure, but it was still a craft nonetheless. And that suggested how it could be accommodated.

Early modern people knew how crafts should be organized, conducted, and regulated so as to take their place in an orderly commonwealth. The practitioners of the press, therefore—ranging from the great scholar-printers of Renaissance Italy to the first denizens of Grub Street—organized themselves into communities large and small, along lines familiar from existing crafts. They established "chapels" of journeymen in their houses, and formed guilds or companies to handle the affairs of the book trades as a whole in particular cities. At the same time, ecclesiastical, academic, and royal authorities devised their own systems to render these communities safe and responsible. To an extent, these too tended to be built on prior experiences. A 1547 French law decreeing that the author and printer be named on the title page of every religious book, for example, was modeled on the long-standing tradition of craftsmen's marks in such trades as silversmithing.[9] Other measures were more original—there was little precedent for the practice of licensing books before they could legitimately be published, and none for the Vatican's Index of Prohibited Books. At each level, and at places ranging from the printing house and bookshop to the bishop's palace and scholar's study, skills came into being and accreted into customs. They took on moral force. In those first generations, as printers, booksellers, writers, and readers jockeyed for position and developed conventions of proper conduct, so the character of printing itself—what printing *was*—emerged.[10]

Uncertainty and the need to make choices dogged this process, to an extent that has tended to be forgotten. To many people of the early modern period the press looked like it *should be* an engine of progress and providence, certainly, and Protestants of the later sixteenth century largely came to believe that it *had been* one in the days of the Reformation. But when it came to their own time and place, they had reason to be less sanguine. There was no guarantee that printers and booksellers, left to themselves, would let the printed book realize what others took to be its potential. Unauthorized reprinting was only one of the problems. There is ample evidence that laypeople's experience of printing included, alongside wonder at its virtues, exasperation at the proliferation of spurious claims to authorship, authenticity, and authority to which it gave rise. The realm of print was one in which the bogus could easily crowd out the genuine, and in which credibility vied with credulousness. Telling the authorized and authentic from the unauthorized and spurious was only one necessary art for thriving in the world of print, but necessary it was. Being a good reader demanded this kind of critical expertise. Writ large, the possibility that print itself might uphold some kind of rational public depended on it too.

The first and greatest of all novels provides powerful testimony to this effect. The entire second volume of *Don Quixote* amounts to a sharp satire on the nature of print a century and a half after Gutenberg. It delights in a recursive humor based on the conditions of life as an author, editor, reader, and even character in a realm of print riddled with such problems. Produced after a spurious sequel had been published in Tarragona, Cervantes' volume has its hero repeatedly encounter readers of the spurious volume and characters from it. Indeed, the plot itself turns on this. Don Quixote alters his course, heading to Barcelona rather than Zaragoza, solely in order to depart from the story of the unauthorized book and therefore prove it inauthentic. Once in Barcelona, he enters a printing house and finds the workers engaged in correcting the impostor book itself. And at the end of the tale Don Quixote dies, just (or so Cervantes says) to make certain that no more bogus sequels can be foisted on the public.

The premise of Cervantes' novel, of course, is that Don Quixote is a naively literal reader of popular print, in the form of chivalric romances. So it is all the more important to acknowledge that the knight-errant is not quite straightforwardly credulous. When challenged, he can uphold his faith. The point is that he does so by appealing to exactly the mechanisms that in the Europe of 1600 were supposed to guarantee a certain veracity in printed books. When told that romances are "false, untrue, harmful, and of no value to the nation," and that they should certainly not be imitated in one's life, Quixote thus has a ready answer. "Books that are printed with a royal license and with the approval of those officials to whom they are submitted, and read to widespread delight, and celebrated by great and small, poor and rich, educated and ignorant, lowborn and gentry, in short, by all persons of every rank and station; can they possibly be a lie"?[11] Licenser and public, elite and people, all concurred. What greater authority could there be?

Don Quixote appeals here to a mechanism that was widely adopted to bring the craft of print into harmony with political order: the license. A license was a statement of approval issued by a state or ecclesiastical officer, and in most countries one was required before any book could be published. In practice the rule was often ignored, and the very fact that Cervantes puts these words in Quixote's mouth demonstrates the difficulty that any licensing system faced if it really meant to impress readers. How effective it was, either in suppressing dangerous or false books or bolstering orthodox ones, is doubtful. But the mechanism operated in close conjunction with two other devices that were to prove critically important for our story: patents and registers. Patents were open letters from a ruler that had been used in the Middle Ages for many different purposes. Within a generation or two of the invention of the press they were being sought to protect titles from unauthorized reprinting; the first is thought to be that issued in Venice in 1486 to Marcus Sabellicus for his history of the city.[12] In every respect, this kind of "privilege" was equivalent to one granted for a mechanical invention, for a newly imported craft, or for a monopoly in a trade. It would continue to be applied to books for centuries. A register, meanwhile, was a book in which printers and booksellers of a particular city entered the titles of works they intended to publish. Its purpose was to maintain communal order, and at the same time to uphold the reputation of the craft community. Contests over particular editions could be resolved by booksellers and printers by reference to these registers, leaving the impression that the trade was inherently orderly. In some cities, entries in registers became secure enough to act as de facto properties, enduring for generations.

All later literary property regimes can be traced back to these two mechanisms. In tandem with licensing, they acted to shape the identity of print and the nature of the book in early modern European commonwealths. But at a fundamental level they were hard to reconcile: one appealed for its authority to the prerogatives of a state, the other to the autonomy of a craft. One aimed at securing interests within the commonwealth, the other at securing interests within the trade. Implicit in the tensions between them was therefore a major unresolved problem of political authority. That problem plagued sixteenth- and seventeenth-century regimes as the first recognizably modern states came into being. It set craft and economic interest against monarchy and conventional morality. In the realm of print, when the clash happened, the invention of piracy would be the result.

PIRATE PRINCIPLES

Piracy and literary property both originated as phenomena of the press. And both would remain deeply entwined with the fortunes of print until new media began to proliferate around 1900. We cannot even ask the right questions of our own culture, let alone answer them, without grasping how they took shape in that earlier age. In particular, the history of piracy is a matter of not just precepts but practices — artisanal crafts, policing strategies, ways of reading, and the like. As we trace these practices through the generations, we often find ourselves in the province of conventions and customs rather than laws, and those conventions and customs sometimes originated long ago. Their impact has been great and lasting even though they long remained largely unwritten. The most important case in point is that of the so-called courtesies that arose in the early modern book trade to govern what was then called "propriety." All civilized book-trade members were supposed to honor these customary principles. They pervaded the realm of print, and shaped that realm along with the more formal practices of licensing, patenting, and registration. Although they had little, if any, legal weight, there is ample evidence that they were respected by printers and booksellers and seen as a basis for harmony in their community. To breach them was not just to violate a particular rule but to dishonor print itself. When contentions over patenting and registration led to the invention of piracy, therefore, the book trade attempted repeatedly to counter the new offense by appealing to its courtesies and updating them. Piracy and propriety evolved together as they did so. The effects of courtesies would persist long after they themselves had retreated from prominence, either by being abandoned or by becoming second nature. Early broadcasting, recording, and digital media all inherited elements from them, and defenders of digital piracy today sometimes unwittingly adopt arguments that descend from the courtesies of Milton's age.

It is fascinating to consider in this light what it takes to become an expert reader (or viewer, or listener) in a piratical environment. What skills equip someone for that role? In some circumstances, the most disturbing thing for authors and owners is that it requires no special skills at all. Reading a piracy may be exactly the same as reading an authorized work. The implications of piracy in such cases are huge precisely because for the user, at least, the fact of a work's being pirated *makes no difference.* This sometimes (but not always) seems to have been taken as true in the eighteenth century, for example, when unauthorized reprints spread enlightenment across Europe. That is interesting because the reprints could in fact differ quite markedly from their originals, and occasionally readers exhibited quite sophisticated forensic skills in appraising degress of authenticity. The same goes for today's global economy. I know from experience that one watches a DVD of *Fanny and Alexander* bought from a street vendor in Beijing without fearing that one may be missing something aesthetically essential, even though the next disk in the pile may turn out to be a completely spurious imposter. In other instances, however, the practices of reception been very different. Think of what it meant in the 1960s for Londoners to tune their transistor radios to pirate radio—casual, commercial, and pop-focused—rather than to the offical, safe, and staid Light Programme of the BBC.[13] Fidelity of reproduction—the ability to replicate an original to a given degree of accuracy—is clearly not all-important. Piracy in practice is a matter of the history of reception as well as production.

It is a matter of the geography of those practices too. Piracy has always been a matter of place—of territory and geopolitics—as well as time. Early modern English law, for example, came close to defining an illicit book by the location of its manufacture. Legitimate volumes were printed in the worker's own home; any printed outside the home were suspect. On a larger scale, until the nineteenth century reprinting a book outside the jurisdiction of its initial publication was perfectly legitimate, as long as the reprint remained outside. The flourishing reprint industries that grew up in eighteenth-century Ireland, Switzerland, and Austria—and that provided for that extensive distribution on which the Enlightenment depended—were entirely aboveboard. As soon as it was reimported, however, the same book became a piracy. That is, piracy was a property not of objects alone, but of objects in space. A given book might well be authentic in one place, piratical in another. Of course, this made piracy a participant in the development of a system of interacting nation-states: where a city in the Low Countries could reprint French books freely in the early modern era, the new country of Belgium found itself a pariah for doing the same in the mid-nineteenth century.[14] The practice itself therefore became a vehicle for national, and nationalist, passions. The Irish reprint trade saw itself as a bulwark of that nation against English depredations, and the American reprinters of the nineteenth century married their practices to an entire political economy on this basis. Indeed, the invention of copyright itself was largely a response to a piracy feud overflowing with national resentments, namely the attempt of Scottish reprinters to compete with London's book trade in the first generation when both lived in a "united kingdom." Today we again see these territorial concerns loom large in our own debates about patenting and bio-piracy, in which they are denounced as forms of "neocolonialism."

Extrapolation from such examples has given us the nearest thing we have to a hypothesis about the development of piracy itself. It sees piracy as essentially a phenomenon of geopolitical thresholds. Piracy's location, on this view, always lies just beyond the sway of the civilizing process. So, for instance, it was reputedly rife in the main thoroughfares of Shakespeare's London, and in the backstreets of Milton's. In the eighteenth century it moved successively to the suburbs, to the provinces, and then to neighboring countries. In the nineteenth its home became America (and Belgium), and in the twentieth it lodged in Japan, followed by China, and now Vietnam. In each case, as it moved further from its original point, laws and norms of intellectual property took hold in the newly un-piratized territories. Piracy emerges, apparently, when developing economic agents live in proximity to great commercial centers. It is therefore identified with the barbarians at the gates, and with what Russians call the "near abroad." It is accordingly destined to be superseded through the civilizing process that leads to a neoclassical, globally integrated economy.[15]

This is all a myth, of course. Piracy has not been superseded in the developed world—indeed, its impact there remains comparable to that in developing nations—and the globe has seen more than one trajectory to more than one way of being modern. Yet the myth matters. The notion of a dissolving frontier between us and them creates real consequences—but consequences that we need to confront, not assume. My hope in devising this history is to suggest ways to do that. In particular, showing that piratical practices have depended on how people understood such things as borders, domestic thresholds, and the nation challenges the axioms on which the geopolitical hypothesis rests. But at the same time it also offers a way of comprehending the appeal of that hypothesis itself. What it cannot do—no one book could—is detail what should supplant it in locally specific terms. It would be fascinating to have a detailed account of the Chinese case, for example, or of Japan, Vietnam, or the ex-Soviet bloc. I cannot supply these. But I can hope to exemplify an approach that we will need to adopt to create those accounts.

The same goes for attempts to address the current crisis of intellectual property itself. Here, perhaps, is where a historical approach to piracy has its most significant consequences. It tells us that piracy is deeply enmeshed in the world we inhabit—and that the same goes for responses to piracy too. Their history is in a sense the history of modernity itself, viewed not quite from below, but from askance. I hope that readers who make it to the end of this book will come to feel that efforts to combat piracy which do not acknowledge this need to be treated with informed skepticism. Being ill conceived, they are generally ineffective. Worse still, they can neglect some historically constituted relationships and damage others. At an extreme, they can even threaten some of the elements of modernity that we most prize, because we take them to be central to life in a decent society. Examples are not lacking of antipiracy practices that pose questions of this order, potentially as serious as those suggested by the fake NEC. When a California company sets up a spurious bit-torrent site in a bid to snare the unwary downloader, the lay observer can be forgiven for failing to see at first which is the real pirate. When a multinational media corporation quietly installs digital-rights software into its customers' computers that may render them vulnerable to Trojan horse attacks, what has happened to the customer's own property rights—not to mention privacy? When a biotechnology company employs officers who turn agents provocateurs in order to catch unwary farmers in the act of "seed piracy," one may wonder where the authenticity and accountability lie.[16] It is not new for problems of privacy, accountability, autonomy, and responsibility—problems at the core of traditional politics—to be enmeshed in those of intellectual property. But to account for that fact demands a specifically historical kind of insight.

In short, the nexus of creativity and commerce that has prevailed in modern times is nowadays in a predicament. Its implications begin with intellectual property, but extend far beyond intellectual property alone. They may well foment a crisis of democratic culture itself. It is hard to see how the situation can be resolved satisfactorily without changing the very terms in which society understands intellectual property and its policing. That is, history suggests that a radical reconfiguration of what we now call intellectual property may be approaching, driven on by antipiracy measures as much as by piracy itself. Such an outcome is not inconceivable. Equally profound changes in the relation between creativity and commerce have certainly taken place before. In the eighteenth century, for example, copyright was invented, and in the nineteenth century intellectual property came into existence. A few decades from now, our successors may well look back and see a similar transformation as looming in our own day. If we wish to delay or even forestall such an outcome—or if we hope to steer the process as it happens—then we will be wise to change the approach we take to piracy. Even to pose that possibility calls for a historical vision. A response will require us to put that vision to use.

2

The Invention of Piracy

To find the origins of intellectual piracy, the place to start is at the heart of London. Stand at the main door of St. Paul's Cathedral. Facing west, walk away from the Cathedral, heading down Ludgate and toward Fleet Street. After about a hundred yards you come upon a narrow alley leading off the street to the right. It is nondescript and easy to miss. Entering the alley, the din of the traffic quickly fades, and you find yourself in a small courtyard. A doorway at the far corner leads into a building of indeterminate age with a stone façade. You pass along a brief, twisting entranceway and into an elegant antechamber. But then the passage suddenly and dramatically opens out, leading into a vast, formal hall. It is richly decorated with seventeenth-century paneling and arrayed flags, all illuminated by stained-glass windows portraying Caxton, Shakespeare, Cranmer, and Tyndale. You are in Stationers' Hall, the center of London's old book trade. And here, beyond all the elegant joinery and ceremonial paraphernalia, lies the key to the emergence of piracy. It sits quietly in a modest muniments room. It is a book.

The Stationers' register is a heavy manuscript tome of some 650 pages, bound in vellum. In fact, several volumes of what was a long series of such registers have survived, dating from the sixteenth to the nineteenth centuries; but the one that matters here was made in the mid-seventeenth.[1] At that time, long before copyright existed, this book was the central element in a practical system for upholding order in London's commerce of print. Someone—typically a bookseller—who wanted to publish a book and was worried about the possibility of a rival trying to print the same work would come to Stationers' Hall and make an entry in the register. This act affirmed a claim to the work, such that nobody else should publish another edition of it. A court of fellow booksellers and printers met regularly in the formal part of the Hall to uphold its authority, which therefore extended, in principle at least, across the literary landscape of the metropolis. In time, entries in the register, dated, guarded, and securely preserved, became tantamount to records of properties. Their importance explains why this volume and its fellows have survived cataclysms like the Fire of London. When copyright eventually came into existence, it did so from a desire to continue this practice and provide it with legal confirmation.

But in the seventeenth century the practice itself was intensely controversial. Some believed it represented an ambition by this community of traders in knowledge to establish its own code of conduct, independent and in defiance of the state itself. Claiming a prerogative to create and defend property in works of culture required denying that prerogative to the king. In a time of deep and well-warranted anxiety about the bloody effects of printed politics, that implication could not go unchallenged. The keystone of order in the realm of publishing therefore came under attack, in what became a profound and far-reaching debate about the very nature of print and its cultural powers.

The contest came at a turning point in European history. It was a time in which medieval forms of politics and culture were being confronted by newer, potentially revolutionary alternatives. A public sphere was coming into existence, based in the proliferation of print. Experimental philosophy was inaugurating what would become modern science, and a mercantile expansion was under way that would trigger the emergence of capitalist economies and commercial empires. Not least—and not coincidentally—the golden age of Caribbean buccaneering was about to begin: the era of Blackbeard and Mary Bonney, of William Dampier and Captain Kidd. Major historical currents, critical to the development of modernity, converged on the book that still sits quietly in its chamber just down the road from St. Paul's. When they did, they ignited a furious and fundamental conflict about politics, property, and print. Its consequences are still with us. The concept of piracy was one of them.

ARTISANS AND INTELLECTUAL AUTHORITY

In declaring that piracy was an invention of the seventeenth century, I do not mean to imply that the misappropriation of intellectual creations itself was anything new in that period, nor that it was regarded with indifference before then. It is easy enough to find complaints of intellectual misappropriation as far back as the ancient world. Galen inveighed against supposititious books attributed to him, and Quintilian bemoaned the unauthorized circulation of his rhetorical works. Vitruvius likewise assailed would-be authors who would "steal" the writings of others in order to pass them off as their own, and recommended that they "should even be prosecuted as criminals." But these acts never seem to have been called piracies, and, Vitruvius notwithstanding, they were not legal offenses. Moreover, the contexts in which they occurred lent them very different connotations from the practices that, beginning in the seventeenth century, *would* be grouped together as piratical. Not only was there no conception of copyright or anything resembling it; when authors expressed distaste for misappropriation, it was sometimes on other grounds entirely. They certainly might object that it misrepresented their opinions, but they also might say that it encroached on the freedom of a citizen, or that it robbed earlier, perhaps heroic or mythical, authors of the appreciation due to them from pious readers. The combination of commercial and cultural ingredients that would produce a concept of piracy did not yet exist.[2]

That concept owes its creation to a moment when major transformations in the social place of knowledge, in politics, and in economic practice converged. They met at just the point when the new craft of printing was giving rise to the first powerful claims on behalf of a literate public to judge issues of common interest. Precisely when authorship took on a mantle of public authority, through the crafts of the printed book, its violation came to be seen as a paramount transgression—as an offense against the common good akin to the crime of the brigand, bandit, or pirate.

The problem that the concept of piracy was designed to address originated in part in the changing culture of knowledge in the Renaissance, and in particular in the challenge to the liberal arts mounted by craft expertise. The Latin Middle Ages had inherited from Rome a categorical distinction between liberal and mechanical arts, such that only the former encompassed the skills appropriate to a free citizen. Artists and craftsmen now challenged this distinction. They saw opportunities to advance themselves in the new civic ferment of the towns by stressing their unique abilities. They announced that they alone could contribute to military success (by building siege engines, for example), economic prosperity (by overseeing mines), courtly splendor (by creating new and remarkable art), and the health of the citizenry (by supplying medical cures). A good alchemist, if one could be identified, might solve the budgetary problems of a prince at a stroke. Guilds, originally associated in antiquity with esoteric "mysteries," now became the guardians of mysteries of a rather different kind: customs, duties, and prerogatives appropriate to each craft. They issued rules to their members decreeing proper conduct and upheld communal courtesies. And they embraced an increasingly proprietary attitude to craft knowledge and skill. The best-known example was that of the glassmakers of Venice, who developed an elaborate series of conventions and bylaws covering everything from the kinds of wood to be used in furnaces to arrangements for electing officials. The Venetian state cooperated by banning glassworkers from emigrating, and it was long rumored that anyone breaking the rule risked death.[3]

From the thirteenth century, with Venice in the lead, this kind of cooperation between state and craft communities began to take more formal shape. One way was by the issuing of *privileges* or *patents*. These were not generally given for inventive originality as such, but, quite calculatedly, for initiatives of all kinds that promised to benefit the local commonwealth. By the fifteenth century, most European regimes were granting them for new devices or enterprises, and for trades merely new to the locality.[4] An inventor had no *right* to a patent, moreover. It was a gift, arising from the voluntary beneficence of the ruler, and its recipient was a beneficiary of state prerogative. Patents continued to be issued, and at increasing rates, for all kinds of things, often having nothing to do with new inventions or trades, simply as a convenient way to reward courtiers or to garner payments. There was thus no patents system as such. But accumulation carried its own weight, and in 1447 Venice passed the first general statute providing for patents covering inventions. It allowed that inventors or introducers of devices new to the Venetian territory would be protected against imitators for ten years; at the same time it formally compelled all inventors to reveal their inventions to the state, which was exempt from the patent restriction and could freely appropriate them.[5] Some quid pro quo of this kind was typical: early modern regimes offered patents as a temptation to skilled artisans to immigrate with processes that were locally new, on condition that they teach their skills to locals. The deal was the ancestor of the rather different bargain of protection for revelation that patents would be reckoned to seal between inventor and public in modern times. Its purpose was to facilitate the introduction of crafts, new or not. And when it worked, it stood both to benefit the community concerned and to deprive its rivals of their own skilled artisans. The fact that a patent involved no court investment and yet rested prominently on the benevolence and paternalism of the ruler only made it more appealing to monarchs who not infrequently skirted insolvency.[6]

As these customs were being worked out, the sciences were in turmoil. At the beginning of the fifteenth century, natural philosophy (loosely, the predecessor to science) was still distinct from the world of mechanical arts. It was a university enterprise, devoted to explaining routine natural processes by means of an Aristotelian causal analysis. It was qualitative (the mathematical sciences occupied a lower disciplinary level), discursive, and disputational. Between the discovery of the New World in the late fifteenth century and the publication of Isaac Newton's *Principia* in 1687, every aspect of this enterprise came under challenge, and most were overthrown. The claims of astronomers, mathematical practitioners, physicians, and natural magicians cast doubt not only on existing knowledge but also on the processes, personnel, and institutions that should be granted intellectual authority. And outside the walls of the universities, itinerant practitioners laid claim to knowledge of nature that yielded not just talk, but power. Paracelsian and alchemical practitioners in particular advanced this remarkably ambitious notion of creativity. They represented the craftsman—not just the artist, but the humble miner, farmer, or baker—as almost godlike in his power to transform and renew. They made such peasant figures into agents of universal redemption, critical to the realization of Providence. More even than the great Italian Renaissance philosophers, they voiced a real transformation in the status of the laboring artisan who knew nature's powers by hard experience. This figure they made into an author of an extraordinarily ambitious kind—one who could transfigure, transmute, *create*.[7]

This was an extraordinarily radical challenge. It extended to basic notions of what knowledge was, who produced it, how it circulated, and why. Artisans produced a practical, powerful understanding that might not be written down but was nevertheless vital. It is only now that we are coming to appreciate once again the subtlety and richness of what Pamela Smith justifiably calls "artisanal epistemology." It may well be that we owe to this epistemology central elements in the concepts of invention and discovery that we have inherited from that period. These include accounts of where new ideas come from, how they are distributed, and their relation to commerce, power, and personal virtue. For example, artisanal traditions posed the question of whether knowledge came as an infusion from God into an individual justified knower, or was capable of being produced by anyone of sufficient skill by cleaving to rules of method. This distinction implied radically opposed conceptions of the nature of discovery, of the transmission of knowledge, and of the very possibility that knowledge could be "stolen." And it was widely circulated in the vernacular, not in the Latin of the schools.

It was a time when learning itself lost its place. Not just artisans, but historians and surgeons, navigators and astronomers—all seemed newly mobile. Mathematical practitioners circulated from town to town, posting problems as challenges to all and sundry. A question of authority in knowledge thus arose and rapidly became acute. Whom should one regard as credible, and on what basis? Contemporaries of Paracelsus and Servetus liked to lament that learning had once resided in the universities, but that self-appointed authorities were now springing up everywhere, generating a dangerous profusion of rival claims leveled at disparate constituencies.

Aspirants to such authority drew upon one craft in particular to advance their claims: that of the printer. The press facilitated appeals beyond the cloister, at first to patrons in the church and at court, and later to a more dispersed and shadowy "public." Printed books became tools with which the enterprising could, if they were lucky and resourceful, lever themselves into positions of prestige. The mathematician Galileo Galilei achieved remarkable success in a series of such moves. John Dee tried less successfully to do the same in Elizabethan London. Paracelsianism itself was a veritable phenomenon of the international book trade, being made up of dozens of tracts, some genuine, many spurious. In artists' and sculptors' studios, in the marketplaces of cities where traveling empirics touted their medical remedies, in the workshops of instrument makers, and above all in the bookshops and printing houses of Venice, Paris, and Amsterdam, artisans and others increasingly laid claim to authority through the means of printed authorship. Their claims came before new audiences, too: audiences that were essentially unknowable, but that stretched far beyond court, church, and university. At a time of Reformation, when religious war loomed across the continent, addressing this confusion was a matter of millennial importance. With the nature, authorship, reception, and use of knowledge all in doubt, the vital need for new ways to articulate the creation and appropriation of ideas—and to distinguish the authentic from the spurious—was evident to all.

LAW, POLITICS, AND PRINT

When and where exactly did people begin to refer to intellectual purloining as piracy? The answer is clearer than one might suppose. It is easy to establish that the usage emerged in English before it did in other European languages. It is more difficult to establish the exact moment the term was coined, but it seems clear that it occurred some time in the mid-seventeenth century. In around 1600 piracy seems not to have carried this meaning at all, except on a few isolated occasions as a metaphor. It appears nowhere in Shakespeare, Ben Jonson, Spenser, Marlowe, or Dekker—or, for that matter, in Francis Bacon, Hobbes, or Milton. This was the first age to see the sustained production of printed dictionaries of English, but the connotation was not mentioned in any of them, whether by Cawdrey (1604), Bullokar (1616), Cockeram (1623), Blount (1656), or Coles (1676). John Donne did once refer to poetic and antiquarian plagiarists as "wit-pyrats" in 1611, and in the early Restoration Samuel Butler likewise called a plagiarist a "wit-caper," a caper being a Dutch privateer.[8] But although these hinted at the later usage, they seem to have been one-off instances. Besides, they addressed not commercial practice, but personal plagiary—a term that itself started to be widely used only around 1600.[9]

At the other end of the century, however, piracy suddenly appears everywhere. It is prominent in the writings of Defoe, Swift, Addison, Gay, Congreve, Ward, and Pope, and *pirate* suddenly starts to be defined in dictionaries as "one who unjustly prints another person's copy."[10] Very soon after that, it can be seen invoked in learned or medical contentions. In a briefly scandalous case of the 1730s, for example, a physician named Peter Kennedy made the provenance of the term clear when he accused a rival of an attempt to plagiarize his discoveries—or rather, Kennedy wrote, "to *downright pyrate him* (as Booksellers call it)."[11] It was a concept that had started as a term of art in the seventeenth-century London book trade, apparently, and was now being appropriated for contests of authorship in other domains. Overall, the evidence for this is unambiguous. And in fact a closer examination indicates that the innovation can be more precisely dated to around 1660–80. At any rate, Donne's seems to be virtually the only example predating the middle of the century, while on the other hand citations start to multiply rapidly in the Restoration. And dictionaries of other European languages published in the late seventeenth and eighteenth centuries then show the term spreading—first to France, then to Italy, and at length to Germany too. Piracy is therefore a legacy of the place and period of the English Revolution, and in particular of the commerce of the book there and then.

Since William Caxton introduced the press to England in about 1471, an institution had arisen in London to oversee printing and bookselling. It was called the Company of Stationers. Although some such fraternity had existed since long before Caxton, the Stationers' Company received its royal charter only in 1557 from Queen Mary. The company was to embrace all participants in the trade, binders, booksellers, and printers alike (such distinctions were in any case rather inchoate at first). It had a remit to police its members to forestall seditious printing. To that end it adopted all of the mechanisms typical of early modern guilds or corporations. In essence, the company created and maintained conventions that together defined what it was to act properly as a member of the book trade. These conventions were many and various—they included, for example, notions of proper dress, deportment, and speech for particular occasions. But the ones that proved especially controversial related to a practice known as *registration*. And that brings us to the book still sitting in Stationers' Hall.

Stationers' Hall was an old castle just to the west of St. Paul's Cathedral. Members were expected to go there and enter into the register the titles of works they were publishing. At first, it seems to have been intended merely to record the fact that each book had been properly licensed. But it soon came to act as the lynchpin of a much more valued system of so-called propriety. That is, titles entered in this volume came to be regarded as restricted to their enterers. By company custom, no other Stationer could subsequently print such a title without the authorization of the original enterer. In the late sixteenth century this became the principal element in Stationers' common notions of right and wrong conduct in the trade. The idea of registering a title would survive to be enshrined in legal notions of copyright for hundreds of years after this, long after the original purpose had been forgotten.

Here is how the system worked. Suppose you were a bookseller and intended to publish a certain book. In principle, your first step would be to get the manuscript licensed, perhaps by a chaplain to the Archbishop of Canterbury. You would then go to Stationers' Hall to register it, paying the clerk a nominal fee to enter its details (title, author, maybe formal characteristics) into the book. Then you would have to invest a substantial amount in manufacturing it. You might finance its printing yourself, although you could ask the author to pay for the paper. You would probably see to its subsequent sale through your own bookshop, but also try to distribute it through a network of other booksellers in London and perhaps beyond. Meanwhile, a lot of capital would be tied up in type, warehousing, and stored copies. More would be exposed in the form of credit extended to other Stationers, and copies exchanged with distant Continental booksellers. So if you found a rival Stationer selling copies of the same work, perhaps even before your own arrived in your shop, you would be dismayed. There were various ways in which a rival might manage to do this. But one was simply to obtain sheets from the printing house itself. Increasingly, booksellers and printers had grown apart, forming distinct groups that lived and worked in different places. This created jealousies and opportunities. Your own printer might well have printed some "supernumerary" copies to make a profit on the side. Or perhaps some journeymen, acting on a long-honored artisanal custom, had gone home with extra sheets, in much the same way that butchers' apprentices were permitted to take home scrap cuttings. Both these practices, and more like them, were to be central to charges of piracy for centuries.

But perhaps no such straightforward appropriation had occurred. It might be that the other work was not *exactly* the same as yours. It might have a different title, for example, or it might be a translation. It could even be a different work entirely, but dealing with the same subject in a way sufficiently similar that it would impinge on your sales. These too might—or might not—be deemed to offend. Deciding what constituted infringement of a register entry was often not straightforward. To resolve the matter, you would go to the experts at the Stationers' court. This court met every month at the Hall. Two senior members of the company would be assigned to investigate. They would examine the register, visit the rival premises, seek out the books, and compare them. They would try to decide whether any impropriety had occurred, and determine an appropriate recompense. Their criteria were two: whether the "substance" of the texts coincided (they need not be literally identical); and whether either infringed on a prior entry in the register. With their report in hand, the court would then decide on a resolution. The offending member would probably lose his impression and pay a small fine. But the aim was not to punish in any overt sense. The court sought to preserve the public character of an intrinsically harmonious craft, the virtues of which were seen to be virtues of print itself. The entire process was thus to be kept confidential. Any Stationer who revealed it could be expelled from the trade—the most drastic sanction that the company could impose.

This regime formed the lynchpin to a largely unwritten code of conduct that extended across the trade in books. A principal task of the companies overseeing trades in early modern cities was to uphold such codes. They monitored the conduct of their members to ensure that they upheld the good reputation of the craft community as a whole. To that end, company wardens enjoyed certain powers, in particular the power to enter members' homes and conduct searches. In London, such a power was greater than any accorded the representatives of the state itself: Crown messengers were debarred by the Magna Carta, or so Londoners commonly believed, from entering properties without a specific warrant. In the case of the Stationers, the wardens—practicing printers or booksellers themselves—could and did conduct routine searches of printing houses, bookshops, and warehouses. They did so to exercise something like what we ourselves might call quality control. What they were searching for were not poorly made clocks, stale beer, or rotten meat, however, as might be the case with other companies, but (as it were) rotten books. A book might fall foul of them in three ways. Two related to the trade's relations with the commonwealth at large: it might have bad type, browned paper, or clumsy proofing, thus impugning the community's craftsmanship; or it might have seditious or blasphemous (or, from the late seventeenth century, obscene) content, thus impugning its citizenship. The third offended against the trade's internal order: it might intrude on the livelihood of a fellow Stationer by violating a register entry. Since it affected the trade community directly, it was the last of these offenses that became in practice the main occasion for routine searches.

The registration system and its attendant customs of policing were central to the practice of press regulation. All books were subject to the searching regime, although most were never licensed. Many were never entered in the register either: it was really a system of insurance as much as of property, providing some recourse in the event of a transgression, and things like pamphlets often did not warrant the expense and trouble of registration. Still, the moral associations of reprinting ran deep partly by virtue of this alliance between state and craft interests. For example, the trade developed a strong association between moral conduct and the carrying on of work in the home. A printing house was to be a printing *house*. At one point the law actually stipulated expressly that presswork could only be done at home. The idea was that activities carried out in a patriarchal household partook of the moral order implicit in that place. By contrast, reprinting, like seditious printing, was said to take place at "private" presses, in "holes" or "corners," free of family bonds and out of sight of polite guests. In such ways did the associations of reprinting track and define the sinews of the book trade as a living craft community within a civic realm.

Until the mid-seventeenth century this system worked well enough. It was flexible, subtle, confidential, and for the most part consensual. The problem was that the community itself was fracturing. The company—and the trade at large—became oligarchic, as booksellers increasingly became a group apart from and above printers. Retailing and, especially, speculation on publishing projects—projects protected by the register—became the loci of wealth, and threatened to relegate "mechanick" skill to the role of a tool. This made reprinting and its countermeasures into fraught political topics. Insinuations grew that the company's leaders had attained their positions by systematically exploiting the system to reprint the books of vulnerable newcomers while securing their own monopoly titles. In one of the most remarkable portraits of the bookseller in this period, one "Meriton Latroon" published a veritable pirate's progress that traced a naive and initially principled newcomer's rise to the top by adopting his seniors' practice of reprinting and appropriation. Its real author, a reprinter of drama named Francis Kirkman, knew very well indeed whereof he spoke.[12] Yet although figures like Kirkman decried its manipulation, and master printers complained of their subjugation, there was as yet no appetite for abandoning the register regime wholesale.

Elsewhere in society, however, such an appetite did grow. The register regime served the booksellers well, but it largely ignored authors and readers. It was deaf to their voices and hidden from their gaze. From quite early in the century authors recorded their own impatience with it. It was therefore fortunate for them that an alternative existed. This alternative rested on the only power strong enough to confront trade custom: the Crown. Royal prerogative could supervene the register by means of a so-called patent, or privilege. The practice of acquiring a privilege giving a monopoly on a certain work actually predated the creation of the Stationers' Company, and it carried on alongside the register. Indeed, it expanded. By the later sixteenth century patents were being used to assign not just individual titles but whole classes of book to lucky recipients. For example, one patentee held the right to all schoolbooks, and another to all works printed on only one side of a sheet of paper. These could be extremely lucrative. The company itself held patents too. Its "English Stock" was essentially an early joint-stock company whose capital lay in privileged books. The original intent was to help bind the trade together by sharing work among poorer printers, thus forestalling seditious work or reprinting. But the Stock grew into a hugely profitable enterprise, and one the management of which many Stationers by the 1640s felt had been hijacked by the oligarchy.

It was perhaps inevitable that the systems of register and patent should come into conflict. The clash could have happened in several European cities, for these practices were common to many; and later generations would see similar contests in France, the German nations, and elsewhere. But it happened first in England. And there, in the wake of civil war and regicide, it immediately became politically explosive. The point was that the issuing of a patent was a moment when the monarch intervened in the life of the nation, slicing through statutory and common law to realize some specific desire. Patents had long been controversial, because before the civil war James I and Charles I had used them to reward courtiers and raise funds by creating monopolies. In 1624 Parliament had passed the so-called Monopolies Act to curtail them. It allowed the issuing of patents only on activities acknowledged to pertain to the Crown (like weights and measures, or gunpowder) or where no trade already existed in the realm to be damaged by the imposition of a monopoly. That meant inventions, or enterprises newly introduced from abroad. As a result, this statute is often reckoned to mark the origin of all Anglo-American intellectual property law. In context, its real target was this proliferation of Crown intervention in the realm's everyday commercial conduct.

On one view, patenting books was a classic instance of the Crown intruding on subjects' liberties. Printers and booksellers had long resented patents. And in practice the Monopolies Act left this resentment unresolved, because Charles I continued to issue them regardless of the act. Long before the civil war, the language on both sides had become that of sedition, usurpation, and rebellion. Under Elizabeth, the Queen's Printer denounced John Wolfe, a notorious reprinter of patented titles, as a sectary and seditionist, while Wolfe proclaimed himself the Luther of the trade. And later the poet and patentee George Wither charged that "mere" Stationers, by elevating their customs above the will of the monarch as expressed in a patent, wanted to "usurpe larger Prerogatives then they will allow the King."[13] Yet something remained missing from such denunciations. It was not vitriol: they were slathered in that. Wither called his Stationer opponents "fylthy," "excrements," and "vermine"; he accused them of "usurpations, Insinuations, Insolencyes, Avarice, & abuses," "fraudulent & insufferable abusing of the people," slander, and in general "abus[ing] the King, the State, and the whole Hierarchy; Yea God, and religion [too]." He charged booksellers with suppressing works, subverting royal power, issuing unauthorized editions while concealing their true authorship, and "usurp[ing] upon the labours of all writers." But he never called them pirates.[14] The same was true of John Heminges and Henry Condell, undertakers of the first folio of Shakespeare, who denounced the previous issuing of "divers stolen and surreptitious copies, maimed and deformed by the frauds and stealths of injurious impostors." Theft, subterfuge, misrepresentation, the corruption of texts—but not piracy. It is striking that until mid-century that accusation of piracy remained unmade.[15] By the end of the century, however, things would be very different. Piracy had become the central accusation in such conflicts. The reason for this lies in the civil wars that wracked Britain in the 1640s and 1650s.

HISTORY, CIVILITY, AND THE NATURE OF PRINT

Between 1642 and 1660, the kingdoms of England, Scotland, and Ireland descended into in a series of bloody internecine wars. The monarch, Charles I, was put on trial and beheaded, and for eleven years Britain was ruled by a sequence of republican systems. For much of this period the old legal and administrative structures that had regulated the book trade were in abeyance. Patents became a dead letter; licensing effectively lapsed with the eclipse of the episcopal hierarchy; and restrictions on the numbers of printers allowed to operate were ignored. The book trade expanded its ranks enormously, feeding on the political and religious controversies of the time. The Stationers' Company struggled to keep order in a trade increasingly composed of men and women who either ignored its rules or were not members at all. The production of popular pamphlets soared, but "propriety" lost its protections. This was the age of Milton's *Areopagitica,* in which the poet hailed the advent of a heroic London citizenry dedicated to the hard work of reading and reasoning through print. It was their right and duty to read, they were told, in order to play their part in Providence. The "True Leveller" Gerrard Winstanley urged that, having freed themselves from "slavery," Britons must now follow the apostle's advice "to try all things, and to hold fast that which is best."[16] Here surely were assertions of what would later become a public sphere.[17] But not all its elements were yet present, and those that were remained insecure. The polite journals and coffeehouse conversation of Addison's London had not yet been dreamed of. There was precious little precedent for ceding political or intellectual authority to a numinous "public" linked by pamphlets and newsletters, except for the most local and transient of purposes. Most of all, perhaps, the very idea that the popular press of the 1640s and 1650s—viciously partisan, violently sectarian, ruthlessly plagiaristic, and often wildly credulous—might be the foundation of *reason* could plausibly have been dismissed as absurd. Booksellers themselves—or rather, a presbyterian group among them—were at the forefront of attempts in the 1650s to reintroduce a licensing system to reduce this anarchy to order.[18] Experience seemed to prove the dangers of unregulated print and undisciplined reading.

In the 1660s, the restored monarchy of Charles II therefore viewed popular print with a queasy mixture of respect, unease, and fear. The Crown was happy to make use of print when it could, but it remained very suspicious of the book trade, and was prone to blame pamphleteering and newsmongering for the great rebellion. Revanchist cavaliers like Sir Roger L'Estrange and Sir John Birkenhead asserted that the exchange of paper bullets in the 1640s had escalated into fusillades of real ones—yet they did so, tellingly, in their own popular newsbooks and pamphlets. The question facing England's rulers was in truth that of all European monarchs: how to accommodate and exploit what was becoming a perpetual sphere of printed argument, in which the rules of knowledge were no longer those of university, court, or palace.[19]

It was in this sphere that the clash between register and patent occurred. It did so at the hands of an impoverished old Cavalier named Richard Atkyns. Atkyns sought to revive one of the most profitable patents of all: a privilege granted by Elizabeth I a century earlier on all books of the common law. This patent had been renewed several times, descending through various inheritors until the civil war had rendered it moot. When the monarchy returned, Atkyns came forward claiming to be the rightful heir to the privilege, and demanded that it be revived. But in the 1640s, with royal power in abeyance, some of the most lucrative legal works had come to be entered in the register at Stationers' Hall.[20] The company had subsequently taken control of these, and now decided to oppose Atkyns's bid in the name of the register system and the trade community as a whole. The resulting struggle rapidly escalated, drawing in the entire regime of the printed book in England. All aspects of contemporary print proved to be at stake: its regulation, its personnel, its social structure and economics, its place in the commonwealth, its past and its future.[21]

The law patent was worth fighting for. The Restoration authorities had resolved to consign the previous decade to "oblivion," such that legal memory would begin again as though Charles I had only just died.[22] New volumes of law were therefore badly needed to replace those that had been printed during the intervening eleven years. Whoever got to produce the new volumes would have to make substantial investments, but the risks would be low and the rewards great. But he would also have to be trustworthy, and there lay a problem. Booksellers and printers were notoriously capable not just of sloppiness but of active intervention in the works they produced—something that in its innocent form was merely one of the duties of a responsible craftsman. In this case the issue was especially delicate, for *accurate* reproduction might now be tantamount to sedition. A printer named Samuel Speed found this out to his detriment, when he was hauled before the authorities for including statutes passed under Cromwell in one of the new law books.[23] Atkyns's fortunes would come to rest on his claim to meet this need for responsible supervision. And that claim was founded on his assertion of what *kind of person* he was.

Atkyns was no printer. He had never touched a press, and showed no inclination to start now. But in his view this was an advantage. Like many in post–civil war England, Atkyns was convinced that the horrifying events of the previous generation had been fomented by the book trade. As

Thomas Hobbes put it in his own history of the early 1640s, at first "there was no blood shed; they shot at one another nothing but paper"—yet it soon became a real war.[24] Atkyns maintained that the explanation for this lay in a shift in the basic nature of the book trade itself—one that the register system had brought about. He proposed to undo that shift and once more make print safe for the commonwealth.

The change Atkyns identified was real enough. It had been gathering pace since before 1600, and would persist for another 150 years after his death. It formed the essential foundation for all the conflicts over piracy that would rage from the Restoration to the early nineteenth century, not just in London but in Europe, and at length in America too. It took the form of a relative decline in the status of mechanical craft with respect to that of financial craft—the craft of speculation and accumulation. The printers in whose name the company had originally been formed were losing influence to a new breed, the booksellers. And the booksellers' prosperity rested not on the exercise of any skill peculiar to print, nor even on retailing, but on the "undertaking"—the publishing, we would say—of editions. That is, they made a livelihood out of entries in the register. These proprietors of "copies," as entries were by now known, had become an elite that dominated the top ranks of the company. According to Atkyns that was a serious political problem, because they were creatures of untrammeled interest. They were prone to the mercenary corruptions that gentlemen routinely attributed to commercial life, without the leavening influence of a craft fraternity to impose some moral limit. And their mercenary interest led them to generate as much public discord as possible, because discord sold books. So social and cultural collapse had been a consequence of the establishment of a property regime in print.

Atkyns proclaimed a solution to this problem. It lay in the figure most trusted in early modern England to uphold truth and act for the common good: the gentleman. The great benefit of patents, in his view, was that they were granted largely to gentlemen, and therefore gave gentlemen powers over booksellers. Patentees must thus be made the lynchpin of a new order of print. They could come to know the trade as well as booksellers, Atkyns insisted, but their knowledge would lead in "different wayes" because it would be guided by the virtuous conventions of polite civility. The relation between undertaker and printer would then be morally renewed. The printer would not be a mere "mechanick," but a servant, incorporated into a civil enterprise.

This amounted to a call for a drastic restructuring of the entire culture of the book, in which the central customs of the trade would be radically degraded. Atkyns recognized this, but argued that the sweeping transformation could be achieved if only the king would agree to cast *the medium itself* as property. Charles II should proclaim that the art of printing belonged to the Crown. In effect, the myriad claims made by booksellers and authors would then become subordinate to this overarching property right, on the basis of which the king could create a new class of gentlemen overseers.

The trouble with this claim was that it was distinctly implausible in the face of received historical knowledge. As Atkyns's antagonists pointed out, everyone knew that printing had been introduced by Caxton, a private subject, and had been pursued for generations as a real, autonomous craft. So Atkyns responded as he had to: by audaciously bidding to reshape history itself. He rediscovered an old book apparently printed in Oxford several years before Caxton's first press, and from it concocted a rival tale. He claimed that in fact King Henry VI had employed Caxton to lure a journeyman from Gutenberg's workshop to England. This worker, whose name was Frederick Corsellis, had then given rise to a community of printers as Crown servants, producing books to royal command. In short, printing was originally an appendage of royal power. But as the numbers of printers had grown, Atkyns related, they had sought to cast off the Crown. At this point "the Body forgot the Head," and, becoming "free," the trade had begun to print whatever generated a profit. The result had been an era of "virtiginous" political upheavals only now coming to a close. And at the same time the trade had coalesced to form its own institution, the Stationers' Company, with the duty of policing print. This, in the new political language of his time, Atkyns denounced as a fundamental conflict of "interests."[25] "Executive Power" had been given to the very people who could offend, "and whose Interest it is to do so." Stationers, in short, became at once plaintiffs, defendants, constables, and judges. A corporation like this, Atkyns concluded, had taken upon itself the role of a "Petit-State." As such, it was fundamentally incompatible with a national monarchy. And that was ultimately why the "paper-pellets" that the trade had issued had grown ever more numerous and poisoned—and profitable—while the policing of them had become ever less stringent, until they became "as dangerous as Bullets." By the eve of the civil war, the grandees of the trade had become impresarios of sedition.

Atkyns consequently saw licensing as a relatively futile exercise, because it did not attend to the real problem. He urged Charles II to take a different course. The true history of the book demonstrated the need for a renewed alliance between royalty, gentility, and craft. The king must create a class of patentees with oversight of major cultural fields. They would then ally themselves with the printers against the booksellers.[26] It would be in these men's interest to suppress books that might rival theirs. The case was analogous, he said, to the contemporary practice of assigning royal land to patentees. Such men did not *own* the land they oversaw. They therefore continued to act to prevent locals poaching royal deer. "Just so is it by inclosing *Printing*," Atkyns explained: patentees in this field too would prevent poaching, in this case of knowledge, precisely because they were *not* owners. Interest would harmonize with honor to underwrite sound conduct.[27] This pioneered an analogy between literary and literal fields that would reverberate for centuries — usually to very different effect. And all that stood in the way of this system, as Atkyns saw it, was the register. So it was the register that attracted his bitterest assaults. He complained to the Privy Council that in its entries "a private propertie is pretended to be gained," and pointed out that that pretence expressly defied royal power. If permitted to remain in being, he insinuated, the register would allow the booksellers to alter the laws themselves, "and cast them into a new Modell of their own Invention." Before long, "the good old Lawes by which Men hold their Lives and Estates, should utterly be lost and forgotten, and new Laws fram'd to fit the Humours of a new Invented *Government*."

It is notable that Atkyns's argument was in principle a very general one. Its ambit was by no means restricted to the book trade. He himself claimed that if it failed then patents for inventions as well as patents for books would fall to the ground. Less speculatively, his complaints applied equally to many other kinds of commercial life, since crafts were generally organized into corporations similar to the Stationers' Company. And indeed, one can readily find parallel contentions being made in different crafts at this time — a moment when old guilds were declining and the future constitutions of trades were in the balance. Atkyns himself drew a parallel with a brewers' company. Such a company, he pointed out, might well insist on its own internal regime, and this too would be illegitimate in principle. But in practice it would be far less damaging than a Stationers' regime. The implications of a mundane craft corporation's autonomy extended only to revenue; but the Stationers dealt in belief. That was what made their assertions of autonomy, epitomized by the register, so dangerous. As he was writing, moreover, Parliament was agonizing precisely over petitions from brewers' companies against royal prerogative in the form of excise duties.[28] "If the Brewers, who at most can but steal away a Flegmatick part of the King's Revenue, deserve the serious Consideration of the Supreme Council of *England*," Atkyns reasoned, "how much more these, that do not onely bereave the King of his Good-Name, but of the very Hearts of His People"? In short, between a brewer and a Stationer "there is as much oddes, as between a Pyrate that robs a Ship or two, and *Alexander* that robs the whole World."

That line marked the culmination of Atkyns's long argument—the crux of his bid to restructure the culture of print in genteel, Tory, absolutist terms. It also marked the beginning of the long history of intellectual piracy.

ENEMIES OF ALL MANKIND

Atkyns himself did not say where his reference to Alexander and the pirate came from. But in fact it had a specific source, and it evoked fears with ancient origins. The word *piracy* derives from a distant Indo-European root meaning a trial or attempt, or (presumably by extension) an experience or experiment. It is an irony of history that in the distant past it meant something so close to the creativity to which it is now reckoned antithetical. By Thucydides' time *peiratos* was being used to refer to seagoing coastal warlords. The great historian began his work on the Peloponnesian war by explaining how the need to limit the havoc caused by pirates had been the key stimulus to the development of the Greek city-state, and hence to that of civilization itself. Before the rise of Athens, Thucydides related, piracy had been seen as honorable. It was in opposing pirates that "the *Athenians* were the first that laid by their Armour, and growing civill, passed into a more tender kind of life." Civilization was the antithesis to piracy.[29]

Ancient writers bequeathed two principal associations of the word *pirate*. Pirates were seagoing thieves, certainly. But there was more to them than that. They were irritants to the civilized order itself. Their very existence amounted to a test of that order. Cicero, for example, invoked the pirate as his *ur*-criminal—he who declined even the honor that supposedly obtained among thieves. The thing about pirates, for Cicero, was that they lay beyond all society. They had no set place, and owed no customary allegiance to legitimate authority. Their existence required that society distinguish itself and its conduct from all that they did. One did not have to honor promises made to pirates, he remarked, since "a pirate is not counted as an enemy proper, but is the common foe of all." This was a telling measure of their outlawry, since Cicero generally held truthful conversation to be the essential foundation for society itself. Indeed, it was their sheer unsociability that for him seemed the defining characteristic of pirates. He routinely identified land-based brigands with seagoing ones on this basis.[30] And that idea came to be formalized into Roman law. As rendered in Justinian's reign, the law accounted pirates *humani generis hostes*—enemies to humankind in general.[31] In this sense, ships were incidental: they simply made excellent instruments with which to achieve this status.

The story Atkyns referred to seems to have been something of a commonplace in the ancient world. It was spoken of by Cicero, and repeated in detail by Augustine.[32] It was Augustine's version that survived beyond antiquity, and undoubtedly this was what Atkyns had in mind. The tale occupied a pivotal point at the heart of the *City of God*. Augustine had finished defending Christianity from accusations of responsibility for Rome's fall, and was moving on to address those pagans who attributed the earlier prowess of the empire to piety for the old gods. He wanted to argue that dominion of the kind attained by the Roman Empire had in any case been no blessing. Life under its sway, he argued, had been characterized by fear, war, bloodshed, instability, and the stress of constant ambition. Joy had been but fleeting, with what Augustine memorably called "the fragile brilliance of a glass." The free had been even more harmed than the enslaved, since the old empire had rendered the powerful Roman a slave to vices. And then Augustine remarked that kingdoms without justice were merely criminal gangs writ large. For "what are criminal gangs," he asked—in words that Atkyns echoed—but "petty kingdoms?" Spartacus's gladiators had flourished as a pseudo-kingdom of precisely this kind, fomenting "acts of brigandage at the beginning, and wars of piracy later."[33] Then came Cicero's anecdote: "For it was a witty and truthful rejoinder which was given by a captured pirate to Alexander the Great. The king asked the fellow, 'What is your idea, in infesting the sea? And the pirate answered, with uninhibited insolence, 'The same as yours, in infesting the earth! But because I do it with a tiny craft, I'm called a pirate: because you have a mighty navy, you're called an emperor.'"[34]

Both Atkyns himself and his intended readers (the MPs of the Cavalier Parliament) must have recognized this reference and understood its significance. It had been much quoted—often, as in Atkyns's case, without attribution—by all sides in the civil war. Indeed, once one is aware of it, one begins to see it everywhere in the politics of the period. The Levellers, for example, had demanded to know whether Alexander and his like were not simply "great and lawless thieves."[35] Milton invoked it. In the 1650s John Dryden, too, described Rome as "That old unquestion'd Pirate of the Land," protected by an Alexander (Pope Alexander VII) but now taught to tremble by Cromwell.[36] And it is even possible that Atkyns got the story from his own printer, a remarkable soldier, political theorist, and pamphleteer named John Streater. It had appeared at the conclusion of James Harrington's *Oceana,* the founding manifesto of English civic republicanism, which Streater had printed in 1656, where it was once again made the occasion for a distinction between virtuous and vicious empire, the latter being "but a great Robbery."[37] And that this was Streater's own view could be seen in his own pamphlets of the 1650s. Indeed, Streater went further and linked the old tale to modern concerns about internal enemies. He maintained a distinction between what he called "Companies" and *"Pyrates,"* on the basis that the former maintained the public good, the latter only a private. "And indeed," he added, "when those that are in *Government* mind but their private good only, they are no better then Thieves."[38]

Too much should not be made of this, but one can occasionally find Streater's notion of piracy in seventeenth-century legal or political writings. On this account, pirates were essentially members of any social institution the civility of which was not integrated with the broader commonwealth's. The point was that most collective groups, such as guilds, companies, or universities, maintained customary practices that both bound them together and secured them as harmonious elements in the commonwealth. A brewers' company supposedly would; so, in its own eyes at least, did the Stationers'. Pirates were then the exception to this rule. A pirate crew was a collective, all right, but it honored no propriety recognizable to the commonwealth at large, and it owed no allegiance to the common good. By these lights highwaymen were as much pirates as Blackbeard or Henry Morgan—and Milton, for one, translated Augustine's story so as to liken kings, not to seagoing pirates, but to "highway robbers." It was perhaps for this reason that unauthorized reprinters too were sometimes called "highwaymen," for example by Defoe, who added that their existence was "a Reproach to a well-govern'd Nation."[39]

Atkyns was drawing on this idea, yet his own argument nevertheless had a unique aspect to it. He was associating the very leaders of the book trade, not with the small-time pirate encountered by Alexander, but with Alexander himself. Like him, they were apparently brigands on the grandest scale: men whose ambition had broken free of the bounds of civility and the commonwealth, and were intent on subjecting "the whole World" —which is to say, culture in general—to their interests. This was the real difference between press pirates and brewer pirates. Because of the nature of what they stole—potentially, any and all culture—printing pirates robbed the world itself. No brewer's community could do that. And that was why he wanted to see the outright eradication of the Stationer from the social world. The realm of print that the Stationer had created was, Atkyns declared, *intrinsically* piratical. He wanted a war on the pirates to be launched on London's own streets.

In opposing Atkyns, the copy-owning booksellers had to develop a similarly sweeping counterargument. They soon did so, and in a way that had lasting consequences. In brief, the booksellers responded to his call for their destruction by inventing a central role for authorial property. They announced that they were essential intermediaries between civility and commerce, vital if polite gentility were to disperse itself without corruption. Gentlemen could achieve authorship with minimal compromise to their freedom only with some such mediating figure to help. The lynchpin of this, they declared, was the principle of property. The author of any "*Manuscript* or *copy*" had, they said, "as good right thereunto, as any Man hath to the Estate wherein he has the most absolute property." This right was then sold to the bookseller, who registered it at Stationers' Hall. There it would be preserved in perpetuity—thanks to the booksellers' policing. This may be the earliest explicit articulation of the idea of literary property—of an absolute right generated by authorship, which could serve as the cornerstone of an entire moral and economic system of print. Certainly, the idea had no clear precedent behind it. It was nowhere referred to in the company's own founding documents, nor in the century-long record of negotiations at its court, nor in the broader legal arena. Only with a lot of interpretive work could it be said to exist *implicitly* in the practice of registration, not least because authors were rarely the beneficiaries of that practice. Our own familiarity with the notion of authorial property notwithstanding, it was just as inventive at the time as anything Atkyns was proposing. And in fact there is precious little evidence that it enjoyed any great appeal.[40] Authorial property and piracy were thus being forged in contest with each other. Each rested on highly contentious grounds, and neither was intrinsically credible. It was the concept of piracy that sparked the articulation of a principle of literary property, moreover, and not vice versa.

In the short term, Atkyns won. The government revoked the company's charter. And this was a key part of a much greater policy: a programmatic campaign to remodel England's political and commercial institutions. Across the country, town and trade corporations of all kinds were soon being reconstituted. On an altogether grander scale, James II at the same time pursued a quite deliberate policy overseas in alliance with grandees in the East India Company, aimed at making international trade a branch of the same absolutist political economy. James's notion was that monopolist trade carried out on the basis of royal privileges by the East India Company, the Royal African Company, and other corporations, would create a caste of merchants whose interests would lie with a strong monarchy. The merchant patentees would create a tributary empire and fund the monarchy sufficiently that it would become independent of parliamentary taxation. This endeavor meant that Atkyns's arguments fitted rather neatly into a grand strategy for creating a new, absolutist English state with global ambitions. It was well supported by contemporary but controversial arguments in the new discipline of political economy itself, and there was nothing intrinsically impossible about any part of it.[41] In the Stationers' case, it resulted in the patenting power of the Crown being expressly written into a new charter offered to a reconstituted company. There would still be a register, but its status must now be explicitly subordinated to, and dependent on, royal "bounty"—not craft custom, let alone authorial property. All talk of an authorial right disappeared. To a man, the booksellers who had opposed Atkyns were purged from the company's offices. At the height of James II's reign in the mid-1680s, a reconstituted commerce and culture of print was in the offing—and this was part and parcel of a bid to transform a commonwealth and found an empire.

Yet the victory was short and pyrrhic. Atkyns himself was dead when it came. With James now on the throne, moreover, the beneficiaries were not the Tories, but the dissenters and Catholics whom James wanted to recruit as allies. And when James was supplanted as king in 1688 this new political economy of print was rudely demolished. The new government of William and Mary restored the old regime in the Stationers' commonwealth. With it returned the conviction that that regime enshrined a natural right of authors. Suddenly, with the political legitimacy of the new regime resting on a sacrosanct principle of property, this conviction was more useful than ever to the trade. What destroyed the absolutist culture of print in London—replacing it with a culture of authorial property that would last far longer—was not refutation, but revolution.[42]

3

The Piratical Enlightenment

The Glorious Revolution ruined the prospects for an absolutist culture of print in England. After 1688, the idea that the medium itself was the property of the Crown, which might administer it through a caste of gentlemen patentees employing printers as their servants, came to seem outlandish. Instead, the book trade's autonomy was reinforced. The trade concentrated on rights in particular works, which a cadre of major booksellers administered as commercial speculations. And the historical tale advanced to promote the absolutist principle likewise lost what plausibility it might once have enjoyed: Corsellis was definitively supplanted by Caxton. The transformation was not inevitable – in France, a system like that advanced in the Restoration endured until the Jacobins swept it away a century later—but it was emphatic. Yet the notion of press-piracy survived. Scholars and Stationers alike had seen the appeal of Richard Atkyns's opportunistic coinage, or perhaps had come upon it independently, and had very quickly made it their own. The bishop of Oxford, for example, defending his nascent Oxford University Press against the London trade, reviled the Stationers en masse as "land-pirats." The Stationer John Hancock complained of "dishonest Booksellers, called Land-Pirats, who make it their practise to steal Impressions of other mens Copies." And within the Stationers' court itself, references to violators of the register as "pirates" began to appear in the 1680s.[1] These usages only grew and propagated after 1688. The postrevolutionary generation gave the term *piracy* the kind of broad, popular currency that it has enjoyed ever since. It did so because it captured important practical realities—realities that would structure the Enlightenment itself.

The Restoration alliance between Stationers' Company policing and state licensing had been based in the so-called Press Act, passed originally in 1662. In 1695 William and Mary's Parliament allowed this law to lapse. It was not the first time this had happened, but the political circumstances were different now, and the law was destined never to be revived. John Locke, whose arguments played a major role in the Commons' debates surrounding the act, repudiated it not only for imposing licensing—which he, like Milton, saw as a legacy of popery—but for fostering monopolies for both individual booksellers and the company at large. In rejecting the statute, Parliament therefore saw itself as upholding Protestant liberty and countering monopolies. But it made no alternative provision for the Stationers' register itself. Suddenly the book trade found itself in a situation in which infringers of registered copies would face no legal sanction whatsoever. And at the same time it became legal to print and publish without being a member of the company at all. Internal regulation might have sufficed to keep booksellers and printers in line in the past, but now, in the speculative and entrepreneurial environment of 1690s London, it was never likely to prove sufficient. This was an environment in which new moral principles seemed to be advanced with every clutch of ambitious "projects"—and those projects soon pervaded the world of the book.

A cadre of oligarchs in the trade now campaigned, if not for revival of the Press Act itself, then at least for a substitute statute to restore the register system. It argued that the natural right of authors—that right that the booksellers had articulated against Atkyns—was being destroyed. How could this accord with a revolution the very axioms of which were property and liberty? But the bid was repeatedly thwarted. And in truth it always confronted a difficult problem of principle. Literary property was a monopoly or it was nothing; but antimonopolism was as fundamental a tenet of Whig politics as faith in property itself. In what was now remembered as a long struggle against Stuart arbitrary government, the fight against royal prerogative in commerce occupied a hallowed place.[2] This intractable confrontation between principles of monopoly and property—between royal power and civil society—ensured that the problem of print propriety remained simmering. Only in 1709–10 did it finally come to a head, and even then the result was notably equivocal. What ensued was a notoriously confused and unsettled piece of legislation. In retrospect it has become known as the first ever copyright act.

It was in these years of no property—between 1695 and 1710—that piracy really became an everyday concept for London's writers and readers. Suddenly it was being referred to everywhere, in poetry, newspapers, novels, ballads, correspondence, and essays. Just as piracy as a *legal* category ceased to exist, so piracy as a *cultural* category blossomed. A major reason for this, of course, was that attention was riveted on struggles with real, seagoing pirates, most notably in the Caribbean. The first Royal Navy expedition had been dispatched to Jamaica in 1688. Since then raw piracy had boomed, fueled by an influx of ex-smallholders unable to compete with slave plantations. In the 1710s, with a temporary peace signed in Europe, the Navy was again sent into action. On the other side of the world, meanwhile, the East India Company struggled against its own "pirates." Like those of the Caribbean, these were often once-tolerated competitors now outlawed under the expansionist and monopolist schemes of the company.[3] On land, the Stationers' Company, like the East India Company, faced a pirate war—and these pirates, too, had until recently known royal favor. The leading "pirate" of the postrevolutionary years was Henry Hills, son of the man who had been James II's royal printer.

The countless legends of buccaneering that came to London from the naval campaigns fueled the war of print piracy. Stories about Edward Teach ("Blackbeard"), Captain Kidd, Mary Bonny, William Dampier, and Bartholomew Roberts filled the London press, where they were themselves pirated. But there they also merged with the kinds of ideas about pirate "companies" on which Atkyns and Streater had drawn. The most influential of all the pirate narratives, Captain Charles Johnson's *General history of the Pyrates,* thus avowedly cast aside "romantic" tales of derring-do in favor of treating pirate crews as commonwealths in the making. The point, its author (thought by some to be Daniel Defoe) said, was to record their *"Policies, Discipline* and *Government."* And as he portrayed them, the pirates did indeed constitute themselves into alternative societies—quite literally so in the case of what is today Madagascar, where they created a nation called Libertalia. Libertalia was in some ways a brutally Hobbesian realm: families retreated into isolated enclaves for fear of mutual attack. But in other ways pirate society seemed to compare rather favorably to that available to London readers. Captains were elected, spoils distributed equitably, crews recruited from all races and creeds.[4] Libertalia probably never existed in reality, yet it drew plausibility from those long-standing evocations of pirate countersocieties. And as with those evocations, the point may partly have been to get readers to reexamine their own surroundings. The elaborate customs of Johnson's pirates looked like parodies of the rituals and conventions trumpeted by companies in their own city with a volume that to many Londoners rang false. A London company might claim to provide for the poor of its trade; Johnson's pirates established rules for the division of spoils and the protection of the injured. Defoe, whether or not he had a hand in Johnson's *History*, was also responsible at this time for advancing the first taxonomy of the "Press-Piracy" then reigning in the streets of the capital.[5]

For just as there were heroic pirate captains in the West Indies, so there were mock-heroic pirate kings in London. Henry Hills junior was only the first. Ned Ward referred to a ruined bookseller "flinging out as many Invectives against *Harry Hills,* and the rest of the Pyrates, as if they had given him cause to think 'em worse Rogues than those that were hang'd last Sessions." (The hanged were, of course, the real pirates, whose bodies were left out to rot *pour encourager les autres.*) John Gay too disdained "*Pirate Hill*'s brown sheets, and scurvy letter." Later, Hills's position would be inherited by Edmund Curll, whom an imposter posing as John Dunton described as a "Pirate" not "frighted from his Trade" even by being thrashed and tossed in a blanket. ("To see Thee smart for Copy-stealing," Dunton is made to say, "My Bowels yearn with Fellow-feeling.") By that time, another victim was vowing rhetorically to "bombard some more modern small pyratical Fortress" that he represented as lying on the coast of Africa, at ancient Carthage. Such figures—Curll himself would yield his place to William Rayner, and so on down to nineteenth-century stalwarts like Richard Carlile and Thomas Tegg—were quite prepared to pose as commonwealthsmen, even Levellers. They claimed that they acted in the public interest by issuing literary work at affordable prices. Sometimes they even projected themselves as midwives of genius, printing work that otherwise might not appear at all. Pleading for pirates "in the Face of Day," as Samuel Johnson would call it, took hold in the post-1688 generation.[6]

In the streets and coffeehouses of London, piracy by now referred to a wide range of sins involving the misappropriation of ideas. The concept became something like a shibboleth of the new society, standing as a symbol of the moral dubiety of "revolution principles" alongside the national debt, projectors, the Bank of England, and standing armies. By 1718 London's theatergoers could even go to see the leading actor of the day, Colley Cibber, playing the role of Peter Pirate, "a Bookseller by Trade, but broke lately," in the latest comedy. Mr. Pirate personified all the associations of his caste, with his obsession with "credit," his claims to have solved the longitude, and his memory of "a dose of Antimony" administered to him by a Wit ("and I have never been my own Man again since").[7] If the Whig defense of 1688 rested on a principle of property—as it largely did—then piracy, like stockjobbing, represented the weakness, amorality, ambition, and transgression that came with it.

The Glorious Revolution therefore left a legacy in this sphere of piracy, the metropolis, as much as it did in the other sphere of piracy, the Caribbean. That legacy was epitomized in the rampant terminology of pirates. Like pirates of the sea, moreover, literary pirates were outsiders against whom a form of propriety could be defined, defended, and upheld as fundamental to order. And that propriety, in retrospect, was one of nascent capitalism. It valued creative individuals' property, and compromised with monopoly, all in the interests of encouraging a speculative practice centered on undertaking what were seen as printing "projects." If a reformed realm of print were to serve as the bulwark of a free Protestant nation, then pirates both had to exist and had to be expelled. By the end of the 1730s, when the first rounds of this battle were culminating, they had made another new term into a household word. That word, nowhere used in the original law of 1710, was *copyright.*

Piracy flourished so scandalously in a city that saw the origins not only of capitalism, but also of the modern natural sciences and mechanical arts. The London of Atkyns and Henry Hills was also the London of Robert Boyle, Christopher Wren, and Isaac Newton. The question of how this could possibly be—of how experimental science could be created in the same place, and sometimes in the same bookshops and printing houses, that saw piracy boom—is the subject of the next chapter. For now, however, it is important to insist that the origin of the concept in struggles of the book trade was never forgotten. That much was made very evident in a spoof of Dante's trip to Hell written by the scabrous Grub Street wit Ned Ward in 1700. Ward's hero finds himself at one point face to face with a crowd of squabbling printers and booksellers—the two camps mobilized by Atkyns. They have arrived at the critical point of their feud:

A Throng of angry Ghosts that next drew near,
Large as a *Persian* army did appear;
Each to the rest show'd Envy in his Looks,
Some Writings in their Hands, some printed Books.
The learn'd Contents of which they knew no more,
Than the Calves Skins their sundry Volumes wore,
Down from the bulky Folio to the Twenty-Four.
As they press'd on, confus'dly in a Crowd,
Piracy, Piracy, they cry'd aloud,
What made you print my Copy, Sir, says one,
You're a meer Knave, 'tis very basely done.
You did the like by such, you can't deny,
And therefore you're as great a Knave as I. . . .
Printers, their Slaves, b'ing mix'd among the rest,
Betwixt 'em both arose a great Contest:
Th'ungrateful *Bibliopoles* swoln big with Rage,
Did thus their servile *Typographs* engage:
You Letter-picking Juglers at the Case,
And you Illit'rate Slaves that work at Press,
How dare you thus unlawfully invade
Our Properties, and trespass on our Trade.

The printers respond to this charge by claiming that the Stationers' Company was originally chartered for them alone, as they had indeed claimed in the Restoration struggle. And as had happened then, all parties are then silenced by the courts. The Stationers are eventually sentenced to an eternal torment. Their fate is to have to read an endless list of Grub Street screeds, all the while being flayed alive by their hack authors, and basting in their excrement atop a pyre of pamphlets.[8]

THE PIRATE SPHERE

By the mid-eighteenth century a slew of improprieties were thought to characterize the rampantly commercial realm of credit in this, the first consumer age. Piracy became their common name. In print, plagiary could be piratical; so could epitomizing, or abridging, or even translating. Edmund Curll's edition of correspondence between Alexander Pope and Jonathan Swift was, Pope said, "surreptitious and pyrated," even though

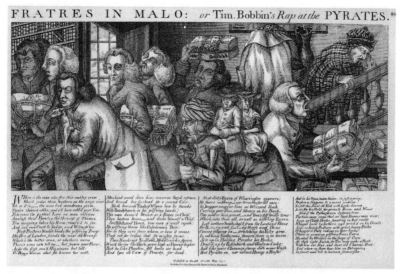

FIGURE 3.1. An eighteenth-century artist's anguish at piracy. "Tim. Bobbin's Rap at the Pyrates," in J. Collier [Tim Bobbin, pseud.], *Human Passions Delineated* (Manchester: J. Heywood, 1773). Courtesy of the University of Chicago Library.

the text had not been printed before. In mechanics, engineers and inventors began to call their rivals "pirates." So did mapmakers keen to preserve their charts from imitators, and artists like Hogarth eager to garner an income from engraving (fig. 3.1 portrays one engraver's anguish at the pirates he encountered). Apothecaries, physicians, naturalists, and poets all shared this rhetoric of piracy in their respective fields.

The moral issues that arose from this were rather profound. For all that writers, scholars, and medical practitioners bewailed its ubiquity, very few were above a bit of judicious expropriation when it suited them. That included getting their own work pirated. Poets eager to avoid seeming ambitious of fame had long taken advantage of credulity about piracy accusations to get their work into print. Isaac Newton took a similar backdoor route to have some of his unorthodox religious texts published, for all that he worried genuinely about the prospect of his other works falling out of his control. That remark by Pope about Curll should not be taken at face value, either: in fact, Pope himself had craftily maneuvered Curll, the most notorious press pirate of his time, into unwittingly serving his own ends by issuing that correspondence. (It seems that Pope wanted to make an edition himself, but feared being caught breaching his correspondents' confidences.)[9] And although authors might rail at the "hacks" and "dunces" populating Grub Street—a real street, adjacent to Moorfields, where many poor writers found lodgings—they were now the mainstay of the trade. A culture of piracy was one that could never be distinguished into two neat camps of the honorable and the dishonorable in the way that antagonists often professed to believe. Everyone involved was, to some extent, compromised.

As a result, it was by no means straightforward to find a secure basis on which to assess the cacophony that was the printed realm. In practice, a panoply of strategies evolved to create, confirm, and contest the authenticity not only of books, but of medicines, machines, textiles, foodstuffs, and other creative goods. What an eighteenth-century citizen could be said to know, feel, or believe might depend on them. People found themselves living amid countless experiments in authenticity.

This world extended far beyond London. It reached across Europe, taking the notion of piracy with it. Everywhere it had its own sustaining legends. The buccaneer of reprinting was one. Another was the sadly heroic artist subsisting in a garret and paid by the line by some such rapacious bookseller. A third, grander in scale, was the idea of a "public sphere."[10] This sphere had its distinctive genre, the journal article, and its representative location, the coffeehouse. Anyone who read journals and contributed back to them could supposedly claim citizenship. It asserted its cultural authority, on the basis that while any individual was fallible, a large enough number of readers could cancel out the foibles and passions of individuals. How far its sway extended into matters of politics or religion, and how legitimately, were matters of much debate. But printers, booksellers, authors, and readers did aspire—sometimes—to the standards explicit in this notion.

The public sphere in practice was riven with distinctions of place, rank, nationality, confession, and gender. Piracy shaped it in several ways. First, it assisted the sheer distribution of books and periodicals, especially beyond the metropolis. Second, it had an impact on the kind, quality, and price of books. Pirates reprinted the most profitable works in smaller formats and at far cheaper prices, mixing and matching contents as they saw opportunity. They therefore facilitated, third, a certain casualness of reading: their books were portable and relatively disposable. Daniel Defoe warned of a world that would be increasingly dominated by hack collections tarted up as treatises, until all learning would dissolve into "a general Rapsody of Piracy, Plagiarism, and Confusion."[11] Finally, and perhaps most saliently, it raised questions of accuracy and authenticity. Generally, pirates sought to reproduce, not to originate. Reprinters boasted of their accuracy. But it was not always safe to trust that boast in particular instances. Pirates did sometimes seek to "improve" an original, if only to be able to advertise their edition as improved. One might silently abridge; another might translate creatively; a third might add material or critical comments. Booksellers competed to claim the latest, best, most complete, most authentic versions. So a culture of the upgrade, as it were, took hold. Piracy of books—but also, as we shall see, of drugs, foods, and other manufactures —paradoxically fostered an ethic of authenticity and completeness. One of the ironies of an age of piracy is that it helped cement print's paradoxical association with both constancy and progressive change at once.

To recognize how reprinting worked and what it meant is to get a different impression of the Enlightenment itself. The piratical Enlightenment was lower-toned, more commercial, more hardscrabble, more various, and altogether edgier than the world of the high Parisian *philosophes* or Scottish philosophers with which we are familiar. Yet that world was never clearly distinct from it. David Hume was caught up in London booksellers' attempts to destroy Scottish "pirates"; Rousseau and Voltaire assailed pirate reprinters of their works and availed themselves of those same reprinters when it suited them to do so; Goethe and Lessing did likewise. Isaac Newton's work was printed by a press pirate, and was itself reprinted without his consent. Stephen Storace's music drifted between opera houses, freely appropriated by rival impresarios. Lawrence Sterne took up a pen and personally signed over twelve thousand copies of *Tristram Shandy* to preempt a pirated edition.[12] To the extent that these men achieved transcendence as authors, it was precisely because they engaged with the pirate realm at a mundane level and mastered its complexities. Those who did not succeed have either been forgotten altogether, dismissed as mediocrities, or consigned to discrete spheres where heroic authorship is deemed inappropriate, such as hackery, pornography, or the newspaper press.

The term *enlightenment* carries connotations of a certain kind of information dispersal. The association is with illumination itself—of light spreading equally in all directions from a central source. But in the eighteenth century the transfer from place to place of texts, ideas, practices, and the like was scarcely amenable to such an image. The kind of ubiquity that happened to certain works and ideas was not one with which we are nowadays very familiar. We are used to living in a world where publishing operates according to more or less common standards; internationalized copyright laws are, among other things, the projection of those standards into the legal sphere. In the eighteenth century, things were very different. Printing was a local craft, addressing local and regional markets. Its legal, conventional, and moral institutions were local too. Printed ideas attained ubiquity not only by distribution from major centers, but also by tension and competition between them and a more numerous set of reprinters, who acted as relays between author and reader. The more the competition, the greater the ubiquity. Locke's works, for example, emerged first from London, but were reprinted in Dublin, Glasgow, Amsterdam, The Hague, Rotterdam, Geneva, Brussels, Paris, Leipzig, Uppsala, Jena, Mannheim, Milan, Naples, Stockholm (by order of the Swedish Riksdag, no less), and, ultimately, Boston. Rousseau's *Nouvelle Héloïse,* appearing first in Paris, was soon reproduced in "Amsterdam" (actually London), Geneva, Lausanne, Neuchâtel, Basle, Leipzig, and Brussels. Montesquieu's work, again first published in Paris, reappeared in all the same countries. Voltaire's appeared initially, sometimes, in Geneva, only to be reprinted in Paris and London. Goethe's *Sorrows of Young Werther,* probably the most sensational single publishing phenomenon of the century, achieved that status by virtue of appearing in some thirty different editions, many of them in translation, and almost all unauthorized. When Italian readers encountered Locke, they were less likely to be viewing Locke's own words than those words as translated into Italian from a French rendering manufactured in the Netherlands. And that is not even to venture into the fascinating but shadowy world of the "radical" Enlightenment, in which tracts circulated in manuscript or in editions with false imprints—the world of "Spinozisme," of John Toland, and of the Illuminati.

Knowledge therefore spread through chain reactions of reappropriations, generally unauthorized and often denounced. Or rather, to use more eighteenth-century analogies, the process resembled not an orrery (a model of central illumination) but the kind of firework that amazed observers by producing staggered bursts across the sky. An initial edition from one location would find its way to a place of reprinting, which would generate a thousand new copies; one of those would then spark another explosion of copies from another reprint center; and so on. Enlightenment traveled atop a cascade of reprints. No piracy, we might say, no Enlightenment.[13]

For the most part, however, this kind of reprinting was not technically "piracy" at all, although it was often denounced as such. That is, it was not illicit. The reason was that it was a cross-border phenomenon. Printers in Swiss cantons reproduced the editions of the Paris book guild; those in the Low Countries reprinted French, German, and English titles; and booksellers in Edinburgh, Glasgow, and Dublin commissioned reprints of London works. In Vienna, most impressively of all, the imperial court munificently supported the huge reprinting empire of Thomas Edler von Trattner. There was no legal reason—and little moral cause—to forbid such activities. Moreover, mercantilist economic doctrines implied that domestic reprinting was to be preferred to the importing of books from abroad. In consequence, it was perfectly likely for a given volume to be either legitimate or piratical depending on where a reader happened to encounter it. Piracy was an attribute of territory. And it followed that the most interesting sites of reprinting were places the territorial autonomy of which—in the century after the Treaty of Westphalia had created the modern nation-state system—remained ambiguous. Scotland was one: it was only subsumed into a "United Kingdom" in 1707, and retained a largely discrete legal system. Ireland was another: a subordinate kingdom with its own parliament. And the German states had an almost metaphysical status vis à vis the Holy Roman Empire. In these places not only did reprinting boom, but controversy blossomed with it. Each produced its own ideology, and even epistemology, of reprinting. All promoted notions of a cosmopolitan "public" served by their reprinting and neglected by centralized, national book trades. Each charted a trajectory of enlightenment.

PIRACY AND PUBLIC REASON

For the reprinters themselves, the problem was that there was not just one case to be made for their practice, but two—and they were mutually exclusive. On the one hand, mercantilist principles emphasized the virtue of replacing imported manufactures with home production. On this score, pirates were vanguards of national economic prowess. But on the other, advocates of laissez-faire began to argue that literary property—that mysterious and novel concept—was just another restraint imposed on a market that ought to be as free as possible. It was, they declared, at once absolutist, monopolistic, iniquitous to the public good, and philosophically absurd. On this account, pirates were exemplars of free trade—

indeed, of freedom in general. Needless to say, while the first kind of argument tended to hold good in metropolitan centers like Vienna, the second sprang from upstart founts of enlightenment like Edinburgh, Dublin, and Philadelphia. (Alexander Donaldson's ringing evocation, as we shall see in chapter 6, found an audience in all three places.) Both stood opposed to metropolitan assertions of authorial property.

Arguments on the other side were equally various. To indicate something of their scope, consider the examples of the Marquis de Condorcet in France and Immanuel Kant in Germany. Each responded creatively to a world of piratical and cross-border reprinting. Each did so by identifying what was perilous about that world. And both advanced proposals for reconstituting out of it a public sphere of reason. But their proposals were notably divergent.

Condorcet wrote as an antagonist to the Paris book guild, and in opposition to Denis Diderot, who had been charged by the guild with defending its interest in literary property. His was a contribution to a long debate in France over privileges, censorship, and "counterfeiting" (*contrefaçon*). His *Fragments concerning freedom of the press* argued that property rights in literary works should not exist at all, because the public's interest in knowledge trumped the author's. Its argument was fundamentally epistemological. Condorcet insisted that knowledge itself originated in sense perceptions, and that since people's sensory apparatuses were essentially alike, its elements were naturally common to all. "Originality" could exist, he conceded, but it resided only in matters of style, not of knowledge. Bacon, Kepler, Galileo, Descartes, and Newton all achieved what they did with no literary property system to encourage them, and the same held true of the works that defined "the progress of Enlightenment" itself— above all Diderot's own *Encyclopédie*. That made the principle of literary property not merely superfluous and unnatural, but actively harmful. To constrain the circulation of ideas on this principle would be to make artifice, not truth, the structuring principle of cultural commerce. Free trade must be enforced in literature. "A book that can circulate freely and that does not sell at a third above its price," he affirmed, would "almost never be counterfeited." Instead, Condorcet proposed creating a realm of printed reason around periodicals, not books. Knowledge should be organized by category, not by author. Readers would return their own contributions to these sources, thus creating a perpetual virtuous circulation. On this view an enlightening realm of print would resemble a vast instantiation of the tree of knowledge prefacing Diderot and d'Alembert's *Encyclopédie,* with each twig being the name of a journal. In the meantime, counterfeiting was simply enlightenment itself, breaking out everywhere.[14]

Carla Hesse has told the story of what happened in the wake of this argument.[15] Briefly, after 1789 the revolutionaries wanted to see enlightenment spread from Paris by its own natural force. They therefore abolished literary property. For the first time, the people themselves would have access to the finest learning and the best literature—to the fruits of genius. What ensued was an experiment in whether print without literary property would help or hinder enlightenment. Before long the very officer responsible for policing the book trade was being accused of piracy, while the most radical revolutionary journal, *Révolutions de Paris,* had declared Mirabeau's letters, as "the works of a man of genius," to be "public property." This was a revolutionary utopianism of the commons. If the French Revolution itself was the revenge of the hacks, as Robert Darnton says, then this revolution of the book was the revenge of the pirates. But as utopias do, it turned rotten. The craft of printing did expand rapidly—the number of printers quadrupled—but what it produced changed radically too. The folio and the quarto were dead. Reprints became first legitimate, then dominant. Even proclamations were pirated. The old world of a few large houses issuing authoritative editions could not survive. Those that endured were smaller, faster, newer. They employed whatever secondhand tools they could lay their hands on, worked at breakneck speed with whatever journeymen they could get, and ensured a rapid turnover by issuing newspapers and tracts with an immediate sale. What books were still published were largely compilations of old, prerevolutionary material. In other words, a literary counterpart to Gresham's Law took hold, and the triumph of the *presses grises* led to disaster. A series of abortive attempts to restore some kind of order ensued, culminating in a "Declaration of the Rights of Genius" that introduced a limited authorial property. But still it took years for publishing to recover from the revolutionary experiment. Only toward the later 1790s did it really do so, and then with the aid of lavish subsidies. In particular, the government sponsored scientific projects, including periodicals designed on Condorcet's lines as "depositories for new inventions."

The context in the German lands was different.[16] Under the traditional system of fairs at Leipzig and Frankfurt, authorship had little economic value, and periodicals, not books, were enlightenment's central vehicles. Condorcet's vision of an authorless public realm was becoming fact in Germany when he articulated it in France. But in the 1760s a bitter, prolonged, and profound debate was ignited about the commerce of print and its role in public culture. Its protagonists included not only the leading booksellers of the time, but its major authors too: Lessing, Kant, Fichte, Hegel, Feuerbach, Schopenhauer, and others. Reprinting was not its only issue. But it was the occasion and principal theme of the debate. So, for example, Jean Paul issued "Seven last words, or, postscripts against pirating," and plays on the topic were staged in Prague and Leipzig. But it was Immanuel Kant who provided the most idiosyncratic and influential contribution. His arguments, like Condorcet's in France, tied the problem of piracy to the very possibility of enlightenment.

Kant's famous answer to the question "What is Enlightenment?" appeared in the *Berlinische Monatsschrift* in 1785.[17] The essay received enormous attention, then and later; it has been treated in recent years as an authoritative description of the public sphere itself. It portrayed that sphere as composed of a vast population of readers of periodicals, whose duty was to practice thinking for themselves. The results of this activity were to be displayed through print to the same realm. Kant insisted on the illegitimacy of censorship to control this realm. He did, however, allow that the state could restrict citizens acting in their capacities as bureaucrats, military officers, clergymen, and so on. In that capacity a subject exercised only what he termed "private" reason. Only in withdrawal from one's professional post, therefore—perhaps in a secluded study—could one really exercise "public" reason. Public reason was therefore produced in (what we would call) private. In public, an author spoke "in his own person." The interaction of such public utterances was what Kant identified as enlightenment.

Shortly after "What is Enlightenment?" appeared, Kant took up his pen again to propose a related thesis in the same journal. By stark contrast, this second paper is nowadays almost completely unknown; yet it was one of Kant's first pieces to be translated into English, in 1798, along with the Enlightenment essay. It took up and extended the claims of the preceding article, and seemed to deal with concerns fundamental to the plausibility of that article's argument. It also reminded readers that Kant himself was thoroughly proficient in the mundane practices of authorship, reading, and publishing—practices on which any kind of public sphere necessarily depended. The piece was entitled "On the wrongfulness of the unauthorized publication of books."[18] We do not know the precise occasion of its composition, but it very possibly arose from the same group of "Friends of the Enlightenment" that inspired the more renowned essay. At any rate, it adopted the argument of that essay as its tacit premise.

The question Kant now addressed arose directly from his conclusion that public reason was a matter of each author writing "in his own person." What if the mediating agents of print appropriated that person—as, in a piratical world, they so often did? Kant observed that a bookseller who undertook to produce an edition must have an obligation to do so faithfully. This fidelity, he added, was facilitated by the provision of exclusive rights. Yet, he conceded, decades of attempts to outlaw reprinting by adducing some kind of property had failed. They would always fail, Kant now claimed, because the author's property, if it existed at all, was inalienable—it was an inseparable extension of the creative self. In any case, a real property right would kill publishing itself, for the simple reason that no purchaser would ever accept liability for his or her copy becoming the basis for a reprint. Instead, Kant returned to his idea that a true author exercised a freedom to speak in his own person. He reasserted this principle, remarking that a book was not merely a passive container of meaning, but a vehicle for a dynamic process of communication. The publisher was properly comparable to an "instrument" for this process—something like a speaking trumpet. It followed that what was wrong with unauthorized reprinting was nothing to do with property. What made it an offense was that it mixed authorship up with mediation. In effect, it was a form of ventriloquism: the pirate hijacked another person's voice. Worse, pirates therefore obligated authors, rather than vice versa —they made them answerable for meanings transmitted without their consent. (Under the reactionary Frederick William II, censorship was once again in the ascendant, and Kant himself fell afoul of the police at just this point.) It was this violation of the author's identity that made piracy potentially fatal to the very idea of a public sphere, and hence to enlightenment itself. The fact that reprinting dispersed learning more widely, cheaply, and accessibly was true but beside the point. Such knowledge would no longer be *public*, because authors would no longer be *private*.

Kant's argument was quite different, then, from Condorcet's, and pointed to very distinct policies. But the Idealist and Romantic contentions in which it participated were no less consequential: they inspired the adoption of literary property principles in the next century. The point, however, is that these are but two of countless attempts made in the eighteenth century to understand and master the piratical Enlightenment. In 1700, as those attempts began, almost nobody spoke in any sustained way of authorial rights. By 1750, many did. By 1800, such talk was ubiquitous. But where those rights led varied widely according to context. In prerevolutionary France, the Crown rejected properties as an encroachment on royal power, and titles remained gifts of "grace" until 1789 — at which point they were abolished altogether. In the German lands, they were at length adopted under the idealist convictions of Kantianism and *Naturphilosophie*. In the English-speaking world an altogether more convoluted compromise evolved. How that happened, and what it meant, will be major topics of the rest of this book.

4

Experimenting with Print

One of the most remarkable aspects of the invention of piracy in the seventeenth century is that it coincided with the culmination of the scientific revolution. This was perhaps not just a chance alignment. The struggles that gave rise to piracy, after all, had to do not just with print, but with the printed. As those involved consistently declared, they impinged upon knowledge itself. In vitally important and lasting ways, what knowledge is taken to be—such that it can be authored, owned, and stolen—emerged at that moment. Even the rise of Isaac Newton to a position of supremacy in the intellectual culture of his day depended on the establishment of practical and principled approaches to that issue.

We are no longer as comfortable as we once were in identifying a scientific revolution at all in the sixteenth and seventeenth centuries. Yet there is no denying that radical changes did occur in that period to Western European knowledge about nature. What emerged was not "science" in our sense, but it was fundamentally different from anything conceivable in about 1500, and our science did emerge in its wake. Since at least the mid-eighteenth century there has been a broad consensus on the momentousness of this transformation. There has been an equally broad consensus that it was fundamentally indebted to the advent of printing. As the great engine of enlightenment, philosophers since Condorcet have thought, the press could have been on only one side in the scientific revolution. But the invention of piracy shows that to sixteenth- and seventeenth-century people themselves the nature of printing was not so evident. The question therefore arises of how this alliance between print and knowledge came about. Who made it happen?

The affiliation between the printing revolution and the revolution in science was real enough. But it was artificial. Scholars, mathematicians, experimental philosophers, booksellers, and others worked hard to make print into a vehicle for knowledge. Virtually all acknowledged the huge potential of the craft, but many cautioned that for it to realize that potential it must be carefully monitored and used. Success was not guaranteed, and there were those—not all of them curmudgeons— prepared to claim that the printed page was actually getting *less* reliable in the age of newsbook vendors and pamphleteers. Two hundred years after Gutenberg, and despite repeated attempts, nobody had managed to establish a lastingly successful scholarly press anywhere in Europe. Authoring knowledge remained a matter of engaging constructively with the world of the printing house and bookshop, in a bid to unite the commitments of their denizens to the interests of learning. The phenomena that society was just starting to call piratical loomed large in scholars' eyes as they labored to produce, distribute, and put to use printed works. In struggling to limit, manage, and exploit those phenomena, they forged a bond between print and knowledge. They also initiated the central elements of what would become the scientific enterprise.

In one sense, to broach this subject is to revive one of the most hackneyed themes of early modern learning: the relation between *words* and *things*. The contemporaries of Newton often proclaimed their revolution in terms of a fundamental recasting of that relation, or even as a discarding of the former in favor of the latter. Abraham Cowley's paean to Francis Bacon is a stark instance:

> From Words, which are but Pictures of the Thought,
> (Though we our Thoughts from them perversely drew)
> To Things, the Minds right Object, he it brought.[1]

Yet in fact natural philosophers could never neglect words quite as conclusively as they liked to claim in their looser polemical moments. Things cannot speak for themselves. And even the most neoteric of new philosophies articulated a view of the textual inheritance of antiquity, if only to distinguish itself from its predecessors.[2] In practice, every experiment was a nexus between the reading of some texts and the writing and printing of others. What the rhetoric about words and things really did was to focus attention on the proper uses of both.

That included proper techniques for reading. There are indeed conventions of reading, in science as in other fields of human endeavor, and they can differ from place to place and time to time. Those of the modern sciences derive ultimately from this period—the period of the first experimental philosophers—when they emerged in tandem with the techniques of experiment itself. Experimenting with print as well as with nature, the experimentalists created the distant origins of peer review, journals, and archives—the whole gallimaufry that is often taken as distinctive of science, and that is now in question once again in the age of open access and digital distribution. Above all, they gave rise to the central position that scientific authorship and its violation would hold in the enterprise.

THE INVENTION OF SCIENTIFIC READING

Experimental philosophy was a way of inquiring into nature that was pioneered in England in the mid-seventeenth century. Its major home, the Royal Society of London, was founded in 1660 and survived to become the world's oldest scientific society. The Society made a point from its earliest days of experimenting with print. It adopted innovative alliances with Stationers, seeking to join forces with a community it could not master. It became a licenser too, endorsing the authenticity and legitimacy of its printed works by means of an *imprimatur.* And, perhaps above all, it pioneered practices of reading. As with all experiments, not all its ventures succeeded. One in particular, the publication of Francis Willughby's *Historia Piscium,* was a notoriously calamitous failure. But together these efforts amounted to a sustained bid to ally craft propriety with learned gentility. To the extent that they did succeed, in later generations the efforts themselves retreated into self-evidence. That was the principal achievement of the Society: to cement together the scientific and printing revolutions so that the seam became invisible.

If there is one thing that everyone knows about the experimental philosophy, it is that that philosophy was indeed experimental. It depended on *doing* things, and on showing the things that were done to other people. That is, the Royal Society created practical demonstrations of natural "facts," the demonstrations themselves being called experiments.[3] But experimental philosophy also rested on repeated acts of writing, printing, and reading. In fact, the Society's practices intersected at every point with the world of the book. For example, the "matters of fact" that it created in its experiments were collected in great register books, which rather resembled the registers of London trade companies like the Stationers, or, in another light, the commonplace books of Renaissance scholars.[4] It then circulated written and printed reports of some register entries both within its own fellowship and abroad. Those reports needed to carry with them a degree of authenticity and authority, in order to warrant the commitment of distant readers. Their recipients would then respond by entrusting their own documents to the Society, which would duly register them, thus creating a perpetual and fruitful circulation. Experimental philosophy depended for its very existence on this circulation continuing and expanding.

Like commonplaces, facts were to be epistemic foundation stones— tools for building a conversation rather than objects over which to dispute. The most dedicated experimenter of them all, Robert Hooke, left instructions for how to lay out a register of experimental facts that owed a clear debt to scholarly note-taking techniques.[5] Yet the registration of experimental reports differed in one respect. For facts to count, they supposedly had to be witnessed by an audience—ideally on repeated occasions. Their registration was therefore part and parcel of learned sociability.[6] And their reading too was consequently not a private act, in principle, but a social gesture. It took place for a group of educated, privileged, and (here, at least) sober gentlemen. Sometimes this meant actually reading aloud before them; on other occasions reading might well be carried out alone, but with an eye to displaying its consequences to the group at the next weekly meeting. In either case, experimental reading took on a rather formal, even ceremonial, air.[7]

Perhaps paradoxically, the individual character of this reading was what made it such a key component of experimental philosophy. It was the diversity of perspectives brought to bear by readers in Arundel House and Gresham College, where Society meetings took place, that mattered. That diversity was what qualified the virtuosi to regard the claims that emerged as robust. So reading was at once a cementer of social bonds—it helped to constitute the Society as a community—and a guarantor that what that community eventually published should indeed be accounted knowledge. (Many later writers would come to characterize objectivity itself in such terms.[8]) While experiments and their reading were indeed collective enterprises—and the former often relied on the labor of anonymous "laborants"—the Society as a whole did not lay claim to authorship. It was to be an arena for debate, not a participant, and had to stay above the fray. But it did validate the appearance of gentlemen as authors, which otherwise might seem immodest. Once approved by the Society, Edward Tyson said, his authorship became an "allowable boldness."[9] This rather delicately balanced position had to be restated many times, and there is evidence that distant readers were skeptical of it, or even affected to find it incomprehensible. But it was useful nevertheless. It was not yet peer review: it was informal, generally oral, and often governed by civility rather than expertise. Yet the distant origins of peer review do indeed lie here.

If being an experimental author was tricky, however, being an experimental reader was no less so. Leading protagonists like Newton and Robert Boyle were quite able to move back and forth between what they acknowledged to be different reading conventions, depending on what kind of knowledge they were dealing with and to whom they were talking. In the Society itself, however, four relatively discrete stages characterized and shaped the conduct of reading. I have called these *presentation, perusal, registration,* and *publication* (which might well take place via correspondence rather than print).[10] Briefly, formal presentations of papers and books happened almost every week, and furnished the Society's major "occasions for discourse." The response often took the form of a "perusal" —a delegated reading, carried out by two fellows who took the work away, examined it for a week or two, and reported back. Many perusals were detailed and creative, leading to new experiments, and some took weeks to deliver. Further conversation and experiment inspired by the perusal would then ensue, and they too might continue for weeks, or even months (and, on exceptional occasions, years).[11] This kind of process constituted the mainstay of the Society's work. Without perusal, it was unlikely that a submission would lead to any conversation at all, and hence to any new experimental knowledge. And a perusal was often characterized after the event as the reading of the Society itself, collectively—not least by authors and booksellers eager to trumpet it as an endorsement in a bid for customers.

Within the Society, registration often accompanied presentation and perusal.[12] The submission was transcribed into a manuscript volume, which was held under lock and key by the secretary. A machine or artifact submitted could likewise be boxed up and deposited. These records were then kept secret, in order to secure achievements from what was called "usurpation."[13] Internally, the register soon built up into an archive of discoveries, to which the Society could lay claim not as author, but as facilitator, securer, and virtual judge of authorship. Defenders of the experimental philosophy thus came to refer to the register whenever they were challenged to show evidence that the activity had achieved any results. But therein lay a problem. The register was confidential. As a result, while it might succeed in securing authorship within the Society itself —and that might be enough to attract some outsiders to send it their discoveries—it could do little for audiences beyond its walls. Nor could it persuade skeptics that the virtuosi were creating useful knowledge. Both reasons help to explain why Oldenburg resolved to deploy a new kind of printed object that would extend the register's reach across London and Europe. Submissions would still be registered at the Society, but some would be called forth as what one fellow called "ambassadors." They would represent their authors, the Society, and the enterprise of experimental philosophy itself in a new "public register" that would be printed regularly and distributed through the European book trade. Invented and administered by Oldenburg, this public register was named by him *Philosophical Transactions*.[14]

The *Philosophical Transactions* has survived to the present as the first scientific journal. It is not always easy, therefore, to remember what a strange object it must have seemed when it first appeared. It started out as a peculiar mixture of correspondence and pamphlet. There was no great precedent for using print to circulate learned claims periodically in this way, although several Continental groups and individuals had advanced ideas along comparable lines. Periodical publication itself was far more widely, and justly, associated with newsbooks and the like—organs as renowned for their claims to truth and accuracy as for their actual peddling of lies and errors.[15] And sure enough, the new journal's footing remained precarious, not least because Oldenburg never managed to produce the Latin version on which his plans for economic independence had depended. At first it often missed its intended monthly appearance (it did not help that the first two years of its life happened to be those of the plague and the Great Fire). Yet as the *Philosophical Transactions* filtered through the channels of the international book trade—being translated, excerpted, reprinted, and reread as it went—so it took with it an image of the Royal Society's conventions, and of the centrality to those conventions of reading and registration. Its success may well have depended, in fact, on the unauthorized reprints that Oldenburg ostentatiously sought to suppress. Continental philosophers responded, both to them and to his original. They embraced the initiative, and their contributions sustained the Society itself as the fervor of its local membership inevitably waned. In those terms the *Philosophical Transactions* proved astoundingly successful.

Register and periodical thus became twin bulwarks of a new form of learned practice, the anchors of experimental civility. Perusal gave rise to conversation; conversation inspired experiments; experiments led to reports and correspondence; and publication then restarted the cycle. Quite simply, this was how the experimental philosophy worked. Early modern science came into being as a self-sustaining process—a kind of social perpetual motion machine that, in some respects, has not stopped turning ever since.

Not every submission to the Society went through precisely this sequence, and departures from the norm were not necessarily seen as transgressions. But sometimes they were, and when that happened the results could be far-reaching. Some of the more violent—and fruitful—disputes of the era hinged precisely on accusations that the Society's reading regime had been subverted.[16] Hooke for one was prone to detecting heinous contraventions of this kind, especially on Oldenburg's part. In the end Hooke carried out what he had long privately threatened, and withdrew altogether from the regime, pending its complete reconstitution. Yet it is at least equally remarkable that such crises did not, in the end, destroy the custom. Very quickly it became so valuable that it was preserved in the face of even the blatant contraventions alleged by Hooke (who denounced Oldenburg as a spy, selling English secrets to the philosopher of Louis XIV, Christiaan Huygens). And the resolutions, too, of some of the most important of those disputes hung on the management of the archives that had been created by the Society's reading practices. The greatest exponent of such management was to be Isaac Newton.

ISAAC NEWTON AND THE REJECTION OF PERUSAL

Newton was, of course, the dominant figure to emerge in English natural philosophy in the late seventeenth and early eighteenth centuries. His emergence took shape through repeated episodes of engagement with the perusal-registration-circulation sequence. The first of these spanned the period from his initial introduction to the Royal Society in early 1672 to his declaration six years later that he was withdrawing and ceasing all philosophical correspondence. From Newton's study in Cambridge, the Society's way of reading had looked less like courtesy than affront. The same cycle of engagement and retreat he then repeated several times — until, that is, he found himself in a position to dominate the sequence himself. At that point he was able to put it to very effective use, to become perhaps the foremost author in the history of the sciences.

Newton first announced himself to the Society by sending a remarkable new telescope "to be examined" by the virtuosi. Based on reflection rather than refraction, his new instrument eliminated chromatic aberration and was a vast improvement on existing designs. Newton also sent a letter to Oldenburg expanding upon his design and requesting a "review, before it should go abroad." The Society acted immediately. The description was read aloud, and entered in the register along with a "scheme" (that is, an image of the telescope). In gratitude, Newton was elected a fellow. Oldenburg wrote him a laudatory reply, assuring Newton that "the society would take care, that all right should be done him with respect to this invention." To ensure that this was so, he simultaneously wrote to Huygens in Paris "to secure this contrivance to the author." Meanwhile the Society ordered the instrument maker Christopher Cock to make its own version of the new telescope.[17]

All this was as it should be, and the reading of the submission duly prompted others to advance their own claims. Over succeeding months contributions came in from all sides. The letters were edited by Oldenburg to make them diplomatic enough, and forwarded to Newton. Meanwhile, at the Society, Robert Hooke did his own duty by pursuing the subject experimentally. He soon proclaimed a discovery of his own that would, he said, allow for the perfection of telescopes. But Hooke refused to reveal it, instead lodging his claim in the form of a cipher. That was a time-honored custom in the mathematical sciences, but one that here may have betrayed a certain skepticism about the integrity of the register system.[18] Then a further letter arrived from Newton describing his new theory of light and colors, according to which "light is not a similar, but a heterogeneous body," consisting of "rays" of different refrangibility. Now the reading conventions came fully into play. The letter was duly registered, and given to Ward, Boyle, and Hooke to "peruse and consider it, and bring in a report of it." Oldenburg further asked Newton to consent to publication, "as well for the greater convenience of having it well considered by philosophers, as for securing the considerable notions of the authors against the pretensions of others." It duly appeared in the *Philosophical Transactions* for February.[19]

As usual, the perusal inaugurated a response. It was this, however, that now caused problems. At the Society's next meeting Hooke stood up and delivered the results of his perusal. They amounted to a set of "considerations" on Newton's letter. Hooke concurred with Newton's experimental reports, but declined to find them conclusive in confirming his theory of colors. He could justifiably have claimed that there was nothing untoward about his comments, since perusals were precisely supposed to suggest interesting queries for future discussion and experiment. But in fact what Hooke said triggered a serious breach. In effect, he claimed that Newton was demanding that excessive weight be given to his—unique and hitherto uncorroborated—experimental facts and reasonings upon them. This implied that in Hooke's eyes Newton was not adequately adhering to the norms of the experimental philosophy itself. He was thanked for his "ingenious reflections," which were registered in their own right and sent on to Newton. He replied courteously, expressing pleasure that Hooke's perusal had confirmed so much of his argument and confidence that its certainty would soon be accepted. But the Society recognized the risk of a clash: Newton's own paper must be published alone, it decided, "lest Mr. Newton should look upon it as a disrespect, in printing so sudden a refutation of a discourse of his, which had met with so much applause at the Society but a few days before."[20]

Hooke continued to perform his duty as curator of experiments. He created a series of experimental variations derived from his original perusal over the course of several weeks. He brought in his own prisms, advanced his own plans for telescopes, proclaimed a better way of grinding lenses, and displayed his own phenomena of colors. He proposed too a way of communicating "intelligence" across great distances by using telescopes and a secret character, and one day the fellows trooped out of

Arundel House to see it tried across the Thames. Once more, all this was just how things were supposed to work. Interestingly, however, Hooke himself now hinted at his own doubts about the Society's protocols — doubts that had been festering for years, as we know from his diary. He declined to register his discourse on the communication device, for example. Such a demurral was not unknown—it usually indicated that a fellow wanted to publish autonomously—but in Hooke's case it reflected a growing skepticism about the integrity of the Society's own authorship system. Soon he had to be explicitly reminded to deliver his account of telescopes "to be registered, to preserve his discoveries from being usurped." And his exchange with Newton on light was registered only when Newton's more formal response arrived for perusal.[21] These were small signs, but together they connoted misgivings as to the whole system.

Yet Hooke was always in demand to do more perusals of the books and letters that arrived so regularly at the Society, so he could not sustain attention on any one topic for very long. As his focus shifted, the incipient confrontation with Newton died down. But it had raised important questions, and in 1675, inevitably, they surfaced again. Newton now found himself challenged by a group of Liège Jesuits — Francis Line, Anthony Lucas, and John Gascoines.[22] This new series of exchanges breached more unambiguously the protocols of reading. Whereas Hooke had accepted Newton's reported observations but denied their conclusiveness, Line in particular denied some of Newton's reported experimental findings. The Society therefore undertook "upon the reading of a letter of his" to perform the experiment itself. Its experimenter was, of course, Hooke. He failed to replicate Newton's result. Occurring just as the Society was reading a second and far more comprehensive letter from Newton himself on light, this experience finally sparked open hostility.

The clash centered on accusations about authorship and its violation. Newton remarked that, on a rare visit to the Society, he had heard Hooke discourse on diffraction. Newton himself had then observed that diffraction might be a special case of refraction. "To this Mr. Hooke was then pleased to answer, that though it should be but a new kind of refraction, yet it was a new one," Newton recalled. "What to make of this unexpected reply, I knew not; having no other thoughts, but that a new kind of refraction might be as noble an invention as any thing else about light." But it led him to remember that "I had seen the experiment before in some Italian author." The author was, in fact, "Honoratus Faber, in his dialogue

De Lumine, who had it from Grimaldo." Newton's implication, which Oldenburg had accentuated by careful editing, seemed unmistakable — that Hooke had elided his appropriation from these earlier writers. Stung, Hooke responded in kind. The core of Newton's own discourse on light, he retorted, was "contained in his [Hooke's] *Micrographia,* which Mr. Newton had only carried farther in some particulars."[23] Newton then declared that Hooke had "borrowed" much from Descartes, and that in his more recent discussions he had done the same from Newton's own work. He added that he himself had always taken care to acknowledge Hooke's authorship of natural facts where he had used them.[24] With that, as it became increasingly hard to see how this contest could be tamped down, Newton broke off correspondence altogether. He had meant to publish a book on light and colors; this he now abandoned, not to return to it until decades later, when Hooke was safely dead. His retreat was not entirely unsignaled — he had already told Oldenburg that he wanted to "concern my self no further about the promotion of Philosophy" — but it was still highly unorthodox. And it seemed that it was the Society's relentless demand for responses that had driven him to the final break. "I see I have made my self a slave to Philosophy," he complained; "a man must either resolve to put out nothing new or to become a slave to defend it."

There was real critical bite to those remarks, because Newton was, in an important sense, right. As a participant in the experimental philosophy he *was* bound to continue engaging with others. The conventions upheld by the Royal Society placed high value on integrating experiments into an endless sequence of conversations, readings, and writings. To that end the experiments themselves should be evident, witnessed, and repeated. Newton had come to disagree fundamentally with this. What mattered, he insisted, was "not number of Experiments, but weight." "Where one will do, what need of many?"[25] By 1678–79 he had therefore arrived at a position that departed markedly from the Royal Society's conventions of experimental philosophy and from the practices of collective reading that they included. And when he retreated back to his Cambridge rooms, he devoted himself to other kinds of reading. Alchemy and scriptural exegesis commanded his attention for the next years. As late as 1724, Newton remembered the moment well, and still defended it as a correct decision.[26]

But in fact what happened was, in the short term at least, a double withdrawal. For Hooke recoiled too. And it was his retreat, not Newton's, that carried the greater immediate peril for the experimental philosophy.

The clash had helped precipitate the final erosion of Hooke's faith in the mechanism of the register and Oldenburg's *Philosophical Transactions*. He had found himself fighting on two fronts, as he sought to uphold his reputation against Newton while at the same time struggling to confirm his claim to a patent for a spring-watch design that might, if it worked, win him a fortune by solving the longitude. It was now that Hooke persuaded the Society's printer to circumvent the Society's licensing procedure in order to append an intemperate attack on Oldenburg to a Hooke lecture entitled *Lampas*. He privately resolved never again to trust his discoveries to the secretary's "snares." Essentially, Hooke had convinced himself that Oldenburg was intent on expropriating for foreigners the designs of English inventors, particularly Hooke himself—and that the register and *Transactions* were really tools to this end. When Oldenburg suddenly died, he moved fast to confirm these suspicions. Hooke rifled his rooms searching for evidence of duplicity, and scoured the journal books in search of "omissions of things and names," drawing lines through empty spaces so that "there may be no new thing written therein." (That is, he wanted to ensure that in future nobody could interpolate reports of later discoveries into the minutes of earlier meetings so as to usurp his authorship.) The traces of this assiduity are still visible in the books today. He and his allies also had the secretary's role redefined, and the *Philosophical Transactions* rethought.[27] All this was in aid of an authorship system that he thought had been profoundly corrupted. Even more than Newton, then, it was Hooke—with the possible exception of Oldenburg, the Society's one irreplaceable participant—who cast the perusal-registration-circulation system into doubt. It is a remarkable fact that the only member to be present week in and week out at the Society for decades distrusted so fiercely what is today our principal source of knowledge of what experimental philosophy was.

Yet in the end Hooke, unlike Newton, could not retreat for long. He remained the Society's curator of experiments, and had to return every week with new contributions. As he did so, he repeatedly reminded fellows of his priority in the discoveries claimed by correspondents. Hooke sometimes maintained that a lecture amounted to a publication for proving this point. His reputation became ever more that of the prickly, defensive claimant, liable to accuse anyone of usurping his originality, and to appeal to some long-forgotten speech to do so.

Meanwhile the conventions of experimental reading proceeded to play a part in the subsequent shaping of Newton's career.[28] The writing and publication of the *Principia* in 1687 is perhaps the paramount example. Halley shepherded it through the perusal sequence, and the Society extracted it from Newton by offering to register it "for the securing [of] his invention to himself till such time as he could be at leisure to publish it." (It was then printed, rather appropriately, in the printing house that John Streater had built up in his alliance with Richard Atkyns to fight for the law patent.) But Newton's subsequent apotheosis into a national and scholarly hero resulted from yet another series of encounters with the Society's protocols of reading and circulating texts. At first, he was subject to them; after the *Principia,* he was their master and their manipulator. That process was not only a result of his success, but also a major component of it. He long continued to sway between dramatic public statement and reclusive silence, as is well known. Historians tend to attribute this pattern to aspects of Newton's own character.[29] But that is a one-sided perception: his decisions were equally shaped by the specific reading, archiving, and publishing practices of the realm into which he was venturing. The Newton who in 1712–13 masterminded the demolition of Leibniz's claim to the calculus—a demolition based squarely in the textual archives of perusal and registration—had learned to be a supreme exponent of Society reading protocols. He was no longer the distant scholar who had been hounded back to Cambridge by Hooke and the Jesuits.

The point of the Royal Society's reading regime was never to *eliminate* disputes like those through which Newton prospered. On the contrary, it was meant to generate them. The intent was to produce fertile engagements between people who thought differently and who might otherwise have had no common ground on which to meet. The Society's civility served first to bring this about, and then to limit and manage the resulting disagreements. Indeed, genteel civility itself—of which Society manners were something of an offshoot—implied not bland acquiescence in what one read, but constructive response to it. A witness at a French literary academy of the time expressed the point well. He "observed in what manner works were there examined," and saw "that it was not a businesse of compliments and flatteries, where each one commends that he might be commended, but that they did boldly and freely censure even the least faults." By this "he was filled with joy and admiration."[30] The Royal Society wanted to operate in much this way. Its practices were meant to create, structure, and sustain disagreement at least as much as to foster consensus. That disputes occurred was not, then, evidence of their failure. On the contrary, that disputes *kept* occurring was powerful evidence of their success.

A very important point needs to be made here. The Society's register, like the Stationers', served to identify not only a form of propriety, but also a characteristic kind of transgression. For the Stationers, the distinctive offense was just then starting to be called piracy. For the experimenters, the corresponding term was not piracy, at first, but *usurpation,* or sometimes *plagiary.* This kind of offense now became the besetting sin of the enterprise itself. Not that there was anything new about plagiary itself, just as there was nothing new about unauthorized reprinting. One thinks of the well-known battles between Tycho Brahe and Ursus, or between Galileo and Marius. But such disputes had been explosive affairs between fractious foes, blowing apart any prospect of collaboration in an escalating welter of accusations, libels, and threats—sometimes including death threats. Time and again, Boyle, Hooke, and others lamented the prevalence *outside* the Royal Society of such malfeasance. They invoked it routinely to their colleagues and counterparts, conjuring images of catastrophic outcomes to encourage them to contribute to the Society's work. Only by registering inventions, observations, and discoveries at Gresham College, they said, could authorship be established and secured. And this line of persuasion worked. The Society did attract contributions from across Europe on much this basis. But as those appeals effectively acknowledged, it did not so much eliminate priority disputes as render them implosive rather than explosive. It used them to force participants into *greater* engagement with each other and with the experimental community. They became structured affairs that followed a prescribed course designed to keep them in train and secure knowledge as their outcome. The perusal and registration system served this purpose. It made the priority dispute into the archetypal scientific controversy.

Whenever a debate arose, therefore, whatever it was at first about, the criteria for victory were now likely to end up being defined by the availability of the register, journal, and *Transactions*—an archive shaped by perusals and anxieties of authorship. So it was almost inevitable that when a figure like John Wallis clashed with Hooke, or Hooke with Huygens, or Newton with Leibniz, they would do so ultimately on grounds of authorship. And it was perhaps just as inevitable that once Isaac Newton took over control of the archive, he would prove unbeatable on that terrain. He took the most sophisticated author-creating device yet invented, and used it to become the greatest author in the history of science.

SEAWATER AND THE POLITICAL ECONOMY OF PATENTS

The Royal Society sought to extend this approach to inventions across the realm. It aspired to oversee the issuing of patents to inventors or introducers of mechanisms, arts, or techniques. Just as it did when venturing into the world of the printed book, however, here it found itself confronting an intractable world of pride and piracy. And it was much less successful in tackling it.

The 1624 Monopolies Act had endorsed the granting of patents for new and newly introduced arts, declaring for the first time in English law that innovation warranted protection. Yet the practice of patenting remained politically controversial, and there was no real patents system for inventors to use. The process of getting and defending a patent was long, expensive, and capricious. The Society sought to intervene in this perplexing practice. Whenever the Crown received a request for a patent, it argued, the Society should be entrusted with appraising the request. In other words, its perusal regime should be extended into the commonwealth at large to regulate innovation in commerce, manufacturing, and the arts.

This ambition arose partly from a long-standing desire to reform the practical arts. In projects like that for a "history of trades," Boyle and his counterparts had sought to persuade the artisans of London to reveal their skills, in return for which the virtuosi promised to improve and systematize them, and then to hand them to the reading public for the common good. Were the Society to become a patent authority, then its role as arbiter of skills would be extended over new as well as existing crafts. The benefits to the Society itself would be clear, and those to the commonwealth promised to be great. Yet its projects to reform the arts had always met with a rather frosty reception. Its gentlemen were not always given the cold shoulder by artisans or master craftsmen, although the belief that they were became ingrained. Robert Hooke, a mechanic himself, conversed extensively with them. But overall the Society's inquiries never came close to realizing its ambitions. To the extent that experimental philosophy engaged successfully with the mechanical arts, it was largely through ventures like Joseph Moxon's *Mechanick Exercises* or John

Houghton's *Collection of letters for the improvement of husbandry and trade*—independent initiatives that began outside the Society and reached into it, rather than vice versa.[31] The situation paralleled in a sense that of Newton in Cambridge: what was deemed civility in one community could look like haughty indifference to another whose livelihood was at stake.

The Society's bids to become a patent referee proved similarly ill starred. These bids, although they were launched repeatedly, do not seem to have been pursued with much determination. Nor is it easy to know how seriously they were entertained in Whitehall—although it seems likely that in the early days at least they were regarded as workable. Charles II himself reportedly affirmed that "no patent should pass for any philosophical or mechanical invention, but what was first put to the examination of the society," and there were certainly cases in which the court did forward applications to the virtuosi. As late as 1713 John Arbuthnot heard that Queen Anne had declared a policy to this effect.[32] But like the practitioners of established crafts, the projectors of new ones may have seen little to gain in revealing their "secrets" to a group of gentlemen who offered in return to secure their authorship. Some even seem to have feared that the Society would make *itself* the proprietor of registered contributions—an impression that did have some support from pronouncements by fellows, including Wallis and Hooke.[33] At one point a proposal was floated in the Society to abandon its vaunted openness in order to reassure such skeptics. But the problem was never really surmounted. The Society's ambition to become an arbiter of authorship in arts and manufactures came to nothing. In part that may have been because its protocols against piracy looked, to craftsmen, like piracy itself.

Nevertheless, the Society did engage at length with patents on a number of specific technologies. When it did so, however, it always found itself in the position, not of an authoritative arbiter, but of one party among many, some of which had access to powerful allies such as the king. One well-known instance is the ferocious dispute over spring watches between Hooke and Oldenburg in the mid-1670s.[34] What made this clash so cataclysmic, perhaps, was precisely that it was a patent dispute, and as such could not be confined within the Society's conventions; Hooke himself appealed to Charles II for support. In general, while the Society was quite successful at dealing with authorship clashes within its community, it found itself on much riskier ground when it was forced to move beyond that community to arenas where different ideals held good. In the courts, at Whitehall, in craft and mercantile companies, and in overseas venues it was often competing with rival claimants to authority, expertise, and even disinterest. And it was doing so on their terrain.

The best exemplar of this predicament was a contest that began, prosaically enough, with perhaps the commonest substance on the planet: seawater. This contest was grounded in the delicate but momentous intricacies of matter theory. But as it proceeded, it brought the Royal Society up against many of the issues and tensions roiling mid-seventeenth-century England, and that we have encountered already: the clash of royal power with commercial custom, the emerging political economy of colonialism, the relative authority of gentility and expertise, and the proper conduct of inventors and scholars in a royal state. And looming over all was the competition for naval supremacy with Britain's great rival as a trading nation, the Netherlands.

Many of the most pressing problems of the age—philosophical as well as political and military—concerned the sea. The problem of the longitude is only the best known of them: anyone who furnished a reliable and portable technique for determining the longitude of a ship far removed from its home port would become rich, and would vastly enhance the power of the nation that possessed the secret. Aspirants to "solve the longitude" included not only men like Edmond Halley but any number of otherwise obscure "projectors." By the early eighteenth century they had become a running joke. But as well as the longitude, the sea presented other issues demanding explanation, including the phenomena of the tides. Alongside these issues, moreover, which were predominantly mathematical and physical, it also posed a set of *chemical* questions. Those questions concerned the origin, composition, and possible utility of seawater.

The motives underpinning such questions were obvious. In an age when military, mercantile, and political power increasingly depended on mastery of the oceans, the problem of provisioning long-distance voyages was scarcely less pressing than that of navigating them. An East Indiaman had to carry a heavy cargo of water just to keep its crew alive. This drastically reduced the amount of cargo, passengers, or weaponry that the vessel could carry. And freshwater tended not to stay fresh for long, so vessels had to put in to shore fairly frequently, which created its own geopolitical demands. Needless to say, a method of desalinating seawater, could it be attained, would eliminate these problems at a stroke. It would give a maritime nation unprecedented ability to project military and commercial power over long distances. "Solving" seawater was potentially as important as solving longitude.

Attempts to tackle the seawater problem dated back at least to the beginning of the century. The ingenious Cornelius Drebbel had advanced one such device in Jacobean times, and his daughter, Catharina Kuffler, tried to interest Boyle and the Royal Society in it in 1663. They seem not to have been receptive, although Balthasar de Monconys reported that the Duke of York (the future James II, who commanded the Restoration navy) had bought Drebbel's secret.[35] Within the Society itself, conversations continued on and off for years on the subject, and Boyle published his own tract on the saltiness of the sea. As a member of the Court of Committees for the East India Company—the managing body of that hugely important corporation—and a participant in the government's Council for Foreign Plantations, Boyle had a personal stake in any technique that could be got to work. He adduced much testimony from sailors to argue that seawater's brackish quality derived from conventional salt, which meant, he reckoned, that it should be possible to make potable water by distilling brine. Boyle proceeded to try experiments, to little obvious effect.[36]

Shortly after Boyle's work on seawater appeared, however, one William Walcot obtained a patent on just such a technique. Walcot was in a sense the Richard Atkyns of the chemical world. He was another ex-cavalier down on his luck and scouting around for a way to make a fortune by staking an audacious and opportunistic claim to a potentially invaluable craft. He had been a page to Charles I, or so he claimed, and had reputedly accompanied the unhappy king on the scaffold, which was a handy if implausible legend to propagate. He had subsequently trained in the law, before suddenly emerging to claim his patent on what he called a desalination machine. The exact nature and origin of this machine are as obscure as Walcot himself; it was not yet necessary to file a detailed description of an invention to get a patent on it, and Walcot probably did not do so. In fact, there seems to be no surviving record of the patent itself, although no one then expressed any doubt that it existed. (At the time, many legal and archival documents enjoyed this kind of existence-by-consensus.) All that can be said with confidence is that his invention was some kind of device for purifying "corrupted" water, probably by distillation. Walcot sought an act of Parliament too to buttress his claim, and boasted the public endorsement of the royal shipbuilder at Deptford. Everything seemed set for him to begin producing his machine in quantity, and reap a windfall.

Yet years passed, and nothing substantial came from Walcot. After his initial fanfare he lapsed into obscurity. In 1683, he found himself cast rudely aside. One Robert Fitzgerald had pointed out to Whitehall that Walcot had done nothing to exploit his monopoly, and demanded to supplant him. Fitzgerald was a nephew of none other than Robert Boyle. He had a rival process, he claimed, which he heavily hinted had been invented by Boyle himself. Fitzgerald's machine apparently cost £18, was less than two feet across, and could produce ninety gallons of water per day, safely and without the oversight of a skilled chymist. Both the treasurer of the Navy and the leading members of the College of Physicians backed it, as did Boyle. Boyle actually conducted demonstrations of the device before the king, using tests he had proposed in his earlier book to show the purity of the water it produced. Walcot tried to protest, but he was completely outgunned. His patent was abruptly abrogated. As compensation the Privy Council granted him only a one-sixth share of Fitzgerald's profits. At once Fitzgerald and his partners published pamphlets announcing their own patented "invention" and appealing for ships' masters to come to a coffeehouse in Birchin Lane to discuss terms for using it.[37] These tracts reappeared in several forms and various languages. Notices also ran in the official *London Gazette*.

But Walcot did not give up. He now began a slow-boiling feud with Fitzgerald that lasted for at least another two decades. It displayed many of the traits that were characteristic of such disputes at the time, when patents could be awarded for other criteria than priority. Walcot thus continued to insist not just that he was "the *first* and *true Inventor*" of the technique, but, more saliently, that he was the only person with the skill actually to make such a machine *work*. He portrayed Fitzgerald and his camp not merely as latecomers, but as corrupt. He charged that they had no real device at all, but were deploying their patronage connections—by which he meant Boyle—to obtain a patent solely in hopes of extorting Walcot's own secret from him. Their real aim, he complained, was to force him "to make a Discovery to them of the Secrets of his Art"—or, failing that, to "Entice his Workmen or Servants from his, to their Service." And others were following suit, seeing their opportunity to set up as "Pretenders" to the invention. Every time such a projector failed for want of skill,

Walcot complained, his own credit was further damaged. All the while, a potentially vital invention lay idle.[38] In each article, this complaint was typical of patentees' charges at the time.

Walcot, Fitzgerald, and Boyle all tried to create and retain "secrets" in the ensuing contest. As they did so, they mapped out the range of strategies that could be adopted to try to enclose technical knowledge in this period, exactly as the Royal Society was seeking to extend its own authority into such matters. Walcot, first, started out by claiming that a special ingredient was added to the water in his device to remove a bad taste that otherwise remained after distillation. As the early eighteenth-century chemist Stephen Hales, who got his information from Hans Sloane, put it, "he kept it a great secret," but Hales heard that it was "some Preparation of Antimony by Fire." Yet Walcot eventually reversed course. In the later stages of the struggle his camp even claimed that a principal virtue of his approach was that it did *not* use such a substance, the lack of proprietary ingredients being a virtue in terms of public utility.[39] Walcot's chymical secret thus melted away as part of a claim about public utility as a requirement for patentability.

By sharp contrast, what Boyle tried to protect only *became* a secret in this struggle. It had previously been openly avowed, and indeed published in print. Much earlier, Boyle had developed a technique for using a solution of silver in aqua fortis (in modern terms, silver nitrate solution) to detect trace amounts of dissolved salt in water. He had published this technique as long before as 1663.[40] But now he suddenly came to account it "a great Secret"—a phrase that seems to have borne some of the connotations that it had in those steady sellers of the book trade, books of secrets.[41] Boyle discoursed of what he now called his "*arcanum*" at the Royal Society, and deposited a sample of it to be kept sealed along with a written description of its use in the register. The sealed deposit was retained, and opened and published only after his death. The registration system thus worked. In fact, Hales believed that this newly achieved secrecy had doomed Walcot's invention. But it perhaps worked too well, because Hales also thought it had imperiled Fitzgerald's. It had denied both of them a way of *demonstrating* that their waters were free of spirit of salt.[42] Certainly, the assaying of substances—the determination of their identity, composition, and medical effects—was a problem for all parties (and a major concern more generally in a context of adulteration, as chapter 5 will show). Although both Fitzgerald and Walcot demonstrated their machines before powerful audiences, including the king, they needed some way to certify the water they produced to those audiences. It was because this problem of authentication loomed so large that Boyle's secret suddenly became so valuable. At any rate, it was evidently possible for something to become a secret long after being published, and without a state restriction being imposed, by being inserted into a secret-registering system like that of the virtuosi.

Meanwhile, Fitzgerald adopted a third tack. Like Walcot, he made cryptic references to "Cements" that had to be used in his machine. What these cements actually were is again unclear—Hales suspected they performed no function at all. But they certainly existed, for Sloane saw them and described them as resembling common brick clay.[43] As a nonmember of the Royal Society, however, Fitzgerald had no recourse to its system of registration. He could not do as Boyle had done. Instead, he put the recipes for his cements in a silver box, added a testimonial handwritten by Boyle, closed it with the king's seal, and lodged the secret with the lord mayor of London. It proved a poor choice, in the absence of a regular protocol like the Society's. Or perhaps it was an all too effective one. For the box vanished altogether. Nobody has seen it since.

These three approaches, alike in some ways yet distinct in their designs and very different in their outcomes, show how mutable the criteria for victory could be in debates about technical authorship. Finding himself stymied, Walcot went abroad. He approached the other great commercial power of the day, and England's major nautical rival: the Netherlands. Here he found more success. Competitive demonstrations of his and Fitzgerald's machines took place before the Dutch authorities, and Walcot's emerged the winner. He persuaded the Dutch that he was "the True Inventor," and that Fitzgerald could do no more than "any Ordinary Distiller." Walcot consequently obtained patents from the States General, the State of Zeeland, and the State of Holland—the last of which, interestingly, explicitly cautioned against "the allowing of Two Grants for one and the same Invention," saying that it would be "a thing contrary to the General Custom of Nations, and would hinder the Practice of Art."[44] Armed with these rights, Walcot felt secure enough to return to England in the wake of the Dutch invasion in 1688. He hoped that a transformed political scene would benefit him, all the more so after Boyle died in 1691. At length Walcot did manage to get a private bill passed through Parliament. In 1695 he finally regained an exclusive right to the art for another thirty-one years.[45]

It did him little good. His machine never seems to have worked very well, and in all probability—it is hard to be certain—no East Indiaman ever carried one in earnest. Projectors continued to propose devices to make seawater drinkable well into the eighteenth century, gaining nothing more than a reputation akin to that of the longitude men for their pains. Still, we should not let hindsight blind us to the point that any one of these machines *might* have proved viable. There was no reason at the time to doubt the possibility, especially with the greatest experimental philosopher of the age supporting one of them. The balance of plausibility was with the patentees. As they imagined vast wealth flowing to them, the Crown hoped for an unrivaled deepwater presence—and the Royal Society dreamed of remodeling the regime of invention in its image.

THE SCIENCE OF SALTS

In testing water-freshening machines, one set of questions loomed large. They meshed issues of knowledge and practice with those of life and nature. How could you tell if you had a "pure" sample of water? How could you decide if the sample were safe to drink? And what *was* drinkable water, anyway? After all, taste only told a drinker so much (and pure water, if it could have been obtained, would presumably have tasted rather nasty). Besides, the latest opinions of physicians and philosophers implied that pure water might well not be the desideratum in any case. Distilled water might lack some dissolved or suspended substance that was vital for health. There was even a plausible candidate for such a substance: the so-called aerial nitre, originally described by Paracelsus, which physicians and naturalists widely deemed responsible for both combustion and respiration. Hooke had developed theories of the aerial nitre in his *Micrographia*, while at Oxford the anatomist Thomas Willis had made it a central part of his project to understand the physiological processes of life. Truly pure water would have been denuded of this substance, and thus would be bad for you. At best, it would do you no good.[46]

The identity of such an everyday substance as water thus became a problem of critical importance for medicine as well as natural philosophy. Boyle worried about it consistently, from both perspectives. It lent the seawater purification debate an added complexity, for it meant that contests of authorship, priority, and property led ineluctably into questions of knowledge of nature itself. But to manage this kind of transition was surely why the Society existed. So could not the virtuosi stake a claim to authority here?

For some at the Society, at least, the problem of water's identity resolved itself into one of the identity of the person vouching for the water. This was a standard move in experimental philosophy, since it tied the credibility of claims to the evident moral authority of the person making them, much as Atkyns appealed to the gentility of his model patentee. Nehemiah Grew, the Society's curator of botanical experiments, took this tack. At the height of the dispute Grew published his own tract of experiments supporting the Fitzgerald camp. To him, the machine should be credited because to vouch for it "we have the Reputation of the Gentlemen who have your Majesties *Patent* for it." At the same time, he suggested that his own experiments should be believed because of his disinterest: "I have no share either in the Profit of it, or in the Credit of the Experiment."[47]

Robert Boyle's name was the most powerful of all to conjure with in this kind of rhetoric. Even decades after Boyle's death, Hales could be heard insisting that "it is not to be suspected that so worthy and good a Man as Mr. *Boyle* was, would impose a Falshood on the World." This last was a particularly interesting declaration, in fact, because according to Hales's own natural philosophy Boyle's testimony about the distillation machine could not be true at all. Fitzgerald's machine could not possibly have worked. Hales therefore struggled to reconcile his own science with Boyle's affirmation that it *did* work. He suggested that Fitzgerald must have distilled water that had already putrefied—a process that, he noted with relief, might indeed have produced drinkable water (he did not say how). Boyle had simply not noticed that his nephew had used an unrepresentative and corrupt sample. Even decades after his death, Boyle's renown for technical competence was apparently a minor loss compared to the need to preserve his good name.[48]

Boyle's testimony counted immensely in the battle itself. It encouraged other Society stalwarts to weigh in, and justified the fellows spending time and energy on further trials. Grew in particular claimed that his experiments at the Society established the purity of the water Fitzgerald's machine produced. The only thing that the water did retain, he argued, was, happily enough, the aerial nitre. But to say this was implicitly to raise that series of further questions about the constitution of drinking water. And it was also to ask what the properties were of the substances that the machine removed. This made the problem of desalinating seawater essentially the same as that involved in analyzing the most popular dietetic and medicinal compounds of the era: spa waters.

The medicinal properties of spa waters were a major topic of inquiry for early modern investigators. They were thought to arise from dissolved "salts," and projectors of desalination machines like Walcot and Fitzgerald sometimes claimed that salt production would be a major ancillary benefit of their own inventions. In Paris, the Academy of Sciences mounted a systematic examination of spas from across France, and this helped spur English efforts. Grew himself presented discourses on spa salts at the Society, while Croune affirmed the properties of the water at Epsom, currently London's most fashionable resort. Sir Theodore de Vaux reported a well at Acton that furnished water two or three times as rich in salt as Epsom's. Perhaps its power could be explained by the nitrous salt observable on the ground around the well itself, he suggested.[49] At the Society, questions about seawater therefore found a ready reception partly because they coalesced with inquiries into the virtues of these other waters and their salts. What resulted was a rich set of investigations extending over decades and involving a vast range of physical, chymical, and medical issues. Some of these issues remained rather tacit in the Society's public representation of its activities, because they fell into the province of chymistry, or even into that of alchemy.[50] But they certainly arose for those closely involved. While modern historians have understandably been captivated by the place of mechanics in the experimental philosophy of the 1680s, it would not be inaccurate to say that the investigation of salts was a more sustained, and in the short term more promising, enterprise.

This work took inspiration not only from the seawater investigations, but also from the original Boylean program. That program had focused on the properties of the air. The most prominent experiments of the Society's first decade had been those performed with the air pump invented by Hooke for Boyle. The air-pump experiments, as is now well known, displayed not only a corpuscularian view of nature, but a way of arriving at natural knowledge that Boyle and his colleagues wished to promote.[51] Now, moving on from those initial sequences, the Society asked questions about variations in the "spring" or pressure of the atmosphere. In particular, the fellows wanted to know what caused such variations. One hypothesis, which Hooke fostered, was that the cause of changes might be substances dissolved in the air, "much after the same manner as water dissolves salt." This led to a general project on the chemistry of mixtures, for which Grew published another long set of experiments. He took Hooke's suggestion further, to argue that the pressure of the air was *in fact* dependent on dissolved salts.[52] Christopher Wren added that perhaps the salts were nitrous, and "impregnat[ed]" the air. If so, that would handily link the spring of the air to the aerial nitre. Boyle was more cautious, suggesting that aerial nitre was only one of a large number of aerial salts.[53] At any rate, the idea of dissolved "salts" became, for a time, common ground between medicine, experimental philosophy, and, because of both spas and seawater, public affairs.

A duel over inventive priority therefore led by this route to a project for new natural philosophy. Grew set it forth in a Society discourse of late 1674. He now argued that "the whole *Business* of the *Material World*, is nothing else, but *Mixture.*" He likened the compositions of *"Atomes,* in *Bodies"* to the arrangements of letters in words, and discussed how to read nature's "alphabet." Experimenters should inaugurate an ambitious program of initiating their own kinds of mixture, he recommended. Salts were central to this program. Like Daniel Coxe, a fellow physician, Grew thought that many bodies contained a *"Saline Principle"* that could provide the key to the core processes of life and nature: solution, agitation, fermentation, putrefaction, and digestion. For instance, he suggested that the salt in seawater originated in rotting animal and vegetable bodies, salt from which was carried downstream in rivers.[54] The proposal had a practical, if visionary, point. Grew forecast that experimenters armed with the knowledge his project would provide might eventually make *"Artificial Bodies* in Imitation of those of *Natures* own production." They could manufacture artificial smells and tastes, for example. If they could capture the saltlike nitre from the air, then they could also use it to *"refrigerate Rooms"* artificially. And above all, they could make medicines artificially— and these would be trustworthy drugs, freed from the natural and human vagaries of spas and apothecaries.[55] Here, finally, was a commercial possibility as great as that offered by seawater. Its founding knowledge and civility alike were to be those of the Society's experimental enterprise.

In this way did a program of experimental investigation inspired partly by a practical attempt to reduce seawater return to the same subject again, after passing through some of the most elemental questions facing seventeenth-century philosophers and physicians. This was how experimental philosophy was supposed to work—by the incorporation of such duels into a regime of reading, registration, and circulation. But by virtue of moving between the Society and other settings where invention and discovery might be adjudicated—the royal court, the naval shipyards, London's coffeehouses—the conflict over the salts of Walcot, Fitzgerald, Boyle, and Grew would end up catalyzing a major change. It would not, however, be a realization of the ambition of the Royal Society to extend its civility over arts and manufactures. That project was never to succeed. Instead they would lead to a transformation in the commerce of medicine. They would inaugurate the age of pharmaceutical patenting.

5

Pharmaceutical Piracy and the Origins of Medical Patenting

The pirating of books causes anger, uncertainty, and disquiet. But it does not generally produce real fear. There are other kinds of piracy that do. Before the industrial age, such fear was an everyday part of life. The question of credit in manufactured words—the question that catalyzed the coining of the term *piracy*—was really only one aspect of a much broader anxiety about credit in manufactured things. People worried particularly about the kinds of things that they took into their bodies: foods, wines, and medicaments. Grocers who bulked up food with flour or vintners who adulterated wine were jailed or locked in the stocks by their peers for public humiliation.[1] But it was medicaments that aroused particular concern. Anxiety about adulterated or forged medicines was endemic and well founded. In focusing on salts—which were key medicinal substances— the Royal Society was therefore venturing into one of the most contentious and consequential areas of early modern life. This chapter considers why that anxiety about medicines arose, and what was done to address it. Its topic is a phenomenon that came to be called *pharmaceutical piracy*—its nature, the countermeasures it inspired, and the legacies of both.

There are urgent twenty-first-century reasons, as well as historical ones, for focusing on medicine at this point. Angry feuds over property and piracy permeate today's culture, but they flare up with especial frequency and passion in the field of biomedicine. The pharmaceutical industry decries attempts to reduce the reach of its patents, while its critics assert that those very patents often represent an "intellectual land grab." At the same time, counterfeit pharmaceuticals circulate with dismaying ease in the developing world, and increasingly find their way into the developed world too. Globalization and the proliferation of online pharmacies have facilitated their dispersal. The World Health Organization's IMPACT initiative has both documented the mortal dangers they pose and revealed the practical and political difficulties of policing pharmaceuticals. The issue such bodies confront is an old one resurrected in a late modern context. Understanding that this is so ought to change not just where we think our current difficulties come from, but what we think they really are.

Contemporaries of Newton and Hooke saw the issue of counterfeit drugs in their own day as one of deadly seriousness, and as related in essential ways to the problematic constitution of a commercial society. Practitioners of all kinds—to say nothing of their patients—confronted real crises of authenticity in medicines, and worked hard to address them. The methods they recommended had much in common with techniques that we have already seen being developed in the realms of print and natural philosophy, and reflected contemporary understandings of commerce and interest. But for laypeople they were much more immediately important. False books could lead you astray, and illegitimate patents could ruin you, but fake medicines could kill you. Partly for that reason, the struggle for authenticity could never be declared won. When today's authorities warn of the dangers of counterfeit and pirated drugs, they are ringing alarms that were sounded in Newton's day. A response, then as now, required addressing the very nature of the commercial world.

Both books and medicines emerged from artisanal crafts organized in broadly similar ways, with apprenticeship systems, ritual calendars, inspection regimes, and the like. Early moderns were therefore quite accustomed to thinking of the problems they posed in parallel. Apothecaries and authors were often portrayed as broadly similar.[2] But in reality the relation was even closer than that. Medicines and books—or, more specifically, newspapers—shared some of the same physical spaces. Bookshops often sold medicines. Printers secured their livelihoods by advertising medicines, and many ran workshops to prepare them. In eighteenth-century England, the printer John Newbery marketed an elixir of his own, the principal ingredient of which seems to have been boiled dog. His counterpart William Rayner's newspapers depended on advertisements for a "pectoral tincture" that could be purchased from his own house. Rayner created what he called an "Elixir Warehouse" near St. George's Church in Southwark, whence he sold what he claimed to be Dr. Stoughton's elixir (but could this notorious press pirate be relied upon to hawk the real thing?). Other printers—in Dublin, for example—maintained their own rival elixir warehouses. This kind of alliance could be found in many cities across Europe, and, as the century wore on, in America too. Physicians told each other that if they want to market a new drug then they ought to go to the booksellers to do it.[3] It all meant that the connection between credit in medicine and in print was not just figurative. The conjunction of media and medica, as it were, was mundane and practical. And when the authenticity of medicines was called into question, the same people and the same places were implicated as those involved in issues of print piracy. It was from this conjunction that pharmaceutical patenting emerged. It did so partly as a mechanism to secure not property, but authenticity.

THE PIRACY OF WORDS AND THINGS

As the seventeenth century drew to a close, Nehemiah Grew should have been a happy and wealthy man. A past secretary of the Royal Society, the compiler of the printed catalogue of its repository, and the author in his own right of a pioneering series of researches in natural history, Grew was a successful physician and a respected naturalist. He owed his elevated position largely to the Society's patronage. But as 1700 approached, all this success was suddenly put at risk. Grew had become a victim of piracy.[4]

Grew's misfortune was representative in many ways of the perils that faced any author in the period: one of his printed works was appropriated by an entrepreneurial rival, who translated it, reprinted it, and published it in such a way as to transform its meaning and quite possibly damage Grew's own name. Equally typical was the fact that both he and his antagonist claimed that their version was the true work. Each labored hard —digging through old papers, reviving long-dormant rumors, spying, threatening, and blustering—to bolster his case. All this was just the kind of tiresome experience that happened all the time to learned authors. Grew even had an advantage over most, in that he had access to the Royal Society's register system. Yet like Walcot and Fitzgerald he also had a major disadvantage. His quarrel, like theirs, did not begin with print, and its ramifications did not end at the bounds of the experimental community. The Society's register alone therefore could not grant him victory. And in this his experience was more than atypical. It was prophetic.

At the center of this conflict stood what was quite possibly the first patent on a manufactured pharmaceutical in the English-speaking world. It was, then, a *substance* that was the real prize at stake. Grew's enemies pirated this substance—a salt produced from spa waters bubbling up in the outskirts of London—before they pirated his book, and the latter piracy took place in the service of the former. As a result, the struggle escalated rapidly, calling into question many kinds of identity at once: Grew's professional identity as a physician, the integrity of medical practice more generally, and even the identity of substances—minerals and medicines, salts and waters, and atoms and powers. Moreover, Grew's preparation had been endorsed publicly by both the Royal Society and the Royal College of Physicians. When it was challenged, that challenge therefore implicated the judgment of Augustan London's elite naturalist and medical communities. The counterfeiters, as Grew's camp called them, not only painted Grew himself as "the Author of a Cheat," but charged the Society and the College with endorsing that cheat.[5] In other words, this became the test case for a would-be alliance of learned print, medicine, and experimental science.

Grew had sought to exploit the roaring fashion for spa waters. That such waters bore therapeutic properties had been known in antiquity, and the Renaissance had seen a flourishing of interest in them. One physician remarked that "Mineral Waters seem one of the greatest as well as the most useful Branches of the *Materia Medica*." But these waters presented embarrassingly knotty problems for physicians keen to display their expertise in nature's causative processes. Their powers, it was thought, derived from salts dissolved as water seeped through the earth. On this account, the properties of a particular water derived from the peculiar combination of subterranean minerals it had absorbed in coming to the surface. Spas therefore exemplified the conviction, forcefully presented by apothecaries and Paracelsians, that mineral medicaments were not only effective, but *local*. Generalized causal explanations were of little use in accounting for them. It was even possible that subterranean mineral conditions might vary so much as to preclude *any* general "knowledge" in this field. At a time when "new" philosophies were everywhere proclaiming the overthrow of Aristotelian and Galenic orthodoxies, waters and their salts therefore stood out as highly visible challenges to traditional medical and philosophical authority.[6] Chymical physicians lamented how little was known of the salts. They recommended evaporating away the water and examining the remaining crystals. Some also proposed using art to reproduce such salts artificially, such as the variety emanating from the spring at Epsom, a village west of London.[7] By the mid-seventeenth century this kind of question was being addressed keenly by both medical and natural philosophers. And the man asked by the Royal Society to explicate spa waters experimentally was, of course, Grew.

Grew's experiments originated amid the long and bitter arguments over desalination machines outlined in the preceding chapter. But his investigations extended far more widely and deeply, to include ideas about the air, the body, and the maintenance of life and health. Having worked in Leyden under the celebrated Paracelsian Franciscus Sylvius, he was well acquainted with the arguments for chymical medicine, and he drew implicitly on these in broadening the ambit of his trials.[8] When he moved to exploit Epsom's water for himself, he thus knew very well what he was doing. His technique was essentially another bid to mechanize the separation of salt and water. But unlike Fitzgerald and Walcot he focused on the salt, not the water; and his market was on land, not at sea.

Epsom's spa had become a favorite destination for Londoners since its discovery in about 1630. The water there had a good but gentle purgative property. Drinking it was supposed to help rid the body of impurities and restore one's humors to balance, thus alleviating a large number of conditions. Perhaps two thousand people, Grew estimated, had gone to the village to drink the water by the time he launched his own enterprise; and nobody knew how many more had bought bottles of it in the city from apothecaries. It was this metropolitan market—and in particular its vulnerability to fraud—that gave him his opportunity. A customer trying to buy Epsom water in London ran two major hazards. One was the tendency of such water to spoil if stored; it would "corrupt and stink" if kept for more than a few days. The other was that the authenticity of the water itself was hard to guarantee. Spring water varied in strength naturally as it emerged from the ground, but the bigger problem was a social one. Apothecaries were known to adulterate their products, either by dilution (to make a scarce supply last longer) or by the addition of new ingredients, or both. The mediation of the apothecary between spa and patient, Grew believed—and this was a standard physician's view—therefore created an intractable problem of credit. Grew realized that he could address that problem experimentally. By converting a social issue into a chymical one, he could also convert it into an opportunity to make a fortune.

Grew proposed to extract the "bitter purging salt" that was the active constituent of Epsom water. This salt could then be stored and distributed safely. He would monopolize its production by using a secret process carried out only by his own trusted operators. All a user need do would be to dissolve it in freshwater to reproduce the original effect. In the early 1690s Grew thus established his own laboratory—not at Epsom itself, but at Acton, another village near London that boasted a spa producing water even better, as he had learned from discourse at the Royal Society, than Epsom's. There he employed a trusted operator named Thomas Tramel to produce the salt in quantity. He used newspaper advertisements to advertise that apothecaries could get the genuine article wholesale from Tramel at an address in St. Paul's Churchyard, the traditional booksellers' quarter. And he affirmed that his salt was even better than the original water. It contained no impurities, did not spoil over time, and could be easily transported and used. Above all, it was innocent of adulteration. "Some who sell these *Waters*," he warned, "when they find their Store begins to fail, will venture to adulterate them with *common Water*." The salt, by contrast, was "always alike." This property of always-alikeness was critical to his plan. It was an ideal of early modern medicaments that they should be so predictable, but one that could almost never be assured. Grew had seen a way to make the salt secure, and safe to use as part of a physician's bill.[9] Thanks partly to such assurances, a market arose that endured long after Grew himself vanished from the scene. We still use his substance today, and we call it "Epsom salt."

To support this venture, Grew wrote his own treatise on the salt and its use.[10] It was the only Latin work that Grew—who was a prolific author—ever published. It detailed his initial experiments at the Royal Society some fifteen years earlier to identify the substance, then indicated its proper use in a range of medical circumstances. This second section in particular was quite carefully composed, being specific, detailed, and extensive. It was intended explicitly to distinguish Grew from a quack or mountebank (as physicians tended to label all irregulars) who might claim some "new-invented *All-heal*." Yet for all its detail, Grew pointed out that he nowhere furnished "an entire *Method of Cure*" for any one condition. A reader could not administer the salt by simply following his examples like recipes. This was quite deliberate. The tract was intended for the use "not of *young Beginners,* but *experienced Physicians.*" Physicians would read it in a certain way: they would know how to fill in its gaps, taking it as offering words to the wise rather than a set of recipes. And in this, Grew claimed, he was living up to the ideals of both the College of Physicians and the Royal Society. His dedication to both institutions claimed as much in a carefully poised display. Neither body claimed any kind of "*Monopoly,*" he maintained; but they did "justly claim the *Custody* [respectively] of *Natural Knowledg,* and of the *Health of Mankind.*"[11] Grew too was affirming an ideal of custodianship, deploying silence to mark the bounds.

As with print, so with medicines: London did not lack for apothecaries prepared to issue their own proclaimed versions of a successful product. Two brothers named Francis and George Moult came forward to compete with Grew. They were by no means unknowns. George Moult was a fellow of the Royal Society, having first been proposed as its operator back in 1685.[12] And in the background to their venture lay a tangled story of ambition and rivalry. At first, apparently, George had agreed to buy Grew's salt legitimately. But Francis had sought to steal a march on George by securing a cheaper price for himself. Grew had refused, at which point Francis decided to make his own salt by "prying into Dr. *Grew's* Method." He went to Acton, observed Tramel's works, and tried to bribe Tramel into breaking his agreement with Grew. When this too failed, he set up his own illicit plant in Shooter's Hill, a demimonde and semirural district southeast of Greenwich, with a retail and wholesale outlet to the east of St. Paul's in Watling Street. He was soon joined by a reconciled George. Their operation quickly ramped up. It became capable of producing enough salt to swamp the market in Ireland and Scotland as well as in England. There was evidently a distribution network for "counterfeit" salts that extended at least that far.

The Moults simply ignored any right that Grew might have as a result of his priority. Legally speaking, after all, no such right existed. But the real question soon became one of chemistry, not law or even morality. How did a customer know if their rival salt was in fact the same as Grew's? For Grew himself reacted by mounting a seemingly self-contradictory argument: that the Moults not merely counterfeited his salt, but produced something that was actually different. Not only did they "invade his Right," Grew said, but in doing so they "falsif[ied] the Medicine." Indeed, in some ways Grew thought them more worrisome if their salt did *not*

89

match his original, since who knew what awful side effects it might then produce? His salt would surely get the blame for them. "Counterfeit Salts," his camp said, put at risk both the propriety of medicine and its political economy—not to mention the health of patients. The contest for authorship thus became a contest for the identity of the substance. Unfortunately for Grew, though, identifying a substance was not easy for anyone to do, let alone a patient. He was left proclaiming that the true salt could be clearly distinguished from "counterfeits" by its bitter taste. That is, you had to *take some*. At that point, your own body became an instrument of piracy detection. The "Authors of any Counterfeits" detected in this way would be prosecuted, Grew thundered. We do not know if any were.[13]

At the same time, the clash also cast doubt on Grew's books, and on his own identity as an author. Francis Moult sought out a copy of Grew's Latin treatise, had it translated into English, and "prefixed such a Title to it, as might induce the Reader, to take it for the Dr's own doing." Then, "that he might the better get the Trade entirely into his own Hands," he printed off 1,500 copies and distributed them gratis to customers who bought his version of the salt. What had originated as a learned Latin treatise for physicians had now become an advertisement for an empiric —and, worse still, an instruction manual likely to be believed and put to use by lay readers. As Moult explained in a preface that he quietly added to Grew's original, medicines very often attained popularity through being introduced with "printed Directions" and "Certificates" of cures. Grew's work served this purpose admirably. He justified appropriating the discourse by claiming that its learning would forestall potentially dangerous misuses of the drug. His was therefore an act of social responsibility.

Grew was horrified by all this. To his eyes, not only was the translation an unauthorized usurpation, insolent and dangerous. It was also full of errors and omissions. For example, it lacked the original's licenses from the College of Physicians and the Royal Society, and it omitted Grew's politic dedication to those two authorities. Not least, that dedication had staked Grew's own claim to priority, pinning it to the Society's record of his experiments at the time of the seawater controversy. Moult's version of the medical receipts also contained a multitude of errors—errors that a lay reader would follow unwittingly, quite possibly killing children. Josiah Peter, a friend and fellow physician, even threatened Moult with a lawsuit not only for "the Wrong he had done the Author" but also for physically endangering the king's subjects. In all, Grew's camp denounced the translation as a "scurvy Libel." It seemed, mused one ex-president of the Royal Society (perhaps Christopher Wren), that "this Shop-Chymist" was "both grossly ignorant, and of an ill Mind." A response was essential to "vindicate the Honour" of the author himself, but also to restore that of the College and the Society. Otherwise readers were likely to conclude that both were "unfit to write or authorize a Book of this nature." Grew even went on to claim that readers might come to distrust *all* such books. They might "suppose there is little Sincerity or solid Truth in any Books of this kind," he warned, "but that Philosophy and Physick themselves are a mere Jingle." In the context of a piratical trade this apparently extreme proposition made a certain sense. And this being so, Grew announced it his duty to rap the knuckles of "this Interloper" so as to forestall such a possibility.[14]

And so he did. Grew issued an authorized version of his treatise, translated by another physician named Joseph Bridges and with new testimonials by Peter. It made clear that the experiments it retailed were "entirely" Grew's own. Of the therapeutic receipts of the second part, it remarked likewise that "it's easy to observe his Property too, in many of these." Even the Archbishop of Canterbury had apparently approved Grew's "very useful Discovery."[15] Bridges took care to restate Grew's caution to readers to consult a physician before using the salt, and drove the point home by reciting at length the "Egregious FALSIFICATIONS" to be found in Moult's version. For example, the spurious version apparently recommended under- and overdoses (physicians of the time often complained that apothecaries confused the numbers sixteen, sixty, and six hundred). And at some points Moult had *failed* to change the original where he should have: Grew had not stated a specific dosage of opiates for cholera, for example, but Moult, "speaking to *all in common,*" should have been explicit. These errors could well do serious harm, Grew and Bridges claimed, because of the tendency of readers to trust printed sources. "Many English Readers take every thing they find in a *pretending Book,* to be *Gospel;* and will swallow any thing, tho it be a *Glyster* [i.e., an enema or suppository] if they are *bid,* or *think they are bid,* to do it."[16] The Moults, Bridges concluded, were akin to currency counterfeiters—no casual remark at a time when such operators were undermining the coinage itself, and when Isaac Newton, as warden of the mint, was hunting them down and sending them to the gallows.

At that, the Moults adopted a new tactic. Accused of both literary and pharmaceutical counterfeiting, they launched into the newspaper press once again, this time to drive home a newly personal attack on Grew himself as a counterfeiter. They reached back in time to charge that he had plagiarized the renowned Italian naturalist Marcello Malpighi in his original natural history work at the Royal Society—work on which his reputation as a naturalist largely rested, in which his knowledge of salts originated, and to which he had appealed in his treatise. It seems that they picked up on old rumors that had circulated in the 1670s. Certainly, Grew had been concerned enough back then to detail painstakingly the differences between their works, and to outline a chronology so that his publishing after Malpighi became a conscious act of civility, not an effort to upstage him. The Moults ignored this and revived the old stories as if they were widely accepted. They even embellished them. Their claim now was that Grew had actually gone to Padua in person, attended the printing house, and "stole[n] it Sheet by Sheet as it came from the Press." It was a standard Stationer's story, here put to newly damaging use. Clearly, this Grew was a literary as well as pharmaceutical opportunist. And the public should infer that it was Grew's own salt that was "False and Counterfeit."

At this point, of course, a reader could have been forgiven for throwing up her hands in despair. How to decide which, if either, of the English books was authentic? Neither was quite the original, after all. If Grew had absconded with knowledge from Malpighi's printing house, moreover, was the original *Anatomy of Plants* his book? For that matter, was Malpighi's fully *his?* Nor could a patient be sure which was the true salt. Even the language both sides used spanned pharmaceutical and print worlds. Just as he stood accused of violating the printer's chapel, so Grew charged Moult with infiltrating his own chymical workshop and attempting to bribe artisans in a bid to "counterfeit" his creation. The language of falsification and invasion of right was the same in both fields. So was the talk of surreptitious access to workshops. It became difficult to tell whether Grew and Peter were thinking of press piracy or drugs when they condemned "counterfeits." And the state of affairs soon became even more confusing, because Bridges's text reappeared in yet another printing, anonymously produced and utterly shorn of its attacks on the Moults. The brothers had presumably seized upon it in the same way they had Grew's original tract, reprinted it, and were brazenly reusing it as advertising for their latest batch of salt. Peter ruefully noted that even physicians and apothecaries were starting to conclude that *all* claims to manufacture Epsom salt, "not only by Pseudo-Chymists, but by Dr. *Grew*'s own Direction," were fraudulent.[17]

Only now did Grew call royal authority to his aid. He finally sought a patent—not on the salt itself, but on his technique for producing it. He got his grant, in 1698, and immediately circulated a letter to the physicians of the city denouncing Moult. It was not the first privilege on a medical device or substance, to be sure—a few earlier patents had been obtained on therapeutic beds and the like, and on the Continent certain medically useful substances like guaiac had been subjected to trade monopolies. But it does seem to have been the first on a medicine *as an invention*. Yet the patent was a response—a tactic, and a desperate one at that. And it did Grew little good. The delay in getting it meant that, as far as the Moults were concerned, he was attempting to use royal power to suppress a craft already in being—that old complaint, explicitly proscribed by the Monopolies Act and earlier leveled by the booksellers against Atkyns. They redoubled their defiance. The lord chancellor found their advertisements "Sawcy," and the secretary of state stepped in to suppress them. But the despairing Grew was at the end of his tether. He entered into desultory peace negotiations, even offering to hand over his patent "for Peace sake, and the better suppressing of Counterfeits." They refused, and promptly seized the opportunity to give out that they were now making their salt "by Dr. *Grew*'s Direction."[18] At this point Grew gave up. He threw up his hands, signed over the patent to the resolute Peter, and retreated to his study.

TRUTH AND MALICIOUS FALSEHOOD

What Peter produced as his last bid to stop these medicinal counterfeiters is a book that is now utterly forgotten, but which deserves a place among the canonical texts in the history of what we now call intellectual property. It went by the title *Truth in opposition to ignorant and malicious falshood.* The work offered one of the first public rationales for patenting inventions in general, and *the* first for pharmaceutical patenting in particular. It did so by underlining fears of counterfeiting, and by arguing that only with security of identity could an *international* trade in medicaments be established.[19]

For Peter, pharmaceutical patents were justified and necessary for four principal reasons. First, he maintained that pharmacy in general, and Grew's work in particular, did indeed produce genuinely new inventions. To claim that, however, he found himself defending the proposition that it was possible in principle for *any* invention to be truly new. The telescope, for example, radical though it had been in Galileo's hands, used knowledge and materials familiar from spectacles. Peter conceded that virtually all inventions were "grounded upon some precedent Invention." Yet he insisted that in some cases the new device gave rise to whole new fields of knowledge or endeavor, and in such cases one could indeed speak of real creation. He cited as an example a proposition in Euclid's *Elements* that had become the basis for land surveying; this proposition had certainly rested on its predecessors, but that hardly invalidated its status as an invention with respect to the new discipline. Similarly, microscopes and telescopes had revealed a new world. And Walcot's desalination machine had essentially been a distilling engine, based on a technique introduced half a millennium earlier; because nobody had thought to apply it to seawater for such public use, Parliament had seen fit to "define, what is a new Invention." The new world it addressed was that of commercial empires. The 1624 Statute of Monopolies itself had exempted a patent in the long-practiced craft of glassmaking in order to help launch an export industry. And Peter accounted Grew's a stronger case than any of these. A few physicians might have performed isolated experiments on spa waters, but none had set up a manufacturing plant to make quantities of the stuff. That was what made Grew's an invention.[20]

Second, the salt produced under the patent was of public benefit. It was purer and safer than even the spa water itself. Its consistent, reliable nature made it preferable. By contrast, the counterfeit salt produced real public harm. Fourteen eminent London physicians had signed a statement for him that, "coming into the Hands of Quacks, Women, and all sorts of Ignorant and Adventurous People," it would surely hurt patients —a statement that possibly reflected their attitude toward unlicensed medical practitioners more than their expertise in the salt. Still, Peter cited evidence that it had caused harm, although it is difficult now to assess this testimony. His examples came from Ireland, where physicians saw in his inquiry an opportunity to assail their local rivals. The late president of Dublin's college of physicians reported that "under the Name of Your excellent Salt, many pernicious Counterfeits are sold, and a great deal of Mischief done to those who take them." He added that to some unfortunates "they have proved Mortal." Thomas Molyneux, another prominent Dublin physician, concurred. The target of such physicians was none other than the lord mayor of Dublin, one Thomas Quine, who happened to be an apothecary. Quine had apparently got Moult's salt from a druggist named Hinde, and given it to such notables as the Duchess of Ormonde. She had been made lastingly ill. A worse fate befell the bishop of Kilmore, who, a Dublin physician reported, had actually died.[21]

Third, a patent would increase the use of the substance—in essence, by accrediting it. Physicians would have no reason to condemn it as a nostrum—"that is, a secret in the way of Practice"—because "every one knows what it is, and may purchase it as any other Drug." And this was critically important, because it could be made the basis of an export trade. Merchants once fooled into shipping a suppositious salt would not risk their credit again by accepting more. By imperiling belief in the authenticity of all such preparations, Peter therefore alleged, "Counterfeit Salts made and sold by Interloping Chymists" jeopardized a potentially important contribution to Britain's political economy. If a patent could truly prevent counterfeiting, on the other hand, then it would uphold the kind of trust at a distance that was essential for an international market in a new manufacture. Not only would the patent itself protect the substance, but so would the wide dispersal that the patent underwrote. Popular familiarity would in time become the most powerful countermeasure to counterfeits, as patients came to know the taste and effects of the genuine article intimately and would be ready to recognize imitations.[22] In a generation, Peter forecast, Grew's salt could become the basis of a huge industry, comparable to that dedicated to conventional salt. He performed a simple calculation, premised on one hundred thousand pounds of salt being made annually in the London area for £10,000 profit. At present, the Moults alone made ten thousand pounds of salt, and the amounts peddled by other "chymists" might well amount to as much again (an indication, incidentally, of the large scale of these enterprises). London consumed two thousand pounds, which, using the political arithmetic of William Petty, implied a potential national consumption of twenty to thirty thousand pounds. This would leave a vast surplus, which could be exported, mainly to Britain's colonies and to the Near East, thus supporting the maritime empire of trade. Grew's salt could become a pillar of the new mercantilism. But this could only come about if "the making of Counterfeits be supprest."[23] Ultimately, the patent was a device to secure trust at a distance. Empires could be built on it.

This was Peter's major contention, but he also had to prove that Grew himself was the proper patentee. He must establish that he "and no other" had been "the Author of this Invention." This was essential because the Moults claimed that his patent impinged on an already-existing craft. The issue was delicate enough that Peter consulted the lord chancellor, Lord Somers, who told him that a patent would be valid as long as the challengers obtained their art illegitimately. Peter therefore had to ratify Grew's priority, in order to allege that he had been pirated by the Moults; the patent might fall if he had *not* been pirated. To do so he resorted to the Royal Society's register regime. Fortunately, Grew retained allies there, especially Hans Sloane. Sloane showed Peter the journal books. He was able to retrieve detailed records confirming that Grew had showed his salt in 1679, "not privately, or to Incompetent Judges, but publickly, to the Royal Society." Christopher Wren and Robert Hooke endorsed the point, and a "Cloud of Witnesses" confirmed it, including authorities from across Europe. The records affirmed Grew's originality in those experimental investigations of the 1670s and 1680s, and bolstered his authorship against the Malpighi myth. Peter thus reconstructed the whole perusal-presentation cycle out of which Grew's work had arisen. His work presaged Newton's employment of the same strategy against Leibniz a few years later.[24]

However, a rather delicate detail now emerged. It seemed that neither Grew's salt nor his original paper about it had ever in fact been registered at the Society. It looked as though he had disregarded the very rules he now wanted others to obey. The aged Hooke stepped forward in one of his last public appearances to counter such an impression. Grew must have declined to register his claim because he had wanted to improve his work in private, he suggested. He doubtless remembered that he had done this himself many times, and that by the time of Grew's work he had had no faith in the register. Still, Peter felt the need to reemphasize that the patent was not premised on Grew's priority in discovering the substance itself; it covered a manufacturing technique. Both the Society and the College of Physicians endorsed his stance, defending their reputations by upholding Grew's. And one of the first druggists to offer it wholesale testified that in 1692 Grew had given him his first parcel of the salt. Interestingly, this man recalled that he had sampled some himself before selling any—a general practice, perhaps, among druggists to guarantee their substances.[25]

Yet even Grew's supporters were uneasy about this revelation. His camp appealed to the Society's civility to justify his reticence; yet it now appeared that he himself had not honored that civility. Since counterfeits were prevalent and dangerous, some suggested, Grew should reveal the secret of his method to deny them their opportunity. If he did reveal it, he would truly "approve himself a Genuine Member of both the Royal Societies." In other words, these supporters came close to charging him with the very monopolism that the Moults alleged. Far from the Royal Society upholding Grew's innocence, it now looked like Grew's monopolism would taint the Society.[26]

Grew seems not to have taken this advice, and in practice the Moults evidently won the contest. There was no trial that we know of, and no indication that they withdrew from their venture. Indeed, a couple of decades later the Royal Society itself would remember George Moult as an honored and respectable fellow. At the advent of medical patenting, then, not only did patenting itself emerge as a tactic—as a challenge to counterfeits, not something challenged by them—but the counterfeits also won out. Claims of strong authorship in medicaments did not prevail, despite the endorsements of the Royal Society and the College of Physicians. We may properly ask, therefore, why those claims endured. The answer is implicit in the degree to which authorship and counterfeiting of pharmaceuticals were bound up with the social constitution of medicine itself. Establishing a secure regime for pharmaceuticals would require a revolution in that world.

MEDICINE IN THE BALANCE

Although the notion of "patent medicines" originated in the early modern period, there is no evidence that seeking actual patents on medicaments was a normal practice. Empirics and apothecaries preferred either to maintain confidentiality about the ingredients of their medicaments or, occasionally, to make a virtue of openness and rely instead on their craft reputation for producing a given drug more reliably, safely, and affordably than their peers. Sometimes they collected secrets and swapped them in a kind of barter marketplace—we know that Boyle did this with medical receipts.[27] New world imports seem to have been the first kinds of drugs for which actual monopoly rights were sought. The Fugger banking family got the most valuable of all, a monopoly on the transport of guaiac bark, in return for a loan to the Holy Roman Emperor.[28] In Venice, meanwhile, one Paolo di Romani obtained a patent in 1594 for a way of rendering a herbal syrup in solid form, but the city's *collegio* of apothecaries persuaded him to share the privilege among his peers.[29] In England, Grew in 1698 was quite possibly the first person to obtain a privilege for manufacturing a pharmaceutical as such. The next such patent (the first on a compound medicine) was issued in 1711, for a substance called *sal oleosum volatile*. It was soon followed by another for Stoughton's elixir, and then by many more in the eighteenth century. So it really does seem as though Grew's bid for protection marked the origin of a trend.[30] Or perhaps it more truly marked the end of one.

Early modern medicine was typically understood in terms of a tripartite structure, comprising physicians, apothecaries, and surgeons. The relatively few physicians were the Latinate elite. They supposedly conducted consultations, recommended dietary regimens, and wrote prescriptions. Ever since classical times, their recommendations had relied largely on regimen and herbal medicaments, tailored, in theory, to the circumstances of individual patients. Polydore Vergil averred that their original bailiwick had been dietetics.[31] Apothecaries made up medicaments to their bills. And surgeons handled bodily manipulations. The reality was much more complex and fluid than this representation implied, however. While this tripartite structure was enshrined in institutions in many cities, and "colleges" of physicians claimed the authority to maintain it, in fact licensing regimes were very incomplete, and members of each rank routinely acted in ways that the others might perceive as intrusions.

Moreover, countless unlicensed practitioners—"irregulars," as Margaret Pelling calls them—serviced the majority of the population. The physicians regularly denounced these irregulars as "empirics," "mountebanks," "quacks," and the like.[32] But they vastly outnumbered the physicians, could sometimes call on alternative licensing authorities (like bishops) for legitimacy, might well appeal to newer kinds of knowledge and experience, and in practice were not infrequently patronized by the physicians themselves. The result was a consistently fraught medical culture, with each group struggling to distinguish and protect itself from the others. It was in this context that the physicians leveled charges that apothecaries and irregulars were tied to base, commercial interests. Those interests, they warned, tempted them to adulterate.[33]

The problem of adulteration was therefore inextricably bound up with contemporary medical institutions and identities. The only case in which a physician could trust to a medicine, it was said, was when he either prepared it himself or supervised its preparation in person. Doing otherwise meant trusting to "as great cheats as are now Extant in the World."[34] The pugnacious physician Coxe added that London's apothecaries were so unreliable "that neither Physicians or the Diseased have reason to repose that trust in them which they challenge as their due."[35] Trusting people and trusting things: this was what was at stake in the interminable battle between the physicians, apothecaries, "druggists," and irregulars. Counterfeiting was what cast such trust into the most acute doubt. Indeed, as the apothecaries grew into a discrete trade, the need for them to expel these "cheats" and police "untrue" drugs was a paramount concern. It loomed large in the creation of the Apothecaries' Company in 1617. The Company took seriously its mission to inspect members' premises and confiscate unsound substances—a practice that paralleled the searches of the Stationers' wardens for unsound books.[36] By contrast, the Company did not stipulate that apothecaries were restricted to dispensing physicians' prescriptions, so there was nothing to prevent them dealing directly with patients.[37] The combination of these concerns—of adulteration and autonomy—triggered a crisis that pervaded London medicine, reaching a head alongside the Grew-Moult clash.

The problem of assessing the authenticity of medicaments was a familiar one. Ancient medical writers had cautioned repeatedly about the need to approach medical substances with suspicion.[38] But as pharmaceuticals became a central element in a nascent consumer society in the seventeenth century, so their credibility had become a newly pressing issue. Adulterating drugs, or "pharmaceutical piracy" (*piraterie pharmaceutique*) as one French investigator called it, proved a booming business.[39] When a vessel arrived at the port of Marseille laden with medicaments, its cargo could be expected to multiply threefold in weight by the time it left the city. London was no better. The hub of a pharmaceutical trade extending across the Atlantic and beyond, London furnished huge temptations to dilute, reconstitute, or downright fabricate. Thomas Corbyn, an eighteenth-century druggist with a prosperous business, remarked that he could have made "100% profitt" by practicing adulteration.[40] Drugs were certainly "pirated" in such ways at least as rampantly as books, and probably far more so.

Yet Corbyn, for one, maintained that he declined the opportunity for a windfall. He realized that lasting security rested on his creating and maintaining a reputation for quality. Makers like him were increasingly conscious that they were selling more than substances alone. This awareness was in all probability sharpened by the ubiquity of fraud. The rampancy of drug piracy—like that of print piracy—actually seems to have created an opportunity for some operators to set themselves apart from and above the herd. They sought to distinguish themselves by ostentatiously *not* indulging in adulteration or counterfeiting. In a marketplace riven with justified skepticism, they profited by making themselves founts of assurance. They sold credibility.

As that implies, drug adulteration affected what might be called the epistemology of pharmacy. As a patient or as a physician, how did you know what a medicine contained, or that it worked? How did you know that you knew? These doubts mattered for more than therapeutic reasons. "Chymical" physicians demanded that their new remedies be adopted, and to bolster their case they challenged Galenists to put them to the test empirically. Grew's own salt was publicly associated with this empirical challenge.[41] Yet their call seemed to go largely unmet. This was not necessarily unreasonable. After all, in Galenic terms it made little sense, because illnesses depended on individual constitutions, so the idea of a single substance having a determinate effect across many patients was intrinsically implausible. Chymical physicians dismissed this kind of reasoning as specious. But they had a much harder time resisting an argument from the nature of medicaments themselves. If adulteration were as real and as commonplace as all knowledgeable writers reported it to be—and if drugs were perishable, to boot—then substances themselves varied unpredictably and undetectably. It was therefore genuinely unclear whether an empirical trial could yield any result reliable enough to be deemed knowledge.[42]

So adulteration was deeply involved in the contest for authority in early modern medicine, and at the same time the greatest contemporary controversy about cures themselves could not be resolved until it was dealt with. Print seemed to offer a partial solution. Pharmacopoeias held up the possibility of disciplining things by words.[43] They were meant to render drugs' identities regular and predictable, irrespective of the particular shop out of which a given dose came. The standardization offered by the printing house would thus produce standardization in the apothecary's workshop. London's physicians produced the world's first national pharmacopoeia, in 1618. Yet the same problems turned out to apply to pharmacopoeias as applied to all other printed books. The London pharmacopoeia itself had to be swiftly withdrawn and reissued, the College explaining embarrassedly that "the printer snatched away from our hands this little work not yet finished." It was then famously expropriated again by the apothecary Nicholas Culpeper, who created an unauthorized vernacular version.[44] Another problem, even harder to deal with, was unauthorized *reading*, of the kind Grew's treatise on salt would get from lay patients. The impression of authority that pharmacopoeias conveyed would encourage readers to miss the actual variability of substances. The relation between print and practice took on acute importance in this sphere, as druggists, herb-women, and apothecaries concentrated on adulterating and fabricating precisely the drugs listed in the pharmacopoeia itself.[45]

Some method for authenticating substances was sorely needed. Since ancient times, so-called organoleptic methods had prevailed: that is, those employing the senses directly, to judge by criteria of taste, smell, appearance, and bodily effects.[46] These techniques remained the norm until the nineteenth century, and they were not necessarily useless. A turpentine adulterant would give off telltale fumes, for example, when a sample was set on fire. The most trusted approach was simply to imbibe some of the drug in question. We know from the diaries of Robert Hooke that he would do this routinely, taking a purge or a vomit and judging its virtue from its felt effects. The body of the patient became the instrument for trying substances, and hence the virtue of the apothecaries and physicians involved in providing them. That was why Grew proclaimed on his title page that his salt was "Easily known from all Counterfeits by its Bitter Taste."[47] Yet the senses could deceive. And "vile Impostors and covetous Operators" were ready with techniques to help them do so.[48] Many alleged bezoar stones were "*forged*," for example, by "a cunning cast of suttle and deceiving merchants . . . who can so exactly counterfeit them, that themselves cannot *know* the one from the other, the true from the false."[49] If these skills existed, then some more powerful technique was clearly called for to counter them. Could experimental philosophy furnish one?

The first writer in English to propose a more sophisticated approach was none other than Robert Boyle. The topic clearly bothered Boyle: in a general critique of medicine that he wrote but suppressed, he complained that nobody had "chalk'd out the possible & practicable way of discovering genuinenes or adulterations of Drugs & Medicins." His *Medicina hydrostatica* offered a solution, based on experiments conducted at the Royal Society during the time that Grew was investigating salts. The book was finally published in 1690, as Grew was setting up his salt works. It proposed using a precision balance to make specific-gravity measurements on drugs and gems to reveal "Whether they be Genuine or Adulterate" (fig. 5.1). Boyle recommended using an oil-based solution for this. Spirit of turpentine was a good option, as it was cheap and therefore "seldom adulterated, as Chymical Oils are too often found to be." Since it was hard for "Counterfeitors" to reproduce a substance's characteristic specific gravity, Boyle reasoned, measurements of this kind ought to furnish "a kind of Standard" for judging both the identity of substances and their degrees of purity.[50]

For the rest of the eighteenth century, and on into the nineteenth, physicians and others continued to express regular disquiet at the state of materia medica. A growing literature on "medical anarchy" spread lamentations about adulteration. But Boyle's relatively sophisticated recommendations seem not to have been adopted in practice. Only in the nineteenth century, with the advent of state-sponsored laboratories for standardizing all kinds of values (weights, measures, currencies, etc.), did they find their use. Meanwhile, physicians, apothecaries, and laypeople alike continued to rely on their senses. But they supplemented them with rules of thumb for appraising the plausibility of the *people* responsible for their medicines. Faith in a medicament ought, apparently, to be subject to a face-to-face assessment of its maker. It was not the case that every user in practice tried to meet every maker, but it mattered that such a meeting should be possible in principle. Again, in the case of Grew this was evident: physicians were asked to "rely on the Author's Veracity" to credit the salt.

The trouble was that this conflicted with the reality of pharmaceutical production. The image was that an individual apothecary cleaved to an individual physician's receipts. The reality was that a system of exchange operated, such that one apothecary made mithridate in bulk, another theriac, and so on. And "druggists" and "operators" maintained a thriving wholesale trade too, on the fringes of Europe's cities. Cox warned that,

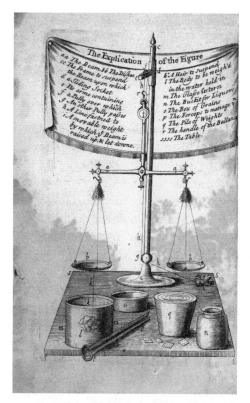

FIGURE 5.1. Robert Boyle's device to detect adulterated
or pirated pharmaceuticals and gems. R. Boyle,
Medicina hydrostatica (London: for S. Smith, 1690),
frontispiece. Courtesy of the University of Chicago
Library.

since they were autonomous even of the apothecaries, "their skill as well
as honesty is liable to be questioned" — and, unlike the apothecaries, they
could not be confronted by customers. They themselves explained their
cheapness by appeal to a peculiar skill or "knack." But physicians were
skeptical, denying that this knack could be anything but the omission of
expensive ingredients or the substitution of cheaper or superannuated
ones. Once more, this was what Grew's camp had in mind when they insisted that he did not mean to "make a noise . . . with a Chymical Knack."[51]
In short, authenticating substances generally meant authenticating
people, and when people could not be authenticated serious problems
arose. That was why setting the credit of medicaments on a sound basis
would demand a social revolution in medicine.

In the event, subsequent medical history would turn on two strategies developed to deal with this. One invoked the constitution of pharmacy; the other, its communication. Physicians maintained that a reformed "Constitution of Pharmacy" was needed to deal with this problem. What they had in mind was that physicians should become direct employers of trustworthy apothecaries—much as Grew did with Tramel, in fact, and much as Atkyns would have gentlemen do with printers. This would produce what, to the eyes of an early modern gentleman, looked like a far safer domain, with the gentleman overseeing the artisan in a kind of master-servant relationship. Christopher Merrett for one claimed that apothecaries had historically originated as servants. The interest that physicians assumed drove adulteration would disappear under such a regime. The making of medicaments would cease to be a "mechanical" enterprise and become an "art." And the physicians should band together into "Societies" to create public laboratories to this end. This, Coxe averred, would not only end adulteration, but encourage the communication of new preparations.[52] In "all well founded Constitutions," he added, "where there is a union of interests, there will be united Counsels and Endeavours." Surely, he inferred, "they who are so tender of every mans propriety, that they account every invasion thereof, an injury done to themselves, will not deny their assistance to Physitians, whose propriety also is strangely invaded, the Usurpers now being almost ready to plead Prescription" (that is, to claim that physicians, like patentees, intruded on an existing craft). Coxe even verged on calling the apothecaries a polity incommensurable with the commonwealth—the core of the pirate concept. He likened them to "Coyners, Robbers, Cut-purses, [and] Sophisticaters of wine."[53]

The apothecaries defended themselves from such assaults much as the booksellers did. Henry Stubbe warned on their behalf of a "dangerous" intrusion on arts that had been practiced for long enough to become "Proprieties."[54] The very existence of the pharmacopoeia, they added, showed the physicians to be would-be monopolists. They neglected "greater secrets" in favor of old medicines, and deliberately withheld their own "magistral" remedies. In the heat of the revolutionary period, Noah Biggs went further still, denying the rationale for licensing and authorship at all in this domain. He argued that the social structure of medicine needed to be overturned altogether, alongside what he saw as other relics of ancient corruption and popery. He likened the licensing system of the College to that of the Crown's press licensers, recently abolished with the Court of

Star Chamber. A collegiate physician, Biggs said, bore "an *imprimatur* on his back," just like a printed book under the old system of publishing. As a Paracelsian, Biggs himself upheld a radical view that medicine must not remain "a kind of staple merchandize." God-given natural knowledge would never multiply if "*Art* and *Ingenuity*" remained subject to property and licensing. Indeed, physic had originated in a spirit antagonistic to authorship. Galen himself, Biggs snorted, had expropriated the doctrines of Dioscorides, "like a *Plagiary* and sneaking *Filcher.*" Pliny had done the same without even understanding them. Later physicians had emulated them so successfully that "the *Art* of *Physick* hath stood a long time at a stay . . . without any progresse made." And so it would remain until practitioners ceased to "deck and polish the Inventions of *Forreigners, Greeks, Barbarians,* and *Ethnicks*" rather than seeking out their own. It seemed to chymical practitioners like Biggs as though "the inventions of our *Grandfathers* had ramm'd up the way of our own *industry.*"[55] In the end, Biggs professed to fear a kind of reverse millennium. God, appalled at the "*Factors* or *Farmers*" who would "monopolize, or monarchize" medical knowledge — who, in pharmacopoeias, "put truth at the bottom of the sack, and their own inventions at the sacks mouth" — might decide to withhold further insights altogether. God might simply "withdraw his gifts."[56] Already there was a devastating contrast evident between the mechanical arts, which "dayly receive *advancement,* and *ascend* by the degrees of *new discoveries,* neerer towards their *perfection,*" and medicine, which remained "*cold, and dull.*"[57]

This was a radical claim indeed: that Providence itself demanded an open field of inquiry in medicine, with the abolition of all properties whether collegiate or authorial. In practice, the range of plausible options was narrower. Physicians wanted the armory of medicaments extended, but they insisted that for this to happen the authorship of physicians both as individuals and as a profession must be protected. That meant adopting degrees of secrecy. Merrett acknowledged the paradox. Physic had improved dramatically in "these few last experimental years," and it was time for the pharmacopoeia to be improved. Yet only someone "well furnished with specificks" would want to launch a new edition; and without some proprietary regime, that would require that the proposer himself "expose" his own specifics "to the whole World." Without some way of securing the authors of new drugs, therefore, the pharmacopoeia would likely remain imperfect. So Merrett urged a campaign to "restore and settle those

Honours ignorant men would usurp, upon the Learned Professors of this Science." The campaign he had in mind would create a counterpart regime of authorial recognition to the Royal Society's register. Until it were in place, he declared, "I see no reason why *Physicians* should communicate their secrets to such persons, who will make use of them, to the ruine of the Inventors."

Here physicians like Merrett and Coxe returned to Galenism and the social structure of medicine. When a physician wrote out a bill, he trusted the apothecary to make a medicine to his instructions—but to do so only once. Ideally, he would return the receipt with the medicine itself to the physician. Certainly, the apothecary ought never to "make use of it as his own when he pleaseth for his own profit, and the Inventor have no further benefit by it." This principle of an inventor's right mapped directly onto the Galenist conviction about pathologies—and therefore medicines—being individuated. Coxe even wanted to insist that the new chymical medicines, which were premised on a denial of that conviction, should therefore not be entrusted to apothecaries at all, but made only in the College's own "publick Laboratory." The physicians on this account constituted a community that advanced not by professed inspiration, unlike Biggs's Paracelsians, but by veracious "communication" in writing and print. For generations they had "faithfully communicated their experiments and observations."[58] Their possession of protocols to provide for this communication was what made their treatments trustworthy. He suggested that many holders of lesser arcana would willingly divulge them if such a sober community was ready to take over their manufacture.[59]

The conflict between Grew and the Moults thus exploited strains that had rent the medical world for generations. Those strains penetrated every aspect of medicine: the identity of drugs, the content of medical knowledge, the nature of discovery and invention, the proprieties of authorship, and the social structure of the entire medical enterprise. Grew knew that he was venturing onto controversial terrain. He may not have recognized just how riven it was, and how far his project would venture onto its most treacherous ground.

A MEDICAL MARKETPLACE

As Grew tried to use his patent to extend the authority of a physician into the province of the apothecaries and druggists, these broad and deep conflicts were approaching their climax. The College of Physicians attempted to recover some authority after the 1688 revolution, while the Society of Apothecaries fought back by, among other things, threatening to reveal the vacuity of the College's presumptions by a pirate printing of its "illogical and unjust" statutes. That it would threaten an action of this kind in search of respectability speaks volumes. At the same time, the apothecaries brought before Parliament what sounds an arcane matter, but was in fact of great significance. The obligation to serve in parish offices was one incumbent on all guilds and companies except the College of Physicians, and the exemption marked out the physicians as a profession rather than a craft. The apothecaries now sought the same privilege. Were they to prevail, they could infer that they too were no mere artisans. And therefore they could engage directly with patients, formulating their own medicaments. To the physicians' shock, the bill passed, and passed quickly. The existing structure of medicine seemed to hang in the balance.[60]

The College reacted as best it could. Conscious as they were of the widespread perception that they were expensive, self-interested, and monopolistic, the physicians resolved to tackle the apothecaries head-on. They opened their own dispensary to provide medicines for the poor. The College also took the internally controversial step of translating and publishing its own statutes, again in order to preempt the apothecaries' plans. And it took the fateful decision to prosecute an apothecary named William Rose for practicing physic. The case was an involved one, but the College won at King's Bench. Rose appealed to the House of Lords, however, where his lawyers represented the prosecution as a strategy of physicians intent on "monopolizing the whole business of physic." The Lords, dominated by Whig convictions against monopolies, took Rose's side and ruled against the College.[61] The result was widely taken to mark the end of a regime. From now on, the old tripartite structure persisted only as an empty shell. A radically entrepreneurial medical marketplace that had long burgeoned in practice was now legitimated.[62]

In the marketplace that ensued, formal distinctions between authoritative and heterodox medicine retreated into invisibility. Patients, as customers, saw nothing questionable in sampling the recommendations of a range of practitioners and opting for the most congenial or most convincing. A vast range of nostrums and "patent medicines" tempted them —many, or so the physicians claimed, pirated from the pharmacopoeia with the addition of some more or less cosmetic ingredient to mask the theft. Or patients might simply self-medicate, following one of a burgeoning range of printed works instructing them how to do so. In being pirated, Grew, in a sense, had helped inaugurate that transition.[63]

It was Grew's generation that saw the first patents issued on compounded, chemical medicaments. Why then, and not earlier or later? The answer rests on the issues appealed to in the Grew-Moult exchange and thrown open with the defeat of the College of Physicians. The old tripartite system had been premised on continuity, not originality. It accorded no special importance to the creation of new medicines and techniques. Discovery and invention occurred, of course, but they were not part of the regular professional identity of a physician or apothecary. As a result, apothecaries, physicians, and operators alike adopted ad hoc measures, and in their internecine struggles articulated rival concepts of authorial propriety and theft. Grew's decision to resort to a patent began as merely one among these tactics. But afterward Grew's patent became something more. The physicians' defeat turned what had been a tactic into a strategy—and then into a structural element fated to form the core of medical culture.

The eighteenth-century medical marketplace lauded the creation and marketing of novelty from all comers and all corners. It emphasized the distribution of professed knowledge to an ever-wider range of readers. It was inhospitable to old authorities who justified their eminence by appeal to Latin learning, or to Galen and Hippocrates. Yet there was at the same time something very Grub Street about it too. In place of those fusty old collegians it fostered a wild free-for-all, with figures like Hans Sloane finding their names attached to nostrums alongside every patent-medicine peddler. The world bemoaned as one of "medical anarchy," in which medicines were faked, counterfeited, and pirated without limit, was also the world in which medical patenting became routine. It was inextricable from the world hailed as enlightened, because it was at its heart the same world.

6

Of Epics and Orreries

Copyright was an invention of eighteenth-century Britain. It was unknown anywhere before 1700, and for much of the ensuing century no other nation had anything like it. Even in Britain, it took until the 1770s for the concept to congeal into roughly its modern form—that of a temporally limited "right" defined by statute and limited to the expression of ideas rather than ideas themselves. Each of those elements was initially hard to articulate and comprehend. All of them remained controversial. Some still do. It is worth asking, then, how such a strange concept came into being at all, and why it was found appealing in the first place.

The answers to those questions lie in how a new political and economic context made the everyday practices of printing and bookselling intensely controversial. In both its nature and its very existence, copyright reflected the fact that it emerged in the generations after the Glorious Revolution of 1688. The exit of the Catholic king James II and his replacement by William and Mary were profoundly traumatic events, which set in motion major changes in the governance and political economy of the British Isles. Invocations of "liberty and property" were commonplace in the long and bitter debate that took place over the revolution's legitimacy. They became, in contemporary terms, "revolution principles." To insist that publishing rested on a system of property, as the major London booksellers learned to do, was therefore astute, since it identified one of those essential principles as being at stake.[1] But in that light "literary property" had a besetting problem too—a problem that few articulated at the outset, but that would become ever harder to ignore as the debate reached its climax: insofar as it was property, it stood at odds with liberty. That is, it set the two principal revolution principles at loggerheads. London's grandee booksellers might see only virtue in entrenching a principle of property, absolute and perpetual, as the axiom of publishing. For their challengers, it was monopolistic, even tyrannical.

The clash over literary property occurred at a time when questions of identity and autonomy were unusually pressing in general. Factory rationality, financial speculation, and machines were combining to challenge craft skill as the basis for authority in enterprises of all kinds. Materialist and deist convictions threatened to uproot clerical authority. Readers were encouraged to suppose that they constituted a public, with a reasoned voice and a legitimate power of judgment. Citizens flocked to see for themselves the powers of nature, as they were produced by virtuosic lecturers and showmen with their electrical machines, air pumps, and orreries. They paid to witness mechanical automata, too, which seemed to reproduce some of the most human capacities with unsettling fidelity. Unsettling too were the conclusions they might draw from these performances about the nature of such capacities in themselves. Were emotions, expressions—even reason itself—matters of wheelwork and hydraulics? In short, the locations of knowledge, authority, and authenticity were unclear in a new way, and the very confusion was for some a commercial opportunity. Out of this culture appeared a "mystery of author-craft" that was at once polite and commercial, reflective and rapacious, and inventive and piratical.[2]

It scarcely needs to be said that the arguments about literary property were long, intense, and finely balanced. They could have ended in many ways, or for that matter not ended at all—which, arguably, is exactly what did happen. At any rate, the copyright that descended to the modern Anglophone world was less an immanent principle of these exchanges than an outcome of them. The moment that defined that outcome came in February 1774. Large crowds gathered at the House of Lords to hear the nation's highest legal authority decide whether literary property existed or not. In the end, the Lords destroyed that property. Copyright, they decided, was not a right of man at all. Indeed, it was almost the very opposite: an artifact, and one that *replaced* a prior right established by an author's work of creation. When a work's copyright expired, it was cast adrift. That represented a huge victory for the pirates—and, arguably, for the public to which they appealed. In terms of revolution principles, liberty won out over property.

CONGERS AND COPIES

The demise of the so-called Press Act in 1695 made "piracy" legitimate. The major players of London's book trade got together to protest. In 1710 they finally secured a new law in answer to their complaints. That statute is always represented as the world's first copyright law. But the term itself did not appear in it, and it left important questions unaddressed as to the nature of any such "right." What it did do was establish a legal focus for contests about the customs of the London trade, such that they would center on claims of property and a doctrine of copyright could indeed emerge from them. In other words, copyright may owe its distant origin to one interested party's response to piracy—or rather, to the *Republica Grubstreetana,* as Swift called it, in which piratical principles allegedly held sway—but it took specific shape through struggles to drive home that response.

Literary property became a highly contested principle because, prior to and largely independent of statute law, a powerful group in the book trade made it into the operating premise of London publishing. It was created and sustained as a mundane reality by alliances among this central corps of booksellers. They had a stake in keeping their projects safe, but they also believed that publishing was only a well-mannered enterprise because it rested on this principle. The alternative was the pirate realm represented by the likes of Hills, Curll, and Rayner. For this small oligarchy, therefore—numbering about twenty to thirty at any one time —conviction, interest, and everyday experience powerfully coincided to establish literary property as the keystone of publishing. That was why, when such property was challenged, they fought back determinedly.[3]

In the aftermath of the Glorious Revolution, this kind of oligarchy took on a new significance. Speculation, risk, and debt seemed in the 1690s to have become central elements in a newly commercial culture, in which credit played a central part. At a national level, the need to maintain a war effort involved a new kind of political economy symbolized by the national debt and the Bank of England. At the level of individual enterprises, it was a time, as Daniel Defoe proclaimed, of "projects." Projects were ambitious proposals for schemes of all kinds—inventions, trade ventures, lotteries, and so on. They were nothing new; a century earlier, Elizabethan London had been full of projectors.[4] But now the projectors sought their investment less through court patronage than in the avowedly public realm of coffeehouse and pamphlet. From treasure-hunting expeditions to new steam engines for draining mines, projects of all kinds sought investment from lay subscribers lured by print and tempted by the promise of future returns. The phenomenon seemed to characterize a new age. And, of course, the book trade depended on projecting too. To propose a subscription for a new atlas or history meant asking others to trust that that project would be brought to fruition. At Garraway's or Jonathan's coffeehouses, customers might find themselves looking at printed proposals for a new edition of the church fathers or a new fen-drainage scheme, and the rhetoric in both would be remarkably congruent. And because many projects failed—editions as much as engines—questions of plausibility dogged the entire culture of projecting. The enterprise of books was credit dependent and risk prone at a time when risk was publicly notorious. It is telling that the most famous of all the swindles of the South Sea Bubble period was rumored to be that of a printer, who pocketed £2,000 from subscribers to his project for "an undertaking of Great Advantage, but no one to know what it is." What is even more telling is that the scam itself seems to have been a figment of Grub Street machinations—there is no substantive evidence that it ever really happened.[5]

It was this concern for credit that led major booksellers to band together to defend their interests. Their alliances began to appear as early as the 1670s and 1680s, and soon became known as *congers*. The original idea behind them was simple. In order to minimize and spread the risk of an impression, each participant agreed to take a certain number of copies.[6] As they became more entrenched, however, so congers took on more lasting and quasi-institutional forms. Some even operated as semiformal joint-stock operations. Their members-only sales—at first of real books sitting in warehouses, but before long of "copies" in the abstract—established the status of certain works as de facto properties. Members were forbidden to trade such works outside these events, and nonmembers were not allowed in. The "trade sales" consequently created a tiny, closed market in the most valuable titles of the book trade. It was secure enough that steady-selling works like *Paradise Lost* could be parceled out into what were effectively shares. No law reserved Milton's poem to anyone, but with "ownership" now distributed among the top booksellers, this elite took on a collective interest in combating any purported "piracy." They never posed the question of whether copies like this were *really* properties, because there was no reason to pose it and every reason not to. Literary property was a social fact. For perhaps fifty years, major works of all kinds appeared under these circumstances (with the partial exception of the novel, for novels were generally issued for a quick profit, with little thought for future editions). By the time the congers started to retreat from view in around 1740, they had done enough to entrench the London trade's reliance on what opponents denounced as "combinations" bolstering an ersatz property regime.[7]

There was no shortage of such opponents. Those outside the central group grumbled that the system was oligarchic and monopolist. Indeed, some charged that in restricting works that would otherwise be open, the congers themselves were piratical. John Dunton, an enterprising and opinionated Whig printer, thus conceded that the major virtue of a conger was in defending against "pirates," but in the next breath denounced the Castle group as a "Pyrat-Conger," marveling that its members could live with their consciences. Another antagonist suggested that the name *conger* had been coined to signify a beast fond of devouring "small fry." The secretive character of the congers was another focus of criticism (one that we shall see Jacob Ilive rehearsing in his later attack on copy owners).[8] These critiques remained largely ineffectual at first, but they would never quite go away.

In 1707–9 it was a group of conger members who succeeded in persuading Parliament to pass a replacement for the old Press Act. Bids for some kind of legal recognition had hitherto been mixed with calls for a revival of press regulation, perhaps by licensing. An alternative was to enjoin that authors must "own" their works in the sense of printing their names on the title pages. The new group did not entirely divest itself of those old arguments, but it focused much more heavily on the issue of property per se. It made the adroit decision to seek protection not for mere "copies"— that is, for a trade custom—but for "properties." Joseph Addison endorsed the idea of suppressing "the scandalous Practices of the *Pyrate* Printers and their *Hawkers*," and issued a furious diatribe in the *Tatler* against them. Daniel Defoe provided its rationale. Defoe proclaimed not only a "Right of Property," but a right of property *created by authors*. This was the booksellers' old retort to Atkyns, revived now in a very different context. A law for regulation and property alike, Defoe said, would be "so agreeable to a Revolution-Principle, so considerable an Article in Defence of Property, that no *Whig* can be against it—without ceasing to be what we call a *Whig*, that is, a Man careful of preserving Property." Even a printer like John How, who charged that the elite booksellers were the greatest pirates of all—and threatened to "publish the whole History of Piracy, wherein the World shall see how the Greatest Men of the Trade have rais'd their Estates"—called for a law so that the trade might have a level field.[9]

In January 1710 the grandees proposed their bill. Envisaging a strict property right in printed works, grounded in the labor of the author and owned, almost always, by a London bookseller, it promised to enshrine the congers' customs into law. But the concept did not survive Westminster. Some critical parliamentarian—it is unclear who—was cautious enough about monopolies to suggest limiting the term of a copy. The idea had been floated before, notably by John Locke, but the booksellers were horrified by it. They rushed out three broadsides overnight, declaring that it would not only undermine "a Right which has been Enjoyed by Common Law above 150 Years," but destroy a "Property the same with that of Houses." Parliament held its ground. Not only did it retain this critically important change, but it also added a further provision that after the first term of fourteen years the right would revert to the author for another fourteen. It then amended the preamble introducing the measure. Where the draft had spoken of the law "securing" a property based in authors' "learning and labour," now the bill described itself as "vesting" a right in proprietors. The distinction between securing and vesting was subtle, especially as the old term remained in the bill itself. But it might well mean that what the booksellers proclaimed as a natural right was something else entirely: an artificial protection, created by Parliament and granted for a limited duration. It might imply, in short, that this was a parliamentary counterpart to a royal patent. And it was in this form that the bill was finally carried. As *An act for the encouragement of learning* it came into effect on April 10, 1710.[10]

NATIONS AND COMBINATIONS

The new statute protected books already published for twenty-one years. In 1731 its protection therefore expired for these works. They were the mainstays of the trade—the prized copies of the London grandees. Steady sellers like Milton, Shakespeare, and *The whole duty of man* suddenly fell out of the statutory fold. It was now, therefore, that those ambiguities in the law took on practical significance. According to the grandees, the end of the statutory term ought not to matter very much. Accustomed to the security of congers and trade sales, they felt that the statute simply provided an enforcement mechanism for what were inherently perpetual properties, created in each case by the act of authorship and sanctioned in general by time-honored customs. Their rivals, however—of whom many more had arisen since 1695—saw things differently. Believing these titles to be fair game, they began to reprint them and to sell them at devastatingly cheap prices.

The Londoners had ways of dealing with local "pirates," or at least of living with them. They could usually be stopped by injunctions in Chancery.[11] Far more troubling were a new cadre of pirates from further afield, operating in a place where Chancery's writ did not run. England and Scotland had united into one nation only in 1707, and they retained separate legal systems. The union had been attended by bitter dissent from the start, and remained controversial among Scots.[12] Central to their concerns were manufacturing and commerce. Contemporary doctrines of political economy mandated protective measures against the manufacturing ambitions of rival nations. But Scotland and England were now parts of the *same* nation, so the Scots demanded that London should endorse printing and publishing in their major cities. But ambitious booksellers in both Edinburgh and Glasgow aimed not only at domestic readers, but at lucrative export markets in provincial England and the American colonies. It was in this context that Scottish reprinting became the flash point of a major struggle.

Piracy therefore became entangled with the peculiar politics of a composite nation. For authorial property to become secure would require coherent answers to questions about metropolis and province, and about kingdom and colony—questions that had already been a major cause of contention in the civil war and revolution.[13] And at the same time it would involve defining the public sphere that ideally traversed these spaces. The Scots defended reprinting as contributing to manufactures north of the border, and as cocking a snook at London's assumption of imperial centrality. Countless advertisements appeared in Scottish newspapers to this effect. And in challenging English "monopolists," they claimed, Scotland's printers and booksellers were advancing the cause of learning. As the Glaswegian printer Robert Foulis declared in 1754 when challenged over reprinting Pope, "I act from principle." Noting with bemusement "the new doctrine" of an authorial property that was prior to all laws, eternal, and illimitable by even the highest "national authority," Foulis insisted that "the most Learned and worthy men in this country, think we do public service in reprinting."[14] In such rhetoric one can see the inauguration of a sustained polemic about print and authorship, certainly, but also about mercantilism and free trade, public knowledge, and the identity of Britain.

Adam Smith, who grew up amid these controversies, declared that "the sole engine of the mercantile system" was monopoly.[15] The reprinters agreed wholeheartedly. They saw themselves as resisting a gang of out-and-out monopolists. The London copy-owning elite laid claim to all works that had ever been printed in England, they noted, excepting only Latin and Greek classics. That looked to them like an attempt to monopolize the book itself. The fact that the Londoners had taken to arguing their case on the basis of a natural—and hence not only perpetual, but universal—right only made their presumption all the more flagrant. London was attempting to stifle a nation's industry and public culture at once, by imposing its own notion of "private Property." So Scottish readers were exhorted to seek out local reprints rather than buy English editions.[16] This was an enormously potent line of attack, and insofar as it latched onto the revolution principle of antimonopoly its appeal extended beyond Scotland. The jurist Edward Thurlow thus agreed that "what was called Literary Property" was aligned with "a scandalous monopoly of ignorant booksellers" who "grew opulent by oppression." The very term "monopoly" was, Warburton and Blackstone agreed, "odious."[17] Merely to mention it was to excite a communal memory of Stuart absolutism and court corruption. Moreover, there was also a real and timely political resonance to this kind of contention. The mid-eighteenth century saw a revival of political controversy over "monopoly," particularly in the form of the East India Company's control of trade with India. London radical Whigs complained against the oligarchic use of state-provided privileges such as the Company's, which outlawed competition and, they claimed, therefore intruded on subjects' abilities to use their intelligence and free will. While the Scottish and English pirate booksellers did not, as far as I know, explicitly link their cause to that of these anti-imperialist radicals, the commonalities were there to be seen.[18]

Needless to say, the London bookselling oligarchs rejected all this. A true monopoly, they insisted, must remove a right to practice a trade that had once been widely shared, but a literary work was something created at a certain point by an author, so this condition could never have been met. "It cannot be said, that an Author's Work was ever common, as the Earth originally was."[19] And they maintained that some regime of literary propriety must exist if everyone, including the Scots, were not to suffer. William Strahan—the leading printer in London, Master of the Stationers' Company, and investor in some two hundred copies, but himself an expatriate Scot—remarked that if the Scots were to win, they themselves would soon discover the need for some equivalent. Francis Hargrave agreed that the pirates would suffer if "pirating" became universal.[20] And some evidence existed to back up such claims. Edinburgh's reprinters were certainly accused of turning on their erstwhile allies in Glasgow by importing "*contraband*" books from Holland and selling them as if they came from London.[21]

As already noted, the Londoners could cope with local pirates by seeking injunctions. But an injunction was a stopgap, meant only to freeze a potential offense until a real trial could occur. It did not represent a formal verdict, and had no impact on doctrine—however much the Londoners liked to imply that a cascade of them did. What they really needed to deal with the Scottish reprinters was a definitive legal endorsement of the principle of a common-law property right, and one that extended it north of the border. In the mid-1730s they therefore approached Parliament for another statute. Westminster turned them down, agreeing only to ban the importing of reprints. But in attempting to legislate for open-ended property, the booksellers had unwittingly opened a Pandora's box. For it was at this point that the real conflict over what was now dubbed "literary property" or, increasingly, "copyright," began.[22] For the next three decades the topic remained constantly before the eyes of readers. In pamphlets, newspaper reports, personal exchanges, and coffeehouse conversations, as well as in a long series of court cases, every conceivable argument for and against such property found a place. The antagonists to a perpetual property right expressly declared that the very existence of public reason depended on the outcome.[23] Collectively, these debates furnished the most sustained examination yet of the principles and practices on which a commercial culture of creative works should operate.

With parliamentary action ruled out, the Londoners had to venture into Scottish law themselves. They did so in earnest in 1743, prosecuting twenty-four Scottish reprinters, including the principals in both major cities, for seven titles. They ended up focusing on one in particular: Ephraim Chambers's *Cyclopaedia*, a key work of the early Enlightenment and the inspiration for Diderot and d'Alembert's *Encyclopédie*. The Londoners were led, somewhat ironically, by an expatriate Scot, Andrew Millar. Millar knew the proprieties of both sides well. Originally apprenticed to an Edinburgh bookseller, he had actually defended the Scottish reprinting of English Bibles in a piracy trial in 1727, only to take over his erstwhile master's London outpost and become a leading copy owner. And he continued to cooperate with Scottish booksellers in undertaking new works, even while leading his campaign against reprints.[24] As Millar knew, the case would have to be made circumspectly. Precedents drawn from English customs before 1707 carried no weight in Scotland, and there was precious little evidence to suggest that anything like a common-law right had ever obtained there. His side therefore phrased its plea carefully. But their antagonists responded fiercely. They did not rest content with court arguments, but, claiming the issue was one of national economic and cultural survival, appealed directly to readers through the newspaper press. The titles they reprinted were in truth open to all, they insisted, and their enterprise was vital to the future of Scotland, and for that matter Britain. Henry Home—later Lord Kames, one of the major figures of the Scottish Enlightenment—took up the cudgels too from the bench. Home announced that Millar wanted to "crush this Manufacture in the Bud" before it could develop an export market in the colonies. He proceeded to use the case to question the political economy of the British Empire itself. If the Londoners won their case for literary property, Home insinuated, then Scotland's book trade would be relegated to a colonial status. The real English plan was to "inslave" Scottish booksellers by restricting them to mere printing and retailing—the fate of the majority of London's bookmen. That would have disastrous effects for enlightenment. With superb irony, he singled out as an example of those effects one of the works cited by the Londoners in their complaint—a *Gardener's Dictionary* originally published in two folio volumes. Only in its cheap and portable Scottish reprint could any real gardener hope to use the book.[25] Faced with such highly charged responses, the Londoners resoundingly lost their case. They appealed to the House of Lords, expecting a friendlier hearing in Westminster. But when Lord Hardwicke voiced his own sentiment that the Act of Anne had really created "a general standing Patent" for books, the booksellers saw the wisdom of discretion and opted not to press the issue.[26]

Edinburgh's "pirates" had won a major victory. In Scotland, at least, an open-ended right to copies definitively did *not* exist. The 1710 statute was still in effect there, but this outcome left the Scots free to reprint any works falling outside its terms of protection. True, they could not send them into England without provoking injunctions and perhaps prosecutions under English law. But they could sell to their own countrymen, and to the colonies too—and the Scots did both with alacrity. From the mid-1740s, exports from Glasgow to America rivaled those from London. David Hall in Philadelphia told Strahan in 1752 that he encountered "a great many Books imported from Ireland and Scotland," and that they came to him "much cheaper than from England." Edinburgh booksellers also exported to the south and east, to Scandinavia, the Low Countries, France, and Spain. And they exchanged their reprints for valued European volumes at the great continental fairs, establishing an all-important circulation of knowledge between Scotland and the Continent. Works of medicine went one way, titles by Montesquieu, Voltaire, and Pascal came back, and reprinting facilitated both.[27] Meanwhile, the setback caused ripples in the metropolis. The lord chancellor was reportedly approached by "Pirats" asking whether it was indeed true that they could freely reprint "old Books such as Milton." When Thomas Osborne with "amazing impudence" had the idea of pirating Chambers's *Cyclopaedia,* Warburton feared it would spark "a settled confusion & destruction of property." And, he added, he was so exasperated at the high-handedness and indolence of the booksellers that he "could, with satisfaction enough, see literary property turned upon the common, to teach those men the baseness of their actions."[28]

At length London was jarred into action. With Scotland almost out of bounds and Parliament still unsympathetic, the copy owners resorted to their own accustomed devices. They entered into a private scheme to eradicate piracy once and for all. At closed meetings, some sixty-odd booksellers signed on to this scheme—an impressive turnout, enhanced no doubt by the fact that those who refused were threatened with blacklisting from trade sales. The plan itself derived from the seventeenth-century precedent of Company searches. The Londoners intended to extend this practice into the provinces, creating a national (or at least English) network of informers and enforcers. And they would then use that network to trigger the legal verdict they needed. They inaugurated a common fund to pay for the campaign, immediately raising the substantial sum of $3,150. Tonson and Millar contributed the most, at £500 and £300 respectively—large sums indicative of the stakes for these two prominent copy owners. The management of the offensive was then entrusted to a committee, including Millar, Tonson, and John and James Rivington.

The campaign proper began in April 1759. John Whiston, a bookseller in Fleet Street, wrote sternly to every provincial retailer in the nation to warn of its launch; he followed this six months later by another letter, still more threatening. The Londoners were resolved on "totally preventing the sale of Scotch and Irish books, which were first printed in England," Whiston declared. He quietly ignored the statutory terms, of course; the whole point was to prevent the reprinting of works outside that limit. In effect, Millar and his corps were trying to stop the "piracy" of almost every book that had ever been published in London. They offered to accept any Scottish or Irish editions that provincial booksellers might have on hand, exchanging them for the same value in their own versions—which would mean fewer actual books, of course, since the reprints were much cheaper. But this offer held good only if all unbound copies were freely surrendered along with a full account of bound ones, and an undertaking never again to deal in "pirated editions." "*Don't you fail to send all* you have," Whiston emphasized. After May 1, he warned, "agents" would be dispatched across the length and breadth of the land to search for offending volumes. Anyone found harboring them would be prosecuted mercilessly. Booksellers should take care, Whiston concluded darkly, "for fear you are informed against."[29]

The threats were soon followed by action. Or so it seemed. Jacob Tonson sued a Salisbury bookseller named Benjamin Collins for selling a Scottish reprint of the *Spectator.* The prosecution displayed a determination to produce a definitive statement. To secure its credibility, the finest counsel were retained for both sides. William Blackstone, probably the foremost lawyer of the century, represented Tonson. Thurlow, a scarcely less renowned orator, defended Collins. And in a very unusual move, all twelve senior common-law judges—from King's Bench, Common Pleas, and the Exchequer—agreed to hear the case. But all was not what it appeared to be. Collins was in fact a correspondent of the Londoners, and one of the few provincial booksellers to be heavily invested in copies. He had been recruited as a willing collaborator. The idea was to contrive a case as advantageous as possible for the oligarchs, out of which would come their required legal ruling. This resolution would then be extended to Scotland on the authority of London's highest courts to sweep the pirates aside. But the suit's contrived character soon became evident. In Edinburgh, Lord Dreghorn (John MacLaurin) dismissed it as a "Mock-trial." In the end the judges declined to issue a verdict at all.[30]

PIRACY, PROGRESS, AND THE PUBLIC

At that point the campaign for perpetual property became even more calamitous. Company searches had been controversial even before 1688. Now they met with real opposition as violating revolution principles. The provinces were not mere extensions of London, Scotland was no colony, and this kind of high-handed treatment provoked resentment in both. One of the Edinburgh booksellers ensnared in the campaign was Alexander Donaldson. Incensed by what he saw as an attempt to maintain a monopoly by intimidation, Donaldson turned into the most convinced and resolute foe the metropolitan copy owners ever faced.

Donaldson had been born in the year when Millar defended Scottish piracy.[31] He had learned his trade as an apprentice to the king's printer in Scotland, and had long collaborated with Millar to issue some of the most significant philosophy and natural philosophy of the Scottish Enlightenment. In Edinburgh he became renowned for the hospitality he extended to local authors, notably Boswell. But Donaldson now developed an implacable abhorrence of the metropolitan trade. What they saw as an essential civility, he repudiated as tyranny. He responded to the 1759 campaign by mounting the first extended campaign ever to claim that perpetual literary property was contradictory to enlightenment and the public sphere. Donaldson pioneered many of the claims made on behalf of a free trade in creative authorship that have circulated ever since.

Central to Donaldson's counteroffensive was an act of pirating. He had got hold of Whiston's threatening letters, and now gave them pride of place in his own devastating little treatise, modestly entitled *Some thoughts on the state of literary property*. The point, he proclaimed, was that "the world" should see "how oppressive, in these lands of liberty, their monopolising schemes have been." The Londoners, defeated in court, had resorted to "combination and conspiracy," using "terrour" to get their way. Booksellers across the kingdom were being forced to submit to their "usurped seclusive right." Donaldson himself had been dragged through interminable prosecutions for "what they call pirated editions," he complained, yet never to any effect, because the Londoners had never dared to push a case to a resolution. A real trial, he affirmed, would lay bear "the mysteries of bookselling" and reveal the vacuity of claims for perpetual monopoly.[32]

Where Tonson and Millar appealed to political economy and law, Donaldson made a point of appealing to the public. Apparently, he told readers, all who reprinted books were now to be denounced as *"pirates* and *invaders."* If so, Donaldson insisted, it was precisely these so-called pirates who were the true bulwarks of the public and of learning. They upheld access to ideas and arguments, in the face of a clique scheming to become monopolists of all printed knowledge. The London trade, he charged, sought to create "the most tyrannical and barefaced combination that ever was set on foot in any country." As Dreghorn had declared, their monopoly threatened to "retard, and, indeed, stop altogether the progress of learning." And it could not be allowed to endure if Britain were to remain "a free country." The very character of Donaldson's tract—a cheap pamphlet, able to be read and argued over in a coffeehouse—exemplified the point it was designed to make.[33]

It is worth stressing that this preeminent "pirate" did not deny that authors deserved to be rewarded. On the contrary, Donaldson recognized that they spent "time and labour" on creating works "beneficial to mankind in general," and acknowledged that the advancement of learning depended on their getting their deserts. But he did deny that their recompense had to come from an "original inherent property" in the work itself. Donaldson suggested instead that an author be regarded in the same light as "the inventor of any art, or the discoverer of any secret in nature." Such an author might well keep his work secret, in which case he or she might be said to retain a property in it. But when it was published, any *natural* right of property ceased. At most, the law might offer artificial protection for a limited period. That was precisely what it did, of course, for inventions. In effect, he advocated a routinized patents system for literature.

Donaldson ended his call to arms with an announcement. Since the Londoners had successfully frightened provincial booksellers into declining his business, he had decided to confront the monopolists directly. He would open his own "shop for cheap books" in London itself, just east of Norfolk Street in the Strand. There he would sell his reprints at 30–50 percent lower than the Londoners' prices. He invited country booksellers and those engaged in exports to trade with him there.[34] At the same time, he also launched a newspaper, the *Edinburgh Advertiser,* that carried advertisements for his trade. They reveal that he also touted Scottish reprints from across the country—and that he acted as a subscription agent for Dublin's leading bookseller, George Faulkner, too. The whole enterprise amounted to a challenge that the London trade could not ignore.

Meanwhile, the Londoners finally got their chance to strike back. A bookseller of Berwick-upon-Tweed named Robert Taylor had taken advantage of Thomson's *Seasons* falling out of statutory protection to print his own edition. Millar immediately launched a suit. For the first time the Londoners won a definitive decision. The verdict was close, and the judges differed significantly in their reasoning, but three of the four—Lord Mansfield, Edward Willes, and Sir Richard Aston—affirmed literary property. And even the dissenter, Sir Joseph Yates, conceded that authorial labor might create a property in an unpublished work, although he believed that the act of publication amounted to presenting the work as a "gift" to the public.[35] It seemed that literary property had finally won the endorsement that it needed. Millar did not live to see the success, having dropped dead suddenly in 1768, but his allies swiftly pushed for a new hearing in Edinburgh. They singled out Donaldson as their target. This time, they chose to center their case on a *History of the Bible* initially prepared back in the 1730s by a Berkshire vicar named Thomas Stackhouse. This was a hodgepodge work. It had been compiled rather than created; one judge expressed disdain at the very idea of being asked to consider Stackhouse an author at all. Still, it was commercially successful, and Donaldson had participated in a reprint. He defended himself stoutly, denying the possibility of a "right to the doctrine contained in the book." His side helped their cause by reprinting *Millar v. Taylor* with a commentary in favor of Yates's dissent and an appendix denying that the verdict applied north of the border.[36] And once more, in Scotland what in London had looked self-evident turned out to be anything but. Donaldson's defense prevailed.

Donaldson was now determined finally to push the whole issue to a resolution. He took a calculated decision to reprint himself Thomson's *Seasons*—the very work on which the Londoners had rested their claims in *Millar v. Taylor.* And he displayed his reprint under their noses in his

London shop. It was a deliberately provocative gesture: the commercial equivalent of throwing down the gauntlet. The Londoners could not possibly allow it to go unanswered. So they as usual sought an injunction, and, again as usual, got it. But Donaldson, unlike previous pirates, was not prepared to acquiesce. He appealed against the injunction to the House of Lords, the highest court in the land and the only one whose jurisdiction extended over the whole United Kingdom. The decades of conflicting customs, practices, and arguments in Scotland and England had come to a head. The decision at Westminster would be, both sides agreed, the crucial experiment that would determine whether or not literary property existed. And for each side the stakes extended to civilization itself.[37]

AUTHORSHIP AND INVENTION

Virtually every issue that has fascinated historians of the eighteenth century found a place in the literary property debates that now approached their climax. This rather cornucopian quality derived in part from the fact that attorneys were accustomed to deploying every argumentative resource they could lay their hands on. Protagonists invoked, for example, the politics of the nation-state, the history and credibility of documentary evidence, mercantilism versus free trade, the nature of a public sphere, the commercialization of genius, and physiologies of sensibility. But one element arose unexpectedly, returned repeatedly, and proved, in the end, pivotal: mechanism.[38] The question on which the fate of literary property may well have turned was that of what distinction, if any, existed between authorship and invention. Was a book like a machine, and if so, in what way? Was an author akin to an inventor? Or were these things in some fundamental way *unlike*—and if so, again, in exactly what way? More subtly, a new theory in astronomy or mathematics, or a table of logarithms, posed critical problems for notions of authorship generated out of poetics. A theory or mathematical table was a textual entity, to be sure, yet one for which independent discoverers might easily exist. It was entirely unclear on what moral basis one discoverer should hold a perpetual monopoly over another.

One reason for focusing on these questions here is that the positions protagonists took on them were, to modern eyes, entirely counterintuitive. Accustomed to living in a world with a strongly entrenched notion of intellectual property, we now associate the advocacy of creative rights with claims for a broad principle underlying them. But there was no such concept as intellectual property in the eighteenth century. And at that time it was the *opponents* of literary property who insisted that authorship and invention were fundamentally alike—that they were varieties of one underlying thing, or, at least, that efforts to prove otherwise made no sense. The proponents of such property, by contrast, sought to demonstrate that they were radically distinct. Their debate proved critical not only to the outcome of the contest itself, but to the subsequent history that that outcome made possible.

Mechanical invention was a child of the projecting age. Attended by the same problems of credit and speculation as stockjobbing and publication, projectors blossomed and crashed as fast as South Sea Bubble companies. We now tend to perceive the first signs of the Industrial Revolution in their schemes, but that perception requires a lot of hindsight. For contemporaries the problem was to discern the plausible—or even possible—from the fanciful or fraudulent. Something of a market arose in expertise dedicated to making such distinctions.[39] In consequence, the meanings, nature, and relative authority of artisanal and theoretical knowledge had to be thrashed out. The most basic terms for the Anglo-Scottish exchange about authorship and property—terms like *skill, knowledge, art,* and *invention*—were therefore not constants in their own right, but remained in flux. Moreover, since around 1700 a polite and commercial enterprise of experiment had blossomed, putting these terms into the hands of a public of readers and customers. Paying audiences flocked to coffeehouse lectures to see men like Jean Theophilus Desaguliers and Benjamin Martin make visible Newtonian "active powers"—powers placed in Creation by God. This was mechanical philosophy too, because its content depended on the artful making, circulation, and use of machines: electrical machines, air pumps, orreries, and, increasingly, automata. One could scarcely adduce the genius of a Newton or a Boyle in this context without invoking the machine work that conveyed the insights of such geniuses to Hanoverian audiences. The impresarios of public lecturing laid claim on this basis to an expertise that deserved to overturn long-standing artisanal customs, so the implications for crafts (including printing) were potentially immediate. To these showmen, the already old distinction between scholars and craftsmen not merely did not hold good any more, but loomed large as absurd, benighted, and medieval. Yet this —or one version of it—was the very distinction that defenders of literary property at this moment felt they had to embrace. They had to insist that mechanical invention was a craftlike, nonintellectual enterprise. Literary creation, by contrast, was the work of the mind.

The reason why the booksellers felt this need was simple. The products of mechanical ingenuity—devices, mechanisms, processes, and models— did not warrant any kind of property other than the banal ownership of a physical object. The only way an inventor could get exclusivity was by applying on an ad hoc basis for a patent. A patent was a privilege, not a right, and its duration was limited by the Monopolies Act of 1624. As Donaldson remarked, patents were therefore "*incompatible* with the supposal of an antecedent right vested in the inventor or discoverer."[40] This explains why it was the opponents of literary property like Donaldson who insisted on identifying a common quality to literary and mechanical invention. In principle, as Blackstone commented at the time, it might have been possible to draw the inference the other way, *from* authorship *to* invention. But to do this would involve questioning the Monopolies Act—a law that had the status of Whig scripture. That alternative was therefore closed off on the grounds of political reality after 1688. So anyone seeking to uphold a natural right for authors had to demonstrate that literary invention was *fundamentally unlike* mechanical. The stakes in doing so were high indeed. If a literary work could be "essentially distinguished from a machine," then the enemies of literary property would see their strongest argument of principle demolished. But if, on the other side, some single principle of creativity underlying words and things could be enshrined in law and culture, then it would destroy the claim of a natural literary property right.[41]

Opponents of literary property therefore maintained that mechanical inventions were "as much the natural Property of the Inventors, as Books are of the Authors"—which is to say, no natural property at all.[42] "A book is a combination of ideas," argued Donaldson's camp; "so is a machine." Both were the result of "invention," and all attempts at distinction were "unintelligible." Both might be kept secret, but as soon as they were published, they were naturally open to all.[43] Yates cited John Harrison— inventor of the chronometer that solved the longitude problem—to confirm as much. "Every Reason that can be urged for the Invention of an Author may be urged with equal Strength and Force, for the Inventor of a Machine," he insisted. "Original Inventions stand upon the *same* Footing, in Point of *Property*, ... whether the Case be *mechanical*, or *Literary;* whether it be an *Epic Poem,* or an *Orrery.*" Harrison had certainly invested at least as much inspiration, mental labor, and money in building his clocks as Thomson ever had in writing *The Seasons.* And, Yates contended, "the *Immorality* of pirating another Man's *Invention* is full as great, as that of purloining his *Ideas.*" Yet the fact was that Harrison had had no natural right. For Yates, the point was powerful but subtle. An author might certainly have a moral claim upon the benevolence of the public. But he had no legal right to demand that benevolence on pain of prosecution.[44] Likewise, Thurlow insisted that "Sir *Isaac Newton* had no greater Property in his *Principia,* than Lord *Orrery* had in his Machine. If the Labour of the Head gives the Right, the Property is just the same."[45] In Edinburgh, at least one of the Court of Session judges declared this question decisive for him. Both books and machines involved "genius and industry," after all, and each had its public utility. And in deciding the important case of *Hinton v. Donaldson,* the lord president made this the primary concern. "Where is the excellence of the invention of a book over that of a machine?" he demanded. "And if there is no foundation for a claim to a perpetual exclusive right in the property of the machine, why should there be one with respect to books?"[46] The same point duly recurred at the climacteric of *Donaldson v. Becket* itself. An orrery, observed the counsel for the Scots, "represents the *Planetary System,*" so it could hardly be devoid of intellectual content. "He, who makes one after the first Model, takes the Science of Astronomy as represented by the *Orrery:* And he, who prints a Book, takes the *Author's Sentiments*—Where is the Difference?"[47]

The opposing position originated with the controversial theologian and literary executor of Pope, William Warburton. In 1747 Warburton published the first defense of authorial property to insist at length on a real distinction between books and inventions. It did so in a simple argument couched in terms of scholastic notions of form, matter, and final causes. Warburton maintained that a book contained what he called "doctrine," in which literary property inhered. By contrast, there was no doctrine in what he called a "utensil," by which he seems to have meant an extremely basic machine like a fork. The only property such a device could sustain was therefore in the material object itself. In other words, to perceive the distinction one needed to consider "the complete Idea of a Book" and recognize it as a "*Work of the Mind.*"[48] Warburton's discussion of books and machines—he clearly had rather high-cultural books in mind, as well as rather banal machines—thus laid out two extremes, characterized by the absolute existence and nonexistence of "doctrine," and hence of natural property. He did, however, acknowledge a complex middle case. This was occupied by what he called "*mechanic Engines.*" Mechanic engines were machines that were partly works of the mind and partly of the hand. Their common characteristic was that they manifested nature's "Powers," which were "regulated by the right Application of Geometric Science."

There was a certain precedent for this idea in the place traditionally accorded in the universities to the mathematical sciences.[49] But Warburton seems to have been thinking specifically of the demonstration devices that commercial lecturers in Hanoverian England used to convey mechanical philosophy to paying audiences. The maker had no *natural* right of property even in such a device, he noted, although "the Operation of the Mind" was clearly "intimately concerned" in its design and manufacture. But a mechanic engine did warrant some *artificial* exclusivity. And that, he said, was exactly why states had stepped in to offer limited-term privileges. In Warburton's view, patents existed because scientific machines occupied an intermediate position between hand works (no property) and mind works (natural property). Their existence paradoxically confirmed the validity of perpetual rights in the latter.[50]

By contemporary standards Warburton's analysis was both simplistic and conceptually dated. Thurlow dismissed it simply as "miserable." Even a simple machine, he pointed out, might demand from its author as much "labour of Head" as an orrery did from its more expert maker, so that "this Ground of Property depends entirely upon the Difference of Heads."[51] But upholders of the right of authorship nevertheless seized on the idea, and from this point on routinely invoked a radical distinction between machines and books. Willes and Aston, for example, insisted on it.[52] More extensively, the anonymous author of *A Vindication of the Exclusive Right of Authors to their own Works* (1762) endorsed a similar commitment. For this author a mechanical invention was properly an "object of trade," and as such should be left unrestricted on free trade grounds. In a machine the working of the mechanism was the only aim, with no further purpose of communicating a doctrine. A printer might well resemble the constructor of a machine in this sense—but nobody thought that a printer merited a natural right.[53]

The great virtue of such contentions was that they took the otherwise rather metaphysical distinctions—between form and matter, or between doctrine and expression—that were always going to be central to any resolution on literary property and gave them tangible form. They did so by specifying the *kinds* of machines at issue. Warburton's invocation of utensils was thus dismissed as "ridiculous" by one antagonist who noticed that it prejudged its outcome. Instead, the real issue lay with "Mathematical Machines, such as Orreries, Microcosms, Clocks, and Watches." An orrery, say, was as much a "composition" as a book.[54] A few specific machines particularly embodied the mixture of doctrine, expression, skill, labor, and investment, and therefore began to reappear repeatedly in the literary property debates. The air pump (fig. 6.1) and chronometer were two of these. A third, and perhaps the most prevalent, was the orrery (fig. 6.2). This was a clockwork device designed to display the Copernican system in motion. It was also, in a literal sense, a model of enlightenment itself, because the point often seems to have been to model the diffusion of light through the cosmos. Every self-respecting experimental lecturer by mid-century had one. A few were enormously sophisticated and impressive devices. They were the prime public instances of a growing fashion for ingenious automata, or self-driven machines.

One particular automaton was repeatedly adduced in the literary property debates. This was Henry Bridges's "Microcosm" (fig. 6.3). An "Elaborate and Matchless PILE of ART," as one showman memorably called it, the Microcosm had originally been constructed in 1741 for the Duke of Chandos, the supreme speculator of the projecting age and Desaguliers's major patron. Since then it had been widely exhibited in coffeehouses. It was a ten-foot-high, six-foot-wide marvel. Built in the form of an ornate Roman Temple, in its fabric it contained musical automata, models of a carpenter's workshop and landscapes with realistically moving figures, and accurate rotating mechanisms showing the Copernican and Ptolemaic systems. It also boasted an orrery for the moons of Jupiter. It played music specially composed for its internal organ—or spectators could ask it to play their own. In all, it combined in one mechanism the principles of architecture, sculpture, painting, music, and astronomy. The Microcosm had taken ten years altogether to build (twenty, it was later claimed) but could be seen for a shilling. That fact symbolized the bargain of rational creativity in a commercial sphere.[55]

Once the preserve of courts, automata like orreries and the Microcosm were now objects of public regard in a world of goods. As they became ever more complex, so they posed ever more pointed questions in that new context—questions about human nature and its relation to

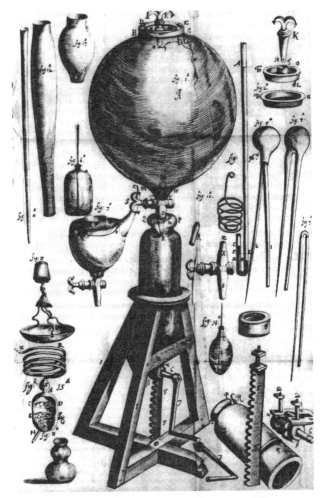

FIGURE 6.1. Boyle's air pump. R. Boyle, *New experiments physico-mechanicall, touching the spring of the air* (Oxford: by H. Hall, for T. Robinson, 1660), end piece. Courtesy of the University of Chicago Library.

mechanism, about social organization (manufactories being envisaged as automata), and, with a *frisson* of infidelity, about the powers of matter itself. Automata became a focus for all the intellectual and social issues of mind, labor, and political organization by which the public sphere was confronted. Clockwork people played music and sighed as they did so; clockwork ducks ate and defecated. By a strange and evocative coincidence, the first writing android was unveiled in 1774, just as *Donaldson v.*

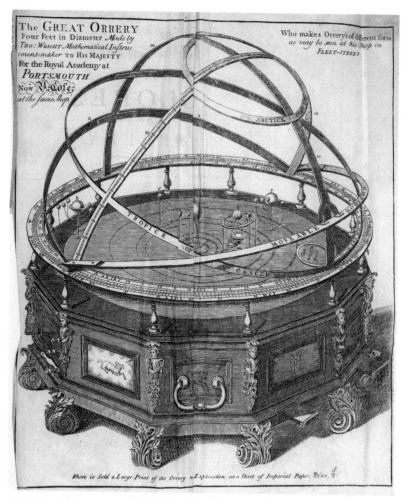

The GREAT ORRERY
Four Feet in Diameter *Made by*
Tho: Wright Mathematical Instru-
ment-maker TO HIS MAJESTY
For the Royal Academy at
PORTSMOUTH
Now B. Cole,
at the same Shop

Who makes Orrery's of different forts
as may be seen at his Shop in
FLEET-STREET

ARCTICK CIRCLE

HORIZON

TROPICK OF CANCER

MOVEABLE

Where is Sold a Large Print of the Orrery w.Explanation on a Sheet of Imperial Paper. Price 2:

FIGURE 6.2. The great orrery. J. Harris, *Description and use of the globes* (London: for B. Cole and E. Cushee, 1763), frontispiece. Courtesy of the University of Chicago Library.

Becket determined that literary production was not mechanical. Constructed in Neuchâtel (that center of reprinting) by the renowned Jacquet-Droz brothers, it was soon being displayed in every European capital, including London:

A figure representing a child of two years of age, seated on a stool, and writing at a desk. This figure dips its pen in the ink, shakes out what is superfluous, and writes distinctly and correctly whatever the company

The Microcosm

FIGURE 6.3. Bridges's Microcosm. E. Davies, *Succinct description of the microcosm* (Glasgow: by R. and A. Foulis, for E. Davies, 1765), frontispiece. Courtesy of the British Library.

think proper to dictate, without any person's touching it. It places the initial letters with propriety, and leaves a suitable space between the words it writes. When it has finished a line it passes on to the next, always observing the proper distance between the lines: while it writes, its eyes are fixed on its work, but as soon as it has finished a letter or a word, it casts a look at the copy, seeming to imitate it.

Another android drew pictures ("the various motions of the eyes, arms, and hand imitate nature exactly").[56] An ex-apprentice of the Jacquet-Droz named Maillardet subsequently built a career in London on machines that seemed to act with "life and reason." According to David Brewster they were "very common" there a generation later, when Charles Babbage certainly witnessed them. To announce such a creature, Brewster opined —thinking of the most notorious of all, the chess-playing Turk—was tantamount to projecting "a mechanical counsellor of state."[57]

That automata and androids exerted such a fascination is now rather well known. But the Microcosm gave solid form to the challenge that they presented to accounts of creative authorship in particular. Could it really be claimed that this machine represented a nullity of intellectual labor, sentiment, ideas, or "doctrine" when compared to Thomson's *Seasons?* Had it demanded less investment of time, work, and money? And were the ideas embedded in it themselves products of mechanical systems— systems of sensation, vibration, and association that human knowledge depended on? It seemed evident that the constructor of any decent orrery, let alone such a wondrous device, must have "a clear Conception of the Planetary System" before actually making the device. Nor could it plausibly be claimed that it was made only for an immediate, utilitarian function. On the contrary, visitors were publicly encouraged to come back and see the Microcosm a second time to *learn* from it. "The End of the Inventor is not fuller obtained in the first individual Machine," therefore, "than the End of the Author in the first individual Book." For Donaldson's side, the Microcosm was the evident proof they needed that inventing involved "ingenuity of the mind." Without exclusivity, it might be that even a machine as prodigious as this could be copied by a crafty imitator relatively quickly, perhaps even quickly enough to invalidate a patent. Surely, if no natural right existed for this, then no literary work should qualify for one either.[58]

The Microcosm might seem to destroy any idea of a radical qualitative distinction between authorship and invention. And indeed, it is hard to find anyone explicitly sustaining that distinction in its case. But by the same token it provided alert critics with a new line of defense against the conclusion that literary property was nugatory. The question became not the nature of original authorship, but the nature of copying. A machine this complex posed the question of what, exactly, the act of copying—of pirating—actually *was*. After all, a copy of the microcosm could never be *exactly* the same as the original. Material always differed to some extent in a reproduction. So did workmanship. In a world that was still largely artisanal, the variations between individual workers' skills and customs mattered. As Blackstone put it, "a Duplicate of a mechanic Engine is, at best, but a Resemblance of the other." But with a book it was different. And in trying to articulate *how* it was different, Blackstone broached what would become a major axiom of copyright. The "Identity" of a literary work, he now claimed, did not reside in its materiality, nor precisely in that "doctrine" that others had vaunted. It lay, rather, in "Style and Sentiment." Paper and type were accidental to this—they were merely "Vehicles to convey that Style and Sentiment to a Distance." Any duplicate that achieved the same transfer was therefore "the same identical Work," irrespective of artisanal variations.[59] This was the origin of the otherwise intractable distinction—which became central to copyright—between idea and expression. Expression, that is, originated in the bid to find a distinction between book and machine. It was that element of a book that required initial authorship but could be copied without mind.

The crucial point therefore lay not in the act of authorship at all, but in the act of copying. A copy of a machine was, as Aston said, always "a *different Work*." That was why the machine's originator could not claim natural property in it. To copy the Microcosm a craftsman would have to reproduce in his mind the ideas of the original maker. As Smythe told the Lords in *Donaldson v. Becket,* a pirate of an orrery would essentially have to be an astronomer, and the copy must therefore be "in a degree an original work." Copying machines consequently had a positive social value. It required investments of expertise, training, and education, and it served progress, because improvements were always integrated into the new device. Some even claimed that progress in general—that is, writ large, the whole stadial history of civilization—depended on this truth.

Ironically, to prove this point Kames instanced "the art of making salt water fresh" as a recent invention that was open. "Was it ever deemed to be a transgression against property, to use that art without consent of the inventor?" But if replicating machines involved "labour of the head," replicating books was mere "labour of the hand." They could be copied by some pirate printer without any attention whatsoever to meaning. Reprinting was mindless, produced no progress, and was therefore valueless. A reprinted book was "the *very same Substance*," replicated by a "*mere mechanical Act.*" That was why it was accounted "theft." Blackstone, for one, said that anyone should be free to "copy and imitate" machines "at Pleasure," in a state of "natural liberty" that ought to be qualified, if at all, only by temporary patents. But replicating books would cripple enlightenment.[60] So pivotal was this point that the Londoners submitted to the House of Lords a special statement describing how books were printed, in order to demonstrate that "printing *of Books* is of a peculiar Nature, and the Manufacture of them totally *different from that of mechanical Instruments.*" By now they were arguing not that the originating of inventions was inferior to the originating of books, but that the copying of inventions was superior.[61]

Donaldson's side therefore had to take a stand on the nature of copying. They did so in 1774, telling the Lords that "*Public Utility* requires that the Productions of the Mind should be diffused as wide as possible." The connotations of monopoly—high prices, shoddy work, the suppression of improvements—applied to enlightenment. They meant that natural freedom must apply to books as well as machines. "Not only the *Manners*, but even *Science* changes in the Progress of Time," they pointed out; with perpetual property in effect, the bookseller who owned Newton's *Principia* could impede later improvements. "All our learning will be locked up in the hands of the Tonsons and Lintots of the age," Camden warned, "'till the public become as much their slaves, as their own hackney compilers are." Sir John Dalrymple agreed, and added disapprovingly that the booksellers "opprobriously termed men who laudably enlarged the circle of literature, by giving new editions of works of merit, pirates." Kames even elevated the right of copying to the level of Creation. Mankind had been created as an imitative being as well as a social one, he announced, precisely to make progress possible. A monopoly for inventors or authors alike would therefore be an error of cosmic dimensions. It would "counteract the designs of Providence."[62]

PERPETUAL MOTIONS

Donaldson's appeal at the House of Lords began on February 4, 1774. With so much at stake, crowds gathered early. Burke, Goldsmith, Garrick, and others were lucky enough to find places in the gallery; hundreds more could not get in.[63] What they came to hear was by common consent the culmination of the most important copyright case in history.

It is not now possible to recapture the exchanges that took place on those days in their entirety. What is known is that Lord Chancellor Apsley boiled the literary property debates down to three central questions. These he posed to the law lords present, requesting, as was conventional, that they cast advisory votes before the Lords as a whole determined the fate of the appeal. They were almost ascetic in their abstraction from everything that had imbued decades of debate with passion and meaning. First: by common law, did an author have the sole first right to print and publish a work? This addressed the fundamental point of whether authorship conferred a right by nature. Practically, this would only arise as a legal issue in cases like the unauthorized publication of correspondence, but its larger significance was that an affirmative answer was necessary if the London booksellers' claims were to be entertained at all. Second: assuming that this right existed, and leaving aside the 1710 statute, did it end with the work's publication? This was equivalent to asking whether an author, in publishing a work, presented it to the public in the sense that an inventor did an unpatented invention. The Londoners assumed that the answer was no. And then, third: if the common-law right did indeed last beyond publication, did the right conferred by the 1710 statute replace it? Only with this third question did the statute itself enter the frame.

The speeches that followed tackled all the themes of the decades-long dispute. Camden in particular added two more queries to Apsley's that restated the problem in such a way that he could mount a vigorous, and later much-lauded, assault on perpetual property. Equally important was the fact that Mansfield, who had earlier upheld perpetuity in *Millar v. Taylor*, remained silent. Mansfield also declined to vote, apparently out of deference to a convention that chief justices not take an active part when the Lords were addressing cases from their own courts. In the event, his reticence mattered as much as Camden's oratory. It left eleven judges registering their views. Question 1, affirming an initial authorial property, passed handily enough by 8–3, although it is remarkable that even this minimalist motion did not pass unanimously. On question 2, asking whether the natural right were lost on publication — or whether authorship equated to invention — the judges advised that it survived, by the narrower tally of 7–4. That left question 3, on whether the 1710 law supplanted the common-law right. This was the real nub of the whole conflict. A vote for the common-law right would endorse perpetual property. And the outcome could not have been closer. The clerk listed the tally as 6–5 against; but it seems that this was an error. In fact, the judges voted 6–5 in favor — and, as Mark Rose points out, it would have been 7–5 had Mansfield voted. The closeness of the tally demonstrates how finely balanced the debate still was.[64]

But these votes were merely advisory. The House as a whole had now to come to its decision, and, the judicial opinion having been recorded, this seems not to have been close at all. The peers decisively rejected the injunction against Donaldson's reprint. Donaldson's *Edinburgh Advertiser* crowed that not a single dissenting voice was heard. Another Scot, John Murray, who had long struggled to break into the London market, told a Glasgow law professor that the decision had dissolved an "illegal monopoly" sustained by a combination of scoundrels.[65] The Londoners had finally got the definitive statement they had so long sought, but what it stated, to their horror, was that literary property did not exist. From now on, copyright would be an artificial, state-created protection. The "pirates" had won. James Boswell told Donaldson that like Alexander the Great — the original pirate of all the world — he could now "sit down and weep that he had no more booksellers to conquer."[66]

What one historian has called "as perfect a private monopoly as economic history can show" had come to an end.[67] What difference did it make? The answer was not quite as clear as the London copy owners feared. They initially portrayed their defeat as a catastrophe. Overnight, they told the newspapers, some £200,000 worth of what they had "yesterday thought property" had been obliterated, and they were therefore "in a manner ruined."[68] They mounted a desperate rearguard action to salvage something out of the ruins, still insisting that literary and mechanical authorship were radically different and petitioning Parliament for relief. The bid provoked another round of vigorous debate, with Donaldson stepping forward again to oppose it. It failed. After that, the bookselling elite decided that it would simply have to live with a world in which literary property had vanished.

The sky did not fall. No metropolitan bookseller went under as a result of the verdict, and literary property itself in some ways proved remarkably resilient. The foundation of such "property" had in any case been customary and practical rather than legal, and all the decision really did was to erase the juridical plausibility of a natural right. London's publishers remained free to maintain their combinations, about which complaints continued to be heard for decades—indeed, centuries—to come. Their first move, in fact, was to moot a huge conger with a stock of £10,000 dedicated to holding the old copies "inviolate."

Yet *Donaldson v. Becket* did have an effect. Rivals sprang up to challenge the London clique, keen to print and reprint in new forms and for new readerships. Thomas Carnan focused on children's literature; William Lane's Minerva Press dominated fiction.[69] The trade enjoyed rapid expansion, with fortunes to be made in hitherto unrecognized areas. Those prepared to experiment and take risks could benefit hugely. Many who did were newcomers to London, like the Scot John Bell, whose 109-volume series of *The Poets of Great Britain*—sold as "the only complete uniform edition of the British Poets"—could only exist thanks to the end of perpetual property. Such enterprises created what was almost a new kind of book business.[70] In a sense, what was happening was that the book trade was taking on the character of an industry. A major marker was the advent of a new social kind, the publisher. The first firm to take that step was Rivington's. Longman had followed suit by the 1810s, and John Murray did likewise, pioneering the system for paying authors that would prevail throughout the Victorian era. Meanwhile, the burgeoning industrial towns became foci of literary productivity in their own right. And in Scotland, Constable created the first modern best-sellers in *Waverley* and *Rob Roy*.[71]

For printers' journeymen, however, the rise of copyright was ominous indeed. How antagonistic the journeymen could be to the oligarchs of literary property had already been revealed in 1762, when a compositor named Jacob Ilive had led a doomed revolt in the Stationers' Company. The grandson of Elinor James—herself a prolific printer, pamphleteer, and petitioner, who had sought to defend the printers' chapels against both copy owners and reprinters in the 1690s—Ilive was something of a Miltonic figure in Georgian Grub Street. He became a virtuoso of pirate strategies, associating with their supreme exponent, William Rayner, and being sued by Alexander Pope as one of the "Pyraters" of the *Dunciad*. Ilive developed over time an elaborate deist cosmology unique to him, according to which humans were fallen angels, interred in bodies and seeking to use reason to reascend through a hierarchy of worlds toward heaven. He added to this a belief that the history of Christianity was one of successive corruptions of books, interrupted occasionally when God "republished" the true bases of faith. And to demonstrate the plausibility of this idea he put his piratical skills to use to produce his own work of Scripture, which he called the Book of Jasher. In short, this was a man who pushed the strategies of the pirate Enlightenment as far as they could go.

Ilive planned to act on his radical convictions. He wanted to reform society root and branch, ridding it of mystery mongers in favor of what he called "bodies or fraternities of artificers living and supporting one another in community"—that is, in printers' terms, chapels. Ilive believed these to be the core of an orderly and moral society. To give them their proper role—the role they had had before the Norman Conquest—he envisaged the "entire abolition" of the oligarchs' governance. He decided that printing itself—the very foundation of a reasoning public—must come first. So he launched a campaign to restructure the core of the craft, the Company of Stationers. Building on an abortive effort by an earlier band of radicals, he issued an unauthorized impression of the Company's founding documents, which revealed the Court of Assistants to be a later interpolation of Stuart times. This *"plain* and *rational"* account should, he thought, lead to a return to *"original Simplicity."* Piracy had cast light where there had been darkness. He now summoned the journeymen to elect their own master and wardens. The rendezvous took place on May 31, 1762, at the Dog Tavern on Garlic Hill.[72] Ilive leaped up onto a table and delivered an impassioned speech proposing that the printers act to "rescue their liberties" from the publishers. They elected one Christopher Norris master there and then, with John Lenthall and John Wilcox wardens—three men who remain obscure but were certainly no copy owners. Ilive believed that these officers would simply walk into their places at the Hall.

Unfortunately for him, the real company was not so compliant. Its officers refused the rebels entry, observing urbanely that Ilive must be "somewhat disordered in his mind." The "rebellious election" proved futile, and a disappointed Ilive himself died shortly after. In the end, far from establishing the chapel as the lynchpin of a revived public culture, his uprising achieved precisely the opposite. It marked the last time that journeymen were ever acknowledged as a voting estate in the industry on which England's public culture depended. For the first time, a fundamental and explicit divide was introduced in the book trade. In effect, property, not craft mastery, was confirmed as the structuring principle by which the trade would be shaped. That future apparently belonged not to the chapel, nor to the pirate sphere, but to copyright—to capital. And the chapels' defeat was not peculiar to the world of print. Similar trends were occurring in many trades. As they did, so journeymen and craftsmen began to see common interests outside their own vocations. A new kind of social classification was in the offing. It mapped allegiances longitudinally, across trades, rather than latitudinally, within them. As copyright and publishing became the defining centerpieces of public culture, a novel way of seeing the politics of craft took root. Its defining element, shorn of the cosmological attributes of Ilive's chapel theodicy, was to be the concept of class.[73]

The contentions about copying and progress that took shape in the literary property furor also coincided with major changes in the practice of patenting, on which the inventive work of industrialization—and therefore class formation—would come to depend. Explicit articulations of some "property" in inventions seem to have appeared only in about 1712 or so—remarkably coincident with the original copyright law—and there was little if any case law before the 1760s. The subsequent consolidation came at almost the same time as Donaldson's challenge, and at some of the same legal hands. In particular, Lord Mansfield—who upheld perpetuity in *Millar v. Taylor* and then doomed it by his silence—presided over the case that established the propriety of patenting changes to machines. His side of the literary property conflict had just been arguing that progress in mechanics was the root of social progress; and this notion he now embedded into patent practice. Mansfield also insisted that the contemporary notion of copying be made the criterion for a patent's specification: a skilled craftsman in an appropriate field must be able to replicate the device from the document.[74] This then became central to the concept that emerged in these years of a patent as a public bargain, with a specification of this kind as the quid pro quo for a temporary monopoly. It also confirmed that "principles" could not be patented. On the authority of Yates's pro-Donaldson view in *Millar v. Taylor,* a principle was now deemed akin to "the sentiments of an author while in his own mind"—pure doctrines, perhaps, unable to be reduced to property until rendered in some published form. Notions of copying, progress, and the public interest thus solidified in the domain of mechanism—of industry—in alignment with the emerging culture of authorship.[75]

It is therefore fitting that one of the few extended responses to the 1774 outcome should come from a Grub Street hack who was also a projector of automata, and that it should address at length the relation between authorship and invention. A leading English translator of Rousseau and Voltaire, William Kenrick made his living as a playwright, a literary pugilist prepared to take on all comers (including Garrick, Dr. Johnson, and even, faute de mieux, himself), and editor of a rather serious critical periodical called the *London Review*. He seems to have been a materialist, a mortalist (that is, a believer that the soul expires at death), and an announced foe to priestcraft; the pages of the *London Review* resounded with his defenses of Joseph Priestley's unorthodoxies. He was also the projector of a perpetual motion machine that enjoyed considerable notoriety.

A Saxon artisan named Johann Bessler, or rather (thanks to a simple encoding algorithm) Orffyreus, had originally invented Kenrick's device in the 1710s. It took the form of a large wheel that seemed to turn unceasingly with no visible power source. The renowned experimental philosopher Willem 'sGravesande had examined Orffyreus's wheel in the Landgrave's court at Kassel and favorably compared it to the latest steam engines, with which it was in competition as a power source for industry. A long debate had then ensued involving Europe's greatest philosophers, as the question of whether such a device were physically possible grew into a no-holds-barred controversy between Newtonian mechanics, which seemed to outlaw it, and Leibnizian *vis viva* theories, which 'sGravesande thought might leave open the possibility. Meanwhile, Orffyreus sought to sell his secret for a huge sum, but found no takers and died in obscurity. Finding himself a decade and a half later in the same castle, Kenrick was inspired to recreate the wheel. After spending another fifteen years on what he called his "rotator," he applied for a patent, only to waver between seeking exclusivity and adapting Orffyreus's old strategy of trying to sell the secret. In the end he announced a new system of mechanics that apparently lay behind the machine, and advertised in print for subscribers willing to pay to be in on the mystery.[76]

Kenrick found that the worlds of print and projecting were inseparable, with the same materialism upholding both. Ideas, the source of knowledge, were explicable in mechanical terms, and as such were in principle available to all. Like Priestley, Kenrick believed in a rational, active public that could be united through the circulation of printed knowledge. A perpetual rotator could be validated by the perpetual circulation of print. But threats of priestcraft and combination loomed over each of these convictions. Even clear, "*sensible* Demonstration," for example, tended not to work when it came to facts that Christians had been told to discount, like that of a continuity between animals and humans; they clung to a conviction that "some unseen, unknown Cause" would appear in the end and "at once confute it all." Exactly the same problem plagued attempts to demonstrate perpetual motion experimentally—witnesses convinced beforehand of its impossibility would refuse to believe their eyes. And he prefaced his account of the rotator with a violent attack on "philosophical criticks" who banded together to reinforce such complacencies, reprinting his tracts at length in order to ridicule them. This was business as usual in the republic of letters, Kenrick sighed; the natural state of that republic was a civil war fought by "pirates by profession."[77]

In Kenrick's view, *Donaldson v. Becket* mattered because it finally made apparent this shared plight of the Grub Street author and the projecting inventor. "The *inventor* of a *machine*, or *art useful* in life," he noted, "is now almost universally admitted to stand precisely on the same footing with the author of a book." *This* was what the long conflict had achieved. And it had the effect of making visible for the first time two problems that impeded progress itself. First, "artists" had no such principle as copyright to protect their interests. They still had to seek patents individually—a time-consuming, costly, and uncertain business. Kenrick therefore urged that a counterpart to copyright be inaugurated for inventors. This would have major social advantages, he thought. By awakening "the curiosity of Genius" and the "spirit of enterprize," it would clarify a natural and proper distinction between the "*inventive artificer*" and the "uninventive artisan" —those qualified to employ others versus those capable only of working themselves. Recognizing the incipient formation of classes around properties meant, he urged, doing something that nobody had seriously proposed before because it would mean scrapping the relevant clause of the 1624 Statute of Monopolies. Kenrick explicitly welcomed that prospect. It would restore to the state the power to patronize ingenuity, and rectify what had in any case been a category mistake, for properties in inventions were not truly monopolies. Far from resurrecting monopolies, his change would help destroy the real combinations that were rife in his own society, like that of the booksellers.[78] In short, a copyright system for inventions would underwrite industrial progress.

The second plight that Kenrick felt the 1774 result highlighted was that of *unoriginal* authors. The previous generation had seen a wealth of debate about original authorship, but almost none (sardonic remarks excepted) about what, after all, amounted to the vast majority of published writing. Kenrick pointed out that the practice of getting injunctions against "pretended pirates" had been used repeatedly against works of compilation. If perpetual copyright did not exist, however, then this tactic became suddenly untenable, because the Statute of 1710 nowhere outlawed these practices. As the Scottish jurist Monboddo had noticed, the Act of Anne forbade only "the mere mechanical operation of printing, without any labour of the mind"; it said nothing against exercising "memory or judgment" upon the original. This mattered enormously. Recycling was, in Kenrick's view, the central reality of eighteenth-century publishing, and therefore of enlightenment. Abstracts, abridgments, epitomes, translations, and compilations were the vast preponderance of the new books published every year. Five hundred "copyists and compilers" existed for every one original author. Moreover, their number necessarily increased as the number of books multiplied, providing ever more fodder for regurgitation. And this—not isolated, heroic creation—was where knowledge and progress truly arose. So the world of printed knowledge was itself a perpetual motion machine, with the power to cycle indefinitely like a commercial-literary counterpart to Kenrick's rotator. That perpetuity of motion had until now been braked almost to a standstill by a false mechanics. A different kind perpetuity—perpetual property—had stopped it spinning. At last, a true mechanics had been given its rein, and the engine of publishing had been freed to accelerate to full speed.[79]

The advent of copyright—and the overthrow of literary property—therefore came about from a violent but fruitful clash between authorship and mechanical invention. The result can justly be called revolutionary for both fields. It was not a revolution in intellectual property, for that concept did not yet exist. But it was, if anything, even more important. Only once it had taken place could intellectual property come into being at all.

7

The Land without Property

Whether... it should not seem worth while to erect a Mart of Literature in this Kingdom, under wiser Regulations and better Discipline than in any other Part of Europe? And whether this would not be an infallible Means of drawing Men and Money into the Kingdom?

GEORGE BERKELEY, *The Querist*

In the mid-eighteenth century, if you wanted to find a pirate you could certainly look to the streets of London or Edinburgh, where you might run into a William Rayner or an Alexander Donaldson. But if you wanted to find piracy pursued on a systematic, overt level—as the epitome of a moral enterprise, aligned with rationality, commerce, and enlightenment —then London's booksellers would shudder and tell you to go elsewhere. They would send you to Ireland. They liked to believe that Ireland was the true pirate kingdom of their age. They thought their Irish counterparts recognized no morality at all, but would grab whatever came their way, produce inferior knockoff copies, and sell them as fast as possible. Their image of Dublin was roughly what *Escape from New York* might have looked like if it had been scripted by Swift.

In truth, the Dublin trade was less anarchic than that. But that meant it was more profoundly threatening to London's grandees. It offered an apparently viable model for the future of print and public culture that cast into doubt everything the literary property oligarchs regarded as indispensable. Certainly, the Dubliners were thriving. Their reach extended across Europe and North America, and they claimed they could print volumes as attractive and as competitively priced as anyone's. And they had produced, they said, a golden age of Irish letters, headed by names like Sheridan, Edgeworth, and Burke. They seemed to think that their disdain for literary property, far from being something to play down, was the foundation of this commercial and cultural success. They claimed to provide the best writing at the lowest cost. That was the real problem they posed.

Reprinting books that had first been published in London, the Dubliners sold them, often at less than half the original price, not only in Ireland but also in Britain and North America. They recognized no obligation to pay for the privilege. This was nothing unusual by the standards of the time, although Londoners sometimes acted as though it were. All nations' systems of literary property were peculiar to themselves. Even the sending of reprinted books across borders—which made them into piracies— did not make the Dubliners really stand out. After all, the Swiss and Dutch were doing this to France, and any number of German statelets were doing it to each other. What made Ireland unique—as viewed by itself and by outsiders—was that there was no authoritative system of literary property *within Dublin itself.*[1] And this was not the Holy Roman Empire, where the sheer size of the region and its multiplicity of jurisdictions precluded any one property regime. It was one polity—really, one city—covering a small area and with a limited population. Yet as the most prominent Dublin bookseller of all, George Faulkner, put it, "there is no Law, or even Custom, to secure any Property in Books in this Kingdom." Faulkner was not being quite honest: there were customary conventions in effect, and he knew all about them. Nonetheless, his trade had no formal rules of property, nor any institutions of enforcement to sustain those rules had they existed. If a Faulkner undertook to reprint a popular book, his lead time over Dublin competitors was likely to be short.[2] At any rate, it was this trinity—a trade of reprinting, an export market, and a lack of internal regulation—that made Dublin exceptional. Even the most routine transactions there took on a strange caste from the perspective of Britain. John Murray, a prosperous and sophisticated trader, found it hard to apprehend the most basic ground rules for transacting business across the Irish Sea.

It seemed that just a few miles of ocean separated the order of London from a place where piracy was the only propriety, and anarchy the only rule.

This posed an evident problem. According to leading authorities across Europe, some form of literary property, however defined, was the bedrock on which public reason had to rest. Print's role in progress depended on fidelity and security of authorship, and those could not be guaranteed without a regime of some kind. There could certainly be dispute about the proper form of such ownership, about where its boundaries lay, and about who should possess it; but little scope existed to deny the need for some such principle. Yet it was precisely this that Ireland scandalously lacked. And it seemed to relish lacking it. If literary property and rules of authorship were so central to enlightenment, why did the Irish model not collapse into chaos and ignorance? Why, on the contrary, did it seem to thrive as never before?

That is a question that merits being asked in the present tense too. The question Dublin's trade posed for eighteenth-century *philosophes* is one that interests us anew today. Our own knowledge industries are united with economists and legal authorities in proclaiming that a formal system of intellectual ownership is a sine qua non. Many historians and critics too have argued that the inauguration of such a system in the eighteenth century represented a progressive transition into modernity. Eighteenth-century Ireland no more supports that position now than it did then. Quite simply, it puts to the test all conventional views conjoining print, property, and progress.

THE CULTURE AND CONDUCT OF REPRINTING

Ireland was a rural, relatively poor society, the bulk of whose population was formally excluded from elite educational institutions. The printed culture of the country was thus largely—and in terms of book manufacturing entirely—the preserve of the towns, and overwhelmingly of the capital, Dublin. The reprint industry in particular was almost entirely a Dublin industry, emanating from the bookshops clustered at the eastern edge of the old medieval city.[3] There grew a craft community small by western European standards (at its peak in the 1780s it numbered around fifty booksellers and thirty printers), and late on the scene, but dynamic and vital. The distinctions that split London's industry between copy owners and craftsmen were slow to take root here. Beyond a small central group, its economic mainstays were not books at all, but jobwork and newspapers —not to mention quill pens, dry goods, and, of course, patent medicines.[4] Archbishop King maintained that would-be authors of books should expect to pay for their own printing and distribute the copies free. Archbishop Synge agreed, telling a friend in 1721 that "there are very few books indeed of which an impression will go off in this kingdom." And as late as 1758 the leading Dublin bookseller George Faulkner observed that his city remained "the poorest place in the world for subscriptions to books," noting that citizens preferred to spend their money on wine and entertaining instead. "More bottles are bought in one week than books in one year," he noted rather enviously.[5]

Yet a literate market was fast emerging, within Dublin and beyond the city too. One visitor to Ulster could already describe finding a population of "rural *philosophes*" there, and the second half of the century would see newspapers founded in a number of towns. A major obstacle to the circulation of books, however, remained price. For most Irish, books were expensive luxuries. The London booksellers, for whom Ireland was a minor concern, had little interest in remedying this. A major point of reprints at the outset was therefore that they were much cheaper for local, Irish readers than their London originals. In 1767 the Irish parliament heard that there was even a standardized retail price, twopence per sheet, and those for whom this was too high might find books at one of the proliferating circulating libraries. Individual buyers remained urban rather than rural, Protestant rather than Catholic. This was the domestic readership that the reprint industry addressed and in turn spurred.[6]

Reprinting took its identity from the politics of the Irish capital. These were politics of fragile prosperity, religious tension, and growing nationalism. On the one hand, the city was a cultural hub. It was the home of the Irish parliament and the location of Trinity College, and the second largest city in the British Empire. Its parliament building, built to the latest neoclassical style, projected confidence in the stability and prosperity of the order it represented—that alliance of parliament, established church, and imperialism known as the "Protestant ascendancy." But on the other hand, that confidence was more fragile than it looked. It never took much to incite fears of a repeat of the kind of massacre many Protestants believed to have taken place in the uprising of 1641, which had helped spark the civil wars. Memories of that event were kept alive by regular ceremonials and publications. Moreover, urban Protestants too were increasingly inclined to chafe at Westminster's rule. They identified restrictions on Irish exports imposed by Britain's parliament—especially by the Woollen Act of 1699 —as a prime reason for the island's relative poverty. Ireland should be regarded not as a colony, they maintained, but as a truly autonomous kingdom, along the lines of the old "three kingdoms" constitutional model of the previous century. Such arguments easily became critical of British rule. And in fact when Samuel Richardson accused Dublin reprinters in 1753 of assuming the mantle of the Irish nation, he did so in the wake of angry agitation in Dublin for this so-called patriot cause. The catalyst was a Dublin apothecary and a pamphleteer for Whiggish reform named Charles Lucas. Lucas and other patriots took as their rallying cry the claim that English mercantile interests were artificially constricting the Irish economy. They fostered a plea that smuggling, used to circumvent English trade prohibitions, could be a virtuous enterprise. By the early 1750s such convictions were common currency in the newspapers of Dublin, especially Faulkner's *Dublin Journal*. A passionate political press appeared. And the book guild itself, up to this point a colorless body, declared for Lucas, associating him with the freedom of the press—which was rather a daring stance for a company that, as the lord chief justice pointedly reminded it, was supposed to facilitate government press regulation.[7]

The reprinting of London titles in Ireland had begun long before this. As early as 1663, London booksellers had accused the king's printer in Ireland of plotting to reprint copies in Dublin for sale in London. And they could be heard warning again in 1702 that printers in Dublin would "strike off and send over" enough copies, "whether correct or incorrect," to ruin sales of Archbishop King's *De Natura Mali*. Their concern was probably not property as such, but the undercutting of London journeymen by cheaper Irish laborers. At that point Ireland's printing industry was still tiny and posed no general threat. Two decades later the situation was different. In the 1720s reprinting became a routine, customary activity. By 1726 the bishop of Derry was reporting that "the Stationers of this Town have lately fallen into a Rappareeing Way of reprinting all Pieces of Note that are published in England"—a rapparee being a renegade soldier of the Jacobite war who had turned bandit. The Dubliners, Bishop Nicholson continued, were "able (as they order the Matter) to furnish their Customers with them at far lower Prices than they can bring them from London."[8] That implied that most reprints were directed at Ireland. But soon the Dubliners turned their attention to more distant markets. By the mid-1730s, if not earlier, reprinting for export was becoming common. The most attractive colony was America—another small market as yet, but one of enormous potential. Benjamin Franklin noticed "piratical" editions arriving from Ireland in 1747, subscribers for which included British army officers. Rather later, the notorious James Rivington would try to build a business by shipping Irish reprints to New York and making himself the conduit for their distribution throughout the country.[9] The real prize was the British market, however. Reprints from Dublin began appearing there routinely too, and soon they could be bought in any provincial town. The fact became so notorious that reprints from elsewhere began to be attributed to Ireland too. A supposed Dublin printing of *The Vicar of Wakefield,* for example, actually originated in colonial Boston. Another Dublin imprint came from Paris; a third from Glasgow.[10] Clearly, the book-sellers in these places believed that Dublin was so strongly associated with reprinting that yet another reprint would not be questioned.

It was now that the London booksellers really began to object. They demanded a parliamentary investigation. It was soon discovered that even quite hefty volumes like dictionaries and Clarendon's and Burnet's histories were readily available in reprinted form. Five years of lobbying later, the inquiry resulted in the passage of a new law prohibiting imports of books first printed in Britain but now reprinted abroad. In other words, it outlawed not the reprinting of books as such, but the importation of the resulting volumes back into England. In theory, this was not much of a change. But its practical consequence was severe. It meant that *all* imported books from Ireland (or Holland) were likely to be impounded, since customs officers had no way to tell whether or not a given title had first appeared in London. And they were indeed seized: to give just one instance, in May 1768 officers boarded a ship with a cargo of Irish goods plus a selection of books including Swift's *Works,* Pope's *Iliad* and *Odyssey,* Rabelais, the *Builder's Jewel,* Anson's *Voyages,* the *Arabian Nights,* and Churchill's poems (presumably the "piratical Edition of these Poems printed in Dublin, under a London Imprint"). They were all impounded as contraband. Irish books were also being seized on arrival in America at this time. In the end the Philadelphia bookman David Hall had to ask for shipments from Dublin to cease altogether, "as there are now always two of the King's Ships at least in our River."[11]

If reprinting English books in Ireland for the Irish was acceptable, however, then so, by the same token, was reprinting Irish books in England for the English. This practice has had none of the attention accorded Irish piracy, but it too began early and became quite routine. In 1694 Benjamin Tooke was already defending it to Bishop King, whose *Discourse on the inventions of men in the worship of God* he had reprinted. If he had not undertaken it, he reassured the bishop, someone else would have. Besides, reprints made his words more widely available, and therefore allowed them to "doe more good"—which, Tooke pointed out, "must be your Lordships intention in printing it." This rather cocksure defense shows that a justification of unauthorized reprinting in terms of dissemination was already available. A generation later Edmund Curll excused his surreptitious edition of Pope rather similarly as a rehash of Faulkner's in Dublin. "All persons in this kingdom have a right to reprint such books as are first published in Ireland," Curll pointed out, and "such as are first published here may be lawfully reprinted in that kingdom." (The point did not escape Hardwick: Curll was rather cleverly insinuating a free rein for pirates, who on this account could purloin any work as long as they arranged for a complicit Irish reprinting first.) "In Ireland the booksellers without ceremony reprint upon the English," John Murray heard later still, "and the English have the priviledge in their turn to reprint upon the Irish." Between 1729 and 1767 the Bowyers reprinted in London about sixty books originating in Ireland, mainly from Faulkner. Usually this was by agreement, but many of the same practical and moral issues attended English reprinting as arose in Irish: the recruitment of trustworthy agents, problems of fake imprints, the knavery of journeymen, and so on. The prospect also gave crafty London operators like Murray leverage over Irish authors, because they could threaten a reprint should the authors refuse to come to terms.[12] However, the London reprinting of Irish titles remained a relatively small-scale enterprise simply because Dublin was never the center for authorship that London was. Formal equivalence meant a substantial imbalance in practice. London, not Dublin, was the cultural and economic fountainhead of an empire.

This was the otherwise obscure context for the best-known instance of Irish "piracy" of them all. In 1753 Samuel Richardson denounced Faulkner for an "invasion of his property" in reprinting his massive novel *Sir Charles Grandison*. He told the story himself. With previous novels, Richardson reported, he had sent sheets to Ireland in advance of publication in London, so both securing a return from an Irish version and forestalling an unauthorized one. He had adopted the same strategy with *Grandison*. After the huge success of *Clarissa*, however, his new novel was sure to be hunted down by Dublin's reprinters, whose ability to bribe journeymen into sending sheets was notorious. So this Englishman's printing house would become his castle. In fact, Richardson arranged for printing to be done at three separate premises, none of which would be given a complete set of sheets. He made sure to employ only "Persons of experienced Honesty." No "Stranger" would be admitted. Every sheet of paper in the building would be accounted for. Workers must not breathe a word during their inevitable sessions at the tavern. He secured from them a declaration—almost an oath—against "Treachery," and handed out printed copies to remind them of their commitment. The sheets themselves were to be taken as they were printed off and deposited in a separate, secure warehouse. The task of taking them there he entrusted to one man only, a proofreader and warehouse keeper named Peter Bishop whom Richardson trusted implicitly. For his part, Bishop reassured him of "the Safety of the Work from Pirates."

These measures in place, Richardson sent twelve sheets to Faulkner as soon as they were ready. What he received back shocked him. Faulkner was abandoning their alliance to join with a group of "pirates." Three Dublin printers—Henry Saunders, John Exshaw, and Peter Wilson—were already hard at work on the novel, with far more of the text than Faulkner himself possessed. These "*honest* Men," as Richardson dubbed them, had "stuck up" title pages to claim the work, and were even implying ("Vile Artifice!") that their version was authorized. Worse still, Faulkner now told Richardson that he had handed over his own sheets, which contained last-minute notations by Richardson himself that were not in his own edition. The confederates could therefore advertise their version as preferable to his. "And who can say," Richardson wailed, that "if they can get it out before him, they will not advertise, that *his* is a Piracy upon *theirs?*"

Richardson now engaged a new Dublin agent, Robert Main, and sent him 750 copies from his own impression of the only volume of the novel that the pirates did not have. It did no good. The Dubliners, determined to "possess themselves of his whole Property," rushed out a "piratical Edition" and captured the market. Main ended up bankrupt. Meanwhile, at home Richardson first dismissed Bishop, only for his suspicion to fall on a compositor, Thomas Killingbeck. In the manner of many print workers, Killingbeck had moved around, and had once worked for a few years in

Ireland. He had been a journeyman for Faulkner himself, in fact, where he had worked largely on copy clandestinely obtained from London. Killingbeck protested his innocence, but refused to sign an affidavit. Richardson forthwith dismissed him too. It seemed he had fingered the traitors. But their violation of domesticity still nagged at him. "Of what will not Men be capable," he lamented, "who can corrupt the Servants of another Man to betray and rob their Master?" The printing house was also the master's home, and the Irish had violated both. They had got their copy "at the Price of making an innocent Man unsafe in his own House." For a society that conceived of itself as a vast collection of patriarchal households, redolent of trust and conviviality, such a crime was of rare enormity. And the loss of integrity was particularly devastating for a printer. By "dishonouring him," the pirates might well persuade London's powerful copy owners never again to "trust their Property in the Hands of a Man, who cannot secure his own from intestine Traitors." Richardson's household and livelihood had both been violated. And all this over a novel overtly intended to impart moral messages to its readers. (Pointing out that a cheap reprint might actually enhance its effect, as one friend did, was scarcely calculated to mollify him.)

Could the Dubliners' conduct possibly be defended? Faulkner thought it could. His defense rested on the primacy of craft custom. For him, such custom was, as it were, both ubiquitously local and locally ubiquitous. It determined good practice within a city, and also showed commonalities and distinctions across cities. His story was that he had discovered the pirates when he "posted" the title, this being in Dublin the "common Practice" of booksellers. What had given them the better claim was the fact that they already had three times as many sheets as he did. By local custom, the right was theirs. Furthermore, it was "an established, invariable, and constant Custom" that those who obtained part of a London work by the same post might opt to collaborate civilly rather than indulging in destructive feuds. In allying with the pirates, then, far from showing baseness, he and they had manifested perfect courtesy. They had upheld "a custom long established" in their trade.

Faulkner then pointed out what to him was the central contrast: the offense Richardson complained of had not been perpetrated in Dublin at all, but in the British capital. The Dubliners had obeyed their proprieties; the Londoners had violated theirs. Richardson's own journeymen were the ones guilty of "villainy and fraud." Indeed, the Irish had noticed the work only because Richardson had had to publish advertisements against a spurious London imitation. He therefore ought to look first to his own "hellish, wicked, and CORRUPTED servants," before seeking to cast out motes in Irish eyes. Faulkner even implied that Richardson *himself* was to blame. Only a negligent patriarch kept "rogues" in his house. It was apparently "constant practice" across Europe for a master printer not only to police his own household but to warn others of delinquent journeymen. Even journeymen rebuffed *"Villains,"* Faulkner added, to the extent of refusing them burial. They would "kick their dead carcases from place to place, as they would dead *cats* or *dogs, rats* or *mice."* That was perhaps over-egging the pudding, but the point was clear enough. Where in Richardson's London was moral probity of anything like such strictness to be found?

Richardson complained that the "Invaders of his property" had "done their utmost to make a NATIONAL CAUSE" of the dispute. They claimed illegitimately to stand for "the Irish nation." This articulation of an association between piracy and nationalism warrants notice, partly because Richardson was, in a sense, right. To the Dubliners, he was a standing enemy. He represented what they saw as a settled English conspiracy to threaten their very existence. They suspected him of having earlier tried to undermine them en masse by importing London-printed copies of *Pamela*—a bid that had been stymied only when Faulkner issued a clandestine version. The *Grandison* affair was to Faulkner and his counterparts only the latest of a series of collective efforts to subordinate Dublin's book trade to London's. Faulkner reinforced this impression by casting Main too as an interloper. The *Dublin Spy* called him a "Scotch pedlar, flying in the face of the government, the Parliament, and the Dublin Society." He was trying to "live independently of Irish stationers," and his importing of English editions was calculated to damage trade and country. Main does indeed seem to have been of Scots origin, and had no guild credentials; he had arrived in Dublin only in 1749. But the broader point is that Richardson's complaint should not necessarily be taken at face value. It was not unknown for a London operator to contract with an Irish counterpart in this way, preventing an unauthorized reprint, only to prevaricate, accuse the ally of piracy, and use that as a pretext to ship over enough copies to flood the Irish market.[13]

Dublin reprinting was not always—nor even usually—clandestine. But it did often have a rather informal quality. For the most part it rested on deals reached between booksellers, printers, and their representatives that were struck in person, over dinner, at the tavern, or in the coffeehouse, and sealed with a handshake. Large-scale projects might necessitate ad hoc partnerships, as with *Grandison,* only for those alliances too to be evanescent in the constantly shifting context of Dublin life. This, more than calculated skullduggery, is why the processes of reprinting have remained obscure. In general terms, though, it seems that major booksellers and printers would often maintain contacts with their London counterparts, and sometimes employ agents there. They were often willing to pay, not for copyrights, but for sheets to be sent to them from the printing house in advance of publication, so that they could be first to reprint the work in Ireland. This could be a distinctly secretive business: when John Millar found his *Observations concerning the distinction of ranks in society* being reprinted in Ireland, his London publisher feigned outrage even though he had himself furnished the sheets for the reprint. It was this ability to get prepublication sheets that gave Dublin reprinting its sometimes startling speed. A Dublin edition might appear less than a week later than its London archetype—or even, as Richardson warned, before the London impression had been published at all. Occasionally telltale evidence from books themselves gives a sense of this speed, as when poet Edward Young changed the title of one of his plays at the last minute and the Irish reprinters could not catch it in time. And it even seems that some Londoners would take the opportunity to play a double game, as in the case to be described in a moment.[14]

Impression sizes for Irish reprints were similar to those for London publications. That is, they ranged from 750 to two thousand, and occasionally higher for a sure seller. The books were usually verbatim reproductions of their originals—and occasionally more than verbatim. Shaftesbury's *Characteristicks,* for example, was reprinted "Page for Page with the English Edition, and upon the same Letter," the salient difference being that the reprint was 30 percent cheaper. Sometimes, however, material might be added, omitted, or altered. Faulkner found one unauthorized reprint of Swift's works omitting *Gulliver's Travels* and the Drapier Letters. William Guthrie's *Modern Geography* was altered to expand the treatment of Ireland (later the Dublin émigré Mathew Carey would add American material too that helped make this one of the most popular books in that country). In the context of a duel between two Dublin theaters in 1760–61, James Hoey craftily substituted the name of Barry for his bitter rival David

Garrick in a reprint of Smollett's *Launcelot Greaves*. According to the *Freeman's Journal*, Hoey was assiduous in editing anti-Catholic views out of his other reprints.[15] Fidelity, as always, was not to be taken for granted.

Dubliners thought their practice worth defending. Their defenses were both specific, upholding particular projects, and general, relating to the nature and purpose of reprinting itself. Faulkner thus pointed out—correctly—that only in a country "whose Booksellers cannot pretend to any Property in what to publish either by Law or Custom" could a complete edition of Swift's works be published. In England too many different proprietors existed for the many individual pamphlets to be compiled into one collection. More general defenses often invoked a combination of textual quality and what was called "nationality." As early as 1710 George Berkeley accused the London trade of attempting to stifle a rising rival that might "bring some benefit to poor Ireland." In 1736 Jonathan Swift told Londoner Benjamin Motte, who had won an injunction to prevent Faulkner from sending his reprints of Swift's works into England, that the treatment of the Dublin trade amounted to "absolute Oppression," entirely of a piece with England's general treatment of Ireland. "If I were a Bookseller in this Town," Swift averred, "I would use all the safe Means to reprint *London* Books, and run them to any Town, in *England* that I could."[16] Later, David Hume, resenting what he saw as Andrew Millar's "false Intelligence" about his *History*, would say that if Millar were still alive, then "I shoud be tempted to go over to Dublin, and publish there an edition, which I hope woud entirely discredit the present one." And James Williams—a pirate even by Dublin standards—boasted of his edition of Goldsmith's *Animated Nature* that it would cause his own name to be "inrolled with those of *Tonson, Millar,* and *Foulis;* who, at the same time that they have enriched themselves, and contributed to propagate science, have done honour to their respective countries."[17] The pseudonymous Roger Spy argued that buying books printed in London would be "instrumental in ruining Ireland." And finally, in May 1785 the speaker of the Irish House of Commons rejected the adoption of English copyright law because it would "put an end to the printing business in this country."[18]

Contemporaries wanting to know more could turn to the Irish press, which regularly defended reprinting on broadly mercantilist grounds. These newspaper arguments could become quite detailed as to the political economy of the practice. George Faulkner thus used his own *Dublin Journal* to defend his reprinting of Smollett's *History* despite paying forty guineas to Rivington for advance sheets. "All the Money of the Dublin edition will be laid out here," he insisted, "among the Letterfounders, Paper Makers, Printers, Rag-gatherers, and other Poor People depending on those Branches of Business." On the other hand, money spent on London editions would "drain this poor Country of so much Cash, and be a means of destroying the above Manufactures, and enrich one London bookseller." Of course, the Dublin printing would also be of better quality than the English, would appear earlier, and would cost half the price. A sympathetic Edinburgh author agreed, arguing that only reprinting enabled worthwhile books like William Robertson's *Charles V* to be bought by "people of middling fortune." (The example was carefully chosen: Robertson had received a famously huge sum for the copyright.) Altogether, Faulkner concluded, thinking probably of Richardson, his endeavor was not only a way to support Irish manufactures, but also served to "frustrate the evil Designs that have been made to destroy Printing in this nation, many attempts having been made for that Purpose."[19]

These kinds of claims clearly took shape and force from "patriot" politics. They came together most emphatically as those politics approached their zenith. At the end of the 1770s the success of the American Revolution exacerbated calls for change. Military weakness and political disarray on the British side encouraged them. When France allied itself with the Americans, so-called Volunteer militias sprang up across Ireland to defend the country from a possible French invasion. These bands soon metastasized into an extraparliamentary political movement that highlighted by contrast the atrophied and unrepresentative character of the parliament. By 1782 it was evident that the British, pressed by defeat at Yorktown, would have to concede either autonomy, union, or separation. London chose autonomy. A deal was pushed through. Suddenly the Dublin assembly could create its own laws. And Dublin's manufacturers could freely export to the empire. Scarcely had the principle of free trade to the empire been conceded, however, when Irish manufacturers began to call for protection against British competitors. A movement for tariffs grew up. Its rationale was not just economic survival, but, at street level, the preservation of a moral order reckoned to be inherent in domestic crafts. The campaign was also associated with attempts—sometimes violent ones—to uphold that moral order, for example, against employers who tried to hire apprentices in place of trained journeymen. Meanwhile a prominent section of the press, including the *Dublin Evening Post* and the

Hibernian Journal, supported the call for tariffs. So, notoriously, did Mathew Carey's *Volunteers Journal,* until it went too far and was forcibly shut down.[20]

This new political situation intensified the moral claims at stake in reprinting. Here was a way to uphold local manufactures and strike back at the cultural heart of England. The most prominent case in point became that of Patrick Wogan and Patrick Byrne, two well-known Catholic printers and booksellers. Wogan and Byrne decided to reprint Thomas Sheridan's *General Dictionary of the English Language.* Their reprint appeared in 1784, dedicated to the Volunteer movement. Advertisements appeared in the press alongside fervent declarations for political reform, freedom of the press, and protective duties. The reprint was a roaring success, selling over three thousand copies. A special impression was made for export to Paris. The London edition had been financed by Sheridan himself, however, at a cost of some £700 to him—and had numbered only two thousand.[21] So Sheridan issued a furious attack on the reprinters in the pages of the *Dublin Journal.* In response, Byrne and Wogan advanced a systematic defense not only of their own conduct, but of reprinting in general. They sought, they said, "to vindicate the Practice of their Brother Booksellers and the Cause of Literature in this Kingdom."

Byrne and Wogan's first point was that they were doing nothing unusual. Ireland was simply cleaving to the norms established by all nations. In the context, however, this was no mere observation, but an argument. They were tacitly insisting that Ireland *was* an "Independent Kingdom," as they called it. They thus embedded the national cause in their case from the start. They then proceeded to declare Sheridan "an Absenter." This was a very insulting title indeed in the context of patriot politics: an absenter was a landowner who decamped to England and left his Irish estate to be exploited by overseers. Byrne and Wogan were charging that the author damaged Irish culture by his absenteeism just as an Irish peer resident in England did the economy in general. On this account it was the height of gall for Sheridan to presume to argue "in Favour of a Work to be printed in and imported hither from England, to the Injury of one published by Natives and in their own Country." They noted that Gibbon, Robertson, Hume, and Johnson had all accepted Irish reprinting with more or less good grace. Moreover, the effective operation of "an Idea of Literary Property" such as Sheridan advocated would in effect mean the imposition of "a *protecting Duty*" by Britain against the publication of any work originally appearing there. It would revive the despised prohibitions that Dublin's parliament had just terminated after so many years of struggle. And finally, literary property would ensure that "the Rich alone" could afford good books. It would guarantee that "the middle and lower Walks of Life would have been deprived of that Entertainment and Information, which have given to the Kingdom of Ireland the Character which it now holds." In every respect, reprinting upheld Irish politics, economics, and culture.

All this was bound up in the booksellers' representation of themselves as individuals. They were, Byrne and Wogan said, plain-dealing, modest, and trustworthy men, whose manner contrasted sharply with the "virulence" of the absentee. They kept their word. Their craftsmanship produced fidelity and honest-to-goodness knowledge, without vain ostentation. Their edition was better printed than the London one, they insisted, and was literally correct. "What they proposed, they trust they have performed."[22] The fidelity and sobriety of their "plain" and affordable book testified to their fidelity and virtue as craftsmen. The reprinting of British titles was a virtuous action in that light. Byrne and Wogan presented the case for the defense at its most confident.

CUSTOM AND CONSENT

These kinds of arguments upheld the reprinting of works initially issued elsewhere. But none of them applied to reprints of works already produced in Ireland itself. This was where the issue of reprinting became difficult. Unlike other places, Dublin had no law or trade-sanctioned bylaw of literary property. But that did not make it anarchic. In fact it had its own conventions—noninstitutional customs—to which Dubliners assigned strong moral qualities. These customs were real and effective. But they were not very old, they lacked a strong legal or institutional basis, they were somewhat imprecise, and in certain circumstances their hold on practice could be tenuous. There were also conventions, of course, about when and how they could be ignored, and about what would happen when they were. If we are to understand how a pirate kingdom could sustain itself, we need to reconstruct not so much the institutional character of the book trade as its moral or cultural constitution.

The principal convention was that of the "posting" of titles. This was an unwritten, but widely recognized, "Rule" (we would perhaps call it a norm) to which members of the trade were expected to adhere. Thomas Bacon—merchant, coffeeman, printer, auctioneer, bookseller, and alleged British agent—described in 1742 how it worked: "There is a Rule among the Booksellers of *Dublin,* established by common Consent and Custom, that whoever shall first paste up Title-Pages, advertising their Resolutions of publishing any Book, the Property then becomes theirs: And this appears to be necessary in a Country where no public Laws have been made in that Respect."[23] "Posting" here meant displaying notice at some common location, such as Dublin's equivalent to Stationers' Hall; or it might also mean issuing a printed advertisement in a newspaper. The bookseller must be ready to produce on demand either the manuscript or the original London edition.[24] Subsequent Dublin editions were then regarded as the prerogative of the original poster.

It is worth stressing that this convention, insofar as it was actually followed, was *stricter* than anything London had ever seen. No such early and easily obtained right had ever been recognized in England. And in fact it was followed, by and large. It even proved secure enough that some did not hesitate to call the result "property." Such property could be bought and sold, as in the case of the £300 paid for Leland's *History of Ireland*—a small amount by London's standards, it is true, but not nothing. Postings sometimes formed the basis for rudimentary share allocations, with shares even descending through inheritance. And, for all that it was not a legal title, "property" of this kind might even hold good in a court of law. Peter Wilson thus won a case to regain the "right" to his *Dublin Directory* after it was sold without his consent in 1781.[25]

But sometimes a Dubliner would breach this custom. A "*Shark,*" Richardson called such a man, who "preyed on *his own Kind.*" And it was the breaching of this norm, not the act of reprinting per se, that the Dubliners denominated "piracy." For example, James Hoey was accused in 1734 of reprinting a Dublin-printed work called *The Toy-Shop* "in a Pyratical Manner, a Method not at all uncommon to said Gentleman." Isaac Jackson's Irish-made *Reading made easy* (a scriptural primer) appeared in "Five or Six Piratical Impressions," such that Jackson was forced to sell off his own impression at cost. Such breaches occurred with a frequency that seems broadly comparable to that in London. Boswell's *Tour of the Hebrides* saw four editions in just one year, some of them queasily disguised with false "London" imprints. By 1778 accountancy books were being produced with the author's signature in each copy to deter such domestic piracies.[26]

Abraham Bradley gave the Quaker Thomas Cumming a blunt piece of testimony as to a Dubliner's helplessness in such situations:

> he had once gave a Sum of Money for a London Copy, and some of his Brothers in Trade came modestly to him and demanded a share in the Sale but absolutely declined being a Farthing Sharers in the Money he gave for the Copy! *Look ye here,* said they, *as you gave so many Guineas for it you must sell it at—or you must be a Loser; but as we shall immediately advertise that we shall publish and sell it at—, you know the Publick will wait till ours comes out; yours will lie on your Hands, and ours will go off, and we, who paid nothing but for Paper and printing, must get Money.*[27]

None of the moral legitimacy that might attach to international reprinting applied to cases like these. They were, and were seen as, major offenses that spoiled the good names of those perpetrating them. More seriously, reprinting a brother's titles contravened the trade's image of itself as a self-ordering craft. So the community felt able to appeal to its own and its customers' moral compasses to reject these "unfair Dealings." Their perpetrators were decried as having expelled themselves from a civil community—Ciceronian pirates indeed. The pirate Hoey was denounced as simply "unfit for Human Society."[28]

As in other European towns, the civil community of the Dublin book trade had an institutional form in the shape of a guild. It was a peculiarly weak one, however. Its weakness derived from its origin in seventeenth-century conflicts. Briefly, prior to the civil wars only the king's printer for Ireland had been authorized to operate there. London's Stationers' Company had taken over that privilege, allegedly so that its booksellers could have a source of cheap labor. At the Restoration, the appointment of new royal printers led to a long, complex, and multilateral struggle between old and new patentees, between monopoly and trade, and between craft and prerogative. It shared many of the characteristics of the patents contest playing out in the same years in London itself. In 1670 the king intervened to call a halt to it. He forced the competing groups into one "body politique," the Guild of St. Luke, alongside the two other "faculties" of cutlers and painter-stainers. This did not really end the feud, but from then on it was the guild that claimed to uphold the craft's order.[29] On paper, it was well equipped to do so. It had many of the powers and responsibilities of such bodies in general, and a "Council of the House," roughly corresponding to the court of assistants in London, met in camera once a month to deal with disputes. But in practice, as far as we can tell, policing was neglected, and most of the council's business involved mundane questions of apprenticeship and freedom.[30] The most persistent problems it faced related to the perennial issue of craft identity (the problem of identifying and eliminating hawkers, "intruders," or "foreigners"), overlain by Ireland's religious politics (Catholics were admitted only as "quarter brothers," meaning that they paid for the "Priviledg" of being allowed to practice their craft).[31] In 1767 it finally gave up trying to stop the unqualified from setting up printing houses, since to do so would be "against the liberty of the Subject."[32]

What the guild did do was confirm the more informal protocols of deportment and civility that were as valued in Dublin as in London for their role in keeping the community intact. Apprentices had to become citizens of "good conversation." They must live with their masters in order to imbibe the correct principles of domestic morality. Members were not to dispute with each other loudly, nor "speak Evill of ye Mr or Wardens." No member was supposed to sue another without first trying to resolve the problem confidentially.[33] And the calendar of feasts and rituals served to reiterate this commonality, especially on "swearing day," the feast of Saint Luke (October 18), when the new master and wardens started office. Finally, and most spectacularly, every three years the trade appeared as one when the lord mayor summoned all the guilds to ride in finery around the bounds of the city.[34] These were expensive events (so much so that from the late 1770s the guild refused to participate), demanding horses, fine dress, gold-edged hats, cockades, yellow gloves with red silk stitching, ribbons, armor, and swords.[35] Carriages and musicians accompanied the printers and booksellers. In 1764, for example, the guild furnished an armored figure of Vulcan, a band of mounted drummers dressed as Turks and Tartars, a "bomb cart" full of "Ammunition . . . for the Belly," and the guild officers themselves, garbed, in a patriot gesture, "in Irish Manufacture only." On most such occasions a press would be dragged along too, borne aloft on a livery carriage and hard at work with a full complement of hack authors, pressmen, compositors, and devils.[36]

Some of the poems produced on these ceremonial presses have survived, and give a flavor of the occasion. They are announced as "printed before the Company of Stationers" — a revealing nomenclature — and articulate the excellence and historic role of printing. Sometimes they take on a local edge—in 1755 a verse referred to printing as a "source of patriot strength"—but usually the terms are more safely conventional. Thanks to printing, declares one, future times will have access to *"Newton,* Entire," and need never "mourn an *Addison,* like *Livy,* lost!" George Grierson, the king's printer, issued a verse written by his wife, Constantia, that hailed printing as a "Mystick Art" enabling readers to dispense with "the hard Laws of Distance" and rule the earth via "the Telescopes of Thought." Other poems lauded the inventors of the press, withholding a verdict on whether Fust, Coster, or Gutenberg deserved the laurel.[37]

It can certainly be argued that this kind of communal expression played an important part in sustaining the civility on which Faulkner and his peers relied. Yet the guild never attained the practical authority that the Stationers' Company had once enjoyed in London. Most pertinently, it never managed to police literary property explicitly. It had no register book, and the terms *copyright* and *piracy,* as far as I can tell, appear nowhere in its records (which survive only in part). Yet the possibility was not entirely remote at the time that the guild *might* regulate property. There were certainly plans to create such mechanisms. Those ambitions did not bear formal fruit, but they indicate that some of its members at least saw it as the proper site on which to build a regime resembling copyright. This may have been because it already regulated the use of a "peculiar mark" by which every cutler was supposed to identify his work. These marks were to be "Entred in the Bookes of this Hall, with their Names Annexed." The guild *did* have a register after all, then—but of trademarks, not copyrights (and even this register seems not to have survived). In 1731 a similar protocol was mooted for print. The guild even established a committee "to Draw up heads of an order to prevent the Inconveniency of Stationers printing over one another."[38] But it seems never to have reported, and the proposal died quietly.

More significant, perhaps, are the individual cases of unauthorized reprinting that came before the guild's council for resolution. As early as 1698, Patrick Campbell and Jacob Milner were summoned for printing the title and preface to Cocker's *Arithmetic* in front of Hodder's quite different text, so that "those were deceiv'd that bought them for Cockers Arithmetick." (John Dunton was quite taken with this "pretty experiment," remarking that Campbell "had a natural aversion to honesty.") The consequences proved less than serious: the next year Milner was elected warden, and the year after that master.[39] Generally, as in London, disputes like this would be delegated to a small group of referees. "According to custome," four individuals, two chosen by each party, would investigate.[40] The referees were to interview the various parties and arrive at a solution. Their negotiations aimed at compromise, not at imposing a rule, and they were never recorded. For that reason we have tended to assume that they never happened. But it would be more accurate to say that we *cannot tell* how often they occurred. An arbitration between the Ewings and Peter Wilson over *The Guardian* is known today only because they themselves published the referees' verdict, and there is no way of knowing how many others there were. It is certainly clear that the practice was still viable well into the second half of the century, when two Catholic booksellers, Patrick Lord and Philip Bowes, resorted to it in a quarrel over Charles O'Conor's *Case of the Roman-Catholics of Ireland*.[41]

What does seem clear is that such refereeing departed from guild authority and became a matter of civility in general. (In London too there are signs of this happening: in the late 1730s, James Watson, pursued by Dodsley for pirating Pope, proposed a booksellers' arbitration, and adhered to it, with no apparent institutional involvement.) Scattered through the various controversies that broke the surface in the press during the century are repeated references to such a process, usually mentioned because one side or the other has refused to abide by its conclusion. In 1751, for example, Oliver Nelson refused arbitration when Robert Main (soon to be Samuel Richardson's agent) accused him of pirating a novel the sheets of which Main had procured from London. Such a refusal was seen as extremely serious—more so than the original offense. In one case a breach like this would prove serious enough to start a pirate war.[42]

A UNIVERSAL HISTORY OF INFAMY

As in London, then, in Dublin what literary property there was rested on forms of trade civility. It was focused in alliances among booksellers, initially ad hoc agreements to protect individual titles, later concords to create and sustain a broader propriety. But the most ambitious of these alliances then became something more. It aspired to set standards in general, as a "company of booksellers" in its own right. Insofar as the Dublin trade developed any institutional system of literary property, this "company" was it. The initiative is significant because it sought to meet a need that in later generations and in many other countries would arise repeatedly: a need to give civility an explicit form, and to codify courtesy. And, unlike earlier counterparts, it did not originate in church, state, or law, but in the mundane practice of the trade.

The roots of the company lay in the most ambitious publishing project undertaken in eighteenth-century Ireland. The *Universal History* was a massive compendium purporting to describe the entire human past. It had first been launched as a speculative project in the London of the late 1720s. Its leading undertaker had been James Crokatt, a bookseller and informant to Parliament against Irish piracies whom Nichols called the greatest literary projector of his age.[43] The intention was that by appearing in regular installments it could build up to four folio volumes while still reaching a wide readership. In other words, it was rather akin to the entrepreneurial works of Rayner, albeit at a much higher intellectual level. But the problems attending all subscriptions plagued this one. The first undertaker went bankrupt, and ended up in prison, whence he wrote pleading letters to the Royal Society bemoaning his involvement in the enterprise. By 1744, when the notorious George Psalmanazar first brought it to some kind of conclusion, it had grown to seven folio volumes and still not managed to move beyond the ancient world. Years behind schedule, it was by now the province of a string of Grub Street hacks. Yet the *Universal History* found readers across Europe, and had an influence even on Diderot and d'Alembert's *Encyclopédie*. Booksellers and printers across Europe sought to reprint it, while in London a new fit of speculation saw it grow again into what eventually became a sixty-six-volume set. And in Ireland George Faulkner saw his opportunity.

Faulkner thought of his reprint of the *Universal History* partly as a national project. It would be, he announced, "the greatest and most expensive Work ever yet attempted in this Kingdom." Issued in folio, it would sell at seven guineas—half the price of the London version. The first volume was duly published in February 1744. But soon it was clear that he would face a rival from the Dublin equivalent of Grub Street. Charles Leslie, a goldsmith, was the principal undertaker of this rival edition. His "great and cheap undertaking" appealed for subscribers to register at the Secretary's Office in Dublin Castle—perhaps an indication of administration support. Either that, or they could attend Richard Dickson, a bookman who ran a Rayner-style "elixir warehouse" in Dublin. The actual printer of the work was to be Margaret Rhames.[44] None of these, it is important to note, was a member of the guild. Their edition was to be issued in octavo, making it much cheaper than Faulkner's folio. Faulkner duly complained of this attempt to "pirate" his edition. But it seemed to him more than a routine piece of opportunism. The pirates, he remarked darkly, were *"itinerant Projectors"*—that is, speculators, akin to hawkers of culture, who were "acting as Agents for People Abroad." Their true intent was nothing less than "to destroy Printing in this Kingdom." They had recently tried their *"Experiments"* in England and Scotland, Faulkner claimed, and had also previously tried, but failed, to undermine the industry in Ireland. If they succeeded this time then they would destroy learning and the arts in his country. He therefore called on "Patriots" to help him to "confound such horrid Devices." Escalating the struggle, he promised to commit all the engravers in Ireland to his own edition. Together he and his compatriots would prove once and for all that Ireland possessed the patriotism, skill, and craft solidarity to complete such a work and eliminate its piratical rival.[45]

Faulkner's rather cryptic remark about foreign agents had a specific target. He was referring to Thomas Bacon—the same man whose testimony about posting we began with. Bacon had established himself in Dublin in the late 1730s. In 1741, the maverick Londoner Thomas Osborne—a fellow participant in the *Universal History*—had introduced Samuel Richardson to him. Richardson had then asked Bacon in Dublin to reprint volumes three and four of *Pamela* for him. Faulkner had got to the work first, however, and Richardson had retaliated by sending Bacon 750 copies of the London-printed impression to sell against Faulkner's. This had caused the Dublin booksellers to suspect that Bacon was a mole—an agent sent by Richardson to undermine their entire trade. They believed that Bacon had received 1,500 copies, not 750—enough to swamp the market. Furthermore, they were convinced that Osborne too had "joined in this detestable scheme" by sending type for Bacon to use in his reprint.[46] Now, when they found that Bacon was in on the rival *Universal History*, they concluded that the publishing project was in effect a new assault on Irish publishing itself.

So Faulkner took an unusual, indeed unprecedented, step. He united the whole Dublin trade against these pirates. He called a meeting with a number of prominent booksellers. They decided together to issue their own version of the *Universal History*, in octavo, not only to stop Leslie but also to fire a warning shot against such insidious plots in general. Dublin's newspapers were soon full of their advertisements. "The Parliament of

England . . . have made several Acts to prevent Books being Pyrated in any Shape," the alliance declared. "And, the Custom of Ireland is, That no Printer or Bookseller shall ever re-print or pyrate any Book or Pamphlet upon another, without his Consent, when the Impression is out." This convention, they continued, was "strictly adhered to," and they were determined to defend it against "a *Sett of Gentry*, who have no Right to their Business."[47] This was why they had banded together to oppose the interlopers. "Being sensible how destructive such Attempts are to so useful a Branch of Business in this Kingdom," they explained, they had resolved "at any Expence, to put a Stop to such Practices for the future."

Thirty-nine booksellers and printers signed on to Faulkner's project. They included the biggest names of all: Risk, the Ewings, Exshaw, Hoey, Nelson, and Wilson. Faulkner also recruited booksellers from across Ireland, who agreed to sell the work in Cork, Limerick, Waterford, Londonderry, Belfast, Newry, and Armagh. They opened their subscription at slightly more than the Leslie version (£5 5s 5d as opposed to £5 0s 0d), but declared that they would match Leslie's price as soon as the latter had actually produced half of his edition. This was an astute challenge: as they pointed out, their own project now had the backing of most of the major booksellers in the country, so its plausibility was far more secure. Subscribers venturing on speculations by "anonymous Undertakers," by contrast, would be risking their money on people of doubtful credit. To reinforce the point, they started calling themselves simply "the BOOK-SELLERS," as though they represented the entire trade.[48]

Faulkner's counterattack generated a skirmish of rival advertisements in the press. He claimed that Leslie had marched into his printing house and threatened in a "menacing and rude" manner to seek massive legal damages. For his part, Leslie replied that he had offered to relinquish his edition if only Faulkner reimbursed his expenses. By now Faulkner was on much the stronger ground, however. He could claim to have "the Body of the Booksellers" on his side, while Leslie was cast as an outsider confronting the civility of an entire trade—again, almost as a pirate in the Ciceronian sense. Faulkner even reinforced the point by printing a letter from Charles Lucas, the patriot hero, repudiating Leslie as an interloper. It proved a powerful enough case to convince Leslie's own printer, Rhames, to abandon her involvement. By September, when Faulkner published a verse satire about Leslie's edition entitled *The Gold Finders,* she was gone. Faulkner's squib ridiculed his antagonists as failed alchemists—the archetypal fraudulent projectors. "A Goldsmith, a Chymist, and Shewman," he called them, Leslie being the goldsmith, Dickson the chymist (he had been convicted of counterfeiting medicines, in a case that Faulkner gleefully recounted at length). The showman was Rhames's replacement, Edward Bate, who was a part-time actor.[49]

The furor over the *Universal History* was widely noticed. It was probably the spur that incited the young Edmund Burke to debate "the necessity of enacting a law against Piracy amongst Booksellers" at Trinity College. And it garnered notice in distant London too.[50] There the booksellers now moved to create their own new octavo edition, which appeared in twenty volumes in 1747–48. Printed by Richardson, its preface spoke of confronting the "base interlopers in a neighbouring kingdom" responsible for "spurious editions." It claimed to have engaged the scholars of England to improve the text and "rescue the most valuable history that ever was penned from the mangling hands of Booksellers." And the Londoners now finally expanded its scope into modern history. This extension, a huge enterprise in its own right, they protected by both a patent and an entry in the Stationers' register. It took years. Volume 1 appeared only in 1759. In the end the publication amounted to some sixteen folio volumes, or forty-four in octavo. After the end of perpetual copyright in 1774 the Londoners would appeal to Parliament for redress by citing the £1,500 that they had invested in it.[51]

The *Universal History* catalyzed the emergence of a new moral agency within the Dublin trade. And a series of disputes in the following years confirmed Faulkner's and others' revulsion at internal "piracy" as corrosive to craft community and nation. A 1747 feud over rival translations of *Don Quixote* was one: Peter Wilson persuaded all major booksellers to subscribe for his version, and the rival disappeared. A tussle in 1751 over Haywood's *Betsy Thoughtless* was another (in which Robert Main, Richardson's Scottish agent, was involved; perhaps Main's status as an outsider lay behind his antagonist's refusal of arbitration). Wilson also engaged in another feud, this time over the *Guardian*. And Faulkner himself fought the most significant of these battles, with the Ewings over Swift reprints. It was something of a personal issue for Faulkner, who set great store by having been a personal acquaintance of Swift. The Ewings had "posted" the title of what he called "their spurious and incorrect Edition," at which point Faulkner notified them that he had the original manuscript; they retorted that what he had were only one or two pages improperly copied years earlier. Faulkner then made the incident a public cause. "For the Sake of Peace, and the Custom of Trade," he ostentatiously offered to refer the dispute "to any one, two, or more Booksellers." But the Ewings "haughtily and insolently" refused, the son declaring that he "would not trust his Property to the Decision of any one Man, or any Set of Men whatever." Faulkner then advertised this refusal as proof of their refractoriness. He published warnings of their attempt to "pyrate" the works "from obscure and incorrect Editions printed in England or Scotland," and urged that "no honest, well-meaning Person" would give them house room.[52] To repudiate this interloping was a matter of the integrity of nation and craft.

The formalization of this process of self-definition occurred in 1767, again at the instigation of Faulkner. He had just been elected sheriff when he found himself facing yet another internal piracy. This time it was an endeavor to reprint Lord Lyttelton's history of Henry II, which Lyttelton had assigned to him; the unauthorized version therefore infringed a peer's honor as well as the customs of the trade. Faulkner responded in what was becoming his accustomed way, by convening meetings with the other publishing booksellers to exclude the offenders. But now he went further than before, declaring a full-scale price war on the pirates. For years, he announced, he had pursued printing and publishing "for the Service of his Country." His efforts had promoted knowledge, encouraged manufactures and trade, and ensured that specie that otherwise would have gone abroad was invested within Ireland. Yet still he found "Malignity, Hatred, Envy and Malice" directed against him. The "insidious People of his Profession" had "pyrated" his books. They had devalued his "Copies," all of which he had procured "in the fairest Manner from the different Authors and Proprietors in Great Britain and Ireland." Nor had their ambitions been restricted to cultural flotsam like almanacs and primers. They had pirated the *Universal History*, "the largest [work] ever undertaken by any Bookseller in Ireland." He and his allies had finally resolved on decisive action. They would drive the pirates out of business.[53]

It was this antipiracy alliance that began to call itself the Company of Booksellers (later the United Company). It acted rather like a conger, attempting to corner the market in the reprinting and import of London books, beginning with *The Vicar of Wakefield* and *Tom Jones*. As so often with the Irish trade, however, how exactly it operated is unclear. It lasted until the end of the century, but it left virtually no written traces. The company certainly hired a London agent, John Murray, hoping to monopolize the supply of new publications from England. Murray duly sent books to what he called the "Dublin Cartel" and declined to supply any other Dubliner. But his rates proved too high, and by late 1778 he was no longer the company's agent. Abandoning the plan of monopolizing the reprint industry, it instead seems to have become something of a substitute guild, a guarantor of trade civility around its participants' copies. It held regular and festive dinners, especially on the anniversary of its founding, when its projection of a staunchly Irish identity was clear. Its members wore only Irish cloth—"the first regular Society that publickly associated to wear the manufactures of this kingdom"—and spearheaded nonimportation campaigns. The company additionally lent its authority to pricing schedules published by the bookbinders, and opposed papermakers' attempts to raise the price of paper.[54] In such ways it began to play the part of a trade body politic. There is even tantalizing evidence that the company sought to create a regime of literary property. At least two surviving books bear title pages with the line "Entered with the Company of Booksellers." Nobody knows if the group ever really adopted a register, but such a line would mean little unless it did. And in 1793, calling for Ireland to pass a literary property law, the periodical *Anthologia Hibernica* described the company as the only bulwark against anarchy. "The invasion of copy right is in some measure prevented in Dublin," it conceded, "by the institution which is called the United Company of Booksellers." Yet the regime remained autonomous of any law, provided no protection either to nonmembers or to authors, and embraced only Dublin.[55]

The company sparked fierce resistance. Rival "pirates" denounced it as a "junto," and offered price cuts of 30–60 percent on their own titles in a bid to survive. What is striking, however, is how far their attacks rested on essentially similar national grounds to the company's defenses. The "pirate" printers and booksellers who fought back—principally Robert Bell (later an American revolutionary), Dillon Chamberlaine, James Hunter, James Potts, and James Williams—justified their actions as encouraging "the printing business in this kingdom, which some of the junto endeavour to suppress, by importation and contracting for books printed in London with their names." In other words, they accused Faulkner and his partners of carrying on the design of Bacon, Osborne, and Richardson by other means. Bell even reprinted Donaldson's *Some thoughts on the state of literary property* with a new preface in defense of Irish reprinting, apparently aiming it as much against the Dublin company as against London's oligarchs. And Bell's group issued a declaration of their own against "Some persons who chuse to distinguish themselves by the title of 'The Company of Booksellers.'" The company, they declared, "having advertised that their property has been invaded," were using this charge to justify selling at below customary prices. Their price war was the real offense against trade fellowship, threatening Irish artisans for the sake of English imports. Bell et al. provided "one instance of their HONOUR" to bolster this claim. They described an edition of Fielding, of which they had published six volumes before the company announced that "their right was invaded." As Bell and his allies told it, they had agreed "in the most solemn manner" to refer the dispute to four "gentlemen of the trade." But when the referees decided against the company, only Faulkner and Ewing had been prepared to acquiesce. The others had proceeded to advertise a spoiler reprint of *Tom Jones,* "in order to deter them from ever daring to attempt printing any new or improved editions in this kingdom, especially while the junto have any old edition on their hands."[56] In other words, the company, while claiming the moral high ground, was violating the principles that truly united the trade. They were turning into Tonsons and Millars.

There was a sharp edge to this confrontation. The company of booksellers was in fact only one of several alliances to arise in these years. Journeymen too formed "combinations" to shield their interests. The binders joined forces to enforce common prices, for example, and by 1791 had created a Company of Bookbinders. Most serious in its intent and consequences was an "Amicable Society of Printers" that appeared in 1766.[57] Its intent was to protect what the journeymen saw as traditional chapel customs in the face of a nascent capitalism that threatened to turn ateliers into factories and reduce craftsmen into hands. It was a complaint arising everywhere in Europe—Jacob Ilive's rising in London being one case in point—and in many industries. But now it burst into the open in Dublin with startling viciousness. As midnight approached on Monday, September 12, 1766, a band of men smashed the door to the home of William Osborne in Golden Lane. Osborne was a journeyman printer, now sixty-eight years old and infirm. He should have commanded some esteem, being reckoned the oldest active tradesman of the entire fraternity. Once inside his house the intruders drew swords and attacked Osborne and his wife "in a most cruel and inhuman manner." He was badly wounded; she lost her hand. The mysterious assailants fled into the night, telling their victims that they had been targeted in retribution for working for John

Exshaw, a pirate notorious for hiring excessive apprentices and eroding the chapel.

Five days later the trade convened to denounce the attack. It issued a public endorsement of Exshaw's "Candour, Integrity & Punctuality" and offered a reward of £50 for the "villains" responsible. At the same time the book trade took the opportunity to declare its general abhorrence of "seditious and illegal Associations" of "idle profligate and insolent Journeymen Printers," who deserted their posts and put craftsmen "in Fear and Danger of their Lives."[58] The attack, it transpired, had followed a campaign of anonymous threats. One letter, to another Exshaw worker named Daniel Donovan, was produced and read.

> Mr: Donovan
>
> As the Care of one's Life, is all the Enjoyment we have on this Earthly Hemisphere, and the Pleasure thereof we seek as much as possible and of such Pleasures you are likely to have but little, I, as your Friend, dear Dan: (tho' perhaps unknown) give you the Design of the Journeymen Printers, in the words following, which I heard from the Sultan's mouth (that is, the Head Man), That if you do not in three Days from the Date hereof, quit Mr Exshaw's House, that They the Printers, will make a horrid Spectacle of you, and as They term it, mark you, by taking at least a Leg, an Arm and an Ear off you, which they hope will be a Warning to Buck, Ellison, Osbourne and the Corkman. Now dear Dan quit the Place, and be assured of the Mens Friendship, and remember three Days from this Date.
>
> I am your Friend
> J. Trueman.

The message had its effect: Donovan would shortly leave Exshaw. Given the professed objective of preserving the chapel community, however, the result for this man at least was sadly poignant. Having deserted his chapel, he found himself following a shiftless path. Donovan ended up an "outcast of almost every printing House in the Kingdom"—almost a personification of the outlaw described by Faulkner in his letter to Richardson.[59]

Secret societies pervaded Irish artisanal life in the last decades of the ascendancy. The appeal to a mysterious "sultan" or "head man" was typical of them.[60] Violence, intimidation, and obscurity were their hallmarks. In the case of the printers the actual violence seems to have died down after the attack on Osborne, but nobody could be sure that it would not return. In the 1770s the Amicable Society of Printers continued to publish a series of less than amicable notices renewing its threats against anyone deemed to imperil the craft's "Bands of conjugal, filial, paternal or social Love." It coupled its calls for fraternity with advocacy of frequent parliaments and protectionism. The guild kept a wary eye on such groups, periodically but impotently resolving to act against them, or at least to encourage the lord mayor to do so. Occasionally it even voiced concern that masters' erosion of chapel life might be provoking their appearance.[61] But there was nothing it could really do. As the 1790s dawned, and Irish politics entered its most dangerous period for a hundred years, such secret societies seemed about to metastasize into something far more dangerous.

Faced with growing dissension in its ranks, the guild finally found its voice. It denounced the administration for opposing "the Protection of our Manufactures, the freedom of the Press, & the Liberty of the Subject." Since the Irish parliament seemed intent on furthering "a foreign interest," the guild resolved, popular action might be necessary to defend "native manufactures." It formed its own committees to work for tariff protection, and honored Grattan with its freedom. In 1795 the guild condemned British interference as "a National Calamity" and called for "the determined and constitutional voice of a united Country." It was not long before the United Irishmen were meeting in Stationers' Hall.[62] And in 1798, as the rebellion broke out that promised to end British rule altogether, the guild finally sat down to draw up a set of rules to govern the book trade. It was about a century too late.

Fomented by the press, the United Irismen's rising was violent, popular, but catastrophic. The French support it had needed never really materialized, apart from a futile gesture by Wolfe Tone, and with the British army no longer tied down in America it was more than sufficient to suppress the isolated rebels. All concerns among booksellers and printers about the constitution of their craft were soon eclipsed. The scheme for a set of rules not only came to nothing, but was physically expunged from the record, with a scrawled comment that any such proposal was "highly irregular." A new order was about to be imposed by the British.[63] Copyright was coming to Ireland.

London had launched three counterattacks against Ireland's reprinters already. The first was in the 1730s, when Parliament passed its law against imports. The second was in 1759, with the ill-starred "conspiracy" to eradicate piracies from the British market. The third effort came in 1784–85, when the furor was part of the general quarrel over Anglo-Irish trade. The initiative was spurred by a declaration in the *Daily Universal Register* that "the piracies so daily practised by the Irish booksellers, call aloud for redress." Almost every worthwhile book published in London was now seized upon, contracted, and republished in cheaper form, "to the great detriment of men of genius and science." Even Edinburgh's booksellers were upset. And William Pitt took notice. An advocate of laissez-faire, Pitt urged the Dublin parliament to adopt English copyright as part of his scheme for a free trade area across the British Isles. But the Dublin press took to the lists once more to decry the plan as an attack on Irish manufactures. Reprints became all the more a form of resistance. Feelings ran high: when the bishop of Killaloe tried to defend copyright in the Irish parliament, he was denounced as a traitor.[64] Within Dublin, it was crystal clear, copyright had no constituency whatsoever. Pitt's plan was quietly shelved. But the reprieve was temporary. Ireland's printers were heavily implicated in the 1798 rising, and they paid the price.[65] After the rebellion London resolved on the drastic step of full political union. The kingdom of Ireland, and with it Dublin's status as a capital, came to an end. A city that had been a nation's center of power, patronage, and fashionable consumption was suddenly reduced to the status of a provincial town. This alone would have been enough to imperil its book trade. But union also meant something worse: copyright. The outlawing of reprints brought the trade to a juddering halt. The press had warned of "disastrous" economic and cultural consequences if union passed, and in its own case it was proved right. Its output plummeted by some 80 percent. Many printers and booksellers emigrated to the United States. Others simply gave up the trade altogether. Not a single one, as far as we know, went to London. In 1806 the remnants voted to seek the dissolution of the union itself.[66]

The extension of copyright to Ireland made what could be called the moral constitution of the nation's publishing industry illegitimate. Its customs had long been decried as piratical, and now they were legally defined as such. Yet it was the end of those customs, and their replacement by a regime of law, that all but destroyed the industry and the literary efflorescence it had sustained. The implications were serious, and not just for Ireland. The transition of 1800 would stand as a test case—or a crucial experiment—for at least the next century.

THE END OF A PIRATE KINGDOM—
AND THE START OF ANOTHER

September 7, 1784. The soldiers at the dockside eyed the coach suspiciously as it drew up to the quayside and halted. They were on their guard, alerted to look out for a desperate escaped prisoner. But it was a well-dressed woman who stepped out and, limping slightly, climbed the gangplank onto a ship that was busily loading in preparation for imminent departure. The redcoats shrugged and let her pass. Later that night the vessel slipped anchor and slipped quietly out into the Irish Sea. Only when she was safely outside territorial waters did the passenger feel safe enough to remove her bonnet and wig. As they came off, they revealed that beneath the disguise was a twenty-four-year-old man. A Catholic wanted for inciting treason in his radical newspapers, Mathew Carey had been arrested too many times already to hope for clemency any more. The ship he had boarded was bound for Philadelphia and exile. Her name was the *America.*

Carey's story has become one of the minor myths of early national American history. Born in 1760, he entered Dublin's book trade over the opposition of his father, apprenticing himself to a Catholic printer-bookseller named Thomas McDonnell. McDonnell was a secret sympathizer with the radical opposition—Wolfe Tone dined at his house, and informers later betrayed him as a United Irishman.[67] Carey recalled him as "a hard, austere master, of most repelling manners." The only virtue he is now remembered for is that of preferring his apprentices to stay alive. In a city brimming with male conviviality, alcohol, and brittle honor, this was something. Duels were routine. But when Patrick Wogan—McDonnell's employer, the pirate of Sheridan, and in Carey's view another "ruffian"—insisted that one of McDonnell's apprentices fight one of his, McDonnell refused to let his appear, and Carey wrote up a denunciation of the custom in general. He delved into history to dismiss dueling as a crude practice with no place in a civilized trade.[68] After this, he launched into writing against the administration, with a first effort radical enough that he had to beat a prompt retreat to France. There he found himself working for the Parisian printer Didot (whom he found reprinting English books), and then for Ben Franklin, through whom he met the Marquis de Lafayette. Back in Dublin, he then launched a newspaper called the *Volunteers Journal.* Its constituency was the paramilitary movement of that name, which paraded for the ancient constitution and a free citizenry. Carey's *Journal* mustered all the rhetorical extremity he could manage to "defend the Commerce, the Manufactures, and the political rights of Ireland, against the oppression and encroachments of Great Britain." It lauded the seventeenth-century regicides and reprinted America's contemporary revolutionaries.[69] The authorities tried to undermine Carey's paper by backing a rival *Volunteer Evening Post,* to little avail (later, rival versions of the *Journal* itself would achieve that end). Before long it was virtually calling for insurrection at home by Irish patriots "*united,* and in *arms.*" But what provoked real action was its advocacy of an apparent assassination plot.

The plot emerged from the popular politics of protection for Irish manufactures in the 1780s.[70] A protection bill was massively defeated in Dublin's parliament, and the fury of an outraged patriot press boiled over. "Oh, Ireland!" wailed the *Dublin Evening Post.* "How are you duped out of liberty in constitution, and freedom in commerce!" Civilization itself had been betrayed. "Are we men, have our intellects been despoiled by our task-masters as well as our property?" Tradesmen with English goods were tarred and feathered, and angry apprentices began "houghing" soldiers (cutting their hamstrings), which was immediately made a capital offense. The mob broke into Parliament itself. A sympathetic lord mayor delayed responding so long that the nervous administration labeled him "little better than an accomplice."[71] The *Volunteers Journal* whipped up the violence. The morning of the riot, Carey published a caricature showing "Jack Finance" (the chancellor, John Foster) hanging from a gallows, with the rubric that this was the will of Ireland's starving manufacturers. The Commons laughed heartily at the cartoon, but then realized that it looked very like incitement to murder—especially when it was widely reprinted in other papers, getting a far broader circulation (this was standard practice, and the *Volunteers Journal* was "the most inveterate robber" of all).[72] A manhunt was launched. Carey escaped his pursuers once by leaping out of a third-floor window, but he could not elude capture for long, and he inevitably found himself behind bars. Meanwhile, the administration pushed through Parliament a new law regulating the press—the strictest ever proposed in Ireland. The *Volunteers Journal* responded with another cartoon, this time with the corpse of Jacky Finance lying discarded under the scaffold, too reviled even for burial.[73]

It seemed that Ireland was descending into rebellion. The *Dublin Evening Post*—not normally a rabble-rousing organ—issued a chilling political catechism that concluded that the English should be expelled by "two millions of Irishmen in arms." Meanwhile Carey was kept in close confinement for fear a mob might rescue him. There he stayed until mid-May. But when Parliament adjourned the lord mayor suddenly found himself with authority over the prisoner and had Carey freed. No sooner was he out than his paper impugned an alderman whose troops had fired on the crowd, and as "reputed proprietor" Carey was threatened with a charge of high treason. Now was the time for a discreet exit. A week after the charge was proclaimed, he donned his disguise and slipped away.

Unlike his previous exile, this one was for good. Instead of fomenting a rising at home, Carey would end up becoming the best-known publisher in the new United States of America. There he contributed to a lasting revolution in public culture. For some forty years Carey would play a major role in shaping the literary, scientific, and political discourse of America. In particular, he was instrumental in fostering a civility that defined publishing. It is notorious that for the better part of a century the United States made a virtue of what the British—and eventually the Americans themselves—called piracy. Carey was one of the founders of that practice. As the United States became home to what one historian has called "the world's most prolific book pirates," his firm was the leader. He not only appropriated London books with alacrity, but also produced works in Spanish for the South American market (he had an agent in Gibraltar sending the latest texts), and in German and French too. He reprinted natural history, natural philosophy, and geography, adapting texts and formats for American readers. Among the authors he reproduced were Wollstonecraft, Condorcet, Lavoisier, Goethe, Byron, Edgeworth, Humboldt, Southey, Scott, Say, Hazlitt, the phrenologist Combe, and Mozart. More to the point, it was Carey's operation more than any other that established the protocols and conventions of international reprinting in general. Its moral, ideological, and anti-imperial character—and its practical basis in allegedly piratical reprinting—could all be traced back to Dublin, and to the paradox of its piratical Enlightenment.[74]

8

Making a Nation

In Britain and Ireland, piracy was controversial. In the American colonies, it was revolutionary. America's small but rapidly growing population of printers, newspapermen, and booksellers was led by immigrants who had learned their craft at the feet of the leading Irish and Scottish reprinters. By the time the War of Independence broke out, some were ready to make piracy a tool of insurrection. For them the very act of reprinting London's books was an act of defiance. It was also an act of definition: their smaller, cheaper, more portable formats defined a public realm befitting a dispersed republic rather than a centralized aristocracy. Incitement to join the revolutionary cause, word of the rising itself, and news of its fortunes all circulated across the colonies by their labors.

Effective as it was, this practice created longer-term problems. With independence won, the new nation would have to build its public culture on the foundations that the revolutionaries had established. It was then that the more profound and implicit questions of a pirate revolution demanded answers. Were the foundations of the new nation's public culture ethical? How could the need to create new knowledge be reconciled with the need to appropriate old? What were the proper shape and constitution of communications to be in a new republic? Those questions had to be addressed in the 1790s and early 1800s, at a time when the nature and future of the United States were still insecure. After the War of 1812, answers began to emerge. By the 1820s, Jacksonian America had a secure and vibrant public sphere—but to European eyes an utterly piratical one.

According to Benjamin Franklin, the advent of a competitive press in the colonies could be dated quite precisely. Its progenitor was a refugee from the first pirate generation in Britain. Samuel Keimer had been a believer in the so-called French Prophets—charismatic Protestant refugees from the Cevennes who made a great impact in London. But he had turned apostate when ordered to pirate a Tory printer's work, and after a spell in prison had left London for Philadelphia. There he hired the young Franklin as a pressman and reprinted English newspapers, issued unauthorized transcripts of assembly proceedings, and created "spurious" versions of the local printer Andrew Bradford's almanacs. The earliest colonial disputes over literary property, in Franklin's view, therefore coincided with the establishment of a viable press. Franklin himself deserted the erratic Keimer, who briefly competed for his erstwhile journeyman's readers (his reprint of Ephraim Chambers's *Cyclopaedia* stalled at the letter *A*) before giving up and moving to Barbados.[1] Franklin, we know, would enjoy altogether more success.

Keimer was unusually brazen, but his activities set the tone for colonial printing houses. No copyright law constrained them, and little by way of trade civilities. For the most part printers had to work out the rules as they went along. One reason for this was the sheer distance between cities, each of which effectively formed a discrete market. Another was the small size and economic fragility of each house. Bookmen had to be jacks-of-all-trades, selling paper, medicines, and dry goods more than books; Benedict Arnold sold both books and drugs. The mainstays of the colonial printer's craft were not books at all, in fact—they were cheaper to import than print—but job work and newspapers. Three-quarters of all printers between 1700 and 1765 were responsible for at least one paper. Newspaper printers eagerly awaited vessels carrying the latest intelligence, and freely reproduced what stories and essays they could lay their hands on. Isaiah Thomas's *Massachusetts Spy* even boasted an emblem of two babes plucking blooms from a basket, with the motto "they cull the choicest." Papers in different cities then reprinted each other's reprints, and since most served local readerships this was not a cause for complaint. Indeed, works like the Whig *Letters* of Cato obtained a remarkably wide coverage thanks to this form of replication. The occasional reference to something like literary property prior to independence—as, for example, when two Boston printers "purchased the copy" of Nathaniel Ames's almanac in the 1750s—stands out as exceptional and rather inexplicable. A distinct kind of public came into existence as a result—one accustomed to regurgitated journalism, collated from distant sources as and when ships made landfall.[2] Not only was Boston not London; it was not even Dublin.

The Stamp Act of 1765, taxing as it did this small and unruly craft's major products, turned the craft itself into a political force. The furor the act created fostered a partisan press that did not disappear again when the law did. Printers from then on knew how to address, manipulate, and profit from the spirit of party. Moreover, their colonist readers increasingly recognized that manufactures in general were essential to protect their place in the imperial order, and that included books. Nonimportation pacts had been central to the anti–Stamp Act campaign, and the mid-1760s saw the first associations for promoting American manufactures of goods like paper. They contradicted what according to London was a colony's role: to supply raw materials to the home nation and buy the manufactures it produced, the traffic in both directions being restricted to British or colonial vessels. That mercantile system seemed rational and mutually beneficial in Westminster, and indeed, the colonies initially resisted London in the name of *preserving* it. But for the colonial book trade it meant that not only books, but type, presses, and skills were all to be imports. Paper was something of an exception, but American mills could not meet demand, so it too had to be shipped in (sometimes illegally, from the Netherlands, or from Spanish ships captured by privateers). As Americans came to perceive the autonomy that might come from an ability to manufacture goods for themselves, everyday objects like books took on a significance in transatlantic politics in addition to their textual contents.[3]

Americans were used to reprints. The Scots began shipping their own in large quantities in the 1740s, the Irish slightly later. By 1752, David Hall of Philadelphia was warning William Strahan in London that "there are a great many Books imported from Ireland and Scotland which come much cheaper than from England."[4] Alexander Donaldson in particular was keen to undercut the Londoners. "He is upon the Pyratical Scheme," Strahan warned, hoping that no "gentlemen" would give houseroom to his books. He was "the Rivington of Scotland." It was a revealingly topsy-turvy comment. More properly, James Rivington was the Donaldson of America. He was London's worst fear: a highly placed, well-informed turncoat. His attempt to corner the colonial market in books showed why an American reprint trade came to make sense.

Rivington was the scion of a clan of London booksellers that had prospered by helping to invent the conger system. He had made his own fortune by speculating on Smollett. Then he split from his peers and embarked on a remarkable scheme to revolutionize the wholesale trade and take control of the transatlantic commerce of books. He hinted to American contacts that London's oligarchy was duping them and only his insider knowledge could secure fair dealing. It seemed to work, for a while. By 1757–58 an alarmed Strahan had discovered that Rivington was exporting as many volumes as the rest of the London trade combined. He was also quietly hiring Scottish printers to make reprints specifically for the colonial market.[5] But Rivington's Achilles' heel was that the vicissitudes of transatlantic trade and finance made him unreliable, in a trade where predictability was all-important. Hall found Rivington's provision of Hume's *History* inconsistent enough to endanger his own credit with his customers.[6] By that point, Rivington's scheme was collapsing. He had indulged too freely in betting at the Newmarket races, and as part of their campaign against provincial and Scottish "pirates" London's grandees had closed ranks against him too. Fearing ruin, Rivington precipitately declared bankruptcy and fled to America. But he took with him a shipload of books, and was soon back in the same business.[7] Hall sent his advertisement straight to Strahan, remarking that it revealed "an ingrossing Disposition"; Rivington seemed to think "there never was a Bookseller on the Continent till he came." Still, some rebuttal was needed, he added, or else Rivington would be believed. The reply duly came from the printer Dunlap, who helped himself to an annoyed Rivington's words "in an ironical Way" to compile a counteradvertisement of his own. From distant London too Strahan tried to counter Rivington by telling contacts that a "great Property in Copies" allowed Strahan to sell as cheaply as any honest man could.[8] But it was the Stamp Act furor that destroyed Rivington's chances. The nonimportation pacts meant that his market dried up. Having also ventured support for the Maryland Lottery—an ill-fated land scheme—he was once more forced into bankruptcy. During the Revolution, Rivington would reappear in yet another guise as a leading Tory newspaperman, serving as king's printer in New York under the protection of

British troops (although rumor had it that he was a spy for Washington). After that he would slip into bankruptcy once more and spent his last years in debtors' prison.[9]

The successive iterations of Rivington's scheme showed the strategic limits of importing. The reading public in the colonies was expanding to a point where it could not reliably be satisfied by shipping quantities of printed books, even at low Scottish or Irish prices. And at the same time the politics of that public shifted profoundly, to discourage importation from anywhere in the British Isles. Printers and booksellers therefore started to think in terms of reprinting in America. The distant origins of the practice extended back to the seventeenth century, but it accelerated markedly in the 1720s. At that point, one observer noted, Boston already boasted "four or five printing houses which have full imployment, in printing, and reprinting books of one sort or other, that are brought from England and other parts of Europe." America's first major domestic publishing venture was a Bible with a false imprint attributing it to the king's printer in London, and Boston booksellers were still falsifying London and Dublin imprints in the 1760s. The relatively few books that Franklin undertook were almost all reprints of works with a proven record in the Old World, the most substantial being Richardson's *Pamela*.[10]

The most prominent reprinter before the Revolution was, fittingly, both a Scot and an ex-Dubliner. In fact, Robert Bell was probably the only prewar American to make book printing the core of his livelihood. Like Rivington, he hated the London oligarchy. But unlike Rivington he also openly hated the imperial system of which it was a part. Rivington had wanted to co-opt it; Bell wished it destroyed. A native of Glasgow, where he had served his apprenticeship before working for the Berwick-upon-Tweed pirate Robert Taylor, Bell had moved to Dublin in 1759. There he had set up a reprinting venture radical enough to offend against the courtesies of Dublin's own trade. Facing concerted opposition within the city, he had responded by reprinting Alexander Donaldson's defense of reprinting with the addition of a diatribe of his own. Then he promptly took ship for America. Landing in Philadelphia, he had revived his reprinting with a vengeance, honing the anti-imperial character of the enterprise. His best-known American project was William Robertson's three-volume *History of Charles V*, which he took on in 1771. It was a calculated and highly symbolic choice. Robertson's book was the most valuable literary property the London trade had ever bought. It was a veritable emblem of the perpetual propriety of the metropolitan trade. Robertson had received the stupendous sum of £4,000 for the copyright. Bell's piracy, accordingly, was easily the greatest commercial publishing project ever produced in the colonies. It sold at roughly 50 percent of import prices. He followed it with Blackstone's celebrated *Commentaries* on English law, and the two books together—Robertson's with its Enlightenment historiography of progress, Blackstone's with its articulation of a common-law tradition of liberty—became major ideological resources for the revolutionaries. But they were only the most prominent of what became in Bell's hands a virtual canon of expropriated literature. He reprinted Samuel Johnson, Lawrence Sterne, and the Scottish chemist William Cullen. Edward Young's *Night Thoughts,* Goethe's *Werther,* and, after independence, Buchan's *Domestick Medicine* all came from his press. Of course, he also reprinted Thomson's *Seasons,* as any self-respecting pirate of the time did. And he even proposed to do Hume, though for once he seems to have failed to follow through. With Paine's *Common sense,* Bell published the first edition, only to fall out with the writer and see Paine facilitate rival impressions across the region—a hoisting by his own petard that saw the tract become the manifesto of the Revolution. In all, his list amounted to a declaration of hostilities against London and London's book trade. And in farming out the actual printing of these books to others, Bell effectively inaugurated in America the role of the publisher.[11]

Bell added his own *Address* to Robertson's history to articulate his purposes. This *Address* was by far the most significant defense of colonial piracy. It was a slight document, perhaps, when set against Donaldson's; but it had a Paine-like directness of its own. Bell first thanked subscribers for what he called "this practical proof of your alacrity to promote native fabrications," thus identifying his piracy with the drive for American manufacturing. He then recommended extending the same approach to books in general. But here he moved to rebut the charge that this was (in his own rendition of the Londoners' position) "an infraction on the monopoly of literary property in Great-Britain." Even if such a monopoly made sense in a land of luxury, "overgrown with riches," it made none in a growing nation. Ireland proved the point. "As soon as any new Book appears in London," Bell remarked, "it is immediately reprinted by the Irish booksellers." They had already reprinted *Charles V* twice, Blackstone three times, and the *Universal History* twice, all "without rendering the smallest pecuniary regard either to Authors or Booksellers." This had fostered an unprecedented reading public eager for "literary knowledge." "This high-born privilege of freely disseminating knowledge," Bell proclaimed, had transformed the Irish nation. It had been "not only Humanified, but almost Angelified." Moreover, Blackstone himself argued that a monopoly like copyright did not extend beyond Britain to any other "country governed by an Assembly of Representatives," which Bell took to include the colonies. The London booksellers had known this when they had paid Robertson his four thousand guineas, so they could hardly complain of injustice now. It would be "incompatible with all freedom" to hold that "an American's mind must be entirely starved and enslaved in the barren regions of fruitless vacuity, because he doth not wallow in immense riches equal to some British Lords." Bell's was therefore an act of liberty. In his proclamation could be discerned a program of piracy that would survive the Revolution and help shape the nation it produced.[12]

IMITATION AND IMPROVEMENT

Robert Bell survived the Revolution to spend his last years as an itinerant and controversial book auctioneer in the new nation. When he died in September 1784, Mathew Carey, having just escaped the redcoats in Dublin, was halfway across the Atlantic. His subsequent landfall was inauspicious. A drunken pilot ran the ship onto the shoals, causing panic among passengers who believed themselves about to drown. When he reached Philadelphia his first efforts to establish himself were not much easier. He had arrived with virtually no resources and absolutely no friends, and only a coincidence that became rather legendary enabled him to start at all. The Marquis de Lafayette happened to be at Mount Vernon at the time, and advanced him $400. Carey invested it in the accustomed fashion for an aspirant Dublin printer: he launched a newspaper. What followed was a sequence of near disasters. The practice of reprinting was central to all of them, as it was to Carey's successful emergence.

The only press Carey could find, first, was that which had belonged to Bell, whose effects were coming up for auction. One Eleazar Oswald, a veteran of the war turned newspaperman, tried to stymie a potential rival by bidding up the price, well aware that Carey would have to buy it at almost any cost.[13] A short, sharp antagonism ensued, in which Oswald reprinted an extract from Carey's old *Volunteers Journal* to impute that Carey had endorsed British repression in Ireland and America. In fact, this was a typical (if deliberate) example of the confusion of meanings generated by reprinting. Carey's old paper had itself been reprinting a British journal in order to rebut it. He now counterattacked by charging in mock-heroic couplets that it was Oswald who made a habit of reproducing British works as if they were his own. Carey's *Plagi-scurriliad* (fig. 8.1) identified his antagonist as a borrower, descended directly from "the celebrated race of Grub-street Garretteers": "Regardless what the world may say," he cries, "Seize ev'ry thought falls in your way." Carey recited an ironic history of such *"privateer"* activities, pretending to laud a tradition of buccaneers who had struggled against monopolists of knowledge. A literary pirate was apparently the true revolutionary of letters, upholding "the liberty of picking, choosing, culling, seizing, and *borrowing*."[14] Oswald took the heavy-handed satire as a public challenge and demanded satisfaction. Despite Carey's earlier repudiation of dueling, he now accepted the invitation—only to discover that Oswald was not only a veteran, but a sharpshooter. The two met on January 18, 1786, close to where Aaron Burr and Alexander Hamilton would face off a few years later. Oswald probably took pity on his rival and shot low. Wounded in the thigh, it took Carey fifteen months to recover.[15]

Meanwhile, Carey's newspaper was proving hard to sell. He needed something to excite readers. The answer he hit upon was to print unauthorized reports of the debates at the House of Assembly, the unicameral body eventually replaced by Congress. It was a "maiden attempt," as he told Franklin, but that meant he enjoyed exclusivity. (Much later, Carey would recall owing his survival to the fact that "the printers had then more scruples about pirating on each other.") The initiative proved his salvation, and he reinvested the profits, first in a collaborative periodical entitled *The Columbian Magazine,* and then in a journal of his own, the *American Museum.*[16] And at the same time he began to build up a substantial trade in imported volumes—science, philosophy, voyages, history—in a bid to don Rivington's old mantle as the intermediary to the old country. By 1796, when Rivington himself showed up offering access to London publications in return for a share in the reprint profits, Carey could afford to spurn him.[17]

The *Museum* found readers across the country, and as far afield as Jefferson in distant Versailles. But such success created its own problems. Subscribers were geographically dispersed, at a time when the infrastructure and credit facilities of the new nation were rudimentary. Signing up

M.ʳ Matthew Carey PRINTER.

FIGURE 8.1. Mathew Carey, portrayed in 1786 as the radical newspaperman he had been in Dublin. M. Carey, *The Plagi-scurriliad* (Philadelphia: for the author, 1786), frontispiece. Courtesy of Brown University Library.

subscribers was easy; collecting subscriptions proved difficult and costly. When, in December 1792, the postal service raised its charges, the *American Museum* closed.[18] But it had already had its effect, acting as a major stimulant of debates about the political economy of manufacturing and commerce. The new nation was weak in both. Its productive resources were rudimentary by European standards, and it had few financial mechanisms to help develop more. In Britain, Lord Sheffield had cast merciless light on the ex-colonies' predicament in his *Observations on the commerce of the American states*. The question for those states was how to address their weakness. Doing so would require a reimagining of commercial, manufacturing, and military strategy.[19] Catching up with and surpassing European industry demanded invention, clearly, but Carey's camp insisted that that must be twinned with the appropriation of machines, methods, and ideas. Carey's periodicals became agitators for nonimportation pacts, tariffs on industrial imports, and programs of "improvement" intended to upend Sheffield's dismal appraisal and challenge British power.[20] The very first issue of the *Columbian* called for a society to be formed to encourage arts, manufactures, and commerce, along with an essay by Carey advocating a new canal between the Delaware and Ohio Rivers—a scheme that would become an idée fixe for the next half-century.[21] And in the six years of its life the *American Museum* not only advocated improvement relentlessly, but adopted a strategy of appropriating knowledge to do so. Explicitly devoted to unoriginality—its motto (like Thomas's old motif) evoked the picking of choice flowers from others' gardens—the *Museum* existed to preserve texts by reprinting them. This it did freely and widely, reproducing both fugitive articles and substantial works like Paine's *Common sense* and the Federalist Papers.[22] By doing so it became the decade's most outspoken voice reconciling a demand for manufactures, natural science, and technology with a republican political vision. Carey prized a remark by George Washington that "a more useful literary plan has never been undertaken in America."

A key component of this project was a scheme for the encouragement of manufacturing devised by Tench Coxe. A merchant with long-standing interests in manufactures, Coxe would be a congressional advisor on the first federal patent law.[23] Manufactures both offered "immense advantages" to the new nation, he believed, and were "full of danger" to the old colonial power. To realize their potential, Americans should welcome imports of raw materials from Europe while imposing tariffs on manufactured goods. And, he added, "we may certainly borrow some of their inventions." Indeed, Coxe argued for a systematic policy to that end. "We must carefully examine the conduct of other countries," he urged, "in order to possess ourselves of their methods of encouraging manufactories." Officials should meet every incoming ship, seek out immigrants who were skilled artisans, and offer them premiums for inventions that might benefit the nation. Perhaps land could be offered in thousand-acre parcels to artisans prepared to become citizens, as a way of recognizing their "merit and genius." (Coxe himself was a land speculator, so this was not exactly a disinterested proposal.) Such a policy, he thought, would also bolster the republican virtue of frugality by curbing the lust for European fashions.[24]

Soon Carey and Coxe had inspired societies for manufactures and improvements across the states, in Philadelphia, New York, Boston, Baltimore, and elsewhere. These associations were linked through a network built partly on Carey's trade correspondence. They were also publicized more broadly through the *American Museum*.[25] In other words, Carey and the *American Museum* became principal agents in developing a republican ideology of appropriating European knowledge while protecting domestic manufactures. Their actual reprinting demonstrated the scope of the enterprise. Carey reprinted cosmology, meteorology, and geology, and made a point of including Benjamin West's call to reject the naming of the newly discovered "planet Herschel" (Uranus) after King George. And at the same time the *Museum* hailed American inventors, and promoted prizes for them. It even offered its own awards for essays on such subjects as the responsibilities of the press and the best policy for manufactures. And Carey undertook to reprint "authenticated" essays on both sides of such debates, arguing that the most fundamental kind of property was a citizen's in "his opinions and the free communication of them," and that this could only be preserved by not "making the printers despots." He also advocated extending this strategy to all other fields. He called on agricultural societies, for example, to reprint "extracts from foreign treatises" that might be useful in husbandry. Medical associations should do likewise. And America needed a "purely moral periodical publication" devoted to reprinting French and English writers like Addison and Steele.

Overall, the idea was for a cascade of reprinting to spread knowledge across the new country. Appearing first in the coastal newspapers, ideas would recur in the inland press, then in magazines, and would at length be preserved in the *Museum*. In this way the *Museum* would become the capstone to a nationwide, reticulated replication *system* dedicated to a rich, secure, and free republic. It articulated a new and aggressive national strategy, with three principal elements: to appropriate European inventions and reward domestic ones; to protect nascent manufactures; and to create a network of canals extending as far as the Great Lakes, thereby creating a truly united set of states.[26]

Prodded by the spread of this movement, Congress commissioned Secretary of the Treasury Alexander Hamilton to compile a report on manufactures in the new nation. Hamilton responded by calling to his aid the societies associated with Carey's journal. Coxe replied in detail, urging the need to build up manufacturing on the basis of "machines and secrets" adopted from Europe. Impressed, Hamilton appointed Coxe his assistant. He now used his new authority to gather much more testimony, from which he drafted a first version of the report.[27] Coxe drew broadly on the *American Museum* to urge that manufacturing would facilitate military and political independence, foster the immigration of skilled workers and capital, and reinforce "individual industry and oeconomy." He not only advocated tariffs and premiums, but restated his suggestion of awarding land to "the first introducers or establishers of new and useful manufactories, arts, machines, & secrets."[28] And he proposed new laws to grant introducers of European techniques exclusive rights—the equivalent of patents, but for introduction, not invention. The government should meanwhile impede the export of inventions developed at home. He finally recommended public investment in three great canal projects, including the Chesapeake and Delaware. A network of communication, Coxe declared, must underpin a successful industrial economy. Hamilton agreed. He took Coxe's text and edited it, discarding the land-award proposal but retaining most of the rest. When he had finished, what emerged was the blueprint for a future industrial, commercial, and financial society.[29]

Hamilton listed a number of specific manufactures that needed protection. Publishing was not among them. Printing houses had proliferated across the nation already. As Coxe had pointed out in the *American Museum*, printing had outpaced any other "branch of manual art" in America, such that even a work like the *Encyclopaedia Britannica* could be produced domestically (it was in fact reprinted with embellishments by Thomas Dobson). But this self-sufficiency should now be put to use. Reprinting must become a lynchpin of the greater project of national development through appropriation. Americans, Coxe wrote, must insist upon "the opportunity of publishing immediately, for the American demand, all books in every European language, within the term of the copy right." They should take advantage of this liberty to issue "plain" editions, affordable by the people, of any worthwhile British works. As London quartos became Philadelphia octavos or duodecimos, republican virtue would be built into the very sources from which national progress would come. It was the first explicit call for international reprinting to be a central part of the project of defining a modern nation.[30]

Carey began reprinting books in earnest at this time. William Guthrie's *Geography* was one target—an old British workhorse already reprinted in Dublin. Carey made extensive changes to the text, completely replacing the section on America and adding his own introduction to condemn the original's bias in favor of Britain.[31] Goldsmith's *Animated Nature* too he reprinted, adding plates from a London edition of Buffon. Political, documentary, and economic works came too. But he also reproduced fiction, especially the Minerva Press's line of sentimental, morally inflected novels by women authors.[32] Carey acknowledged no copyright in any of these, of course, because there was in fact none to acknowledge. But he went too far when he ventured to reprint natural philosophy from the American Philosophical Society, in a bid to circulate it too in an accessible form. For Carey, the Society was guilty of "aping the quarto volumes of the Royal Society," and should shift to cheap octavos of the kind that he, Coxe, and Hamilton were advocating for international reprints. What was "public" in the 1660s was nothing of the sort in the 1790s, and a different politics of readership demanded a new kind of publishing. The aged Franklin stepped in to put a stop to this, telling Carey that he risked fatally undermining learned journals in general. But Carey remained sure he was right, and returned to the fray three decades later, by which time the APS would have issued only seven volumes of its journal in fifty-five years. It would have been faster and safer in the interim for authors to submit papers to Calcutta, he would point out.[33]

In truth, what Coxe and Carey were proposing was deeply controversial, and the federal government never did invest in the appropriation of manufactures from Europe. But private associations—beginning with the societies of the 1790s—repeatedly sent agents to Europe with orders to scout out the latest engineering designs or to seek potential emigrants with the skills to aid in canal or, later, railroad building. Coxe and Hamilton collaborated in one of the earliest and most ambitious of these ventures, aimed at creating a model manufacturing town around machines and skills adopted from Britain. An agent went to the United Kingdom to collect industrial secrets on the quiet, while Coxe recruited a group of émigré Britons already in America who claimed to possess knowledge of key machines. One George Parkinson, for example, was given a U.S. patent to replicate the mill machinery of Richard Arkwright. But Hamilton and Coxe made the fatal error of entrusting the directorship of their scheme to William Duer, a financial speculator then maneuvering secretly for a controlling interest in the Bank of New York. Duer inflated the new nation's first financial bubble. When it burst in March 1792, he was left facing $3 million of debt, and the project for a manufacturing town collapsed with his bankruptcy. A strange mixture of the visionary and the furtive, the whole project became for Hamilton's enemies a symbol of speculative recklessness and amorality, and a cautionary tale against the very idea of industrial appropriation.[34]

Shortly after this, an altogether grander crisis transformed the politics of appropriation. Britain had begun impounding U.S. cargo vessels bound for Jacobin France. Over two hundred vessels were seized, their crews pressed into serving in Britain's cause. At the same time, the British also connived at the depredations of pirates from North Africa who attacked American shipping. The resulting crisis made partisans of all stripes reconsider their positions. Hamilton wanted peace, but Jefferson and his supporters argued for action, and Carey plunged headlong into their camp. He published his own *Account* of Algiers explaining why. In contrast to many, Carey did not condemn the corsairs as such. Instead he drew a moral about mediation: an African reading a Western depiction of Algiers, he said, would treat it with as much "disdain" as an American coming across a "frothy" book about the United States published in London. But Algiers was a military dictatorship and a kingdom—"an epithet which might, without regret, be expunged from every human vocabulary"—and it colluded with Britain in "the general conspiracy of the Domitians and Caligulas of Europe" against Jacobin France. The United States should deploy a navy to deal with it for these reasons, not because its piracies reflected some deep-seated moral flaw.[35] In the event, President Washington appointed Chief Justice John Jay to negotiate a solution. When Jay returned with a treaty, Carey supported those who denounced it as a capitulation to a reactionary power. Moreover, he believed that the treaty implied a drift to aristocratic governance in the United States, because it required only presidential and senatorial confirmation. Carey sought to prevent ratification, not least by reprinting the treaty and circulating it through his established network with a long list of criticisms. He and Coxe then went on to campaign for the Jeffersonians. His correspondence network became a tool for anti-Federalist coordination, and his premises in Philadelphia a clearinghouse for campaign communications.[36]

The transatlantic crisis not only transformed Carey's own political associations, but helped reprinting as a practice emerge as a conventional custom, Hamiltonian but not narrowly Federalist. The relative costs of manufacturing and importing shifted. "For many years," as striking Phila-delphia printers later recalled, "books could be imported into the United States and sold cheaper than they could be printed here." The crisis evened the field. A little later, the introduction of copyright to Ireland tipped the balance even further by destroying the Dublin reprinters. Europe was at war, the seas were perilous, a duty had been imposed on imported paper, and now the Irish competition was gone.[37] Organizations like the Charles-ton Library Society began to order American reprints in quantity because their traditional sources were cut off. Moreover, Americans increasingly felt that they *should* not look to Britain for books. A society formed for the importation of books in 1805 was not a success, and in 1807 importing editions was actually made illicit by a nonimportation law.[38] Reprinting grew into a standard practice. It was a way to make knowledge affordable, accessible, and useful—in a word, republican.

The fortunes of the enterprise remained fragile, however. As was customary, nodal figures like Carey guaranteed the debts of many trade counterparts, some of them in towns far distant from Philadelphia. Doing so cemented bonds and sometimes allowed Carey to wangle lower rates when he hired those obligated to him. (We do not know if he repeated the initiative of another firm, which imposed a requirement not to pirate its books.) Even in the 1820s, his firm would still have eight hundred active engagements in hand, for clients scattered across the nation. But "endors-ings" were not typically accounted as debts in a firm's books. A default might therefore have unforeseen and devastating consequences—with the potential to multiply into a cascade across the industry. Carey repeat-edly lamented this "vile system." He could have been ruined, he later recalled, had just one creditor called in a debt on the wrong day, and twice he approached George Washington to borrow cash lest that happen. But to refuse to guarantee another's debt was almost unthinkable; it would show discourtesy, and might itself prompt a collapse. The memory of just one bankruptcy that Carey triggered in this way continued to haunt his conscience for years.[39]

The risks posed by attacks on one's credit were constant and real. And they were exacerbated in febrile times like the late 1790s—the years of the Alien and Sedition Acts—by xenophobia. William Cobbett chose this moment to denounce Carey as a member of a secret Masonic-Jacobin cabal known as the American Society of United Irishmen, dedicated to importing the French Revolution. Once again, reprinting was to the fore, with Cobbett seeking to erode Carey's credit by charging that he exemplified a general Irish nonchalance about *"mine* and *thine,"* and Carey retaliating by displaying Cobbett's own borrowings from John Ward Fenno. Carey denied the conspiracy charge vigorously (but not entirely ingenuously), but for a moment he stood on the brink. He even announced publicly that he was selling up. But Jefferson's election as president came just in time to save him.[40] Carey reaped the rewards of political patronage. He obtained a reliably lucrative contract to print laws, and became a director of the Bank of Pennsylvania, securing access to financial credit. Having lived at continual risk of bankruptcy, suddenly he need never face that peril again.

By now Carey was a leading figure in the book trade, successful enough to export to Europe. He could also afford to invest. A large dollop of capital went into a Bible, the type for which he bought from Hugh Gaine and kept standing for almost two decades. As that implies, the crisis had prompted him to take another momentous decision. He decided to sell his printing operation and concentrate his energies on publishing alone. From now on his ventures—both republications and originals—would be manufactured by printers hired for the task. In prospect was a profound reconfiguration. As in Europe, publishers were beginning to set themselves above artisans and retailers. By the same token, printers were beginning to see themselves as sharing more with artisans in other trades than with grandees in their own. The new publishers themselves, too, had to design novel ways of acting at a distance, including new approaches to credit and obligation. Most booksellers had hitherto dealt with predominantly local markets, connected, if at all, by precarious exchange agreements; but Carey's reach already extended far afield, especially to the south. He now built upon the networks he had established for the *American Museum* and from his own prodigious travels. From peripatetic agents like Mason Weems, through the many printers of Philadelphia, to prison inmates hired to make cartons, Carey's operation became a web of broad span. By about 1810, he thought, this style of operation had almost entirely replaced old-style subscriptions.[41]

As it expanded, however—as, in general, publishing became a national endeavor—so this kind of web triggered conflicts. The claims of publishers to particular titles and genres came into conflict when their markets merged. The result was a proliferation of piracy charges across the United States. The fragile and interweaved nature of credit made it essential, not just for individuals, but for the trade at large, that some mechanism be created for resolving these conflicts. The question that confronted Carey's peers after 1800 was thus one of political formation. How could they wrestle their various local practices, customs, and roles into a coherent, well-mannered national trade?[42]

"THE CONSTITUTION OF OUR LITERARY REPUBLIC"

Carey's journey from Ireland was far from unique. Since 1720, over a hundred thousand had made the same voyage. In mid-1784 three hundred artisans and their families left Dublin in one ship alone, and similar numbers were on board two more that weighed anchor within a week or two of Carey's. He had done his bit to spur the exodus, issuing from his cell an exhortation to emigrate. The United States, he thought, offered land and freedom. And for a bookman there were other incentives too. The London booksellers were exploiting the end of perpetual copyright in their own kingdom to create cheap editions, narrowing the field for Dublin's reprinters. Even before the Act of Union, the Irish industry was in decline.

So it was that Dublin's reprint trade was resurrected in Philadelphia and New York. Robert Bell made unauthorized reprinting a revolutionary act; the loyalist Thomas Kirk reprinted Dugald Stewart and the Romantic poets; and Hugh Gaine did the same to Addison, Burke, and Chesterfield. Irish émigrés built American publishing. They naturally based it on what they knew best: the customs of the Irish trade. But those customs could not simply be reasserted in such a different setting. The first generations had to invent principles for regulating propriety across a landscape with several centers, not just one. They also had to determine how those principles could be promulgated, upheld, and defended. This involved developing sustainable, practicable customs for exchange, credit, and communication across distances large and small. It also meant building up the habits that would embed such frameworks into everyday life at the level of the printing house, bookshop, and home. As in Ireland, therefore, reprinting did not mean abandoning civility—on the contrary, it made civility all the more important. For Carey in particular, the policies he advocated for print were part and parcel of campaigns promoting philanthropy, moral reform, temperance, the abolition of slavery, the shipping of freed slaves to Liberia, the relief of Greek refugees, and "internal improvement" (the building of canals, and later railroads). Creating a self-perpetuating engine of culture was part and parcel of establishing an industrious, independent, moral, free, and resilient nation.

Copyright was a consideration here, but at first a distinctly peripheral one. America had had a federal copyright law from 1790, to be sure. But it protected only authors resident in the country, and in practice was of limited appeal even for those. Of roughly thirteen thousand titles published in the 1790s, only about five hundred were registered for copyright. And periodicals were not covered at all.[43] The law could certainly be invoked—Thomas Dobson told a nervous author in the mid-1790s to register a work to prevent its being reprinted "in such a manner as you would not wish to see"—but it did not yet have a central role. That author did not take Dobson's advice, and only from a later date do the archives of publishers begin to fill with certificates of registration. In the meantime, to some the very principle remained (perhaps conveniently) obscure: Isaiah Thomas caught a rival red-handed, only to be told that copyright did not protect "a *complete* work."[44] There had never been much need for it, in truth. Reprinting in different cities had generally been uncontroversial because markets were overwhelmingly local. But no longer. Thomas fought to restrain what he called the "phrensy" of new piracy complaints, reckoning it "a duty I owe the trade" to uphold good order. He exhorted his peers to maintain "harmony and a good understanding" for the sake of the trade's public reputation. Thomas even told one printer tempted to patent a work (and hence to defend it aggressively) that doing so would be "unworthy of a man of honour." Space must be left for enterprising projects, he insisted, "or Genius, in America, must lie dormant." He considered proposing a referee system to that end, à la Dublin. But ultimately he acknowledged that the clashes were beyond his control. They proved "the necessity of a regulation in our business."[45]

The American trade had no guilds, but assertions of moral community —of "companionship" among journeymen, for example—had been heard long before the Revolution. As early as 1724, Boston's booksellers had considered a call to "establish themselves into a Company."[46] Only after independence did such moves lead to anything substantive. Beginning when Franklin tried with Isaiah Thomas in 1788 to establish "regulations for the benefit of the trade," associations repeatedly appeared, not all of which evaporated quickly.[47] The initiatives tended to take one of two forms: alliances of printers (masters and/or journeymen) to protect artisanal values, and alliances of booksellers to secure publishing. Both sought stability, and both faced domestic and international reprinting as central concerns. In their more rhetorical moments, each claimed to stand for the place of print itself in the progress of civilization.

The printers' associations sought to enshrine a moral economy of printing as a craft, not as a form of capitalism. One of the first was the "association" of masters called the Company of Printers that appeared in Philadelphia in 1794. It aimed to deter nonmembers from practicing printing, and to monitor members' compliance with craft rules.[48] It was followed a year later by the Typographical Society of New York, and then by the Franklin Typographical Society, launched specifically for journeymen in 1799. Another group, the Asylum Company of Journeyman Printers, appeared in 1800, only to change into the Philadelphia Typographical Society. A Boston equivalent also arose, and in 1808 took the name of the Faustus Association. All of these were essentially artisanal—the journeymen's groups were among the first workers' associations in America. Yet their views of their role could be quite broad. Both the Baltimore and Philadelphia societies called for protective duties on imported books, for example, while the Faustus Association listed the protection of printing houses from fire as one of its principal raisons d'être.

It was, however, the second kind of association that more directly shaped piracy and property. This was the society dominated—and often launched—by booksellers, and specifically by publishing booksellers, Carey being their doyen. Such groups aimed to maintain prices, the integrity of editions, and proprieties for intercity commerce. The "courtesies" of the trade were their province; they tried to organize trade sales and book fairs, and to achieve the quiet resolution of disputes. They typically proclaimed a "harmony of interests," as it would become known, between printers, publishers, booksellers, and authors, although some formally excluded artisans from their ranks. The first of these bodies was the Philadelphia Company of Printers and Booksellers. It convened for the first time on Independence Day in 1791, with Carey a moving force and a regular participant.[49] Somewhat akin to an old London conger, its intent was to distribute the risks of publishing both by formalizing a share system and by preventing piracy. It also sought to fix prices so that members need not compete against what they saw as underselling.

In setting up the society, Carey declared, he hoped to achieve two ends. First, he wanted to encourage the publication of works otherwise beyond the means of individual booksellers. And, second, he hoped to "secure the copy-rights of the members against invasion by printers at a distance, or by the associators individually." The venture lasted five years before Carey abruptly resigned, triggering its collapse. It had "utterly failed" to meet its first aim, he explained. The company's choice of works to publish, interestingly, had proven less judicious than that of any individual. And at the second aim it had done even worse, proving actively "pernicious." Books the company had undertaken in Philadelphia had been seized upon for that very reason as sure things and reprinted in New York, Boston, and other towns. Had he been acting individually, Carey said, he could have made exchange agreements with those reprinters and benefited from their work. But the company's own principles had ruled that out. So the adoption of a compact against reprinting had, in practice, been self-defeating. The Philadelphia Company had been a very costly "experiment," and it had failed.[50]

A major reason for this failure was that the Philadelphia Company was based in just one city. The problems it was formed to tackle arose, increasingly, from trade between cities. In 1800, therefore, Carey was interested to hear from a correspondent named Littlejohn a more ambitious scheme that would operate at that national level and thereby underwrite the emerging customs of American publishing and international reprinting. "I am told that in general 500 copies of any book will pay the expenses and a decent profit," he observed; "if so, what a vast number of books must be reprinted if booksellers would only be punctual and honest to each other." Littlejohn urged that the major booksellers of Philadelphia, New York, Boston, and other cities coalesce into what he called a "Company of Stationers of North America." The company would provide a mechanism for alliances to produce editions otherwise too costly or risky to be viable. But it would also go much further. It would create and sustain an entire

moral system of print. At a Stationers' Hall in each state, respected practitioners would uphold regulations to "prevent interference in the same
work"—that is, to forestall piracy. At the same time, they would police
membership of the fraternity, threatening expulsion for "infidelity" to its
customs. "The present State of the morals of Booksellers in the United
States requires something of this kind to keep them honest punctual
& willing to serve each other," Littlejohn concluded.[51] Carey agreed; he
scrawled "An Idea" on top of the proposal and got to work.

Littlejohn's was but one of several suggestions aired at this time. The
Baltimore trade, for example, coalesced to urge the federal government
to impose a levy on imports of books. This prompted a Boston bookseller,
E. T. Andrews, to suggest to Carey that associations be formed in major
cities to regulate the trade, to "prevent the importation of all such Books
as may be printed by each association." If a member of such a body reprinted a European book, no other member would be permitted to import copies except in a more expensive format. What all such suggestions
shared were three convictions: the paramount importance of reprinting
European works; the consequent need to eliminate domestic reprinting
and rival importing (in their terms, piracy); and the requirement that a
solution to these problems come from the trade itself. And practical
moves soon began anew. In 1802 a New York Association of Booksellers
convened, its principal purpose being to reprint European schoolbooks.
The Company of Printers of Philadelphia reconstituted itself, significantly,
as a Booksellers' Company, complete with a trade journal, and elected
Carey its president. Similar organizations appeared in Boston and Lexington. At Carey's urging, the Philadelphia company proposed a register
system to "settle the Priority of claims to new works." And in December
1801 Carey circulated a letter to major publishers across the United States
proposing that they harmonize all these emerging bodies into one whole,
in a "patriotic spirit of fostering domestic arts and manufactures." By
coalescing, as the German trade was then doing, into a single community,
the publishers could further to an "incalculable" degree the achievements
of "American genius."[52]

So it was that in summer 1802 New York hosted at Carey's initiative
the first publishers' trade fair in America. He intended it to emulate the
great fairs of early modern Germany, at which the booksellers of Europe
had gathered to barter sheets, make contacts, and sustain trust across far-
flung networks. Like them, Carey's fair was for booksellers engaged in

long-distance publishing projects in a loosely federated polity. Its purpose was to foster the development of a coherent national enterprise. He therefore used the occasion to launch what he called an "American Company of Booksellers." In part a realization of Littlejohn's scheme, it also attested to a continuing ambition to improve "arts and manufactures" and keep specie within the country by supplanting imported books. The new company would revive a civility that Carey believed had obtained in early modern Europe. The pioneers of publishing in the United States were about to forge a national enterprise by inventing an American equivalent to the Stationers' Company of Shakespeare's London.

The American Company was in practice dominated by Irish émigrés. Its first president was Hugh Gaine, who had come over in 1750 and was now "the oldest printer and bookseller in the United States."[53] Carey persuaded Gaine to make an opening address. The old loyalist spoke at length, using his oration to urge the creation of nothing less than a new "social compact." The elimination of internal pirating would be its keystone. Its objectives would be the refinement of national morals and the advance of science in the republic. Carey's project, Gaine told the gathered booksellers, added "a dignity to our avocation before unknown." Fittingly, he turned to history to articulate its importance. "The mind," he said, "is led, by a natural transition, to the first rise of our manufacture in this country." As with other industries, Gaine remarked, Britain had until recently been the origin of almost all major print initiatives. "Her manufactures enabled her, without the expense of government or protection, to reap all the benefit of our labours." This was very much Carey's view, but it was significant that Gaine voiced it, given his own history. Now, he continued, the expansion of papermaking and printing had finally made it possible to turn that subservient relationship upside down. To do that, however, the trade needed a moral structure. Most of all, it needed some principle to guide interactions between cities. Such a principle had never existed before, and the law of copyright alone was not sufficient to furnish it now. The great task of the era was therefore to establish this principle. Only with that achieved would it be possible to talk meaningfully of publishing as an *American* enterprise, different from and superior to its British competition.

Gaine did not condemn all domestic reprinting. Some works, he conceded, were "calculated for more partial spheres," and these could be reprinted in small editions for particular locales. Reprinting per se was not evil, then. But it was "unsafe" and "ungenerous to the last degree" when applied to publications of a larger reach. The new association proposed to counter the practice by making it "unsafe" for the reprinter too. It banned reprinting within the States, and announced that it would try to stop titles being imported if the works were available from American publishers.[54] With exchange through Carey's fairs supplanting local reprints, a national market would finally come into being, and with it a national public. This was the heart of what Gaine called "the constitution of our literary republic."

The American Company proclaimed its actual constitution two years later. By this time Carey himself was president. Echoing the U.S. Constitution, he intended his own version to "form a more perfect union" in the realm of print. To that end, it set out to "establish rules for the transaction of business—to promote the Manufactures of our country—and to promote the great interests of Science and Literature." As forecast by Gaine, the very first article outlawed "the republication of Books already printed in the United States"; the second forbade the import of works already being made in America. These two principles were to be the foundation on which the American book should develop. The Company created a "board" from the three great centers of Boston, New York, and Philadelphia to adjudicate such matters. It would maintain an annual register of all American publications, and could "impeach" any offender against rights, who, on being "convicted," might be censured or even expelled; anyone publishing work of "immoral tendency" risked the same fate. It would also uphold workmanship in general, offering prizes for the best printing, binding, ink, and paper (much as Carey had long done for other manufactures). But piracy was its principal concern.[55]

Carey remarked that his plan for the American Company of Booksellers was based "on a deliberate study of society in the United States." No doubt it was. But it nevertheless found its task daunting. In practice the trade could come to no consensus on even its most pressing questions —those of reprinting and of a tariff on imported books. Revealingly, even Carey's own Philadelphia company seems to have claimed a right to reprint works formerly owned by those who became its members. And then there was the problem of figures like the John Brown who declined to join because, as he ingenuously put it, he preferred to be free to reprint others' titles. Brown's objection clarified a major disadvantage with this kind of strategy in general: that it could only be effective for those within the company's ranks. Brown and his like might become rogues, effectively free to pirate at will provided they were prepared to endure blacklisting. His case therefore spurred renewed efforts "to settle the Priority of claims to new works" in general. Meanwhile the company exhorted members to "discountenance" bringing into Philadelphia books to which its members already laid claim, including those hitherto brought in openly through the exchange system. The company's authority was evidently rather frail. Eventually it found itself in the humiliating position of receiving an offer from an outsider to sell it copies of one of its own most highly profitable titles, Aesop's *Fables*. It summoned up enough pride to reject this offer, lest it "encourage the printing of any work, the right whereof, belongs to this Company." But soon afterward it shut its doors for the last time. On a larger scale, much the same fate overtook the American Company too. For a couple of years it seemed to thrive, but far-flung booksellers soon learned to use its channels to distribute reprints of major publishers' titles. The very system that Carey had inaugurated to prevent piracy turned out to have facilitated it. This "evil that had not been foreseen," as he called it, outweighed all the company's advantages. Both company and fair collapsed.[56]

Not everyone was distraught. It is interesting, given their grand aspirations, that Carey's companies and fairs encountered real opposition, not least from some who might have been expected to be enthusiastic. Andrews in Boston, for example, feared that they would "do more harm than good."[57] And at least two Philadelphians other than Brown refused to join Carey's company. One was Robert Campbell, who specialized in cheap reprints of English books. Campbell almost certainly saw in the association a threat to his mode of business, and refused to have anything to do with it—prompting the company in a moment of bravado to adopt a policy of reprinting on anyone who pirated a member's works. The other was William McCulloch, who bluntly told Isaiah Thomas that all such institutions, especially Carey's "peculiar hobby horse" of the fair, were "useless, if not pernicious." McCulloch refused to believe that a customary regime could work, and disdained arguments for it as mere moralism.[58] Yet another Philadelphia opponent was John Bioren, who made his living by reprinting other booksellers' titles and declined to recognize any institution that claimed the authority to stop him. The company blacklisted Bioren. It proved an ineffective sanction: he did indeed go bankrupt, but not until a decade and a half after the company itself had expired.

Most consequential, however, were perhaps the radical attacks in the press that cast Carey's efforts as a "conspiracy" of monopolists and capitalists—a "combination of rich *booksellers* against *authors and printers.*" That is, he found his schemes cast as the successors, not to the great German fairs, but to the very force he most violently despised—the perpetual-copyright conspirators of London. Both the existence and the terms of this opposition mattered. Carey's camp was beginning to trumpet what would become a broad political-economic ideology, hugely important in antebellum American politics, based on a supposed "harmony of interests" between agrarian, manufacturing, and mercantile classes. The artisanal critique threatened to give the lie to that idea, in the very area that its major advocate might have been expected to know best.[59]

A NETWORKED SOCIETY? ASSOCIATION AND ITS FAILURES

When mid-nineteenth-century British authors like Wilkie Collins inveighed against American piracy, what so offended them was not the reprinting itself so much as the systematic and proud manner of its pursuit. The Americans, Collins said, made "robbery" into "the basis of national aggrandizement." In essence, he was right. Since before the Revolution, reprinters had stressed the propriety of their enterprise, arguing that they were spreading enlightenment in the face of corrupt and monarchical monopolists. After 1800, the practice had become part and parcel of the so-called American System. This system became a leading candidate for economic orthodoxy in the wake of the War of 1812. Its central element was an insistence that manufacturing, properly considered, exhibited a "harmony of interests" with agriculture and trade. But whereas trade and agriculture were relatively well developed in the United States, manufacturing remained vulnerable to European domination. Policy should therefore be directed to enhancing manufactures and resisting European—that is, British—depredations. Three means should be used to this end. The first and most important was the appropriation of ideas, machines, men, and skills, by any and all means, while protecting American industries by tariffs on imports. British artisans would take any opportunity to come to America, Carey thought, and he even issued his own guidebook for those considering the move. The second was the provision of financing for new projects. And the third was the promotion of "internal improvements," especially canals. In every respect this program was radically opposed to the orthodoxies of British political economy after Adam Smith. It was anti-laissez-faire, anti–free trade, and orientated toward factory rather than agrarian production. And Carey was acknowledged as its leading architect. He authored treatises, badgered possible converts, encouraged the formation of new waves of societies, and traveled up and down the coast in pursuit of the cause. He also sought to reform the publication regime to circulate such knowledge.[60] It was this effort that not only embedded "piracy" as national political economy, but created the political economy itself.

By the mid-1810s, Philadelphia manufacturers were acutely anxious that Britain, emerging from the long years of Napoleonic war, was about to launch a determined effort to destroy them. At Westminster Lord Brougham confirmed their fears when he called on British factory owners to sell at a loss in America so as to stifle the manufacturing that, "contrary to the natural course of things," had grown up there.[61] American newspapers seized upon Brougham's impolitic avowal, and as it circulated from reprint to reprint it created a furor amid a population suffering a serious economic downturn.[62] Carey in particular responded, redeploying print in the cause of the American system—a cause he declared as important as any "since the organization of the government." It amounted to "the mighty question, whether we shall be really or nominally independent." He handed over his business to his son, Henry, and threw himself into organizing and authorship. Carey cajoled readers to support a phalanx of associations: the Philadelphia Society for the Promotion of National Industry, the Pennsylvania Society for the Encouragement of American Manufactures, the Society for the Promotion of Manufactures and the Mechanic Arts, and more.[63] A Society for the Dissemination of Useful Knowledge would seek out, reprint, and circulate gratis British (and a few American) tracts "calculated to advance the best interests of society." And his Pennsylvania Society for the Promotion of Internal Improvement— yet another band—sent an engineer named William Strickland to Britain to gather techniques for building railroads and canals. Strickland's *Reports* were published (with copyright, for once) by Carey's firm, as much to bolster a jaded "public opinion" in the possibilities of improvement projects in general as to convey specific technical information.[64]

Carey gave his commitment to internal improvement a name. This was a habit of his; as a political economist he would write as "Hamilton" or "Colbert," and in politics he had sallied forth as "Harrington" (after the seventeenth-century author of *Oceana,* James Harrington). When writing on canals and improvement Carey adopted the persona of "Fulton." The choice was in homage to Robert Fulton, the Pennsylvanian credited with inventing the steamboat. Carey saw in Fulton a salutary lesson about improvers. The engineer had died while still fighting to protect his steam vessels — the latest of which was called the *Olive Branch*, after Carey's hugely successful tract from the War of 1812 — from what he called "pirates who have clubbed their purses and copied my boats." In Carey's view America had never witnessed "a more infamous and outrageous attack upon mental property."[65] Moreover, Fulton had also been an adept at industrial appropriation from Britain, with Joshua Gilpin, by now Carey's closest ally, as his surreptitious sidekick. Above all, however, he had been a visionary proponent of canals as the keys to a great future society. Since the beginning of his engineering career, he had envisaged canals (not just a few grand waterways, but scaled capillary networks) facilitating a commercial utopia of free trade, public reason, and open knowledge that would extend from metropolis to deepest province. He had told Napoleon that canals would complete the French Revolution, George Washington that they would complete the American. Thomas Mifflin, governor of Pennsylvania, heard they would "bind the whole country in the bonds of social intercourse."[66]

Carey shared this vision. For him too canals were the Western world's first network technology. He hoped to use them in America to "unite her people in one indissoluble bond of prosperity and sentiment, to make all *parts* of the commonwealth one flourishing and inseparable *Whole*." The rhetoric was utopian. With the publishers issuing forth knowledge, canals promised to spread that knowledge and thus eliminate ignorance. They would turn the harmony of interests from a theory into a reality. In its very first issue, the *Columbian Magazine* had carried a "Philosophical Dream" by Carey that envisaged the United States in 1850 united into a single political and economic body by canals. The *American Museum* had played the same tune, repeatedly hailing canals as "binding the union with the most substantial and certain cement."[67] After 1812, this might actually be achieved. So Carey threw himself into what he saw as an essential component of a network that would eventually extend from the Atlantic to the Great Lakes. First dreamed of in the seventeenth century, and seriously projected in the eighteenth, the Chesapeake and Delaware Canal would finally be built in the nineteenth.[68] It would cut the distance between Philadelphia and Baltimore by three hundred miles. But its engineer, John Randal, was a fellow visionary, later responsible for a utopian community along similar lines to Robert Owen's in Britain. Before long Randal fell foul of the canal's financiers. He was dismissed, much to Carey's outrage. The lawsuit he subsequently filed saddled the canal with debts so massive that it could never be made viable.[69]

Carey was tireless in pursuing canals and the idea of a networked nation. He slogged up and down the country, to New York, Boston, Salem, Hartford, New Haven, Providence, and Baltimore, seeking commitments for societies for manufacturing. In Washington he buttonholed the secretary of war. His words poured endlessly from the press—constitutions, open letters, advertisements, appeals, denunciations, defenses, treatises, polemical essays, replies to polemical essays, replies to the replies. He would rush his views into print on an almost daily basis, sending them page by page to be printed (on American-made "machine paper") as fast as he could write. He then sent them to every postmaster in the nation, distributing them gratis and pointedly declining to register them for copyright so that others could reprint them—which did happen, albeit not with the alacrity that he desired.[70] His diary conveys something of the intensity involved: he would rise at around six, write for the press for four hours or more, compose letters to wavering allies for as long again, and at night, after the theater, return to the grindstone again, often staying up well past midnight. He took laudanum to keep going when he fell ill, or indulged in a faddish water cure. Even in his seventies he kept to this punishing routine.[71]

Alexis de Tocqueville famously marveled at the propensity of Americans for forming associations of all kinds. At first glance, Carey's string of almost indistinguishable initiatives seems to fit Tocqueville's image. He was constantly launching projects, or societies, or committees within societies, for causes that ranged from Sunday schools to the settling of freed slaves in Liberia. He fretted when he was *not* included on committees; one such occasion led to two pages of private agonizing about his unpopularity, concluding with the thought that "Mankind are not worth the sacrifices I make." Yet what leaps out at a modern reader of Carey's diary is how far his America *failed* to live up to the Tocquevillian vision. His circulars received minimal responses, or, later, none at all. He was dismayed by how infrequently his works were reprinted in New York and Boston—and then on "paper only fit for ballads." He circulated notices to manufacturers, but found that he "might as well have sought to raise the dead." He collected his own works into a 550-page volume on political economy and sought to publish it, but few subscribed and he lost $300. A weekly paper, the *Political Economist,* devoted largely to reprints, likewise failed. Reprints of Hamilton's *Report* also ended up being charged to him. His proposed societies found few backers, and his argument with the secretary of war proved fruitless. In 1824 he came up with a plan to reprint thirteen key works in favor of the American system, and to have them stitched into twenty thousand almanacs destined for readers in the refractory southern states. The cost would be less than $2 per hundred, he thought, and if each were read by twenty people, they "could scarcely have failed to revolutionize public opinion." But again he found no sponsors. (Such ventures tended to fail even when funded, in fact, as southern post offices would find ways to lose the tracts.) Although his tracts were initially "republished with flattering encomiums in most of the newspapers," after a while the appetite died. Even his beloved canal project succeeded, to the extent that it did, only in the face of "apathy, torpor, and destitution of public spirit."[72] Carey privately expressed himself "disgusted" at the refusal of wealthy men to support a cause in their own interest. "Why should I waste my time," he wondered, "labouring to serve a community, in which there is not the shadow of public spirit"? Several times he resolved to withdraw from the fray. But that was one resolution he could never keep. And when he did withdraw from one society, it promptly collapsed.[73]

The problem, at root, was that Carey believed publishing was what a Tocquevillian association was *for.* He consistently gauged influence by measures familiar to a publisher: numbers of editions, sizes of impressions, rates of subscription, steadiness of sales, and manner of distribution.

Of the Boston Report, a flimsy, frothy, superficial publication of 198 pages, there were three editions printed, of (if I am correctly informed) 2000 copies each, within a few weeks, one in Boston, one in New York, and one in this city. . . . Of Smith's Wealth of Nations, and Say's Political Economy, there have been four editions printed in this country, 4750 copies in the whole. The first edition of Say, of 750 copies, was sold in three years; the second, of 2000 copies, has been sold in four. The tendency of these works is to paralize our industry, and, to a certain degree, to render the United States virtually colonies of the manufacturing nations of Europe. Of Raymond's Political Economy, a work far superior to either, there have been only two editions printed, both amounting to 1250 copies. Of the first, a large number, probably one-third, were sacrificed at auction, and the sale of the second has been very slow and limited.

What chance did the American system have? (He forgot to mention that one of those editions of Say had been issued by Carey himself.)

By these lights the one essential thing for any campaign, on any issue, was funding the press—all the more so in political economy, for in this field tracts must be distributed free, so unappealing were they to paying readers. "Nothing more was necessary" for his arguments to win the day, Carey thought, "than to give them free and general circulation."[74] By *circulation* he meant reprinting as well as distribution. Copyright, he maintained, must be actively repudiated so that they would propagate from town to town across the south. His tracts and reprints frequently exhorted all and sundry to republish them.[75] The trouble was only partly that this was a crudely quantitative approach to a problem that was significantly qualitative. It was also that the sheer costs of such a practice were substantial. And Carey's frenetic pace militated against sponsorship because he could not wait for editing. A society with Carey in it was a society that had to vest its trust in him implicitly. Increasingly, they seemed reluctant to do so. He was left lamenting that half the projects that came to nothing, in all fields, did so because of "beggarly parsimony as to the expense of printing."[76] The very manufacturers he claimed to defend seemed to regard him as "a wretched Grub-street garreteer." He was gaining a reputation as a hack, without even the lucre that might compensate for such a title. The last straw was the failure of one of his "societies for publication" —in this case a "Society of Political Economists" designed to get "sound doctrines" to southerners. It attracted only two subscribers. Carey finally gave up, signing off with a prediction that the world's greatest "experiment of free government" was set to fail amid "insurrection, civil war, and anarchy." And yet, he sighed, "all this evil might have been prevented, by an early and copious distribution of essays and pamphlets."[77]

THE AMERICAN SYSTEM OF INFORMATION

The effort took its toll. Carey burned through some $95,000 in a decade, more than half of it on his various campaigns. He found himself paying for the printing of pamphlets on credit, and passing on the embarrassing

IOUs to the firm while insisting that his family make ever-greater econo-mies. He even decided in effect to disinherit his children, believing that the family name could better be preserved through some public project. His son Henry grew convinced that something must be done. The fortune of a publisher still rested on reputation, and this Mathew was endanger-ing. Worse still, in transferring the company to Henry, Mathew had grossly overvalued its large backlog of warehoused law books—a form of albatross that many publishers still bore around their necks before stereotyping— and this made its finances all the more vulnerable. The family entered the 1820s in desperate need of money. That need would persist and perhaps helped to drive its ventures in international reprinting.

The storm broke in 1830. Henry confronted his father in a series of letters that revealed the domestic side of the pirate utopia with an angry directness hard to parallel in its time. "You think your family a happy one," Henry declared bluntly: "It is certainly not so." Maria and Susan, Henry's sisters, could barely get by and suffered from "depression." The damage that the family and firm would suffer should their public persona lapse was catastrophic, and the risk very real. Money was being drained by Carey senior's quixotic authorship. Mathew should retire from writing in order to preserve the family name.[78] Seeking to impress the rationality of this policy, Henry composed an economic and emotional balance sheet. Parodying the kind of table Mathew Carey had long presented in his po-litical-economic tracts, it compared the costs and benefits of devoting himself to the public sphere as against family life. The accountancy was poignant and rhetorically devastating (see table on p. 210).[79] He hoped that this would persuade his father to stop giving away "any more of your property." "For Heaven's sake—for your own sake—for my sake, take my advice."[80]

Mathew did nothing of the kind. Instead, it seems he wrote a scathing denunciation of Henry for filial treason, rushed it to a printing house, and had it printed. Henry was incensed. His own father had printed a "mon-strous libel, containing charges which, if true, would render me unfit to associate with gentlemen." Worse, he had entrusted this document to "a parcel of journeymen," who would surely already have circulated its con-tents among their counterparts across the city. In the world of printing there was more than one kind of publicity, as both Careys knew, and Mathew had "added to the scandal" by submitting the firm and family to the mercies of the chapel. "You cannot now be certain that there are not

Two Pictures

INCOME	$6000	INCOME	$6000
House	1200	Home	1800
Maria & Susan	300	Maria & Susan	500
Other house expenses	500		
Baird	250	Baird	500
		Other family expenses	500
Horses & Carriage	500	Horses & Carriage	500
Pamphlets & type, &c	3250	Charities &c	600
	6000		

Vexation at printers—annoyance with correspondents &c &c	Money plenty
Want of money	Reading—travelling—amusements for yourself to spend a few
Maria & Susan distressed	hundred dollars
Myself in same situation	Family happy
Baird & Eliza. Ditto	Baird ditto
&c	Myself ditto
	Bright faces—cheerful hearts— Love & affection
	&c &c

500 or 5000 copies in circulation," Henry protested—a statement that constitutes a significant piece of evidence about the social uncertainties of publishing. He had "done me injury for which you can make no amends." Now that he had been brought before a new variety of judges, it was "necessary" that he be "fully cleared of the charges." There is no mistaking the tone. Carey's public career in America had begun with a duel; now it looked like ending with one, and the challenge came from his own son. The prospect was unthinkable. A lawyer negotiated a fragile reconciliation, and the tract was withdrawn (no copy is now known to exist). When Mathew Carey died a few years later, his final publication was a set of "practical rules for the promotion of domestic happiness."[81]

Reading his complaints of the lassitude of manufacturers and improvers, it is easy to get the impression that even his allies treated Carey by this time rather as Franklin seems to have been treated by some younger politicians of the 1780s: as an embarrassing old codger. But he remained a respected figure whose opinions carried the heft of a veteran, and if anything it was Carey who had less of the Nestor about him. When tariffs were in fact imposed, he was chaired in triumph through paper mills in Ohio and greeted in Pittsburgh with cannonades and choruses of "Hail to the Conquering Hero." His funeral in 1839 provided a massive demonstration of his public status; nobody since the revolutionaries themselves had commanded such a huge attendance.[82] What they were saluting was not really Carey himself, however, but the rise of a distinctive American industrial ideology, which denied class distinctions in favor of the "harmony of interests." After half a century, international reprinting and industrial appropriation had a secure place in this protectionist "American system."

That created a situation without precedent. In the eighteenth century, international reprinting had flourished, to be sure, and conflicts over cross-border "piracy" had flared up repeatedly. But in each case the struggle had been between a major power and a relatively minor rival on its periphery: between England and the Scottish reprinters, between Britain and the Irish, between France and the Swiss, or between rival German states. Now, for the first time a clash over reprinting was about to be triggered between two major industrial powers. And it was central to the self-image of one as a modern, united, virtuous republic of industry. When Americans reprinted, what they reprinted came largely from the world's financial, imperial, and manufacturing center, London. And London publishers were already accustomed to seeing their reach in global terms. In terms of capital, organization, and markets alike, their interests stretched across the colonial and Anglophone world. The combination made reprinting politically volatile in a way it had never been before. The next generation would see an internationalization of the question of piracy, as calls multiplied for a unification of literary property across borders and oceans. The implications would extend from the intimate, as in Carey's own case, to the global.

9

The Printing Counterrevolution

Does printing entail progress? As the eighteenth century drew to a close, that question began to be asked again with renewed urgency. The assumption that enlightenment and print were natural allies, never universal in the first place, began to fall apart. Faced by the radicalism of the Jacobins, the idea of the public sphere suddenly seemed not only a polite fiction but an implausible one. The diversity of readerships became fearsomely apparent as political pressures arising from events in France lent prominence to alternative audiences. Corresponding societies and radical publishers fomented opinions with no place in genteel conversation, and in London Pitt's government reacted by taking unprecedented powers to police the press. At the same time, understandings of creative authorship and its relation to commerce were once more in flux. Romanticism challenged them in terms of the concept of genius. If an author imbued a work with some inimitable emanation of individuality, as theories of genius suggested, then the proprieties of public knowledge needed to be rethought once again. In Germany, genius became the principle behind authorial property laws early in the nineteenth century.[1] Yet in Britain the conjunction between genius and copyright remained somewhat artificial and post hoc. After all, with its relatively short duration, a copyright was not much of a recognition for this unique human property. As a result, it was quite possible to argue that prevailing copyright principles were incompatible with genius itself.

Throughout the modern era, we have tended to assume that the ruling in *Donaldson v. Becket* set the terms for literary property once and for all. This is simply untrue. Quite soon after the verdict, opposition to it and its implications was beginning to appear. Such opposition has since taken different forms—some advocating for perpetual property, as Wordsworth did in the nineteenth century, others for a "free trade" in ideas—but it has never been definitively defeated. In the first decades of the nineteenth century it mounted its first considerable effort. A campaign arose to abrogate the law of copyright on the grounds that it was antithetical to genius, scholarship, and genuine property. Its leading protagonist was himself a Romantic par excellence: a poet and novelist who revered nature, hailed the virtues of melancholy solitude, analyzed the character and processes of creative genius at great length, and retraced the steps of Byron, Shelley, and Keats in their travels across Europe. As well as fighting his battles in Parliament as an MP, he created his own printing house to contribute directly to reshaping the contemporary culture of print. He was also, perhaps—it is impossible to be sure—a forger, embezzler, and self-deluding impostor of extraordinary proportions. His name was Sir Samuel Egerton Brydges.

Brydges was in some ways an eccentric character, and his campaign can in retrospect look quixotic. Moreover, the passionate commitment to antiquarianism that led him to fight for it is a devotion distinctly alien to modern sensibilities. But his concerns were by no means unique at the time, and his cause found powerful support from a number of constituencies, not least the leading London publishers of the age. Moreover, Brydges was an antiquarian at the moment when antiquarianism enjoyed its greatest authority as a form of knowledge. Claiming to be an extension of Baconian approaches to the study of local and national customs, it had become a flourishing enterprise in the mid-eighteenth century, and in Romantic guise attracted devotees from across the nation in the revolutionary era. No one political meaning attached to the activity—for every Walter Scott, publishing his Tory-leaning researches with Ballantyne in Edinburgh, there was a radical like the publisher William Hone. Hone used his own antiquarian work to argue in court in the 1810s, at the peak of Brydges's campaign, that the Bible had been a common property in the Middle Ages, freely appropriated and rewritten by lay communities. Overall, Romantic antiquaries in these decades collectively created the first sense of a long, various, and dynamic cultural history to be investigated in the British localities that stood apart from urban homogeneity. Theirs was thus a vital enterprise of great consequence. Brydges certainly thought that contemporary copyright law represented a mortal threat to it. And although he did not succeed in his quest, in a fittingly antiquarian sense neither did he entirely fail. One lasting consequence of the assault he mounted was to be the creation and preservation of a mass of facts —the "novel antiquities," as it were, of publishing itself. Archived in Westminster during the parliamentary inquiries Brydges provoked, they were quietly stored away for years, until the information pioneer Charles Babbage rediscovered them. For at least the next century these archived facts would then be dusted off and re-exposed to view, informing a series of challenges that would define many of the terms of modern intellectual property debates.[2]

In Brydges's own eyes, the publishing industry that was coalescing around the copyright principle was a monstrous mechanism for the triumph of commerce over true genius. But his campaign was never targeted at authorial rights per se. On the contrary, he and his allies insisted that by this time nobody would deny the legitimacy of such rights, and they claimed to be upholding them. Their quarry was copyright itself—a distinct and much more equivocal target. In particular, they opposed the practice known as *legal deposit*. This was a requirement that a number of copies of each book published in Britain had to be turned over to select libraries for their collections. It was written into the statute law of copyright—which is why we still call the beneficiaries "copyright libraries" to this day. The rule had long been something of a dead letter, but the libraries had recently attempted to collect on it. The Brydges camp maintained that this aggressive demand was a real infraction on property, and that if successful it would kill off all Britain's most valuable publishing ventures. In principle, the deposit promised to realize the potential of print for enlightenment by creating universal libraries; in practice, Brydges's side argued, it was an "evil" doomed to destroy that potential. They maintained that in late Georgian London copyright had given rise to a plot for public-interest piracy on a massive scale. And so they concluded that the law underpinning that plot—the law of copyright—had to go.[3]

UNIVERSAL LIBRARIES AND THE ENDS OF ENLIGHTENMENT

The ideal of the universal library has a long history, extending back to the Library of Alexandria and forward to utopian visions of the Internet. In some ways, ironically, its nadir was reached just when the ideology of enlightenment placed greatest weight on it. Plans for a *Bibliotheca Universalis*, envisaged in the early decades of printing and pursued doggedly by Conrad Gesner and others, had fallen ever further behind the exponentially increasing number of printed works. Library science originated in a doomed attempt to master the range, if not the population, of books. And notions of a physical library with pretensions to universality became Enlightenment dreams, for which visionary architects like Etienne Louis Boullée even created bombastic designs (fig. 9.1). The logic was simple, compelling, and impossible. If printing was what made progress and enlightenment possible, then its products must be collected and organized in order to preserve knowledge and facilitate progress. They must be made accessible, too—no more priestcraft and mystery of state. The appeal of the idea was evident. Only slightly less so were the economic, political, and epistemic problems attending it—problems that Borges and Eco would famously allude to in modern times.[4]

In England, however, the approach to creating a universal library was more pragmatic. It rested on the ancient universities and the principle of deposit, which dated back to 1610. In that year Sir Thomas Bodley had come to a private agreement with the Stationers' Company by which the Company agreed to provide a copy of every new book its members printed for Bodley's library at Oxford. By way of quid pro quo, the collection would be made available as a source of copy for subsequent editions.[5] Despite annual reminders, however, the Stationers had observed the agreement only patchily, and instead of the Latin treatises he had expected Bodley found himself receiving pamphlets and other English-language "riffe raffe" such as Shakespeare. Eventually Oxford's curators appealed to Archbishop Laud for help, and he incorporated the deposit agreement into a Star Chamber decree of 1637 establishing licensers of books. Void during the Interregnum, in 1662 it was then restored again as part of the new monarchy's Press Act that reinstituted the licensers. At that point three copies of every publication were required, to be lodged at Oxford, Cambridge, and the Royal Library in London (which in 1759 would become the library of the British Museum, and much later the British Library).

FIGURE 9.1. The universal library. Etienne-Louis Boullée, design for the royal library, in *Mémoire sur les moyens de procurer à la Bibliothèque du Roi les avantages que ce monument exige* (Paris, 1785). Courtesy of the University of Chicago Library.

But the Stationers remained desultory, and occasionally worse: in 1694, Tory bookseller Thomas Bennet rejected the impost in front of the king's own librarian, the renowned classicist Richard Bentley, with the remark that he "knew not what right the Parliament had to give away any man's property."[6]

Barely a year later Bennet's implicit wish was realized. Licensing lapsed for the last time, and with it the requirement to deposit copies. The result, as we have seen, was fifteen years in which "piracy" was legal. In 1710 the first copyright law was finally passed to meet the trade's complaints. As well as instituting the innovation of statutory copyright, it quietly restored and extended the deposit requirement. Now, after Anglo-Scottish union, six more libraries were added to the list of those entitled to volumes: Sion College, the Faculty of Advocates in Edinburgh, and the university libraries at Edinburgh, Glasgow, St. Andrews, and Aberdeen. A total of nine copies were now liable to be demanded, all on the best paper used in each edition. Booksellers obtained their statute against piracy, but at the cost of this benefaction to learning.

The trade proceeded to interpret this new law rather ingeniously. The booksellers decided that it represented a bargain. They rationalized it as a fee levied by the state in return for its safeguard against pirates. Logically, they then reasoned, the fee ought only to be paid for those works that they registered at Stationers' Hall for such protection. They concluded that they were perfectly free not to register a given book, opting instead to risk its being pirated. In such cases they need not deposit the nine copies. And this became their standard practice. As a result, the books deposited were those most likely to be registered, and hence those most likely to be pirated: almost all in English, not Latin, and much of it hackwork. It was these, and not prized works of scholarship, that piled up at the universities. For more valuable works — and law books, for example, could be very expensive indeed — the booksellers reverted to trade civilities rather than statutory copyright, and, as Edmund Law put it, resolved to "trust one another." Declining to enter these titles, they escaped the need to provide free copies. Or in the case of series they might register just one volume, guessing that that would be sufficient to deter pirates. They would then offer to deposit just that one volume, effectively compelling the libraries to pay full price for the rest. Either way the effect was the same. The linking of deposit with copyright threatened to turn the university libraries into repositories not of learned and significant scholarship, but of the piratable. Attractiveness to pirates seemed to be the de facto axiom of Enlightenment archiving. In practice the proffered works were often so unpromising that the libraries did not even bother to collect them.[7]

Thus the deposit was inscribed into press regulation and propriety long before the Enlightenment, and its history had been checkered. Nevertheless, by the late eighteenth century the principle of deposit had become part and parcel of the broader representation of print as the motor of enlightenment. Enlightened nations, it was said, should furnish national libraries aspiring for universal coverage. Those libraries must be efficiently organized and publicly accessible, in order to facilitate the open conversation on which progress was acknowledged to depend. The provision of books for such libraries was, then, a matter of fundamental importance, as was their subsequent classification.[8] As Basil Montagu, a Cambridge law don, put it explicitly, the practice promised to create "an universal library" — "a library approaching to such perfection in its arrangement, that a student may instantly find all the treatises upon that subject, either of general literature or of any particular science, to which he is directing his attention." A universal library would have signal benefits for "the progress of medical science" alone, Montagu pointed out, and the same would be true of other sciences.[9] But the British universities were not state bodies, and lacked resources. Only deposit could feasibly turn them into arks of universal learning. In the 1790s the actual practice of deposit therefore began to cause rumblings of resentment, falling as short as it did of this utopian ideal. So the universities finally considered asserting their claims in earnest.

In 1798 the court of King's Bench unintentionally brought the incipient issue to a crisis. It suddenly and unexpectedly ruled that a bookseller could claim a property right in a title even if it were not registered at Stationers' Hall.[10] At a stroke, this removed the one incentive that had existed for registering books, and hence for depositing them. The libraries' already slim pickings looked to be falling to zero. Worse still, when copyright was extended to Ireland in 1801 two more libraries were added to the list of beneficiaries. With Pitt's Act for the Suppression of Seditious Societies (1799) also demanding that a copy be retained for policing, a total of twelve copies had now to be reserved from every registered title. This was now a tax—small for normal editions, but real enough—which there was no reason to pay. Unsurprisingly, the number of titles deposited fell sharply. In 1803, a year for which the online Short Title Catalogue lists well over four thousand publications, Cambridge received just twenty-two.[11] If universal libraries were really an essential tool of enlightenment, this could only be a serious crisis for civilization.

A struggle to revive the deposit therefore began. It was initiallly spearheaded by the law professor and barrister Edward Christian. Finding to his chagrin that Cambridge held none of the most recent law books because they had never been delivered, Christian devoted two years of his life to researching the issue, and then published the results as *A vindication of the rights of the Universities*. In truth, he aimed higher than at mere vindication. Christian argued that the libraries had a far more extensive right than had ever been appreciated: he reckoned that they could legally claim a copy of every book published, irrespective of registration. He called for this right finally to be enforced. Obviously, the prospect was going to be alarming to London's publishers. Moving fast, however, the MP John Charles Villiers organized a series of meetings between Christian and the booksellers at his London house, hoping to broach an agreement. His idea was to offer the booksellers an extended copyright term in return for the deposit. He came very close to success. The publishers conceded that a "universal deposit" could be accepted, in return for a blanket extension of the copyright term to twenty-eight years. (That may have been a concession too: at least one writer had thought it "essentially necessary" to revoke *Donaldson v. Becket* and reintroduce perpetual copyright.)[12] Villiers swiftly advanced a bill to this end in the Commons, arguing that it was vital to the future of education and learning. But there it met with unexpected opposition. Sir Samuel Romilly in particular rose to protest against its unanticipated implications for the most expensive of books—books that were practically immune from piracy given the costs of their production. Faced with his opposition, the bill stalled.

As the attempted compromise collapsed, the libraries and the publishers faced the prospect of a long conflict. Cambridge University's Syndics resorted to a test case in a bid to forestall it. To considerable public surprise, they won.[13] Suddenly it looked as though the publishing industry faced a comprehensive, legally enforceable, deposit requirement. The publishers and their allies were aghast, and the bibliographical antiquarian Joseph Haslewood wrote that the verdict was "fatal to literary property." Thrown onto the defensive, they immediately clamored to revive a parliamentary solution. This time they got their new law. But, as had been the case almost exactly a century earlier, the result was not at all what they had sought. The bill they proposed would have enshrined a twenty-eight-year copyright in return for deposits partially paid for by the libraries, and would have permitted publishers to renounce copyright protection altogether in return for depositing only one copy. Christian was determined and unyielding in his opposition to this measure, and succeeded in killing it. Instead, the new Copyright Act of 1814 incorporated most of Christian's own claims into law. The publishers found themselves subject to blanket demands for eleven copies of all works, copyrighted or not. It was this measure, therefore—the first clear legal provision for a universal library—that provoked the real crisis.[14]

GENEALOGY AND GENIUS

Who was Sir Egerton Brydges? The question is a key one, if only because he himself posed it incessantly from the 1790s through to his death in 1837. The problem was that his own answers bore little relation to any acknowledged by his contemporaries. Brydges's own view was that he was Baron Chandos of Sudeley, a title that he claimed *per legem terrae*—by common law, rather than by the normal criteria of the college of arms. What he meant by this was that the House of Lords had denied him the noble rank that he felt was his due. It was a contradiction that plagued his life. A convinced Burkean, Brydges exalted the peerage as the country's senate—the only body capable of deciding grand issues in circumstances of quiet, disinterested reflection, secluded from the sirens of urban cunning and political faction. But he found his own identity destroyed by that very institution. Even his "Sir" had a certain taint about it: it was not a

British honor at all, but a privilege conferred by the Swedish order of St. Joachim, and was in conventional terms worthless (he finally became a baronet in 1814, resolving that particular problem and taking what his friend Francis Wrangham called a small step "toward the ancient honours of your ancestry").[15] Resenting the peers' refusal as an injustice founded in corruption and national malaise—as serious as their lordships' reception of Byron—for decades everything Brydges did, said, and wrote was tinged with indignation at personal honor affronted.[16] Ironically, his peerage did come to define Brydges, but by its denial rather than its possession.

Brydges was at least a gentleman. He came from a relatively prosperous Kent farming family and was educated at Cambridge, which he left in 1782 without a degree. Although qualified as a barrister, he declined the profession in favor of living the life of a rural squire. He lived first in Hampshire, where he rented a parsonage from George Austen and indulged Austen's teenage daughter, Jane, in amateur dramatics. It is tempting to see him as a distant archetype for *Persuasion*'s Sir Walter Elliot, in fact, especially as Brydges's sister, to whom Jane was especially close, was named Anne.[17] Then he moved to his childhood surroundings near Canterbury. There Brydges devoted himself to agricultural improvements, conversations with rural gentry, and polite literary games with the military officers stationed nearby. But nothing he did succeeded. The agricultural projects lost money (despite crop prices being at record levels), the local squirearchy despised him as a snobbish arriviste, and after a brief period of enthusiasm even a cavalry officer's life proved distasteful.[18] What Brydges really liked to do was write—and this liking he indulged freely. Decades later, when well into his decline, he remained capable of composing two thousand extempore sonnets a year; we still have at least ten manuscript volumes of them.[19] Before that he proved himself an indefatigable author of novels, essays, and topographical and genealogical works. He also served as editor of a slew of literary and antiquarian pieces ranging from Margaret Cavendish to Milton.[20] The labor proved devastating, not least because, like his aspirations to nobility, his claims to genius received none of the acclamation he thought they deserved. The effect can be seen in two portraits that he incorporated into his autobiography in 1834. It is hard to imagine a starker "before and after" contrast illustrating the sheer enervation of aristocracy denied (figs. 9.2 and 9.3). For it was aristocracy of land and mind—nobility and genius—that defined Brydges and his campaigns.

Beginning in September 1789, the so-called Chandos case mushroomed

FIGURE 9.2. Samuel Egerton Brydges as a young man. S. E. Brydges, *The Autobiography,* 2 vols. (London: Cochrane and M'Crone, 1834), vol. 1, frontispiece. Courtesy of the University of Chicago Library.

over four decades. The Lancashire herald, George Beltz, called it "the most extraordinary attempt ever made to attain the summit of a British patrician's ambition."[21] The dukes of Chandos had been one of eighteenth-century England's most prominent noble families, renowned for their patronage of the arts and sciences. One of them had been responsible for the Microcosm, that device so central to arguments about creative property.[22] But the last duke had just died without issue at the age of fifty-eight.

FIGURE 9.3. Brydges as an old man. Brydges, *Autobiography*, vol. 2, frontispiece. Courtesy of the University of Chicago Library.

It was assumed that the line had become extinct. Within a month, however, Brydges had persuaded his elder brother, Edward, to petition for the barony. Their claim was that they were descended from the third son of the original Baron Chandos, one John Brydges, who had been granted the rank back in 1554. (They could not claim the dukedom because that was a later creation bestowed after the family branches had diverged.) The coincidence of names aside, Brydges's conviction was at first based on sheer Romantic inspiration. He believed that the old duke had died just as he himself had been poring over old funerary inscriptions in the Chandos vault, and to his mind the coincidence could only be portentous. He also remembered hearing his mother speaking about a link, and avowed that as a child he had been surrounded by heraldry and portraits of Gibbon, Hardwicke, and Lord Chancellor Egerton (a real ancestor, on his mother's side).[23] But more evidence than that would be needed to convince others of the claim. So Brydges hired the Windsor herald for what became seven long years of researches, retained the finest London lawyers, and launched his campaign.

The resulting case became one of late Georgian England's more diverting causes célèbres. It centered on questions of genealogy and documentary evidence. The opponents of Brydges's claim proposed an alternative family tree, according to which he was in fact the descendant of a quite separate line—a humble family hailing from the nearby village of Harbledown. But there were at first no records to distinguish which stemma was genuine. So Brydges turned to musty church records, and to a secure chamber in his family home that held a disorganized pile of old deeds and parchments. Eventually he emerged with "new evidence of an extraordinary nature" to buttress his case. This evidence included a transcript of a long-lost parish register, plus other documents purportedly linking his genealogy to the Chandos's in the mid-seventeenth century. At first glance these were conclusive. Unfortunately, however, on close examination the crucial entries appeared to be in recent ink—and checks of the original church records revealed mysterious obliterations at important points, again apparently made after the fact. Had the documents been doctored, or even fabricated? The attorney general certainly came to believe Brydges untrustworthy. What had begun as an affair of honor in one sense thus became one in another, even more personal. From now on, if Brydges were not a peer, then he must be a forger.

After its first hearing in the House of Lords in June 1790, the case descended into a morass of heraldic and genealogical complexities. Finally, in 1803 it came to a vote. It was a narrow one. But Brydges's brother—the actual claimant—made a crucial strategic error. He circulated a printed exhortation to the peers on the eve of their vote. The action was seized upon as a breach of privilege, and catalyzed opposition at a critical moment. Brydges's own former counsel, the heavyweight Tory Lord Eldon, now decided not to cast a vote at all. This proved decisive. The peers rejected the claim by one vote. Not only was Brydges's status denied; he was implicitly concluded to be a fraud. He retreated to the country in a fit of despond. "My mind at this period was active," he later recalled, "but I do not think that it was in its soundest state."[24]

Worse was to come. As the Chandos claim was inching its way slowly and expensively toward disaster, Brydges sought to create for himself the daily life of a peer as he imagined it to be. He had developed elaborate theories about the role of the landed nobility in the moral life of the nation, making them central to its political economy and civilization. He tried to put them into action in anticipation of his imminent ennoblement. So he bought up and renovated a dilapidated old Elizabethan mansion in Kent, establishing its manorial sway over a number of local farms and parishes. With this base he sought to engage in all the polite activities of a peer. Money hemorrhaged through these projects as fast as through his legal campaign. By the beginning of the new century Brydges was in serious debt—at just the moment when the failure of the Chandos claim made an escape through elevation impossible. So he took an even more calamitous decision. He resolved to buy the old Chandos seat of Sudeley Castle—a spectacular ruin that had stood uninhabited ever since Cromwell reduced it in the 1640s. He moved to his son's home of Lee Priory, about five miles south of Canterbury, in preparation for this grand move. But the reality was that Sudeley was far beyond his means. Brydges found himself stranded at Lee. It became his last English home.[25]

There were worse places for a bard to live. Lee Priory was well suited to seclusion and melancholy. It was surrounded by extensive grounds and rolling hills in which the poet could freely wander, and was rich in historical associations. The gardens contained the remains of Iron Age quarries, a ruined chapel close by was rumored to have been constructed by the Knights Templar, and a local river was said to mark the high point of the Viking invasions. The house itself was built on ancient foundations (it had been the home of royal physician George Ent in the seventeenth century), and had been extensively rebuilt by the architect James Wyatt to a high Gothic design. It housed an extensive collection of books, art, and antiquities. Its grand library was a renowned model of "extreme elegance and chastity," and a "Strawberry Room" had been erected to provide Horace Walpole with a home away from home. (This room is almost the only part of Wyatt's building to survive today, incidentally; it is lodged in a storeroom in the Victoria and Albert Museum.) Proudly crenellated, Lee Priory had become a handsome country seat. Already, on an earlier visit in 1791, its features had inspired Brydges's first novel, *Mary de Clifford*. Now it, and its library in particular, became his intellectual retreat.[26] It also became the headquarters from which he plotted a revival of literary genius.

As resentment of the Chandos defeat festered, so did Brydges's genealogical sense of his own identity. He refused to accept the Lords' verdict— on the contrary, he continued to lay claim to the title—and he campaigned to have the case retried before a jury. At the same time he threw himself into prodigious genealogical researches. From these he emerged convinced not only that he was indeed a descendant of the original baron Chandos, but that his family line could be extended far further back. His real ancestors, he now concluded, were Charlemagne and the Merovingian kings. Brydges now laid claim to a descent from all but half a dozen of the 144 noblest houses of Europe (and although he did not draw attention to this, we may note that the Merovingians had claimed descent from Christ). He designed an extraordinary coat of arms for himself combining the emblems of every one of them. (See fig. 9.4, which the Lancaster herald Beltz described as "HERALDRY RUN MAD!")[27] Brydges printed his argument in a lavish folio designed to "open and trace the streams of royal and illustrious blood which have flowed into the Compiler's veins." The work contained a total of 252 tables of descent—"and yet," he threatened, "the subject is not half exhausted."[28] In short, Brydges now boasted of a descent more refined than that of any contemporary royal family. "I am not merely contending for equality," he insisted, "but for superiority."[29]

In an age of antiquarianism and genealogical research, this was perhaps the most extreme manifestation of their ambitions. On its basis Brydges now built both an argument against the expansion of the peerage and a theory of the descent of virtue—even genius. The first of these rested on a simple demand: what title did those without noble blood have to privilege, and if noble blood were not a title, why have a peerage at all?[30] It was a reactionary but pointed question. Recent years had in fact seen a "profusion" of new peers, sufficient to change the very character of the House. Altogether 209 new lords would be created between 1776 and 1830, after three-quarters of a century when the number of peers had been almost constant. Brydges expressed revulsion at what he saw as the industrialization of the House of Lords. He decried this intrusion of capitalist grandees as a calamitous dilution of principle in favor of capital. "The aristocracy of *money* is the worst in the world," he cried, "and that rank and title bought with new wealth is quite intolerable." The oldest male-line

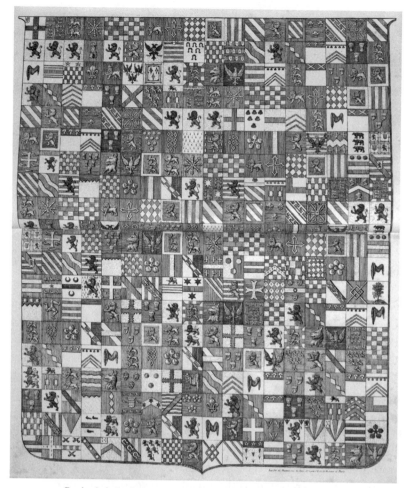

FIGURE 9.4. Brydges's design for his coat of arms. S. E. Brydges, *Stemmata illustria* (Paris: printed by J. Smith, 1825), facing p. 4. Courtesy of the University of Chicago Library.

peerage now dated back only to 1442, while new peers shut the door on legitimate claimants. This amounted to a substantive change in the constitution.[31] What had originally been a "senate," in which a virtuous, landed aristocracy had steered public affairs in an atmosphere of secluded contemplation based ultimately in the countryside, had fallen into the world of commercial interest. The peerage was becoming "blended with the people." Placing his genealogical facts in competition with the political-economic fact of industrial capitalism, he pronounced the latter wanting.[32]

Brydges's genealogy of genius was twinned with this. "Perhaps the most influential aristocracy of the present day," he declared, "is the aristocracy of literary genius." But as defined by the literary marketplace, at least, this was not the aristocracy of ancient families; it was instead an apocalyptic "aristocracy of the Stock-Exchange and new wealth" standing alongside that of Pitt's peerage.[33] He therefore believed it imperative to furnish "the utmost preciseness and clearness in the analysis and constituents of genius" in order to distinguish the real thing from this impostor. And he spent years in pursuit of that analysis even as he tracked the minutiae of his Merovingian bloodline. Genius, like nobility, turned out to rest on an analysis of what he called "the Value of Historic Pedigrees." His contention was that "genius or moral virtue," while not exactly inherited in a deterministic sense, tended in general to follow bloodlines. A knowledge of authorial heredity might not be essential to judge the worth of a poet's work, but "if we are interested in his genius," Brydges remarked, "we always desire to know his history." A descent like his—which purportedly included Lord Chancellor Egerton, Princess Mary Tudor, William Cavendish, "the whole race of Plantagenets," the Tudors, Charlemagne, the kings of Jerusalem, Sir George Ent, all the lords Chandos, Gibbon, Lord Chancellor Hardwicke, and many others—gave him a better chance than most of manifesting genius.[34] His own love of literature, he conceded, was not solely a product of this "hereditary infusion." But it had sprung from "the intrinsic qualities and colours of my mind and temper."

One aspect of this that deserves note is that genius was not always marked by originality. In general, Brydges thought that new opinions were ipso facto unlikely to be true or (therefore) good. A true genius might be someone who restated truths already known, perhaps since ancient times. The significant thing was *how* they were restated. True authorship was a kind of spontaneous re-creation, possible only from a mind created genealogically. This drove Brydges to formulate a discipline dedicated to examining how "the rank, habits, and character of his ancestors" conditioned a genius. He called this "imaginative biography." It amounted to an attempt—by his standards a systematic one—to capture the characteristics and sources of genius by exploring the inner lives of authors in genealogical terms.[35]

What imaginative biography revealed was that genius was utterly incompatible with the world of print in late Georgian Britain. The printing press was the very icon of enlightenment, and the image of a free press was central to Britain's national pride. But Brydges maintained that works of genius were unlikely to be favored by a publishing industry shaped by copyright, and hence devoted to satisfying popular tastes. Authorship had become a matter of prostitution, "a mere piece of dull mechanism" serving party interests or motivated by demand to sell "vulgar stories suited to feeble intellects." "The most profitable parts of authorship are the mechanical and the servile," he declaimed; "to make large profits, therefore, is certainly no proof of genius or of talent!" And the rise of steam-printed periodicals with anonymous reviews accentuated this. An author had no chance against such a creature: "it is mechanically dispersed every where, and read by every one, — read, as newspapers are read, — to qualify a man to join in the conversation of society: its circulation is multiplied at least thirty-fold beyond the average sale of separate publications; — and a single copy on the table of a large reading-room affords perusal to hundreds." Contemporary publishing practices had thus become a matter of "intrigue, faction, and combination" — practices utterly incompatible with genius. Merely the need to live in London in order to engage with these mechanisms was destructive enough, ruining the very solitude and seclusion that genius required.

Seclusion was a paramount principle here. It pervaded Brydges's discussions of politics, creativity, and reception alike, defining his representations of nobility, virtue, authorship, and reading. He was convinced, for example, that readers unable to enjoy tranquility would be unable to exercise freedom of judgment, and since this was true of the vast majority making up the public sphere, that realm practiced not thought, properly speaking, but reflex. It was a slave to passion. That was a major reason why the "modern doctrine" of determining issues by reference to public judgment was mistaken.[36] The same principle applied a fortiori to authors, who needed seclusion in order to recognize and articulate sensations. A central aspect of the literature of the 1790s was this resort to pastoral solitude. Faced by an increasingly fractured and faction-ridden public realm, many writers — radicals like Godwin as well as reactionaries like Brydges — made idyllic retreat into their source of authority. In effect, authors became publicly private. Yet Brydges insisted that it was the *combination* of solitude and what he called "artificial society" that was truly productive. The "bard" — a category in which he certainly included himself — should occupy the same place in the field of literature as the landed nobleman did in politics. In both cases retreat lent the space and time for disinterested observation and reflection. But it must be retreat from a bustling city to which the artist/noble returned in order to act, and within which literature could flourish.[37] While genius was antithetical to the kind of "cunning" needed to get ahead in the metropolis, engagement with the cultivated arts of the city remained essential if the sublimity of nature were to work its magic. So any author possessed of genius was probably doomed to a life of frustration and poverty. All the more so, indeed, "so long as the voice of the multitude is to rule," and "every mechanic thinks his own councils ought to govern the State."

Brydges was emphatically not an Enlightenment man. He disdained notions of human perfectibility as simply "false," and denied that knowledge progressed. Even political economy, by many reckoned to be the new science of its age, had in his view made no advances since Charles Davenant in the late seventeenth century. The issue of progress in the natural sciences he evaded (as would Coleridge) by declaring that those sciences had been professionalized out of profundity. And above all the press, commonly seen as the engine and guarantor of progress, was in Brydges's eyes not a "vehicle of reason" but of passion. It pandered to the hasty and capricious judgments of the mass of readers who could not retreat to seclusion.[38] "If the merit of a literary work is to be tried by the number of readers," he asked, "what work of genius can be put in competition with a NEWSPAPER?" Brydges therefore maintained that literature had become a subject of the same political economy that underlay the mass press and the decline of the peerage. With the new aristocracy came an "aristocracy of *false Genius*" that was at least as bad. It operated by "combinations," and rendered futile all individual expression. Press and Parliament were in "exactly the same state."[39] In opposing "the sect, the propagandists, the *Illuminati,* who talk about '*the March of Mind,*'" he saw himself as opposing popular "despotism and tyranny."[40] Significantly, in printing his own case Brydges was careful to stipulate that he was *not* appealing to the public as a tribunal; only a properly constituted court could legitimately decide such arguments.[41]

Brydges labored ever more frantically on his genealogical researches, forlornly seeking the one manuscript that would secure his own character. That character was in turn central to his arguments about print culture, and to his attempts to overturn it. More broadly, the role of the genius author, he believed, had largely disappeared with the advent of modern industrial culture, along with that of the senatorial peer. Genius and print had parted company.

THE PRINTING COUNTERREVOLUTION

What was to be done? Brydges pursued two strategies. One was a parliamentary campaign. This involved challenging copyright law—the lynchpin of the commercial publishing community. The other involved a more direct intervention in printing itself. This strategy took shape in Brydges's secluded retreat of Lee Priory. It involved reshaping English literature by physically remaking its elemental objects: books.[42]

Brydges was already a much-published author of poetry, novels, and "literary antiquities" by the time he moved to Lee Priory in 1810. Now he began to think in terms of a more direct intervention in the practice of publishing. In the late 1790s he had become fascinated by the enterprise that contemporaries were learning to call *bibliography*. Today this is an established field of knowledge, essential but somewhat dry. Such was not the case in Brydges's day, when it was unsettled and very fashionable. Since the seventeenth century *bibliographia* had come to mean the knowledge of books, by analogy to *geographia*. Such knowledge typically took one of two forms. One was discursive, embracing the state of a particular branch of learning; the other, which proved more lasting, was taxonomic, addressing the classification and knowledge of books qua books. It centered on lists, called *bibliothecae* (libraries), which had multiplied after the invention of printing. The question they posed was how to organize, classify, and represent the world of printed knowledge. Answering it called for a new science. This science developed alongside those for classifying the natural world. Linnaeus—and Gesner before him—produced both. By Brydges's day the dream of a single universal reference source had long proved unrealizable, however. Even bibliographies of bibliographies were obsolete before they could see print. In response, bibliography came to mean a classificatory science not so much of knowledge as of the book: of typography, binding, and paper. The shift was partly a response to the upheavals of the French Revolution, which resulted in the dispersal of many collections and therefore a need to specify the details of particular volumes closely and systematically.[43] Out of two revolutions—the printing revolution and the French Revolution—thus came a new, systematic science of the book.

Brydges was at the forefront of bibliography, but—as always—in an idiosyncratic sense. He was a founder-member of the Roxburghe Club, which originated after the famous sale of books from the Duke of Roxburghe's library in 1812, and a regular interlocutor with Thomas Dibdin and other bibliophiles. But his version of the enterprise was not quite what others conceived it to be. Above all, his bibliography would not be a *science* at all. He professed distaste for the minutiae of typography and binding—and especially the idolatry of sheer scarcity—that motivated most contemporary bibliophiles. He thought such details "petty," and confessed to finding them "revolting." Instead, his object, he said, was not merely rare books, but neglected books. The distinction was all-important. He wanted bibliography to be an endeavor of recovery—the literary equivalent of today's rescue archaeology, perhaps—devoted to literature that would otherwise be obliterated beneath the commercial structures of the public sphere. Brydges was utterly unconcerned with analyzing typefaces, characterizing bindings, and developing rules of bibliographical description.[44] What mattered to him were inscriptions of creativity—fragments of a lost antiquarian idyll of genteel authorship.

This was the literary equivalent to the antiquary as activist. Brydges wanted the bibliographer to be an active participant in a cultural conflict. He wanted to hold up to judgment "the casual prevalence of momentary fashion" that prevailed now that copyright reigned. This he would do by confronting it with the different voices of the sixteenth and seventeenth centuries—and, later, by those of Renaissance Italy and France too. His ultra-Burkean hope was to put elite opinions to the test (he despaired of popular ones) by confronting them with previous wisdom. The paradox was that he believed the very practice of publishing and reading in his time to be incompatible with such a project.

So Brydges adapted to this paradox. He pursued his campaign, not by co-opting the existing publishing industry, but by creating his own. In 1813 he established a press at Lee Priory, engaging two printers from the same London house, John Johnson and John Warwick, to operate it as compositor and pressman. Warwick, intriguingly, had a background of commitment to printers' chapels reminiscent of Jacob Ilive's, having been jailed at the Old Bailey in 1798 for projecting an artisanal "parliament" in opposition to the master printers.[45] And Johnson was fascinated by "typographical antiquities" in his own right, later authoring his own *Typographia* (1824) in praise of chapel skills. For some nine years their press remained in operation, ending in 1822, four years after Brydges himself had moved overseas. In that time it produced more than fifty works, plus a hundred individual sheets containing poems, electoral addresses, and the like. (Lee Priory volumes became collectors' items shortly after the press closed, and remain so today.)[46] Some were Brydges's own compositions, others antiquarian and poetic efforts by his friends. But the majority were reissues of forgotten poetry and prose from the Elizabethan and Stuart periods. Not all of these, Brydges thought, were works of genius, but they did exemplify a realm of authorship in which genius could still be manifested. The point was that they were incompatible with the print culture of his day. So he printed them in small runs, never more than one hundred.[47] That was never going to produce a runaway commercial success. But popularity was never the intent.

The Lee Priory press may be seen in terms of a long history of "private" presses extending back almost to Gutenberg.[48] Such operations were sometimes mere playthings, as was the case, for example, with Horace Walpole's in the mid-eighteenth century. But often serious motivations underpinned them—motivations that have been belittled because of their small size and short duration, as well as their denomination as private. They belong in a history of experiments in making print into a force for learning, scholarship, and civility.[49] Brydges's in particular arose out of a conviction that the contemporary culture of print was hostile. Like earlier projects, it aspired to restore the past to view. Regiomontanus in the fifteenth century had wanted to print ancient mathematics; John Fell in the seventeenth had wished to restore patristic texts. Brydges wanted to republish old poetry. His choices were in part inspired by genealogy— he began with Margaret Cavendish, to whom he claimed to be related. But otherwise he simply preferred neglected poets of melancholic bent, dedicated to pastoral retreat. Raleigh he portrayed as someone who could have been great if not distracted by affairs. By stark contrast, the invention of copyright in 1710 counted as a tacit watershed: none of his reprints was of an author writing after that date. Pope, for example—the greatest property of the eighteenth-century book trade—he found trivial and artificial. Collins he approved of, but only as an Elizabethan *après la lettre*.[50]

Brydges's project of bibliographical antiquarianism therefore had a point. He was convinced that genius was incompatible with contemporary print, because such print was built on copyright. While even a mass readership would salute genius in the long run, in the short term it was irremediably blind. A "leading principle" in selecting pieces for reprinting, Brydges therefore declared, was the assumption that prior to the commercial age, "popularity" had tracked authorial merit, but the two were now radically distinct.[51] What was needed was a different kind of print—one as independent as possible of the metropolis, of commerce, of Grub Street, and of mass reading. Lee Priory was the exemplar of this new practice. What it produced was in effect an alternative genealogy of literary genius, extending from the invention of the press to the adoption of copyright. In sum, Brydges's press was a gesture toward the undoing of a print culture.

GENIUS, HISTORY, AND COPYRIGHT

As a principled despiser of the world that copyright was creating, and as the proprietor of a press dedicated to small impressions, Brydges had a double interest in the developing issue of universal libraries. Universal libraries represented enlightenment itself, and the way they were to be collected was, he thought, fatal to small experiments like his. He therefore became the leader of a campaign against the deposit, and against copyright.

Brydges mounted his campaign by pointing out that at the last moment in its parliamentary progress the bill for Christian's universal library had been subtly altered. The universities' right now extended not only to all new works, but also to reprints. This threatened to cripple the entire antiquarian enterprise, of which the verbatim reprinting of old materials was an essential part. Moreover, not only did the universities now deny publishers the right to waive piracy protection; they also extended the deposit tax to cover titles for which there had never been piracy protection in the first place.[52] It thus made a nonsense of the supposed link between protection and deposit. This extension was, to his mind, all-important, since it threatened to "extinguish" antiquarian publishing altogether. The purported compensation for acknowledging the libraries' claim was the extension of copyright terms to twenty-eight years, but to him the very connection between copyright term and deposit now stood revealed as spurious. The one was a matter for the author and the public, and in any case extended from a preexisting and natural "property in the fruits of their own intellects"; the other was a subject for authors and libraries.[53] After all, as he and several other critics pointed out, libraries like the Bodleian were *not* public institutions in any but the most legalistic sense: they remained closed to "the publick at large," and in many cases even to students at the universities themselves. But at the same time he warned that one aspect of the case was an implicit threat that the libraries might *become* public, developing into circulating libraries and therefore removing from the market not just nine or ten readers at a time, but ninety or a hundred.[54] This would simply destroy the market for scholarly works. Creating the Enlightenment's universal libraries would in practice kill off the very books that such libraries existed to collect. After all, even if the deposit actually did serve a public interest, that did not mean that it should not be paid for. Without payment, he declared, the universities' demand amounted to "the plea, not of the beggar . . . , but of the robber!"[55]

By this point the debate had broadened to include several major London publishing houses, as well as lawyers, authors, poets, and the reading public. Disagreement reigned even on as apparently objective an issue as the actual cost of the tax to publishers. The universities maintained that the real burden was zero. They argued that at most it could be the cost of the paper on which the deposited copies were printed, but this could always be made up either by raising the prices of the remaining copies or by printing eleven more. For Brydges and the publishers, the calculation was equally simple but very different. They argued that the tax stood at a hefty 22 percent of the total price if the print run were fifty copies, 11 percent if it were one hundred, and so on. In these terms, what was an insignificant imposition for popular works produced in vast numbers became a major deterrent against the publishing of specialized works in small runs. That is, it militated against what Brydges's camp assumed was the most worthwhile literature in favor of the most popular—which made its integration with copyright rather fitting. As evidence, they produced extensive and detailed lists of books demanded by all eleven libraries, totaling a "tax" of £2,722 yearly solely on works retailing at £1 or more. Dibdin's antiquarian *Bibliographical Decameron* represented a particularly good example: its deposit had cost the publisher over £100, for which he received no benefit in return, "since it is a work of a nature which renders any piracy of it quite impracticable."[56] In addition, Thomas Longman supplied evidence of twenty-three books (mostly reprints, and hence until now exempt) published in impressions of 100–250 copies each. In these cases the tax aggregated to over 6 percent. Longman testified that a prestigious volume of South American botany by Humboldt had been cancelled because of the mere prospect of the tax being imposed. Humboldtian exploration was perhaps the most important and influential enterprise in the sciences of the Romantic era, and yet it was being suppressed. Here, then, was real evidence of the deposit stifling knowledge.

In part these contrasting estimates of cost reflected the extent to which the economics of genius, far more than those of mass print, were still at the mercy of chapel customs. "By an invariable ancient custom" pressmen charged by units of 250, and refused to subdivide such units; so if an impression stood at 250 before the deposit, to print eleven more copies would be as expensive as printing another 250, and thus prohibitively costly.[57] The universities' estimates always ignored this. Worse, according to Longman and Brydges, prices could not be raised to cover the deposit, not least because a universal deposit itself removed from the marketplace a substantial number of potential purchasers who now had access to library copies.[58] Moreover, by reducing the appeal of rarity it "absolutely" nullified the "ardour" of the private collectors who otherwise might pay elevated prices. For works of learning of such a nature, the combination threatened to prove decisive. Only by charging high prices to the discriminating few could a true author of genius be adequately remunerated for producing a specialist work. That was why testimony before a Commons committee on the subject concentrated on the deposit's effects on "Natural History or Science"—subjects that in many cases had to be published at the author's cost, and for a miniscule market. Brydges and his allies argued that the deposit would curtail their production altogether.

Needless to say, such an argument rested on fundamental assumptions about genius and readership. Brydges assumed that genius was rare, individual, mysterious, and above all incompatible with the appetites of a mass audience. The most important literature was therefore at little to no risk of outright piracy, because true genius was at best incommensurable with a publishing system based on copyright. Despite this, he nevertheless believed the very possibility of literary creativity to be at stake. Both points rested on what he took to be a profound difference between learned publishing in Queen Anne's day and that a century later. Given the old custom of optional copyright registration, the reciprocity of copyright and deposit had not been a serious concern. Small-circulation specialist works could simply remain outside the system altogether: no protection, no deposit. "How utterly different then," Brydges declared, "in their very essence are the grievances of the late act!" By the 1800s, publishing was divided into specialisms. Learned works enjoyed far smaller print runs, and were targeted at niche markets. "There are a few works of great genius adapted to the general reader," Brydges conceded, "of which probably the demand for copies exceeds that of any former time." But most works of genius were not of that kind.[59] It was axiomatic that "whatever is deep, whatever is abstruse, whatever appeals to the highest qualities of the mind, or the most difficult subjects of intellectual acquirement" was ipso facto "fitted to interest a very limited number of readers." Therefore, for such works "a very small impression supplies the utmost demand." Two hundred copies might easily exhaust the readership for advanced works of mathematics, antiquarianism, botany, or bibliography. But this scarcely negated the cultural value of such works—indeed, it confirmed it, with a logic no less beautiful for being circular. The real reason why the deposit would kill learned culture was therefore that true genius was incompatible with popularity: with a readership small and fixed, the effects of the deposit "tax" were maximized. With the current law in effect, Brydges demanded, "Can any Author or Publisher be insane enough to embark in an expensive publication, at the certainty of the frightful loss which would thus be inflicted on him?" Clearly the answer was no. So "the man of genius, or of science, or learning, dies in obscurity; and his talents or acquirements are buried with him in the grave!"[60]

It seemed obvious to Longman, Brydges, and their allies that universal deposit must therefore be an evil even for the libraries. In practice, universal libraries would be infinitely large reservoirs of triviality. The realization of the Enlightenment ideal would mean its own degeneration. And it would get worse over time, as the libraries became "overgorged" with frivolous and unimportant books, costing prohibitive sums to house, arrange, and bind—money that might otherwise have been used to fund purchases of worthwhile works. And they could never escape from the commitment to stockpile more and more. This would have knock-on effects on future scholarship. It was human nature to be depressed by excess, Brydges noted. A crammed library catalogue provoked in any sensitive soul "a temporary depression of spirits, and an ebb of that energy which in the limited furniture of his own little library has carried him through years of fatigue and self-privation." Even those determined enough to persevere would find their minds rotting under the influence of so many worthless books. One certain effect of universal libraries therefore would be to concentrate damaging books in such a way that they would do their damage most effectively. Authorship would die out, as potential geniuses, confronting this dispiriting mass of scribble, decided not to take the trouble. "If the reverence and celebrity which in enlightened ages have attended Authorship are destroyed, by giving equal preservation and the same place of distinction to whatever the Press vomits forth, who will foresake the inviting pleasures of youth, and the enjoyments which court the senses, for the solitary lamp, and the anxious and abstracted toils by which the capacity for the higher sorts of literary composition, or success in the more difficult branches of science, is cherished and attained?" Deposit thus not only threatened present genius and corroded that of the next generation. It also extended into the indefinite future the slew of mediocrity that popular print now produced.[61] The real effect of a universal library would be to render eternal what might otherwise be a regrettable but transient cultural predicament. Anachronism aside, the lament remains today very recognizable. Its value lies in directing attention away from sheer accumulation and to issues of taxonomy, classification, and selection.

So what should be preserved, and how? Properly, according to Brydges, preservation should be a gesture of civility, not copyright. It should be shorn of commerce and reserved for those works that at least *might* warrant it, "otherwise the honour of the palm fades to nothing."[62] But Brydges acknowledged that no transcendental criteria existed by which to determine such desert, so he conceded that it might be useful to have *one* repository of all books published. It should simply not be *public*. Decoupling access from accumulation, he revealingly suggested that the copy presently required by anti-Jacobin legislation be used for this. The resulting collection should be confined "in special custody" at the British Museum. It looks very much as though what Brydges had in mind was that the Enlightenment's universal library and the "private case" of the British Museum Library should swap places.

It remained to correct the law itself, and somehow reconcile collection, copyright, and culture. Brydges and his allies proposed four principles. First, nothing should have to be deposited if the impression were smaller than a given threshold. They did not stipulate a number, but probably had 100 or 250 in mind. At least, in such cases the libraries should be required to pay part of the cost. Second, raw reprints must once more be immune from deposit demands. This would protect antiquarian ventures. Third, the libraries must request books by citing their specific titles —

they must not simply issue blanket demands for all publications.[63] This was partly to ensure that they actually wanted what they got—Brydges claimed that the libraries currently discarded many of the volumes passed on to them. And, fourth, publishers should again have an explicit right to decline protection from piracy in return for not being subject to the deposit demand at all.[64]

Brydges advanced a bill to this effect. Not surprisingly, it proved intensely controversial. Christian remarked that if it passed "the whole civilized world will sustain an irreparable loss, and science will for ever droop and mourn." Cambridge University weighed in to support him. The university even revived and endorsed Richard Atkyns's old story of Corsellis, the purported predecessor to Caxton, in order to bolster its case. Christian added that the universities' right to collect copies of all published books had been granted in 1710 as compensation for the loss of an earlier right to *reprint* all books: between Corsellis and copyright, Oxford and Cambridge had been empowered by royal patent to act as universal pirates. Brydges was now accused of trying to "invade the rights and property" of the ancient universities and to wreak "the greatest possible destruction to the diffusion and extension of learning."[65] Glasgow University and the Bodleian likewise issued petitions, noting that Brydges's arguments had been "very widely circulated." The contest had now raised, they noted, "the great question of LITERARY PROPERTY."[66] Amid angry scenes in Parliament, Brydges told MPs that the concept of copyright itself was at issue. It had been invented to address "piracies," but that original aim had been abandoned in 1814. As a result, Humboldt's science had been "crushed," and antiquarian reprints threatened with extinction. The fundamental question was now simply this: "Had authors and publishers—or had they not, a title to this property?"[67] If they had, then contemporary copyright had to go.

It almost worked. Brydges's bill failed by just one vote.[68] That was enough to initiate a major parliamentary committee investigation into the whole issue—the first of what became a sequence of such panels throughout the nineteenth century. The committee heard witnesses on all sides, amassing a tranche of evidence concerning the little-known customs of the publishing trade. In this dossier it left behind what amounted to an evidential time bomb under the foundations of publishing. And in the meantime it was itself convinced. It reported that the eleven-copy requirement was indeed excessive. It recommended that only the British

Museum retain its right; the other libraries should be given allowances in lieu of their claims. Failing this, it proposed several intermediate remedies, including compelling the libraries to pay a share of the costs. But Parliament moved slowly, and in 1818 was dissolved before anything was done.

The dissolution destroyed Brydges's chances. His resources had run out. He skirted bankruptcy in his reelection campaign, and when he lost he immediately fled the country to escape his creditors. A year later, when the new Parliament convened, attempts were made to revive the cause, but they got nowhere without him. For another generation the publishers would continue to complain about the deposit. Eventually, in 1836, a new set of debates would arise, culminating in a law depriving six of the eleven libraries of their right. Brydges's own campaign might have failed, then, but the motives driving it had not gone away.

SMALL SCIENCE

In many respects Brydges's observations of his surrounding culture were massively questionable. If genius was really doomed not to be recognized by a mass audience, then why did piracies of Byron's work attract such huge readerships in the late 1810s? Why did Scott—with whom Brydges collaborated in bibliographical projects, and of whose genius he was convinced—achieve such success?[69] In his critical judgments, for every Wordsworth Brydges got right, he got a Southey wrong. For the most part his alternative genealogy of printed bards (Wither, Greene, and so on) seems, and seemed at the time, a parade of insipid second-raters. Above all, perhaps, Brydges had little to say about the rise and consolidation of scientific discovery and invention as modes of creativity, generally disdaining them as mere techniques. Later, as the Decline of Science debate raged, the distant Brydges did condescend to contrast literary and scientific claims to genius in potentially intriguing terms:

Discoverers in science may be useful;
But all their merits are transmissible:
They are, like money, things of circulation,
And equally available to all.
But the fine essence of imaginative
Genius eludes transmission, and thus lives

And breathes alone in the identical words
Of its creator. Therefore poets live
Forever in the presence of posterity.[70]

But this too went nowhere.

Yet as the sciences underwent their own upheavals in the era of Romanticism—upheavals that would culminate in the formation of modern disciplines and the invention of the scientist—strategies close to Brydges's heart had a place. His own associations may have been with country rather than city, lords rather than commons, and patronage rather than profession. But in some intellectual and technical fields, too, small-run publishing made sense. (After all, the average impression of an academic monograph today is about 250–400 copies, which would be at the high end of Brydges's domain, and that number is falling fast.) With this in mind, Thomas Fisher—antiquarian, pioneer lithographer, and passionate antagonist to library deposit—claimed that "the union of the Arts of Design with Literature" had given rise to a new kind of book. This new medium incorporated finely rendered images that were not merely aesthetically beautiful, but epistemologically essential. They were necessary, Fisher noted, for "conveying ideas with a minuteness, accuracy, and force, unknown to the book prints of former times." He listed the major disciplines that stood to gain: not only topography, local history, and antiquarianism, but botany, zoology, conchology, natural history, architecture, astronomy, and the mathematical sciences. In all these endeavors, knowledge could for the first time be presented with precision, accuracy, and impact—with objectivity, it might be said. But these objects were expensive to produce and addressed very small, dedicated readerships. It was because the deposit imperiled them that the issue was urgent in the extreme. It stood to suppress knowledge itself.[71]

Two brief examples may suggest how this kind of publishing could work in practice in the sciences. The first is one of the works directly imperiled by the deposit: John Sibthorp's *Flora Graeca* (fig. 9.5). An elegant work of Levantine natural history written in Latin, this mammoth project was inching its way into publication by fascicles as the deposit became a live issue. In all, it would consume some thirty-four years and ten volumes. Its small run (about thirty copies) and enormous cost made it highly vulnerable. In 1825 the British Museum actually sued for its free copies—a deadly threat, since producing back issues at that stage would have cost

FIGURE 9.5. Small-run publishing in natural history: Sibthorp's *Flora Graeca.* J. Sibthorp et al., *Flora Graeca,* 10 vols. (London: R. Taylor for J. White, 1806–40), vol. 1, frontispiece. Courtesy of the University of Chicago Library.

another £3,000 and delayed the enterprise by a decade. After prolonged arguments, the Museum lost because the courts determined that such a bijou publication was not a *book* at all.[72]

The second example is that of the Sussex physician, poet, antiquarian, and fossil hunter Gideon Mantell. Mantell was an early pioneer of paleontology, devoting himself to seeking out in quarries the remains of what looked like giant reptiles. Adopting the Brydges style of publication, he reported his findings in small-circulation works of local history, aimed at procuring noble patronage rather than commercial success. His publisher was one of Brydges's campaigners against the libraries, Lupton Relfe. It was Mantell who named one of his ancient creatures *iguanodon,* because its tooth resembled that of a modern iguana. But these were the very years in which the British Association for the Advancement of Science came into being, betokening the emergence of a new practice of scientific authorship quite distinct from the antiquarian conventions to which Mantell cleaved. His work at first enjoyed little attention in this scientific community, and Mantell did at length turn to more commercial publishing, not least in hopes of royalties. However, with his reputation among the scientists still precarious, he found himself confronted by the power of their own mode of publication. A long-running feud with the notoriously ambitious Richard Owen reached its peak when Owen gave a famous lecture at the British Association in 1841. Mantell believed that Owen had silently appropriated his work. He denounced the talk as "base piracy." But the Association voted to subsidize Owen's publication anyway. And his would not be a work of geological antiquarianism aimed at one or two patrons, but a professional publication directed to a transnational research community—a work befitting the newly defined role of the scientist. It was in this context that Owen, partly to cast a distinction between his work and his rival's, coined a new name for the class of creatures they were both studying: *dinosaurs.* And it was his version that gained lasting influence. This was certainly not due solely to Mantell's devotion to a small-circulation, antiquarian style of authorship and Owen's to a more successful alternative. But the difference in authorial strategies was nevertheless as consequential as it was stark.[73]

GOTHIC GENIUS

Just as his twin strategies against the contemporary culture of print seemed to be reaching their culmination, Brydges found himself cast out of Parliament. Facing insupportable debts, he fled first to Paris, then on to Geneva. Apart from a lengthy poetic tour of Italy in 1819–21 and a second sojourn in Paris in 1825, Brydges resigned himself to a fitful but Romantic seclusion in the shadows of the Swiss Alps. There he worked late into each night writing endless sonnets, pamphlets, bibliographical and genealogical screeds, and self-righteous defenses of his cause in the Chandos case. Night after night he railed silently against Beltz's "impudent and libellous" demolition of his Chandos claim, his "pure wickedness," his "false representation," and so on.[74] Meanwhile the Lee Priory press struggled on, finally closing its doors in 1821. Its most expert operator, Johnson, left somewhat earlier in high dudgeon.

In exile Brydges returned to his bibliographical endeavors. The "almost mechanical" enterprise of bibliography, he said, suited a wronged outcast incapable of deploying real imagination. Incapacitated from exercising genius himself, he preferred to reprint the works of others rather than resort to claiming as his own "thoughts borrowed from others." His reprints appeared in minute print runs from Naples, Florence, Rome, and Geneva. In one he "registered" more than a thousand ideas from previous centuries that in his own day were hailed as novel. In others he expostulated on the nature of genius and its neglect by a gluttonous public.[75]

The one intermission in this effort came from a brief but calamitous return to Lee Priory. Seeing his old haunts again made Brydges more melancholic than ever. And he embarked on a byzantine scheme to pay off his debts that ended up ruining everyone who still tolerated him. The scheme involved Lee lands that were currently mortgaged. The mortgage was paid off, and they were sold to the bibliographer and mediocre poet Edward Quillinan. Quillinan then sold them back for three times as much, generating a paper profit of £15,000. This was divided between Brydges, Brydges's lawyers, Quillinan himself, and Brydges's family. But the one-time lenders soon heard of the miraculous rise in value. They sued, starting a legal struggle that would last eleven years and prove disastrous to all involved. Brydges's eldest son, the actual owner of Lee Priory, fled to the Continent and died in a lonely fishing cottage in Brittany. His youngest was jailed for debt and went mad. For years Quillinan could not afford to marry Wordsworth's daughter. Even the lawyers went bankrupt.[76] Only Brydges himself escaped, apparently unchastened, to Geneva. He was soon assisting from afar in an ultra-Tory plot to unseat the Duke of Wellington as prime minister, on the grounds, of all things, that his economics were imprudent.[77]

Brydges's copyright campaign, like that plotting, can seem in retrospect willfully idiosyncratic. But he came closer to success than one might initially have supposed, and he thought of it as his proudest moment.[78] And we should also remember that he had many allies—including much of the highest echelon of the London publishing industry. He was in practice quite able to make common cause with commerce in its oligarchic form. Moreover, many of his antagonists' arguments were in fact no less outlandish than his own. After all, it was the *defenders* of copyright who resurrected Corsellis and proclaimed a pre-1710 right of universal piracy. And the factual relics of his campaign would survive it to be revived by later critics of publishing monopolies, starting with Charles Babbage.[79]

But there is more to be said than that. The outlandish character of Brydges's campaigns was in fact a central element in them. His understanding of his own nature was forged in the late 1780s and 1790s through the Chandos campaign and his early attempts at novel writing. What lasted from those years was a conviction that he was essentially (whatever his outward appearance) aristocratic, sensitive, secluded, poetic, and temperamental. It was as such that he wrote himself into his Gothic novels — especially *Fitz-Albini,* in which he appears as a reclusive lord given to poetic insight (the name of the work comes from combining two elements of Brydges's purported family tree). When he himself was not their hero, characters from his elaborate genealogical past served the turn, displaying traits that he thought he had identified in his pedigree. But the point is that as much as he inserted himself in Gothic and Romantic narratives, at the same time he inserted Gothic and Romantic narratives in himself. Brydges lived his life from one lightning-limned discovery in a ruined crypt to the next. Such glimpses inspired both his general genealogical faith and his specific discovery of the true descent linking himself to Gibbon. In these glimpses, in his recurrent need to define genius, and in his impassioned proclamations about aristocracy, popularity, and originality alike Brydges aspired to the identity of a distinctly tragic Romantic hero. And it was this aspiration, more than argument, faith, or need, that drove his campaigns. Indeed, throughout the years of the copyright conflict he never ceased to issue restatements of the Chandos claim in such terms. The claim recurred in every imaginable literary form: poetry (from sonnets to multivolume epics), novels, imaginative biographies, periodical essays, and edited works. Brydges even endured six years of "drudgery" to edit Collins's peerage in nine volumes, apparently in order that a few pages might "transmit a record of his family wrongs to posterity." In all of this, as Beltz rightly said, his life became a gothic novel. For one dizzying moment, at the fag end of old-regime Britain, the identity and role of printed authorship looked like becoming merely one more subplot in "the eternal *Chandos Romance.*"[80]

10

Inventors, Schemers, and Men of Science

Victorian Britain prided itself on standing at the summit of industrial, economic, and scientific achievement. Its factories supplied the world, its ships held sway on the oceans, and its engineers, naturalists, and electrical researchers ranked with the best in Europe. Inventors and discoverers were the heroes of the age. Yet in the decades from 1850 to 1880 every aspect of the relation between invention, industry, and society came under the harshest examination it had ever undergone. Critics charged that the mechanism that had evolved over centuries to recognize, encourage, and reward inventors—that of patents—was outdated, inefficient, and even fundamentally ill conceived. They were at first few in number, but soon appeared in every class and all regions of the country. They claimed that it profoundly misrepresented the nature of invention, the social identity of inventors, and the place of both in a modern industrial economy. They insisted that it be not just reformed or updated, but abolished outright. And they almost won. Our own loud contests notwithstanding, the Victorian campaign against patenting—which expanded to embrace copyrights too—remains to this day the strongest ever undertaken against intellectual property.

Yet there was more to it than that. As we have seen, it had come to be accepted in the late eighteenth century that literary authorship and invention were not radically distinct kinds of thing. Both were manifestations of some common power. By an import from the German language, this common power gradually came to be called *creativity*. It carried with it the implication that regimes of property in creative work ought themselves to be emanations of some common underlying principle. As formal systems they should therefore interlace coherently. When patenting came under attack, hard-pressed defenders of the system found that it was only by appealing to this commitment that they could head off the assault. They saved patenting by insisting that it was but one aspect of a deeper, sweepingly fundamental principle—one with clear, distinct, and adamantine political overtones. They called that principle *intellectual property*.

The debate about patents was not unique to any one country. Similar contests took place across Europe. In France, leading politicians, political economists, and savants weighed in on both sides. In Prussia—later the German empire—the campaign encouraged Bismarck to pronounce against the practice of patenting, which remained at a low level for decades in the German lands. In the Netherlands, the campaign actually led to the abolition of the entire patents regime. And in Switzerland, it long dissuaded the authorities from establishing one at all. Only America among the industrial powers seems to have been largely unaffected by the furor, for a combination of particular reasons: thanks to the proselytizing of Mathew Carey's generation, the inventor had long been seen as a virtuous republican type; the patents system there had been adumbrated in the Constitution; and it was a relatively easy and affordable system for Americans to make use of.[1] These conditions, however, were peculiar to the United States. In all other major powers the fate of patents became very much an open question. And the controversies that raged in this generation set the terms in which almost all later debates about creativity and commerce would be posed.

Great Britain was the foremost industrial power of the time, so it was in Britain that the conflict over patents was carried on most fiercely and with the most important consequences. It split the country's professional elite. Proponents and antagonists included many of the most prominent engineers and men of science, as well as lawyers, authors, philosophers, and gentlemen. And rival camps rarely ceased to badger Parliament for action. Beginning in 1829, a long series of parliamentary committees and Royal Commissions investigated the law and practice of patenting in increasingly broad terms. At first, the issue was one of reform, very much along the lines of the broader political movements beginning in the 1810s to reform structures of governance and administration that had remained essentially unchanged since the seventeenth century. In 1852 one such attempt proved successful, producing a sweeping change that in effect created the country's first patents *system,* as opposed to the rather ad hoc cluster of conventions that had obtained before that. But the success proved double-edged. It triggered the emergence of a full-blooded campaign, not to update patenting, but to abolish it altogether—and then, some of its more bullish protagonists urged, to destroy copyright too. What had begun as an effort at reform had become something far more serious and far more fundamental. And the abolitionist campaign rapidly won influential converts, among them the engineer Isambard Kingdom Brunel, the electrical researcher and jurist William Robert Grove, and several of the nation's highest-ranking legal officials. Above all, the arms magnate Sir William Armstrong and the sugar capitalist Robert MacFie acted as the leaders, icons, and organizers of the movement. There were spells during the ensuing decades in which draft legislation was being introduced almost every year.[2] Many in the 1860s and 1870s believed that the abolitionist forces were on the verge of triumphing. Had they done so, then the world's dominant imperial and industrial power would have taken the initiative to extend radical laissez-faire principles into the very activity of invention. Industrial creativity would have fallen to free trade. And subsequent scientific, industrial, and economic history would surely have looked very different indeed.

Not only were the stakes in these patent debates very high, but the debates themselves ranged more widely than might have been anticipated. They embraced prolonged exchanges about the nature of discovery and invention, about how the propensity to make discoveries was distributed in the social order (in particular, whether a "class" of workman inventors existed or could exist), about whether "inventors" could be distinguished from fraudulent, deluded, or opportunistic exploiters (often termed "schemers"), and about the rewards that any such inventors might or might not deserve. At the same time they probed the use and abuse of scientific expertise to bolster or question claims in the law courts in general, not just in patents cases. From that point, they extended to issues of the nature of scientific evidence, culminating in suggestions that Britain should create a discrete court machinery to deal with issues demanding scientific testimony. It was partly in this light that the struggles over patents converged with others to redefine the very identity and authority of the scientist as a recognized social species.

We should begin with a patent. In mid-1817, the Scottish evangelical naturalist and editor David Brewster (1781–1868) filed an application for one, setting in train events that would culminate in the climactic contest almost exactly half a century later. It applied to a new optical device that he christened the kaleidoscope. This was one of many instruments that Brewster had devised or improved in the course of years of painstaking research on light, some of which he had earlier patented. But the kaleidoscope was a different kind of device. It was not intended for scientific researches by philosophers, but for what Georgian England called "rational amusement." In other words, it was one of countless machines made and marketed at this time to middle-class consumers to provoke wonder and encourage reflection by the user. Such machines circulated in a dynamic, entrepreneurial, and very competitive world of goods. Emerging out of the world of mid-eighteenth-century lecturing that had created the orrery, the automaton, and the Microcosm—and that had been so pivotal to the advent of copyright—they too made use of spectacle, artistry, and revelation to sell themselves and the reputations of their makers. But they were also meant, and taken, seriously as instruments. Brewster himself believed that he was contributing to the education of a popular discernment in sight. For example, he thought the kaleidoscope would illuminate principles of symmetry that pervaded the natural world and were central to good neoclassical art. It would inculcate a kind of "eye for admiring and appreciating the effect of fine forms" that was the equivalent of an "ear for fine music," and that might have a similarly emancipating and cultivating effect. He described his kaleidoscope as an "ocular harpsichord" that produced harmonies of color. Artists and architects could use it to try out symmetries before fixing them in their creations.[3]

The kaleidoscope was an immediate and spectacular popular success. Within a few months, perhaps two hundred thousand had been sold, in Paris as well as London. It was a sensation on a scale with no real precedent in the eighteenth century. Brewster told his wife that "no book and no instrument in the memory of man ever produced such a singular effect."

But this very success became a major source of disgruntlement for Brewster. Thousands of "poor people" were making and selling the devices — none of whom was paying him for the privilege, and none incorporating the precise scientific elements that Brewster insisted upon (such as the ability to change the angle of the internal mirrors). As a result, not only was he losing out, but his intended aim in promoting the device was being betrayed.

Brewster's decision to get a patent was nothing very unusual by this time. The practice had grown in the eighteenth century as the Industrial Revolution accelerated, and the first printed survey of patent law had appeared in 1803.[4] It was about to be instrumental in the elevation of what had once been called (and denigrated as) "projectors" into an admired class of "inventors." That elevation was at least as consequential as the far-better-known shift from "natural philosophers" to "scientists." Indeed, it could be said that the Industrial Revolution emerged as a transition from the age of projects to the age of invention. The pivotal figure in this transformation was James Watt, who had staunchly defended his patented steam engine and was apotheosized after his death in 1819. Yet there was still not really such a thing as a patents system in Britain. Each grant was still an individual grace proffered by the Crown out of its goodwill. Obtaining one was an expensive and dauntingly bureaucratic operation. It took at least ten discrete steps, and applicants had to go through a long series of clerks' offices with fees levied at every one; the process had originated in Tudor legislation intended to secure an income for clerks.[5] The application took months and cost about £350 even in uncontroversial cases. Specialist "patent agents" made a living by shepherding claims past the various hurdles; they were usually engineers and projectors familiar with the intricacies from their own experience. Perhaps only these agents really knew the entire process. By the late nineteenth century they would receive a royal charter, making theirs a recognized profession.

Furthermore, a patent once obtained was often nothing more than a license to litigate. It provided no protection for a successful invention unless the patentee were prepared to defend it in lengthy, costly, and risky court battles, often against competitors with vastly greater resources. By the mid-nineteenth century, campaigners for reform could cite examples in which a patentee's legal costs had risen above £10,000. Even successful patentees were fairly likely to find themselves ruined, or at least tied up in court for years, enmeshed in a tangle of precedents and procedural arcana that had accreted over a long period. Worst of all, they complained, issues that were often highly technical—to do with the design of a steam engine, say, or the properties of a smelter—would be subjected in court to the ill-informed opinions of lay judges. It became commonplace to liken the whole thing to that most eighteenth-century of plausible swindles, a lottery. Some patentees won, others lost; nothing much more than chance seemed to govern which. The problem was therefore moral as well as scientific and economic. Patents made workaday inventors into "speculators," gamblers, or "schemers," staking themselves and their families at long odds for an even smaller chance of success than the regime seemed to promise. "If the private history of schemers could be gone into," William Robert Grove would soon suggest, then all would see that "the delusive ignis fatuus of a patent" constituted "a delusion, more honourable, but not less exciting, than that of the gambler."[6] In this respect patenting became part of a much wider debate in the nineteenth century about the proclaimed "demoralization" of industrial society, much of which employed the language of gambling.

At any rate, Brewster obtained his patent. But, as his daughter put it, "as it often has happened in this country, the invention was quickly pirated." It seems—at least, this is what Brewster thought—that the craftsman he had employed to manufacture the device took a sample to the major London artisans to solicit orders. They immediately made versions for themselves, perhaps assuming a customary prerogative to do so. And so the design leaked out. At that point, countless "tinmen" and "glaziers" began to make component parts for kaleidoscopes "in order to evade the patent," while others simply manufactured and sold entire instruments in blissful ignorance that a patent even existed. Much to its inventor's chagrin, it came to be widely assumed that the patent itself had been declared void. Brewster guessed that less than 1 percent of the kaleidoscopes sold in those heady months were produced under his patent and therefore "constructed upon scientific principles." As a result, not only had he been deprived of a fortune, but of the millions who had seen a kaleidoscope, "there is perhaps not an hundred who have any idea of the principles upon which it is constructed, who are capable of distinguishing the spurious from the real instrument, or who have sufficient knowledge of its principles for applying it to the numerous branches of the useful and ornamental arts." For decades he would continue to complain.[7]

Brewster's experience with the kaleidoscope had ramifications beyond his own pocket. Lacking a university or clerical position, he depended on diverse and often unreliable sources of income, such as the £100 or so he received for each issue of the *Edinburgh Journal of Science*.[8] Had his patent held, he could have escaped at one bound the chains of drudgery and worse that held him down—his interminable editorship of the *Edinburgh Encyclopaedia* embroiled him in potentially ruinous lawsuits. He could have attained the leisure and freedom of action of the gentleman. A breached patent blocked his path to advancement into the ranks of gentility. His experience, he therefore decided, indicated the existence of an enormous social problem that needed to be solved if society itself were not to atrophy.

Brewster does seem to have met with all the misfortunes that reputedly bedeviled nineteenth-century inventors. His patent specification was called into question; his workman purportedly leaked details to others; and the prospect of going to law was so intimidating that he simply declined to defend his patent at all. All these experiences were reportedly widespread. He resolved that something must be done. By 1821 Brewster was already instrumental in forming two associations in Edinburgh, a Society of Arts (named after London's own Society), dedicated to promoting Scottish inventors, and a School of Arts, which was to be the first of Britain's many Mechanics' Institutes. Throughout the 1820s, he continued to use his editorship of the *Edinburgh Journal of Science* to promote calls for state support for inventors and men of science. And at the end of the decade, when Charles Babbage published his *Reflections on the Decline of Science in England*, Brewster not only helped behind the scenes to compile its arguments but sallied forth in public as Babbage's most prominent supporter. Babbage's book appeared in the context of Parliament's first major investigation of the patents regime—an investigation that revealed widespread disillusionment but resulted in no action. Brewster told Babbage that he had observed those 1829 hearings with "astonishment," and was flabbergasted that nobody had advanced his own view, which was that patents should be akin to copyrights, obtainable easily and "*without any expense whatsoever.*" "Why should not an invention be property at common law," he asked, "like a book, which is protected by statute only to enable the author to recover more summarily?"[9] His conviction was no less consequential for being ill founded (copyright did not in fact have this legal status at this time). And Brewster went public with his opinion in his long review of Babbage in the *Quarterly Review*—a review widely seen as a distinct manifesto for the so-called declinist camp. Brewster even went beyond Babbage in several key respects, the most important of them being patenting. He would later admit that the review had in fact been commissioned by the editor precisely to serve as an attack on the "iniquity" of the patent laws—and that it had been so influential as to become "an integrant part of their history."[10]

Brewster fully concurred with Babbage in diagnosing British science to be in "a wretched state of depression." Other nations had used the years of peace since Waterloo to renew their long-standing devotion to the arts and sciences, he noted, often through state sponsorship and the awarding of honors. The institutions of science in France, Prussia, and Russia boasted munificent state and aristocratic support, and Brewster delved back into the past to recount the ways in which natural philosophers and mathematicians from Galileo to Volta had benefited from such patronage. Britain, by contrast, had done nothing. Since 1815 it had chosen rather to rest on its reactionary military laurels. The universities had no positions for researchers, the Royal Society and its counterparts in Dublin and Edinburgh had no funds for stipends (they even charged their members fees), and not a single philosopher currently enjoyed a state living. Britain had even recently abolished its one state scientific body of any consequence, namely, the Board of Longitude—a highly symbolic act that had helped provoke Babbage's alarum.

Brewster warned that this indifference had a direct impact on research. Prominent scientific figures were compelled to eke out a living by low-level teaching, or else, as at the University of Edinburgh, by lecturing to paying audiences—an activity that reduced them to showmen in competition with itinerant lecturers. "In this age of extended and diluted knowledge," he remarked bitterly, "popular science has become the staple of an extensive trade, in which charlatans are the principal dealers." The horror of it was revealed by the fact that professors were even "devoting themselves to professional authorship." A lecturer was forced to be a "commercial speculator," a role that left no place for original researches. None of the great inventions and discoveries of the past century had originated at the universities, Brewster claimed, and, he added mischievously, "there is not one man in all the eight universities of Great Britain who is at present known to be engaged in any train of original research." Such a charge exceeded even Babbage's high standards of tactlessness, and

INVENTORS, SCHEMERS, AND MEN OF SCIENCE

Brewster soon had to scramble for a face-saving account of what he had meant in the face of the formidable William Whewell.[11]

Brewster now launched in earnest into his assault on the inadequacy of the patents regime. With the sciences left to languish, British economic power rested on the mechanical, chemical, and agricultural arts. But these he thought had been not just neglected but actively oppressed. Brewster had told Brougham two years before that the patents regime was "horrid."[12] Now he declared the whole thing not merely a lottery but a fraudulent one, "which gives its blanks to genius and its prizes to knaves." It robbed inventors to fill the pockets of state officials. The system enshrined "vicious and fraudulent legislation." It furnished an inventor with a "factitious privilege" of no genuine value, and charged an exorbitant "tax upon his genius" of £300–£400 for it. There was no possible justification for this tax, Brewster maintained, since patents offered no real protection, and could only be affirmed as property by surviving hugely expensive lawsuits. The contrast with copyright was stark. A literary author obtained protection straightforwardly, and so, Brewster affirmed, "piracy is almost unknown" in the realm of print (an implausible view, incidentally, but let that pass). The inventor of a machine, on the other hand, must labor long and hard, "either in the dark or with the assistance of tried friends, lest some pirate robs him of his idea, and brings it earlier into use." The cost of applying for a patent, and still more that of defending it against such pirates, counted as an absolute barrier to poor inventors. Even if it had not, it would be a lucky man indeed who evaded the "pirates who lie in wait for the poor man's inventions." Far from encouraging invention, consequently, the system in fact served to debar "nine-tenths of those individuals who are most capable of advancing the interests of the arts." Whitehall's clerks and judges, on the other hand, benefited handsomely from their fees. The whole thing, Brewster concluded, was itself piratical: it cast the state's officials as "a legalized banditti."

Brewster thought that this bandit law threatened British industrial power. "Bribed by foreign gold," he warned, Britain's artisans were departing for foreign nations, taking with them their inventions and skills. The kind of invitation extended by Mathew Carey and others from America was, Brewster believed, all too effective. Britain's continued industrial might therefore depended on dealing not just with the decline of science, on the one hand, but, on the other, with the deeper "evil" of the patents regime. For the sciences, he wanted chairs established at universities for "men of genius," honors for scientific practitioners, and the provision of financial rewards through learned societies that would become "the scientific advisers to the crown." For patenting, more radically, he argued that privileges should be as easy to affirm as copyrights. This would effectively mean abolishing application fees altogether. One of three "scientific boards," based in London, Edinburgh, and Dublin, would instead appraise each application, and if the specification were deemed adequate and the invention judged to be new then the inventor would get absolute protection for fourteen years. An inventor could still take out a patent even without such approval, but at his or her own risk. With all this put in place, Brewster affirmed, the "inventive genius" of the nation could spring forth once again and the temptations of emigration could be countered.

But constructing a modern patent system would be hard work. Brewster's manifesto was itself prompted partly by the failure of the 1829 parliamentary committee even to issue a recommendation. He therefore reasoned that what was needed first and foremost was political agitation. He nurtured the hope that the Royal Society would undertake this task; but before it would do so it would have to be reformed, and there seemed little chance of this happening. He therefore called for a new body to take up the cause—an "association," as he called it, "of our nobility, clergy, gentry, and philosophers." It would be modeled on a contemporary German congress for natural history and *Naturphilosophie,* a meeting of which Babbage had attended. Brewster hoped that a new association of this kind would both impel the reform of patents and, almost as important, inspire the nation's aristocrats to take up their proper role as "patrons of genius."

Brewster's call for a new association, as is well known, marked the origin of what became the British Association for the Advancement of Science. Agitation about patenting was one of the new body's prime purposes. He wanted it to launch itself forthwith into a campaign for reform, telling allies that since Brougham was now lord chancellor they could expect a favorable reception. Yet the Association as it in fact emerged in 1831 was not the body Brewster had wanted. In fact he played little active part in steering the nascent group, and before long a powerful Cambridge cohort, led by the still smarting Whewell, moved to the fore. Under Whewell's oversight the Association moved away from Brewster's preoccupations. It devoted itself to mechanical *science,* not mechanical *arts*—the distinction being that science was theoretical, whereas arts were learned by personal contact and often had industrial aspects to them. The idea of campaigning on patent issues was quietly abandoned. The BAAS was not to return to the political activity that Brewster had envisaged until the mid-1850s.[13]

Still, one well-known achievement of these early meetings deserves to be noted. This was the coining of the term *scientist* to connote the new kind of specialist expert to whom the Association appealed. Whewell seems to have proposed it himself. He referred to it in print anonymously in the *Quarterly Review* of March 1834, and called seriously for its adoption in his *Philosophy of the Inductive Sciences* six years later.[14] Whewell saw that active researchers were devoting themselves increasingly to what were becoming discrete technical fields, and that, as they did so, so they grew "estranged from each other in habit and feeling." As a result, it was no longer clear what investigators of nature should be called collectively. They paid little attention to general or philosophical questions, it seemed, and therefore Coleridge had "properly" denied them the title of philosopher. There was a sorely felt need for a new name for the specialist, technical, and professional pursuer of natural knowledge. The new word was intended from the start to mark out real cultural distinctions, in a society increasingly characterized by mechanized industry. And in that light, one distinctive attribute of the scientist was a propensity to make discoveries. Earlier figures (Newton, Boyle, Priestley, and others) had certainly discovered things, but in general early modern natural philosophers had been charged with explaining nature in its usual course; they had not been charged with pursuing novelty. Discovery was not a central and defining aspect of the natural philosopher's role. For the scientist's, it was. This was a major reason why the issues of patenting and the scientific practitioner arose together and were to remain inseparable.

The invention of the scientist took place in a generation when major changes were occurring in other realms of professional and vocational knowledge, most notably engineering and medicine. In each case, one can identify a pivotal role played by activities decried — or praised — at the time as piratical in forging a new identity and authority for the practitioner. Medicine is the best-known instance, in which the British Medical Association acted as a radical union in support of the new "general practitioners" against the licentiates of the old Royal College of Physicians. Thomas Wakley's agitation was as much a contribution to this fight as his launch of *The Lancet*. Run with the help of Cobbett (long after Mathew Carey denounced him as a corsair), *The Lancet* built its reputation on the serial piracy of medical lectures, and frequently had to defend itself in court for its actions. When it did, it gleefully printed the court cases too. It combined this with a consistently acid tone in opposition to conservative forces in medicine and society at large. *The Lancet* became the house journal of the radical general practioners—until it was usurped in the early 1830s by the *London Medical and Surgical Journal,* which undercut its price and usurped its sources. These organs (there were more, not now remembered), and the camps they appealed to, fought bitterly with accusations of piracy and counterpiracy. The struggles over professional identity in medicine in this era were as affected by such accusations as those over identity in science. And both were much less clearly distinct from the realm of radical and materialist pirate printers like Richard Carlile, William Benbow, and Thomas Tegg—the nineteenth-century successors to Hills and Rayner—than their denizens liked to admit.[15]

FROM REFORM TO ABOLITION

Agitation to reform the operation of patenting can be traced back a long way. As early as the 1780s, in the midst of fears aroused by Pitt's proposed free trade arrangement with Ireland, James Watt and his friends had banded together to urge major changes. Among the themes Watt articulated were a number that became key to the subsequent century's debate. Should patents be admissible for merely introducing a device from abroad, for example? Watt thought so, and this practice had in fact long been accepted, but increasingly others rejected it. Should one be able to patent a principle as well as a device? Again, Watt thought one should, but his was not a majority view; and in any case the concept of a "principle" was anything but evident. Most important, should some tribunal be created that would vet an application for novelty before a patent could be granted at all?

This idea of a patent tribunal encompassed many of the trickiest problems with a patents regime. Since the 1730s, applicants had had to submit "specifications" of their inventions. The idea that a patent represented a bargain between society and the inventor—a temporary monopoly in return for revealing the invention—rested on this requirement. But patent specifications often concealed as much as they conveyed. This was not necessarily the result of incompetence or inexperience. Rather the reverse: there was a distinct art to composing a patent specification so as to reveal just enough to sustain the claim and identify the invention, but not so much as to make the claim overly specific or to enable others to replicate it. This finely calculated ambiguity frequently caused problems for patentees in the face of later challenges. Watt himself had fallen foul of it. A tribunal, he suggested, might ensure that a specification was indeed an adequate description of the invention. It might also go further, and judge the novelty of a claim, thereby reducing litigation. But Watt preferred that any such opinion should be merely advisory. And he rejected altogether the suggestion that it should rule on the utility of an invention.[16]

Proposals for some kind of tribunal proved tenacious. They were repeatedly resurrected in the nineteenth century, and their potential scope did not end with the application process. Perhaps a tribunal could also replace the conventional law courts in hearing challenges to existing patents too—a possibility that Brewster, for one, favored strongly. Only this, advocates claimed, could end the lottery of patent litigation. They proposed that a special court be convened solely to decide patent challenges (and perhaps those relating to copyright too). Such a court too was not in fact instituted, but the idea that it could be returned time and time again. But any such plan immediately posed the problem of who should sit on such a body. Judges and advisors would need to be at once impartial, objective, technically expert, and practical. Watt suggested a panel of three Fellows of the Royal Society and two artisans. Others advanced different combinations, and the question recurred incessantly. It gave rise to a sustained and very widely publicized set of exchanges on the qualifications, social role, and credibility required of anyone who could authoritatively decide such matters. Debates on the subject could be heard at mechanics' institutes, chambers of commerce, and literary and philosophical societies across the land. One of the most powerful forces pushing for a public recognition of the "man of science" as a juridical figure was consequently this: that such a figure was needed to serve as a gatekeeper into the commercialization of creativity in industrial society. Moreover, to replace the royal will with the verdict of a "man of science" would implicitly supplant the authority of the monarch in this critical area by that of the scientist.[17]

These were the kinds of complex and tangled questions that in 1829 led to the formation of the first select committee to examine the regime. Although it led to no firm proposals, the committee did manage to record widespread disapprobation of the prevailing practice. Calling witnesses from engineering—especially Marc Isambard Brunel—as well as the patent agents, it heard about a wide range of problems. The existing regime found almost no support outside the ranks of those most closely invested in it. Brunel for one remarked that "patents are like lottery offices, where people run with great expectations, and enter any thing almost." Opinions on how radically to reform it, however, differed widely. Some witnesses urged a reduction in the cost of obtaining a patent, for example. But it is important to note that most, including Brunel, resisted this. They feared that it would foster too many patents on "trivial" or "frivolous" devices, which would then have a stifling effect on industrial progress. Some proposed having a panel of examiners vet candidate inventions, perhaps doing away with the requirement for a specification altogether. Others merely thought that a longer time should be allowed to file the documents. Some proposed that the specification should be kept secret; most thought that it should be open, but not actually printed and published. For his part, Brunel remarked that it would be impossible both to make a specification sufficiently public to avoid others unwittingly "pirating the invention" and at the same time sufficiently private to prevent infringement by real pirates. He also wanted specially selected juries to try challenges to patents, proposing the Royal Society as arbiter, because with a regular jury one "might as well toss for the fate of a patent." The idea of a panel, of course, immediately gave rise to questions about how to populate such a body. Who could be trusted to act impartially? Whom, more to the point, would the public trust?[18] So intractable were all these problems that in the end the committee petered out in the face of them without producing any recommendations at all. And successive committees and commissions throughout the century would find themselves hearing similar opinions repeatedly. Broad consensus clearly existed on the need for *some* kind of reform, but none at all on *what* kind. When Brewster's attempts to mobilize the scientific community failed, the whole issue languished.

In the end what compelled action was the Great Exhibition in 1851. The Exhibition was meant to display British and colonial inventive prowess. But manufacturers had a long-standing record of skepticism about even smaller-scale events of this kind, suspecting that their secrets would be revealed to competitors. Now they feared that the absence of effective protection would permit British contributions to fall prey to foreigners, who, as the ultra-Tory MP Charles Sibthorp told the Commons, would "come and pirate the inventions of our countrymen."[19] After much agonizing, at the thirteenth hour Parliament did pass a temporary law to extend special protection to exhibits at the Exhibition; it came into effect a few days after the Crystal Palace itself had opened.[20] The experience made it clear that something more permanent and considered was sorely needed. The Society of Arts, the Exhibition's original champion, now called for a new system, and the BAAS finally stepped forward to make the case too under the presidency of Brewster himself; he told the Association's Edinburgh meeting that the patents system currently did nothing to help inventors against "remorseless pirates." As a result, in a two-year period no less than three parliamentary select committees investigated the law of patents. They found, to almost nobody's great surprise, that it was radically dysfunctional. For example, one chief clerk had not performed any of his duties for almost fifty years since being appointed in 1801.[21] The committees recommended sweeping reform, including the lowering of fees and the establishment of a "scientific" board of examiners. Two failed bills followed in 1851, one of them promoted by Brougham. The following year a new government proposed a third, and this one was finally successful. It passed into law as the Patent Law Amendment Act.

The 1852 law really represents the beginning of a patents system in Britain. It swept aside an antiquated machinery. England, Scotland, and Ireland were consolidated into one area. The application fee was reduced to £180. A single Patent Office was created, with a staff of commissioners and clerks—most notably the tireless Bennet Woodcroft, who devoted himself to establishing a functional system. Above all, perhaps, Woodcroft instituted a reliable and accessible *archive* of patents, with indexes, lodged in one location. From now on an applicant would receive provisional protection from the moment of application, thus closing the window of opportunity that pirates like those of Brewster's kaleidoscope had previously enjoyed. But not every measure favored by Brewster and his allies found favor. Some witnesses, for example, had opposed the lowering of application fees, for fear of unleashing a flood of trivial patents by over-ambitious factory workmen. And most had opposed the notion of a panel of "men of science" to vet applications, preferring to leave patentees to defend their own claims. The result was that fees, while reduced, remained substantial, and it remained the responsibility of patentees to defend their patents. Although an application would be examined by the commissioners before any patent was granted, the examination remained rather pro forma. There was to be no tribunal, and the process remained free of "scientific" input except in the form of ad hoc advisors (who in practice were rarely consulted). Nor was there to be a special court for judging patent disputes.[22]

As remarkable as the creation of a real patent system, however, was the simultaneous advent of real and sustained calls for patents to be abolished altogether. Among the first of those prepared to voice this possibility was the MP John Lewis Ricardo, nephew of David Ricardo, the great political economist, and himself a convinced opponent of the Corn Laws. The younger Ricardo was the chairman of one of the early telegraph companies — telegraphy being by far the most advanced and exciting commercial science of the day. He had found himself forced to buy up patents to forestall litigation, and was therefore inclined by his own experience to see them as monopolistic obstacles to laissez-faire. He pointed out—as many would repeat in the next generation—that patents had not been required to stimulate the invention of printing, gunpowder, or paper. Only "trivial" improvements tended to be patented, he claimed. In the end, Ricardo denied outright that patents accelerated invention. He maintained instead that they were an unnecessary impediment—the equivalent, in effect, to the navigation acts or the Corn Laws themselves.[23]

Ricardo's was at first a lonely view. But soon it attracted more support. In fact, it was the process of vetting the new law in 1851–52 that sparked the emergence of a movement dedicated to the cause of abolition. This movement would last a generation and of find backing from all sectors of society. In part, this was because, by abolishing the administrative problems of the old regime, the inauguration of a rationalized system brought deeper, intrinsic problems into sharper relief. Those problems had to do with the nature of invention itself, the social identity of the inventor, the relations between science, the public, and progress, and the political economy of laissez-faire. More immediately, however, what triggered the ensuing controversies was the fact that the practice of patenting now took effect in a realm of commerce and manufacturing that increasingly saw itself as international in scope, and taking effect in an empire of free trade. That is, it introduced a problem of space, at precisely the same time as it focused attention on attributes of patents that were deemed to be essential. The combination proved incendiary.

In the mid-nineteenth century a growing impetus behind patent reform —as also in the case of copyright—was the aspiration to extend what had always been a purely national practice into the international realm. Since the 1830s, Britain had sought to reach agreements with European and

American governments on patent and copyright treaties to do this in limited ways.[24] The principal rationale lay in contemporary economic doctrine. According to the tenets of political economy, the royalty that users of a patented technology paid to the patentee could be seen as a kind of tariff on domestic manufacturers. Since the existence, terms, and rates of such royalties varied across borders, national patent regimes violated the principles of free trade. For this reason, European powers sought (with qualified success) to create harmonious, or at least reciprocal, patents and copyrights rules. For free trade to operate, the costs of patents to users — including their accessibility, terms, and restrictions — should be uniform across nations. Abolitionists would soon proclaim that the only way to achieve this was to do away with such costs altogether. It is therefore slightly ironic that what gave the initial spur to the antipatent campaign was a move by the British government to do just that in one instance. Specifically, the immediate cause of tension was a new relation that the 1852 law defined between Britain and its colonies. The 1852 law expressly excluded the colonies of the British Empire from having to honor patents filed in the home country.[25] Colonial manufacturers could now adopt the latest technologies from Britain without paying royalties.

This decision derived in large part from earlier struggles over slavery, especially in the West Indies. The West Indian colonies had been slave-plantation economies until emancipation in 1834. The owners of sugar plantations there had then faced the prospect of addressing labor costs for the first time. Rivals in Brazil and Cuba still used slave labor, however, and the colonial owners claimed that this put them at a disadvantage, especially after 1846, when London's equalization of tariffs meant that they could no longer count on preferential treatment. The sugar producers attempted to maintain their position by mechanization — many adopted steam-powered mill machinery — but nonetheless a severe depression took hold in the West Indian sugar trade.[26] It was in this context that Westminster decided not to extend patent protection to the colonies. The hope, in effect, was that the ability of sugar manufacturers to adopt modern steam machinery without paying royalties would serve as a positive subsidy to help them against their slaver rivals. There were other considerations too, of course. Not least, the sheer variety of legal subsystems across Britain's haphazard empire made it hard to envisage them coordinating in any one patents regime. And the effort of creating such a scheme seemed scarcely worthwhile, because many colonies were deemed incapable of inventing on any sustained level in any case (Whitehall did obtain reports on this from all the colonies). But it was the West Indian refiners' interest that was decisive. It effectively persuaded Parliament to leave the colonies outside the new patent regime.

As a result, the patent system that came into existence in 1852 incorporated for the first time an avowed spatial distinction when it came to the empire. It embraced a fissure between the home country and the colonies that was quite unlike what had existed in the previous century. The combination meant that the new, modernized patents system led to a radical debate that embraced international trade and politics, and in the end the constitution of imperialism.

THE ABOLITION CAMPAIGN

The 1852 law provoked a furious reaction from Britain's own sugar refiners. In particular, it provoked that reaction from one among them: a Glaswegian sugar magnate and president of the Liverpool Chamber of Commerce, Robert A. MacFie. MacFie was already a known skeptic about patenting. He had given evidence against the practice prior to the passage of the new law, petitioning against the multiplying number of patents and allying himself with Ricardo's position. Now he became a determined and relentless campaigner against it, dedicated to abolishing the whole system. If the antipatenting campaign of the Victorian period needed a leader, MacFie would be it.[27]

Two other figures besides MacFie stood out as leaders of the antipatent campaign. One was William Robert Grove, a well-known electrical researcher turned barrister. Grove's voice carried authority. He knew very well the most lucrative new science of the age, telegraphy, and the one in which patents promised to be most influential. He often presented himself as more a skeptic about patenting than an out-and-out abolitionist. In 1860, most notably, he published a well-regarded proposal for an entirely new court dedicated to both the granting of patents and the trying of cases resulting from them; he envisaged that it might also extend its remit to copyright, and to all cases "of a scientific character." It was probably the most plausible such proposal among the many put forward in these years. In some ways it was daring: Grove's court would have the authority to reject patents for trivial improvements, for example, and to determine how long each patent should endure based on the needs and worth of the invention, both of these powers being anathema to the pro-patent camp. But he also insisted that its judges should be barristers, not men of science, and that it should have a jury—in both respects adopting a more conservative view than many of the reformers, let alone abolitionists. (His jury would be composed not of laymen, but of "manufacturers, chemists, engineers, &c.") The point, for Grove, was that his tribunal promised a return to "the spirit of the ancient patent law," as enshrined in the common law of Coke and articulated by the Statute of Monopolies. But such a court was not forthcoming, and Grove gravitated increasingly to the abolitionist camp. He at length became even more radical than MacFie. Or perhaps he was merely more fatalistic. Whereas MacFie wanted to introduce a system of state awards for deserving inventors, Grove denounced even this possibility, insisting that the state should refrain from intervening at all. He seems to have thought that the cause of the lower-class inventor would inevitably be hopeless in the face of big capital.[28]

The most reliable, authoritative, and powerful antipatent campaigner of all, however, was the engineer, arms manufacturer, and inventor Sir William Armstrong (1810–1900). Armstrong was an iconic figure of high Victorian imperial invention (fig. 10.1). Legends circulated about him, in the way that they did figures like Watt or Isaac Newton. The press pronounced him a "wizard," and he was said to have proved his inventive genius as a child to Robert Stephenson by building mechanical models. Originally trained as a lawyer, Armstrong had become an engineer in the 1840s, inventing and building hydraulic cranes for dockyards. Then the Crimean War revealed woeful deficiencies in Britain's artillery, which was still using guns similar to those of the Napoleonic era. Armstrong saw a chance to capitalize. He rapidly developed a new design of cannon. With a breech-loading mechanism and a rifled barrel, the Armstrong gun promised a radical advance (fig. 10.2). He secured a contract with the navy, on the basis of which he rapidly accrued a vast fortune. He then went on to supply many of the world's other powers too, with heavy weapons built at his vast Elswick works near Newcastle (fig. 10.3). At the end of the century he would employ twenty-five thousand workers there, and his hydraulic devices would be central to the development of the Royal Navy's turreted dreadnoughts. He ploughed part of his wealth into a magnificent hydroelectric-powered mansion in Northumberland. Named Cragside, it was an astonishing edifice—an industrial Neuschwanstein. It was the single most ambitious private architectural expression ever built of high

FIGURE 10.1. Sir William Armstrong (First Lord Armstrong of Cragside). Portrait by Henry Hetherington Emmerson (1831–95), Cragside. Reprinted by permission of The National Trust Photograph Library. The Armstrong Collection (acquired through the National Land Fund and transferred to The National Trust in 1977), © NTPL/Derrick E. Witty.

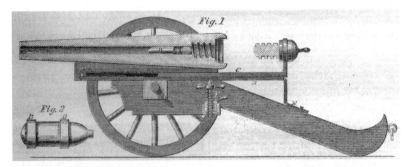

FIGURE 10.2. The Armstrong gun. *Scientific American*, n.s., 1, no. 1 (July 2, 1859): 16. Courtesy of the University of Chicago Library.

FIGURE 10.3. A huge machinery shop at Elswick. "The Elswick Ship-Building Yard. VII," *The Navy and Army Illustrated* 6, no. 73 (June 25, 1898): 314–16, at 314. Courtesy of the University of Chicago Library.

Victorian scientific-industrial enterprise (fig. 10.4). With Armstrong on their side, the antipatent campaigners boasted one of the most charismatic personifications of industrial invention. But he was also one of the most controversial—for there was another side to his story of wizardry, entrepreneurship, and perseverance, as the ensuing debates would reveal all too clearly.[29]

But Armstrong, Grove, and MacFie were only the leaders of a movement that had representatives in every class, region, and profession. Laissez-faire ultras, many of them veterans from Cobden's anti–Corn Law campaign, were one constituency; Ricardo was one of these, and another J. E. Thorold Rogers, professor of political economy at Oxford and of economic science and statistics at King's College, London. Such figures created a political economy of antipatenting. And powerful allies arose in the legal, manufacturing, engineering, and scientific fields too. In the law, Sir Roundell Palmer, soon to be solicitor general and lord chancellor, was a somewhat wavering supporter. Glasgow manufacturer James Stirling

FIGURE 10.4. Cragside. Reprinted by permission of National Trust Photograph Library. © NTPL/ Rupert Truman.

represented the manufacturers. Isambard Kingdom Brunel, the greatest of all Victorian engineers, came forward to make that profession's case for abolition. And J. A. Wanklyn, professor of chemistry at the London Institution, represented the "men of science" by maintaining that patents were obstructing science itself.

More broadly, antipatent arguments were rehearsed in countless forums across the country, and in the press too. Literary and philosophical societies and mechanics' institutes held debates, and then petitioned Parliament for reform or, less frequently, outright abolition. Many chambers of commerce did likewise; MacFie's in Liverpool was an especially prominent voice for abandoning patents altogether as equivalent to a lottery. In most cases such bodies were split on the issue, however, with abolitionists proving a vocal minority of around 30–50 percent. The National Association of Chambers of Commerce held a whole day's debate on the issue in 1864, which revealed it too to be divided. So was the Institution of Civil Engineers, although its president, William Cubitt, favored abolition. Its counterpart body of mechanical engineers heard a highly controversial statement of the case for abolition by Armstrong, who was its president in 1861. MacFie also appeared frequently at the National Association for the Promotion of Social Science, founded in 1857 on a similar model to the BAAS, and the Society of Arts, which charged a committee with exploring the issues.[30] Meanwhile Rogers made another strong abolitionist statement to the London Statistical Society in 1863.

Most notably of all, perhaps, the BAAS now returned to the fray, probably because of the growing presence in its ranks of civil and mechanical engineers. MacFie himself addressed the Association, of which he was a member. And in 1863, at a key moment in the national debate, Armstrong even served as the BAAS's president. He duly took the opportunity once again to regale its members with his own, almost miasmatic account of creativity. It bears interesting comparison to the organicism of Kant and the earlier Romantics: "As in the vegetable kingdom fit conditions of soil and climate quickly cause the appearance of suitable plants, so in the intellectual world fitness of time and circumstances promptly calls forth appropriate devices. The seeds of invention exist, as it were, in the air, ready to germinate whenever suitable conditions arise; and no legislative interference is needed to ensure their growth in proper season." Whereas for Englightenment figures like Kant an organic account of creativity had upheld a strong notion of authorship, for Armstrong a discrete kind of organicism implied the very opposite. (Evidently, Brewster acidly replied, for the great arms magnate inventions were "the result of something floating in the air, a kind of epidemic.") Propelled by the controversial reception that such addresses encountered, the Association promptly created a succession of committees of its own devoted to the patents question, with contributors including Grove, MacFie, and Armstrong, as well as

Henry Bessemer, Lyon Playfair, and William Siemens from the pro-patent camp.[31]

The antipatent campaign also made the most of the press. The *Economist* was a reliable ally, and all the major quarterlies published papers detailing their positions. Furthermore, MacFie circulated many of the speeches, papers, letters, and debates that he and his allies authored, in the form of fat printed volumes.[32] These books were deliberate experiments in their own right in the manipulation of authorship. They comprised slanted compilations of material drawn from all over the country and beyond. For example, MacFie included extensive extracts from Henry C. Carey's American arguments against international copyright. And he even helped himself to a translation of Kant's argument against counterfeiting, which here was pressed into service in the opposite cause of *eliminating* authorial property.[33] Each of these volumes was sold at five shillings, a price low enough that "all classes of the community" might be able to buy them for circulation among their neighbors and through their associations. A hundred copies were set aside to be distributed gratis to public libraries. Moreover, MacFie positively exhorted readers to extract and reprint whatever they needed of their contents, as long as they acknowledged the original sources—that is, the sources from which he himself had taken them. "The Compiler feels that he has dealt very freely with what he has found in various quarters," he conceded, "and craves that the same liberty shall be taken with what he here presents."[34] Like Mathew Carey's, this was a new kind of polemical publishing—avowedly "open source," to put it anachronistically—that had few precedents outside the demimonde of radical politics.

The abolitionist campaign found converts very rapidly. Perhaps most striking of the early ones was the very sponsor of the 1851 bill in the upper house, Lord Granville. Granville now announced in Parliament that he had been persuaded by the critics: there was no "absolute innate right of property in ideas," and Britain no longer needed to pursue a "bargain" between inventor and public to stimulate making and revealing inventions. The whole patent system was, he concluded, "unadvisable for the public, disadvantageous to inventors, and wrong in principle."[35] More conversions followed when the administration changed and what had been a Whig measure became a Tory one. By 1862 a Royal Commission could produce a remarkably ambivalent report, culminating in a much-quoted remark that the flaws of the system were intrinsic to the very nature of patenting. Its chairman, Lord Stanley, moved to an abolitionist position too. Then, at the most damaging of moments, a scandal hit the Patents Office when a clerk was accused of embezzling fees; the outcry reached high enough to force the resignation of the lord chancellor himself. At much this point the *Times* also executed a sharp volte-face and declared against patenting. It was this conversion, more than any other single event, that convinced many that the entire system faced imminent destruction. The real choice, it suddenly seemed, lay between radical reform and outright abolition. And many, including now the *Times,* not only preferred abolition but thought it inevitable.

Why this dramatic upsurge of support? The antipatent case rested on a number of claims about invention and the inventor, and about their place in industrial society, that many in Victorian Britain could recognize. Most fundamentally, it involved a commitment to an understanding of invention (and of progress more broadly) as being gradualist, collective, and methodical in nature. The antipatent camp insisted that invention was a process of reasoning, or of rule following. Almost anyone could, in principle, be an inventor, by following methods that in a modern industrial society like Britain were widely understood. Inventors were not heroes at all, but everymen. Had Watt not built his steam engine, someone else would surely have made its equivalent before long. And the inventor, like the scientific discoverer, drew on a universal reservoir of knowledge—one that was available to all, "like air, or light." This shared field of knowledge resembled a commons. And a radical distinction had to be made between the act of mechanical or chemical invention, utilizing this commons, and the act of literary or artistic authorship. The distinction was clear, MacFie and his allies claimed, from the fact that simultaneous or near-simultaneous invention was by no means a rare event, whereas the very idea of simultaneous authorship was absurd. Almost every significant invention since the printing press had been claimed by several rivals; by contrast, it was ridiculous to imagine that any two authors could have "invented" the *Divine Comedy.*

According to the abolition camp, industrial-age humans in general (although not all humans in all ages) possessed a built-in urge to invent. There was therefore no need for a patents regime to stimulate them. If anything, the system risked overstimulating the inventive faculty, and leading unwary artisans into excessive speculation, monomania, debt, and ruin. This contention reflected a proclaimed commitment—one common to both abolitionists and defenders—to the so-called workman-inventor. This much-debated figure was reputedly each side's major intended beneficiary. The main problem was distinguishing genuine worker-inventors from "schemers." The latter were workers who rashly neglected their vocations in a quest to develop a single, spectacularly successful invention to lift them out of poverty at one stroke. The patenting system, abolitionists claimed, encouraged this gambling mentality, which all too often led only to the workhouse. Isambard Kingdom Brunel was particularly outspoken on this theme. Even when such figures did create genuinely patent-worthy inventions, they were said to find themselves locked into a "racing system" to get a patent, competing with unscrupulous rivals who would do anything to appropriate their achievements. In those circumstances, should the patent system really encourage the unrealistic belief that inventing could substitute for a profession, or a business?

The antipatent campaigners historicized this account of invention and progress. They typically claimed not that inventing *was* (in and of itself) a cumulative, collective, and methodical process, but that it had *become* one. Grove, for example, conceded that patents had been broadly successful "in the earlier period of the history of invention," but claimed to see "fundamental objections to its efficient working in the present state of civilisation." "In an early period, when the patent law first grew into existence, inventive genius was rare," he explained. "Now the case is widely different; inventors are so numerous, the progress of physical science has made such vast strides, that it is, at all events with regard to a great number of inventions, a question only of weeks or months when an invention is to be made." Modern inventing had come into being only with the development of modern scientific methods and rapid communications by steamship, railway, and telegraph. This implied a quasi-positivist account of history, in terms of progressive stages. Patents might have been useful once—so those who revered the 1624 Monopolies Act as a major step in political progress were not wrong—but a modern industrial nation had left them behind. It not only had no more need of patents, but would in fact be impeded by them. If British industry were not to decline—a threat that all sides commonly represented as imminent—then the nation needed to extend the principles of laissez-faire and free trade to the realm of creativity. It must cut the "tax" of patent royalties as fast as, or faster than, its rivals.

Patents were therefore charged with several offenses at once. They projected an artificial idol of the single inventor, radically denigrated the role of the intellectual commons, and blocked a path to this commons for other citizens—citizens who were all, on this account, potential inventors too. They thereby denied the progressive character of industrial society. Patentees were the equivalent of squatters on public land—or, better, of uncouth market traders who planted their barrows in the middle of the highway and barred the way of the people.[36]

The question of the inventor, finally, led straight to a corollary that was less often voiced explicitly but remained critically important nonetheless. Where did "the public" stand—and what was "the" public anyway? Defenders of patents had claimed that they represented a bargain between inventor and public, such that the inventor got protection for a limited period in return for not just making the invention but revealing it, and giving it to the public at the end of that period. In that light, a patent was not an untrammeled private property held in defiance of the public, as MacFie liked to say, but actually *included* a public interest. But abolitionists denied that this was true in practice. To them, the interest of the patentee was in practice dominant. Patentees were under no obligation to charge reasonable royalty rates, after all, nor indeed to issue licenses at all. Some even preyed on existing manufactures. They acted, in short, as monopolists. The abolitionists claimed that the public interest was being eroded drastically, as property rights were proclaimed across more and more of the intellectual landscape encompassed by the industrial arts. At the very least, some representative of the public should be introduced into any process determining the granting and contestation of patents. Henry Dircks tackled such claims head-on in his *Inventors and Inventions,* published in 1867 as a direct riposte to the antipatent campaign and dedicated to Bessemer "as an Inventor and Patentee." The abolitionists' references to the public referred, he said, "not to the *public* at large, but to the manufacturers of Sheffield wares and Birmingham wares." No member of the general public was inconvenienced by patents, "for it is to patents that the public are indebted for many luxuries and necessities unknown to our forefathers."[37] Replies like this suggested that rival definitions of the public were in operation, but the abolitionist camp at first simply disdained such distinctions.

If patents were abolished, however, what would replace them? Some, like Grove in his more sanguine moments, wanted nothing at all, favoring what they saw as a true free trade in intellectual talents and products.

Their bracing view was that the worker in a manufacturing plant who came up with a genuine improvement would always be rewarded by an enlightened capitalist; if he were not, he would become much more valuable to competitors, and would find his proper place in the intellectual marketplace. This was very much Brunel's view too. Empirical evidence in its favor was, it must be said, sketchy. And, perhaps for that reason, MacFie himself was not prepared to go so far. He wanted patents replaced by a system of rewards—both honors and cash "bounties"—to be awarded to worthy inventors by the state. He reckoned that such a system would be far cheaper to administer, and would avoid all the perils of monopoly that came with patents. As we have seen, Brewster had long wanted the state to create something of this kind, although he wanted it to supplement patenting, not supplant it.

What was convincing about all this, in the end, was its conviction and sweep as social theory. It allied the worker-artisan, the public, and the new nature of science and technology, tying all of them to the doctrines of political economy. And out of the mix it conjured a kind of utopia. Should the campaign fall short of absolute success, moreover, the abolitionists were prepared to countenance intermediate steps on the way to their promised freedom. The most noteworthy—although MacFie was reluctant to endorse it wholly—was for so-called *compulsory licensing*. This idea seems to have originated as a serious proposition in the 1830s, although predecessors can be traced back into the eighteenth century. The idea was that, after a few years of exclusivity, a patentee would be obliged to grant licenses to all who requested them, at a royalty rate decreed by a government agency. In fact, the British government already practiced a kind of compulsory licensing for itself, in the sphere of military procurement. Having found patentees' demands excessive, since the Crimean War the War Ministry had insisted on setting its own royalty rates. More than that, it often effectively laid aside the "rights" of patentees—including, significantly enough, Armstrong's. By what hypocrisy, the abolitionist side asked, could the state adopt such tactics for itself while denying them to the citizenry? Compulsory licensing schemes of one kind or another (generally rather vaguely worked out) were therefore examined by almost every inquiry to look at patents, and the BAAS recommended that they be adopted. The most plausible version was one identified with a MacFie ally, engineer John Scott Russell, that was modeled on the monopolies that Parliament gave to railway companies on certain routes. In return for exclusive rights, rail companies guaranteed to run trains for working passengers, at appropriate times and affordable fares. Russell proposed that this principle of access and maximal pricing be adopted for patents too.[38] But no compulsory licensing policy was in fact adopted until after the end of the century, and even then on a very limited scale. The biggest pitfall was held to be the need to evaluate inventions' worth in order to assign a royalty rate. This, it was thought, presented insurmountable problems of equity and epistemology, since nobody could predict the value of an invention ahead of the market. Russell's idea therefore went nowhere—but it would be resurrected, as we shall see, by a later and altogether shiftier "king of the pirates."

THE INVENTORS' INSTITUTE AND THE
INVENTION OF INTELLECTUAL PROPERTY

The appropriation of free trade political economy to an antipatenting cause was not inevitable. All of the principal earlier political economists had been prepared to reconcile free trade and laissez-faire doctrines with an endorsement of patenting, even if some had done so through gritted philosophical teeth. Adam Smith had done this, as had the elder Ricardo, Bentham, Babbage, and McCulloch. John Stuart Mill maintained this position into the 1860s. Mill spoke out briefly but strongly: to abolish patents, he declared, would "enthrone free stealing under the prostituted name of free trade." It would leave "men of brains" helpless in the face of "men of money-bags."[39] These positions, as much moral and class based as political or economic, would eventually become the basis for a desperate and determined defense of patenting.

The strength of the movement to abolish patents came as a surprise. Defenders of patenting were slow to mobilize. But at length a small band, determined to stem the tide, convened a body that they christened the Inventors' Institute to fight back. The Institute's moving force was none other than the now aged Sir David Brewster. Brewster's nostalgic remarks in these years about his failed early plans for the BAAS sometimes seemed to imply that he thought of the new Institute as everything he had always wanted that earlier body to be. At first it had only three members. But by 1866 that had grown to five hundred, and it was angling to become a permanent chartered body, to stand alongside the Royal Society and the BAAS as a new trinity at the pinnacle of British science and technology. (1866 was also the year that saw the founding of the first English university research laboratories in experimental physics, in Oxford and London; ten such laboratories would appear by 1874, to pursue this industrially consequential science.) It launched its own journal, the *Scientific Review*, which Brewster employed liberally to assail the abolitionists. Significantly enough, he often did so in language lifted directly from his articles of more than thirty years before: the lines about the patent laws being "vicious and fraudulent" and turning legal officials into a "banditti," for example, returned verbatim. In every monthly issue the *Scientific Review* carried on the fight. For example, it lamented the Admiralty's decision to appropriate patented weaponry under a compulsory license scheme as a form of "Fourierism" that threatened to justify state robbery in general. It saw this as heralding a concerted campaign to abolish patents on the quiet, and warned that more than half the patents commonly supposed to exist had already been quietly obliterated.[40]

Brewster and the *Scientific Review* did not argue that the patents system should be preserved unchanged. On the contrary, he called it a "monster evil," that taxed genius and submitted it to the whims of "utterly incompetent" judges. It needed "radical change." But whereas the abolitionists thought it a burden on the public that must be swept away, Brewster and his allies thought that what made it evil was precisely its weakness and expense to the inventor; they wanted it strengthened and its reach extended. They maintained a view of the issue that was if anything higher and more uncompromising than anything deemed plausible since 1774. Inventors, they held, had a *natural* right to their inventions; so too, they sometimes added, did "men of science" to their discoveries—that is, researchers should be able to patent facts. Because of the risk of "pirates," this right should get legal protection for at least twenty-one years, and preferably the inventor's lifetime. It should be obtainable without any fee at all, like copyright protection. Once ratified by a scientific panel, it should be "absolutely secured" from legal challenge. And it should be sustained across the entire empire. Civilization itself was at stake. Brewster ventured into an apocalyptic mode to make that point. "Withdraw from circulation the secular productions of the press that are hoarded in all the libraries of the world," he argued, "and society will hardly suffer from the change. Withdraw the gifts with which art and science have enriched us—the substantial realities through which we live, and move, and enjoy our being—and society collapses into barbarism."[41]

The fundamental stance of the *Scientific Review,* however, was that intellectual creativity, whether literary, scientific, or technological, was essentially *one thing.* It therefore merited equal treatment whatever its manifestation—and that treatment was the strong, readily obtainable protection exemplified by copyright. The magazine reprinted Trollope's call for international copyright with the United States, for example, not because it wanted to enter that particular battle, but because it wanted to demonstrate that Trollope's cause was essentially the same as its own. "Viewing all intellectual rights as equal," Brewster proclaimed, "and regarding them as sacred and unalienable as any other species of property, we maintain that they should be put upon the same footing." The *Scientific Review* in fact—along with like-minded organs such as *The Engineer*—became one of the very first forums in which a reader could consistently encounter references to such a universal and uniform kind of property that existed across media. It called this entity, in Brewster's own words, "intellectual property."[42] And "intellectual property," according to the *Review,* must be as sacrosanct in the new industrial economy as landed property had been in earlier, agrarian societies. Copyrights and patents alike should therefore ideally be absolute and perpetual. And a threat to either imperiled both.

The *Scientific Review*'s rhetoric against abolitionists was correspondingly uncompromising. The magazine denounced Armstrong in person as "traitorous," while MacFie was "the arch-enemy." Another man convinced by the abolitionist case was labeled a "pervert" (a term carrying the same overtones then as now). And the magazine increasingly cast the whole struggle—which it defined as one over intellectual property in general—in the strongest political terms. Brewster declared that violating this "property" would be akin to the monarch violating Magna Carta. It would therefore legitimize "extreme resistance"—a very charged phrase, on which he did not dilate. Elsewhere, he added that MacFie's proposed alternative of a bounty scheme was akin to a proposal to reform the system of political representation by returning to the pre-1832 reign of rotten boroughs.[43]

Brewster's journal buttressed such assertions by developing an alternative political economy of invention that turned the arguments of the abolitionists on their heads. According to this scheme, the patentee was the real free trader. The real monopolists, therefore, were the "great capitalist manufacturers" like Armstrong and MacFie. Like all monopolists, these magnates feared new competition—competition that might well come from the brains of inventors. Indeed, according to the *Review,* what inventors *did*—their essential nature—was to "break down the monopoly of capital." That was the core of their progressive function in civilization. The magazine defined that function in class terms. The magazine stood, it declared, for the "workman inventor" in particular. Such a figure needed secure property if he were to fulfill his antimonopolist function. "If the security of brain-craft property should be taken away by the abolition of patents," the journal warned, "this work would cease, and stagnation would be the rule." And then, it added, "we should have a tendency to become Chinese." It was therefore the inventors who were "the true advocates of free trade." By contrast, the line of MacFie, Grove, and Armstrong was antagonistic to all property. It amounted to "the wildest socialism," if not the philosophy of Bill Sykes. The sympathy they so frequently expressed for worker-inventors was "crocodilian." A Dr. Thomas Richardson supplied one of the strongest evocations. "If the truth be told," Richardson averred, "this opposition of capital against the patent laws is closely allied to the battle which now agitates most communities, under the more familiar title of *Capital* versus *Labour,* and might be properly termed the claims of *Brains* versus *Capital.*" He quoted an iron manufacturer to the effect that "'brains are more abundant in the world than capital, and ought, therefore, to be had cheap.'" As ever, Sir William Armstrong was his exemplary case. When it came to Armstrong, indeed, the charge carried new force in the 1860s, because his giant enterprise was seeing its first major industrial strife, as a relative glut of engineers encouraged his personal decision to dismiss some 2,700 striking experts. (It suggests something about Armstrong's style that the foreign labor he hired to replace the strikers soon went over to their side.) In the end, the journal announced, the abolitionists' case came down to the stark message conveyed by Armstrong's management at Elswick: "Labour, whether mental or physical, is to be the slave of Capital." That was a doctrine that could lead only to "rabid communism and uncompromising revolution."[44]

ARMS AND THE WORKMAN

Who were these alleged "pirates" against whom patents protected the worker-inventor? It was here that defenders of patenting pulled out a trump card. They identified the pirate king as Sir William Armstrong himself.

Pro-patent campaigners had long singled out Armstrong as the eminence grise behind the whole abolitionist movement. MacFie might have
been its most loquacious protagonist, but he had none of Armstrong's
prestige as an inventor in his own right. Recognizing the authority that
Armstrong wielded by virtue of his renown, they therefore increasingly
sought to defile and destroy that image. Having profited by patents himself, they charged, he now sought to deny others the chance to do so.
Worse still, they accused him of preaching what he practiced: for this was
a man who, far from coming up with his own inventions, had in reality
made his fortune as a "compiler of other men's." The *Telegraph* quipped
that he was adept at more than one kind of rifling. He had stolen the inventions of Whitworth and Krupp, *Scientific American* charged, "without
scruple, or even the polite 'thank you, sir' of the highwayman." *The Engineer*
likewise devoted several editorials not only to a rebuttal of Armstrong's
arguments but also to a demolition of his reputation as an inventor. Far
from being one of the country's greatest inventors, it concluded, Armstrong had invented "nothing; absolutely nothing." To count him an inventor was "an injustice to the great body of inventors," to whom he was
in fact a deadly enemy. His whole reputation and fortune were built on
"plagiarisms." Not content with "appropriating the ideas of others right
and left," concurred *Scientific American,* Armstrong was now seeking to
"have the larceny legalized by the world."[45]

In particular, the *Engineer* and like-minded organs asserted the claim
of a Royal Artillery captain, Alexander Theophilus Blakely, to be the real
inventor of the rifled cannon. To see the point of this, one needs to return
briefly to Armstrong's own history, and especially to his recourse to it as a
kind of mythic foundation for his antipatenting claims. Armstrong liked
to say that it was Brunel's withdrawal from his artillery experiments that
had given rise to his own convictions against patents. As he told the BAAS
in 1861—in a speech repeatedly interrupted by applause—the two had
found their work obstructed by a patent that an opportunistic rival had
filed only a few weeks earlier. This patentee stood to deny the British
public the benefits of their experiments. The experience demonstrated,
Armstrong said, the "impolicy and injustice" implicit in a regime that gave
a monopoly to whichever claimant happened to get to the patent office
first. And he claimed to have found that the example was representative,
because, as he put it, "similarity of circumstances will constantly suggest
similar ideas to different minds." A contract he had later won for a set of

railway wheels, for example, had been blocked by another patent, this time one filed fourteen years earlier and left dormant ever since. A patents system not only subjected inventors to a race in which the winner took all, but provided an opportunity for avaricious projectors of "schemes"— "pen-and-ink inventors," as he called them—to extort money from real inventors, or even to block inventions from appearing. "This readiness to give protection to mere schemes is the bane of the system."[46]

In endorsing Blakely, the pro-patenting camp was challenging head-on this story of Armstrong's, and hence both his image as the wizard inventor and his fable of patenting in general. Blakely was in fact the patentee complained of by Armstrong as having stopped his and Brunel's experiments. Far from obstructing their work, however, he and his supporters produced old correspondence indicating that he had offered to facilitate it. Having independently invented a weapon virtually identical to what became the Armstrong gun, he had wanted to submit it to military trials, and, it seemed, had approached Armstrong with a request to build a gun to his design. Armstrong had allegedly entertained the idea, but then declined, only to proceed with his own virtually identical cannon. When Blakely wrote to request royalties, Armstrong had immediately filed a patent claim with trivial differences that, as Blakely put it, seemed designed solely to "evade the words of my patent." Blakely had thought of suing, only to be warned off by government officials. According to his camp, therefore, it had been Blakely who had been stymied, and not just by a patent but by Armstrong's corrupt resort to influence in high places.[47] His company had been forced to give up on Britain and sell its guns instead to powers like Japan and China. Meanwhile Armstrong handed over his patents to the state, which kept them secret, and he became superintendent of the Royal Gun Factory and the government's engineer for rifled ordnance. He served in these positions until February 1863, enjoying substantial oversight of the testing of his own and rivals' guns. At the artillery range in Shoeburyness, military officials dealt with "inventors" every day—a class of whom even journalist Patrick Barry, who wrote an exposé of the range's management, remarked, "I have always found it prudent to disbelieve them in nearly all they said." But Barry charged that it was the behemoth of Armstrong (and, to a lesser extent, the other great Victorian arms magnate, Sir Joseph Whitworth) that forced the "struggling inventor" into deceit and subterfuge. The military and Armstrong himself, Barry reported, made a practice of rejecting any invention submitted to their testing, only to appropriate to themselves any that were in fact worthwhile. Armstrong, in short, regarded inventions either as challenges to be suppressed or as raw materials out of which to "cobble" together his own designs. Even his original patents had derived from research subsidized by the state, and as such "ought to be public property."[48]

Authors in both Britain and America were thus not slow to accuse Armstrong of using his position to waste public money on his own, allegedly inferior, artillery solely to protect himself against rivals like Blakely and a whole class of "inventors" in gunnery. In other words, he was the true monopolist—and, at the same time, the true pirate, reigning over an institution that provided him with an endless stream of new ideas to seize upon. Patentees, by contrast, were brave individual inventors (even if their businesses were in fact large and sophisticated) who in general tested monopolists. Armstrong's cynical treatment of inventors in the patent struggle reflected his contemptuous exploitation of them on an everyday basis at Shoeburyness. In the heat of the antipatent campaign, Blakely himself even took to turning up at occasions where Armstrong was due to speak—including the BAAS in 1861—and publicly heckling him. Each time he did, he sparked loud and passionate exchanges.[49]

Others too now came to light who had patented similar guns before Armstrong. Foremost among them was a Harvard engineer, Daniel Treadwell, who had built and patented a gun to a similar design in the 1840s. Details of his design had been distributed to British military officials in 1848, and the patent itself had been published in 1854, shortly before Armstrong's own appearance on the scene. Treadwell entertained no doubt as to what had occurred. He told the U.S. secretary of war in 1860 that Armstrong's gun was "a close imitation" of his own. He enterprisingly turned Armstrong's "denunciation of patents" before the BAAS—the speech that Blakely had attended—against its author. That speech proved, Treadwell pointed out, that Armstrong was thoroughly versed in the archive of patents. He therefore must have known of Treadwell's own earlier filing. On this basis he flatly accused Armstrong of theft, and called upon Britain's engineers to repudiate his "piracy."

By the mid-1860s, then, Treadwell, Blakely, and the pro-patenting camp had created a countermyth of Sir William Armstrong. According to this countermyth he was not an inventor at all, let alone a wizard, but a corrupt oligarch of the old school. Armstrong reigned supreme only in his piratical dominion over what was one of the defining industries of the age.

At this moment the patents controversy came to a head. In 1868 Mac-Fie was elected to Parliament amid a general victory for Gladstone's Liberals. He was now in a position to pursue the cause of abolishing patents in Westminster itself. This was the first general election in which all male householders could vote, a fact that MacFie regarded as confirming his mandate for radical change. He swiftly introduced a bill for abolition, supported by Stanley and his ally Roundell Palmer, now the attorney general. The immediate consequence was another round of impassioned debate. As well as the Inventors' Institute, the Institution of Mechanical Engineers, another relatively new body, also now campaigned against abolition. Petitions arrived from many provincial associations too. With reform and abolition locked in contest, the battleground became very confused. Several groups well disposed to patents actually campaigned against reform bills, suspecting them to be stalking horses for the abolitionists. And yet another round of inquiries commenced.[50] This one, however, in a bid to deal with the conflict once and for all, took a much wider remit than its predecessors. It was charged with considering not just how best to administer a patent system, but whether such a system should be maintained at all. And abolitionists were well represented on it, with William Robert Grove participating alongside Palmer, Armstrong, and MacFie. The *Scientific Review* feared that it was stacked against the inventors — who were, it pointed out, almost completely unrepresented.[51] The end of intellectual property, it warned, was in sight.

But the 1871 and 1872 inquiries did hear from two very prominent engineers. Both were immigrants. Henry Bessemer (a contributor to the Inventors' Institute) and William Siemens were extraordinarily important figures in the steel and engineering industries, and both testified to the importance of the patents system in enticing people like them into Britain from overseas.[52] At a time of renewed concern about the emigration of skilled workers, this testimony packed a very powerful rhetorical punch. On the other side, the arguments of MacFie and his allies proved vulnerable when empirical evidence of actual hardship caused by patents was demanded. Their campaign waxed indignant about patentees' obstructionism, but when confronted with Bessemer and Siemens, MacFie failed to point to concrete, empirical instances of either suppression or extortionate royalty demands. The antipatent case suddenly seemed to rest on a rather abstract extrapolation from political-economic theory. MacFie was ultimately maneuvered into admitting that he was seeking legislation to forestall problems that were more theoretical possibilities than actual, documented issues.

The same modernization and bureaucratization that had triggered the abolition campaign in the first place also counted against it now. The background labors of Woodcroft—who was an inventor as well as clerk to the Commissioners of Patents—were of critical importance. He had by now catalogued the previously unusable masses of patents, collected thousands of models, and instituted regular filing, indexing, and printing routines. For the first time, the patents regime became a usable archive. It did for the realm of invention and the public something like what Oldenburg had done for that of experiment and a much smaller community two centuries earlier. Along with the publishing of treatises defining the field and the chartering of patent agents, these measures made patenting a routine convention, imbued with moral as well as economic value for a large and growing community.[53]

Still, patenting might well have ended but for the general election of 1874. The election saw Disraeli's Conservatives replace the Liberals in government. MacFie lost his bid for reelection, and Palmer moved to the Lords. Overnight, the Commons therefore lost the two most active proponents of abolition. And the agenda of the new government was toward imperial consolidation and domestic social reform, not patent legislation. Eventually, in 1883, a new law did pass, but it was a law for the reformers, not the abolitionists. That law marked the passing of a generation when patenting might have ended and free trade in knowledge established in law. MacFie and his allies continued to murmur against the practice, but they recognized that without representation in the Commons there was little they could realistically do. Palmer bit his lip and endorsed the new law as a lesser evil than the status quo.

IMPERIAL PROPERTY

"We read of 'intellectual property,'" MacFie sniffed in the last of his antipatenting and anticopyright books in 1883. "Whatever else is comprehended under this name, it extends to *invention*."[54] But it already extended much further than that, as he well knew. It united invention with literary and artistic creativity, and, indeed, with industrial and corporate symbols in the form of trademarks, by providing an underpinning concept. One could now say that invention and authorship were tied together as aspects of intellectual property. That was the point of the concept. And by sub-suming these previously disparate areas of law under the same conceptual identity, it paved the way for the multiplication of protections that the twentieth century would create.

Yet MacFie ended this last volume by drawing attention to a different way in which "intellectual property" extended previous conventions. It not only made them conceptually deeper and wider, but also underpinned their extension across geographical space. In the 1880s, just as the anti-patenting campaign faltered in Britain, two great international conferences took place, at Paris and Berne, that would set in train the international harmonization of "intellectual property" that has proceeded ever since. It was therefore both fitting and challenging that MacFie's book ended by posing the problem of the relation between this new kind of property and global politics. But it did so in a political context distinct from those of Paris and Berne, albeit one more closely related than we tend now to remember. MacFie's grandiose peroration was imperial, not European. It called for a radical reconstruction of the entire British Empire.

We tend to forget this now, but in the high Victorian era, before the race for Africa really got going, it was not self-evident to Britons them-selves that the empire was worth preserving. Doctrinaire advocates of Manchester school political economy were not particularly inclined to see any rationale for colonies. In a free trade world, Britain, as the globe's greatest manufacturer, would continue to export goods whether or not colonies remained under its control. People would continue to want the cheapest products, and those came from the United Kingdom's factories. At the same time, colonies drained British resources because they had to be defended against attacks by rival powers. This made for a hugely demand-ing worldwide burden on the Royal Navy, at a time when it was spending heavily on rearmament (with Armstrong guns, very often). Furthermore, it was not clear why the colonists should want a continued imperial con-nection, since it made them tempting targets. Around mid-century, there-fore, Whitehall made a number of moves to reduce the British military commitment to the colonies and to require colonial administrations to fund their own defense. And highly placed London politicians made state-ments that the ties between colony and metropole were entirely volun-tary. Any colony that desired to leave the empire could do so on amicable terms. The combination seemed to imperialists to carry a clear message: that the empire was a fragile and friendless entity soon to dissolve.

The empire itself was apparently in peril. Proposals to shore it up began to appear in response. Those proposals soon coalesced around a concept first articulated in the *Quarterly Review* in 1853: that of "imperial federation." This was a proposal—the details of which varied widely—to reconfigure the empire as a single polity, centered on an assembly or council to convene in London. This would be a new body altogether, sitting atop the British parliament, that would deal with issues of imperial scope: war and peace, treaties, and common legal systems. The idea made little headway at first. As late as 1868, Gladstone's government was inclined to be skeptical about the worth of the colonies. But in the early 1870s it rather suddenly revived as a serious political possibility, principally because events overseas seemed to converge on a demonstration that federation was the path of the future. The Prussian defeat of France, followed by the creation of a federal German Empire, was one powerful signal. Another was the unification of Italy. A third was the victory of the North in the American Civil War. The first and last of these created powerful international rivals, both of them federal in structure.[55] Moreover, the development of telegraphy and efficient steamships meant that communication with Australia was now potentially as rapid as it had been with Britain's own provinces at the time of union in 1707. At the same time, Britain fell into an economic slump that called into question earlier assumptions of prolonged industrial dominance. Calls consequently began to be heard for free trade policies to be qualified.

In the midst of such events, MacFie became the first politician to propose imperial federation in Parliament.[56] He recommended that all the colonies must be represented alongside the home country in a single Council of State, which could bring political unity to the empire. But what would ensure that this unity ran deeper than politics? MacFie announced that only the abolition of "intellectual property" could meet that imperative need. By building a publishing industry that sold large editions cheaply, rather than, as the London publishers then did, small ones at high prices, the empire could be saturated with literature. Abolishing copyright would "let British literature diffuse itself naturally and acceptably throughout the Empire, the mother country becoming at length, what easily it may be rendered, the grand fountain-head of useful information and wholesome influences, from which the whole family draws refreshment."[57]

MacFie now returned to his magpie mode of authorship, issuing collections of materials in favor of an imperial federation that would extend and complete the unfinished project of a United Kingdom. An "imperial representative council" should be created to serve as the legislative and executive body for the empire as a whole. In effect, MacFie's proposal was to create a "United States of the Britannic Empire," along the lines of the United States of America. This created a potential problem akin to that faced by Mathew Carey in America, of creating unity out of diversity. For MacFie and the imperialists, however, the answer was organic (that is, racial) as well as public. "We should feel, and speak, and act," he declared, "*everywhere* as *one people.*" The colonies should coalesce into one body, populated by emigration from Britain. And in this light he tied his continuing distaste for copyright and the patents system to his new imperial polity. Settler colonists should become full citizens in every sense, he insisted; but to achieve that Britain must destroy "the copyright monopoly, a monopoly which appears to neutralise the statesmanlike policy of sending the healthy throb of vivifying influence from the nation's heart in the largest possible measure to its remotest extremities."[58] And in manufactures, similarly, he called not for free trade, now, but for "*fair* trade." That is, he demanded "a small import duty on manufactures, to give a slight tilt to the safe side," in compensation for the "invention taxes" that patents represented.[59] Short of some radical reconfiguration to politics and intellectual property, he warned, the colonies would surely secede and the empire collapse. "There has been a portentous change," MacFie concluded darkly. "If we do not direct it aright, it will culminate in revolution."[60]

This kind of conviction—which was often frank in its espousal of racial superiority—was central to the movement for imperial federation that now appeared. By 1884 it had given rise to an Imperial Federation League, aiming at the creation of a worldwide imperial constitution based on representation, information, trade, and blood. A particularly interesting literary manifestation came from the historian J. A. Froude. Froude wholeheartedly shared the movement's rather Carlylean denunciation of the moral and physical effects of domestic industrialization. Rather than seeing large numbers of Britons escape those effects by emigrating to America, however, he wanted to see them given subsidies to move to the colonies.[61] In 1884–85 he undertook a voyage to Australia and New Zealand, returning through the United States. He published his observations as a book pointedly entitled *Oceana.* The title came from James Harrington's work of the 1650s, which had envisaged a fantasy version of England becoming an eternal "commonwealth for increase." Froude's point was that, properly organized, Victorian Britain could create Oceana in Oceania. "Anglo-Saxons" carrying "the genius of English freedom" would, he thought, bring this about by unifying these places into a single commonwealth united by an "organic and vital" tie.[62] In 1887 the first of a series of "Colonial Conferences" met in London to consider such federalist ideas, and the possibility of establishing uniformity in patents was raised. But "consciousness of national unity" was not enough to carry it, and the idea went nowhere. It continued to be raised in later conferences, but proved intractable. It was this kind of problem, as well as the more obvious issues of viability, that in the end doomed federalist imperialism. The League closed its doors in 1893.

MONKSWELL'S DEMON

In 1891, the jurist Robert Collier, Baron Monkswell, lamented the state of contemporary copyright law. It seemed, he told Parliament, as though ever since 1709 it had been "the sport of some malignant demon." The same point could have been made of patents in the Victorian period. Indeed, for much of the nineteenth century patents had been in a far worse state than copyright. But what Monkswell's remark equally implied was the extent to which coherence and logical order themselves had come to be seen as virtues intrinsic to sound law. This had not always been the case in these fields, at least. But by now it was reasonable to assert that if there was such a thing as "intellectual property"—and there was—then its legal manifestations should be consistent. Patent and copyright law should be species of this larger body, as too should be design and trademark law. Instead a mischievous sprite had seemingly rejoiced in taking what should have been a logical structure and reducing it to a confused, inchoate, self-contradictory mess.[63] Monkswell's demon was thus the legal antithesis to James Clerk Maxwell's more famous demon of 1871: it produced disorder without any visible expenditure of energy. But in the cosmos of the new, self-consciously modern legal mind, it was equally paradoxical.

This was new. The concept of "intellectual property" was a creation of the decades immediately preceding Monkswell's remark. It took a generation or more to coalesce. Those battles forced defenders of patents to articulate hitherto discrete bodies of legal doctrine as aspects of one deeper concept. They largely succeeded, but the legacy of their success was a perception that, insofar as the branches of intellectual property law and administration were inconsistent, they were also flawed. Consistency would from this point on be identified increasingly with two kinds of attribute. One was intrinsic: it had to do with the nature of invention, and with the identity of the author, inventor, or discoverer. The other was extensive: it asserted universality, across time and, more emphatically, space. The reason why the invention of intellectual property in the mid- to late nineteenth century mattered was that it brought both into contact and insisted on reconciling them.

As a result, the Victorian patent war mapped out for the first time what remains to this day our range of options relating to intellectual property. Those options extended all the way from the outright abolition of patents and copyrights to their confirmation as absolute "rights." The abolitionist case reflected laissez-faire strictures against "monopolies" of all kinds; the absolutist embraced convictions about the intrinsic justice of rewarding labor, originality, and creative genius—and insisted on a sometimes utili- tarian imperative to support creators for the sake of the common good. Between the two extremes stood many plans for mitigated property re- gimes. Some proposed compulsory license schemes, for example, which would permit others to make and distribute a creation, but compel them to pay a predetermined royalty when they did so. Others suggested some kind of state-appointed panel of experts to reward inventors for their creations. Every side laid claim to support from the nature of science, but represented that nature differently. Was the scientist a positivist revealer of God-given facts, a heroic discoverer possessed of unique genius, or an everyman laboring for meager rewards? Or was science properly a collec- tive practice in any case? And were discovery and invention heroic acts, or human ones indebted to common knowledge? The clash over such ques- tions led straight to the most contested political conceptions of the age, including free trade, colonialism, and political order.

Meanwhile, "intellectual property" became spatial, but in a different way. At root, MacFie had campaigned not so much for the abolition of copyrights and patents, but for what he called "assimilation." The idea was to harmonize such levies internationally, ideally at zero, but, if zero could not be attained, at some shared level. And so this foe of all intellec- tual property ended up becoming a respected contributor to the interna- tional movement for extending such protections across borders. Freeing them from national specificities, this movement helped solidify the very notion that both patents and copyrights were aspects of a single entity—

"intellectual property"—that transcended pragmatic and local jurisdictions. So far from being abolished, in other words, the succeeding years saw patenting embedded in international law and practice—a process that attained its authoritative expression in the Paris and Berne conventions. These remain the bases of international patent and copyright law respectively to this day. In the same way, major international meetings in the same generation promoted scientific universalism, medical procedures, and trade policies.

In the end the two countries that abolitionists had pointed to as thriving without patents gave up and fell into line. Switzerland adopted its own patent law in 1888, and modernized it in the early twentieth century. The Netherlands, which had abolished patenting in the free trade moment, created its own new patent law too. For both countries, it was not a lack of invention or innovation without patenting that forced the change. In fact the evidence was ambiguous on that score. Rather, both feared being excluded from the international club now being formed around the Berne and Paris conventions. They passed patent laws to head off that possibility. Their concession marked an epoch: the ascent of intellectual property as a species of international politics.[64]

11

International Copyright and
the Science of Civilization

In summer 1871, as the inquiries into patents reached their climax, a near-blind traveler from New York stepped quietly from the train at Euston. It was cold and rainy, and with London full of French refugees from the siege of the Communards lodging was hard to come by. He eventually found a bed in a tiny bedsit in Queen's Road. The stranger slept all of three hours before forcing himself up again and venturing forth. He immediately launched himself into an extraordinary tour of scientific luminaries. First, he went to Herbert Spencer's lodgings; they played a hurried game of billiards, then set out for the Royal Institution and John Tyndall. Thomas Henry Huxley came next. From Bain to Lubbock to Galton, the visitor went lame from the distance he walked.

What merited these labors was the chance to realize a great nineteenth-century dream: that of making the ideal of international scientific collaboration into a sustained practical reality for the first time in history. The stranger so dedicated to this vision was Edward Youmans, probably the foremost advocate of public science in contemporary America. His friend John Fiske declared Youmans the John the Baptist of the scientific era (Darwin, he thought, was its Christ). Through a long association with a huge New York publishing firm, D. Appleton and Co., he labored to ease the entry of scientific works into American culture. He edited compilations on the correlation of forces and on scientific education, as well as masterminding journals and personally lecturing on topics such as evolution and social science. Now he wanted to take the idea of a universal realm of science and make it a reality. As Herbert Spencer told him over the billiard table, Youmans's "movement" promised to "revolutionize" communication, and hence civilization itself.

The trouble was that the realities of communication were far from congenial to such an ideal. Vast problems stood in the way of any attempt to create a universal culture based in printed communication, even in the sciences. Each country had its own publishing system, and with none prepared to give ground, transnational "piracy" was a major obstacle. For Youmans, overcoming this was a matter of evolution. He was convinced that modern societies were poised to develop into a scientific stage of civilization. But the advance was currently stymied because the medium on which it depended was so riven. It was currently impossible to produce a successful work in one realm and prevent its being pirated in another, often in a cheap, disreputable, and above all unfaithful impression. The nationalism of copyright thus inhibited what Youmans called (in his own reprint of European scientists' views on education) "the culture demanded by modern life."

Youmans's plan to tackle this problem rested on establishing a vast collaboration between scientists and publishers across the major powers of the day: Britain, America, Germany, France, Italy, and Russia. In the absence of universal laws of authorship, honor would have to be made its foundation—the honor of publishers themselves. His idea was for publishers to promise to reward scientists at the rates due in their respective countries, giving an undertaking that would hold fast as a matter of civility, not law. Only in this way could a field of universal reason, long envisaged but never attained, finally come into being: a scientific spirit transcending state, nation, and language.

Youmans had proposed grand schemes before, however. None of them had borne fruit. So his reputation was one of visionary failure. Some of the scientists he met voiced doubts about his ability to succeed now, while others regretfully told him that they were already tied to publishers and could not politely break away. Given the dependence of his own plan on civility, Youmans could hardly gainsay that principle. But his labors did begin to garner support. Spencer vouchsafed a public letter extolling it. Huxley endorsed it. So did Lubbock. Tyndall volunteered a recommendation to the most prestigious scientist in the world, Helmholtz. And in mid-July Youmans got the chance to dine with Charles Darwin himself, who expressed great enthusiasm and insisted that the scheme be publicized at the BAAS's great annual jamboree in Edinburgh. Youmans and Spencer forthwith took the train for Scotland, where Huxley, Carpenter, Balfour Stewart, Bain, and Lindsay all helped spread the word. Youmans circulated a printed manifesto announcing that his scheme would offer British science "the practical benefits of an international copyright law." And at the same moment Appleton himself published a carefully worded letter in the *Times* lamenting American piracy of British ideas. Youmans left Scotland convinced that his scheme would succeed. He and Spencer sailed for Paris in search of French scientists to recruit, and Youmans then proceeded alone to Germany, where he met Helmholtz, Virchow, and DuBois-Reymond. Huxley's name carried the day, and a major German publisher and a prestigious editorial committee signed on. Elated, Youmans declared that his scheme stood ready to produce a hundred volumes.

The first of what was dubbed the "International Scientific Series" appeared soon after. Tyndall's *The Forms of Water* inaugurated what became an enduring sequence, its most famous titles being John Draper's *History of the Conflict between Religion and Science* and Spencer's own *Study of Sociology*. Spencer's work—a classic in the development of social science—was in fact the ideological keystone of the ISS, which aspired to unify science around a scheme of universal evolution. Yet Youmans had to "bully" the book out of him. That bullying reflected a continuing uncertainty about the entire project. The initiative had made Appleton some "ugly" enemies in the United States, who saw it as a Trojan horse for an internationalization of copyright. He warned Spencer that they meant to retaliate by pirating his titles — "and when that thing begins there is no knowing where it will end." The "courtesies of the trade," as Youmans called them, were real but brittle; once violated, "the spell dissolves." Sure enough, two announced editions of the *Study*. Terrified of his ideas being stolen—and dropping hints that he deserved priority as discoverer of evolution over Darwin and Wallace—Spencer was not about to take the threat lightly. He had his London publisher hasten plates to Appleton, who issued saturation advertising for a nonexistent pamphlet edition in order to buy time for the real volume. This he rushed out to "forestall piracy." Moreover, the threat was systematic enough to warrant a new periodical for science being created to counter it. It was "vital," Youmans said, that this venue exist if scientific authorship and authenticity were to be secured in the face of "the temptation to reprint." The new counterpirate journal came into being, and was called *Popular Science Monthly*. For the rest of the century and beyond, it stood alongside *Scientific American* as America's foremost vehicle for general science.[1]

The International Scientific Series and *Popular Science Monthly* were designed to spearhead a transformation in public knowledge by tackling the culture of international "piracy" that Mathew Carey's generation had bequeathed. Spencer spurred it on in hopes of destroying what he called the "utter viciousness" of the "piratical system." So ubiquitous was the practice that Youmans repeatedly warned European scientists about the pitfalls of engaging, not with reprinters per se—for that was unavoidable —but with the wrong kinds of reprinters. For example, if one Blanchard, a doctrinaire positivist, succeeded in pirating Spencer's *First Principles,* then the public would inevitably identify Spencer's project with the "gang of obscene, prurient, and scoffing authors whom he patronizes and advertises." It was largely by virtue of heading off such threats that Appleton became instrumental in the introduction into American public culture of virtually every contemporary British and German thinker of note.

Yet Youmans was quite capable of exploiting the possibilities of the pirate system himself. He changed works for new audiences, giving even Spencer's essays a new title and editing them at the level of paragraphs and sentences. His efforts substantially shaped Spencer's reputation in America, not least by distinguishing his views from positivism.[2] When he helped himself to the work of the leading British Comtean, Frederick Harrison, Harrison responded in the *Times* by accusing Youmans of "a new form of literary piracy." Youmans could only agree that American reprinting was "a scandal to civilization," but he pointed out that Harrison had been paid a royalty, and that his reprint had shielded him from worse pirates. So he had been "'plundered' by being protected against plunder." He stood his ground on the fundamental point that British writers had no right to stop their works being read. "His consent was not asked," he remarked, "because it would have implied control of that over which he had no control." The *Times* lamented that the American attitude applied Hobbes's state of nature to science. Youmans would have called it Darwin's.

THE RULES OF "THE GAME"

Both the problem science faced and the strategy Youmans adopted to confront it were firmly rooted in the practices of mid-nineteenth-century publishing. Transatlantic reprinting became an incessant and frantic competition in the 1820s. Mathew Carey's successors in Philadelphia and New York found themselves in an endless contest to obtain the latest London works—novels, memoirs, travel books, even law and science—as quickly as possible, so as to be able to reprint them first and beat their rivals to the marketplace. Rival publishers whipped up excitement about the sheer speed of the enterprise, hoping to catch customers who otherwise could wait a week for cheaper reprints of their reprints. For more than half a century the practice of reprinting shaped what was published in the United States, how it was published, where it was published, and how it was read.

American reprinters took full advantage of print's industrial revolution. Mechanized papermaking was introduced in 1816, and Fourdrinier machines appeared from Britain just over a decade later. The machines made the raw materials of the business cheaper and massively more plentiful. For Mathew Carey they exemplified the ambition of America to become a land of manufactures; his late tracts proudly proclaimed that they were printed on "machine paper." By the mid-1840s, when almost all papermaking was mechanized, the mills were producing ten times as much as in the early years of the century. Rail then brought these massive quantities to the major printing centers, where steam presses devoured them. They churned out books and newspapers in huge numbers—numbers that Henry Carey always cited as proving the vibrancy of America's literary republic. Book production increased eightfold in a generation.[3] And rail also brought print to new markets—passengers even found novels by Dickens serialized on the reverse of their timetables. Meanwhile, stereotyping allowed publishers to escape the burden of keeping huge amounts of type locked up in forms and books stored in warehouses. By mid-century virtually all popular reprints were being stereotyped. Once one publisher had stereotyped a work it was rarely worthwhile for others to do so. Instead they might rent the plates or buy sheets from the first, appending their own title page. The technology therefore helped secure trade courtesies, and some authors too embraced it as securing faithful editions. Thoreau complained that the Harpers, by seizing on the technique, had become dictators of public taste.[4] It also accentuated the sheer importance of being the first to get one's hands on a work, however. So the enterprise of transatlantic reprinting became more febrile than ever.

The transatlantic reprint business came to be called "the game." It really dated from the craze for Scott's Waverley novels.[5] To spectators it looked like a free-for-all, as publishers raced each other for every new and promising London book. Carey's firm (now run by Henry) fought tooth and nail with the Harper brothers in New York, while both took on upstarts like Grigg. Carey started out with the largest operation, and had extensive distribution networks, good international contacts, and a record in medicine, science, and engineering that the others did not share.[6] But the New Yorkers gained ground because they had newer equipment, and their city enjoyed both better shipping links to Europe and faster transport routes to the interior. Before long Carey was begging for the last sheets of new books to be shipped from London in manuscript before they could even be printed, pointing out that his "opposition" had a large market on their doorstep and so could publish as soon as they had printed off a few copies; he, with a vast hinterland to address, could not publish "until we have at least 2000 or 2500," so he desperately needed "a few days start."[7]

As this implies, the difference between victory and defeat in the game might be measured in hours. When news arrived of a promising book to be published in Britain (or elsewhere, but Britain was the major source), the rivals would mobilize agents in London to track down advance sheets. If possible, they would secure an agreement with the original publisher and/or author for early access. They would then strive to outdo each other in getting the sheets to the United States. Multiple copies would go on different ships, in hopes that one would get there ahead of the rest. James Gordon Bennett's *New York Herald* would even charter small boats to intercept incoming vessels and save precious hours. Whoever won that race could then claim the work. The winners might then take one of three routes. First, they could make amendments to the text in a bid to claim legal copyright. This was tried by Darwin's American publisher, and in some cases led to important changes or additions to major works; but it was an expensive and risk-prone strategy. Second, they could rely on what was generally—but not always—acknowledged by the major houses as a "courtesy of trade." Or, third, they could simply accept that rivals were inevitably going to pirate the book within a few days anyway, and try to make as much profit as possible in the brief period of exclusivity. In practice, the risk was sufficient in many cases to make the third of these the least worst option.

Sheer speed therefore remained all-important, even after landfall. Once a volume was out on the streets of Philadelphia or New York, a publisher had scant days—sometimes hours—to capitalize on it before competitors issued their own impressions. Henry Carey thus complained to the secretary of state himself about the precious minutes his cargoes took to clear customs. And haste had textual implications: sometimes reprints omitted chapters, or substituted sections by other authors, or even included chapters that the author had drafted but intended to delete. Carey once had to issue an apology in the newspapers after publishing an incomplete text of Scott's *Pirate*.[8]

Major publishers retained agents in London to play the game. Their charge was not only to look out for new books in general, but to obtain by hook or by crook advance sheets of the best ones. Henry Carey was the first to hire such a figure. In April 1817 he wrote to Longman requesting a standing arrangement for new works. He especially wanted works by a string of specific authors, some of them readily recognizable nowadays (Byron, Edgeworth, Scott, Dugald Stewart, and the "Author of Waverley" —Scott again, of course), others more obscure. He offered to pay £250 a year for prior access to copies, which must be sent by the "first and fastest" ships. Longman declined the offer, but passed the request on to a wholesaler and small-scale publisher named John Miller. Miller now became Carey's agent, a role he kept until 1861. He had a broad remit to seek out promising works. Only Scott stood outside his purview: after Scott's Edinburgh publisher, Constable, accused the Careys of appropriating proof sheets stolen from the printing house, they agreed to pay him directly for access.[9]

Agents like Miller were empowered to negotiate for sheets, which meant that British authors, if they were lucky, might be offered payment for American reprints. The Careys offered Dickens £100 for *Nicholas Nickleby,* and Scott would get £75 for one of his novels. Decades later Wilkie Collins got less than £1,000 for *The Woman in White,* and conceded that even that had been generous, "with the pirates in the background, waiting to steal."[10] Such sums were, the Americans insisted, ex gratia payments, not purchases of copyright. What a player of the game was paying for was time: a brief and unpredictable moment of de facto monopoly. As a result, the payments were also very small, at least by the standards a wildly successful author like Dickens came to expect in London. For example, two years after Carey and Hart took a risk by reprinting the first four numbers of *Pickwick Papers* when Dickens was still a relative unknown, they sent the author £50 in acknowledgment of the huge success they had enjoyed. By comparison, the copyright due to an American, James Fenimore Cooper, was about $4,000.[11] The Harpers justified paying Bulwer only £100 by arguing that his popularity in the States was substantially created by their efforts, not only in publishing the books but in orchestrating reviews and responses. The very name of Harper on the title page, they informed him, mitigated criticism. But then they added a sting. Their very success would inevitably encourage piratical rivals—they sent a pirated *Last Days of Pompeii* to prove the point—and they warned that if Bulwer were to approach any other American publisher then they too would pirate his works to destroy their market. The threat laid bare for a moment the raw reality behind the proclamations of civility that the trade liked to make in more public settings.

At its peak, the efficiency of reprinting was awe inspiring. Distributing a work to ten or more printing houses, an experienced American publisher could have an entire three-decker novel on the streets in two to three days. In 1822, Henry Carey employed nine houses to rush out Scott's *Fortunes of Nigel* overnight—and was only just ahead of a rival in New York that was set to appear two days later. Competing piracies, ranging down to a tiny 18mo, appeared just after that, killing Carey's sales. In 1825 the firm printed Byron's *Don Juan* at thirty presses in thirty-six hours. And when Carey received Scott's *Quentin Durward,* he had 1,500 copies of the three-volume novel printed, bound, and distributed in twenty-eight hours. At that speed, he crowed, he had "the Game completely in our hands." "The Pirates may print it as soon as they please," for he expected to have "complete and entire possession of every market in the Country" for the all-important first forty-eight hours. "Independently of profit," he added, it was "in the highest degree gratifying to be able to manage the matter in our own way without fear of interference." In New York, meanwhile, the Harpers managed to issue the three-volume *Peveril of the Peak* in twenty-one hours. If an original work were in another language, then translation slowed the process down—but only by a little. A German original could be Englished, printed, and published in a matter of days. As Carey explained to a London publisher, he could not possibly purchase anything resembling a copyright in such circumstances. "The only advantage we derive from the purchase," he pointed out, "is the sale of 3 or 4 days until another Edit. can be printed in New York, Boston, and here."[12]

This was a cutthroat business carried out by people who saw themselves as gentlemen. Just as Mathew Carey had sought to establish a civility in the early years, so Henry too attempted to mitigate its wilder aspects. The immediate trigger for this effort was the first serious attempt by British forces to counter American piracy. It took place at a critical time. The economy had hit a slump; Carey confided to Miller that it had cost the firm some $30,000 and added that Andrew Jackson "ought to be hanged." At this moment, the London publishers Saunders and Otley launched an office in New York to challenge the reprinters. Frederick Saunders, son of the proprietor, crossed the Atlantic in person to see off the upstarts. That threat by the Harpers against Bulwer reflected their concern: they realized that they were now in a fight on two fronts. First they struck at Carey. Carey had signed William Beckford's *Italy* the previous summer, but the sheets had disappeared en voyage. By a mysterious coincidence they now turned out to have fallen into the Harpers' hands, and the New Yorkers fed them to a Philadelphia reprinter who rushed out an impression. Meanwhile the Harpers moved to pirate the very first book that Saunders produced in New York, Lucien Bonaparte's *Memoirs*. They persuaded Saunders's printer to hand them the sheets, then rushed out their own edition several days before the complacent Londoner could finish his. They hailed this victory for "American enterprise" with street placards and press advertisements across the city. At the same time, cheap periodical pirates attacked Saunders's market from the bottom, reprinting his titles at a third of his prices. Saunders's pleas on behalf of "personal property" fell on deaf ears, and he soon gave up the fight. A decade later he could be found working as an editor at the Harpers'.[13] Carey proved more robust: receiving Bulwer's *Rienzi* on the same January day that the Harpers did, in less than two days he had five hundred volumes in New York retailers' hands. But this was war, and priority for once could not be allowed to win the day. The Harpers leaned on reviewers to ignore the Carey edition, and issued their own at only 50¢—a price he could never match.

The outcome was a pyrrhic defeat for all sides. Not even the Harpers could make a profit at that price. So it was this sobering experience that forced the two American rivals to recognize that the game was driving them to mutual destruction. Carey used the occasion to cajole the Harpers into participating in what had long been his pet scheme to formalize a civility. The New Yorkers had always refused to participate, but now agreed to help define the "courtesy of the trade." Such a courtesy would be, Fletcher Harper testified, their only "protection against piracy." By "piracy" he meant not international reprinting—the courtesies were meant to *preserve* that—but conflicts within the United States itself.

Courtesies always had a protean and situational quality. Indeed, that was one of their strengths. A generation earlier, Mathew Carey had proposed institutions—companies and fairs—to establish harmony, only to see them fail. These hopes never quite disappeared, Henry Carey himself continuing to dream of a single company upholding "Union."[14] But experience implied that less institutional approaches might work better, if only because there was no authority for populist reprinters to resist. And they suited a generation concerned to forge a collective sensibility through ceremonies and invented traditions. Trade dinners now became regular and ornate affairs, for example, with every kind of food cooked in all possible ways. Participants sat through speeches and toasts—sometimes upward of fifty—hailing the transcendent importance of printing and publishing for civilization. *Ars artium omnium conservatrix* was emblazoned on countless banners and floats in civil processions. Almost any excuse would do: Washington's birthday; the completion of an aqueduct; the return of troops from the Mexican War; the building of the University of Nashville; the laying of the transatlantic cable in 1858; and, of course, the supposed four hundredth anniversary of printing itself in 1840.[15] It was in this context of relentless public representation, then, that courtesies took on real force once more.

Negotiations between Philadelphia and New York now articulated a few major customs. All hinged on priority of some kind. In order of increasing controversy, the list ran as follows:

- *Priority of publication.* If a publisher issued an edition of a foreign work, that publisher acquired a right to it, for an indefinite period.
- *Priority in periodicals.* If a periodical obtained advance sheets, this also gave an exclusive right to publish them in book form.[16]
- *Priority of receipt.* The first to obtain advance sheets gained an exclusive right. But this was usually coupled with an obligation to announce an intent to publish; that is, it was subsumed into:

- *Priority of announcement.* The first to announce publicly an intent to publish a given title acquired an exclusive right to it, provided that the firm actually had the complete work in hand. This was the first and most important convention in debate between Carey and Harper. It was sometimes called the "Harper Rule," although it resembled a custom that had operated in some European cities, notably Dublin. Because it begged the question of what a *complete* work was—did proof sheets count?—it gave rise to fierce battles.

- *Priority in authors.* A publisher who had republished one work by a foreign author gained an exclusive right to all that author's subsequent works. This had no known European precedent and was always contested. Carey complained loudly that the Harpers infringed it by reprinting Marryat, and the Harpers regarded it as threatened by Saunders and Bulwer. Carey at length distanced himself from it, preferring to negotiate on an ad hoc basis for each new title.

- *Reprisal.* There should be a schedule of "reprisals" against trespassers on these courtesies. This idea was advocated by the Harpers. It is not clear what the proposed reprisals would have been, but in all likelihood they would have comprised some kind of blacklisting, and even of reprinting on the reprinters. Cases are certainly known of individual publishers retaliating in these ways. But Carey rejected a formal scale, so none was adopted.

The first five of these conventions became core to the mid-century American publishing industry's understanding of itself. They were still being cited in the 1860s as the only basis for stability in what otherwise would descend into "chaos." Only the idea of a prescribed schedule of reprisals went nowhere. The Harpers, coming to the trade after Mathew Carey's generation, had wanted a regime of principle, aiming at justice. Carey was aghast at the idea: he preferred a regime of custom, aiming at peace.[17]

Courtesies could be effective. To cite just one example, a rival conceded a law book to McCarty and Davis with the remark that "this circumstance alone as I conceive (viz. the priority in receipt of the Copy from England) can give you any right over the publication of an English work."[18] And transgressing invited retribution, which might well take the form of piracy. Thus a reprinter eager to take on Spencer's *Evidence of Man's Place in Nature* "ventured upon the ruse of announcing it from advance sheets," as

Youmans reported, only to find Appleton, who had advertised it first, threatening to pirate the reprinter's own copy of Lyell's geology. A similar conflict attended Mill's *On Liberty,* Appleton this time losing out to Ticknor and Fields. Such examples could readily be multiplied. But at the same time, courtesies remained negotiable, up to a point. One rather brazen transgressor tried to claim that pirating did not infringe "customary rights" if demand exceeded supply, but for the most part the distinctions were subtler and less nakedly self-interested. The Harpers used the New York press to advertise, for example, but Carey preferred that of Philadelphia, so disputes arose over what exactly constituted a "public" announcement. Neither was it entirely clear how much of a work one needed to possess to justify announcing it. Packages from London invariably contained less than an entire book, and, as Mathew Carey had told his son in 1821, it might be "impossible to tell with precision" what the texts they did contain actually were. The Careys certainly advertised before they had complete novels in hand—and occasionally when they had not even been written. The Harpers then adopted a policy of announcing *all* likely-looking titles that they came across in the London reviews, deciding only later which to actually republish. Carey followed suit. Eventually both sides were seeking out copies of *Blackwoods* and the *Athenaeum* with as much haste as actual books. Courtesy creep, as it were, had set in. And this would at length bring the approach into some disrepute. "All this chaos and uncertainty," said James Parton in 1867, "all these feuds and enmities, have one and the same cause,—the existence in the world of a kind of property which is at once the most precious, the easiest stolen, and the worst protected."[19]

Like all games, therefore, this one had rules—or at least, proxies for rules. Copyright was not one of them, for the most part, because of the game's transnational playing field. In place of law the publishers advanced a system of civility, based on courtesies. But the increasing variegation of what was now an industry would put that idea to the test. And when it did, it would foment a crisis that provoked a fundamental reexamination of the place of creative property in modern society.

LEVIATHAN

As the reprint industry grew, it developed a hierarchy. A Dickens novel might appear first in a good-quality reprint by Carey or some other respectable firm; then in a cheap piracy of that reprint; then in chapbooks; then in serialized forms; then in provincial newspapers; then in 25¢ "railroad" editions; and finally as chapters printed on railway timetables. As this happened, distinctions between propriety and transgression became increasingly blurred. Reprinters who ignored the courtesies issued popular works in enormous quantities and at very low prices. A five-volume Macaulay appeared in sixty thousand copies, at 15¢ per volume. Reprinters also issued science (Liebig's *Chemistry*) in impressions well into the tens of thousands. And just as the Careys and Harpers justified their own reproductions as moral enterprises, so these "pirates" (as Carey called them) openly defended theirs as exemplifying republican values. Here, after all, was an endeavor that distributed improving literature and authoritative ideas in unprecedented quantities and at extraordinarily low prices. It arguably did more to make America a truly lettered republic than any number of polite Philadelphia publications. It was in monarchical England, one pirate observed, that special societies had to be created to *push* useful knowledge out; here, entrepreneurs of knowledge responded to the pull of the masses.[20]

The sensational climax of this piratical arms race came with the advent of the so-called story papers. Issued on newsprint, and initially forming supplements to actual newspapers, these organs took the republic of piracy to its logical conclusion by abandoning the book altogether. Their raison d'être was to take advantage of preferential postage rates to reach enormous readerships. They first arrived on the scene in 1839, when another banking crisis had precipitated a depression in the publishing world. Commitments to courtesy threatened to dissolve under the strain, while Carey responded by withdrawing from the reprint business altogether to concentrate on science and medicine.[21] The best known of the story papers that now appeared were *Brother Jonathan* and *The New World,* both edited by the partnership of Park Benjamin and Rufus Griswold. They were published weekly, using the massive capacity of industrial printing to produce in large numbers and low prices—*Brother Jonathan* sold for 6¢. They scored an early victory by getting the first *Nicholas Nickleby* via the brand-new steamship *Great Western*. From then on, they promised, they would capitalize on such advanced technology to beat the old guard to the latest works.

From these grew the bizarre objects called "leviathan" papers. *Brother Jonathan* created the genre, claiming to employ "the largest folio sheet in the world." One Christmas special measured more than six feet by four. To modern eyes their close-printed sheets are almost unreadable, and in fact they were soon replaced by more manageable formats that readers could bind up to form their own books. But with no copyright fees, no binding, no storage, no bookstores, and no tied-up capital, they were ultra-cheap to produce. By 1843 the *New World* was selling twenty to thirty thousand copies a week. Only the biggest-selling conventional newspapers came close to such figures. Publicity stunts helped—Benjamin had street vendors march in cacophonic processions through central New York when a new title arrived. As a correspondent told London's *Athenaeum,* the phenomenon reached to every kind of literature: in one week this witness had seen a history of Ireland, the *Edinburgh Review,* d'Aubigné's account of the Reformation (translated from French), Liebig, and Froissart. The story papers hailed it all as "a great literary revolution," "truly democratic," and utterly subversive of "intellectual aristocracy."[22]

The story papers pillaged European periodicals, reprinted old works under new titles, and, at a pinch, stole from each other. With a premium on speed, their texts were often defective—or deliberately altered. A Dickens novel might be augmented with a smidgeon of Thackeray. But the reprinters claimed that they had a right to make such changes, because they were retrofitting the cultural products of monarchies for readers in a republic. The *New World* in particular campaigned loudly for this right to remove insidious traces of aristocracy. It even criticized the *Knickerblocker* as aristocratic for trying to register copyrights.[23] This being so, the papers also brought back to the fore the epistemic implications of piracy. So rapid and so various had reprinting become that it might be unclear where original authorship lay, let alone if it conferred any rights.

This was dramatically demonstrated in the case of an author who was not only a creature of the reprinting system, but one hailed as the first great American writer: the mysterious Charles Sealsfield. Originally a Carey discovery back in 1829, Sealsfield eventually authored a total of eighteen novels, many set in the frontier regions of Louisiana and beyond. When a prominent German critic nominated him as proving the advent of a valid American literary culture, the *New World* took to pirating him. But in March 1844 the *Boston Daily Advertiser* ventured a public guess that Sealsfield was a model author in a very different sense. So perfect a creature was he of the pirate sphere that the man himself did not exist—he was a product of the same sensationalist publishing economy that produced the notorious Lunar hoax and Edgar Allan Poe's balloon caper. Proponents of literary property immediately began charging that "some publisher who lives by stealing the brains of foreign authors" had simply invented "Sealsfield" from a farrago of materials purloined here and there from periodicals—this being a common practice of the story papers. The *New World* responded by adducing frontiersmen's testimony that his works must reflect firsthand experience of conditions out west, and by the time-honored tactic of putting his original manuscripts on display, but to little avail. What ensued demonstrated a deep, pervasive uncertainty about authorship itself. Perhaps Sealsfield was British, some wondered; perhaps he was a European who had plagiarized American writers; perhaps he was a phantom. Britain's *Blackwood's Magazine* began to publish Sealsfield's work too, and this complicated matters still further. Some American critics assumed that the *New World* was reprinting *Blackwood's* material, rather than vice versa —at which point Poe himself condemned the whole thing as a "laughable or disgusting instance of our subserviency to foreign opinions." The question of the author's very existence, and implicitly of American literary prowess, seemed to hang absurdly on the contingencies of transatlantic shipping.

In point of fact, Sealsfield did exist. But he was a shadowy and evanescent character, in the manner not just of American piracy but of middle-European political intrigue. An escapee from a Prague monastery, he had taken on a false name, offered his services as a spy to Metternich, and, after traveling widely in the western states of America, settled down in Switzerland and become a behind-the-scenes operative for Louis Napoleon.[24] Even so, there was a real sense in which the anxieties over his reality represented a confirmation of Kant's point about the corrosive power of piracy as ventriloquism, updated for in an industrial and nationalistic age.

In 1839 a story paper called the *Corsair* appeared that seemed to represent a *non plus ultra* of the pirate sphere. A rival summed it up as "a total infringement on the decencies of civilization." For once, its province can unambiguously be called pirate publishing, because the paper itself eagerly embraced that label. Distributed by mail to around 2,500 subscribers—and therefore a minor example of the genre—it assumed the rhetorical identity of a buccaneering vessel. Its crew was entirely composed of previous victims of piracy, including a French surgeon and a German philosopher. They made prize of any worthwhile literary vessels they came across, every issue containing extracts from major British and Continental authors. Its crew professed to fear none but the barque *Boz* (Dickens's pen name, of course)—"a queer craft, *all-of-a-twist.*" (As the *Corsair* elsewhere put it: "Why will the next story by Boz be like the invention of the laurel crown? Because it belongs to the *first seizer.*") It also followed phrenology and animal magnetism, profiled Ada Byron, and revealed an interesting commitment to proletarian creativity by denouncing the pedagogic initiatives of the "march of intellect" as "penny-magazining [the masses'] way to scientific dullness." But the paper was also exemplary in not being what it seemed.

The *Corsair* was the brainchild of the flamboyant N. P. Willis. Willis went to London himself to establish its sources, where he quickly made the acquaintance of Charles Babbage, John Stuart Mill, Harriet Martineau, Captain Marryat (with whom he fought a duel), and Thackeray. This last became the *Corsair*'s London correspondent. Meanwhile Willis reported discovering a British piracy of his own work. But he denounced this as resulting from the scandalous state of *American* law. "See the effect of our robberies of English authors," he declared: such larceny existed only because of "our defective law of copyright." This betrayed the real purpose of the whole venture. In fact, the very egregiousness of the *Corsair* was supposed to prove how morally irredeemable American practice was. It thus launched frequent broadsides against what it called, with only apparent paradox, "the piratical law of copy-right." Willis actually thought copyright should be both universal and perpetual. His paper existed to prove the need for its own destruction.[25]

Writ large, Willis's venture succeeded. The newsprint pirates gave reprinting a bad name. Harper led the counterattack, prompted partly by a conviction that *New World* spies were trying to steal works the firm had in press and partly by suspicions about the setting of a fire at its premises. A short but bitter price war ensued. Meanwhile, the Post Office, fearing that the mail might collapse under the strain of the reprint papers, abruptly reclassified them as pamphlets. This jacked up the postage rate from about 2¢–3¢ per issue to 12¢–18¢ and eliminated at a stroke their economic viability. The papers denounced the postal service as for betraying their ideal of "universal diffusion of information." But it did no good. *Brother Jonathan* folded quickly; the *New World* followed soon after. The genre expired with them.

FOR AND AGAINST TRANSATLANTIC COPYRIGHT

Fresh from their humiliating defeat in New York, Saunders and Otley turned to Harriet Martineau to organize a petition of British authors to the U.S. Congress. Martineau complied. The resulting document was signed by fifty-six writers, including Bulwer, Carlyle, D'Israeli, Edgeworth, and Southey. Along with Charles Dickens's notoriously undiplomatic comments while visiting in 1842, it inaugurated what became a decades-long struggle for international copyright between Britain and America.

The rather nonplussed addressee of Martineau's petition was Senator Henry Clay. Clay had been Mathew Carey's most prominent ally in developing the American system. But in the wake of his marginalization by the Whig Party he needed a new cause, and he swiftly moved to adopt this one. Creating an international system would not be an easy task, he realized. The internationalization of copyright was itself an unprecedented idea. Not even the German states had a common literary regime at this time (although it was commonly believed in America and Britain that they did). The only real precedent, moreover, was that resulting from the union of Ireland and Britain, which was hardly an auspicious example given its effect on the Dublin industry. And many publishers, and especially printers, would be against it. Philadelphia's in particular protested that it would price "honest farmers" out of America's "reading community," destroying the nation's republic of letters.[26] Clay hit upon the strategy of a "manufacturing clause" in a bid to head off their opposition. He would make the prompt printing of an edition in America a condition of a foreigner's holding a U.S. copyright. This, he hoped, would align the copyright quest with Careyite political economy. Much of the contest that ensued derived from this attempt.

Two manifestos issued at this time set the terms for that contest. Saunders's, attributed to an anonymous "American," was thought to have been written by Washington Irving and Grenville Sackett.[27] It denounced the typical American publisher as a "Literary Pirate" who not merely appropriated works but "dismembered" them. Yet the tract also upbraided British copyright as inadequate. It maintained that literary property should be perpetual, and condemned *Donaldson vs. Becket* as "an unheard of stretch of legislative tyranny and injustice." The linkage of deposit to copyright (Brydges's complaint), it added, had further raised "piracy" over property. The point was to take existing arguments for American reprinting and trump them. In terms reminiscent of Mathew Carey, it aligned authorship with improving means for "the conveyance of intelligence," such as canals, harbors, and railroads, all of which produced "moral and intellectual improvement" for the populace.[28] The United States, it affirmed, was pioneering a new kind of society. But a "depraved" moral sentiment could play no part in that. "Robbery has in no code of modern, political science been made the basis of national aggrandizement," the tract warned, "and those nations of antiquity who resorted to such means soon found that the tenure of their property was rather precarious." Moreover, in a pirating domain readers were forced to imbibe aristocratic "stimulants," and not the "Spartan broth" suited to their hardier constitution. Only with universal rights could authors uphold an interest in plain and virtuous truth. That is, only international copyright could sustain a distinctly Kantian ideal of public reason, on which a nation might build its future.

The initial public champion for the other side was one Philip Nicklin. But Nicklin was a front man. He had been Carey's agent up to 1829, and he dedicated his riposte to Henry Carey. His should therefore be read as the answer of the long-dominant American reprinter to Saunders's challenge. Appropriately enough, it was largely composed of reprints: the British petition, Clay's bill, a speech by Talfourd, even an article on copyright from the *Encyclopaedia Britannica*. Along the way, Nicklin pointed out what he claimed were blatant contradictions. For example, the authors complained that their reputations suffered by reprinting; yet imposing copyright would reduce readership. Complaints of "mutilation" were equally far-fetched, he thought, because "sharp competition" upheld accuracy.[29] Nicklin professed to concur on the need for copyright to be perpetual, and he too endorsed Brydges's campaign against the deposit. But he would subject literary property to a compulsory licensing system similar to that advocated by the British antipatent campaigners. This he thought essential in order to open books to the "energy" of real free trade. Getting rid of monopoly was the only way to make "pirates and piracies" disappear. And this "abolition of literary piracy" was surely the "consummation" wished by all. A true harmony of interests — that iconic phrase — would then bind societies together.[30]

Both sides therefore began by presenting this as a struggle for the soul of the republic, with, on the face of it, a good deal of common ground. Yet within a few years this would metastasize into a conflict over fundamentals: protection versus free trade, manufacturing versus commerce, democracy versus oligarchy, Philadelphia versus New York. It would address central questions of modern culture as that culture came into being. What was knowledge, and how were its development, transmission, and storage best secured? This radicalization emerged because the question of cultural property became a problem for a new intellectual discipline—"societary science." The person who made it that was Henry Carey.

CIVILIZATION AND SOCIETARY FORCE

The United States has now lived for longer with international copyright than it did without. As a result, the case for it is familiar. The case against is far more counterintuitive. But there was indeed an argument against transatlantic copyright. It upheld not just piecemeal unauthorized reprinting, but a system, and thereby a society. The figure most responsible for it, Henry C. Carey (1793–1879; fig. 11.1), created the most influential arguments ever mounted for an alternative to universal literary property.

Carey's role was grounded in experience. As Mathew Carey's son, he enjoyed deeper familiarity with the world of publishing, in all probability, than any American contemporary (except perhaps the Harper brothers). He had been a publisher most of his life, having first managed a branch of the firm in Baltimore at the age of twelve. Between 1821 and 1835—the glory years of the reprinting system—he ran what was one of the largest publishing houses of all; in 1824–26 its sales aggregated to over $500,000. During that time he masterminded the consolidation of the reprinting industry itself. He knew the culture of reprinting so intimately because he was largely responsible for its existence.

Carey began an authorial career at the moment when he was badgering the Harpers into framing the courtesy system. At first he was a free trader—a commitment that his father reviled. But in the late 1830s something happened to overturn his views. At that point his own firm was leaving the frenzy of reprinting behind. As it did so, Carey, retiring from active involvement, wrote a volume entitled *The Harmony of Nature*. The book apparently argued from natural science to a version of classical political economy. We cannot know for sure, however, because he abruptly withdrew it and destroyed the entire impression, saying that he had experienced an economic epiphany. A sudden conviction that orthodox

FIGURE 11.1. Henry C. Carey. H. C. Carey, *Miscellaneous Works,*
2 vols. (Philadelphia: H.C. Baird, 1883), vol. 1, frontispiece.
Courtesy of the University of Chicago Library.

political economy radically misconstrued the natural world had transformed his views. He now embarked on a remarkable new career as a
political economist and developer of what he called "societary science,"
in which antagonism to free trade was almost axiomatic. Carey spoke,
wrote, campaigned, and published in this cause without cease for the rest
of his life—a period of some forty years. During that time he became
probably the most famous and influential American economist of whom
we today have never heard. His views were adumbrated in a three-volume
Principles of Political Economy (1837–40), proclaimed in *Past, Present, and
Future* (1848), and then consummated in the *Principles of Social Science*
(1858–60). In the interstices of these projects he issued an unending tor-
rent of letters, tracts, pamphlets, and editorials on every topic of his day,
from slavery to currency reform. Crowds of thousands came to hear him
speak. He played a leading role in the formation of the Republican Party,
and in 1860 was instrumental in defeating Simon Cameron's bid for the
presidential ticket, thus paving the way for the nomination of Lincoln,

whose favorite economic thinker he was thought to be. Meanwhile he also traveled widely in Europe, meeting John Stuart Mill, the scientists Liebig and Humboldt, and Cavour, the Italian politician. And at home "Carey's Vespers"—regular occasions for wine and conversation about social topics—would later be remembered as foundational for the enterprise of social science. While John Stuart Mill may have pronounced Carey the worst political economist he had ever read, for every Mill there was a Marx, who lined him up alongside Bastiat as the only one worth refuting. And the lawyer and economist Erasmus Peshine Smith found Carey's writings so revelatory that he was led to repudiate the very notion of intellectual property and elaborate a history of civilization itself in terms of piracy.[31]

In Carey's hands, piracy and copyright became elements in a massive and ambitious would-be science that encompassed the natural and social worlds. He sallied forth several times on the topic, but his *Letters on International Copyright* represented his most important effort. The *Letters* appeared first in 1853, at the peak of his agitation in the shaping of Republicanism. Written to oppose a treaty that the secretary of state had negotiated with Britain, it became the single most influential tract against the establishment of copyright between Britain and the United States. In part, it rested on the specific constitutional question of whether a treaty could legitimately determine domestic policy, since it need not be ratified by the House of Representatives—high-handedness that he associated with "centralized" governments.[32] But Carey credited it with almost single-handedly preventing such copyright being adopted in any form. In 1872 he published a sequel, *The International Copyright Question Considered*. These together formed the *fons et origo* of the anti-internationalization camp. Read alongside Carey's "societary science," they provided an authoritative and apparently scientific argument not only against the internationalization of literary property, but for its strict limitation even at home.

In challenging free trade, there is a sense in which Carey wrote so much because he had to: he was confronting the central orthodoxy of classical political economy. Free trade, as he remarked, had the status in London, Manchester, and Glasgow of "unquestionable scientific truth." To confront it successfully therefore required more science—and different science. This was what Carey set out to produce. He tried to supplant Ricardo's political economy with a societary science that would overturn most of its axioms, methods, facts, and prescriptions at once. He aspired to produce a unified system of knowledge that extended, in principle, from the most basic natural facts to the highest laws of society. His opposition to what he always insisted on calling "British free trade" would then be based on "societary laws" as certain in the social world as that of universal gravitation was in the natural. And what was at stake in discovering those laws, Carey insisted, was the "great question" of his age: "that of civilization." There is no denying that the answers he produced were peculiar—not to mention extremely convoluted. But his presumptuousness in advancing them was typical of his age, when many proposed sciences just as presumptuous: Bagehot in Britain, Tarde in France, even Marx himself. And that age took Carey very seriously indeed.

Where did Carey get the idea for a unified system of sciences? He got it, quite simply, from reading. That is, he gleaned it, in part at least, from products of the American reprinting system. In particular, Carey devoured Auguste Comte's *Course of Positive Philosophy* in Harriet Martineau's translation as soon as it appeared in America, which it did in a reprint by none other than Appleton. Carey inhaled Comte, and circulated copies to his acolytes along with his own anticopyright tracts. Positivism convinced him that a social science must be created, and integrated as the highest level of a coherent and universal system of knowledge. In his own work he was not a positivist in the strict Comtean sense, however, and he reacted strongly against Comte's later moves to create a new religion. But he remained certain of the need for a unified science based on "positive knowledge." For him that meant two things. First, the investigation must begin with observations—with facts—and not with theoretical pronouncements. This, he believed, placed him in stark contrast to Manchester-school political economy, which paid no attention to "the great laboratory of the world" and dealt in terms so abstracted as to be actually false. And, second, there was a hierarchy of natural laws, and hence of sciences to address them, extending from the most basic to the most exalted. These laws must be common to both natural and social realms, and Carey would be their discoverer. He thus projected himself as nothing less than a nineteenth-century Copernicus, fated to overthrow the monstrous concoction of epicycles that was contemporary political economy. Hence it was that a *Manual of Social Science* designed to feed his doctrines to students opened with a rhapsody from Kepler about the harmony of the world, and hailed Carey as "the Newton of Social Science."[33]

Carey's prime example of the blindness of political economy was an axiom that he attributed to Ricardo, although in fact it dated back at least to Adam Smith. According to this axiom, societies always began by farming the most fertile soils. Later, as population pressures grew, they spread into less fertile lands, so their agricultural output tailed off. Carey took this axiom to be central to the reputation of political economy as the "dismal science," because it not only assumed that wealth ultimately derived from agriculture, but also asserted that humanity faced an ever-worsening future. That is, it was the basis for Malthusian despair. Carey maintained that history showed it to be false in every single factual instance (fig. 11.2). Marshalling examples from ancient Assyria to modern Chile, he tackled "this atrocious theory," as one eulogist put it, with "a demonstration of its falsity that has scarcely a parallel in the history of science, physical or moral." Carey asserted that *in fact* societies did the precise opposite. They always began by cultivating uplands with thin soil (A), and only moved on to richer, lower country (B) as wealth and technology permitted. And this made sense, he thought, because their sheer fertility would make rich lands hard to farm with primitive machinery. Carey thus asserted that history showed a common thread of *progress:* from poorer to more sophisticated roads, from simpler to more complex commerce, from primitive to more powerful tools, and from subsistence to productive farms. It was almost certainly this conviction that inspired him to seek out Liebig, who was the leading proponent of an agricultural chemistry that promised to shatter Malthus's pessimism.[34]

Carey's social science developed from this fundamental observation into a huge mass of empirical specificity and principled generalization. At the same time it came to resemble more and more explicitly a certain image of natural science. It began from the point that man was, as Carey declared, "the molecule of society." Our basic need (because definitive of humanity itself) was for "association" with other humans. One only

FIGURE 11.2. Carey's pictorial retort to Ricardo. H. C. Carey, *Principles of Social Science,* 3 vols. (Philadelphia: J. B. Lippincott and Co., 1858), vol. 1, 138. Courtesy of the University of Chicago Library.

became properly human through association, because humanness consisted largely in knowledge, knowledge depended on experience, experience was collected and communicated through language, and language came into being collectively. A completely isolated human being would therefore not be fully human at all. Thus this latter-day Newton proclaimed what he called his "great law of molecular gravitation": that human beings naturally gravitated toward one another, forming social groups. Moreover, larger groups exerted a correspondingly stronger "attractive force," cities having more pull than small towns. As Carey concluded (with a distinctly shaky grasp of Newtonian principle), social gravitation was "as everywhere else in the material world, in the direct ratio of the mass, and in the inverse one of the distance."[35]

What resulted from this law was a society resembling a collage of planetary systems. People gravitated toward centers, large and small, and small centers congregated around large. To explain why these systems did not collapse in on themselves, Carey hit upon on what he dubbed "societary circulation." This now became his central concept. Such circulation, he argued, was essential to the development of "all those faculties, mental and moral, by which the human animal is distinguished from the brute." It was an old idea dressed up in nineteenth-century clothes—Harringtonian republicanism had rested on a similar principle in the seventeenth century, and Harrington could almost have dictated Carey's contention that "with societies as with individual men, physical and mental development, health, and life, had always grown with growth in the rapidity of circulation and declined as the circulation had been arrested or destroyed." What was new in Carey's version was what did the circulating. This was an entity that he called "societary force." Societary force was by all accounts to be taken as real, not metaphorical. Carey wanted it accepted alongside the other forces—magnetism, gravity, electricity, and so on—the interactions between which so excited naturalists in the 1840s–1850s. Figures like Faraday and William Robert Grove had become famous for suggesting that forces were somehow interlinked, and proposed various visions of the "correlation," "conversion," or "conservation" of "force," "power," or "energy." Carey vaunted this as nothing less than a "new philosophy." It promised to resolve all "subtle agencies" into manifestations of "one and the same force." That force could never be created or destroyed, only converted into some other form. By exercising such conversions, one could produce effects in the real world. In retrospect this sounds like early energy science. But in the 1850s substantial differences existed between these rival schemes, Carey's among them. His was, in essence, a contribution not to the physical science of force, but to the social. If "unity of law" unified the sciences, that was because it was itself based in a more fundamental "unity of force." Societary science was the discipline devoted to analyzing this unity of force in all its provinces.[36]

In other words, power came about through the artful guidance of a circulation of force through its various forms. To ask about the nature of this force was in a sense to raise a *question mal posée,* since no one form was more fundamental than the others. But for Carey the best candidates were electricity, first and foremost, and money a distant second. Electrical force appeared in the nervous system and in plants no less than in inorganic matter; it flowed freely through conductors with, he thought, no loss of efficacy. Electrical circuits furnished the easiest form of force circulation to imagine, the most powerful, and the most modern. Electrical force in motion therefore became his archetype for societary circulation. It was not an absurd idea; on the contrary, it was distinctly up to date. In Carey's generation, researchers like Alfred Smee were trying to develop an American science called electro-biology to display forces implicit in social communities. But there is no sign that Carey directly encountered electro-biologists. Instead he built his vision on what little he himself knew of electrical circuits. He asserted that every individual in a social system exhibited a certain polarity, analogous (and perhaps more than analogous) to the terminals of a battery like Grove's. Which polarity one displayed depended on one's role at a given moment. As "giver and receiver, teacher and learner, producer and consumer," he wrote, each citizen could be considered "positive and negative by turns." As a result, when citizens combined in different configurations they could collectively constitute "a great electric battery to which each individual contributes his pair of plates." Societary force would then flow from and through this battery. Such a model suited a notion of money as this force, too, making capital into a circulating, fluid-like entity in some ways similar to Marx's concept. "As it is with electricity in the physical world," Carey told the treasury secretary on one occasion, "so it is with money in the social one." Both electricity and money were powerful and invisible—traits that led him to predict that society would eventually adopt a form of money free of all "material representation."[37] At any rate, if all the "plates" could be arranged properly, then Carey felt that "perfect circulation" would be the result. And at that point, he concluded, "economic force flows smoothly through every member of the body politic, general happiness and prosperity, [and] improved mental and moral action, following in its train."

This idea of social batteries had prescriptive implications. The question it posed to policy makers was how to create and maintain such batteries in the number and arrangement that would maximize the flow of societary force. The key to this lay in the polar character of electricity. Carey thought that just as real batteries depended on a difference between plates, so societies depended on distinctions between social plates, or citizens' roles. It was therefore crucial in order for circulation to take full effect that a society exhibit *diversity*. Specifically, there must be real "difference of employments." Without that there would be no "positives and negatives" to provide the opportunity for force to be converted and power to be obtained. Moreover, such distinct individuals must not only exist, but also be in at least close proximity (this being half a century before long-distance power transmission). In other words, diversity and interaction had to obtain *at the local level*. So Carey despised institutions that acted at a distance and the "middlemen" who served them. Middlemen were "traders" of all kinds, who charged for the transfer of goods and people across distances and therefore imposed a tax on association. They were like insulators interrupting a circuit. By contrast, he spoke admiringly of the class of the "converters" in a community—the makers of cloth, iron, books, instruments, ships, houses, mills, and furnaces. They acted, he said, as "the solvents of the electric battery." This class constituted "a body of conductors of an electric force whose action becomes more and more intense as societary positives and negatives, producers and consumers, are brought into closer relations each with every other." Without them, the battery would cease to work. Like Tocqueville before him, Carey thus hailed the American tradition of "civil corporations," but for the different reason that he thought civil society was the institutional form of social circuitry. And he also argued that maintaining social variety might depend on government action to sustain diversity within communities. Such action would uphold the operation of a free market locally, by intervening to prevent its homogenization under distant factories (a demand redolent of one that eighteenth-century artisans had made on different grounds).[38] This being present, he enthused, "the power and the habit of association [would] become more and more confirmed." Every "societary atom" would find its place, and "an enlightened feeling of self-

316

respect gradually supersedes that blind selfishness which so generally characterizes ignorant and isolated men." Morals, tastes, feelings, and affections would improve, and the people would qualify for the liberty of "freedom of speech." Progress would prevail.

Carey's conclusion was thus that civilization—intellectual, moral and economic progress—depended on the maintenance of a diverse and de-centralized set of circulations. This involved local free markets protected by strong barriers against distant monopolies. His prime example was the German *Zollverein,* the customs union produced in post-Napoleonic Europe that regularized trade across the German states. "Under it," Carey declared, "the positives and negatives of a whole nation were brought into communication with each other, and thus has been created a great battery of 40,000,000 pairs of plates throughout which there is a rapidity of cir-culation scarcely elsewhere on so large a scale exceeded." France and the state of Massachusetts, likewise, managed to preserve social variety; as a result, the powers of their people developed daily, and they were free. The same thing was happening to America at large. Thanks to Lincoln's policy favoring national production, "almost perfect circulation having been established throughout a gigantic battery of 20,000,000 pairs of plates," activity had succeeded paralysis, and society was stronger than ever before.[39]

But it had been a close run thing. In 1860, Carey had thought the coun-try subject to "a paralysis of the body politic, an arrest of the circulation, and a waste of physical and mental force." This stagnation had been the consequence of a neglect of societary force, usually to the benefit, again, of so-called middlemen. Much of Carey's occasional writing was more or less directly devoted to attacks on this class. He blamed the chronic prob-lems of the period on their existence, charging that they created "forced" trade and called it free. The slave states of the American South were one case in point. (Carey was convinced that the Civil War was attributable to free trade and British perfidy.) But it was in Britain and the British Empire that Carey perceived the effects of middlemen to obtain in their purest form. Britain displayed decreasing association and advancing slavery, in effect if not literally. Being devoted to trade, he argued, the British system elevated the interests of distance above those of juxtaposition, and of class above diversity. Britain's vaunted "machines" of the Industrial Revolution were all industries for acting at a distance: ships, railways, telegraphs, and roads. They were never machines of locality. And they culminated in mere display and pomp, meant to pull in the gullible. "Her whole energies are now devoted to getting up a show," Carey declared of the Great Exhibition. "Thus is the nation converted to a gigantic *Barnum*, with a gigantic museum, a new description of *machine*, invented for the purpose of attracting visitors." Meanwhile, beneath this gaudy show positives and negatives could never come into true contact because the laissez-faire system had destroyed local distinctions of person. With no opportunities for fruitful juxtaposition, force remained "latent," circulation "sluggish," and the people "enslaved."

Carey identified this phenomenon with *centralization*. This was for him the ultimate end of free trade and laissez-faire. Wherever it obtained, free trade led to a small class of the very rich, and a mass of the very poor who were effectively enslaved. Like Carlyle and Engels (and the British antipatent camp), Carey made much of the demoralizing effects of this "involuntary association," in which workers' lives were rife with fraud, drunkenness, and gambling. The colonies were in an even worse state. India had been laid waste; invoking Liebig, he predicted the utter exhaustion of its soil. In terms of societary science, free trade imperialism ensured that positive and negative plates were kept far apart, which prevented "any development whatsoever of mental force." Relentless exploitation for distant factories would lead inexorably to a kind of heat death of the empire.[40]

The way to fight back was by the hackneyed policy of protection. But Carey gave this policy a new, more fundamental purpose. "Without it, men cannot combine together," he declared. The Union would go the same way as Ireland, India, and Carolina. With protection in place, however, "there must be daily increasing economy of muscular force." With that would come the increasing development of "brain power" (another variant of societary force), leading to the enhanced use of machines. Civilization would triumph. "Centralization and civilization have in all countries, and at all periods of the world, been opposed to each other," he reckoned, and the way to civilization was by decentralization.[41] The implications of protection were therefore millennial.

Carey therefore saw classical political economy as a false science concocted in the service of centralization, and hence of tyranny. It seemed to work only because British policies really did reduce humans to machines, producing the very objects that the science described. His societary science was to be its nemesis. In truth, however, Carey was no scientist. He never performed experiments or did any but the most perfunctory mathematics. His work was devoid of statistical analysis, instead parading endless "facts," each of them treated as self-sufficient and self-explanatory. Instead, he made reading into his scientific practice. He collected and regurgitated massive amounts of historical and economic information from printed books. Having honed his skills in long years spent as a reader for his father's publishing house, he co-opted a way of reading that in private he called his "'copy-book' plan."[42] This "plan" was in essence a version of the commonplacing used by earlier generations of scholars to cope with the daunting flow of books produced by printing. Commonplaces constituted Carey's version of scientific "observations." For Marx this was his fatal flaw: he lambasted Carey for an "uncritical and superficial" shuffling of numbers, for "spurious erudition," and for an "atrocious lack of the critical faculty." But what to Marx was a maddening weakness was for others an impressive empiricism, much needed in the arid field of political economy.[43]

In particular, Carey relied for his observations on the reprint system. None other than Edward Youmans's edited collection *The Correlation and Conservation of Forces* was a key resource for his societary science.[44] This volume was the first account of "the new philosophy of forces" to enjoy large exposure in the United States. It comprised reprinted essays by Grove, Helmholtz, Mayer, Faraday, and Liebig, all of them arguing for the correlation of "forces" between various branches of physical phenomena. An additional reprint by the physiologist and proponent of animal magnetism William Carpenter went further, to indicate rich interchanges between physical and vital forces. Carpenter's extension of this "new philosophy" to the internal dynamics of the human body was deeply controversial in Britain. But as Youmans remarked in his introduction, if he was right then the principle of correlation "must also apply to society." And it was there, he continued, that "we constantly witness the conversion of forces on a comprehensive scale." "The powers of nature are transformed into the activities of society; water-power, wind-power, steam-power, and electrical-power are pressed into the social service, reducing human labor, multiplying resources, and carrying on numberless industrial processes: indeed, the conversion of these forces into social activities is one of the chief triumphs of civilization."[45] Carey's reading of the book followed these leads, which bore fruit in his own force-based societary science. He well knew Youmans's views—he once showed up at Appleton's premises and launched into a tirade against him for promoting Spencerism and "British free-trade"—but his use of the edition was radically antagonistic to them.[46] In short, Carey's defense of reprinting would rest not only on reprints, but on those designed to destroy reprinting itself.

TWO IDEAS OF PIRACY

Carey became the universally acknowledged "high priest" of protectionist ideology. His polemics enjoyed huge support in the Northern states, especially Pennsylvania. The press, Horace Greeley's *Tribune* in the van, lauded them; Greeley himself wrote a treatise endorsing much of Carey's program (its protectionism, that is; he supported international copyright).[47] As a result, two ideas of piracy confronted each other in contemporary literary politics. One was that of national rapacity. The outraged British accused America of this, charging wholesale theft not only of books but also of designs, theories, technologies, and industrial techniques. Carey willingly conceded that to the British Americans were "little better than thieves or pirates." The other was what his camp saw as the *real* idea of piracy: that exemplified by Britain's endorsement of colonialist exploitation across the globe. In support of free trade, Carey's side pointed out, the British were quite prepared to hail maritime pirates as free trade pioneers. They regarded the smuggler who violated other countries' tariffs as "'the great reformer of the age.'" In the opium wars the British had grabbed Hong Kong solely to use it as a "smuggling depot." They would surely act similarly toward America, if given the chance. Already, they had tacitly supported "pirate ships" fighting for the Confederacy. It was all part of a global racket known as empire.[48]

Only one of these two forms of piracy could survive. The other would be identified forever as outlawry, and consigned to a discarded stage of historical development. In the 1840s–1880s which would suffer that fate remained an open question. The answer, in the view of many in Philadelphia and places like the Lehigh Valley, would determine the fate of modern civilization. It was also what lay at the root of Carey's angry performance at Appleton's publishing house.

For the publishing industry was one place where Carey's social cosmology took effect. It provided a key measure of civilization, for example. He tracked the decline of association in Spain in terms of the falling number of presses in operation.[49] Similarly, he repeatedly employed a simple diagram (fig. 11.3) to display his core argument about the United States. It represented a schematic cross-section of North America, running from the Rockies to Massachusetts, with paper and rag prices forming its vertical axis. This stark pair of lines, indicating the convergence of prices between raw and finished materials, mapped the impact of association and thus represented an index of civilization. Moreover, he conceived of the book trade in general as the ultimate solvent of his societal battery— "a body of conductors of an electric force whose action becomes more and more intense as societary positives and negatives, producers and consumers, are brought into closer relations each with every other." Withdraw printers and publishers, and circulation would cease, with the calamitous results visible in Ireland after Union. Carey urged any reader curious about what societary science might be to watch the movements by which people manufactured a newspaper.

> That there may be progress, there must be motion. Motion is itself a result of the incessant decomposition and recomposition of matter, and the work of association is but the incessant decomposition and recomposition of the various human forces. In a heap of penny newspapers we find portions of the labor of thousands of persons, from the miners of ores and coal and the collectors of rags, to the makers of types and paper, the engine-makers and engineer, the compositor, pressman, writer, editor, and proprietor, and finally the boys by whom they are distributed; this exchange of services going on from day to day throughout the year, each contributor to the work receiving his share of the pay, and each reader of the paper receiving his share of the work.[50]

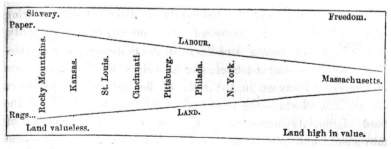

FIGURE 11.3. Carey's diagram of America. Carey, *Principles of Social Science*, vol. 3, 93. Courtesy of the University of Chicago Library.

Similarly, the book trades exhibited the importance of juxtaposition. A printer who worked for a publisher was not free, because the latter intervened before the public, while bookbinders, of all people, endured "the nearest approach to serfdom that I know to exist in civilized life." "Precisely so is it with nations," Carey promptly added. A colony's predicament was "precisely that of the printers."[51]

Carey's accounts of Ireland displayed the real implications of this. The island's brief period of legislative independence in the eighteenth century had allowed it to impose protective tariffs, he observed. That had been the great period of prosperity for what the British had denounced as its piratical book trade. It had also been a period marked by "development of the intellectual faculties," as vouched for by the fact that "the demand for books for Ireland was so great as to warrant the republication of a large portion of those produced in England." In other words, eighteenth-century Irish piracy had been the measure as well as the source of public knowledge. But British centralization had decreed the imposition of copyright. With that, the book trade had "entirely disappeared," and the country had become a land of famine and deprivation—of "slavery, depopulation, and death." Westminster had never again permitted "Irish positives and negatives to come together in such order as was required for production of any societary force whatsoever." It was no surprise, then, that "half a century of international copy-right has almost annihilated both the producers and the consumers of books."[52]

This was why Carey led the opposition to transatlantic copyright—and why his opposition took the form it did. To him this was an epochal clash between "centralization and civilization." Centralization had produced in Britain a book trade concentrated in London, where booksellers and newspaper producers operated in combination. Dickens personified this centralization in authorship, to the extent that he even sold advertising space in his serialized novels to less fortunate writers. The consequence was a real erosion of intellectual quality. British knowledge, Carey thought, was in decline. "Science, whether natural or social, is not in demand." The knowledge that *was* pursued there was mere empiricism; since the system could not be defended in principle, British science eschewed the search for principles. The United States followed a different model. There, decentralization made every citizen a reader. "The whole mind of the country" was improving, generating more and more inventions. Already

American farmers used machines far more powerful and more efficient than their English counterparts. That was one reason they could afford the time and money for books. This domestic progress therefore both financed and required the republication of foreign works. On a national scale, the reprint industry was one with the rise of American manufactures. "The rapid advance that has been made in literature and science is the result of the *perfect protection* afforded by decentralization."[53]

Carey therefore denied that the true cause of any British author's hardship was a lack of transatlantic copyright. The real problem lay in Britain. Authors were seeking relief not because of a real grievance to do with America, but because they had fallen into the same political-economic system as British industrial workers. Under centralization, the local demand for "information" dried up, and with it the local demand for authors. British weeklies, Carey declared, "require little of the pen, but much of the scissors." All who wanted to write professionally had to move to London—centralization again—where they encountered publishers acting in monopolistic combines, and of course the notorious deposit demanded by libraries. Even popular authors were published in editions of fewer than 2,500 copies—piddling quantities by American lights.[54]

An author like Macaulay or Dickens, therefore, was "precisely the same" for Carey as an industrial manufacturer who made cloth from cotton in a British factory. The great publishers were the equivalent of steamship or railroad magnates. They had the same autocratic, imperial tendencies. "Transporters and publishers are alike middlemen," he urged (with the example of the Camden and Amboy Railway in mind, which he had publicly assailed for its monopoly behavior). The only thing restraining them was "a salutary fear of interlopers." If some kind of compulsory license scheme could be adopted, then "much of the difficulty relative to copyright would be removed." But publishers opposed that idea as contravening the "respectability of the trade"—the very ideal of courtesy that, ironically enough, Carey had been so instrumental in embedding.[55] There was thus no way in practice to decouple the "*double monopoly.*" Carey's position here approached that of the antipatent campaigners who reprinted his arguments. For both, the question of copyright was a matter of the fundamental politics of industrial society.

But here Carey went further, and resorted to a frankly positivist view of knowledge itself. "Positive knowledge" rested in facts, and in facts there

could be no property. "Men who make additions to science know well that
they have, and can have, no rights whatever." Empirical discoverers (Carey
seems to have had explorers in mind) might labor to produce such facts,
but facts themselves were "the common property of all mankind." Moreover, a discrete set of workers arranged and compared facts to arrive at
laws, and finally entire sciences, and these too attained no property. "Newton spent many years of his life in the composition of his *Principia*," Carey
remarked, yet had gained no right in the "body" of the work—not that it
would have been worth anything anyway. Yet these were the only authors
who really produced knowledge. The class of writers who *did* benefit from
copyright produced no new facts or ideas, but merely "clothed" what
others had worked so hard to achieve. Robert Chambers was a case in
point: his hugely successful *Vestiges of Creation* had "appropriated" La-
marck's science and "reclothed" it. Walter Scott had likewise "filled his
mind with facts preserved, and ideas produced, by others, which he reproduced in a different form." Carey likened such writers to arrangers who
made bouquets from the flowers of other people's gardens. They deserved
some remuneration, certainly, but never a monopoly. Those pressing for
"the interests of science" in the international copyright campaign, he
pointed out, were in reality almost always "literary" men of this type—the
users, not the creators, of science. Had "a single man who has done anything to extend the domain of knowledge" signed the petitions? And yet
writers paid nothing for the facts they appropriated and exploited. Were
the Senate to consider a bill to give *discoverers* monopoly rights, Carey
hinted, it might merit examination—but it would never do so, because
these same literary clothiers would howl at the elevation of the real hewers
of wood and drawers of water.[56]

So Carey endorsed independence from copyright as essential to civilization, and did so on the basis of a sweepingly ambitious social science.
He attributed the Union victory in the Civil War partly to "the universal
development of intellect among our people," and warned that future
progress would depend no less on developing "the national mind." Knowledge must remain available to all, "old and young, poor and rich, black
and white." Universal copyrights, he roundly declared, were a relic of the
ideology of the slave owners. "The enfranchised black, on the contrary,
desires that books may be cheap." The "greed" of a Dickens or a George
Eliot stood out as in that light as not only wrong, but shameful.[57] The
choice was that stark:

Protection to the farmer and the planter in their efforts to draw the artisan to their side, looks to carrying out the doctrine of decentralization by the annihilation of the monopoly of manufactures established in Britain; and our present copy-right system looks to the decentralization of literature by offering to all who shall come and live among us the same perfect protection that we give to our own authors. What is called free trade looks to the maintenance of the foreign monopoly for supplying us with cloth and iron; and international copy-right looks to continuing the monopoly which Britain has so long enjoyed of furnishing us with books; both tending towards centralization.

That was why embracing international copyright would be, as Carey told the Speaker of the House of Representatives in 1865, "suicidal."[58]

UNIVERSALITY AND EMPIRE

In the nineteenth century, proponents of authorial property sought to deepen and extend the principle across time and space. Wordsworth wanted literary property made perpetual; Dickens wanted it to span oceans. It was the second effort that proved the more richly controversial, because the more promising. It coincided with the age of imperial expansion. Eventually, the proponents had their way. In the 1890s Washington did indeed legislate for international copyright (although the United States did not sign the Berne Convention until almost a century later, in 1988). That did not end unauthorized reprinting—far from it, as writers like Conan Doyle found out to their cost.[59] But it did bring to an end the period in which America made piracy a system. From then on, it was merely a crime.

In the generation-long struggle over reprinting that preceded this moment, skeptics based their antagonism on a refusal to abstract a principle of authorial property from the spatial extensions of power that it would in practice require. That is, they insisted that a universalization of authorship must be imperial in more than a metaphorical sense. That is why Appleton and Youmans had to base their plan for a transnational scientific community on the fragile basis of courtesies—and why such visionary endeavors provoked passionate opposition. The reasoning led in a direction diametrically opposite to that of the otherwise similar arguments leveled against patenting in Victorian Britain. The antiproperty camp in Britain proclaimed that the integration of the empire depended on the eradication of copyrights and patents; the antiproperty camp in America proclaimed that independence from that empire depended on the same deed. A link between empire and intellectual property—as it now came to be called—underlay both.

12

The First Pirate Hunters

It is the beginning of a new century, and the music industry is facing a crisis. New technology, new media, and innovative business practices are challenging the copyright principles that have underpinned the industry for as long as anyone can remember. Taking advantage of a revolutionary process that allows for exact copying, "pirates" are replicating songs at a tremendous rate. The public sees nothing wrong in doing business with them. Their publicity, after all, speaks of a mainstream music industry that is monopolistic and exploitative of artist and public alike. The pirates, by contrast, are ostentatiously freedom loving. They call themselves things like the People's Music Publishing Company and sell at prices anyone can afford. They are, they claim, bringing music to a vast public otherwise entirely unserved. Many of them are not businesses on the traditional model at all, but homespun affairs staffed by teenagers and run out of pubs and even bedrooms. In reaction, the recently booming "dot" companies band together to lobby the government for a radical strengthening of copyright law—one that many see as threatening to civil liberties and principles of privacy. In the meantime they take the law into their own hands. They resort to underhand tactics, not excluding main force, to tackle the pirates. They are forced to such lengths, they say, because the crisis of piracy calls the very existence of a music industry into question.

If this all sounds familiar, it is not because it is a description of the troubles facing today's entertainment goliaths as they confront libertarian upstarts online. This is a portrait of the early twentieth century, not the twenty-first. It was a time when the music industry faced a piratical threat more serious than ever before or—until recently—since.

At the beginning of the twentieth century the music industry in Britain and the United States was an enterprise devoted to the sale of printed sheet music. The publishers producing such music did so on a truly enormous scale. Copyright registrations between 1880 and 1901 came to over eight thousand a year, and the actual number of titles issued was much greater.[1] Perhaps twenty million copies a year were printed in Britain alone. The best-known pieces sold in the hundreds of thousands. The small number of wildly successful songs, like Stephen Adams's *The Holy City*, became major cultural icons (Adams's song, perhaps the most pirated musical piece prior to the Internet, would find a place in Joyce's *Ulysses*). As the industry was fond of pointing out, such hits cross-subsidized the many songs that were only modestly successful or that failed outright. To create them, publishers spent money on what they called "advertising," which included paying "royalties" to well-known music hall and vaudeville singers to perform particular songs. Those songs could then be marketed with the singers' endorsements—they were called "royalty ballads." It was a practice of which the industry was never very proud, and there were periodic attempts to change it, but they never succeeded because of fears that competing companies would take advantage of any that observed a moratorium. It explains why a leading *proponent* of musical copyright could tell MPs that he roundly denounced the paying of royalties.

The publishing companies were family firms, proud of their cultural mission. Not just concerned to exploit commercially the value of "dots," as the printed notes were called, they saw themselves as nurturing personal as well as professional relationships with artists like Stanford and Elgar. They sold sheet music at about a shilling and fourpence for each song. The details of how that pricing was calculated were kept confidential, however, and this encouraged rumors that the publishers colluded with each other to keep prices high. A pirate could get you the same song for twopence.[2]

Whether or not they were aware of this, the Edwardian pirates built on practices that had been pursued for centuries. The illicit reproduction of musical scores had existed since at least the seventeenth century, and probably earlier. But it had never been a systemic *problem* before, because

the enterprise of music publishing had not centered on a property principle. Until the 1770s music was regarded in England as lying beyond the
purview of statutory copyright, so piracy as such did not exist. Publishers
simply issued unauthorized reprints freely. They also arranged, trans-
posed, and otherwise altered works for paying clienteles, sometimes in
periodical form, as in Harrison and Drury's *Musical Magazine* of the 1780s.[3]
Meanwhile opera companies in the London of Handel and Arne thought
nothing of sending agents to each others' opening nights, transcribing
striking melodies, and reusing them in their own dramas. There was no
great sense of impropriety attached to this until later, when Romantic ideas
of authorial genius became commonplace and a composer like Hector
Berlioz could lambaste amenders as thieves, libelers, and assassins. Yet
Berlioz also reported that the arts of appropriation were still alive and
well in the nineteenth century: he recounted meeting a rascal named
Marescot who crowed about the fortune he had made by applying them
to Weber's *Der Freischütz*. (So brazen was his act, Berlioz added, that "I
feel pretty sure that you will take me for a historian and hence not believe me.")[4]

Almost every moderately successful composer knew the exasperation
this kind of thing could lead to, not least at the hands of the omnipresent
—and by all accounts extremely irritating—organ-grinders who filled city
streets with deformed versions of melodies like the toreador song from
Carmen.[5] Any fan of Gilbert and Sullivan knows of the furious, convoluted,
and sometimes ludicrous struggles they pursued in Britain, America, and
elsewhere over publishing and performing rights. Their early *Thespis* was
already garnished with a printed "Caution to the American Pirates," and
they once shipped an entire company of players to America under assumed
names to forestall a rival impresario. *The Pirates of Penzance* was composed
in a blurred rush of all-nighters (culminating in an interpolation of music
from *Thespis*) to stymie pirates in New York.[6] All this was simply the nature of musical life. What were unprecedented in the years around 1900
were the size and audience of the pirate boom. And in that context the
fact that music only *existed,* in a sense, in performance complicated its
plight beyond anything familiar from books and images.

Two profound changes underlay the extraordinary growth in music
piracy, one technological in character and related to production, the other
cultural and related to use. The first was the development of photolithog-
raphy. This process allowed pirates for the first time to make what were to

all intents and purposes exact copies. Some piracies took an expert to tell them from the genuine article. Paper quality might differ, but in terms of legibility a piracy was typically flawless.[7] This ability to produce practically exact copies at very low cost revolutionized piratical possibilities. The other change was the late Victorian phenomenon of "piano mania." As middle- and lower-class incomes rose, and consumer credit became an everyday experience, so money became available for leisure. In the last quarter of the nineteenth century a number of novel ways of spending it came into being, ranging from professional football and cricket to seaside holidays and the *Daily Mail*. Pianos were among the most successful of all. Suddenly every aspiring family wanted what one commentator called "that highly respectablising piece of furniture." By 1900, the proportion of Britons buying pianos (generally German imports) was far greater than that of French or Germans, and was exceeded only by the rate among Americans. In 1910 there was a piano to every ten or so people in the country. The boom created a completely new market for music.

Where pianos went, piano music had to follow. Middle- and lower-class amateurs created a huge new demand for cheap sheet music. Music publishers used all the tools of late Victorian commerce—newsagent networks, railways, and telegraphy—to distribute their wares to what was becoming the first musical mass market. One of the largest even branched out into making pianos itself. At first the publishers concentrated on piano reductions of operas and symphonies—you could even buy a transcribed *Tannhäuser*. But soon they saw the chance to create a new kind of celebrity for some of the songs they "plugged," and began fostering Grub Street composers dedicated to the rapid-fire production of pieces playable by mediocre performers in front of inattentive listeners. The social practice of music changed quite substantially as professional virtuosity diverged from, and increasingly disdained, this burgeoning realm of amateurs, who were trained by an equally burgeoning crowd of unregulated so-called professors. No wonder that at the height of the piano boom serious musicians could be heard condemning the instrument as "an evil influence upon home music."[8]

By the late nineteenth century, legislation had largely eliminated the kind of freedom that had made the earlier wholesale appropriations of music above board. But the new mass market threatened to make enforcement in practice virtually impossible. The new piracy began to take off in the late 1890s, and really exploded at the start of the new century.[9] At first it manifested itself mainly in metropolitan thoroughfares like the Strand and Fleet Street. But it was soon "all over the place."[10] It became ubiquitous, large scale, and sometimes breathtakingly insouciant. Nor was piracy solely restricted to "popular" music-hall fare and the like. Contemporary lists dating from the 1880s to the Edwardian era show that alleged piracies included works by Massenet, Sullivan, Gounod, Puccini, Mascagni, and even the occasional Wagner, as well as countless marches by a reliably indignant Sousa. The pirates copied any music that would pay, and as performance was democratized and domesticated this came to mean a very great deal of music indeed.

If it was a new mass market that drove piracy, what made it almost respectable was a widespread if intermittently expressed sense of resentment at the traditional music publishing companies. Like the eighteenth-century grandees attacked by Alexander Donaldson, they were seen as nepotistic, unimaginative, monopolistic, and secretive, and in the economic culture of the late Victorian era these were worse sins than they had been a century earlier. In 1899 composers even took the same step that authors had tried so many times, forming an association to publish music on their own behalf. It aimed to secure for its members "the full benefit of any financial reward" from their efforts. It seems to have been a failure, but its message was clear enough. Moreover, retailers too complained about the publishers. They objected to high prices, secrecy about the setting of those prices, and a practice of supplying material directly to music teachers at reduced rates. There was, then, a receptive audience for the claim that there was something seriously awry that the rise of the pirates was merely making manifest.

The publishers reacted to the pirates both individually and collectively. Chappell and Co., one of the main music publishing firms, seems to have been the first to take a strong stance. Its William Boosey was in the process of expanding the company's interests into the ballad market, in conjunction with regular ballad evenings at the Queen's Hall, and therefore had a new concern for the protection of copyright. The other major publisher to be concerned was the firm of Francis, Day and Hunter. This firm had evolved out of a minstrel act and now published large quantities of popular song (along, rather appallingly, with do-it-yourself minstrel kits). The most important alliance forged by such companies was at first the

Music Publishers' Association, created as early as 1881 by Boosey. The MPA encompassed not only all the major London publishers, but also a number of authors and composers, including Gilbert and Stanford.

The problem these firms and composers faced was not one of legal right. The law clearly decreed that copyright in printed music existed. The difficulty lay in translating that principle into practice. The law accounted copyright violation a civil offense, not a criminal one. This meant that tracking down perpetrators was largely a matter for their victims. They had no right to enter private premises to search for pirated music, however, unless the householder admitted them. No self-respecting pirate was ever likely to do that. Even if they did succeed in getting hold of pirated music, moreover, the most they could hope for was its destruction. Any award of costs was likely to prove futile, since the hawkers they usually apprehended tended to disappear before hearings, or else to plead poverty. The publishers would find the pirates back on the streets within hours, clutching fresh bundles of stock. This kind of problem existed for all publishers, of course. But it was not a great problem for books, since a book represented a relatively substantial capital investment and its seizure was consequently a serious matter for the pirate. With music, each copy amounted to only a sheet. Printing replacements was therefore cheap, fast, and easy. Pirates freely allowed them to be seized en masse, regarding it as a minor inconvenience—or, as one said, a small tax on their operations. Such a tax was certainly no deterrent given the profits to be made. No wonder, then, that some among the publishers came to the conclusion that they needed to go beyond the law.

TO CATCH A THIEF

In January 1902 the publisher David Day, of Francis, Day and Hunter, resolved upon more direct action. Day was already known for his staunch opposition to piracy: in 1897 he had been described as "the mildest mannered man that ever cut the throat (so to speak) or scuttled the ship of the piratical song printer." But what he planned now was far more risky than any strategy previously undertaken. He hired the services of a detective agency and raided a piratical warehouse himself, seizing five hundred copies of pirated sheet music. The raid was almost certainly illegal, but the astounded pirates offered no resistance. Encouraged by the success, Day and his men then moved on to "attack" a cottage in the north London suburb of Dalston, where hawkers were gathering to pick up pirated copies to sell on the street. They pretended to be hawkers in order to gain access, and nabbed fifteen thousand copies more. An unfortunate barrow boy yielded another four thousand. Yet another eight thousand came from a hawker's premises, twenty thousand from a room near Mansion House. Elated, Day retreated from the field and waited to see what the pirates would do.[11]

What they did, as it turned out, was nothing. The Dalston men had summoned a policeman, but when he declined to get involved they did not resist Day's raid. He had got away with it. Word of his success soon spread. An anonymous "Anti-Pirate" spelled out to the trade press its message: that the publishers should systematically recruit "commandoes" modeled on Day's raiding party, each group comprising twenty or so men ready to target marketplaces in London and beyond. It was a grimly appropriate word, coming as it did from the Boer War, because many of the songs being pirated were jingoistic ditties associated with the South African campaign. Before long the leading firms were embarking on such a policy. To further it Day inaugurated a new, single-purpose alliance that he called the Musical Copyright Association. He plucked a junior clerk from Francis, Day and Hunter, John Abbott, to be secretary of the group. Abbott found himself charged with spearheading a new offensive against the pirates—an offensive that would skirt the fringes of illegality, that would pursue tactics soon disowned even by the MCA's own lawyers, and that would depend for its success on the reluctance of the pirates to have recourse to the courts.[12]

Abbott proved a good choice. He went about his task with alacrity, recruiting and drilling a small army of what he called "ex-police officers and others with some knowledge of the pugilistic art." The intention was to "clear the streets."[13] As his campaign against the pirates began in earnest, hawkers were confronted on the streets, distributors challenged in their premises and pubs, and printers raided in their cellars and garrets. The numbers of copies seized mounted into the hundreds of thousands. The MCA even mooted prosecuting an unsuspecting member of the public who had bought a piece of pirated music, "with a view to making an example." That idea was quickly discarded, but in general the MCA was so successful that a year later the MPA was considering disbanding itself in its favor.

But not all pirates were as quiescent in the face of the MCA as those encountered by Day at the beginning. Faced by self-appointed troops, some of whom insinuated that they bore firearms, a few of the pirates did challenge their legal authority to act. Hawkers brought assault charges against the commandoes, and sometimes won. In August 1902 a home-owner was confronted in his doorway by half a dozen MCA men, who bullied their way into the house and threatened to "drop" him if he re-sisted. Even though they found three thousand pirated sheets, the case that came before the local magistrate was of assault, not piracy, and the MCA men found themselves rebuked. The MCA's policy was one of "orga-nized hooliganism," declared the magistrate. The remark rapidly gained notoriety, being picked up by opponents of the campaign and widely cir-culated in succeeding months. As such cases mounted, it began to appear that the offensive might backfire. After all, to the general public it might well seem that assault was a more serious matter than piracy. And this perspective was shared by some in authority too. One Leeds judge la-mented that as the publishers pursued their vigilante war, assuming guilt before innocence and trespassing on thresholds across the land, "the liberty of the subject is becoming of no regard at all."[14]

Moreover, substantial skepticism existed among retailers and their public that the publishers were acting in anyone's interest but their own. Perhaps British music lovers might even be better off with the pirates. Piracy was a blessing, remarked one music retailer with a plague-on-both-their-houses tone of resignation: perhaps, "now that the publisher is in his death grapple with the pirates," the London firms would finally be forced to listen to the retail network.[15] Another, writing anonymously from Liver-pool, blamed the trade for maximizing profits by flooding the market with commercial "rubbish." Only if a "system of 'weeding out' the poor and shoddy songs" were organized, he thought, could piracy be "dealt with." The *Yorkshire Post* reported that the major reason for piracy was that the publishers circulated only expensive editions, demanding a stiff 18d profit per item. After all, the success of the pirates in selling vast numbers of copies ought to convince the publishers that selling cheap could pay. And the fact that the MCA had had to resort to "a sort of police" scarcely indi-cated confidence that it had the public on its side. Stories of scandalously underrewarded composers now began to abound. The *Evening Standard,* for example, recalled how, at a time when "pirated craft cruise through the main and other thoroughfares of the metropolis," Strauss's *Blue Danube* had made £100,000 for its publisher in just one year, but Strauss had pocketed only £40. Through 1904, as the pirate war intensified, such stories resounded with increasing frequency and piquancy. Skeptics complained that even people who went out of their way to help the MCA against the pirates were treated shabbily. Embarrassingly enough, in several cases pirates brought before magistrates turned out to be ex-MPA or -MCA agents who said that they had been forced to turn pirate by the excessive prices charged by the legitimate publishers. "I can't help myself," said one. "The publishers charge such an enormous price for their copies." Their insider knowledge had only helped them become better pirates.[16]

Still, one of the main objectives of the campaign was being realized, albeit at a high cost in terms of public repute. As well as running to ground individual pirates, the MCA wanted to make piracy an issue on the national political stage. In this it succeeded. In October 1902 a new musical copyright act came into force. Intended to strengthen the hand of the publishers, the new law permitted the police, on being given a written request by a victim of piracy, to seize illicit sheets without first obtaining a special warrant. For the first time antipiracy raids could become official police actions. And the police moved fast to put their new powers into practice. In London the acting commissioner circulated a printed warning to hawkers that piracy would not be tolerated. At the same time Day and the MPA deployed their own force, numbering now perhaps a thousand men in the capital alone, to capitalize on this official backing. With letters of authorization from the major publishers, more MPA agents spread out across the country. The level of seizures went up dramatically. In the following three months alone 750,000 copies were lodged in police stations, awaiting the bonfire.

But that very volume betrayed a fatal weakness in the campaign. The seizures sounded impressive, but after a short time it became clear that the flow of piracies was not being staunched. Worse still, none of the pirated music seemed to be going to the incinerators. Police stations were simply becoming warehouses for hundreds of thousands of copies of pirated music that nobody wanted, and their cells were fast filling up with paper. Something, the police realized, was wrong.

The problem was that the same legal system that outlawed piratical invasions of intellectual property also treated the copies as objects of *physical* property. Therefore they could not be wantonly destroyed. Soon after the campaign began, a magistrate in London made this explicit. He insisted that the pirate from whom copies had been seized must always be heard from before they could be destroyed. The police lacked the power to arrest and detain pirates summarily, however; the only way to get them to court was by serving a summons. And because almost all hawkers either lacked a permanent address or refused to give it, a summons rarely worked. Of five to six thousand summonses issued in the ensuing period, only 287 were successfully served.[17] Almost always, the men disappeared into the city's backstreets, leaving no trace of their presence. They simply abandoned the seized copies, which promptly fell into a legal limbo, neither property nor nonproperty. Meanwhile the hawkers obtained more copies from their suppliers and returned to work. In other words, the 1902 law failed, as one magistrate said, because it did not oblige the pirate to defend himself.[18]

The mere amassing of pirated music was therefore impressive but futile. On February 1903, only four months after the new law had gone into effect, the Metropolitan Police suspended its enforcement. Eventually a compromise would be reached whereby the police held copies for a year before destroying them. But the new law was ineffective for other reasons too. In particular, it had been initially envisaged to provide strong powers to enter pirates' lairs and detain suspects, but these clauses had been removed in its passage through Parliament.[19] With no power to detain, no power to force one's way into private premises—magistrates were still ruling in favor of the pirates on this—and no power to fine offenders, the police and publishers still stood no chance of inflicting more than glancing damage. The MCA even tried to prosecute hawkers as unlicensed peddlers, drawing on laws that dated back to the seventeenth century; but this tactic too could do nothing to hurt the real pirates. The only other option was to go after pirates for not printing their names on title pages, which was illegal under newspaper law. But the publishers needed the permission of the attorney general to pursue this course, and four times he refused on the grounds that the law was intended against sedition and blasphemy, not to uphold a private interest. Eventually they gave up.[20] The campaign's futility had in the end drawn public attention to the weaknesses of the publishers' own position.

With criticism mounting, some in the trade saw a need to change direction. Day himself was the first to break ranks. The pirates were right in claiming that there was a demand for cheap music, as he admitted later, adding that he was "not above taking a lesson out of the pirates' book in that way."[21] In the *Daily Mail*, the organ of lower-middle-class cultural aspiration, he now announced the launch of a new sixpenny music series. Francis, Day and Hunter would issue at 6d songs previously sold only at 18d or 2s. The new price was far more competitive with that of the pirates. The first issues of this series, comprising both new and old music, appeared in October 1903. A direct result of the combination of pianos and piracy, the new venture was a radical departure for the orthodox trade. Leslie Stuart, whose *Soldiers of the Queen* was a mainstay of the sixpenny editions, remarked that it amounted to "an admission of the claims made by the defenders of the pirates that publishers have been robbing the public."[22] And the publishers' critics were, if anything, delighted to be vindicated in such an emphatic way. This was the "day of cheap music at last," hailed the piratical Popular Music Stores of Doncaster in the local press. For once, "the elect in the musical world must recognize the increasing desire of the masses to share in the refining pleasures of high-class music." Even the staunchly pro-publisher trade journal *Musical Opinion* proclaimed a "Revolution."

The campaign against music piracy was unraveling. Rather than forcing the pirates into line, Day's own firm had broken ranks and accepted their pricing levels. It seemed to acknowledge the increasingly widespread perception that the mainstream publishers had not been acting in accord with the popular interest. Even the new sixpenny series soon looked as though it would fail to undermine piracy, however, because the pirates quickly learned to use the legitimate pieces as "cover" for their own (that is, the hawkers would tout a pile of pirated music beneath a top copy of one of the sixpenny pieces).[23] Meanwhile the MCA, by now far less confident, had fallen strangely silent. So successful, so enterprising were the pirates in building up networks of manufacturing and distribution that, as one songster warned, they seemed to be "becoming publishers in their own way."[24] If that actually happened, then they would truly have won their war.

ARTHUR PRESTON AND THE PLACES OF PIRACY

For want of a better strategy, the publishers now decided to return to what Abbott called their "'smash and grab' method." With Day and Abbott's

MCA rather discredited, the MPA, previously rather dormant in the campaign, came back to the fore. And with it came the MPA's new agent in the fight against piracy, William Arthur Preston.

Arthur Preston—otherwise known as Willie, or, mysteriously, as "Nigger"[25]—had, like Abbott, been an employee of one of the big music publishers. In his case it was Boosey and Company, where he had worked since about 1890. He was deputed to the MPA in 1901, however, and from late 1903, if no earlier, enjoyed effective command of the Association's antipiracy efforts. In this capacity he traveled the length and breadth of Britain and Ireland, seeking out pirates and dragging them through the courts. Apparently indefatigable, Preston single-handedly revived the publishers' campaign, extending it to the furthest provinces and eventually seeing it through to victory. Remarkably, he kept a detailed scrapbook recording his successes—and his failures—along the way.[26] This scrapbook has survived, along with his archive of the music most vulnerable to piracy. Together they make possible a detailed reconstruction both of the practice of piracy and of the strategy by which it was defeated.

Preston ran three distinct campaigns against pirates, which may almost be thought of as circuits on the traditional English judicial model. The first was a sweep across the north of England and the Midlands, beginning in Liverpool in December 1903 and inaugurating an effort that would continue beyond Preston's own return to the capital. Among other towns, this campaign took in Manchester, Glossop, Doncaster (where the patron of the Popular Music Stores, one Joseph Cartledge, was the chief target), Sheffield, Barnsley, St. Helens, Leeds, Preston, Birmingham, Walsall, Leicester, Burton-on-Trent, Nottingham, and Middlesbrough. In each place hundreds, and often thousands, of copies of pirated music were seized. The second circuit then concentrated on London and its suburbs, including Enfield, Greenwich, and Walthamstow. It was this circuit that would culminate in the decisive breakthrough, as we shall see. Preston's third circuit, finally, took in the south, ranging from the Medway towns in the east to Plymouth in the far west. And as these proceeded, he continuously kept an eye on other regions, traveling to Dublin, Belfast, and Londonderry to hunt down pirates in Ireland, and even making a detour to the Isle of Man. Altogether he masterminded some 240 raids in three months (that is, an average of two to four a day), grabbing about forty thousand pirated items.[27] There can have been few men who saw more of the British Isles in 1904–5 than Arthur Preston.

Preston developed a standard approach for dealing with his antagonists. He would arrive by train, having been alerted to the possibility of a raid by his local agents (the descendents of Abbott's commando force, plus any music sellers prepared to support the campaign). Often he would bring with him a second-in-command, William Muffey. Claiming that he had been summoned by the complaints of copyright owners, Preston would also carry along certificates of copyrights lodged at Stationers' Hall in London. These were the essential proof on the basis of which he could obtain an order from a magistrate for a search. Sometimes he would go to the pirate himself and place an order as if he were a routine customer. The order obtained, Preston would then take with him at least two plainclothes police detectives. Sometimes he might take more, as at one notorious Birmingham house where both Preston and Abbott ran into trouble; after a sergeant expressed fear about going there, it being "such a rough place," Preston took two plainclothes men, one inspector, and five constables. They were confronted by an angry crowd of 150.[28] But even here they did eventually gain entry. Afterward, in court, Preston would say that he had personally examined the haul to verify that the sheets were pirated (sometimes he would concede that a few were not), and give a speech about the profundity of the threat posed by pirates to musical culture. Then, his purpose achieved, he would go on to the next town and the next case.

To understand these tactics, we need to go back to the reasons why the 1902 law had failed. The main one relates to a major theme of this book, namely, the relation between space and piracy. The law inherited a belief associating morality and place that had been ingrained in British society for centuries. This was the conviction that the home was the primary site of sound morals. In the late sixteenth and early seventeenth centuries, when vagrancy acts were first instituted, it had been taken for granted that secure, patriarchal households were the basis of a stable society. Streets, fairs, and markets, on the contrary, were notorious for their licentiousness. When piracy was invented in the late seventeenth century, it was at first associated with printing carried on in "holes" and "corners," rather than in homes. Laws requiring peddlers to obtain licenses, which the publishers had already sought to exploit against sellers of piracies, were another reflection of this idea, the tenacity of which it would be hard to overestimate. A principal reason why the 1902 act provided no right of forced entry into houses, then, was that it assumed a priori that piracy was a street-based crime.

The consequence became immediately visible in one of Preston's first cases, in Liverpool in late 1902. In this industrial city some two hundred separate songs were reputedly available as piracies, and the legitimate trade complained of a 60 percent decline in business. So Preston arrived and immediately moved to seize piracies from "street sellers." Then he and three detectives armed themselves with court authority and raided the home of one John O'Neile at 50 Hunter Street, seizing seven thousand copies of pirated music and causing a "sensation" in the neighborhood. They had found the top floor of the building "literally covered with music," they told the subsequent hearing; even more stacks of copies were under a bed in another room. The defense, however, contended that there was no evidence that the music had actually been *sold* there—something that Preston's attorney had to concede. "The act is rather weak," he observed; "It would have been better to leave us alone and let us proceed under the old act." The reason was, as the defense claimed, that "the act refers to street trading and not to anything in a house." So O'Neile was apparently warranted in storing music in his home. Stymied, Preston's lawyer had no option but to abort the prosecution. Tellingly, a moment after O'Neile walked, a barrow boy who had had far fewer pirated sheets in his possession came before the same judge and found himself with no such recourse because he had been operating in the street. He, by contrast, was punished.[29]

Preston's struggle with the pirates thus came to focus on questions of place. Was the location of a raid a home, or a warehouse? Was it a place of sale, or of storage? To what extent could police or MCA men obtain access? And, at a broader level, how was piracy distributed geographically across the country? The pirates' tactics adopted the same focus. They began to appear in courts and in the press as heroic defenders of domestic privacy, and as upholders of provincial autonomy against the monopolizing tendency of the capital. Newspaper reports increasingly tended to classify piratical villains according to their place of work. This culminated in a social taxonomy. Pirates were classified into four broad but distinct kinds, reflecting their relation with private and public spaces.

The first class was that of men who sold sheets "in the public streets." Generally termed hawkers, these were the small fry of the trade, who often reappeared with new stock mere hours after a confrontation, refused to betray their sources, and rarely yielded more than ten to one hundred copies at a time—sometimes they carried as few as one or two.[30] Preston and his men cornered innumerable such "travelers." They were everywhere, to the extent that in 1903 one legitimate publisher bewailed the fact that "all the business is now in the streets."[31] While there was inevitably a feeling of futility to such encounters, in fact the hawkers did change their practices as a result of the campaign, increasingly abandoning the thoroughfare as a place of trade. They instead went house to house, dropping printed catalogues through mailboxes and returning later to deliver any desired music to the householders. (In an example of the anti-Semitism occasionally evident in this struggle, Preston claimed that "alien Jews" specialized in this part of the trade.)[32] The pirates eventually took this strategy to its logical end by circulating their catalogues by mail, eliminating the vulnerable figure of the street seller altogether.

Something of a midpoint between street and premises was represented by the market stall. Markets had long had this ambiguous status, back into the early modern period, and continued to display it in the industrial era, even after the major fairs were no more. Much prized by their operators, stalls had a strange and ill-defined status as both private and public at once. This meant that Preston had to argue repeatedly for his right to seize materials on stalls, even though they might be visible to passersby—or might be only thinly concealed. In Cardiff, for example, he was accused of trespassing, which led to an open debate in court about whether a stall was "as sacred as an Englishman's private house." "That one spot is," it was affirmed.[33]

People with real addresses—shopkeepers, coffeehouse men, publicans, and so on—were an altogether more serious matter. Their fixed premises meant they could often act as local centers of distribution. Generally, hawkers would be supplied from some such house, pub, or other outlet, with the actual warehouse being a small distance away down a back street. Two examples stand out as notable. One was the Manchester shop of a young man called by the press "Himie Cohen," where Preston found thirty hawkers collecting piracies to sell (some of them escaped out of a window). He also seized a memo book detailing average takings of £12 to £24 per week—an indication of the proceeds to be expected from a middle-of-the-road piracy outfit. The other was the Rose and Crown, a pub in East London. This was probably the most notorious of all pirate hubs. A man known as Tum Tum, or Tubby, held court here, handling the distribution of copies from a nearby storehouse in Compton Passage. Tum Tum and the backstage "wholesale man" were two examples of the kind of figure Preston particularly wanted to catch.[34] Seizures from such men might come to five thousand or so—up to a thousand times what a hawker carried. Indeed, the numbers were large enough that they sometimes created problems of their own, as when Preston was told in a Sheffield courtroom to verify that every single sheet in his haul was pirated. It took hours; one bored spectator suggested that they pass the time by singing the songs.[35]

Preston also sought the printers who actually produced the piracies. But these were not as crucial as one might suppose. Like the hawkers, they were often, in Preston's much-repeated phrase, "men of straw." Frequently "foreigners," they worked in garrets or cellars, and used rented equipment so as to minimize capital risk if they were detected. Since they owned nothing, nothing could be taken from them in punishment or to pay costs. Even if they did own something, they often handed it on to a spouse or relative, who would continue the business.[36] By January 1904 Francis, Day and Hunter had pursued about three dozen injunctions against such figures, but had recovered costs in only three cases, all of which involved people with their own premises.[37] Still, more can be said about their locations. Printers of pirated music seem to have been concentrated overwhelmingly, and as far as Preston was concerned perhaps exclusively, in London. The poor, overcrowded East End was their principal manor. But plates could be distributed anywhere a willing worker could be found, so there were also raids in, for example, the relatively salubrious precincts of Kensington. From temporary and shifting workshops copies could be produced at astonishing rates—five thousand per man per day, according to one informer—and distributed across the rest of the capital by means of a secretive network employing railway station cloakrooms. And from London the rail network took them quickly and efficiently across the country, to Leeds, Liverpool, Manchester, and the great railway nexus of Doncaster. There, local organizers distributed them back down the social hierarchy of piracy, first to the local distributors, both in the regional centers and in lesser towns like St. Helens, Barnsley, Leicester, and Nottingham, and then through their rear windows to the hawkers.

But all these, too, were in the end of merely secondary importance. The real catch was the mastermind, the pirate himself. This figure was the publisher's illicit doppelgänger. He was the criminal capitalist, the musical Moriarty, the piratical patron of the arts who oversaw the whole enterprise while never getting his own fingers inky. The pirate might be a highly visible public figure, yet one able to move from place to place with apparent ease. And the pirate was the one figure that Preston, Abbott, and their men had never managed to nab. He seemed to be, as the *Sheffield Telegraph* lamented, "ungetatable."[38] For all its dynamism, Preston's offensive would not be a true success until it trapped a real pirate.

Then, on Christmas Eve, 1903, it did.

THE KING IN PARLIAMENT

Away to the cheating world go you,
Where pirates all are well-to-do;
But I'll be true to the song I sing,
And live and die a Pirate King.

THE PIRATE KING, IN GILBERT AND SULLIVAN'S
Pirates of Penzance

The great Victorian railway termini of London give rise to lines that snake out across the city atop stolid brick viaducts. The arches under these viaducts have often been converted into warehouses and workshops. Today, for example, the rare pedestrian who wanders onto Link Street, a few steps from the traffic that roars by incessantly on the main road between the east London boroughs of Hackney and Homerton, will find a line of such arches occupied by a taxi firm, a repair shop, and a used-car dealer. Hundreds of London's distinctive black cabs are parked there nose to tail, awaiting mechanics and drivers. There is nothing to show that this is the place where, a century ago, music's first pirate king held court.

For some time, Abbott, still pirate hunting, had had one of the Link Street arches under observation in what he called "the best Sherlock Holmes manner." Finally, on December 24, 1903, he was ready to launch his raid. Armed with an order from Hackney Police Court, he and two plainclothes policemen entered the archway. There they garnered a huge haul: almost seventy-five thousand sheets of pirated music that had been about to be dispatched down the Great Western Railway to the pirate network. It was a big enough discovery that for once the pirate turned up to contest it. His name, apparently, was James Frederick Willetts.

Not much is known about Willetts. Even his name is a little uncertain. As pirate king, he often used the alias John Fisher, coined apparently because he had at one point been a fishmonger of some kind; and he also had a number of other monikers, among them "the colonel." His mother had been a printer, and he had served an apprenticeship, probably in her house. He was experienced in the business, having worked in newspapers for fifteen years. But since then he had tried out various other trades, including that of traveling salesman. He had once been imprisoned for embezzlement, which he defended as appropriating what were rightfully his wages when his erstwhile employer went bankrupt. Since the 1902 law, however, he had seen an opportunity to earn a windfall from his original trade, and had become the nation's leading music pirate.[39] His business card (for J. Fisher and Co.) listed his address as the Rose and Crown in Goswell Road, which made Tum Tum his agent. Willetts coordinated some half a dozen printers, and a distribution network that extended across the nation. Dealing in huge quantities of music, it was he who so insouciantly dismissed a seizure of forty-five thousand copies as "a little tax." With grudging respect, Day—who seems to have spoken with him personally—called Willetts "a most energetic man with a thorough business training." He was, Day allowed, "a model pirate."[40]

The Christmas Eve raid was the first of a series of spectacular attacks over the next eighteen months. They progressively revealed a network of piratical manufacturing and distribution, run, to all appearances, by Willetts. In early 1904 Abbott raided a cottage in Finchley and found a printing operation with twelve thousand copies of pirated music. (Its overseer, one J. Puddefoot, complained in Gilbertian terms that the searchers were "straining at a gnat and swallowing a camel," since "they do worse on the Stock Exchange every day.") In March, Francis, Day and Hunter sued James and Arthur Childe of Islington, who had printed ten thousand copies in Hoxton and Islington. In October, a raid in Hackney yielded nearly 240,000 copies. In July 1905, another in the north London suburb of Dalston yielded over 280,000 from a warehouse rented by George Wotton on behalf of the king of the pirates. Subsequent raids across north London and the east end resulted in further big hauls: 6,500 in Devons Road, 150,000 in Upper Holloway. Off Goswell Road, a warehouse operated by William Tennent on behalf of "J. Fisher and Co." and selling by catalogue yielded 160,000 copies.[41]

Such numbers commanded attention. Parliament once again had to turn its attention to music piracy. January 1904 saw a series of hearings before a special committee convened to address the issue. As far as the facts of piracy were concerned, the committee heard little that was new. Those testifying before it included leading publishers, who attested to the extent and intensity of the problem. Both Abbott and Preston appeared, as did police officers, lawyers, and magistrates. But what was remarkable was that the "king of the pirates" himself, Willetts, volunteered to appear alongside them. He did so in his capacity as manager of the People's Music Publishing Company—a front organization that was based in the venerable book-trade center of Paternoster Row. His testimony was recorded verbatim, and reported at length by the press across the country under headlines that repeated his claim that piracy was beneficial (even "good for piano trade," as one asserted).[42] It was the first—perhaps the only—comprehensive defense of piracy ever to be voiced by a self-proclaimed pirate king in a major center of political power.

Willetts seized his opportunity to the full. His defense addressed both the structure of music publishing as it then was, and the broader principles of musical culture to which it appertained. He began from the position that no author or composer should be given—or in fact had—a freehold on gifts that were God given for the public benefit. This was in principle non-controversial. For the first time, however, musical works really did redound to the general good. Willetts reminded the MPs that educational reforms in late Victorian society had only recently made musical proficiency part of the cultural makeup of every artisan and factory worker. This and the piano boom had created a market for sheet music that simply had never existed before. More than that, the new market (which Day had called the "number 2 market") remained fundamentally distinct from the more traditional market to which the legitimate publishers remained devoted. Unlike their purchasers, Willetts's were working class. They simply could not afford music priced at 18d per song—a price that he considered "extortionate." But they did not necessarily desire different and inferior *kinds* of music. Artisans as well as gentlemen, he insisted, bought music from *Tannhäuser, Carmen,* and *William Tell* (all of these being out of copyright). And in this he was right; Day had conceded that the pirates sold "a good quantity" of Chopin, Beethoven, and Wagner.[43] All they wanted was music that was affordable. Willetts therefore argued that piracy of such songs at 2d had no significant effect at all on existing publishers' sales, because the pirates addressed a sector of society that they neglected completely. Indeed, piracy might even *increase* the sales of the legitimate publishers, since it amounted to free advertising. Willetts claimed that David Day had confessed as much to him privately (both of these enemies occasionally hinted at remarkably candid conversations between them, as though the leading policeman and the leading pirate could have no secrets from each other). In other words, he insisted on the fractured character of the new mass culture at a time when others were content to extol its size.

But why were legitimate publishers insensitive to this enormous new market? Because, Willetts continued, they had evolved into a cozy, familial trust—a "ring"—dedicated to maintaining high and uniform prices by means of confidential collaboration.[44] In order to maintain their place, the publishers made much of the importance of the authors and composers having sacrosanct rights, but it was not the authors and composers who decided how those rights were exercised; nor did they decree their rates of return. The publishers determined how the system worked in practice. In other words, they were implicitly acting in the tradition of the trade assailed by Babbage two generations earlier, by Donaldson in the eighteenth century, and by Atkyns in the seventeenth. And they had made their ruthlessness crystal clear by their illegal and violent actions against the pirates (Willetts liked to tease his opponents with that magistrate's line about "organized hooligans").[45] But, Willetts now added, Parliament need not accept their conventions. For the sake of the new public interest that had now come into existence, changes must be made. The publishers' combine threatened "to really stop the musical education of the country."[46]

Willetts also advanced his own view of the nature of musical property itself, merging older criticisms of literary monopolies with his new notion of a mass public interest. Copyright was not a freehold, he insisted, nor a natural right. It had originally been a "liberty" or "privilege" conferred on an author by Parliament for the public's good, and it must return to that status. The proper analogy was not with real property at all, but with the kind of monopoly that Parliament might grant to a supplier of any public good, like a rail operator or a gas company. Such a monopoly did not give the operator an unrestrained right to charge whatever fares it wished, or willfully to restrict access regardless of the public interest. A rail company, for example, could not refuse to operate trains for all but the wealthiest portions of society, even though this might be the best policy for the company. In fact, Parliament routinely decreed that train companies *must* run services at prices that the people could afford, and at times they needed, in return for granting the monopoly. This was an extremely significant point for Willetts to make. It showed that he was versed in the antipatent campaign of MacFie and Armstrong a generation earlier, which had appealed to exactly the same practice in arguing for a form of compulsory licensing. (Ironically, cheap excursion trains now provided the ideal way to distribute Willetts's pirated music across the nation.)[47] So this, Willetts maintained, was precisely what Parliament should do for copyright monopolies now. Where it had fostered the concept of cheap travel, so it should now foster the concept of cheap music, in the same quest for a cultured citizenry. There should be first-class and third-class editions of musical pieces, just as there were first- and third-class railway carriages. Both would get the punter to the same point, but with varying comfort levels en route. They would have different appurtenances (bindings, typography, and so forth) and would appeal to different markets. This, he pointed out, was precisely what Francis, Day and Hunter was already doing with its cheap music series—an idea that Willetts claimed had originally been his. (Interestingly enough, media conglomerates have been tempted to try similar market-segmentation strategies to counter music piracy in our own day.)[48]

If this idea were to work, however, then existing copyright practices would need to change radically. Willetts wanted to decouple two central components of literary property. On the one hand, the pirate king professed strong and unequivocal support for the principle of rewarding authors or composers through income from sales—indeed, he pointed out that because it did not maximize sales the existing system often failed to provide a livelihood at all, citing the case of one composer reduced by the publishers to such straits that she died in a lunatic asylum. He insisted that composers would benefit more from the massively higher sales a mass-market cheap-publishing regime would produce. On the other hand, however, he defied the usual assumption that linking authorial incomes to the market must imply a power to restrict a piece's circulation. Instead he proposed that Parliament decree a statutory royalty. This would take effect along the lines proposed in MacFie's patents furor, and in fact recently enacted in qualified form in a new patent law.[49] Anyone could reprint and sell a piece of music, on this account, but all who did so must pay the composer and author at the required rate. Only the most abysmal flops would fail to cover their own printing costs.[50] Essentially, Willetts was arguing that a piece of music should be regarded as analogous to an invention under the antipatent campaigners' understandings. Or, more saliently perhaps, he was arguing that it was akin to a performance. In fact, the principle would at length be adopted to deal with the new technologies of recording and broadcasting.

In this context Willetts suggested that piracy had an important social function beyond serving the public interest directly. Not only did it bring cheap music to the commonwealth. Not only, too, did it employ thousands, at a time when "work is wanted." (The pirates liked to claim that copyrighted music tended to be printed abroad, whereas everyone accepted that theirs was done in London, although the mainstream publishers countered that it was done there by foreigners.) He also argued that it was a catalyst for legal change. Willetts maintained that such change was always slow and overdue, and tended to come about only through what he called "agitation"—another point learned, perhaps, from the patent wars. In Edwardian England piracy was the agitation that made the problems of mass musical culture manifest. It forced the need for new law into the public eye. When a mass market for cheap music was legitimated, the people would have the pirates to thank.

Day grudgingly conceded that the pirate king had a defensible-sounding ideology. "The pirates say that times have changed," he remarked. "They say they have been doing good work for the nation for the spread of music by doing what publishers ought to do."[51] In testifying to Parliament, Willetts wanted to make piracy into orthodoxy. His campaign—as he saw it—would recalibrate commercial propriety around a new kind of mass market and a new kind of moral norm. Day could see the appeal of all this. But Willetts went too far. He did not want it to stop at music, but urged the parliamentary investigation to extend to books too. And it seems that others outside Parliament wanted this connection made too. At any rate, in a strange incident the significance of which is hard to judge, pirated versions of Kipling, and, more strikingly still, of Prime Minister Arthur Balfour's *Economic Notes on Insular Free Trade,* appeared on the streets at this very moment, the latter announcing itself as an educational initiative aimed at enlightening the masses. The book piracies were widely noticed and everywhere linked to the music debates. But if the intent was to provoke a revisiting of copyright in general, they had no immediate success. Willetts's own attempt to draw parallels was swiftly silenced, while his parliamentary allies suspected that the proposed extension to books was a scare tactic fomented by the industry in a bid to create enthusiasm for a stronger bill.[52]

The parliamentary committee was not about to accept any of this. Willetts was subjected to aggressive questioning about the personnel involved in his operation (in stark contrast to the representatives of the established publishers, it may be noted, to whose customary confidentiality the committee enthusiastically deferred). Understandably reluctant to reveal such sensitive details, Willetts ended his testimony in some disarray. With his departure the investigations came to an end. The committee then brushed him aside in its report and recommended that a stricter antipiracy law be passed. Unremittingly hostile to Willetts's claims, the report argued that piracy threatened the future of the music publishing industry and had to be combated. It urged giving the industry everything it wanted.

Yet Willetts's testimony did find some sympathetic hearers. Even the music publishers' own trade press conceded that it was a mistake to be so secretive. More significantly, the pirates had a major sympathizer in Parliament: a Glasgow MP named James Caldwell. Caldwell was a Radical who had made a fortune from calico printing—an industry with its own rich history of conflict over copyright piracy. He had been responsible for watering down the earlier law against music piracy, and had talked out two stronger bills in 1903–4. Now he once again mobilized to the same end, threatening to stymie the publishers' desired law.[53] He used the hearings to advance his own report, explaining why the practice had arisen and what should be done about it. His account matched that of the king of the pirates at almost every point. Piracy was a substantial problem, Caldwell conceded, but it was driven by the "lawless and high handed" actions of the publishers acting as a trust. Their combination upheld high prices, producing a situation analogous to that of London's book publishers a generation earlier with respect to the United States. In each case the result had been entrepreneurship denounced as piracy. He endorsed the existence of a vast new working-class "number 2 market," and charged that the existing publishers were entirely neglecting it. This being so, Caldwell agreed that piracy might even serve to *increase* legitimate sales, because it demonstrated the popularity of a piece without appealing to elite customers.[54] Caldwell wanted this belief written into copyright itself, ideally by a compulsory-license clause similar to that in the patents statute. In effect, this would disaggregate copyright into two rights, of authors and sellers. The former would be protected while the latter was opened up.[55]

Caldwell and Willetts stood in profound conflict with everyone else represented. They alone maintained that copyright was not simply a matter of the private interest of the owner—a property likened repeatedly to that which a gentleman had in his watch. Preston for one endorsed this very high (and legally untenable) notion.[56] The result was a pronounced desire to bring legal protections for copyright up to the same standard as those for more conventional theft—to raise piracy to a form of larceny. This would not be merely "natural progress," as one London magistrate had suggested, but, Caldwell insisted, a real transformation.[57] He pressed witnesses again and again about their views of the nature of literary property itself, only to be told again and again that it was solely a matter for the owner. The public had no stake in it, pricing in particular being entirely a matter for the publishers. To Caldwell this high-handedness was the real explanation for why the industry was experiencing such difficulty. It would always be hard to enforce a law, he pointed out, to which "the general public sympathy" stood opposed.[58] At the same time, Caldwell insinuated that the "illegal proceedings" of the MCA had themselves increased piracy by "advertising" both the money to be made and the impunity of the pirates. Everything combined to persuade him that Parliament should be chary of giving even greater powers—powers of detention and entry in particular—to the publishers.[59]

By this point the authorities had taken upward of three million copies of songs from the pirate king and lesser operators, to no obvious deterrent effect. On the contrary, the popular legitimacy of their enterprise seemed only to increase. The *Daily Mail* told its middle-class readers that the pirates had wrought a "revolution in the publication of music"—and announced the launch of its own series of cheap songs to take advantage of it.[60] In early 1905, moreover, the pirates took a further ominous step when Willetts formed a limited company. From now on he was personally insulated from many liabilities. However many copies the MPA and police might seize, he could be back in operation almost immediately.

It was at this point that the publishers resorted to desperate measures once again. Boosey's ran a socialist candidate against Caldwell in his Glasgow constituency, in an attempt to split the vote and get a friendly Conservative elected in his place. That tactic failed. The industry then held a huge protest in central London to voice the antipirate cause. Parry and Elgar went along, joining with the publishers to launch a new alliance called the Musical Defence League. Then, in April 1905, the mainstream publishers took the most drastic action of all. They announced that the problem of piracy had grown so severe and so endemic that they would no longer invest in publishing any new works. In effect, the entire music publishing industry shut down. "Mr Caldwell's triumph," it seemed, was "all but complete."[61]

THE CONSPIRACY

Alongside Willetts's sensational testimony and Caldwell's mischievous maneuvers, the House of Commons committee on music piracy also heard a new suggestion to counter the pirates. It was voiced quietly on January 20, 1904, by the veteran barrister Sir Harry Poland. Poland remarked that it might well not be practical to pursue the pirates for breaching copyright, for all the reasons that the publishers had articulated. But in the very act of banding together to perpetrate their deeds the pirates were, he thought, committing a real crime. They were engaging in a conspiracy. Although piracy was a merely civil offense, the law regarded conspiracy as a far more serious matter—one subject to severe penalties, including prison. It should certainly be possible to prosecute them for that.[62]

This comment by Poland reappeared as an almost casual aside in the committee's final report, submerged by its general recommendation for a new copyright law.[63] But the line that the pirates might be "engaged in a common law conspiracy to infringe on rights of property" caught the attention of a lawyer named Percy Beecher. Beecher then mentioned the remark to William Boosey, chief pirate catcher of Chappell and Company. Boosey immediately saw a chance to damage the pirates. The evidence was already available, after all, from all those raids carried out over the past eighteen months. It had simply never been regarded as *evidence* before, because nobody had thought to pursue the act of organization in itself. Now it gave an opportunity for a real victory. And this possibility arose at a time when the pirates' use of a limited-liability company rendered even the existing strategies even more futile. Boosey decided to make the attempt.

The resulting trial began in December 1905. The alleged conspirators included many men who had been the subject of raids in the previous eighteen months, and whose operations had proved to be linked. George Wotton, William Tennent, John Puddefoot, and William Wallace were charged with conspiracy to print, publish, and sell copyrighted material— but the main target was their leader, Willetts. Together they had worked as James Fisher and Co., a company name registered in January 1904 under the names of Puddefoot and Wallace, plus several others who seem to have been entirely fictitious. There was no doubt that Willetts was the real force behind the organization. Their hearing took seven weeks, with over fifty witnesses participating. Willetts chose to mount what has been described as a token defense. He first remarked that the songs in question might not be copyrighted at all, as few of them were registered at Stationers' Hall. Then he maintained that the legitimate publishers themselves depended on secrecy, consistently refusing to reveal the terms under which they operated. In fact this defense may not have been intended as token at all, since it echoed complaints leveled consistently since the seventeenth century that the enterprise of publishing was itself conspiratorial. In any case, Willetts may have been hoping that parliamentary legislation would render the case moot. It did not, and his own defense proved futile. Willetts was sent to prison for nine months.[64]

Willetts's sentence marked a fundamental shift. For the first time, the pirates faced severe penalties. They could no longer hope to resume operations a day or so after a raid. Soon after the Willetts trial, a second conspiracy case, this time against the "Leeds Pirate King," a man named John Owen Smith who had done extensive business with Willetts, resulted in a similar victory for the publishers. Then, in August 1906, the new music copyright law was finally passed by Parliament, over the objections of Caldwell and his few allies. It had been championed by the senior parliamentarian T. P. O'Connor, with the all-important advantage of government support (fig. 12.1). Even so, it passed only on the evening of the last day of the parliamentary session, and with the aid of a special sitting of the Lords. The new law confirmed the sea change brought about by Willetts's dethroning, because it ended any hopes that he might have harbored that piracy would be decreed legitimate retroactively. Willetts never recovered. But the king of the pirates had scarcely been deposed when sheet music prices suddenly rose by 50 percent; middle-class musicians might have been forgiven a brief twinge of regret at his downfall.

THE RISE OF THE PIRATE HUNTERS

The music publishers had survived. In the wake of Willetts's defeat piracy did not vanish completely, but it was drastically reduced in scale. Willetts himself was finished, and Caldwell's arguments seemed forgotten—

A PIRATE CRAFT.

T. P. O'CONNOR *(Captain of War Sloop in chase).* "THE ROGUES! THIS OUGHT TO SINK 'EM!"

FIGURE 12.1. T. P. O'Connor fires a music copyright cannon at the pirates. "The rogues! This ought to sink 'em!" *Punch* 131, no. 1 (July 4 1906): 11. Courtesy of the University of Chicago Library.

although when gramophone records were included in copyright law a little later it was on terms similar to those proposed by Willetts for popular songs, and compulsory licensing would be embraced for books, too, albeit on a limited scale.[65] The Music Defence Department of the MPA was disbanded. Arthur Preston retired from the MCA; he went on to manage Margaret Cooper, the resident light entertainer for Chappell's ballad concert series at the Queen's Hall, and died in 1926.

In 1944, four decades after Preston's pirate war, it underwent a strange revival when Britain's Ministry of Information decided to recall these events to public view. The Ministry was eager to exploit nostalgia to rebuild public morale as World War II drew to a close. It recruited a film company called Gainsborough Studios to produce a series of movies. Some of the resulting films were based on music-hall themes, and one in particular centered on Abbott and Preston's pirate war. It was entitled *I'll Be Your Sweetheart*, after a song that had been pirated in those days. Shot in between V2 strikes, the film starred Margaret Lockwood, at the height of her notoriety for her "wicked lady" roles, and the then unknown Michael Rennie, who would soon go to Hollywood and find stardom as the alien in *The Day the Earth Stood Still*. It told a simple love story tacked onto a one-dimensional account of the piracy crisis from the publishers' perspective. The movie was no masterpiece, and it understandably made a negligible impression both at home and in its U.S. release. But, looked at today, it is a rather extraordinary document because it incorporates substantial tranches of dialogue closely culled from the actual raids, court cases, and arguments of 1900–1905. How it came to do so is not entirely clear. But it is certainly the case that Gainsborough had recruited many ex–music hall stars in the 1930s to appear in its screen comedies. One of them was the screenwriter and director of *I'll Be Your Sweetheart*, Val Guest. Guest had begun his own career as a songwriter for one of the music publishers in the wake of the Willetts episode. It seems that in devising his film he wrote up the stories that he had heard told in its corridors. And he transformed them, somewhat bizarrely, into propaganda. The music industry's first pirate war thus became a tale of the solidarity of commerce, creativity, and public-spiritedness against black marketeers and spivs.[66]

Guest's moralized retelling suggests the longer term significance of the campaign against the music pirates. The last-gasp victory of the publishers had rested on what was virtually a redaction into legal argument of Preston's pilgrimages across the land. The publishers won by finally confronting the fact that piracy was a matter not just of immorality, but of complex social networks with their own channels of communication and their own ideology. The conspiracy charge succeeded, not by challenging the content of the pirates' networks, nor by seizing their products, but by identifying them *as* networks. So all those raids and seizures had not been so futile after all. They had yielded something immeasurably more valuable than a million or two sheets of paper. What really counted were the tiny scraps of knowledge they had yielded. Together those scraps could be combined into a detailed understanding of piracy as a collective practice—and it was only when they were so combined that the pirates met their nemesis. Preston and Abbott had defeated Willetts, in effect, by replicating his own social knowledge.

In that light Preston and Abbott's historical significance lies in the institution they created: the first ever private police force dedicated to fighting piracy. There had been precedents for this, to some extent—one thinks of the agents sent across the land to track down piracies in the mid-eighteenth century. But nothing resembling their drilled "commandoes" had ever been put into the field before. They took this initiative at the very moment when private detective agencies such as Pinkerton's were coming into their own in America and Britain as entrepreneurial counterparts (and sometimes more) to the professionalizing police forces. Like them, Preston and Abbott had hit upon an opportunity that was not to go away. Their initiative marked the beginning of an alliance between business, intelligence, policing, and intellectual property that would endure long after their victory. Today, private antipiracy policing is a growth industry. It recruits ex-policemen, as Preston and Abbott did, and it too has been known to pursue its quarry not just as pirates but as criminal conspirators. The modern pirate hunters propel policy and legislation too. In the early years of the twentieth century, the private antipiracy police raised serious questions about everyday rights and freedoms—questions that many at the time, including prominent legal officers, viewed as seriously as any concerning piracy itself. How far those questions remain pertinent today, in the context of a vastly larger and more powerful antipirate industry, is something that should give all of us pause for thought.

13

The Great Oscillation War

Since the last years of the nineteenth century, new forms of communication and recording have proliferated as never before. Society has found
itself having to accommodate not just one or two potentially revolutionary
technologies, but an accelerating series of them: sound recording, radio,
television, audio- and videotape, computers, digital media, the Internet.
We are naturally accustomed to invoking the revolutionary importance
of the most recent of these. But in the history of piracy there is a strong
case for saying that the most transformative of all was an earlier device:
radio. Radio *broadcasting* in particular was something entirely new when
it arrived in the 1920s. The power to transmit instantly and openly to an
ill-defined but massive population demanded a change in assumptions
greater, in its day, than that required by the Net today. It was this that triggered radically new forms of piracy—and new strategies to fight them.
Many of today's piracy concerns can be traced back beyond digitization,
to seeds sown at that time.

During the 1920s "pirates" were seen as a potentially mortal threat to
the nascent enterprise of broadcasting itself. But two kinds of piracy were
at issue, exemplified in the United States and Great Britain. Everything
in the different systems adopted by these two nations—ownership, financing, technology, policing, and cultural impact—coalesced in the problem
of piracy as each defined it. In America, piracy was a form of *transmission*.

Pirates were broadcasters who interfered with each others' signals. Often, these were originally legitimate operators pushed to the margins by the increasing might of the networks. Theirs became the relatively familiar kind of pirate radio that would return to prominence in the 1960s and that still exists today. Their story is relatively familiar and fits neatly into the long history of piracy as a practice of reproduction or circulation. In the United Kingdom, by contrast, something more interesting happened. Although such challengers did exist, the more dangerous pirates were not transmitters at all. They were *listeners*. That is, "pirates" were members of the public who "listened in" to broadcasting without contributing what was reckoned to be their fair share to its costs. This was a radically new kind of piracy—a receptive practice, not a productive one. It came into being, significantly, at the time when the concept of "information" started to emerge. The subsequent histories of receptive piracy and information were to be quite closely related. But in the first place the practice of pirate listening imperiled the very existence of broadcasting in the British realm.

PATENTS, POLITICS, AND A NEW KIND OF PIRATE

Just as America experienced a "radio boom" in the early 1920s, so too did Great Britain. In mid-1921 Britons had held just four thousand licenses for "experiments in reception." A year later there were seven thousand, along with 286 for transmission. That June, the *Daily Mail* sponsored a broadcast of Nellie Melba, announcing the moment when "listening in" became an aspiration of its huge middle-class readership. After that, thirty-five thousand receiving licenses were issued in 1922, followed by 1.1 million in 1924, and 2.2 million in 1926—an increase of 55,000 percent in five years in licensed sets alone. A 1924 guide also contained well over one thousand call letters of amateurs engaged in transmission.[1] In this short, euphoric period radio had become part of everyday life. John Reith, the British Broadcasting Corporation's first director general and the dominant figure in broadcasting before WWII, declared that roof aerials were now a ubiquitous sight in the urban and even rural landscape.

Authority over the transmission and reception of radio signals lay with the Post Office, by virtue of earlier legislation giving it control of telegraphy.[2] It took the responsibility seriously, and until the early 1920s issued licenses on the assumption that they would be for scientific activities. Even the Marconi Company—the dominant player in the nascent industry—

had to apply for permission to transmit from its experimental station in Chelmsford. In 1920 the Post Office actually denied Marconi a license, on the basis that its "frivolous" signals were not true experiments and might interfere with military communications. But it soon received a rude shock. By this time thousands of private enthusiasts had already begun to experiment with receiving and transmitting devices of their own, setting up "stations" and stimulating a literature of wonder that invited ever more to join in. Dozens of wireless societies had sprung up across the country, starting as early as 1913 and proliferating after the war. As in America, this community was made up of citizens who had either begun tinkering before World War I or, in many cases, been trained by the military. And as in America, too, they saw themselves as upholding an ideal of the "man of science" with full research freedom. Their "first and constant" campaign was therefore for the granting of receiving licenses "with complete freedom." "Every Englishman," the amateurs declared, "is entitled to hear what is going on in his aether provided his listening apparatus does not annoy his neighbours" (an important and, as it proved, consequential proviso).[3] Moreover, they saw the ether as a natural commons across which such free researchers could roam in search of discoveries. So when the Post Office suspended Chelmsford's transmissions, more than sixty societies, boasting some three thousand members, protested against the decision, and did so in the name of science. It was an unexpected declaration of strength, before which a startled postmaster general backed down. It signaled how central the identity of the scientific experimenter would become as the enterprise of broadcasting got under way.

At much this time, several companies began to seek licenses for "what is called 'broadcasting.'" Marconi alone proposed to build six powerful transmitters across the country, which would have been enough to make the ether a private preserve. But Marconi had challengers, and if more than a few of their proposed stations were built, it seemed that "interference and chaos" would surely result. The problem was already looming large in America, where stations routinely drowned out each others' signals, threatening a level of "ether chaos" that might make listening unbearable in major cities. The Post Office heard that Washington was girding itself to impose "very drastic" restrictions. A secret report by an assistant secretary named F. J. Brown not only brought home the scale of the problem in the United States, but also noted that the economic viability of broadcasting remained unproven. It looked as though Commerce Secretary

Herbert Hoover would address both issues, Brown reported, by instituting a hierarchy of stations assigned to discrete bands.[4] Some equivalent regulation must clearly be considered in Britain. Permission to use radio "for experimental purposes" had always been granted readily enough, but the question facing the Post Office now was how to forestall "chaos" on an American scale.[5] Moreover, the government was wary that the new medium might be used for what it called "communistic or other seditious propaganda." The two fears combined to inspire a conviction that only "reputable commercial organizations" should get licenses to broadcast.

By mid-May 1922, several large transmitters were already in operation. Marconi had plants in Chelmsford and London; Metropolitan Vickers ("Metrovick") had one in Manchester; Western Electric had another in Birmingham. The risk of ether chaos was growing fast, and the Post Office decided to call a halt. It forthwith deferred proposals for nineteen or twenty more stations, declaring that "the ether is already full."[6] As Postmaster General F. G. Kellaway told MPs, it would be "physically impossible" for so many to operate at once. The laws of nature forbade it, and ignoring those laws would lead only to "a sort of chaos." Some recipe had to be arrived at for both funding the enterprise and avoiding chaos. Marconi believed that it had one. It advanced what it called a "revolutionary" proposal. The plan envisaged that the government would oversee programming, and even keep a list of all purchasers of receiving sets. The company would build and run the transmitters. It would transmit free broadcasts for licensed receivers, and in addition would offer a paid service for weather and financial information restricted to those with special sets tuned to receive it. Discrete wavebands would be set aside for the free and paid broadcasts, along with more for amateur experimenters. Receiving sets would then be sold as sealed boxes, pretuned to the appropriate wavebands. The government seems to have viewed the scheme sympathetically, not least because it would "discourage" ordinary folk—"as distinct from experimenters and serious amateurs"—from listening in to signals on other frequencies. As Marconi's engineers noted, there "seems to be no reason for making it easy for the general public to listen to everything that is passing in the ether."[7] Such sentiments hinted at the combination of public concern, technical possibility, and hard imperial politics that would have to go into forming a system.

On May 18, twenty-four of the leading manufacturers of receivers met with Kellaway to hash out the issue. Sparked by Marconi's proposal, the meeting set in train a series of negotiations—intricate, delicate, and often angry—that would culminate in the creation of the British Broadcasting Company. To see why piracy became a major concern, it is necessary to delve a little into this process. From the start, it focused on the prospect of a single overarching institution. Two concerns pointed this way: that of possible ether chaos, and that of violating intellectual property.

It was Marconi's Godfrey Isaacs who proposed a single conglomerate. His major rationale at first was not chaos, but patent ownership. As the holder of more than 150 relevant patents, Marconi believed that no other concern could build a transmitter without trespassing on its rights. Isaacs declared himself willing to cede those rights, but not to competitors; he would only countenance a single body operating in the public interest.[8] He therefore proposed that the major manufacturers meet at Marconi House to decide among themselves the shape of this institution. In the event, the more neutral venue of the Institution of Electrical Engineers was adopted, but the manufacturers did indeed meet. They immediately delegated the details to a committee of the "big six" manufacturers— Marconi, Metrovick, Western Electric, the Radio Communication Company, General Electric, and Thomson-Houston. Just one representative of the many smaller manufacturers was added to their number, and that at the insistence of the Post Office. During the ensuing weeks this committee met frequently, at times on a daily basis. Its exchanges were often sharp, in particular when Isaacs confronted Archibald McKinstry of Metrovick, who became the standard bearer of an anti-Marconi bloc. The problems they addressed were in their eyes "fundamental."[9]

We can tell what topics preoccupied these men because an agenda for their first meeting has survived. It was drawn up by Frank Gill, president of the Institution of Electrical Engineers and chairman of the committee. Several of the issues that Gill listed as central were destined to remain constant themes in the subsequent history of British broadcasting. Should it be the preserve of a single institution, for example, or should there be competition? How should it be financed—should advertising be permitted? What about the handling of news and politics? But what is striking is how unproblematic these perennial issues proved at the time. The preference for a single company, for example, was clear. It would avoid "confusion and interference," circumvent patent clashes, facilitate oversight, make for "efficient and stable" programming, and provide a coherent system for "national use." And nobody wanted unrestrained advertising, so the need for some public provision was also uncontroversial. The problems lay in the implementation. In particular, such a plan would necessitate both restricting the market for receivers and imposing a license fee, both of which were politically problematic and therefore constituted "considerable obstacles" for the Post Office. The committee realized that a "united front" was essential if it were to succeed. What imperiled that prospect were three problems, critically important at the time, that have since dropped out of sight. Gill identified them explicitly: patents, protectionism, and piracy.

First and most urgent was the issue of intellectual property. Both patents and "know-how," as the participants called it, would need to be pooled somehow for any single entity to be feasible. How this might be done proved an almost insurmountable problem, on which the whole proposal for a single company nearly foundered. Isaacs wanted to insist that Marconi alone, as the dominant patentee, build the transmitters. It alone could furnish "uniform" standards, he declared. But the others denied this "absolutely," retorting that their own patents might be fewer but were just as necessary. They wanted the future company to pick and choose apparatus on grounds of quality, "regardless of the patent situation." McKinstry in particular complained that Isaacs would make Marconi a monopolist. Metrovick, he said, refused to proceed "on the basis of operating by leave of somebody else." Isaacs responded by challenging the others to place their own designs on the table, saying that anything in them that seemed preferable would be incorporated by Marconi in its apparatus. Scarcely an inviting suggestion, it found no takers, and the all-important unity disintegrated.[10]

Some way must therefore be found, as Gill put it, to proceed "unhindered by patents." It was a measure of the seriousness of the crisis that Gill himself proposed simply abandoning them altogether. McKinstry agreed, saying that a "composite station" could then be built with "the best of everybody's patents." He even recommended that the manufacturers indemnify the future company against patent-infringement suits. But Isaacs would have none of it. He dug in his heels and insisted that unless all stations were built by Marconi it would scupper the whole plan. "We are not going to give you the opportunity of learning what we have learnt," he insisted. McKinstry, exasperated, repeated his charge of monopolism. If Marconi was set on vetoing the scheme if it did not built all the stations, then he would veto it if Marconi did.

McKinstry now proposed a desperate course. He suggested scrapping the entire one-company scheme and instead creating two rival bodies, centering on what had emerged as the two patent pools. The first would be the British Broadcasting Company; the second, a new entity provisionally called the Radio Broadcasting Company. Manufacturers would join one or other company as they preferred, and each of the eight proposed transmitting stations would then be allocated to either the BBC or RBC. A third corporation would divide up license revenues between the two.[11] It was a workable if ungainly idea, and the postmaster general grudgingly agreed to support it as a last resort. But Isaacs still vowed that he would prevent the second company from using Marconi's patents. It now seemed that *any* proposal would fall afoul of his intellectual property absolutism, and that broadcasting itself might be stillborn. In despair, the group reported that not only could they not agree, but they could not even arrive at a wording to describe their disarray.

With the crisis at hand, McKinstry and Isaacs met privately over several days and hammered out a compromise. Nobody knows the course of their arguments—they must have been intense—but by July 19 they were back to talking in terms of one company.[12] Perhaps Isaacs saw that unless Marconi compromised, it risked losing its patent rights anyway by state intervention. Precisely that had recently happened in the United States at the end of World War I, when the company had seen its patents allocated to U.S. companies, especially RCA. At any rate, Marconi relinquished its demand to build all the stations. It would construct six, but the other two were to be allocated by the board of the new company, and Marconi agreed not to restrict their use of its patents. Gill had been right: only when intellectual property was abandoned could the roadblock be passed. The *way* in which it was set aside, however, would have lasting consequences.

Finally a viable scheme was in the offing. The new company was to be a conglomerate, open to all "genuine British manufacturers employing British labour." They could buy in by purchasing shares at the nominal cost of £1. The company would gain free access to its members' patents in building and maintaining its equipment. While nothing explicitly guaranteed that it would be the sole broadcaster, in practice its monopoly was everywhere assumed. For all its eventual rationale of public service, therefore, the company was constituted initially as a combine cemented by patent sharing, and was bound up with a protected market.

The Post Office opted to fund this enterprise by a combination of two sources. One was a royalty charged on every set sold to the public. This would pay for capital expenditure on transmitters and plant, and would expire once those costs were met. Rates varied for different sets, but were substantial: they ranged from 7s 6d for a crystal set to 45s for a three-valve set.[13] Partly to secure this income, for at least eighteen months only British-made receivers were to be sold, and only BBC members could make them. They must be manufactured to designs approved by Post Office engineers, and an official decal must be displayed on each set to confirm this. Certain components too—valves, headphones, and speakers—had to bear this mark. Kellaway had been reluctant to exclude foreign competition, fearing charges of protectionism; and the move did prove controversial. But he finally endorsed the arrangement. It seemed "reasonable and defensible" in the face of cheap imports from European countries with devalued currencies, and from an American trade brought to a juddering halt by ether chaos. And there was a major technical rationale too. The requirement served the need to minimize an annoying resonance effect known as *oscillation*. When oscillation occurred, a listener's equipment experienced what later would be called positive feedback. The aerial would then reradiate and produce interference for receivers across the surrounding area. Much more than interference by unlicensed stations, it was the characteristic "howl" of oscillating receivers that in practice threatened ether chaos in the United Kingdom. If oscillation derived from poor-quality or mismatched parts, then, it was surely appropriate to empower Post Office engineers to counter the menace.[14]

The second funding source was a license fee paid annually by all owners of receivers. This income was to be devoted to programming costs, so the policy was open-ended. The new "broadcast licenses," as they were called, could be bought at Post Offices anywhere for 10s, half of which would go to the company. They authorized their holders to use approved receivers to listen in to signals transmitted by BBC stations. They did *not* authorize the use of non-British components, nor non-BBC sets. A license holder could not legitimately use the equipment for other purposes, nor for other listening. And while the combination of stamp and license did not expressly forbid people from opening up their sets and tinkering with them, the intent was certainly to convey the impression that doing so was frowned upon.

In planning for the new system, officials assumed that two hundred thousand of these broadcast licenses would be sold in the first year.

Everything depended on that figure being met. But how many Britons would pay for authorized receivers if German or French imports cost much less? And, more importantly, how many would buy licenses—especially if they were being asked to stump up higher prices for receivers too? Nobody knew the answers to these questions. If the population were indeed to prove recalcitrant, moreover, then enforcing either rule would be extremely difficult. On the answers to these questions—and especially the second—would depend the fate of British broadcasting. Looming over the whole scheme, in short, was the third problem that Gill had identified at the outset. He had signaled it in the agenda for that first meeting by an entry consisting of three cryptic words: "as to pirates."[15]

PIRATES AND EXPERIMENTERS

The first broadcast licenses went on sale in November 1922. At much the same time the new company came into being. The BBC was initially capitalized by the big six, all of which were represented on its board.[16] As it began broadcasting, however, and as set manufacturers sought to sell receivers to its fast growing public, so its ranks rapidly grew. From an initial membership of about twenty companies, it grew to over five hundred within the first year. On the face of it, it was a roaring success. Yet within the BBC and Post Office, officials remained justifiably apprehensive. Grumbling about the scheme had been heard even before it got off the ground, and the conservative press was assiduous in fomenting discontent. At times the *Daily Express* in particular—which aspired to its own broadcasting station—ran hostile stories almost daily in the name of what it called "free air." So the potential for popular resistance was real. And it was not long before reports started to reach the company of citizens refusing to buy licenses.

Anyone determined not to buy a broadcast license had two options. The first was simply not to get one at all. This was the possibility that Gill had signaled by his reference to "pirates." A fear of piracy was thus explicit in the very origin of British broadcasting. The piracy Gill spoke of was not an illicit reproduction of information, however, but its illicit reception. For the first time, large segments of the population stood to be labeled as pirate *listeners*. The problem was that nobody had any inkling of how many would actually turn pirate in this way and "listen in" without a license. The temptation was certainly real enough, not least because there was no practical way of identifying the culprits. Prior to November, the scheme's backers had preferred to assume and assert that the British were good sports. The whole enterprise depended on that educated guess about national character. The problem was that it soon became clear that the British character was not so docile after all. Sales of broadcast licenses fell far short of hopes, and the gap increased by the week. By mid-1923 the number of unlicensed receivers was widely estimated at one to two hundred thousand. One hostile newspaper even put it as high as five hundred thousand, and the postmaster general conceded publicly that this was not an unrealistic figure. Such numbers were more than high enough to call into doubt the viability of broadcasting.[17]

If outright piracy had been the only problem, then perhaps the authorities could have conjured up a solution to it. But the second option open to a thrifty public vastly complicated the situation. This was the option to seek a so-called experimenter's license. The experimenter's license was essentially the same old permit that had existed before the BBC was ever mooted. It cost 10s, the same as the broadcast license, but holders were exempt from the royalty on sets and could use whatever equipment they wanted. This freedom was essential for research. But it also permitted soi-disant experimenters to listen to the BBC at substantially lower cost (and, some said, with better equipment) than the hoi polloi. When the broadcast license went on sale, therefore, the number of Britons claiming to be experimenters suddenly began to rise. In February 1922 there were just under seven thousand reception licenses in use; by July, that number had grown to eleven thousand. Already one MP had forecast that "they will be 100,000 before long," and he proved close to the mark.[18] By December, thirty thousand claims for experimenters' licenses had been received. The Post Office expressed itself "greatly concerned" about the rate at which they were coming in. Two months later, fifty thousand had accumulated, and the procedure for appraising them had seized up. On New Year's Day, 1923, the new postmaster general, Neville Chamberlain, stepped in. Chamberlain announced an immediate moratorium on experimenter's licenses. Before any more could be issued, the government would have to be sure that they went only to *real* experimenters. The survival of the system depended on it.

The existence of experimenters combined with the phenomenon of listener piracy to cut a swathe through the suppositions on which the broadcasting regime was based. By the time the crisis came to a head in spring 1923, the number of experimenters in Britain had apparently increased by some 10,000 percent, with unknown hundreds of thousands of outright pirates too. The number of broadcast licenses sold was meanwhile only eighty thousand—a long way short of the two hundred thousand initially envisaged. Sales of new BBC receivers had meanwhile slumped by 75 percent, which far exceeded anything attributable to market saturation. Everyone assumed that the missing purchasers were buying unlicensed sets. It was a calamity, and it was clearly due to pirates. But nobody had any way to identify the out-and-out license evaders. So attention focused instead on the people who had licenses but claimed to be experimenters. These could be found, certainly, but the question they posed was one of authenticity. The fate of broadcasting now hung on the deceptively simple problem of telling a true experimenter from a piratical imposter.

That problem was a very delicate one. The experimenter's license encapsulated what were seen—not least by the Post Office—as freedoms both useful and powerfully symbolic. Those who proclaimed the right of science to access the ether did not lack for powerful friends. After all, until broadcasting came along, *all* licenses had been for experimenting, and officials valued their role in supporting what they now distinguished as "bona fide experimenters." Originally the question of bona fides had not arisen at all. "Experimenters" had simply been amateur enthusiasts who built their own sets. They had been motivated not by the desire to listen to broadcasting, which had not existed, but by curiosity about the properties of wireless, the ether, and the future of communication. The development of wireless had taken place largely at their hands. Moreover, the figure of the experimenter as a modest, plainspoken, virtuous worker of wonders commanded widespread respect—before Big Science, it seemed that not much separated the radio researcher from a figure like Ernest Rutherford, who had risen from colonial origins to the pinnacle of scientific achievement. Not least, that figure was seen as a peculiarly *British* individual, personifying hope for the empire's future in the face of German discipline and American teamwork. Indeed, Kellaway had found himself facing parliamentary challenges on this score even before the BBC plan was finalized. Rumors about sealed sets, restrictions on equipment, and a monopoly on transmission had all aroused fears for the future of science, and therefore for that of Britain. "Why are not the British public permitted to obtain the best instruments science and brains can produce?"

one MP had demanded to know. Another alleged that "if they shut out foreign inventions from coming into this country, the development of science may suffer."[19] It would be "perfectly absurd," agreed the laissez-faire advocate and publisher Sir Ernest Benn: "what people want is the freest intercourse of the scientific ideas of all the nations of the world."[20] MPs liked nothing better than to hail the "large and enthusiastic and important body of scientific men, chiefly young men, in this country, who are deeply interested in amateur wireless telegraphy." Experimenters' licenses should be not only available, some thought, but free, lest the authorities hobble "this new and very interesting scientific development." In the end Kellaway had had to commit himself publicly to the experimenter's license in order to get the BBC launched at all. The freedom of science was apparently at stake.[21]

There is even evidence that the prospect of an outcry over experimenters may be what frightened the radio companies into setting aside their patent feuds so suddenly and coalescing around the BBC plan. The big six companies had realized from the outset that they must make special concessions for what they too called "bona fide" experimenters.[22] But as negotiations proceeded Sir William Noble secretly learned that several manufacturers of components—allies of the wireless experimenters and antagonists to the prescribing of complete sets—had approached the *Daily Mail* to run a "propaganda campaign" against a royalty system on the basis that it would impede experimental science. Noble was concerned enough to press the big six to "rush" the formation of the BBC to head off the possibility. They did. The propaganda campaign went ahead anyway, however. The mass press now set itself up as the defender of participatory science. "It is intolerable," the *Express* thundered, "that tens of thousands of scientifically inclined British subjects should be prevented from carrying out experiments." It was impossible to predict which citizens might make crucial discoveries, it charged. "The more experimenters, the more discoveries." According to Fleet Street, "an amateur who makes his own set is an experimenter in the truest sense of the word. He is constantly manipulating it, probing mystery after mystery, and the whole history of great inventions has shown that it is in this way that discoveries are made." Thousands of amateurs were working to find a cheap alternative to crystal, for example: "Surely this is experimenting." This being so, "the mere *intention* to make a set should entitle any one to an experimenter's licence." And the *Mail* ran a series to help laypeople qualify as experimenters so as

FIGURE 13.1. The anti-BBC press. "Kitten on the keys." *Daily Express,* April 11, 1923.

to "enjoy the full freedom of the ether."[23] The conservative newspapers' campaign for "free air" did not let up throughout the difficult early years of broadcasting (figs. 13.1 and 13.2), and this evocation of the lay scientist was central to it.

CITIZENS AND SCIENTISTS

How many "bona fide" experimenters did Britain really contain? Nobody had any idea. Originally, estimates had been of the order of five thousand. No one had supposed that there were even ten thousand "genuine experimenters" in the country—the very idea had been dismissed as "extreme."[24]

FIGURE 13.2. The anti-BBC press. "Open the window." *Daily Express,* April 7, 1923.

But as the license system came into being, such estimates fell by the wayside very fast. Increasingly anxious, the BBC told the Post Office that 80 percent of the applicants for experimenters' licenses could not possibly be "bona fide." It urged resolute action against supposititious experimenters, and a stiff rise in their license fee. Without at least a threefold increase, it warned, *everyone* would soon be claiming to be an experimenter.[25] Noble suggested that "the great bulk of the high grade amateurs" would surely accept such an increase, since it would "eliminate many of the amateurs who are not bona fide experimenters." The police might well need to get involved too, the company warned darkly. But its pleas met a frosty reception. The Post Office agreed to dispatch inspectors, but without enthusiasm or optimism, and Chamberlain "scoffed" at the very idea of enforcement. The government dismissed outright the demand for an increased experimenters' fee, despite signs that the Radio Society of Great Britain was indeed willing to entertain the idea. "Out of the question," a Post Office official scrawled flatly on the memo proposing a 300 percent increase.[26] Panicking, the company then demanded an outright moratorium on experimenters' licenses. But this was even less likely to happen. One MP reacted by proposing that the licenses be issued to *all* applicants, however unqualified, in order to "encourage the attainment of a scientific acquirement by the people." An exasperated postmaster general would eventually threaten to do just that—and to authorize a second broadcaster to boot. That would have terminated at a stroke the economic, political, and technical justifications for the BBC's very existence.

What qualified someone to be counted an experimenter? The BBC was revealingly equivocal on this question. With its very survival at stake, it declared itself "quite certain" that the true number of experimenters was but a small fraction of the fifty thousand applicants. It guessed perhaps five thousand at most, insisting that the Post Office was witnessing "a wholesale effort made by boys of all kinds to call themselves inventors."[27] Yet it refused to say *why* it believed this. A "machinery" for "finding out who are genuine experimenters and who are not" was beyond its remit, it declared. Only the state had the legitimacy to establish such a mechanism. And as it happened, the Post Office did have a criterion for identifying experimenters. The problem was that the advent of broadcasting had rendered it completely useless.

The Post Office's standard had been adopted as part of the deal introducing the broadcast license in the first place. It was called the "liberal" criterion. It held that *anyone who built a receiver* was both qualified and, presumptively, motivated to do experiments. This was the definition that the postmaster general had upheld in winning Parliament's approval for the broadcasting plan, and until now the Post Office had tried to maintain it in practice. But finer-grained definitions were considered and sometimes implemented piecemeal on the basis of the Post Office engineers' experience of appraising how "fit" applicants had been for transmission licenses prior to 1922. Applicants had to show themselves "men of good character," for example—one Harold Butler being "an Honest,

Hard-working and Industrious Man, . . . very Intelligent among Machinery." One possible qualification was a declared commitment to some specific program of experimental work, such as a study of the effects of weather on reception. Another, seen as much more plausible, was the ability to use a receiving set without oscillating. But none seemed workable as a general rule. The press would surely raise hell about more constraints on science, and constituents were already complaining to their MPs of being denied experimenters' licenses. Why was a Mr. Dwyer of Pengam denied a license, for example? Because, his MP learned, experimenters' licenses were issued "to all applicants who furnish evidence that they have a definite object of experiment in view and possess sufficient qualifications for the purpose." Dwyer had been deemed to have no scientific qualifications. A similar query revealed that military officers were generally assumed competent to be experimenters. These were touchy subjects, however, and the postmaster general made haste to affirm that he could see no better way than the liberal rule to distinguish "bona fide experimenters, whose license fee he would not desire to increase." Perhaps a "boy" who assembled a set from parts was not really a "bona fide experimenter," he conceded, but rendering any finer distinction as a matter of consistent policy was impossible.[28] He even denied that listening to the BBC disqualified one from claiming the title of experimenter. After all, an experiment in reception might depend on receiving the broadcast signal, in which case the distinction would lie in how the recipient experienced it. As one scientist put it helpfully, "the experimenter may listen to the 'Beggar's Opera' purely for the purposes of comparison, but he must not listen to it for purposes of enjoyment."[29]

It soon became clear that the basic assumption behind the "liberal" definition of the experimenter had ceased to make sense anyway. The assumption had been that someone skilled enough to make a set would be capable of experimenting with it. But what it meant to "make" a set had changed. Companies had sprung up to supply parts that users could simply bolt together. Some manufactured their own, others imported them, this being all too tempting for "the pirate in the trade who stops outside the B.B.C. and 'takes his risk.'" These enterprising parts makers were generally not specialist radio firms, but, as McKinstry put it derisively, mechanics capable of making "a small nut, a small screw, or a bit of wire." He called them "pirate firms," and meant the charge in at least three senses. First, as they were not radio manufacturers the BBC would not admit them to its ranks, so they were not authorized to sell parts at all. Second, they pirated—in the old sense of unauthorized reprinting—the "British Broadcasting Company" decal and slapped it onto substandard parts that they then sold for genuine. And, third, they violated Marconi's patents. (Complaints on this last score lessened somewhat, it must be said, when it turned out that Marconi itself was quietly importing headphones from Central Europe under a shell company called British Danubian Imports.) The general problem they presented, however, was that they provided an escape clause to the license system. Any literate person could now construct a receiver by following their instructions. Such instructions circulated very widely, appearing on cigarette cards, for example, and told how to make radios out of everyday items like whisky bottles (fig. 13.3).[30] Inherent in the liberal criterion for experimenters' licenses had been the assumption that building a set was *hard*. That was why it was a good proxy for expertise. But now everyman could cobble together a radio. The clients of the pirate firms thus committed both listener piracy and patent piracy at once, and could get away with it by claiming to be experimenters

FIGURE 13.3. Bottled wireless. *Daily Express,*
April 25, 1923.

on a definition that no longer worked. If not stopped, complained Western Electric, this practice would "spoil the whole thing."[31]

Invoking the rise of this market in parts, furthermore, the press now insisted—and the company conceded the point—that a large proportion of so-called pirates were in reality victims of their own consciences. That is, they were not buying licenses because no license applied to them. They built their own sets, and therefore met the old "liberal" definition of experimenters; but they used their sets only for listening in to the BBC, and so did not see themselves as experimenters at all. The *Express* estimated that fully 75 percent of all set owners fitted this bill. These pirates were actually the most enterprising and principled class of Britons, added the *Mail*. They were "so keen that they have made their own sets," but at the same time were ethical enough to resist a false characterization and defy an overweening state. "If it comes to the two choices they would rather choose being a pirate than having their name given and being subject to arrest."[32] The system was thus creating tens of thousands of criminals of conscience. The press began to call on the Post Office to create a third kind of permit, therefore, which it dubbed a "constructor's license." As the *Daily News* put it, if "an ingenious amateur" could make a receiver using parts, then this "amateur with experimental leanings" must be accommodated in a way that did not offend against the very virtues of honesty and plainspokenness that experimenters ought to possess.

Creating such a license would mean acknowledging that the liberal definition of the experimenter was dead. It would require a new, more substantive definition, involving the pursuit of experiments *after* building a set.[33] The company saw an opportunity here. If a much smaller set of experimenters could be identified and set aside, then it could pursue its true targets with much less political trouble. Maybe experimenters' licenses could be restricted to what Chamberlain called, in a meeting with Reith and Noble, "scientific research wireless workers."[34] In March 1923, hoping for such an outcome, the company submitted its own proposal for a £1 constructor's license that would still restrict its holders to parts of British manufacture. But the Post Office remained opposed, still fearing condemnation for imposing a tax on the curiosity of the "boy, or young person, or poor man."[35] And the parts manufacturers responded with outright hostility. They launched their own full-blooded campaign against the BBC, denouncing it as a combine squatting on an industry that had outgrown any need for monopoly. The result, they declared, was "the chaos at present existing in the trade," in which "piracy is encouraged." Apparently a regime designed to prevent ether chaos was creating social chaos. Convinced that the system had broken down—or rather, it had never worked in the first place—Ramsay MacDonald demanded a parliamentary investigation to ascertain how such a disastrous agreement could ever have been signed. And the question of the experimenter had come to subsume all of the problems facing the new medium.[36]

The company realized it was in a pickle. Strong action against spurious "experimenters" and outright "pirates" might save it in the short term, observed its chief engineer, but such action would require policing so aggressive as to be politically disastrous. It would therefore doom the organization anyway.[37] Before more than a few months of broadcasting had passed, the experimenter and the broadcaster were at loggerheads. Either the ideal of the amateur scientist must be jettisoned, or the broadcasting compromise would die. This was the legacy that the initial patent feud had left behind—a kind of social, political, and epistemological booby trap lodged at the heart of the broadcasting system. One postmaster general confessed to struggling for "days, and almost nights" with it, and called it the most difficult problem of his career.[38]

It is worth pausing to ask why. What made the identity of the experimenter so prized? In large part, the answer has to do with the anxieties of the 1920s, when technocracy was the utopian politics of the day and an entire generation that might have secured a scientific future for the nation had been lost to war. It was now that the League of Nations proposed an international law allowing for the patenting of scientific facts, precisely to encourage a new generation to become scientists.[39] But there were also deeper historical currents at work. The question of the experimenter had roots extending back to the seventeenth century, and had been revived by the Victorian debates about industry and invention. By the early twentieth century, at risk of oversimplifying, three broad types existed for the authoritative knower: the older ideal of a gentlemanly, generalist amateur, distinguished by disinterest and purity of motive; the scientist proper, distinguished by expertise and professional qualifications; and the lay experimenter or inventor, distinguished by experience and originality but impossible to identify by any rule.[40] Radio crystallized these distinctions. Here was a technology that was at once a popular hobby, a tool of utopian change, and a branch of technical knowledge—one built on the dauntingly difficult physics of Maxwell, Hertz, and Heaviside. Its founding figures were often not academics or industrialists, and scientists had initially dismissed Marconi's own claims as either exaggerated or commonplace. In this light, broadcasting was bringing about a public reckoning between the social identities of the scientist, the researcher, and the lay inventor.

When Chamberlain imposed his moratorium on experimenters' licenses, it was supposed to remain in place until a definition of an experimenter was settled upon. The Post Office declared its resolve to restrict such licenses to what it called "persons with unquestionable qualifications." But what exactly it meant to be qualified as an experimenter was, of course, entirely unclear.[41] The question was already urgent, and was getting more so by the day: the BBC thought that two hundred thousand more "infringers" would take out experimenters' licenses if they could, making for a total far in excess of the original hopes for broadcast licenses. One possible answer lay in examinations. The Institution of Electrical Engineers was the best-known instance of a body that used formal exams to create a profession. But one reason why the identity of the experimenter was such a problem was precisely that such systems had, to an extent, failed. Measuring mastery of a stable body of existing technological knowledge was one thing; measuring the potential to master and transform a fast-advancing field was quite another. The Radio Society of Great Britain maintained no examinations or professional diplomas, and in any case the Post Office resisted imposing any such "standard of importance" to distinguish between experimental programs.[42] In the parliamentary inquiry that eventually looked at the issue, the idea of basing experimental identity on formal scientific qualifications was considered and rejected. It recognized experimental potential as too protean to be captured in formal examinations. An attempt by McKinstry to limit licenses to members of technical institutes similarly expired, when it was pointed out that Edison himself would not have qualified by that criterion. "You are in danger of nipping in the bud all sorts of semi-genuine people," one witness warned: they "cannot *prove* their ability for anything of this kind and yet might be useful investigators or inventors."

A. A. Campbell Swinton, FRS, drove home the same point to grander effect. Swinton, who spoke for the Radio Society of Great Britain, roundly declared that radio "owes its existence to amateurs," and cited Marconi and Oliver Lodge—as well as Sir William Armstrong, the Victorian enemy of intellectual property—as proving the point. No rule could exist for identifying experimenters like these. In practice, Swinton thought, "you have almost to let anybody experiment who wants to." The more people were encouraged to experiment, the more likely it was that the crucial discoverer would turn up. This was to Swinton a matter of national survival. "In our modern electrical civilization," he warned, "our commercial survival depends upon the attention given to electrical subjects." The big new U.S. industrial research laboratories could swamp any British rivals in their field. The only way to compete with them was to do something *different*—and the way to do that was to take advantage of the putatively British virtue of individuality. The stereotype of the British eccentric suggested a real strategy to set against the spirit of teamwork manifested in American industrial research. The empire might depend on this virtue. Swinton—and his was a widespread view—was therefore arguing that Britain must protect the lone experimenter lest the nation become beholden to another power's intellectual property. Broadcasting policy must be subordinate to that paramount need. "From the point of view of the future of the country," he insisted, "the experimenter is a more important person than the broadcaster." Far from worrying about experimenters interfering with broadcasting, he warned of the dangers should broadcasting be allowed to interfere with experimenters. Swinton wanted the BBC silenced for regular intervals every day to let them work.[43]

Just as the BBC thought things could get no worse, the stakes were suddenly raised once again. Yet another new postmaster general arrived on the scene. William Joynson-Hicks ("Jix") was a populist Conservative of robustly reactionary moral views, but a free-trading gadfly when it came to technology. He was pronouncedly out of sympathy with a monopoly system. Jix announced forthwith that the government could not legally continue to deny licenses to bona fide experimenters. The moratorium therefore had to be lifted. *Some* selection process had to be put in place, therefore, and fast. A group of Post Office engineers was hastily convened to root through the backlog of applications and determine once and for all which claimants were "honestly experimental."

The result was an attempt at a quantified social taxonomy. The engineers produced a table classifying the applications into sixteen ranks, according to what they called their "character" (fig. 13.4). This table was an attempt to resolve the question of the population of experimenters, on the basis of four distinctions: whether one's home-built set came from a kit; formal qualifications or experience; an announced program of experiments (or at least a theme for one); and self-identification as a listener to

Analysis to 8 May 1923.
CLASS I. Home Made Sets (Not ready made parts so far as is known)

A	B	C	D	E	F	G	H
With experience or qualification.	With experience or qualification.	With experience or qualification.	With experience or qualification.	Without experience or qualification.	Without experience or qualification	Without experience or qualification	Without experience or qualification.
Giving indication of nature of experiments	Giving indication of nature of experiments	Giving no indication of experiments	Giving no indication of experiments	Giving indication of nature of experiments.	Giving indication of nature of experiments	Giving no indication of experiments.	Giving no indication of experiments.
Not expressing desire to receive Broadcasting 743	Expressing desire to receive Broadcasting 2362	Not expressing desire to receive Broadcasting 183	Expressing desire to receive Broadcasting 915	Not expressing desire to receive Broadcasting 1069	Expressing desire to receive Broadcasting 4603	Not expressing desire to receive Broadcasting 1298	Expressing desire to receive Broadcasting 5760

CLASS II. Purchased (Non B B C) sets and "home assembled"
from ready-made parts

As above	As above	As above	As above	As above	As above	As above	As above
73	318	29	126	132	539	201	916

Class I	16833
Class II	2334
Total	19167

FIGURE 13.4. Post Office engineers' analysis of experimenters and listeners-in, compiled in May 1923. Sykes Committee minutes, POST 89/18, vol. 8, item 8. Courtesy of the Royal Mail Archives.

broadcasting (true experimenters presumably did not listen in). It is difficult to be sure, but my sense is that this was the first attempt by state officials anywhere to measure how many experimenters their nation really contained. On their answer hung the shape, practice, and impact of the most powerful mass medium of the age.

At the same time, Joynson-Hicks appointed a committee of inquiry to reexamine the whole enterprise of broadcasting from top to bottom. To encourage the company's cooperation in this unwelcome endeavor, he floated hints that if it were to prove recalcitrant then he might simply accept all applications for experimenters' licenses. Defining the entire nation as experimenters in the making, this would completely undercut its economic and cultural foundations. He wanted the BBC at least to accept a constructor's license at 10s—half its own proposed price—and was prepared to take it to the brink of destruction to force this through. The company called an emergency meeting and denounced his "threat" as a "serious breach of faith."[44] But there was nothing it could do. Less than six months after the BBC's launch, Jix had decided it was time to reform broadcasting root and branch. The crisis had come. There were other concerns too—the music publishers, for example, were up in arms against the company because they saw it as a reincarnation of the old sheet-music pirates.[45] But the matter of the experimenter and pirate, everyone agreed, was "the all inclusive and great question" of the day. Everything else was "unimportant."

Joynson-Hicks's committee of inquiry met under the MP Sir Frederick Sykes in mid-1923. By now, as well as the thirty-three-thousand-odd applications for experimental status that were still in limbo, the BBC also feared that there were four or five unlicensed sets in use for every one licensed. Publicly the Post Office put the latter proportion at 1:1, but even that was bad enough to be fatal. In private meetings Jix acknowledged the true scale of the problem, and named it frankly: he "mentioned 200,000 and called them 'pirates.'"[46] The BBC remained convinced that almost all "experimenters" were in truth Jix's pirates in mufti. Although it wearily reiterated that it did not want to restrict "genuine experimenting," it wanted the Post Office to deny most of the applications it had already received, once more guessing that the number of real experimenters might be about five thousand. It suggested referring the applications to "any qualified technical authority"—its own engineering department would do—to certify them. In effect, it would rest its future on the professionalizing ethos of the engineers. By what criterion should such certification be carried out? "I can suggest a method," Noble said tartly: "A very cursory glance." Ninety percent of the applicants were *obviously* unqualified, and a standardized refusal form should be sent to the rest. Brown agreed, saying that most applications were "camouflage."[47] But few others were prepared to be so bluntly skeptical.

It soon became evident why. Dismissing applications was by no means as simple a task as Noble believed. Of the thirty-three thousand sorted by the Post Office engineers so far, "a considerable proportion" did cite some potentially relevant experience. As the panel probed Noble and McKinstry further, even they began to flounder in the face of hypothetical cases, and even undoubted experimental geniuses, who would not have made the grade. What about "a young man who is not yet a competent investigator or an experimenter," for example, "but who desires to become so, and may become so?" Noble suggested that such a person should buy a broadcast license and a BBC set, and get a "period of experience." But, as the panel quickly pointed out, the set would be boxed, so such a person could hardly do much experimenting to qualify himself. And from this emerged a further tricky problem. Everyone agreed that experimenters had to be free to access the entire range of available parts, to combine those parts in new ways, and to roam across the ether.[48] Constructors needed none of those freedoms. Yet they too needed parts to build their sets. A real stumbling block in the way of a constructor's license derived from this: it seemed to open the door to bunglers with substandard parts, threatening horrendous oscillation that would drown out broadcasting. Both the Post Office and the BBC balked at mere constructors being let loose for this reason. They mooted providing lists of approved, standardized parts, to which constructors would be restricted.[49] But what was a "part"? Many were things like solenoids, batteries, and accumulators that had multiple nonradio uses. Noble finally conceded defeat when pressed for a definition. Even McKinstry could offer nothing better than a revealing tautology: a component part, he proposed, was a part entered on a list of components drawn up by an expert.[50] It was harder still to see how to standardize such parts—let alone how to charge a royalty on their sale, as the BBC wanted. Furthermore, to *construct* a set should mean to make it from "raw materials," the broadcaster insisted; merely "assembling" it was "a totally different thing." Yet components were bought ready-made, and were hardly "raw." Even if a list of standard parts could be created, therefore, nothing would prevent entrepreneurs from producing lower-level parts for making those parts. This was exactly the kind of conundrum that had led engineers in the first place to throw up their hands and argue that they should "box everything."[51] Boxing the radio—or even its "parts"— was therefore indelibly linked to defining the experimenter. Neither was practically or politically feasible.

As a result, the answer to the question of the experimenter turned out to be at once the simplest and the most complex of all. There was *no way to tell* who was or was not an experimenter, nor to count how many there were. Or, to put it another way, *everyone* was an experimenter, at least potentially. In that case, radio took on a different role. It might be the trigger that could turn potential into actuality, taking dormant talents and enticing them into use. "The listener may perhaps become an experimenter," as the Sykes committee reported, and "the experimenter may possibly become an inventor." It was not that there was no distinction to be made, but that there was no consistent rule sure enough to stand as a reliable basis for making that distinction in advance. It was beyond the capabilities of bureaucratic assessment systems. Something essential in the nature of science had apparently been resolved.

There was nothing else for it. If experimenters were not a discrete class, then the experimenter's license had to go. Until the end of 1924, the

Sykes committee concluded, two kinds of license should be issued: the broadcast license at 10s, and a constructor's license at 15s. The latter would disappear at the start of 1925, when the royalty on equipment would also be abolished. Everyone would then buy the same license, and protectionism would cease. In that case, piracy would surely plummet. The recommendation was adopted, and the panel was proved right. The problem of evasion shrank so quickly that the constructor's license was relinquished six months early.[52] Just as important was the fact that doing away with the experimenter's license had relieved the Post Office of "the difficult and somewhat invidious duty of determining whether applicants are genuine experimenters or not."

The British Broadcasting Company did not long outlive the crisis. A second parliamentary committee, chaired by the Earl of Crawford in 1925–26, marked its end. It was wound up and replaced by a new entity, the British Broadcasting Corporation—the organization that has survived and grown into today's BBC. This was more explicitly a public body, with the basis of the old group in patent pooling and protection retreating into obscurity. Henceforth, British broadcasting would be funded by a uniform license imposed on all users of receivers, on the assumption that all benefited from the service. From now on, the distinction between listeners and pirates would be stark, with no experimenters left in the middle to blur things. Meanwhile, the new-form BBC was soon seen as not just a new kind of media organization, but a model for the management of any major resource for the common good. This "public interest corporation," a novel hybrid of state ownership and independent management, offered the promise of a future social order built on wisely paternalist consensus, rather than imposed by totalitarian statecraft or exploitative capitalism. Before long John Maynard Keynes was pointing to the BBC to argue that his age was witnessing "the end of *laissez faire*."[53]

THE WAR ON OSCILLATORS

Every piece of evidence submitted to the Sykes and Crawford committees shared the assumption that interference was a defining problem of wireless, and therefore that nature itself made monopoly an unavoidable choice for broadcasting. Every piece except one, that is. The exception was the dossier of an obscure company calling itself Secret Wireless. Secret Wireless had a technology that it claimed could eliminate the need for monopoly and destroy listener piracy at a stroke. The brainchild of a bicycle mechanic and amateur inventor—one of the thousands of experimenter-pirates the BBC suspected to live in the engineering city of Coventry—the company's device split a signal between three separate wavelengths (fig. 13.5), which at the receiving end a special set would recombine into one. The original aim had been for confidentiality—an old dream of wireless engineers, back when radio had been in competition with telegraphy—but now the gadget took on a new purpose. It could lock up a signal and deny access to anyone without a license. By this one simple machine, it claimed, the "'pirates' would be wiped out." Moreover, several broadcasters could operate without mutual interference. Even a wireless telephone system might be possible. Ether chaos would be forgotten. Out of the entire mass of evidence considered by the government in the 1920s, this was the only testimony that seriously questioned the fundamental assertion that the physics of the ether dictated a monopoly. It is striking that the radical proposal came from the world of the experimenters—the very world disdained by the Post Office and BBC as piratical.

There was only one problem: Secret Wireless's invention did not work. Post Office engineers were steadfastly skeptical of the company's claims, on cultural as well as technical grounds. A broadly tuned receiver (as many were) would simply catch all three wavelengths, and in any case the community of amateurs, given its character, would surely publish circuit diagrams for a decoder within weeks of any launch. There could be no justification for using three valuable wavelengths for the system. The company failed to get approval for a testing station, and without that facility could do nothing. In the absence of a working alternative, authorities therefore remained convinced that the only way to preserve the public good was to purge the ether of laissez-faire. Wavebands must be parceled out as "a valuable form of public property." Systems descended from that perception would dominate broadcasting for the rest of the century, even though critics protested many times that the axiom was fragile. Only with digitization would the kind of possibility suggested by Secret Wireless seem plausible once again.[54]

So the BBC remained a monopoly funded by licenses, and pirate listeners continued to threaten it. But an insight gained from the controversy about experimenters now returned to suggest a way of defeating them. Both pirate listeners and experimenters were liable to open their sets and

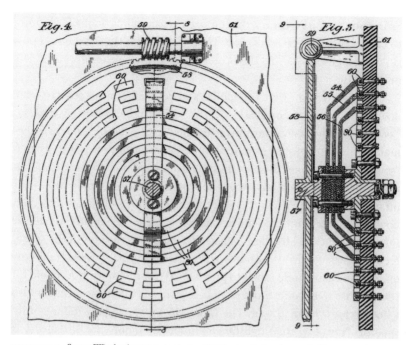

FIGURE 13.5. Secret Wireless's antipirate device. UK Patent 261,847 (1925–26), "Improvements in or relating to means for wireless communication." Crown copyright.

meddle with them. In particular, they tried to boost reception by adopting an electronic resonance technique known as reaction. This would tend to cause the aerial to oscillate, however, drowning out the broadcast signal for everyone in the neighborhood by a piercing ethereal howl. The standardizing of sets and parts had been partly intended to reduce this plague. But pirate listeners were of course unaffected by such standardization, and experimenters were explicitly exempt from it. So a "policing of Amateurs," as Gill called it, was essential for broadcasting to find its audience at all. It had to tackle oscillators and pirates at the same time. Otherwise, Parliament heard, "the whole of broadcasting will fall to pieces."[55]

Oscillation was a real problem and a perennial complaint. It could make the experience of listening intolerable. The BBC retained files full of complaints about it from towns across the country. Indeed, senior staff had several embarrassing experiences when they tried to demonstrate radio in provincial towns, only to find oscillation drowning out the signal. All they could do on such occasions was wait as patiently and apologetically as they could until the unknown offender got bored and switched off.

From soon after its creation, the company began calling on the Post Office to take action against oscillation. The problem was that of the four possible strategies to address the problem, all seemed either impracticable or impolitic.

The first strategy was to use police and Post Office inspectors to track down perpetrators of oscillation. If the oscillator had a license, that was easy, because the license authorized officials to inspect the holder's equipment. Noble suggested mounting a demonstration, on the basis that "sometimes [Britons'] honesty must be stimulated by a prosecution." But the assumption was always that the worst oscillators would be license pirates. Countering them therefore involved sending officers into their houses without prior consent to conduct searches. That threatened the same constitutional freedom as had exercised press pirates in the seventeenth century and music pirates in the Edwardian era. It would take only one or two cussed individuals to proclaim a trespass on the household for the exercise to become more trouble than it was worth—especially with a hostile press lying in wait. The *Daily Mirror* was already talking of inspectors "invading the Englishman's home" to snoop into all aspects of life—food, clothing, dogs, leisure, literature, and now wireless. And the *Daily Express* quickly picked up on the possibility and took delight in printing cartoons portraying the "wireless pirate" as a defenseless little everyman victimized as a serious criminal (fig. 13.6). Components manufacturers chipped in too, explicitly aligning the broadcasting police with the Stuart absolutism of the seventeenth century against which parliamentary rule had defined itself.

House-to-house inspections were inconceivable, the authorities quickly conceded. They were "outside the pale of practical politics." But to refrain from enforcement altogether was impossible too; it would amount to reviving the "dispensing power of the Stuart Kings."[56] So the Post Office did in fact try policing. Trial runs took place in January 1923, right at the beginning of the moratorium on experimenters' licenses. Bournemouth was the first place chosen.[57] This effort produced the evidence cited before Sykes as to the numbers of unlicensed receivers. But detection of violators proved tricky, and nobody wanted a trial.[58] According to the law, "pirates" were liable to up to a year in prison with hard labor, but only one case had gone to court by mid-1923, and the culprit was fined £2.

The few accounts of piracy prosecution that did appear showed the need for caution. One concerned a J. W. Sheriff, of that epitome of respect-

FIGURE 13.6. The wireless pirate as everyman. *Daily Express,* February, 18, 1925.

able suburbia, Cricklewood. In March 1923, at the climax of the crisis, Sheriff wrote to the postmaster general declaring that as a "student of history" he believed the restrictions on radio sets to violate the Monopolies Act of 1624. Legally, Sheriff was on thin ground, but the solicitor general advised that it might be better on the whole not to press the issue, and he was not made a martyr.[59]

The second case was more serious. It arose in 1924, at a time when the *Evening News* was warning that "the day is not far distant when wireless pirates will be prosecuted." It centered on a Londoner named Robert Ford. In lieu of a license for his son's receiver, Ford sent the BBC one guinea for its service, claiming that he listened largely to overseas stations. Then he challenged the postmaster general to prosecute. When nothing happened, he concluded that licenses were evidently not required. But at length a warrant was issued, his home was searched, and he was arrested (fig. 13.7). He insisted on being jailed, which allowed him to proclaim himself "the first individual in history . . . to be imprisoned as a result of the use of one of his five senses in his own home."[60] After he got out he published a rambling attack on the entire broadcasting system.[61] Ford claimed that the license was an unconstitutional tax, imposed without parliamentary authorization. Even the Post Office's authority to license reception was in his view groundless — he pointed out that the 1904 Telegraphy Act, on which that authority rested, referred only to *transmission* and not to reception. (He was correct, and the assertion was much ballyhooed by the *Express*; the government responded by quietly passing a law that redefined the term "transmission" to include the whole process.)[62] Finally, nobody could prevent ethereal waves from crossing the threshold, and a listener merely attended to them; why should the act of listening render the home subject to forcible entry? It threatened what he called "the 'castle' principle." Ford could even quote unfortunate statements by Reith and the postmaster general that a right to enter homes was essential to maintaining the Post Office's "control of the ether." This was exactly the prospect most trumpeted by the conservative press, which was given to declaring that it would be better to "abolish wireless" than forfeit liberty. For Ford the whole license system rested on a "piratical presumption" to "proprietorship of the universal ether," not to mention to "authorship of 'wireless' itself." He ended up indicting the postmaster general as a "self-confessed pirate" — the one "Real Wireless Pirate," no less. His book culminated in a Gilbert-and-Sullivan-style mock opera in which this buccaneer stood aboard his vessel *Transmizzione* gloating that "it is a glorious thing to be a Pirate King," as he fleeced the headphoned passengers of the *El Publico* (fig. 13.8).[63]

If overt policing was an unappetizing option, there remained the possibility of delegating oversight to local communities of amateurs. This was the approach preferred in the United States. But groups like the Radio

90   THE WIRELESS "LICENCE" RAMP.

threatens to apply, could have been found, *if searched for.*

But, of two assumptions, one. Either the members of neither House realized that the clause was included in the Act they were passing, or they realized it and knew that the

THE P.M.G. VIOLATES THE FLAG.

To the eternal disgrace of the British Post Office the house of a private citizen is forcibly entered by Post Office police because the P.M.G. " supposes " that the owner owes him ten shillings.

Photograph of the preliminaries to the Police Raid upon the author's house on September 29th, 1925.   Two Post Office emissaries (centre) are seeking admissions from the author (left).

Act did not apply to the reception of broadcasting. I may choose, and with reason, the latter assumption, which the wording of the Act itself substantiates. It still remains, therefore, to be seen if broadcasting shall be endowed at the expense of the liberty of the subject, or if, indeed, with strong and sufficient commercial interests attached and dependent, endowment is, in fact required. A monoply may be advisable, though not essential. But even if a monopoly be essential, the need of

FIGURE 13.7.   Arresting a pirate. R. M. Ford, *The Wireless "License" Ramp: "A Lesson in Bureaucracy"* (London: St. Giles Press, 1929), 90. Courtesy of the British Library.

FIGURE 13.8. The postmaster general as pirate king. Ford, *Wireless "License" Ramp*, 117. Courtesy of the British Library.

Association were apprehensive. The overtones of vigilantism were all too evident.[64] In America, they knew, the custom had not been entirely above controversy. Herbert Hoover once asked the leader of one amateur association—possibly Hugo Gernsback, the pioneer of pulp science fiction magazines—what his members did when they found an interferer, and he ingenuously replied that "we just take the fellow out and beat him up."[65] Nothing so vulgar happened in Britain, as far as is known, but nevertheless the prospect of lay surveillance made many uneasy. Ford called it a "system of universal espionage," and it was widely suspected that the BBC orchestrated such a system.[66] But in fact the BBC and Post Office were unenthusiastic—because they had tried this kind of thing and found it wanting. Their engineers had found lay informers' testimony to be unreliable, despite efforts to standardize it by the use of questionnaires, and their "spy system" had produced very mixed results. Ten percent of complainants had turned out to be producing their own oscillation. In the end the "self styled voluntary inspectors" were suppressed, not as sinister, but as useless.[67]

The third possible solution lay in education. Since oscillation came from poorly tuned equipment, it ought to be possible to educate users out of the practice. The BBC produced countless pamphlets on avoiding oscillation, which it circulated widely with the aim of reaching every household. Its mass-circulation *Radio Times* and *BBC Yearbook* also included regular sections explaining the phenomenon and how to eliminate it (fig. 13.9). Cartoons drove home the message, contrasting the model citizenship of proper reception with the prospect of alienation that faced listeners-in who oscillated (figs. 13.10 and 13.11). The company even tried to get its point across by likening broadcast licenses to dog licenses, the oscillating receiver being the rabid rottweiler of the airwaves. The parallel was widely ridiculed as absurd. Still, unlike policing, the strategy of reeducation actually seemed to work somewhat. By March 1925 complaints of oscillation were decreasing for the first time. But they showed no sign of disappearing altogether, and in many locations oscillation remained a plague.

The fourth possible strategy was the most significant. It was to develop a technological device to track down perpetrators of oscillation. It ought to be easy to use a direction-finding antenna to do this by triangulation (fig. 13.12). The idea of an oscillation detector was accordingly one that surfaced early. In March 1923, one aggrieved listener had already advertised in the national press for an "expert with direction-finder to detect experimenter, probably near Hyde Park."[68] This frustrated citizen wanted to track down an oscillator destroying his own listening. The Radio Association told the Sykes committee that its members could, in principle, use a direction-finding receiver to locate interferers.

But the real beauty of a detection device became evident a little later. Once experimenters and pirates were disaggregated, by a simple but powerful logic it could be used to solve the deeper problem afflicting the broadcasting system—that of listener piracy. Such piracy had been

TWELVE DON'TS FOR LISTENERS

DON'T run your aerial parallel to other aerials near by.

DON'T connect your earth to the same point as that used by your neighbour.

DON'T try and communicate with your neighbours by making your receiver howl.

DON'T use a longer aerial than necessary if you have strength to spare.

DON'T vary your strength of reception by distuning your receiver. It spoils the quality and is liable to increase interference in your own set.

DON'T try to work a loud-speaker from a plain single-valve set.

DON'T "fiddle" with your set if the results are satisfactory.

DON'T forget that it is impossible practically to get true reproduction when receiving in the "silent point."

DON'T forget that the B.B.C. is prepared to send a copy of a special oscillation pamphlet to anyone, free of charge.

DON'T forget that when you oscillate you are running the risk of having your licence cancelled by the Postmaster-General.

DON'T use a super-heterodyne receiver on an ordinary aerial. A frame aerial is essential.

DON'T compensate for the running down of your batteries (both low and high tension) by increasing reaction. If you do this your set may oscillate when switched on after standing idle for a few hours.

THERE ARE SOME "ODD" EXPLANATIONS FOR OSCILLATING
(Drawn by H. M. Bateman for the B.B.C. Anti-oscillation Pamphlet)

FIGURE 13.9. "Twelve don'ts for listeners." BBC Handbook (1928), 262.

THE GOOD LISTENER DOES NOT OSCILLATE

FIGURE 13.10. "The good listener does not oscillate." *BBC Handbook* (1928), 227.

impossible to police because there was no way to tell who did not have a broadcast license. But pirate listeners and experimenters, all things being equal, were reckoned to be the two prime producers of oscillation.[69] And the whole point about oscillation was that it was hard *not* to detect it. The debate about experimenters' licenses now made this into the key to enforcing the license system, by removing legitimate experimenters from the equation. The prime culprits of oscillation were now supposed to be listener pirates. An oscillation detector would therefore ex hypothesi detect those pirates. It promised to furnish the BBC with its savior: a scientific pirate detector (fig. 13.13).[70]

At one stage engineers envisaged a fixed national system of detectors. But that would be prohibitively costly, and perhaps politically impossible. So they devised a scheme to use vehicles carrying direction-finding

SUSPECTED! FRIGIDITY ON THE 9.15

FIGURE 13.11. The suspected oscillator suffers ostracism. *BBC Handbook* (1929), 352.

DETECTIVES LOCATING AN OSCILLATOR

FIGURE 13.12. "Detectives locating an oscillator." *BBC Handbook* (1929), 350.

FIGURE 13.13. "Now then, where's that crystal set?" *Daily Express,* February 16, 1925.

apparatus instead. In "very favourable circumstances," they hoped, such a van might be able to zero in on an oscillator's house. Two trial vehicles were ordered from a French company in early 1926, but it was not until July that the first was ready to begin testing. It was a dark, cramped vehicle, like a smaller version of the "Black Marias" used by the police to ferry prisoners around. On its roof was a large circular frame aerial. This could be rotated by means of a shaft descending into the rear of the van, where sat an operator and a "pilot." The procedure was to stop the van somewhere within range of the interference, tune the antenna to receive the distinctive howl, and rotate the aerial until the signal reached a minimum. The operator could then plot a line on a map of the locality, yielding one bearing on the source. The pilot would then use a compass board (war-surplus submarine gear) to direct the driver to a second point, from where a new reading would be taken; and then to a third. These three readings together identified a triangular region about two hundred yards on each side, which operators came to call the "cocked hat." At this stage the van would proceed to the edge of this triangle and begin "combing out"—that is, repeating the triangulation procedure to isolate a single stretch of road. Finally, by driving down the road slowly the operator might even identify the actual house from which the oscillation issued. The men could then knock on the door of the "howler" to inform him or her of the antisocial behavior.

The BBC identified the region around Windsor as a good testing ground for the technology. A Commander Carter had already done local investigatory work, and he helped the London team with the lay of the land. On December 21 the van drove down from the capital. After much initial frustration, it did eventually succeed in identifying a perpetrator. The first ever victim of a detector van was a Miss Pritchett of Slough. Whether this was such a great triumph could be doubted, however: she lived in the same street as the person who had complained of interference, so "detecting" her by conventional means would have been straightforward. Moreover, she was not a pirate. Her set was licensed, but had simply never been properly adjusted. So the test did nothing to show the worth of the vehicle for identifying a serious oscillator, let alone a piratical one. And the expedition culminated in a minor accident that put the van out of action for weeks.

Nonetheless, a milestone of sorts had been reached, and a public demonstration was soon scheduled. It had to be carefully stage managed, since the van could only localize a source of oscillation if the interference persevered for several hours while it trundled through the streets performing its triangulation. Most real listeners-in, needless to say, were not obliging enough to leave their radios on for so long. A member of staff therefore quietly volunteered his house in North London for the carefully rehearsed event. None of this was revealed to the press, which treated what it saw on January 17 as a genuine detection. Representatives of the Press Association, Central News, and Reuters traveled with the van as it drove north from Aldersgate Street and followed the procedure for tracking down an interferer. When it zeroed in on the suburban house from which the howl originated, the journalists were duly impressed and hailed a revolutionary advance. Newspapers across the nation echoed their enthusiasm. A "wonder car" had arrived, they announced—a "Sleuth Van which Cannot Fail." The Post Office had "declared war, scientific war, on all who oscillate," declared the *Yorkshire Evening Post,* reporting that the van would replace the monitoring of local enthusiasts. Perpetrators were duly warned that the "oscillation war" (as the *Western Mail* called it) could now have only one winner. "The effect is as good as if we had entered the house," the van's engineer was quoted as saying. Most howlers were unaware of their offense, newspapers were careful to point out, and welcomed being told of it when they were detected. Three cases of such ignorance, all of them women, were widely reported (fig. 13.14).

FIGURE 13.14. Post Office van for detecting oscillators. *BBC Handbook* (1928), 184.

With this success under its belt the Post Office proceeded to inaugurate its second detector van in the Manchester area in mid-1927. Two years after that a third followed. How successful they really were is rather unclear. Some oscillators were certainly detected, but very few were deemed worthy of more than some tactful advice, and by 1932 only half a dozen licenses had actually been revoked. All were cases of what the Post Office called "cantakerous" people.[71] But as the merely uninformed were educated, and as equipment improved in sensitivity, so the purpose of the vans shifted exclusively to the detection of unlicensed receivers—ones that were not giving rise to any listener complaints at all. That is, they became true pirate detectors. The long career of the "detector van," a symbol of Britain's broadcasting culture for the rest of the century, had begun.[72] It would be punctuated by poster campaigns against "pirates" every time a new way of listening or watching broadcast media appeared (fig. 13.15 is one of a long sequence of such images).

To Americans, detector vans have always seemed incipiently totalitarian. As early as 1933, when schoolchildren across the United States were told to debate the rival systems for broadcasting, it was the detector van that counted decisively against the British. I have myself heard NPR announcers in more than one city remark during pledge drives that the alternative to giving money would be to have Orwellian detector vans snooping around listeners' neighborhoods. In truth, they were never effective enough to be that sinister. Internal memos spoke more about the importance of publicity than about their actual successes. Advocates had pointed out even before their deployment that their "psychological effect" would be important even if they never actually worked, and rumors about their impracticality always circulated. When television was introduced after WWII, a senior engineer told the director of television that a popular account of the new generation of vans was needed because with the original radio equipment people had come to believe "that the van was completely bogus." He then added the revealing comment that the vans "used to work wonders in producing licenses some twenty years ago and of course it need not be bluff nowadays." He still only had two of them. It seems that for decades what vans there were spent most of their time cruising the streets in a bid to be visible. As late as the 1970s, one appeared on the children's show *Blue Peter* in hopes of convincing people that it really worked.[73]

FIGURE 13.15. "Don't be a pirate!" Courtesy of the Royal Mail Archives (PRD 1005).

CULTURAL AUTHORITY, PIRATE LISTENING,
AND THE NATURE OF A MEDIUM

The BBC was never just an expedient response to the threat of ether chaos. It was also designed to be an instrument of cultural improvement. As Reith put it, it tried to give the people slightly better than what they wanted. Listening to its programs was supposed to be *work*. Its own popular publications insisted on this point. Listening must not be done while pursuing other activities, for example. One article declared that if any one listener enjoyed a whole evening's programming, then something must be going badly wrong. The organization also sponsored listening clubs, trying to make the practice into a collective one. The ambition seems to parallel those of the reading and authorship clubs that flourished in the same years, but the effort was less successful; the listening groups seem to have died out quite quickly once BBC sponsorship ceased.[74] A very interesting history of listening could be excavated from such attempts.

The problem of listener piracy was accordingly not only financial and technical, but also cultural. Pirate listeners might listen to *something else* and in *some other way*. They might migrate to private stations intruding on the ether, for example. Several of these appeared over the years, the most notable prior to WWII being Tory MP Leonard Plugge's Radio Normandie. After the war this threat would revive in the form of Radio Luxembourg, and later the 1960s North Sea pirates like Caroline. Even if listeners remained with the BBC, moreover, they might listen merely for enjoyment, or for escapism, or inattentively. Programs might be juxtaposed in unpredictable ways, leading to unanticipated meanings and criticisms. In this they might be assisted by the various relay or wired-broadcast operations that arose in the 1930s and, the BBC feared, mixed its programming with that of commercial rivals. The BBC's first chief engineer, Peter Eckersley, championed a grand national scheme for wired broadcasting after he was forced from the corporation for being cited in a divorce—a scheme that was inspired in part by Secret Wireless's ambitions in the twenties. But he did so in hopes of providing a media vehicle for the British fascist Sir Oswald Mosley, who was secretly his employer. At any rate, the practices of pirate listening undermined the BBC's prized concept of "balance," which, as the economist Ronald Coase demonstrated in his powerful mid-century critique, had always been its real raison d'être.[75]

That put in question the nature of broadcasting as a medium. In a realm of listener piracy, the messages put out might differ radically from those being received. Pirate listening threatened to create a nation of autonomous, individualized agents—modern Menocchios, as it were, ready and able to listen as unpredictably as the now-famous Italian miller had read in the sixteenth century.[76] Just as the rediscovery of Menocchio later forced a profound reexamination of the nature of print and the power of the page over readers, so the discovery of pirate listening militates against the early, utopian vision of broadcasting as producing a modern enlight-enment. And at the time, too, the ideal of a nation of responsible, self-improving listeners leaked away through the cracks created by this form of piracy. As it did so, it made way for very different ideals—ideals of heterogeneity that in succeeding decades would shape the politics of media, communication, and information itself.

14

Intellectual Property and the Nature of Science

Piracy was central to the emergence of the information society. This was true not just in the obvious sense that radio pioneers pirated each others' inventions and unauthorized transmitters competed for bandwidth. At a broader and deeper level, the identification of new forms of piracy—and the actions taken to fight them—required articulating what mass communication and information themselves would be in a democratic society. That imperative affected no aspect of modern culture more, perhaps, than the definitive enterprise of Western industrial society: science. In the mid-twentieth century, disputes over piracy and intellectual property triggered a reappraisal of the relation between research and the common good. A distinct vision of the scientific enterprise—its nature, purpose, legitimacy, and authority—came into being as a result. It proved immensely influential. In the postwar years it was put into action to shape the administrative and institutional structures of the sciences. It continues to shape what we ourselves take science to be.

One reason why this matters is that the nature and place of science now seem remarkably unstable once again. Among the more prominent convictions about science in our own world is that, just as it has become global in scope, so it has obliterated long-honored boundaries between public and private, between interest and disinterest, and between academy and industry. Science seems to tunnel through the gothic walls of academia with greater ease than ever before. Intellectual property is the engine that drives it to do so. Patents "incentivize" inventive originality, claim supporters—and annual increases in the number filed apparently testify to their success in doing so. For antagonists, a "rush" to patent is a corrupting force at the heart of scientific culture. As proprietary conventions flow "upstream" from the commercial world to pollute—such language is quite common—that of research proper, so biomedicine in particular is portrayed as betraying an older tradition of "open science."[1] And if science simply *is* open knowledge, then science itself is in peril. Meanwhile, it goes without saying that many see an explosion taking place in the extent, scope, and volume of piracy accusations swirling around the sciences. This conjunction explains why today's conflicts about the commercialization of research and the corporatization of education are so bitter. All sides see the essential character of the scientific enterprise as being at stake. They are not necessarily wrong. But if that essential character is in reality a legacy of mid-twentieth-century piracy debates, then the consequences either way may not be what we have all supposed.

INDUSTRY, SCIENCE, AND THE COMMON GOOD

In interwar America, as now, industry and science were joined together by patents. Major corporations owed their existence to their creation, purchase, control, and manipulation. They had begun to create major laboratories out of what had previously been patent divisions, and in truth (although not always in rhetoric) these labs remained dedicated primarily to creating more patents. They also notoriously sought to "fence off" their economic territory from competition by deploying patent rights, and to buy up any such rights that they did not create—although the extent to which this really cramped competition was endlessly debatable. Two broad kinds of question came to dog the enterprise of industrial research as a result. First, was the work done in an institution like Bell Labs— founded in 1925 and effectively owned by AT&T—really *science,* and if so, by what definition? If the answer seemed relatively clear for Bell Labs, it was far less so for the other 1,500 or so industrial laboratories in existence by the late 1930s, many of which made none of the same claims to encourage open-ended inquiry. The second question derived from this. Were patent practices socially beneficial at a time of widespread hardship—indeed, they were legal at all? If the answers to these questions were no, then the patent system might need radical reform, or even obliteration. And science and its relation to the common weal might be at stake.

The favorite proposal was not for outright abolition, however—although a vocal minority did seek that—but for some form of compulsory licensing. This was a conscious revival of the idea developed in nineteenth-century Britain. It had long attracted support in the United States, despite the objection of patentees like Edison that stories of patent suppression never stood up to scrutiny. In 1919, for example, an economics professor at Brown University named Floyd Vaughan investigated the uses of patents at great length, and concluded that the evils of the system might well offset the benefits. Every industrial power except the United States now embraced compulsory licensing, he pointed out, recommending that readers seek out MacFie's old arguments to see why. Others added that there was ample precedent, extending back to Elizabethan England, for overturning patents that were not being "worked." By the 1930s, after years of such arguments, Congress was actively considering legislation to impose compulsory licensing.[2] If it did not pass, critics threatened, then the system should be done away with.

The literature comprising this "patents question" grew to be immense. Its very size testifies to the importance of the issues at hand. In fact, the renewed battle over the principle of patenting had become a focal point for a perceived crisis of capitalism, democracy, and science themselves. Its background lay in the rise of "trusts" before World War I. The Pennsylvania Railroad and Standard Oil were the iconic examples of these mammoth corporations, which emerged initially in fields involving the distribution of materials or messages across large distances, for which standardization on a continental scale was a prerequisite. Rail pioneered the gigantism, followed by telegraphy, telephony, oil, and electricity. New forms of organization and economic rationality appeared in these immense companies, which employed mundane communication and storage devices like memos and file cards, and a new "science of management," to hold themselves together.[3] Moreover, after a period of antitrust politics, in the 1920s concentration had once again been vaunted as a natural and beneficial process in the new media of the day. Radio and telephony supposedly required its virtues of standardization and "efficiency." (The local and amateur radio practitioners left outside the "radio trust" might disagree, but they were increasingly defined as pirates.) But the Depression impugned the credibility of such claims. It threw rule by experts into doubt. As it lingered on into the late thirties, it was scarcely necessary to endorse Nazi or Soviet claims about the "decadence" of liberal democracy to fear that, with so many unemployed amid such plenty, *something* was not working right. Perhaps monopolistic trusts were to blame—and intellectual property was their foundation. If so, then their stifling of inventions must be fixed if democracy were to survive.

The Depression also sparked a crisis in the public renown of science itself. It seemed both too powerful and not powerful enough—or else both too responsible and too irresponsible. On the one hand, unemployment was blamed on reckless and unaccountable science, which created new technologies with no regard for consequences; on the other, scientists were condemned for cleaving to an ideal of "pure" research, and refusing to conform their questions to public needs. The British railway magnate and Bank of England director Sir Josiah Stamp came to be particularly associated with the former charge when he reportedly advocated at the BAAS a moratorium on scientific research in order to give society and ethics a chance to catch up. Stamp himself denied proposing any such thing, saying that what he really wanted was a reallocation of resources from the physical sciences to the social—including eugenics—and an "inventions clearing house" where the impact of technology could be managed by scientists, industrialists, and bankers. Like many Britons, he thought the BBC an excellent model to follow. But it was the cruder point that was widely taken.[4] The socialist group around J. D. Bernal was the loudest advocate of the second claim, although the opinion was in fact widely shared, and had affinities with industry's own advocacy of entrepreneurial science. The problems of society had never called out so clearly for scientific attention, and to assert the prerogatives of pure science looked awfully presumptuous when so many were destitute. Influential scientists themselves called for an end to the "ivory tower." In 1933 the sociologist Read Bain issued a particularly outspoken demand that scientists accept their responsibilities as citizens, arguing that society's future depended on it. "Racketeers are running sores on the social body," Bain pronounced, "but unsocialized scientists are a foul corruption in the very heart's blood of society." The "pure" scientist was "a moral eunuch."[5]

In fact, the ivory tower was something of a myth. University research was a far smaller affair in the 1920s–1930s than it was later to become. What there was of it was in any case tempted to follow the lead of the industrial research laboratories. The conviction that science and property were antithetical, too, was far from universal. In 1923 the League of Nations seriously proposed instituting a property right in scientific discoveries, arguing that this would attract a new generation of young citizens into the sciences to replace that lost in the trenches.[6] By the 1930s American academia had taken several steps in that direction—steps that today we often wrongly assume were not taken until the 1980s. Several institutions created initiatives to encourage faculty to produce patentable work, the benefits of which would be channeled back into their facilities; others garnered patents, in a practice approved formally by the AAAS in 1934. Ernest Lawrence's Radiation Laboratory at Berkeley depended on patent royalties administered via the University of California's Research Corporation, which was essentially a patent pool (the arrangement encouraged the marketing of ever-larger instruments as medical devices). At Stanford, the university's patent attorney barred radio pioneer Lee De Forest from visiting a research group for fear of piracy. Yet at the same time, the University of Pennsylvania resolved that its faculty should *not* patent inventions related to public health, and Harvard and Johns Hopkins adopted similar policies. The American Medical Association pondered establishing a corporation to control all medical patents in the public interest, fearing impediments to progress. In short, a broad spectrum of positions existed, from the high-flyers to the communitarians. Proprietary science might be as genuine as nonproprietary, depending on where one worked.[7]

What triggered intense debate about patenting and the place of science were a series of federal inquiries into the communications industries. The major focus was on the American Telephone and Telegraph Company, AT&T. AT&T at this point held the largest accumulation of capital by any private company in history. It had $5 billion of gross assets, and annual revenues of $1 billion. It oversaw two hundred nominally separate "vassal corporations" with a total of over 300,000 employees—itself a drop of 150,000 from the peak in 1929. This "Bell System," as it was called, provided 80–90 percent of local telephone lines, 98 percent of long-distance lines, and virtually 100 percent of the wired links on which radio broadcasting depended. The conglomerate also had a monopoly on radio-telephone communications across the Atlantic and Pacific. In addition, it manufactured more than 90 percent of the equipment used in American telephony, by virtue of its wholly owned subsidiary, Western Electric. And Western and AT&T jointly owned Bell Laboratories, the world's leading industrial research institution. Bell Labs conducted scientific research in all subjects related (sometimes loosely) to electricity, communications, and acoustics, and was the exemplar of industrial science. All this rested on AT&T's patent portfolio—"the Bell System," the FCC declared, "is built on patents"—which derived from research and purchases alike. That portfolio extended far beyond wired telephony, embracing radio, the sound equipment on which the movie industry depended, therapeutic devices, PA systems, and timing equipment for sports events. In effect, the system held an effective monopoly on all "communication by wire and wireless."

The Roosevelt administration's inquiry into this behemoth grew into the largest of all the antimonopoly investigations of the age. It lasted two years and produced sixty volumes of transcripts, two thousand exhibits, seventy volumes of internal briefings, and two reports—as well as more than forty volumes created by the Bell System itself in its defense.[8] And it offered a perfect occasion to appraise "the adaptation of scientific discoveries to the purposes of production." As one official put it, the AT&T investigation became the era's principal venue for debating the consequences of patents in general for society, science, and industry. Roosevelt insisted on this broad remit, having declared in his second inaugural that the government ought to "create those moral controls over the services of science which are necessary to make science a useful servant instead of a ruthless master of mankind." He had recruited MIT President Karl Compton to head a Science Advisory Board, encouraging supporters to believe that such moral oversight might actually happen. The AT&T inquiry was the battleground on which the fate of that idea would be decided.

The telephone empire had always been the subject of peculiar public resentment. As early as 1891, its own legal adviser had warned that it held "a monopoly more profitable and more controlling—and more generally hated—than any ever given by any patent." Challenges had loomed up continuously at first, and the company's culture still reflected its early experiences fighting off "piratical opposition." Only once, however, in the early twentieth century, had "independent" telephony posed a real challenge. At that time operators had cropped up everywhere, even though the trust had ensured that "nothing relating to the science of the telephone art should become public"; some even made use of farmers' barbed-wire fences to carry calls. They had seen themselves as mounting an "uprising of the people" against Boston Brahmins and big-city Bosses, and as embodying "the spirit of American independence." But an attempt to unify the independents into a rival system failed in 1902, and Wall Street promptly abandoned them. AT&T had then agreed to end its designation of them as pirates. Instead it moved to monopolize the long-distance market, buying up patents and filing its own so as to keep this province to itself. Two critically important examples were the loading coil and the audion. AT&T bought Columbia engineer Michael Pupin's patent to the coil in 1900 and, thanks to successive minor improvements, held it inviolate until 1935. During that time not a single license was issued for the device, which was essential to any long-distance operation. De Forest's audion (a triode amplifying valve) played a similarly central role in radio communication, which meant that AT&T became a pivotal player in the "radio trust" too. So dominant was the company's patent position that from 1908 to the outbreak of World War II it did not need to launch a single lawsuit against a pirate.[9]

The Bell System therefore represented in its purest form a "philosophy" of "the place of science in industry." The lynchpin of this philosophy was the eponymous Bell Labs. The origins of this institution lay in existing laboratories within the system, all of them created to secure patents. Research at those labs had aimed at piecemeal improvements, not radical inventions—the chief engineer had once reassured the company's president that "no one is employed who, as an inventor, is capable of originating new apparatus." But once the independents were out of the way the company poured money into more systematic and radical research. It spent about $250 million on science between 1916 and 1935—an amount larger than the total operating budget of Harvard University—in pursuit of all kinds of projects. It represented itself as devoted to open-ended investigation. But in practice only the most prominent scientists enjoyed such freedom. The major aim remained to "occupy the field" by patents.[10]

The FCC's interpretation of all this was deeply unsympathetic. It concluded that the Bell System was a monopoly based on an "extensive and unremitting" pursuit of patents. The trust lavishly underwrote a version of science to bolster this pursuit, the Commission argued, and it identified that version with science tout court. But its science created tools of restriction. Moreover, those patents covered minor improvements rather than real inventions, and many were in fields only marginally related to wired telephony. And although relatively few of its patents were nowadays bought from outsiders, those few included the ones on which the entire system rested. Since 1876, in fact, by hook or by crook the company had managed to secure the rights to *every* development in telephony, with the short-lived exception of automatic exchanges. Rumor had long assigned it an "underground railroad" to the Patent Office allowing it to appropriate others' ideas for itself. The FCC claimed that about two-thirds of AT&T's approximately nine thousand patents were dormant, and useful only for "suppression." AT&T staunchly denied this, of course, saying that the true figure was closer to 50 percent, and pointing out that the need for standardization meant that many patents would inevitably end up unused. The impression remained, however, that patenting as a tool of suppression, once a theory of the Victorian campaigners, had become a massive reality. According to Roosevelt's FCC, patent monopolies really were blocking progress, suppressing inventions, and oppressing the public. The Commission believed that the history of telephony and radio demonstrated the sheer range of abuses to which patents were prone. Intellectual property appropriations and piracy accusations had distorted an entire modern economy. In AT&T's world, it concluded, "research, inventions, and patents appear less as sanctified brands of public service and more as weapons of industrial warfare aiming at monopoly." It urged Roosevelt to make sure that America was never again subjected to this kind of strategy, by creating a compulsory licensing system.[11]

AT&T responded with the indignation of a mugger's victim. The Commission's proposal was tantamount to a policy of "confiscation" by the state, it declared. It imputed that the FCC had simply misunderstood the nature of patents in the first place. The commissioners apparently assumed that "all the possible means of communication are, and always have been, available resources in the possession of the public," like public lands. This allowed them to infer that patents in the field were attempts to "filch something from the public possessions." But an invention simply did not exist prior to its being invented, so no "public lands" were being fenced off by AT&T. On the contrary, by mandating revelation a patent guaranteed that the public gained. But while a patent endured, the company insisted, "there is no reason why others who have contributed nothing to the result should be permitted to pirate the invention." Yet the FCC was now proposing that kind of piracy become federal policy.[12]

The question of research and the common good therefore came down to claims of rival piracies. The acquisitive piracy of the Bell System stood against the expropriative piracy of the FCC. This "patent question" lay at the heart of what was acknowledged to be a looming crisis in relations between science, industry, and society. And in 1938 Roosevelt poured gasoline on the fire. The president launched the Temporary National Economic Committee, a panel of advisors charged with investigating corporate monopoly, and called upon it to endorse compulsory licensing. At the same time, he appointed Thurman Arnold, a determined antimonopolist, to run the Justice Department's Antitrust Division. With Justice and the TNEC both on the case, it looked like radical change was in the cards. The New Deal was about to extend into science.

By now the enemies of patenting had a new focus. The TNEC feared that patent monopolies might prejudice strategic resources ahead of a coming war. For example, Britain needed beryllium, an essential component in the alloys used in military aircraft; but the German company Siemens held patent rights that could prevent its American licensee from filling the order. What if Standard Oil, which managed the U.S. patents on synthetic rubber for I. G. Farben, found itself similarly hobbled in meeting the American military's demands? (After Pearl Harbor, Standard would be forced into cross-licensing to preclude such a possibility.) Yale professor Walton Hamilton revived the FCC's charges against the Bell "imperium" in this context. An alternative, the TNEC pointed out, existed in the most iconic of American industries, that of automobiles. Patents held little sway in Detroit, which had long maintained conventions of "free use."[13]

The TNEC extended these questions into the heart of scientific research. It posited that industry required moral compromises of the scientist. The head of Bell Labs, Frank Jewett, admitted that Michelson had told him when he left academia that he was "prostituting my training and my ideals." But Jewett and most others rejected any such moral distinction. Not for a long time, they remarked, had the researcher really been an isolated gentleman. In the laboratory, academic or corporate, "a collective discipline replaces the freedom of the individual." The "individual phase" in the history of science, Vannevar Bush concurred, was being supplanted by the "group phase." Jewett defended the principle of patenting —and AT&T in particular—in these terms. The Bell System did not fear others using its "stuff," he affirmed: "we are a natural monopoly, we don't care, let them use it if they want to." What he did fear was the secrecy that would prevail if there were no patents to buy. Similarly, Bush credited patentees with upholding a "pioneering spirit," and with securing a high standard of living for Americans. He declared himself "decidedly opposed" to compulsory licensing because an invention that was "thrown open" would not be developed at all. A skeptic about the New Deal, Bush soon became the principal witness on science and patenting. He had substantial experience himself, not least in launching Raytheon in the 1920s to make thermionic tubes for radio sets. (Raytheon had run up against both the radio trust and AT&T.) Bush had also chaired a committee of the Science Advisory Board dedicated to the relation between patenting and new industries. To the TNEC he recommended a reformed patents system, insisting that no deep moral divide existed between industry and academia.[14]

Jewett and Bush made explicit the stakes of the TNEC investigations. They stood to reconfigure the relation between research and the economy. In that context it is remarkable that AT&T, Jewett, and Bush all abandoned the most long-standing arguments for intellectual property. The old claims about labor and first occupation vanished. More significant still is the fact that none resorted to the traditional alternative to such arguments, namely, the figure of the Romantic author. On the contrary, they insisted on the demise, or at least the terminal decline, of this figure. They occasionally invoked "the inventor," but almost always in elegiac fashion, as someone made obsolete by the great industrial and institutional laboratories with their team-based practices. The nature of science —of knowledge—was different now. Patents existed, apparently, to sustain these new, collective institutions. Indeed, it was the antipatent camp that made much of the individual inventor. In the twentieth century the Romantic author had to be *protected against* intellectual property. Harvard economist Alvin Hansen, for example, condemned patenting on this basis as threatening the national character.[15]

The committee concluded that the patent system had enabled monopolists "to control whole industries, to suppress competition, to restrict output, to enhance prices, to suppress inventions, and to discourage inventiveness." New Dealers like Walter Kaempffert, a prominent antipatent voice at the *New York Times,* agreed, demanding that America "abandon" a science defined by capitalist incentives in this way. But by now it was too late for mere administrative measures. War was at hand. The imperatives of military mobilization trumped all. Roosevelt consolidated the AT&T investigation and the TNEC—along with several other bodies—into a single National Patent Planning Commission. He charged it with a fundamental revision of the culture of research.[16]

Daniel Kevles has traced in detail the process that led from this point to the inauguration of a postwar scientific order. Briefly, leadership of the antipatenting camp fell to a West Virginia senator, Harley Kilgore, who proposed a "Science Mobilization Act" to create an office empowered to override patents in the national interest. The agency would also coordinate grants to research institutions, which it would distribute partly in accord with social needs. Thurman Arnold proclaimed the plan a "magna carta of science." But it met with bitter enmity from industry, from the military, and even from the sciences themselves. Bush, by now leading the Office of Scientific Research and Development, was especially antagonistic. He decried the prospect of laypeople judging research proposals — the very element that most exemplified New Deal ambitions to entrench the social responsibility of science. Moreover, Kilgore wanted private rights to be void if *any* public funding had been used in a project, which to Bush reeked of the radical antipatenting sensibility of the FCC.[17] His own vision for science rested on corporate collaboration with the state, and he believed that patents were essential if this were to become a reality. Their confrontation eventually gave rise to the institutions definitive of postwar American science.

Kilgore retooled his proposal into what he called a National Science Foundation, retaining what he regarded as his plan's most important elements: commitments to guide science for the common good and to patent the products of federally funded research on the public's behalf. Bush responded, however, with an astute administrative maneuver. He engineered an invitation from Roosevelt to propose his own suggestions for sustaining the successes of science and technology in the coming peace. Bush's report dusted off all the rhetoric that he had employed before the patent panels of the 1930s, rededicating it to the cause of asocial science. The public should get at most a free license to use the results of research, it insisted, not a patent, and the public should have almost no role in deciding research priorities. *Science—The Endless Frontier* became the foundational covenant of postwar American science.[18]

Bush's scheme was not immediately successful, however. Truman was inclined to favor a more social model along Kilgore's lines. Commerce Secretary and ex-Vice President Henry Wallace too pushed for this. Wallace mattered because he was responsible for the assets of what was then the largest patent holder in the United States: the Alien Property Custodian. The APC held rights seized from German concerns, comprising in total some 5 percent of all America's active patents. Wallace's idea was to take these and make them the basis for a revived commons, jump-starting the culture of public science that the old New Dealers had envisaged when fighting AT&T. He wanted to grant royalty-free licenses to all who requested them, and even to mount special advertising tours around the country to draw the attention of small businesses to the possibilities. The assets involved were considerable, especially as at the same time large quantities of material were being requisitioned from Germany itself. Boeing, for example, benefited, the design of a new jet bomber being heavily indebted to German wind-tunnel data. Dye and chemical patents were given to a new Chemical Foundation, while German imports were banned as infringing these patents. But the Republican Congress cut Wallace's funding. His scheme stalled, and he left the administration in frustration.[19] In 1950 Congress and the White House finally settled on a National Science Foundation that would be based on Bush's design, not Kilgore's or Wallace's. Pure science, expert appraisal, and a patent-based structure of public and private research prevailed as policy. The scientific commons shrank into an ideal.

INTELLECTUAL PROPERTY VERSUS INFORMATION ECONOMY

The years of these conflicts saw the inauguration of a series of disciplines dedicated to understanding the sciences and their place in society. Between 1920 and 1945 one can see the beginnings of, for example, sociologies of invention (in S. C. Gilfillan's *Sociology of Invention*), science (in R. K. Merton's classic papers), and technology (in W. G. Ogburn's work). There also appeared a psychology of creativity (with patent officer Joseph Rossman's *Industrial Creativity*), and a grand theory of technology and society (with Lewis Mumford's *Technics and Civilization*). In some cases these initiatives were closely related to each other. Gilfillan, for instance, dedicated his *Sociology of Invention*—originally a Columbia Ph.D. thesis—to, among eight friends, Ogburn, Rossman, and Merton; another dedicatee was Kaempffert. The questions they conceived—about the role of the researcher, the nature of invention, the relations between creativity and society, and the responsibilities of science—were to a large degree shared, and took shape in the context of this crisis. Ogburn actually chaired Roosevelt's Committee on Technological Trends and National Policy, which focused on invention and was eventually subsumed into the National

Patent Planning Commission. Kaempffert for his part authored a sweeping historical argument condemning industrial and military secrecy as inimical to technical progress.[20] The contests over patents were both spur and foil not only to a new science policy, therefore, but to an array of new approaches to the nature of science.

Take as an example the most influential of these efforts in the medium term, Robert K. Merton's. Merton's sociology has typically been seen as motivated by the need to counter totalitarian claims to scientific support. It was, but Merton acknowledged that it also reflected the discord about communications and patenting. He preceded his famous account of the norms of science by an analysis of the relation between social order and inventive activity—an analysis stimulated by British economist Arnold Plant's attack on intellectual property, which we will encounter again below. From 1941, moreover, Merton worked with Paul Lazarsfeld at Columbia's Office of Radio Research, a group seen by the industry as allied to the critics of the communications monopoly. Lazarsfeld and Merton developed methods for studying radio as a social agent, which they subsequently took pains to discuss with Norbert Wiener's cybernetics group. *Social Theory and Social Structure* (1949), the book that made Merton's name, proceeded sequentially from the sociology of media to the sociology of science—something we miss today when we read only the latter sections. In fact, he had pursued the two fields simultaneously. Mertonian sociology of science thus appeared in the guise of an outcrop of communications work. His insistence on a norm of "communism" deserves to be seen in that light. Merton insisted that scientific research was subject to a form of common ownership of its products. He built from that a model in which scientific advance was driven by reputational capital, not economic. And, he added, this enterprise was "incompatible with the definition of technology as 'private property' in a capitalistic economy." Plagiary was true science's counterpart to piracy. The model would be hugely consequential as the basis for attempts to rejuvenate the scientific culture of the nation after Sputnik, becoming established in the process as the most influential general image of science.[21]

In the meantime, not all skeptics about intellectual property were progressives like Merton. At least as influential a critique came from the so-called liberal movement in economics that was determined to resurrect laissez-faire. Although it is usually now recalled in terms of the later development of neoliberalism, in fact intellectual property—and cultural property in general—was a nagging concern for this movement. If monopolies were always bad, as the economic liberals assumed they were, then on what basis could *information* monopolies be defended? Copyrights and patents were artificial—indeed, state-created—monopolies of this kind, so should they be defended at all?

In Britain, with the BBC vaunted as representing the future of culture itself, the import of those questions was especially pressing. It was nowhere more so than at the institutional home of 1930s economic liberalism, the London School of Economics. Probably the prime mover there of this kind of argument was Arnold Plant (1898–1978), an engineer-turned-economist. Plant never published very much by the standards of professional economists, and most of his later career was spent as a Whitehall apparatchik. He has been far less renowned than colleagues of the time like Friedrich von Hayek and his own one-time assistant Ronald Coase. But he was extremely influential behind the scenes, not least by virtue of being personally associated with many of the economists who chafed at Keynesian orthodoxy after the war. In papers that he did publish on copyright and patents in the 1930s, and in later ones addressing public broadcasting, Plant laid out a template for their attack. He did so on the basis of what was, in fact, an extensive and intensive excavation of the archival and statistical evidence on the history of copyrights and patents. He even seems to have tried to discover the origin of the usage in the context of intellectual property of the word *pirate*. Almost none of that labor broke the surface in print. What was evident, however, was his rediscovery of the arguments of the Victorian campaign against intellectual property.[22]

But Plant began his assault on copyright in 1934 with another forgotten figure: Henry Carey. He reread the Philadelphia protectionist's attacks on international copyright, and noticed that Carey—who had explicitly endorsed the unauthorized reprinting of his own works—was one of very few writers to acknowledge his own interest as an author. Plant admired this candor. Authors were interested parties, he agreed. Readers would therefore be wise to treat the overwhelming public consensus on the benefits of copyright with a dose of cui bono skepticism. Continuing to excavate the lost tradition of resistance to intellectual property, Plant arrived at the conclusion that copyright was simply a monopoly. It elevated prices, provided an entirely indiscriminate and unjustifiable encouragement for ventures that did not deserve pursuit, and was in many cases unnecessary (the frequent republication of classics in many different formats provided abundant proof of this). Perhaps, he mused, it should be abolished.[23] Nor did he shrink from advancing the thought experiment of a publishing realm lacking any copyright. After all, for many genres — academic monographs, say, and poetry—it was simply irrelevant. And in the sixteenth century the book trade had thrived without any copyright law. A culture of reprinting—of "piracy"—had existed that Plant likened to that of knock-offs in the modern world of high fashion. Milan's fashion houses did not fold simply because high-street chains imitated their designs, and high-street chains in turn did not fold when street vendors imitated their imitations. What developed instead was a hierarchy of discrete markets. Something similar had obtained in transatlantic publishing in Carey's day. The need to be first in a market, coupled with a "tacit understanding" that a book issued by one publisher "should not be pirated by another," had been sufficient to keep it all going. If a respectable rival transgressed, then the big publishers would produce "fighting editions" in retaliation; but penny-dreadful versions circulated in their own world. Plant likened these to the "fighting buses" that London operators in the 1930s used against pirates on the capital's streets.

Plant claimed to find in scientific research a modern version of that Renaissance marketplace. It implied that patents should go the same way as copyright. Invention could clearly proceed apace without them, and where they existed, they blocked discoveries from being made. In biology, for instance, plant breeding flourished independently of intellectual property (an example that today seems distinctly ironic); so did medical research (ditto). Besides, patents, where they were granted, created a false authorship that could be fatally alluring to workers. Dredging up testimony from the MacFie campaign, Plant cited Brunel to prove this point. Discoveries and inventions were in fact collective achievements, and a vibrant world of science and technology could easily be created under tacit norms rather than overt monopolies. For many research scientists it would even be preferable. They simply wanted their creations dispersed as widely as possible, and intellectual property actively hindered that dispersal.

Abolition being an unrealistic proposal, Plant returned to the nineteenth-century debates once more and proposed the alternative of compulsory licensing. The principle had often been condemned, he conceded. But it had been tried in Italy in the 1860s, and Britain too had adopted it in limited form in 1911. Plant approved. The system avoided the perils of authorial monopoly while still providing for authors' livelihoods. He proposed that the period of monopoly in patents and copyrights alike be reduced drastically, to about five years, and the compulsory royalty period correspondingly extended. But the British economy was by now not isolable, and such a proposal ran afoul of its international commitments. The Berne Convention enshrined a commitment to French legal notions of a moral right of the author, to which compulsory licensing was anathema. International harmonization, in this case, served not just to standardize intellectual property but to redefine its nature. Yet the idea refused to go away. The reason for this was not that Plant's arguments about patenting were, in themselves, new. They were not. But Plant was the first economist to address science as part of a general issue. That issue was how to deal with cultural property in what he forecast would be a new kind of economy, grounded in information.[24]

TACIT PROPERTY

Claims that research is intrinsically inhospitable to rules and doctrines therefore emerged repeatedly in the mid-century furor over patents, science, and the public good. Shorn of their ties to intellectual property anxieties, such claims today bring to mind the work of the chemist and philosopher Michael Polanyi, who maintained that research rested on tacit knowledge and therefore could not be subjected to planning. But his work should not be shorn from those ties. A chemist and refugee from Nazism, in Manchester Polanyi had become increasingly exercised by the questions of the nature and public role of science, and devoted years to answering them.[25] His principal target at first was the crystallographer and Marxist, J. D. Bernal. Bernal and his allies — including J. B. S. Haldane, Lancelot Hogben, and junior partners like Dorothy Hodgkin, Eric Hobsbawm, and Rosalind Franklin — maintained that science must be a socially engaged activity, with scientists taking responsibility for what they wrought. The enterprise ought to be overseen — "planned," in the term used by Polanyi's side — for the common good. Bernal extrapolated a future in which the natures of research and capitalism would prove incompatible and be supplanted by a harmonious union of science and society. But realizing the "social function of science" in this way must, he believed, involve repudiating "scientific property." Citing the American debates, Bernal insisted that a patents system perpetuated the subordination of science to an increasingly superannuated capitalism.[26] Polanyi concurred in demanding an end to the association of science with property, but for a diametrically opposed reason.

As it became clear that the war would be won, realization dawned among opponents of state intervention like Plant that the "threat" loomed of a Labour government in Britain. Clement Attlee's party was committed to nationalizing key industries and creating a socialized health service. Friedrich Hayek's *Road to Serfdom* and Karl Popper's *Open Society and Its Enemies* became the two best-known statements of the position against such policies, Hayek in particular warning of a slippery slope from state planning to totalitarianism. *The Road to Serfdom* backfired at the time, being widely read as hyperbolic. When Labour did take power, Hayek and his allies retreated and formed themselves into the Mont Pèlerin Society, a group dedicated to economic liberalism in what they perceived to be a hostile world. Polanyi was a founder-member. His view of science was an integral part of this commitment, and his transitory Society for Freedom in Science had had parallel aims. He conceived of the scientist as the exemplary practitioner of what he called "public liberty." That is, the scientist's independence from social control was at root the same as that of the witness, judge, and voter. Their conduct in such roles corresponded to no articulable principle or method beyond the practice itself, and must be unpredictable. But their freedom in those roles redounded to the benefit of all.

Polanyi insisted that research itself was similarly not a matter of methodological rules, but rather of "tacit knowledge." That is, it rested on ineffable techniques, preferences, and norms that together resembled a tradition more than a rational system. For that reason, while Hayek warned that planned research was tyrannical, Polanyi believed it impossible. Research, to be genuine science, must play out in something like a marketplace, characterized by "the Liberal conception" of freedom. He insisted on the distinction between this and "applied" science—a distinction that the ill-fated Soviet physicist Bukharin had once denied to him existed in a socialist society. Planning could only inhibit and corrupt knowledge, resulting in disasters like Lysenkoism. Polanyi passionately upheld this view of what he called "pure science," in almost religious tones (and he was a noted theologian). Bernal's camp, he concluded, had "surrendered" to a philosophy that would destroy science. He was as opposed to science with a social purpose as Hayek and Popper were to industry with a social purpose.[27]

Polanyi's assault on patenting was all the more remarkable in this context. "Patent Reform" appeared in the *Review of Economic Studies* in autumn 1944, shortly after *The Road to Serfdom.*[28] It seemed to mark a sharp departure from everything he and they defended. Polanyi certainly contended that patents misrepresented creativity and corrupted research — that was unsurprising. But he argued that the distortions were so great that they outweighed even the dangers of state intervention. The system could only be fixed by change so radical as to amount to its destruction, he maintained. It should be replaced by both a comprehensive state system of administration and a massive provision of state subsidy. That is, in order to free science from its bondage to intellectual property Polanyi was prepared to do a deal with what he regarded as the devil. Why?

Polanyi acknowledged the strength of support for patenting. A broad consensus in its favor had existed ever since "the very earliest days of the Free Trade movement" (by which he meant the early modern agitation that had produced the 1624 Monopolies Act). Without patents, backers felt, industrial research would lose the stimulus and guidance of market profitability. Speculative capital would dry up. Inventors would be left at the mercy of rapacious corporations, and could not afford to seek backing for fear of seeing their creations expropriated. Research would stagnate amid a reversion to craft secrecy. Polanyi thus recognized the strength of the assumption that "pioneer" inventions needed patents.[29] But that assumption, he insisted, was false. If research was truly a matter of tacit knowledge, then no algorithm could exist to predict even probabilistically which candidate discoveries or inventions would succeed. There was *no such thing* as "commercially justified" investment in pioneer ventures, therefore, with or without a patent system. This being so, there was nothing to offset the "grave difficulty" of patenting, namely, the truism that "the full benefit of knowledge is only reaped when its circulation is free." Monopolies militated against the progress they were supposed to uphold. In recent years, Polanyi claimed, their harmful effects had even increased. The TNEC had proved this: "floods" of patents, often of dubious validity, constrained whole fields of inquiry, while fear of litigation quelled innovation. The system was one of millionaires' justice, as radio pioneer De Forest had found to his cost. Like Plant, in the end — to whom he sent a review copy of the article—Polanyi believed that patents were dubious extrapolations from a false understanding of creativity itself. They presumed to "parcel up a stream of creative thought into a series of distinct claims, each of which is to constitute the basis of a separately owned monopoly." In reality, discoveries were not atomistic in this way, but drew on "the whole network of human knowledge." The system failed because it sought "a purpose which cannot be rationally achieved." Intellectual proprietorship was irrational and corrupt. "The nature of knowledge" demanded "the abolition of patents."

"In order that inventions may be used freely by all," Polanyi urged, society must "relieve inventors of the necessity of earning their rewards commercially." But here was where things got tricky. Pure science could not be self-supporting. As a first step, Polanyi helped himself to Plant's idea for compulsory licensing. But this was merely a way station on the path to the total abolition of intellectual property. In its place Polanyi recommended what he called "a system of appropriate governmental action" that would replace patents with rewards from the public purse. His idea was a descendent of the scheme that MacFie's antipatent camp had proposed seventy years before. No longer would scientific authorship be individual, indivisible, and proprietorial. Polanyi instead envisaged tribunals of experts evaluating inventions' worth and disbursing money according to a graded scale of authorial contribution. He estimated (it is not clear how) that a total disbursement of 10–30 percent of the appraised economic benefit from a given invention for the prior year would cover this. This, he thought, was a price well worth paying to spur innovation, eliminate piracy, and end "the last vestige of control which a patentee could exercise over his competitors."

This was on the face of it an astoundingly interventionist proposal. It had no counterpart anywhere else in Polanyi's voluminous writings. But he argued that eliminating intellectual property in research was so important that it justified extreme measures. The need outweighed even "the danger of corruption and arbitrary oppression" that he felt was intrinsic to government subsidies. He tried to distance his idea from notions of state planning, saying that it merely involved streamlining an existing distribution rather than reallocating resources between rival institutions. Its task was already being performed badly, he pointed out; the target of doing better would not be hard to hit. But he conceded that to avoid corruption the appraisal system of his tribunals would have to be "rigid" and that government agents, not peers, would have to staff it. They must exercise a perfect oversight of the field of industrial creativity. That might seem distinctly Bernalian, and, moreover, to conflict once more with Polanyi's stipulation against predicting research outcomes. But the important distinction, perhaps, was that between retrospection and prediction. The tribunals' valuations would be of an invention's previous value, not (as with a patents system) its future worth.

This tension draws our attention not to Polanyi's final view of science and society, but to what was in fact a difficult internal struggle that he waged during the war years to articulate that view. He struggled with a series of projects, the remains of which are to be found among his papers today. Each one incorporated sections from its predecessors. In the intellectual progress that they trace, the issue of patenting turns out to have been central. Briefly, he first projected a book to be called *Science,* directed squarely against the "planning of science" movement. This he pursued for three years, in 1940–43, only to abandon it and move on to another work provisionally called *The Scientific Method in Society.* This in turn gave way to *The Autonomy of Science,* which advanced a sweeping three-stage view of the history of science extending back centuries. Elements of this then reappeared in what might seem a radically different text, on *Economic Planning.* Finally, Polanyi turned the book on planning into a volume named *Full Employment in Theory and Practice.* And this last did appear in print, as *Full Employment and Free Trade,* in 1945—constituting the third part of a triptych with Hayek's *Road to Serfdom* and Popper's *Open Society.* Only much later would fragments of the other projects resurface, most notably in *Personal Knowledge.* Throughout these pivotal years arguments about patents formed one of the few common threads, linking each new project to the last. Even the full-employment work culminated with them: their abolition was central to creating a moral form of free trade that it claimed was essential to sustaining low unemployment.[30]

One reason for this ubiquity was that Polanyi believed that the ideology of free trade had originated in opposition to patents. Economic liberty dated from the Monopolies Act of 1624. But more important was the fact that in the 1930s–1940s many hailed patent pooling as the basis of internationalism and objectivity in research. The idea was that patent pools created internally open research communities extending across industries and nations. Bell, GE, Phillips, and Osram were all exemplars. (Osram was a subsidiary of Marconi, and had been a subject of complaints in the radio pirate debates.) Theirs was hailed as model science—rational, managed, team based, and beneficial. Patents were thus the lynchpin of a domain in which planned science seemed an achieved and admirable *fact*. Polanyi had little choice: if his critique of planning were to hold good, he had to attack the system at this point.

His own experience told him that the image was a mirage. At ICI, he recalled, he had been prevented from speaking openly to others even in the same factory. In his drafts one can see him working up from this kind of personal experience to his well-known views on the nature of science. He insisted that even in the combines real originality came not from teams, but from individuals. Often they were only hired into the team *after* they had made their important discoveries. This made sense, because no rational firm would give an inventor the leeway needed for all the failures necessary to produce a success. Combines thus betrayed science because, he wrote, "there is no mechanical, safe rule to discovery." If analysis could be centrally guided, he added elsewhere, it was "not research but surveying; no originality." "*Very Important*," he noted at one crucial point: "Usual argument: Invention, progress, is logical, determined, therefore foreseeable. While in reality: *because* it follows the evolution of inherent logic in steps, *each of which is a maximum step of human intelligence*, therefore unforeseeable."[31] In other words, it was not that the process was inherently irrational, but that each step took one to the limits of predictability at the moment of its being taken. And here one book manuscript ended abruptly.

The book on *Scientific Method in Society* took this point further by focusing on the role of secrecy in constricting the marketplace for ideas. Polanyi identified two kinds, created by states and companies. He rather wistfully considered proposing that military research be made illegal under international law, before proceeding swiftly on to the corporate kind of secrecy, which he thought more damaging to the general welfare.[32] This was where patents came in. In industrial capitalism, he said, patents were really tools for cartel building. Radio was the case in point. Going further than Plant, he insisted that inventors must retain their autonomy in the face of both military secrecy and patent cartelism. It was here—a context lost from his published argument—that he started to consider their remuneration out of public funds. To the same end, moreover, Polanyi also mooted having the state roll back copyright, while subsidizing libraries and scientific publishing. Scientific progress would rest on reprinting too.

What he called "habits of publicity" would become part of the normative culture of industrial research—indeed, of capitalism itself. "It will be considered as a feature of decency and dignity in industrial life," Polanyi predicted, "to let everyone benefit freely from knowledge which is obtained in the firms' research laboratories." Altogether, these moves would "pervasively refresh the intellectual atmosphere in which individual scientists spend their lives."[33]

Behind Polanyi's view of science was therefore a sustained and even rather agonized engagement with the fate of the researcher in a realm dominated by patent pools. It was the centrality of this concern that led him to his convictions about the central importance of tacit knowledge. It also led Polanyi to argue that science and intellectual property were fundamentally incompatible, and that patenting must be abolished. Taking up claims from Plant, the Roosevelt inquiries, and the Victorian anti-patent campaign, Polanyi developed for himself a sophisticated, libertarian ideology of open-source science.

THE PATENT AS JAMMING DEVICE

When the British Post Office used oscillation to detect pirate listeners, it was making pioneering use of what a generation of researchers in the 1930s–1940s came to recognize as a general class of physical phenomena. These phenomena occurred across a range of systems the outputs of which "fed back" into the system itself: gun-control devices, engine governors, electronic circuits. All could in principle be treated as mathematically isomorphic. Tackling them as such, mathematicians and engineers like Claude Shannon, Warren Weaver, and Norbert Wiener developed a theory of what they called *information*. Piracy and patenting took on new and central roles in that theory.[34] Wiener in particular took the commitments to openness voiced in the AT&T furor and by proponents of liberalism like Plant and Polanyi, and articulated for them a place in the creation of an information age.

From his arrival at MIT, an institution closely allied to AT&T and Bell Labs, Wiener devoted himself to research in electronics and communications.[35] He developed a theoretical approach that he termed "generalized harmonic analysis" for resolving signal and "noise" in amplifiers and wave filters. He and a Chinese doctoral student, Yuk Wing Lee, used the approach to develop a filtering circuit that could be used in telephone systems, recording devices, and broadcasting (where it promised to eliminate interference). Its fate was to prove symptomatic. Wiener and Lee filed patent applications and licensed their device to a subsidiary of Warner Brothers called United Research Corporation. Lee took a job with URC to bring it to market, parrying increasingly angry demands from MIT, in the person of Vannevar Bush, that he conform to scientific norms by publishing his design.[36] Warner was considering using the device in moviemaking; but Lee already talked more ambitiously of "wired radios." The latter was an AT&T project, akin to P. P. Eckersley's vision in Britain, to use carrier waves in coaxial cables for telephony or even television.[37] It all proved premature. Warner was in poor health, the Depression was relentless, and URC went to the wall. Lee took to calling it "United Research Corpse." The pair looked to Europe, hoping that Siemens or Telefunken Klangfilm (an audio and movie company) might take up their invention. But the prospect of piracy and endless litigation deterred them. In the end, their circuit suffered the iconic fate of inventions in the contemporary patents conflict: Bell Labs bought up the rights as part of AT&T's strategy of sweeping up all relevant patents, and it was never heard of again.[38] The experience made the conflict a matter of immediate experience for Wiener, and he never forgot it.

It was reinforced after Lee, now unemployed, returned to Shanghai. There he operated a radio service for the Ministry of Finance for a while, and then took a professorship at Tsing Hua University in Beijing. Wiener paid him a visit, and they designed a new, multipurpose wave filter circuit —one flexible enough to be mass produced and used throughout a telephone network, as well as in amplifiers, televisions, and phonographs. AT&T bought it, of course. But the giant paid only $5,000—hardly the fortune they had hoped for—and never put it to use. For Lee the sale still proved crucial. Stranded behind Japanese lines, he used his share to buy an antiques store and survived the war that way. But Wiener felt confirmed in his conviction that the corporation had bought their patent solely to suppress it.[39]

Back in America, Wiener embarked on the research in antiaircraft systems that famously led him to project a science of control and communication in general. He came to recognize that "oscillation" could throw many different kinds of mechanical or electronic systems into chaos. For example, a device to predict an aircraft's flight path might go into "violent oscillation" if the target changed course. He already knew all about oscillation in "howling" radios, and had heard that oscillation could have destructive effects in ships' gun turrets too. The neurophysiologist Arturo Rosenblueth later told him of human symptoms that seemed similar once again. In general, oscillation was a problem that arose when "information" produced by a given system fed back into that system. As general as it was, any solution to it would demand a convergence between hitherto discrete branches of engineering, and other disciplines too. Wiener gave the name *cybernetics* to the highly technical enterprise that ought to result.[40] Its central pillar was a theory distinguishing "signal" from "noise" in networks. This theory posited information as an entity separable both from particular material instantiations and issues of meaning or content.[41] It would become central to telecommunications and computing.

Wiener concentrated after the war on extending and diversifying the influence of this "theory of messages." At its most ambitious, the "cybernetics group" that met in these years argued that cybernetic principles should influence all social decisions: how to design machines, what values to embrace, what actions to take or avoid. In the age of the concentration camp and the atom bomb, they were acutely conscious of the moral implications of such an ambitious science. Wiener introduced cybernetics to the public with a warning of a "modern industrial revolution" that might well devalue the brain as emphatically as the first Industrial Revolution had the hand. "It cannot be good for these new potentialities to be assessed in terms of the market," he cautioned, if they left the majority with nothing to sell. He made desultory efforts to interest the labor movement in agitating for political intervention to forestall such an outcome.[42] Concerns about the appropriation and blockage of information equally haunted his evangelizing.

Wiener was convinced that intellectual property was obstructing the potential of information science. In large part this conviction originated with his own experience of dealing with AT&T. But he had fallen foul of state secrecy too, having submitted a proposal for a digital computer only to see it neglected. In 1944 he therefore noted with some pride that his collaborators on a pivotal computing endeavor were "unanimous" in repudiating the corporate patentees RCA and Bell Labs (that is, the old radio trust and AT&T). These convictions appeared both in the relatively technical announcement of the new field in Wiener's *Cybernetics* (1948) and in the more popular account he published as *The Human Use of Human Beings*

(1950). *Cybernetics* was one of those publications that exemplifies its own argument, in that it was commissioned by an associate of the Bourbaki collective (an antiauthorial collective of mathematicians), Enriques Freymann. Freymann wanted it for a new publishing venture "as nearly free from the motive of profit as any publishing house can be." And Wiener voiced increasingly strident denunciations of secrecy as incompatible with science. He was removed from the government's list of scientists approved for classified work for his pains.[43] His "rebellion," as he characterized it, soon became irreversible, as Wiener ostentatiously began declining government funds for research. From the early 1950s he increasingly laid aside research to concentrate on exposing what he saw as the corruption of science by intellectual property. He intended to issue a third and much longer expression of his convictions in a book he entitled *Invention: The Care and Feeding of Ideas*.[44] It assailed the practice of patenting on which corporate science rested. He largely completed it, but then left *Invention* unpublished.

Wiener developed a historical account of invention itself. It centered on information, and in particular on the *flow* of information. He insisted that it was theorists, and not "gadgeteers," who produced truly radical departures. His paradigmatic inventors were figures like Newton, Maxwell, Gibbs, and Wiener himself. His own work with Lee, indeed, counted for him as an exemplary case of a "change in intellectual climate." It had made manifest what had previously been implicit in the theories of Gibbs and Fourier. This was a remarkable contention given that their device had, in Wiener's view, been a victim of the patents system. But it reinforced his broad claim, which was that what really mattered were the channels by which information could flow between two basically distinct social kinds, akin to the mechanic and liberal artists, or scholars and craftsmen, invoked in earlier centuries of debate about creative rights. He called them thinkers and makers. Before a new technique could "pass from the intellectual to the artisan," as he put it, society must provide these two quite distinct types with adequate contacts. Thus, for example, Hellenistic Greece had been a golden age of invention because Archimedes and Hero could "communicate with kings and learned men." This principle had reached its acme in the late nineteenth century in a "synthesis" of science and craft. The age of the "science lords" like Kelvin had seen the "pure scientist," the "craftsman," and the "industrialist" combine into one.

But then had come disintegration. Research had become a corporate enterprise. Edison had created the industrial laboratory, in which teams of workers approached invention as a business. Following his lead, AT&T had built its own massive machinery to churn out patents. Business needed science as never before in this age of communications, and the Bell System encapsulated their convergence. It had cultivated a new kind of "adventurer-scientist" who, in Wiener's eyes, betrayed science in pursuit of power and profit. "Megabuck science" was his contemptuous name for the whole enterprise. Laboratories—whether Soviet or American, private or public—came to resemble the enormous machines that it required. Like Polanyi, Wiener dismissed these institutions as good at rote work but unsuited to radical discovery. To them, every problem was a task to be tackled by a team, and teams were tools of mutual concealment. Secrecy and fear thus pervaded modern scientific life—fear of subordinates, competitors, and rival nations.[45]

The reason why megabuck research killed science, therefore, was that it mistook the nature of information. Information was properly more process than substance. It existed as a flow through a network, not an accumulation in a reservoir of some kind. The fallacy of large-scale laboratory science was its ambition to hoard knowledge in one place (the team, or the lab itself). The patent system was the counterpart of this in legal terms. That was why Wiener's career culminated in an attack on the patents system. Intellectual property, he proclaimed, impeded the flow of information in the great network that was society. Worse than interference, it was a kind of deliberate "jamming."[46] It had to go. Whatever policy might replace it, he believed, must make the recognition of authors conditional on open publication. It must be a policy of counterjamming. The verdict with which *Invention* culminated was explicit. "The truth can make us free," Wiener concluded, "only when it is a freely obtainable truth."[47]

Wiener's history of invention singled out AT&T for attack. Its long-distance network, Wiener implied, was the material extrusion of a patent pool, snaking out to entwine America.[48] The creation of that network had marked the conjunction of patenting and capitalism to concoct the adventurer-scientist, the model for whom had been Columbia engineer Michael Pupin, patentee of the network's crucial component. Wiener discarded *Invention* because he wanted to focus all the more on Pupin's story. He had decided to write, of all things, a novel about patenting. Entitled

The Tempter, it would explain the rise of AT&T and the fall of science in terms of a fatal Faustian bargain. He told his publisher that it would be "a treatment in fictional form of my ideas on invention in the modern world."

Wiener's tale turned on the electrical engineer Oliver Heaviside (1850–1925). Heaviside's story had long fascinated him—longer, in fact, than any other single topic, cybernetic or otherwise. Wiener's own earliest work at MIT had been an attempt to reformulate his work for electrical and communications engineers.[49] An increasingly reclusive figure, who, as Wiener put it, "was born poor, lived poor, and died poor," Heaviside had lacked powerful allies in academia and the Post Office. In Wiener's view this made him "sincere, courageous, and incorruptible." He had devoted himself to a problem of attenuation that plagued long telegraph lines, insisting against orthodoxy that they should be "loaded" with inductance coils at regular intervals. In correspondence he had dubbed this idea "heavification," a term that both expressed the principle and encapsulated "just credit to its inventor." But the Post Office—with a monopoly on telegraphy—had denied him experimental facilities and, in Heaviside's view, attempted to suppress his papers. He had responded by denouncing scientific secrecy as "one of the most criminal acts such a man could be guilty of," and had refused to patent his contributions.[50] Pupin had then become the first to mount a real test, announcing his success to the AIEE and securing his own patent on the technique, defeating a rival researcher from AT&T to do so (with the company's connivance, Wiener thought). AT&T then bought Pupin's now-robust patent for a rumored $500,000. The suddenly rich Pupin had given scant credit to Heaviside, preferring to credit his own childhood experiences with Serbian shepherds (who apparently communicated by banging knives stuck into the ground). His autobiography became a best seller, helping to legitimate the image of the industrial scientist. Meanwhile the loading-coil technique became the basis of the entire long-distance network, and hence of the culture of research that Pupin so served. This in turn had led to Wiener's own early research foci, because AT&T wanted to add "repeaters" (amplifiers employing a negative feedback technique) at points along the lines and find a way to transmit several signals at once.[51] The possibility rested on the "wired wireless" concept for which Lee and Wiener had intended to sell AT&T their own circuit. To make matters worse, just as Wiener and Lee were in the midst of their frustrating patent experience, Pupin publicly hailed AT&T as the harbinger of a future utopia "more just and generous to the worker than any which the world has ever seen." "One of the great services which the telephone has rendered to this nation," he maintained, "is its demonstration that an industrial monopoly, wisely administered, can be a national blessing." A perpetuation of small science would only have "paralyzed progress." In demonizing Pupin, therefore, Wiener was not attacking a figure from the past, but one who personified the current glorification of intellectual property.[52]

Wiener believed that this piece of piracy had been a turning point in the history of communications science—and of science in general. By 1930 at the latest he was convinced of the need to vindicate Heaviside against his "plagiator." He worked to track down papers in Britain and urged the project on a journalist so passionately that he recoiled.[53] Ten years later, amid his intense work on antiaircraft systems (he took Benzedrine to keep going), Wiener made the time to write Orson Welles a long letter urging the director of *Citizen Kane* to make his next film about the Pupin affair. It would address the "feral" period of modern industrial science, he said, and its origin in piracy and soul selling. He added that Appleton, that advocate of science communication, had pulped Heaviside's authorized work, only for "at least three pirated editions" to follow, "one in China," and for them to become canonical.[54] Welles is not known to have replied, but Wiener did not relinquish the idea. In *Invention* he remarked that Pupin's autobiography was in reality "a cry from Hell." *The Tempter* then took this conceit to its limit. In his own terms, the novel merged Prometheus with Faust. Heaviside, obviously, was Prometheus. Pupin was the ambitious but shallow scholar who sold his soul to a monopolist Mephistopheles. And the patent system was the mechanism—the cosmos, as it were—structuring this modern Faust's temptation and downfall.[55]

Invention and the Heaviside novel were products of a period of personal and collective strain. Far from providing a path for civilization's future, cybernetics was on the brink of collapse. And it was Wiener's fault. As he became increasingly fervent about openness in science, he grew more protectively authorial about his own endeavors. In 1951 he finally exploded. Wiener ferociously denounced McCulloch for appropriating his reputation as the author of cybernetics, calling him a "picturesque and swashbuckling" usurper. The evocation of a pirate was all but explicit.[56] Accustomed to such tantrums, the president of MIT, James Killian, sent the usual mollifying response. But this time Wiener was resolute. Whether his fear of usurpation were really the motivation, or whether, as has recently been claimed, his wife contrived the split by concocting bizarre tales of sexual impropriety, this time his resolution lasted. The rift proved permanent, and his erstwhile collaborators were devastated. Cybernetics disintegrated. *Invention* and his two volumes of memoirs were written amid the wreckage.[57] When the crisis of information came, it arrived with an accusation of piracy that blew his community and his vocation to shreds. If Pupin's book was a "cry from Hell," one may ask, what was Wiener's?

WHY, THIS IS HELL

We still live amid the legacies of these mid-century debates about science and society. We inherit their terms, and the culture of science that shapes our world is the one left to us by them. If we think "information wants to be free," then we voice a sentiment championed by Wiener, Polanyi, and Plant. And when we worry that the resurgence of patenting and commercialism in research may be betraying science—as many do—we appeal to a quasi-Mertonian image of the enterprise that was itself framed by a debate about those very themes. Merton himself, not incidentally, seemed less sanguine in the late 1980s about the chances of surviving the change than he had been in the 1940s.

What is happening to science today is in one light an example of what is happening to all other creative practices. But there is a very important difference. In all other realms, globalization is represented as replacing localisms of various forms: musical styles, literatures, fashions, and so on. In the sciences, something different is at stake. An apparently new, market-oriented ethos of universality is seen as replacing, not an accumulation of localisms, but an older—and, many think, nobler—form of universality. That older form was, on this view, real science itself: an objective, ideologically neutral endeavor, that yielded knowledge independent of the place of its creation precisely because it was kept apart from the market.[58] It is this difference that lends critiques of patent-oriented scientific culture their real bite. It turns their complaint from one of deterioration into one of betrayal. What we are left with, apparently, is an empty simulacrum of a noble enterprise. That is the central contention behind the most angry, even violent, debate to swirl around the sciences today. It should be clear by now that the premises of that debate are poorly understood. In particular, the image of proper science that it appeals to is by no means historically adequate. Contrary to popular belief, there was in fact no quantum leap in scientific patenting in the 1980s. In the 1930s, some research institutions sought patents just as avidly as the likes of MIT and UCSD do now. And as Steven Shapin has demonstrated in detail, industrial and academic practices of science in the mid-twentieth century were not in practice distinguishable on any such stark moral grounds.[59] More to the point, the image itself is a relic of earlier conflicts precisely about the patenting of research and the enclosure of intellectual and technological "commons." In other words, it is not so much that pure science never existed, as that the idea that it *could* exist is one we owe to debates about intellectual property and piracy. In the light of history it is hardly surprising that the resurgence of scientific property in our time should uncork such passions.

To calm those passions we need a different historical understanding of science. Until the recent rise of the life sciences, the received view was that the epochal episode in modern science was the Manhattan Project. Out of that project came big science and the postwar institutions of the NSF and NIH. While it would be absurd to deny the importance of the bomb, it is nonetheless the case that an alternative view is conceivable.[60] On this view, the history of modern science would turn not on physics, nor even on biology, but on communication and computation. Such a recalibration would involve revising the chronology, focus, problems, and sources of the history of modern science. Its epochal moment would come earlier, with broadcasting and long-distance telephony in the 1920s. Its central problems would involve the changing character of the scientist and the fate of scientific norms amid the emergence of corporate, team-based, and managerial science. The vexed story of patenting and its enemies would offer a way both of getting at this history and of apprehending its importance. If we want to get out of hell, this may be one possible exit route.

15

The Pirate at Home and at Large

In the last quarter of the twentieth century piracy was at once domesticated and globalized. It was the occasion, on the one hand, of sleepless nights for suburban parents harried by the recording industry interested in their children's file sharing. On the other hand, it became a perennial bone of contention in the geopolitics of world trade. Together those two trends marked the entrenchment of information as a structural element of late modern life. Digitization, with its promise of perfect copying— inevitably dubbed "cloning"—accentuated this process. But it did not begin it, and it did not determine its nature. What did were perceptions, practices, and convictions that had coalesced earlier—sometimes much earlier. They came into sharp focus during the 1970s and 1980s, ready to be put to use when a digital revolution became an imminent prospect. What brought them together was a practice that spread rapidly from being a niche activity of hobbyists and aficionados to a mass phenomenon. It had its own moral economy. It inspired real devotion, and, in consequence, affected how the new digital devices would be put to use. Many called it *home piracy*.

Piracy has frequently cast the political status of the home into sharp relief. From the seventeenth century to the twentieth, controversies repeatedly rested on perceptions of what went on in homes and expectations of what *should* go on in them. Piracy conflicts demanded some specification of the roles of home and state in creativity and commerce. They also required some account of how to police domestic activities in a liberal democracy. But home copying terrified the culture industries in their formative years of the mid-twentieth century more than prior piracies because it implied a radical decentralization of cultural production. What made this possibility plausible was the reception accorded to one of the technologies appropriated by America from the ruins of Nazi Germany: magnetic tape. Reel-to-reel tape machines became a presence in many U.S. households by the late 1940s. Although cumbersome by the standards of later incarnations, they made recording and copying far easier than they had ever been before. As domestic habits of use developed, they made it possible to visualize a revolutionary shift occurring in the place of reproduction, and even creation, from factory to home. Or perhaps it would be better to call it a counterrevolutionary shift, because before the Industrial Revolution all such work had taken place in household settings. At any rate, the cheapness, portability, and reusability of tape made it a perfect vehicle for communities that were already seeking some such tool—communities like that of amateur radio experimenters, for example.[1] It was conducive to their moral commitments to exchange, sharing, and distributed creativity. And that had practical implications. It was relatively straightforward to defend a principle of intellectual property in a world of industrial copying, because such copying took place in policeable places. But once those imperatives became both domestic and universal, intellectual property itself would come in for fresh skepticism.

HOME PIRACY

That piracy, broadly construed, should occur in the home is nothing new. Print pirates worked out of London's houses in the seventeenth century, sheet-music pirates dealt out their copies of popular songs by the thousand from terrace houses in Liverpool and Manchester in the 1900s, and listener pirates could be detected in their homes in the 1920s. Yet such a thing as "home piracy" always seemed counterintuitive. This remained true in the 1960s and 1970s. European and American authorities alike consistently attempted to distinguish "home copying" or "home taping" from piracy per se. Piracy, they insisted, was a commercial enterprise, and *therefore* not domestic. "Private" taping was for personal use, or at most for sharing among a few friends on a noncommercial basis. But as the practice proliferated, so that distinction eroded. In the presentations of industry lawyers, in the less cautious statements of trade associations, and above all in the press, "home piracy" became a reality for the first time. The taping of radio broadcasts, then records, and finally television programs and movies came to be called piratical whether or not it had market motives. By the late 1970s the music industry was describing it as the greatest threat it had ever faced—an existential peril that might destroy music itself. That rhetoric would later be reiterated by Hollywood and the broadcasters with the advent of VCRs, and the entertainment industry en masse with the coming of digital networks. What many citizens saw as an inoffensive practice—indeed, a constructive one, around which sociability cohered, and from which new art emerged—took on ominous significance. Every time they pressed *record,* citizens were told, they contributed to "the death of music."

The history of the home itself inflected the meaning of this proclaimed piracy in two principal ways. The first had to do with understandings of moral and political order. The household had long been accounted the essential unit out of which society was formed. Since early modern times, the political nation had been construed as a huge concatenation of households. Moreover, the household was reckoned a peculiarly powerful site of moral propriety when most crafts and trades were carried on there. The craft or retail space on the ground floor of a Renaissance city building had been a mixed space, combining the public world of the street and the private one of the home. The guardianship of the patriarch extended from the family to manufacturing and commercial conduct across this space. Books, as we have seen, were made and sold under that authority; but so were all other goods. Many cases in which seditious or libelous books were prosecuted in the early modern period hung on the distinctions between parts of the house: who could go into particular rooms and what they could do there. Surreptitious, illegal, or simply bad work was associated with other spaces. It might happen upstairs, in the definitively private part of the house, which implied concealment. Or it might go on outside the house altogether, in "corners" or "holes"—language that still cropped up in descriptions of radio piracy at the early BBC. This implied something dangerous, or otherwise unfit for family morality.[2] Of course, pirate printing did in fact happen in conventional printing houses, but when it did contemporaries struggled a little to grasp its nature. They often portrayed the households in question as disordered, to the point of not being true homes at all. They might be topsy-turvy, with servants lording it over masters; or riddled with adultery, as reputedly with some of the more notorious Whig and Tory printers of the Restoration. Samuel Richardson's denunciation of "intestine treachery" viscerally captured the fear of a master whose domestic world turned out to be not domestic at all.

In practical terms, piracy in a house was all but impossible to police. The domestic threshold constituted a line of demarcation between the street and the home, which was supposed to be impervious to surveillance. In early modern London, tradesmen and -women asserted that this autonomy originated in the Magna Carta, and was thus a matter of the highest constitutional importance. They appealed to it consistently to deny constables permission to enter and search their premises, and not infrequently they won their cases when they did. There were few more incendiary requests in that incendiary age than the Surveyor of the Press's for a general warrant that would have trumped the householders' claims. This association of domesticity with propriety and autonomy survived the Industrial Revolution, moreover, when work is usually reckoned to have been displaced out of the home. It was still at issue in the Edwardian era, when Arthur Preston's agents muscled their way into houses in search of pirated music. Pirate listeners in the 1920s invoked the sanctity of the home too. In each case they raised the specter of state officials barging in and arresting children. This prospect was everywhere identified with tyranny. In the mid-twentieth century the association became still more frightening: it was a sign of totalitarianism.

Home piracy thus remained something of an oxymoron. Classically, if something took place in the home, then it was not piracy. Yet the home was of course not a static entity. It was increasingly identified as a female sphere, and one open to colonization by new technologies—washing machines, air conditioners, refrigerators, telephones, and radios.[3] By the seventies the home had been reinvented and proclaimed the site of some technological utopia or other many times over, while never losing its moral centrality. But it was a domesticity of leisure now. Even the highest utopianism of the era never envisaged the home recovering its old, early modern place as a locus for creative production. That distinction between home and work—central to definitions of modernity since at least Max Weber—remained sacrosanct. But it became entirely conventional for domestic technological sublimity to come with a Stepford-style sting in the tail, or a Midwich cuckoo or two. Invasion and insurrection lurked there. Home piracy would take on aspects of both.

In the early 1970s the oxymoron began to dissolve. It did so, paradoxically, because of a sudden *decrease* in music piracy. Organized, commercial piracy—the large-scale clandestine copying of recordings for sale—had suffered a series of defeats at the hands of police forces. As it retreated from prominence, so the extent and impact of casual domestic copying was thrown into sharper relief. The music industry decided to move against home tapers as quasi-pirates. But home copying had already acquired a distinct halo of civic virtue. It came only partly from the status of the home itself. An expressly moral enterprise of rerecording had appeared a generation earlier among two distinct but related groups of connoisseurs. Their efforts had fostered a perception among a small but dedicated community that the industry was hopelessly addicted to "big business" practices, and that those practices endangered the creation, circulation, and above all preservation of art. They had made piracy an exercise in conservation, sanctified by the amateur virtues of dedication and disinterest. The assault on home taping would have the ironic effect of reviving that conviction and raising it to the status of conventional wisdom.

THE MORAL ECONOMY OF MUSIC PIRACY

The perpetrators of this moral piracy in the 1950s were aficionados of two musical genres at first sight as different as could be: jazz and opera. But the genres shared two major characteristics. First, each was catered for not just by huge record companies (principally the duopoly of RCA-Victor and Columbia) but by many smaller "independents," staffed by dedicated enthusiasts. And, second, both their audiences, while relatively small, were intensely devoted to the music. They were also expert about it, sometimes obsessively so. They were collectors as much as listeners. They foraged in yard sales for obscure Jelly Roll Morton discs or Lauritz Melchior performances, dreaming the Enlightenment dream of building "libraries" that might attain universality and completeness within their chosen spheres. They recognized canons of "classics" in those spheres, which required pristine pressing and special handling. In both jazz and opera, pirate recording was aimed at this peculiar kind of audience. The pirates themselves, moreover, were members of the same audience and shared its predilections. They wanted to make money, but they were in business for more than profit alone. They justified their actions in terms of furnishing a public archive of classics. The major companies, they charged, had neglected these classics so severely that an artistic heritage risked disappearing altogether. That corporate neglect furnished moral legitimacy for their own actions.

That said, however, jazz and opera manifested significantly different justifications for piracy. In the case of opera, the major pirates sought to create access to performances that were either new—broadcasts of live occasions—or unknown because they had been lodged in East German or Soviet bloc archives. (One or two advertised their refusal to pay royalties as striking a blow against communism.) In the case of jazz, the issue was largely one of *restoring* access to classics that were out of print. Jazz aficionados charged that the large recording companies adopted a "dog in the manger" attitude to their own backlists, not only declining to republish existing great art themselves but refusing others permission to do so. (Their complaint bears a pronounced resemblance to that of scholars today faced with the similar attitude of book publishers to their own out-of-print titles.) The so-called battle of the speeds that erupted in the late 1940s between seventy-eights, forty-fives, and LPs was central to this accusation. As the new formats came in, so recordings published as seventy-eights would have to be reissued. The major labels were reluctant to undertake the task. The battle was proving disastrous for them, as consumers hesitated, awaiting the outcome, and sales slumped. They saw no reason to invest in reissuing music that they knew could not be profitable given their overheads. So the pirates did it themselves. Accusing the major companies of betraying a "public trust," they made and sold their own re-pressings. In their eyes, their piracy was principled. It was a service to civilization.

Jazz

Unauthorized copying of records was almost as old as records themselves. As early as 1898 a police raid in Chicago found cylinder-duplicating machines concealed in a room behind a door marked with a skull and crossbones.[4] For decades such practices benefited from a peculiar quirk about copyright in recordings that endured from 1909 until the 1970s.[5] While a song's words and music—the written composition—could be copyrighted, and a disc could not legally be "duped" (directly copied), a recorded song could be reperformed, recorded, and sold, provided a compulsory royalty were paid. In practice the status of recorded music as property was even more unstable than that implies in the 1920s–1940s, being highly contingent on factors like race and region. Independents like the Chess brothers in Chicago paid little or no attention to copyright (or performing right, for that matter). Nor, for black artists, did the performers' collection society, ASCAP. The expropriative relations that prevailed between companies and African American artists are today notorious. Only in the 1950s did Chess and other companies realize what they were missing, and scour their lists to copyright everything they could. Similarly, the industry long turned a blind eye to unauthorized copying. Insiders jocularly referred to the after-hours work of pressing plants as "nocturnal emissions." After World War II, however, the crisis brought on by the battle of the speeds compelled it to pay attention.[6]

The motor for change was the dramatic growth of independent labels in the mid-1940s. Often owned by the proprietors of bars or clubs, or by record retailers, these labels focused on newer musical forms that they knew firsthand. Jazz was the outstanding example, followed by the urban, electrified blues of Howlin' Wolf and Muddy Waters. Independents were soon springing up across the country, in Memphis and Detroit as well as New York and Chicago. The luckier ones stood to profit immensely from their local knowledge and risk taking. As they did, so they developed broad distribution systems with remarkable speed, taking records and the music they bore across the nation. At the same time, urban radio stations began to diversify away from the homogeneity of the networks, targeting African Americans and white teenagers adopting African American music. The term *rock'n'roll* was coined by a Cleveland station chasing this market. The independents began to appear on *Billboard*'s charts, and by the mid-1950s to dominate them. By 1960 some three thousand labels existed, 80 percent of which were one-off efforts created to record a single session and sell perhaps a thousand copies of the disc. After a period of hoping that this new market would disappear, the majors lumbered in, signing the independents' artists or hiring white musicians to cover their songs in safer forms. The period was one of radical disaggregation, in which creativity was strongly associated with local expertise and almost domestic production.[7]

But production was not in fact done at home. Pressing discs remained

almost entirely the preserve of manufacturing plants. In the 1930s domestic record-cutting machines had been sold for a while, and there was
an equally short efflorescence of recording technologies a decade later,
led by the wire recorder. Some musicians—most notably, experimental
modernists—were eager first adopters of such machines.[8] But the technologies were fiddly and expensive, and in the case of wire acoustically
unsatisfying too. More to the point, there seemed to be no desire for
home recording. Pressing remained an industrial enterprise. Plants were
autonomous firms, or else semiautonomous units of the big companies
mandated to bring in contract work from outside. That would make the
conglomerates both police and pirate at once.

The musician and aficionado Charles Smith ascribed the origins of
record piracy to an ethos of collecting jazz records that dated from the
twenties. Sometimes, Smith recalled, in order to get a final classic to
round out one's collection, one had to get acetates made from a friend's
copy. These acetates were called *dubs,* and the practice therefore came to
be called *dubbing.* One of the first to make it into a commercial enterprise
was a record retailer named Milt Gabler, who created United Hot Clubs
of America. He was soon followed by others. As Gabler's chosen name
suggests, early discs were often meant for circulation within "clubs" of
like-minded enthusiasts, rather than for open sale. The record companies'
own machines were put to use to make the discs—"on the level, open and
above board." And they would give their records titles like "classic swing,"
reinforcing their emergent sense of a canon.[9] The practice languished in
the Depression and the war, but revived smartly in the late 1940s, when
it suddenly became prominent in the context of the battle of the speeds.
Several labels emerged to reissue out-of-print jazz in the new formats.
They had names like Hot Jazz Clubs of America (HJCA), Blue Ace, Jazz
Panorama, Zee Gee, Jazz Time, and Viking. All were small concerns, and
some were still professedly devoted to specific clubs—although how genuine these clubs really were is unclear. More ambitious than most was the
self-consciously named Jolly Roger. The creation of a twenty-three-year-
old New York enthusiast called Dante Bolletino, Jolly Roger rapidly
became the most controversial of these labels, and the catalyst for their
destruction.

Bolletino had become impatient that RCA and Columbia were not
transferring their treasury of old jazz seventy-eights onto microgroove
LPs. He began to do it himself in 1948, under the fictitious authority of

the "British Rhythm Society." Jolly Roger appeared shortly later. By 1951 Jolly Roger was publishing discs by, among many others, Louis Armstrong, Jelly Roll Morton, Sidney Bechet, Benny Goodman, Fats Waller, Artie Shaw, and Bessie Smith. By the middle of that year Jolly Roger was easily the most prominent of all the "pirate" labels. It brought to a head what had been a simmering controversy among connoisseurs about all this "bootlegging" or "piracy"—two terms that were to be distinguished from each other only at the climax of this clash.[10] At its center was a magazine called *Record Changer.*

Record Changer was a connoisseur's journal, edited by a collector named Gordon Gullickson in the Washington, D.C. suburbs for a readership extending across the country. It consistently took the pirates' part. As long as the big companies let "classic" performances gather dust, Gullickson believed, they were "betraying a public trust." Pirates were not personally moral, *Record Changer* maintained, but they nevertheless performed a public service. Accordingly, it insisted that those who pirated recordings that were already commercially available—and such people did exist, as the magazine was soon informed in no uncertain terms—should desist. Others should carry on. Its larger point was that the moral identity of piracy depended on the moral economy of the music industry. That economy, Gullickson felt, was an uneasy mix of two incompatible systems, art and capitalism. In practice, the industry operated solely to maximize profits. But *Record Changer* insisted that record companies, whether they acknowledged it or not, had to be more than businesses. Theirs was a "moral and artistic burden," donned when they undertook to record and distribute "material that 'belongs' (by virtue of its cultural significance) to the people as a whole—or to that portion of the public that recognizes and insists upon the aesthetic importance of jazz."[11] Bootlegging, therefore, was only trivially a matter of individual pirates' greed. Its deeper cause was the companies' denial of their custodial responsibility. The magazine proposed the creation of an association of small recording companies—no giants admitted—to deal with issues of piracy according to this moral economy, shunning recourse to law. It was yet another in the long line of proposals for a trade civility. In late 1951, however, this was a controversial idea. A time of retrenchment was no moment to represent the pirate as "a Robin Hood of the waxworks."

The big companies were now looking far more aggressively at bootleggers. RCA-Victor took the lead. It would target not only the pirate labels, it declared, but also the plants pressing their discs for them. Embarrassingly enough, however, it immediately turned out that one of the biggest factories manufacturing pirate discs was in fact RCA's own Custom Pressing plant. Worse still, it had been making records for none other than Bolletino's Jolly Roger. *Record Changer* revealed with no little schadenfreude that Bolletino had even hired RCA's plant to pirate RCA's own records. The most blatant pirate of them all had been operating in the very bowels of the "sworn enemy of disc piracy." To Gullickson this amounted to an "almost grotesque" proof of how unfit such corporations were as custodians. They clearly treated a pressing plant as a mere "robot," the sole purpose of which was to make money by manufacturing discs, content being irrelevant. The well-tempered robot obeyed, studiously ignoring questions of meaning, ethics, and even law. It did not even have enough nous to notice a pirate flag, which surely ought to have given the game away. The whole episode revealed "the wide gap that exists between 'their' world and 'ours,'" *Record Changer* concluded. If RCA really wanted to prevent a Jolly Roger exploiting it routinely, it had to place genres like jazz in the control of custodians—people who *knew something about it.*[12]

The implications of RCA's humiliation were potentially far-reaching. Its willing involvement in what were *clearly* piratical pressings might well make it impossible for the company to prosecute the pirates. Since only a "gentleman's agreement" kept record companies from preying on each other's catalogues, the prospect of chaos loomed. Bolletino himself recognized and lamented this rather outlandish possibility. In the event, however, a very different crisis ensued. The American Federation of Musicians decided to blacklist Bolletino's holding company, Paradox Industries, for not paying royalties to the artists whose records Jolly Roger pirated. Paradox truthfully (if amorally) pointed out that most of the performances had been cut at a time when royalty contracts for mainly African American jazz musicians had been virtually unknown, so there were no agreements to honor. Besides, it claimed to use its revenues from piracy to fund new recordings for which it *did* pay royalties. But the AFM held firm. The boycott cemented Paradox's identity as solely a bootlegger. In early 1952, Columbia and Louis Armstrong (who, very unusually, had earned royalties since 1924) took the opportunity to file a suit against the company. Bolletino at first wanted to fight. Since records were not copyrighted, he believed, they must be "essentially public domain."[13] But he soon thought better of the idea, and on February 7 he surrendered.

That day, the entire culture of jazz piracy collapsed. The three main organizations—Bolletino's Paradox, the Century Record Company, and Jazz-Time Records—all announced that they would cease bootleg operations forthwith. At one stroke all the recognized pirate vessels—Jazz Panorama, HJCA, Blue Ace, Jazz Classics, Anchor, Viking, Emm-Ess, and Zee-Gee—were scuttled.

Opera

Just as *Record Changer* revealed Jolly Roger's coup against RCA, the middle-brow magazine *Saturday Review* published its own scoop about record pirating. It involved the first nationally prominent case of piracy in classical music. The recording was of Verdi's *Un Ballo in Maschera.* The label, Classic Editions, claimed it to be an Italian performance, but the *Review* exposed it as an imposter. In reality it was a "pirated reproduction" of a Metropolitan Opera House radio broadcast made in 1947. Strangely enough, this set too had been pressed at RCA's Custom Pressing unit, presumably at much the same time as Jolly Roger's jazz discs. However, it was not the piracy as such but the subterfuge about attribution that seemed to anger the *Review*'s writer most—principally because of the "contempt" it implied for music critics.[14]

It soon turned out that the pirate *Ballo* was not an isolated case. Operas were appearing on pirated discs fairly routinely. But the practice had significant differences from that in the jazz world. Unlike jazz, opera recordings generally did not derive from existing American records. They came instead from obscure European sources—or, more often, from radio broadcasts. The practice depended on a different technology too. "Pirating has been given a big boost by magnetic-tape recording equipment," reported *Time.* Tape permitted pirates to record broadcasts and have their discs on the street in days, to be sold through secondhand record stores—thus effectively creating an environment similarly febrile to, though much smaller than, that of the reprint industry of a century earlier.[15] Often, as with Classic's *Ballo,* recordings derived from transmissions of performances at the Met. In any case, pirated operas frequently disguised their origin by bearing attributions to unknown European artists. The practice became the particular habit of a concern calling itself the Wagner-Nichols Home Recordist Guild, which issued about twenty Met performances in all. Some piracies even came from radio stations' own acetates of such transmissions, which could yield surprisingly high quality.

As with jazz, there was an economy at play in opera piracy at a time of technological transition, and that economy was moral and aesthetic as well as economic. Small, dedicated operators could profit from opera issues where major labels could not. It cost about $1,000–1,500 to press a two-disc opera in a run of a few hundred copies, which meant that an outfit like Wagner-Nichols could break even on sales of perhaps one hundred. A company like RCA or Columbia, on the other hand, with much larger overheads, would have had to sell more than five thousand to make an issue worthwhile. That alone made it unlikely that a major corporation would publish works like Meyerbeer's *Roberto il Diavolo* or (naturally) Bellini's *Il Pirata,* both of which appeared from so-called private labels. As with jazz, moreover, the market was made up of cognoscenti who prized every performance and every pressing, and the pirate enterprise built on that fact. More standard repertoire did sell better, of course. Callas, especially after her American debut in Chicago in 1954, was a must; and the most celebrated performance of all was Montserrat Caballé's in *Lucrezia Borgia.* On the other hand, a few particularly arcane items apparently sold so badly that they strained even the pirates' margins to the breaking point. But theirs was a niche enterprise, and a certain esoteric quality was embraced. In explaining why, one pirate with a revealingly acute historical sensibility invoked the spirit of Lionel Mapleson, who had been the Metropolitan Opera's librarian at the turn of the century. Mapleson had made a series of cylinder recordings of star singers in performance that later became celebrated among aficionados. He had done so with the House's permission, but for the opera bootleggers he provided a foundation myth. He was "the first pirate," they believed, and the tones of Caruso had been preserved for posterity only because of his efforts. "We 'pirates'—if you must call us that—are the custodians of vocal history," his later epigone declared.[16]

The opera pirates generated their biggest coup by taking on the most daunting project in all music. They produced the first commercially available recording of Richard Wagner's *Der Ring des Nibelungen* in its entirety. Today, opera mavens tend to recall Sir Georg Solti's Decca *Ring* as the first complete recording to be sold, although other cycles were recorded earlier and have been published since Solti's first appeared in 1965. But Decca was preceded—and, it was feared at the time, preempted—by the pirates. The first published *Ring* was advertised—in the *New York Times,* no less—by the label Allegro in 1954. It cost $56 for nineteen discs. Its announced origin lay with performances in Dresden led by an otherwise mysterious conductor named Schreiber. Music critics pounced on it eagerly. When they listened, however, what they heard immediately made them suspicious. The recording quality was atrocious, with what sounded like radio interference plaguing the sound, and breaks every thirty minutes—precisely the length of a tape recorded on a domestic deck. Someone had clearly recorded the operas from broadcasts, and had done so amateurishly, perhaps at home, with a single tape machine. A little more work revealed that the actual performance had come from Bayreuth in 1953, and the real conductor had been Joseph Keilberth. It was an "indecent travesty," said one critic; "the most brazen and daring case of out-and-out piracy that we have yet come across," added another. The Wotan and Sieglinde, Hans Hotter and Regina Resnik, took to the press to condemn it. Resnik sued. Allegro was forced to destroy the stock.

The underlying story to the recording came out during Resnik's suit. It had come from a company calling itself "RCA." This was not, of course, the real RCA. The letters stood here for "Record Corporation of America." Such imitative tactics had been used by print pirates for centuries, but this "RCA" was one of a number of operators bringing the technique up to date. Such outfits began producing classical LPs in 1951 and continued in "RCA"'s case until at least 1957. During that time the pirate RCA published a large number of discs, all claiming to have been recorded in Europe by orchestras, conductors, and soloists who turned out to have been either misattributed or entirely fictitious. The company's owner, however, was a known figure, who had in fact been a major player in the orthodox industry. Elliott (Eli) Oberstein was a one-time manager at the *real* RCA; he has plausibly been identified as the first artist's agent. After being eased out by internal rivalries he had gained access to troves of recorded performances by German musicians of the war and immediate postwar years, along with newer off-air recordings and some Soviet and Czech performances. Most were stored in what was now East Germany, often in the vaults of radio stations. They formed the basis of the discs that Oberstein's ersatz RCA now issued haphazardly in America. The *Ring* was his most ambitious feat, but he also undertook other grandiose projects, including a complete *Boris Godunov.* The details have never been traced, but there are hints enough of subterfuge and shadowy go-betweens, and of a network of musical espionage that would probably now be impossible to reconstruct, to evoke Le Carré.[17]

The record piracy of the 1950s was a commercial enterprise, but it was not *only* commercial. It arose from circles of expert enthusiasts forming distinct social groups—publics, as it were. They kept in touch by correspondence and through small-circulation subscription publications that were full of expert reviews and arcane information about pressings, performances, and personnel. They cultivated a sensibility of shared devotion to the higher cause of musical art. They created canons and the criteria to judge quality by. There was something very eighteenth-century about them: opera and jazz connoisseurs pursued what were, in effect, microscopic Kantian Enlightenments. Both indicted the record companies for being merely capitalist institutions, when they should and must be archivists in service to art. Their archives should be in public, where "public" meant their own communities: they demanded that the companies issue or license the discs, not that they market them to the masses. In short, opera and jazz buffs were prepared to countenance piracy or bootlegging because they held a normative view of what recording *was.*

When the companies clamped down, as far as they were concerned they observed a firm distinction. Piracy henceforth would mean the mass production of forty-fives, and be associated with payola, the Cosa Nostra, and, inevitably, loaded jukeboxes in New Jersey. In 1970 they supplied data implying that criminal piracy of these kinds had become a $100 million per year industry. But what had happened earlier left the industry with a problem that this sharp distinction was not sufficient to remove. They were susceptible to revived charges that they disdained originality, merit, and heritage, and that someone should step forward to perform the custodial function they neglected. Such perceptions were not always accurate or disinterested—the jazz pirates had preyed on independents' lists too. But they endured.

THE LINGERING DEATH OF MUSIC

After 1951–52, the record industry changed tack on piracy. It had always endorsed extending copyright to recordings, but now it coalesced to form the Recording Industry Association of America (RIAA) with an avowed antipiracy mission. The RIAA would both lobby for copyright and intervene in its own right to deter, prevent, and detect piracy. The manner in which it did this was from the outset similar to that of Arthur Preston. It hired its own agents, who operated largely outside public oversight or

FIGURE 15.1. Record counterfeiters caught by New York police in the early 1960s. *Stereo Review* 24, no. 3 (February 1970): 60.

control, and used any legal tools it could think of. There might be "good pirates" and "bad pirates," as one interested party affirmed—only the bad ones were truly clandestine—but the RIAA went after both. As its campaigns gathered steam, meanwhile, a federal law criminalized out-and-out record counterfeits. In 1966 New York outlawed the unauthorized commercial copying of recordings (fig. 15.1), and mandated that discs must display their manufacturers' details—a clause that could have dated from the seventeenth century. California soon followed suit.[18] All these tactics would become more sophisticated and familiar as music entered the digital age, and are of course still with us today. But by the late 1970s the RIAA thought it could claim substantial success. Commercial piracy seemed to be on the decline.

It was replaced by home copying, made possible by cassette tapes. The cassette was not only a recording medium but a convenient, portable, and durable means of *displacing* music. Cassette players were as ubiquitous in homes as transistor radios. They had become a fixture in cars too, and in 1979 the Sony Walkman signaled their imminent ubiquity. Such devices transformed the place and practice of listening, at the same time as they facilitated rerecording. Some commercial outfits were quite brazen in exploiting the possibilities: in Chicago, a store called Tape-A-Tape successfully defended itself against Capitol Records. But with cassettes it was really *non*commercial copying that troubled the industry. There was no precedent for understanding this practice, or for quashing it. The RIAA lost no time in warning that home copying was a bigger threat than commercial piracy.[19]

As early as the 1950s, audio manufacturers had tried to sell the idea of home recording as a hobby akin to photography. But only when cassettes arrived did a mass market emerge. From the outset Phillips adopted a policy of openness for the key patents, making the cassette a de facto universal standard. Teenagers adopted them wholesale, using transistorized, battery-powered recorders.[20] Capitalizing on affluent teen culture, cassettes made possible a dynamic domestic world of constant recording and rerecording, swapping and reswapping. Someone could buy one copy of an LP, and a circle of friends each make a copy of it; or records could be borrowed from public libraries and copied. Or, of course, one could record one's own LPs for preservation purposes. And makers of "mix" tapes could feel themselves to be exercising a certain authorship. The problem of home taping was thus akin in some ways to that of pirate listening to radio in the 1920s. It was a subtle, unostentatious practice that left few traces and allowed for a certain creative freedom on the part of what were otherwise seen as recipients. It could not easily be stopped without disproportionate police actions, and legislation offered no easy solution either. It was a problem at once of technology, place, and moral economy. Tape recorders were small, cheap, and simple to use. Recording could now be done in a garage, bedroom, or den. The cassette thus overturned the basic distinction between home and workplace so distinctive of the modern era. This was why the home came into focus in piracy conflicts once again.

All of these practices generated moral quandaries. But they were indeed quandaries, not unambiguous sins. In 1972 the magazine *Stereo Review* asked its in-house philosopher and "demon tapester" to clarify the ethics of what it called this "great tape robbery." The tapester agonized that advocacy of home taping was symptomatic of a general malady of the day. Perhaps home tapers should be aligned with moral relativists and believers in "situational ethics" (a distant echo of Ruth Benedict's famous anthropological explanation of Japanese conduct in the war). Maybe they resembled the antiwar "radicals" who thought that shoplifting was virtuous because they equated property with theft. Certainly, many of the magazine's own readers regarded the record industry as a claque of "robber barons" who deserved what they got. The tapester's own analysis—

complete with academic references and a nod to Kant—was that copying could rank anywhere from the benign to the criminal, depending on the circumstances. But when it mattered, he came down in favor of the practice. Like the 1950s pirates, the tapester concluded that it was indeed justifiable to rerecord material that the companies had permitted to lapse from the catalogue.[21]

Radio broadcasters were the first to complain of home taping, back in the days of reel-to-reel units in the 1950s. It took until the late sixties for the record industry to initiate its long sequence of jeremiads warning that it was a mortal threat to music itself. Of course, as critics like the tapester pointed out, it was more plausible to say that the practice was a threat not to music per se, but to music of a certain kind: that produced in an industrial mode, with a small number of technologically sophisticated and highly capitalized corporations mass-producing "hits." This was a model of culture that dated back to steam printing.[22] As with steam printing, it often proved tempting for critics to focus exclusively on the homogeneity to which it gave rise. In that light home taping—like bootlegging, and, especially in Europe, pirate radio—came to represent the antithesis to this perceived blandness. Its social character—its conviviality and its reliance on sharing and swapping—implied a critique, if not an alternative. *Rolling Stone* subjected the industry's claims to particularly withering skepticism. Its claim to have lost $1 billion to home taping—a claim advanced by Alan Greenspan, then an industry economist—turned out to rest on an assumption that 40 percent of home copies would otherwise have been sales of discs. But in fact home tapers bought *more* albums than average. Home tapers were not "freeloaders" after all, therefore, but the industry's most dependable customers. Monopoly and mediocrity were to blame for the industry's problems.[23]

By this time, Congress had yielded to the RIAA's urgings and launched hearings into home taping. It swiftly passed a new law.[24] As so often, however, the statute was not exactly what the industry had desired. The new statute did bring audio recordings under the wing of copyright for the first time, rejecting the idea of compulsory licensing. But on the other hand it also explicitly foreswore restricting "home taping." Noncommercial copying was not, after all, to be treated as a transgression. Although this was in large part merely an acknowledgment of the inevitable—to stop home taping was both impractical and impolitic—it was an important statement nevertheless. The measure acknowledged explicitly a distinction between (commercial) piracy and (noncommercial) "home" copying. Later, too, Congress preferred to leave it to the industry to counter the latter by creating an anticopying technology—the effects of which are evident today.[25] At any rate, it came to be widely believed that a "home taping exemption" existed in the law. Congress, after all, had discussed precisely this when Representative Edward Biester had evoked "a small pirate in my own home." Biester's son habitually taped records, and the boy became an unwitting proxy for an entire population of home tapers. The assistant registrar of copyrights, Barbara Ringer, had made the obvious explicit. "I do not see anybody going into anyone's home and preventing this sort of thing," she had testified, "or forcing legislation that would engineer a piece of equipment not to allow home taping." Judges tacitly and tactfully cleaved to this principle, and acted as though an exemption for home taping existed. The principle of the home took primacy over the principle of intellectual property.

LIBRARIANS AND TIME BANDITS

The crisis of home taping remained a relatively confined, slow-burn one as long as only audio recordings were at issue. That changed when video came into the home. Hollywood and the television industry were far larger and richer than the music companies, and enjoyed a global reach. They now saw a threat to their interests. Home piracy was about to become a geopolitical flashpoint.

Videotape had a history several decades long by the time it entered American homes. That history adumbrated many of the coming problems. It involved transnational allegations of piracy and the concoction of a tradition of U.S.-Japanese rivalry. An upstart California company, Ampex, had developed the technology in the mid-1950s as a tool for television studios, at that time still mainly constrained to live broadcasting. Video had enjoyed a rapid success in that market, even though machines cost $50,000 each. Ampex had applied for patents in Japan too. But there it ran into a company called Totsuko. Totsuko developed and patented audiotape systems, the profits from which it was reinvesting in novel transistor designs licensed from AT&T's arm, Western Electric. It was adapting the transistors for high frequencies and deploying them in small, portable radios for which it coined the name Sony. The radios sold in the millions. So successful were they that the American market was soon awash with

knock-offs bearing nameplates like Sonny—the first of many U.S.
tions of Sony devices (and something forgotten amid the 1980s c
of Japanese industrial imitation). As Totsuko negotiated, the Japanese
Ministry of International Trade and Industry (MITI), aghast at the prices
Ampex was charging TV studios, inaugurated its own program to produce
a videotape technology, beginning with straight copies of Ampex machines. Sony, as it was now called, trumped this in 1965 with what it claimed
was the world's first home VTR—a monochrome reel-to-reel machine
that, Sony said, householders would buy to record programs while they
were out. Soon a rather more practical unit called the U-matic was on sale,
followed by the Betamax. Ampex's inevitable piracy suit went nowhere.[26]

In America, by this time the press was widely predicting the imminent
arrival of some kind of home video recorder. Several manufacturers had
designs in the offing, all of them mutually incompatible: CBS's EVR,
RCA's SelectaVision, the independent Cartrivision, and several others.
Universal's ally MCA invested in a video-disc system to which it gave the
very seventies name DiscoVision. Cartrivision was the only one really to
reach the market, appearing in 1972 as a machine for recording TV programs and watching rented tapes (which employed the simple intellectual
property–protection device of being impossible to rewind). When it arrived, therefore, Betamax landed into a receptive environment, and one
rich in potential competitors. Its name reflected that: it derived from the
Japanese for a satisfyingly rich brushstroke in calligraphy, and referred to
the fact that the Sony technology alone used the whole width of the tape.
There were those who suggested that the real reason why Universal now
decided to assail Betamax was to protect its partner's stake in Disco-
Vision.[27]

Soon after Betamax arrived, Universal and Disney decided to fight it.
They filed suit against Sony, a number of its retailers, and one token Betamax user (a volunteer named William Griffiths who was an employee of
the plaintiffs' law firm). The Hollywood behemoths sought damages and
an injunction against the sale and use of the technology. For the first and
defining time, home taping itself was to be placed in the balance. At the
initial trial in California, District Court Judge Warren Ferguson dismissed
their contention. Home taping was fair use, Ferguson decided, and even
if it were not it would scarcely warrant an injunction against an entire
technology. But in October 1981 the Ninth Circuit Court of Appeals overturned Ferguson's decision and made Sony liable for massive damages.[28]

By now the clash was already set to become the greatest "communications squabble" of the age, and "one of the biggest knock-down, drag-out legal wars in American history." The only point of comparison anyone could find was the mid-century contest over AT&T and patent pooling. The potential consequences of a victory by either side stirred huge public controversy.

VTRs were by now commonplace, and home recording was a routine practice in hundreds of thousands (soon to be millions) of American homes. Yet, as the *New York Times* declared, the court had discovered it to be "piracy, even in the privacy of the home." The *Chicago Tribune* added bluntly and resonantly that the verdict made "Everyman a copyright infringer." It meant that "three million Americans . . . are little more than modern-day pirates," warned columnist Philip Shenon—adding for good measure that "the average American" was probably now an offender. Lawrence Tribe even told Congress that home taping was forbidden by the Constitution. Arthur Levine, a Washington lawyer, identified the changing *place* of productive and creative technologies as the focus of the issue. Tape recorders, he pointed out, and imminently computers too, allowed citizens to "become their own printers and publishers, their own television producers and record recorders." Countless millions risked being defined as "instant criminals." Entrepreneurs bought advertising space to encourage panic buying of VCRs and tapes.[29] Outlawing video would be tantamount to enacting Prohibition in the cultural sphere.

Sketches and op-ed pieces proliferated warning of some prospective video police force (fig. 15.2 is just one example), many of them unconsciously indebted to a long tradition of invoking teenage pirates. "Gray men in greatcoats" would break into your house to arrest toddlers, Americans read; AWACS planes would be deployed over suburbia to erase their tapes en masse by electromagnetic fields. (The Reagan administration was mired in a controversy over selling these aircraft to Saudi Arabia, so the conjunction leaped readily to mind.) G-men appeared in countless cartoons, "breaking down the bedroom door in search of contraband *Mork and Mindy.*" Inconsequential as they may seem today, these parodic warnings had an effect. One commentator thought the prospect of such home invasions would provoke a backlash against big government in general, and bring about "the final collapse of American liberalism." More modestly, the industry lobbyist Jack Valenti was later heard to blame the RIAA's defeat on them. In the short run, they certainly helped prompt

"Metro police, Betamax squad. We'd like to ask you some questions."

FIGURE 15.2. The video police. "Metro police, Betamax squad." *Chicago Tribune,* November 10, 1981, sec. 1, 17. © Tribune Media Services, Inc. All rights reserved. Reprinted with permission.

two bills to appear in Congress aiming to exempt all households from piracy charges, one representative having scribbled out a draft on the spot.[30]

But what really did go on in the home? The perennial problem of answering that question loomed large and early. Universal quickly tried to tackle it by getting hold of a list of Betamax buyers in Los Angeles and dispatching private investigators after them. A judge swiftly intervened to stop this. Both sides then retreated to survey research of the kind pioneered by mid-century radio researchers. They identified two ways in which householders apparently used their video recorders. These were soon dubbed *time-shifting* and *librarying.* Time-shifting—recording a program for watching later—was the more benign. Librarying was more controversial, because it involved the preservation, not just the rescheduling, of programs. The implicit claim to a curatorial or custodial prerogative in librarying was also pertinent. In its higher forms it evoked a moral economy similar to that of the pirates of the fifties. (The copyright expert for Sony, it is worth noting, had cut his legal teeth in those opera cases.) Both practices played a part in the Supreme Court's two examinations of the issue, the first of which was on January 18, 1983. By then it had attracted more amicus briefs than any other case in history, including one from the American Library Association. The studios lost no time in asserting that householders' routine practices were "no different than tape piracy." "The fact that it is at home," they insisted, "makes no difference."[31] But with so many homes involved—it was forecast that videos would soon be in 40 percent of U.S. households—location made all the difference.

In their private deliberations the Supreme Court justices returned to the congressional hearings prior to the 1971 measure against home audio taping. They did so because prior to that the law had effectively permitted "record piracy," and the hearings, impelled by the rise of large-scale piratical enterprises, had been a turning point. They had rendered the prospect of home searches moot by permitting noncommercial, domestic taping. But this permission was not explicitly reiterated in the subsequent Copyright Act of 1976.[32] Moreover, unlike sound recordings, movies had been protected by copyright ever since 1912. In their case there had never been an explicit allowance for noncommercial copying. The only refuge of the video taper seemed therefore to lie in the fuzzy, almost ineffable notion of "fair use."

Long recognized as a peculiarly difficult and controversial subject—as it still is today—fair use represented a compromise central to the conundrum of intellectual property. There clearly must be occasions when the principle of property has to leak a little. The use of quotes in criticism or research is an evident example. The conventionally accepted origin of a concept of fair use to address such occasions occurred in 1841, when W. W. Story decided that a 350-page excerpt of George Washington's published correspondence did *not* qualify. It was "piracy," he ruled, not "justifiable use" or (in British Lord Chancellor Eldon's phrase) "fair quotation."[33] But Story famously remarked that the question of how to tell fair from unfair use was almost metaphysical, involving distinctions "very subtle and refined, and, sometimes, almost evanescent." Only in 1976 did a statute attempt such a definition. It listed four "factors": the purpose and character of the use (profit or nonprofit/educational); the nature of the work; the "substantiality" of the extract; and the consequences of the use for the market of the original. Even these were to be *included in* a decision about fairness, not *decisive for* that decision. The House report of the time contented itself with noting that fair use was "an equitable rule of reason," for which no definition was possible.

The major contention in the Court therefore arose over whether home copying was "fair." John Paul Stevens thought it was. Home-produced copies had never mattered until taping came along, he pointed out, and the 1971 hearings had then resolved the issue. This being so, the threat to privacy involved in any attempt to "control conduct within the home" must take precedence. Furthermore, holding Sony liable for contributory infringement would leave the corporation with a "truly staggering" bill: the statutory amount of $100 per copy would add up to billions of dollars. Such an absurd punishment would discourage the development of new technologies—hardly the purpose of copyright.[34] Thurgood Marshall, however, claimed that while fair use quotation in a review or critique served the public interest because it was productive, home taping was intrinsically unproductive and therefore should not qualify. Moreover, the letter of the law stated that use need not affect an *actual* market value in order to be disqualified—it was enough to show that it impinged on a *potential* value. The industry had never yet been able to show a real loss from home taping, rather to its embarrassment, but it had shown the potential for loss. Advertisers might well refuse to pay the same fees if they thought that viewers were pressing *fast forward* to skip through ("zap") commercials. As Marshall clung to this view, it became clear that a consensus was going to be hard to find. After "many late nights," the justices decided to start again.

A very unusual second hearing took place in a crowded courtroom on October 3. Universal's parent had just announced record results, and the judges seemed more worried about policing millions of homes than about industry revenues.[35] That impression was confirmed when the final decision was announced on January 17, 1984. Splitting 5–4, the Court decided in favor of Sony, with Stevens writing the opinion. The VCR did have substantial noninfringing uses, they concluded, of which time-shifting was one. Stevens particularly noted that the complainants made less than 10 percent of the programs that came into households, and that others had declared their openness to this kind of duplication. In a "rule of reason" balance, a positive benefit outweighed a speculative harm. Marshall dissented, along with Blackmun, who decried a blow against copyright itself. The opinion, if it were applicable to books and other media, would imply a potentially radical expansion of the fair use criterion.

The outcome reinstated the domestic threshold in intellectual property. There was definitively no basis for "extending commercial copyright law into private homes." It ended any prospect that citizens in general might be denounced as "pirates." From now on, the *Washington Post* declared, when companies sent film and music into your house they had no right to tell you what to do with them. Some felt a profound shift in the moral and political economy of creativity was in the offing: "artists," it was said, "are going to be paid once for the work and then all humanity will have access to it."[36] These implications would become clear when digital media arrived. File-sharing and peer-to-peer networks like Napster and MP3.com would exploit them in the first Internet generation, followed by Grokster and Kazaa in the second, and the Pirate Bay in the third.

SAMURAI IN THE DEN!

With the prospect of outlawing home copying as piracy now ruled out, the MPAA followed the RIAA's lead and tried to tax it. A lobbying campaign lurched into action for a levy on tapes. Even the *New York Times* came out in support. Banding together as the Home Recording Rights Coalition, video manufacturers and others countered with their own claims of restrictive practices and price fixing (prerecorded videos then sold at $70).[37] What ensued was an early example of the kind of lobbying arms race that has since become familiar. As in later cases, the tactics quickly descended to a brutal level. A quickly notorious example was a direct-mail letter sent over the film star Charlton Heston's signature to constituents in key congressional districts. The letter urged them to exhort their representatives to support the culture industries. But it did so by appealing crudely to nationalism. "A group of wealthy, powerful Japanese electronics firms" had "invaded" the country, it warned. They were "trampling" laws and "threatening one of America's most unique and creative industries." The levy was vital to hold them back. Nationalistic overtones had always existed in the home taping contest, but they had grown markedly louder as the Betamax case wound on. Almost routinely, now, one side was identified as "American" and "creative," the other as Japanese and, implicitly, imitative. Valenti announced that as the United States lost its global economic and technical lead, "the American movie is the one thing the Japanese with all their skills cannot duplicate or clone"; presumably his implication was that if Sony won, householders would clone it for them. He also likened video recorders to "tapeworms" in the body politic. The American people apparently faced the prospect of surviving in a postapocalyptic "entertainment desert."[38]

Remarks like these sound hyperbolic in retrospect, but at the time they played upon an anxiety about economic and technical decline that was almost universal in the United States. In the wake of the oil crisis, and facing huge and growing trade deficits, the country convinced itself that it was about to be eclipsed. And Japan was the most plausible candidate to supplant it. A sizable literature of jeremiads fueled fears that an imminent contest for supremacy with Japan was already as good as lost. Chalmers Johnson's *MITI and the Japanese Miracle,* published in 1982, sounded the first of the warnings, with a relatively well-researched investigation culminating in the testimony of Sony's own chairman. It was at length joined by Clyde Prestowitz's *Trading Places: How We Allowed Japan to Take the Lead* (1988), Pat Choate's *Agents of Influence* (1990), and journalist James Fallows's widely cited article in *Atlantic Monthly* (1989) proposing that the U.S. adopt a cold-war-style strategy to "contain" Japan. The foremost management theorist of postwar America, Peter Drucker, argued in *Foreign Affairs* that the Japanese were the first developing nation to rise by being "imitators," not innovators. Drucker defined Japan's strategy as one of "adversarial trade," based on a premise that imitating other nations' technologies must lead to a zero-sum game. Michael Crichton's *Rising Sun* fictionalized the contention. By the early 1990s Americans had heard of a *Coming War with Japan,* and learned that *Zaibatsu America* was doomed to become a colony of Tokyo.[39]

The Japan jeremiads mattered because they professed to explain Tokyo's inevitable victory in terms of culture. The peculiarly Japanese institution of the *keiretsu* was a favorite explanatory device. Laissez-faire was obsolescent, the argument went, and would be replaced by a social model embracing keiretsu-like characteristics of cooperation, cartelism, and vertical integration. The United States had hitherto been able to hold its own only because its individualist culture favored innovation. But the Japanese had now obviated this advantage by piracy—by helping themselves to Western scientific and technological advances. (The irony of this claim in light of earlier American appropriations of European technology was not widely appreciated.) MITI, allegedly the mastermind of the strategy, was reputed to focus on robotics, computing, telecommunications, pharmaceuticals, and biotechnology. In a case that enjoyed enormous exposure and was seen as proving the point, Fujitsu was caught trying to purloin IBM's innovations. Drucker even maintained that the Japanese grand strategy was itself an imitation of an American invention—the industrial research pioneered by AT&T and Bell Labs in the 1920s. A hoary representation of Asian culture as essentially imitative took on new force here, and publishers' complaints about the piracy of engineering textbooks found a new and receptive federal audience. The same senator who legislated for home taping also sponsored legislation to strengthen patent laws against supposed Japanese pirates. Washington, he proclaimed, must help companies "protect themselves from the foreign manufacturers which steal American-owned technology."[40]

The analyses of keiretsu and the like that appeared in these works were of course only ostensibly about Japan. They were really about the United States itself. They redeployed tropes from cultural anthropology (sometimes quite dated ones) to articulate by contrast a series of anxieties about American social and economic culture. Thus, for instance, Japan's alleged culture of farsighted planning furnished a contrast to domestic capitalism's self-defeating short-termism. Harmony stood in opposition to social disintegration. Today it may seem that the keiretsu were never more than a "myth"—albeit one in which Japanese themselves believed. But in the 1980s American politics needed them.[41]

Home piracy thus metastasized into an element in a narrative of national malaise and cultural difference. In every little act of "home piracy," on this account, Japan's ascent was furthered one more step. Newspaper cartoons again drove home the point, as ferocious samurai did battle on the home front (fig. 15.3). Nobody had ever tried to convey the dangers of Phillips's audiocassettes by publishing caricatures of threatening Dutch burghers, but suddenly lurid images cropped up everywhere of warriors menacing the living room. Such images rendered the putative link between the domestic and the geopolitical starkly evident. And Reagan Commerce Department official Clyde Prestowitz made explicit the identification between home video, the appropriation of science, and the end of American economics. MIT, the very model of academic/industrial science, now had nine chairs funded by Japanese corporations that "tapped directly into the scientific source." Prestowitz claimed that "the Japanese" stood ready to expropriate new American technologies while shortsighted U.S. corporations declined to patent them. "The best example is the VCR," he explained. But when told of the peril, citizens' first concern was still whether and how to buy one. The hardware of home piracy came out of Japan, of course, perhaps by appropriation from California (nobody recalled the German origin of tape). But so, it was implied, did its historical

FIGURE 15.3. Samurai in the den. D. Sherbo, "Video Wars." *Washington Post,* May 2, 1982, f1. © The Washington Post. All rights reserved. Used by permission and protected by the copyright laws of the United States. The printing, copying, redistribution, or retransmission of this material without express written permission is prohibited.

role. It threatened what was otherwise the last remaining bastion of American supremacy, and the one field of the economy that could not be beaten by geopolitical piracy: the business of culture. It made the home-owner not only a producer, but a producer of "cheap copies"—another stereotyped Japanese trait. Indeed, between the two Supreme Court arguments Senators Robert Dole and Lloyd Bentsen had tried to resolve the Betamax case by treating it as a matter of trade. They wrote to MITI suggesting a compromise in the style of recent U.S.-Japanese deals covering car imports. This crisis for Hollywood posed "a potentially serious threat to US-Japanese trade relations," they pointed out, and if Congress were to step in it would surely do so "in the context of a large Japanese trade surplus." Hearings on U.S.-Japanese economic relations did actually take place alongside those on home taping. Only the likelihood of a Sony court victory dissuaded MITI from taking up the senators' idea.[42]

Sony's victory in the Betamax case proved pyrrhic, of course. Betamax was soon overtaken by the rival VHS standard. Reflecting on the failure, Sony came to a momentous decision. It decided that it resulted from a basic rift between technology and "content" in the electronics and culture industries. That is, in an emerging information age the divide between industrial and creative properties could be fatal. Implicit in the Betamax experience, therefore, was a message about how international capitalism and creativity intersected—or failed to. It was on this reasoning that Sony launched what became the largest Japanese acquisition of all. It first bought CBS Records for $2 billion. Then, in September 1989, it moved to buy Columbia Pictures, priced at the time at $3.4 billion ($5.6 billion including debt). The rationale was to connect together intellectual properties in technology and creativity.

Needless to say, the bid stirred up intense controversy, involving all the issues of the previous half-century of piracy debates: public responsibility, curatorship, canonicity, and nationalism. Columbia's huge backlist of classic films represented something close to the American "soul," it was said. What did it mean for a nation to sell its soul? Moreover, the deal happened to come to fruition at a moment of extraordinary global uncertainty. It culminated just as the Berlin wall fell. With the Soviet bloc in terminal disarray, a fundamental reconfiguration of global politics was in the offing. Washington's anxieties about the place of Japan in that process found a focus in the Sony bid.[43]

What epitomized the fear was a pirated book. The original had been published in Japan back in January and swiftly sold five hundred thousand copies. It was entitled *"No" to ieru Nihon* (*The Japan That Can Say No*). Its authors were Akio Morita, Sony's chairman, and the novelist-cum-politician Shintaro Ishihara. Morita's contributions were relatively sober. They voiced a critique of American capitalism that was, if not exactly welcome, at least familiar. Ishihara's, on the other hand, were intensely controversial. Then fifty-six, Ishihara's views were idiosyncratic but often extremely nationalist, and he was about to launch a maverick but startlingly strong bid to lead the LDP. Japan should feel free to flex its muscles, Ishihara exhorted, and could afford to do so. The United States' nuclear deterrent had become entirely dependent on Japanese technology; were Tokyo to withhold this technology—or even offer it to the USSR—then it could engineer a tectonic shift in global power. Ishihara singled out for praise the strategist behind the Pearl Harbor attack, presumably for grasping such opportunities. He identified the shifting economic fortunes of Japan and America with intrinsic racial natures, while at the same time decrying American concerns about trade imbalances as themselves rooted in racism. It seemed that Sony was endorsing what was effectively his manifesto.

Word of all this arrived in Washington as the fate of the Sony bid for Columbia had to be decided. Samizdat copies of a mysterious translation began to appear on Capitol Hill. Michigan Representative Sander Levin had the entire text inserted into the *Congressional Record*. Thousands of photocopies were soon available. The "pirated" text became "the rage of Washington." Like pornography, remarked Harvard's Lawrence Summers, the authors' reluctance to allow publication "only served to increase the demand for it." Scandalized politicians, savvy journalists, worried executives, anxious citizens — all who could get hold of a copy of "the bootleg," as it was called, did so.[44]

Like so many piracies, *The Japan That Can Say No* raised an issue of authenticity. In this case it was taken to expose a secret truth — a hidden national strategy behind Sony's appropriation of American cultural property. It served to crystallize all the fears undergirding Japanophobia. The *New York Times*'s science reporter Nicholas Wade took Morita and Ishihara to task over it. Summers weighed in too, publishing a remarkably explicit open letter warning America to open its eyes and act to counter the threat it outlined. He called for a drive to secure supremacy in industries like semiconductors for national-security reasons. The fundamentals of economics should be abandoned, Summers urged, because "there is little to be said for a laissez-faire attitude toward industries upon which our future security depends." Suddenly aware of how damaging this might become, Morita swiftly withdrew from a planned English translation — thus ensuring that the only version to circulate in English was the bootleg. Ishihara flew to Washington in person to denounce it, determined to counter what he called "the vile, error-filled pirate translation." Once there he cannily presented himself as "one of the latest victims of intellectual property piracy."[45]

The incident encapsulated the continued potential of an act of piracy to shape the state of play at the most critical juncture since the end of World War II. As Ishihara prepared to fly back to Tokyo, the last mystery was solved: the source of the bootleg itself. A spokesman let slip at a press conference that it was the work of the Defense Advanced Research

Projects Agency (DARPA)—a branch of the Pentagon charged, among other things, with bolstering technological projects related to national security. The Pentagon hastily announced that it had been intended for internal use and had therefore not violated copyright. Ishihara pounced, pointing out that anyone could photocopy it at a public library. It had become a "best non-seller." He demanded that his government file charges against the United States as a national pirate.

The DARPA "piracy" had focused debate at a potentially critical moment. It had seemed to reveal the motives actuating the buyers of America's soul. But after the revelation of its source—and Ishihara's defiant intervention—it was overtaken by the rush of events in that time of upheaval. Threats of Washington intervention receded. Sony's acquisition of Columbia proceeded, to enjoy distinctly mixed fortunes in the 1990s. But there was a certain irony in the fact that the home piracy debates, having been elevated to the level of geopolitical scandal, had culminated here. As the old order disintegrated and the world changed course, the institution responsible for defending the nation itself was reduced to publicly denying it was a pirate.[46]

TAPE WORLDS

Home piracy was the American and European wing of a worldwide phenomenon. When any home could be a production center, production itself scattered into a distinctly postindustrial multiplicity of places and forms. Everywhere, the advent of tape cassettes internationalized cultures, but at the same time shrank and disaggregated them. Styles of music, for example, ramified down to the level of the street and precinct, but then circulated globally. This was certainly the case with some American R&B, and with British house music too (which was also associated with pirate radio). In many countries quasi-monopolist cultural industries, often identified with the nation, found themselves challenged by proliferating clusters of independents and alternatives. One could think of them in terms of "tape worlds," by analogy to Howard Becker's "art worlds."[47] Occasionally the challengers won out: in some African countries (Ghana, for example) the multinational record companies withdrew from the marketplace, complaining of rampant and unrestrained piracy. When they did, the results were by no means utopian. But more often the companies stayed, banded together with independents, and fought for new laws and police actions. Piratical and other copying were never eliminated, but they took on a symbiotic role. We are only beginning to understand the complexities of these processes of the last analogue age.

Home taping was thus the first truly global piracy, paradoxically enough, and it was global precisely *because of* its domesticity. Cassettes were cheap enough to spread rapidly even in the developing world. In many places, casual copying eclipsed commercial piracy. Tape made debates over creativity and commerce truly ubiquitous. Commercial piracy itself had become a vast enterprise, equal to any of the great multinationals. In the EEC (now the European Union) alone, 21 million pirated cassettes appeared every year, and video was set to be the next step in this "bonanza for pirates." The public often took their low prices as an indictment of the "immoral" margins sustained by the legitimate industry. Yet home taping was seen as the greater problem. Well over 85 percent of West Germans admitted doing it, and unlike commercial piracy it stood for a moral economy that threatened the "death of copyright.". Its expansion therefore posed direct challenges to "the cultural life of each country."[48] In India, meanwhile, as Peter Manuel has shown, cassettes transformed what had been a connoisseurs' moral economy of bootlegging rather like that of the jazz pirates into something much bigger, more corporate, and more culturally various. Pirated tapes cornered 95 percent of the market and became an international industry. A 1979 start-up calling itself T-Series was widely claimed to pirate the backlist of the old colonial company, HMV, which had failed to keep its own copies — and in its turn T-Series denounced pirates who faked its labels. A veritable "pirate network" — or rather, a network of networks — came into being, with its own equivalents of majors and indies. Practices of parody and reinvention central to much Indian music took fresh inspiration from the proliferation, giving rise to a burst of new creativity. Digital media would later take advantage of these networks to produce the dizzying array of media cultures that compete on the subcontinent today.[49]

In other regions the implications were more directly political. The banner case was Iran, where Khomeini's speeches circulated in huge numbers of cassettes under the noses of Savak. No less a figure than Michel Foucault, who reported from Tehran for an Italian newspaper, called the cassette the tool par excellence of counterinformation: "if the Shah is about to fall," Foucault pronounced, "it will be due largely to the cassette tape." In Africa, a vibrant culture of oral poetry seized upon cassettes to renew and revivify itself under the Somali dictatorship of Siad Barre. Multiplying sequences of poems, adapting and responding to each other, recreated the flow of oral performances. Somalis took the tapes, recopied them, and passed them on. Listening took place in prescreened groups that formed the basis for opposition cadres.[50] One could go on listing examples indefinitely, from Ireland (the IRA purportedly ran a pirate videotape business at one point) to the USSR. The point is that in so many places different groups saw a piratical potential in the cassette for subverting centralized industry, authority, and culture. It threw together the intimate and small scale with the boundless and the visionary.

That would have lasting consequences. For as teenagers swapped mix-tape compilations in London and poets competed with each other in Africa, in Northern California cassettes were being pressed into service to build a similar kind of community of recording, sharing, and copying. But the content that interested this community was intriguingly different. The first home computer hobbyists took the principles of home copying and applied them to digital data.

16

From Phreaking to Fudding

The word most often associated with piracy at the turn of the twenty-first century was probably *software*. Software piracy, an arcane concept before about 1975, became a ubiquitous one in that generation. In the press it rivaled and then subsumed the lamentations emanating from the entertainment industry about pirated music, movies, and books, as they came to be redefined as subspecies of software. With the growth of the Internet, fears of identity theft, phishing, and the like—culminating in spectacular feats like the pirate multinational NEC—merged with those of piracy proper to make problems of credit and authenticity central to the very constitution of a global "new economy."

By the late 1970s, a fundamental fault line was emerging around digital creativity and intellectual property. Digerati themselves disagreed profoundly about the place of property in the new digital realm, and as that realm became increasingly a networked one those disagreements metastasized. At one extreme, some pioneers urged that intellectual property be built into the very code structuring the networks. At the other, some advocated its abandonment as an anachronistic barrier to creativity and community. These positions cut across conventional political affiliations. As a result, polemics about piracy came to stand as proxies for fundamental convictions about the cultural, social, and technical character of the digital domain. Images of pirates, buccaneers, Robin Hoods, and the like that had permeated expert communities in programming from at least the 1960s now took on a more serious tone as they opened a set of rifts between various proprietary regimes and some nonproprietary ones. The moral and practical realities of the digital realm evolved through the ensuing exchanges.

When contemporaries sought to understand what was happening in this transition, they often appealed to an ethos of antiproprietorial creativity that digital networks supposedly favored. That is, they sketched a cluster of morally consequential "norms" to which true digerati were supposedly committed—norms of sharing, access, and technocracy—and which characterized the emerging culture. The perspective made sense not only because it captured something about the technical properties of digital networks, but also because it evoked a widely believed account of the nature of true science. But that understanding, we have seen, was itself a consequence of mid-twentieth-century conflicts about patenting. Patent strategies in the telecommunications industries in particular had triggered the articulation of this normative account of science, which included a conviction that real research was ultimately incompatible with intellectual property. What is more significant here, however, is that alongside what may loosely be called an ideological inheritance was a practical one. Two closely related kinds of "piratical" interloping had survived the contests of the 1920s–1950s and would now play important roles in shaping the digital revolution. One was unlicensed radio. Amateur ("ham") transmission and reception remained a popular activity throughout the century, and in the 1960s pirate broadcasting enjoyed massive audiences, especially in Europe, for its laissez-faire, libertarian, and antimonopolist messages. The other, however, was older still, and its influence was to be more direct. This practice had originated in the early days of telephony, back in the nineteenth century, only to revive and acquire a new prominence, along with pirate radio, in the sixties. It was called *phreaking.*

PHREAKING

How did the digital world come to be riven between rival conventions of property and responsibility? The answer involves a history extending back beyond the development of digital technology itself, to ideals of science and media that were forged in the days of the radio and telephone trusts.

It also derives from underground practices seen by their proponents as upholding those ideals in the face of industry and monopoly. Take radio. All the principal participants in the making of the home computer either had backgrounds as ham radio aficionados or came from whole families of them (as did Stewart Brand, founder of the first online community, the WELL). Before their experiences at MIT, Stanford, or any of the other canonical sites of the computer revolution, these figures were *already* acculturated into norms of open access, technical meritocracy, libertarianism, and the sharing of information. These were the values bequeathed to amateur and pirate radio from the 1920s–1930s patent fights against AT&T and the radio trust and, in the UK, from those around the BBC, and identified, thanks to those fights, with science itself. It was consequently easy for those early digerati to see the disputes about openness and property that arose in home computing as disputes of a certain kind, for which precedents existed to suggest the stances they should adopt and the actions they should take.

The case of telephony is even clearer. Independent ("pirate") telephony survived, just as independent radio did. In the late 1960s and early 1970s, radicals revived this tradition of expertise. Ripping off Ma Bell took on an added charge for them as a statement of antagonism to the state and to capitalism. Phreaking—telephone network "piracy"—was a way to thumb their nose at the iconic leviathan of corporate America.

Nobody seems to know when the hobby began of gaming AT&T's networks. Its conventionally accepted origin was long placed in the late 1960s, when the term "phreaking" appeared in the press, and others mentioned MIT in the early part of that decade. But the practice certainly has a history a lot longer than that. Even before 1900 teenagers were caught fiddling free calls, and later in Al Capone's Chicago gangs would tweak the phone system to register an illicit bookie's line to some harmless householder. Interviews with leading phreaks in the 1960s revealed that they had learned the habit earlier, sometimes in the mid-1950s—and often in quite uncosmopolitan places too, like Kansas or Mississippi. Britain's Old Bailey had heard a conspiracy trial in 1953 against a London chemical company director who made long-distance calls by tapping the receiver rest. And MIT's phreaking could be tracked back to that decade too, as key Tech phreaks had learned the craft before they ever arrived in Cambridge. In short, the phreaks of the early 1970s were the tip of a historical iceberg. And that is interesting because in the 1950s, 1930s, or 1890s telephone piracy could not possibly have had the political meaning attributed to it in San Francisco in the Vietnam era. Instead, it starts to look much more like the enterprise of exploration that arose around early radio.[1]

Telephone piracy was certainly something portrayed by its practitioners in ethical terms long before 1970. They professed to disdain mere mercenary motives. Instead they proclaimed that they were dedicated to research, and to sharing the insights that resulted from that research. They maintained that the knowledge gained by exploring the network was justification enough for doing so without constraint. That knowledge must, of course, be made openly available — even (and perhaps especially) to AT&T's own staff. Many had a love-hate relationship with AT&T, similar to that which trainspotters cultivate with rail companies. A devotion to technical expertise irrespective of professional affiliation; the intrepid exploration of a network; the discovery of knowledge; the free sharing of discoveries with the priesthood of experts: these were the elements, to coin a phrase, of the phreaker ethic. Doubtless many phreaks stretched the point, simply wanting to place calls gratis. We know that some sold their services to homesick GIs in Vietnam. But their ethical self-portrait was nevertheless impressively consistent and specific.

Two innovations lay behind the popularization of telephone piracy in the 1960s, which seems to be when it first came to be called phreaking. First, AT&T had recently changed to a new long-distance switching technology known as multiple frequency (MF). MF used audible tones at discrete frequencies as an instruction set to tell the network's switches how to channel each call. The tones were transmitted on the same channel as the telephone conversation itself. Knowing their frequencies, it was therefore possible in principle to blaze a trail through the network simply by playing them into a receiver at the right moments. This was what phreaks sought to do. A few could whistle the required notes, but most used an electronic tone generator, perhaps embedded in a "blue box" device. The phreak simply dialed a free 800 number and then sent a tone at 2,600 Hz down the line to trick the exchange into believing that the caller had hung up. "Tandems" (switching devices) in the system emitted this note when they were inactive. Sequences of different tones could then route a call anywhere the network reached — to South America, Asia, Europe, or the Soviet Union. From the mid-sixties cassette tapes became the ideal tool for recording and exchanging these tones, making phreaks into natural allies of home tapers.

The difficulty lay in finding those other frequencies, of course. For years, the only way to discover them was by trial and error, or by asking a more experienced explorer. But in 1960 a house journal of Bell Labs, the *Bell System Technical Journal,* published them in an ill-advised moment of scientific openness.[2] By coincidence, much the same thing happened a little later in the British Post Office's counterpart journal. Alert readers realized that they had found the equivalent of "open sesame." (That there were amateur readers poring over these abstruse journals, incidentally, confirms that a community already existed.) A legend subsequently arose that Bell Labs tried to recall all the copies of the issue. True or not, it was too late. Following the revelation, phreaking grew into a widespread activity.

As it grew, phreaking developed its own pantheon. Perhaps the most admired member was a blind African American, Joe Engressia (who died in 2007 under the name Joybubbles). Engressia had briefly hit the headlines while a student at the University of South Florida, because he had discovered that he could whistle the crucial MF tones into a receiver with perfect pitch, and thereby maneuver through the network without the need for electronic gizmos. He became the focus of countless urban legends, some of which were true (or true-ish). It became a rite of passage for phone explorers all over the United States to place a call to him using their homemade MF devices and cassette recorders. He would put them in touch with each other, and so an underground network grew.

Northern California became a major node for this network under the leadership of an ex-military technician named John Draper. Draper was one of the many who had been involved in radio before he turned to the telephone system. He had been a radar and radio engineer for the air force, stationed in remote Alaska, where free telephoning proved invaluable. After that he had worked at a variety of technology companies, including Cartrivision, the Palo Alto company that had tried to market a videotape device ahead of Sony's Betamax. He also engaged in pirate broadcasting, calling himself San Jose Free Radio.[3] It was because of his pirate radio work that he came into contact with Engressia's phreaks, one of whom heard his signal and got in touch. When it turned out that a plastic whistle distributed free with the breakfast cereal Cap'n Crunch happened to produce exactly the 2,600 Hz tone needed to initiate a phreaking odyssey, Draper adopted the moniker as his *nom de phreak.* As "Cap'n Crunch" he became another legendary presence.

In the early 1970s phone explorers coalesced with a counterculture keen to make ostentatious gestures against the mainstream broadcasting and entertainment industries. The best-known declaration of war was perhaps that by the so-called Air Pirates, a group of San Francisco cartoonists who published skillfully rendered imitations of 1930s cartoons portraying Disney's icon taking drugs and having sex (the corporation pursued them so humorlessly that it provoked a backlash from another outfit calling itself the Mouse Liberation Front).[4] In the same year, Abbie and Anita Hoffman's Youth International Party—the "Yippies"—seized upon phreaking as an ideal tool for a parallel effort. Not only would it help connect fellow Yippies together, they reasoned, but the practice itself suited their ambitions for media. Their point was that underground media must be a commons, with any organ free to reproduce the contents of any other. Hoffman's own guide for would-be revolutionaries, *Steal This Book*—published by "Pirate Editions"—advocated "outlaw" radio and TV stations, which should be linked through (unpaid) telephone lines to form a nationwide "people's network." They would form "the vanguard of the communications revolution." "One pirate picture on the sets in Amerika's living rooms is worth a thousand wasted words."[5] To make this pirate revolution work, experts ("technical freaks") would be needed, and Hoffman recommended that readers find them in the world of amateur radio. He also directed them to *Radical Software,* a periodical emanating from a New York group of artists in the brand-new home-production medium of videotape. Operating oxymoronically as the Center for Decentralized Television, *Radical Software* was heavily influenced by Marshall McLuhan and Buckminster Fuller, and also by Norbert Wiener's antiproprietorial vision of information. The magazine proclaimed in the first lines of its first issue the imperative to universalize access to information, not least by abjuring copyright. It included what it called a "pirated" interview with Fuller, and invented a symbol to represent the "antithesis" of ©. The symbol was a circle containing an *X* (for *Xerox*). It meant "*DO* copy."[6]

Phreaking thus became a fixture of the counterculture. The Fabulous Furry Freak Brothers experimented with it (fig. 16.1). More than that, it promised to provide a means by which the counterculture might achieve two ends at once: it could counter mainstream media and achieve coherence in its own right. After all, what better way to combat Ma Bell's "improper control of the communication" than by merging phreakdom with the Yippies' characteristic combination of practical jokery and earnestness? Even as *Steal This Book* hit the streets, Hoffman and a New York

FIGURE 16.1. The Fabulous Furry Freak Brothers try phreaking. A. Hoffman,
Steal This Book (New York: Pirate Editions, 1971), 137. Reprinted by
permission of Gilbert Shelton.

phreak going by the pseudonym Al Bell began to publish a regular underground journal entitled *The Party Line*. Their intent was to proselytize
about "the phone company's part in the war against the poor, the non-
white, the non-conformist, and in general, against the people." In practice,
each monthly issue was devoted to encouraging the mass adoption of
phreaking. It twinned technical notes with screeds, reciting "Corporation
ripoffs, establishment fucks, healthful hints, names and addresses of our
friends who wish to be known, new services, new devices and plans for
them." The journal endured for over a year until it was renamed TAP,
for Technological American Party—or, later, Technological Assistance
Program, apparently because banks refused to open accounts under the
earlier name. It became a principal nexus for phreaks at large and continued to appear into the 1980s.[7]

By about 1971—and in practice well before that—phreaking constituted
a self-conscious community that "met" in the virtual space of the network
and had global reach. It was, as the anthropologist Christopher Kelty has

said of more recent open-source communities, a "recursive" public, in that it solidified around expert interventions in its own basic infrastructure.[8] The community ostentatiously embraced the claims of the old radio amateurs to openness and knowledge seeking. They aspired to be, and by training often were, practitioners of science. "Like scientists conducting experiments," it was said, "the phone phreaks report results to each other." In Britain, evidence of a similar community surfaced when the Post Office considered adopting a technology akin to that of the Bell system; a public-spirited Cambridge undergraduate cropped up to warn of its vulnerability. It soon turned out that details of the entire British telephone network had been lodged in Cambridge University's mainframe—evidence that these phreaks were computer adepts. In 1973 an Old Bailey judge, faced with a dockful of such reprobates, remarked that the temptation seemed similar to that of heroin addiction. He acquitted the lot, but only after asking them for the access codes to his local exchange. One of the lucky perps—a recent Oxford physics graduate—went home and wrote the episode up for *New Scientist* (fig. 16.2).[9]

The Party Line may have had one unintended consequence that was very significant indeed. That October, phreaks suddenly found themselves in the limelight thanks to an exposé published in *Esquire*. "There is an underground telephone network in this country," the magazine revealed.[10] Journalist Ron Rosenbaum introduced readers to the major contours of the phenomenon, and even interviewed the supposed inventor of the blue box himself—who recalled that he had been "fooling around with phones for several years" before he came across the *BSTJ* at his university, "a well-known technical school." Rosenbaum hinted at connections to Yippie-style political activism, but did not pursue them, noting Cap'n Crunch's anxiety lest he reveal secrets to a "radical underground" that he claimed was on the verge of learning how to freeze the entire U.S. telephone network. The focus was instead on phreaks as explorers. Many of them had apparently come to phreaking from dabbling in radio experimentation. As one put it, "any idiot in the country with a cheap cassette recorder" could blaze a trail anywhere in the world. Phreaks apparently explored the network, discovered knowledge about its properties, and swapped their knowledge (and tapes) with each other. Discoveries, they held, must be shared between those recognized by the group as experts. The phreaks presented themselves as a kind of technical vanguard, liberated from bureaucratic protocols and free to follow where their expertise

FIGURE 16.2. "Are phone phreaks just telephone addicts?" *New Scientist* 60, no. 876 (December 13, 1973). © *New Scientist* magazine. Reprinted by permission.

led them. They seemed to see their role as akin to that of pop-culture heroes. They would spring up wherever there was a problem, reveal it (and its solution) to the amazed gratitude of the plodding Lestrades of Ma Bell, and then disappear again into their secret identities. They abhorred the system for its conformity, inelegance, and complicity with the government, while at the same time admiring its scale and complexity and wanting to "perfect" it. The attraction lay in solving technical problems—in playing the game—and not a few could envisage acting as anti-phreak detectives, were they to be asked. There was more than a little self-consciousness about such protestations, of course, yet they were impressively consistent.

Now, *Esquire* revealed, the phreaks were headed in a new direction: into the world of computers. Affirming as usual that the mere possibility of making free calls had never interested him, Draper claimed that what *had* attracted him to phreaking was the possibility, dangled before him by the Californian phreaks, that it was a way to contact a computer. By the early seventies he was veering between flat denials that he ever practiced phreaking any more and professions that "if I do anything it's for the pure knowledge of the System." He elaborated: "I do it for one reason and one reason only. I'm learning about a system. The phone company is a System. A computer is a system, do you understand? If I do what I do, it is only to explore a system. Computers, systems, that's my bag. The phone company is nothing but a computer."

Mark Bernay, another pseudonymous phreak, similarly attested that he had "gone beyond" telephony and was now "playing with computers more than playing with phones." He had found himself a programming job, only to be fired for carrying out phreak-like explorations in the company's computer system as the Midnight Stalker. An informer had turned him in (he seemed more upset by the low-tech banality of this than by the fact of being caught). The possibility had briefly been raised that he might be rehired as an investigator of other intruders, but it had been swiftly vetoed, and, Bernay admitted, justifiably so. "My personal thing with computers is just like with phones," he ended by remarking. "The kick is in finding out how to beat the system, how to get at things I'm not supposed to know about, how to do things with the system that I'm not supposed to be able to do."

The crux of the *Esquire* report was that many phreaks were taking this same step. They had found to their delight that they could use the simple computers now appearing on the hobby market to extend their phreaking explorations into new zones. They could dial up other computers, out there in the corporate or even military sphere, and discover a further class of terrae incognitae connected to the Bell network. This extension of phreaking into digital systems was set to be "the wave of the future," Rosenbaum guessed. And the implications if he was right might well be considerable. The phreaks' philosophy of sharing, access, technical virtuosity, and a buccaneering disregard for rules might do to the computer—still at this point a symbol of high-modern bureaucratic rationality—what it had tried to do to telecommunications in the 1920s–1960s.

Rosenbaum concluded by trying to coin a name for this new level of exploring. He suggested *computer freaking*. The name made sense, because, as he put it, the activity "suits the phone-phreak sensibility perfectly." But it never caught on, for the simple reason that the practice already had a name. It was called hacking.

HACKING

When asked where phreaking had originated, many in the early 1970s suggested that it came from the Massachusetts Institute of Technology. The notion revealed the extent to which hacking and phreaking had already converged, for MIT was well known to be the *fons et origo* of hacking. Yet it also had a basis in fact. Small numbers of students arriving at MIT in the late 1950s and early 1960s had enjoyed phreaking, and they were the same students who originated digital hacking too. They found their intellectual home in the Tech Model Railroad Club (TMRC), which maintained a train set in one of the Institute's buildings. The layout included an extraordinarily elaborate electronic communication system, built from components donated by Western Electric, the manufacturing arm of AT&T. Model locomotives at MIT were therefore controlled by the same switching technologies that the phone phreaks exploited. It did not take these students long to discover that they could explore MIT's own phone network using TMRC techniques. By 1963 a TMRC acolyte named Stewart Nelson (who had experimented with phones and radio in Poughkeepsie before arriving at MIT) had made the obvious next step, using a PDP-1 computer to sing MF tones into the AT&T network. Soon the students had made their way into systems across the nation. Department of Defense contractors were a particular target.[11]

The subsequent trajectory of hacking from Cambridge to Palo Alto and beyond has been well known since Steven Levy's classic *Hackers*. Originally a term for a practical joke of the childish but technically neat kind long popular at places like MIT and Caltech, it now came to mean the virtuoso feats of computer cognoscenti—those who neglected every other aspect of life in order to tweak digital systems to create elegant solutions ("hacks") to tricky problems. At a time when computers were still largely the preserve of specialist technicians, these young virtuosi held a basic commitment to direct "hands-on" experience in order to produce their hacks. Emulating the communities of radio amateurs and phone experimenters, they insisted on the importance of freedom to engage directly with the technology itself. Accessing technologies and sharing the resulting knowledge was in their view essential for technical and even social progress. Moreover, when even the most basic tools—like an assembler—had to be concocted by the group itself, asserting proprietorial authorship made no sense. They upheld the (Wienerian) view that their work should resemble the unimpeded flow of information inside the system. The computer game, Spacewar, that emerged from this conviction has been called the first piece of open-source software.[12]

Hacking took on a different form in Palo Alto. It did so because the Bay Area had a history of its own in radio and telecommunications, which extended back to the AT&T patent conflicts and the culture of radio experimenters. In the 1920s–1930s, local companies there had fought the big East Coast combines. The best-known of them, the Federal Telegraph Corporation, employed amateur radio enthusiasts even before WWI; Lee De Forest developed vacuum tubes there that became central to the broadcasting industry. In the twenties FTC continued to defy the radio trust, recruiting radio amateurs to assist in circumventing patent restrictions while winking at local emulators of its own technology. A Palo Alto industry dedicated to advanced technologies developed alongside it that was antithetical to patent pools.[13] The cluster of research institutions that subsequently emerged in the area drew on this tradition. The three principal sites—Douglas Engelbart's Augmented Human Intellect Research Center, ex-MIT professor John McCarthy's Stanford Artificial Intelligence Laboratory, and, a little later, Xerox's Palo Alto Research Center—embraced an understanding of the computer as another key to a liberating democratization of thinking and acting. The commitment to openness therefore shifted from a technocratic maxim to a democratic one. It became a mode of emancipation at once practical, self-improving, and utopian.[14] Achieving a broad level of access for "the people" to networked computers, under an ideal of democratic research, was more important than the MIT ideal of deep access for a small cadre of technical adepts.

What emerged from that shift in emphasis was a new kind of computer. The "home computer," as it was christened, was as alien and unsettling a thing as the home pirate, and for similar reasons. As in Cambridge, however, a merger of phreaking and hacking was central to defining the new technology. It occurred at a range of extramural and sometimes transient social settings, including various homes, Kepler's bookstore (a place reminiscent of the bookshops and coffeehouses of Restoration London), and a Free University that offered courses on "How to End the IBM Monopoly."[15] In print, there was of course Stewart Brand's *Whole Earth Catalog*, a guide to "tools" useful for readers impatient with the conformities of American consumerism. Launched in 1969, the catalogue touched on an extraordinary range of topics, from cybernetics and communication theories to agriculture and medicine, with an eclectic individualism purportedly inspired by Buckminster Fuller. It grew with successive editions until by 1971 it was almost 450 pages long. Its influence was demonstrated by the People's Computer Company, a project overseen by Brand and Robert Albrecht (whom Ted Nelson hailed as the "caliph of counterculture computerdom"). The PCC was both a publication and an institution. As a publication, it was produced on the same printing equipment as the *Whole Earth Catalog*, using similar pagecraft to proselytize for a cognate message. It even reprinted *Catalog* material verbatim. As an institution, it developed from an older project, "Community Memory," that had deployed public terminals linked to a mainframe, the hope being that they would become both communications devices—pathways by which citizens could establish links with each other—and portals to information. Community Memory had been the project of one Lee Felsenstein, a computer enthusiast with an upbringing full of radio experiments. PCC offered a more concretely social site: a storefront center where people could come in to learn about and use computers, with regular gatherings and events.[16]

The PCC made it a proclaimed principle of its operation that software should be available free to the participant community, and that their further uses of it should also not be constrained. The group's programming language exemplified this conviction. The PCC created a "Tiny BASIC" for the most popular kit computer, the Altair 8800. The language was a "participatory project," announced in the PCC newsletter and published there in full as it developed. Readers sent in their own suggestions and modifications, which were incorporated to improve the code. Soon a photocopied Tiny BASIC newsletter was being circulated to a mailing list of four to five hundred readers. This grew into an authoritative magazine entitled (by its printer) *Dr. Dobb's Journal of Tiny BASIC Calisthenics and Orthodontia,* launched as a vehicle for "the design, development, and distribution of free and low-cost software for the home computer." Like the PCC itself, it was the manifestation in public of a community defined by its sharing of information and code.

Meanwhile, Brand had begun to find the demands of running the *Whole Earth Catalog* wearisome. He decided to end it, and to do so with a bang. He threw a "demise party" for 1,500 guests at the Exploratorium. The event became one of the most storied moments in countercultural and computer history alike. At the height of the party, Brand, cloaked in a black cassock, announced that $20,000 remained in the kitty and invited the attendees to come up with a way to spend the money. There followed hours of argument, by turns utopian, angry, and desultory. The exchanges were still going on inconclusively as dawn broke. The choice seemed to boil down to some kind of communications project—radio or print—or a donation to Native Americans. It was then that a bearded man stood up, introduced himself simply as a "human being," and told them they were all missing the point. His name was Fred Moore. An enthusiast for computers as educational tools, Moore was currently teaching classes at the PCC after a spell of aimlessness in the wake of a prison term for draft resistance. What really mattered was not the money, he now declared, but the sharing of skills and knowledge for the common good. The "union" of partygoers was far more significant than any cash they might distribute. Money actually got in the way—a point Moore drove home by setting fire to a fistful of dollar bills. It was an inspired intervention, although not necessarily in the sense that Moore wanted. The survivors of the party were so impressed that they decided to hand the cash over to him. He suddenly found himself in charge of an unwanted trove that amounted, all told, to some $30,000. Moore took it away and buried it in his back garden.[17]

From then on Moore and a few comrades would meet periodically to lend parcels of this money to worthy projects. Their meetings were long and tortuous—"a kind of verbal *Whole Earth Catalog,*" one participant said. Moore found the process excruciating. He took to circulating missives to his fellows imploring them to show "cooperation and trust." His pleas also posed the question of how best to define property in a new technology, such that the rules for their venture might be comprehended—a problem that was becoming more pressing in the PCC itself. As the operation began to divide into two camps—one more interested in advancing technology, the other dedicated to using computers to empower communities—Moore joined with an engineer named Gordon French in a bid to revive what they recalled of the original sensibility. Moore and French posted notices everywhere they could think of inviting like-minded enthusiasts to what they called an "amateur computer users group—Homebrew computer club ... you name it." It would be open to anyone who was both interested in building a computer "or some other digital black-magic box" and enthusiastic about sharing information, working together, or "whatever."

The first meeting of the new group, on March 5, was a success. In subsequent months turnout increased by leaps and bounds. Before long more than four hundred people were coming, and the group had to relocate to SLAC's auditorium.[18] Lee Felsenstein—the pioneer of Community Memory—became its unofficial compere. The Homebrew Computer Club, as it was soon called, fast became a principal center for Californian hacking.

For the committed, like Felsenstein, norms of information sharing and hands-on invention were more than just countercultural platitudes. They related rather specifically to the kinds of convictions voiced by Ivan Illich, the one-time Catholic priest whose Centro Intercultural de Documentación in Mexico served to facilitate conversations among skeptics of technological and corporate modernity. Running through Illich's work was a call for individuals to retain creative autonomy in the face of the cultural homogeneity that he believed corporate technologies tended to foster. He wanted to develop an "autonomous and creative" interaction, as he put it, both among people and between people and their surroundings. "Conviviality" of this kind implied living "a life of action," and one full of active creativity rather than receptive consumption. Books, media, and machines were all to be regarded as "tools," not as delivery devices. So society should seek to design and adopt "convivial" technologies. For Illich the telephone network was a prime example of a convivial technology, as long as the charges were low and access free. A still better example was the audiocassette. In Bolivia, Illich lamented, the government had established a television broadcaster at great cost, which reached some seven thousand sets spread among a population of 4 million. The same money could have been used instead to provide cassette recorders to eight hundred thousand citizens, along with blank cassettes and a huge library of recordings. Not only would far more people have benefited, but the resulting "network" would have been of a radically different, decentralized kind. Input by citizens, literate and illiterate alike, would have been normal. Its principle would have been creativity, not receptivity. That was what it was to be convivial—and in Illich's terms freedom required conviviality.[19] Illich likewise believed that conventional education was receptive and commoditized, and therefore illiberal. He proposed replacing schools by "webs"—computer-based "reticular structures for mutual access"—that would facilitate open-ended and creative interactions. They would resemble enthusiasts' clubs. Some might establish "skill exchanges" at which laypeople could gather to learn about technical tools, perhaps in storefronts. In a city like New York, convivial computing of this kind would permit a culture of reading to be created democratically, rather than on the basis of a "selection by some Chicago professors."

The problem was that modern industry did not produce convivial technologies. It preferred "a world of things that resist insight into their nature." Concealed inside closed boxes—or inscribed in silica—technology was becoming ever less convivial. The prime example was radio. Boxing radios had commoditized know-how, he thought, producing "a noninventive society." But in its early days radios had been open and convivial, Illich recalled, and a radio enthusiast (what the BBC had called a pirate listener) had often made every set in the neighborhood "scream in feedback." For Illich that howl was a sign of a kind of freedom that had then been widely distributed, had survived for a while in science ("the one forum which functioned like an anarchist's dream"), but was now almost extinguished there too. He wanted to return to the culture it had signaled. In short, Illich proposed that the "the principal source of injustice in our epoch" was not Vietnam, Soviet communism, or South American dictatorships, but "tools that by their very nature restrict to a very few the liberty to use them in an autonomous way." The possibility of establishing a convivial society rested on opening boxed machines to revive the spirit of those pirate listeners. Intellectual property of this kind must be superseded in order to build the "web-like structures" essential for a free society. Illich was not sanguine about the prospects of achieving this—he mused that only Mao's Communists had the clout to do it. But he nevertheless maintained that "while democracy in the United States can survive a victory by Giap, it cannot survive one by ITT."[20]

Illich defined a vision for some early digital pioneers, like Felsenstein. Yet, contrary to much hacker mythology, enthusiasts in the early days were never united in opposing intellectual property per se. Ted Nelson's *Computer Lib/Dream Machines* of 1974, the foremost example of counter-cultural computer literature, is revealing of the tensions involved — tensions that would end up shaping digital culture itself. A visionary manifesto for the power of engagement with computers, Nelson's book was in one sense a clear articulation of the principle of computer conviviality. It was also, as he put it, a "blatant" imitation of "the wonderful *Whole Earth Catalog.*" Yet at the same time it condemned phone phreaks and copyright radicals alike. "Why is it always the guys with the cushy and secure jobs who tell you tweedle de dee, ideas should be free," Nelson asked. He advocated applying copyright to programs, and advised readers always to append a copyright symbol to their own code. So strongly did Nelson feel on the subject that his Xanadu project — a prophetically grandiose plan for a kind of designed hypertext web — incorporated into its design a form of com-pulsory licensing. Had Xanadu succeeded, it would have built a particular kind of intellectual property system into the very infrastructure of what became the Internet. It would have solved the network piracy problem by making piracy technically impossible — even while mandating openness at the same time. There was a distinctly Victorian air to the idea. "You publish something, anyone can use it, you always get a royalty automati-cally," Nelson proclaimed: "Fair."[21]

THE DISINTEGRATION OF CONVIVIALITY

The enduring fame of the Homebrew Club derives from its having been the location where phreaking combined with hacking to create a new kind of computer. All participants were welcome to adopt copies of soft-ware or hardware designs, as Felsenstein said, on the condition that they brought back more. One passionate advocate named Dan Sokol would even give out handfuls of new chips at meetings. Software was swapped and shared on cassettes, with similar norms to those of home taping. Later, when the Club developed its own relatively formal library of tapes, it had to create artificial rules covering the proprieties of collection and circula-tion. "The library is really a software exchange," it advised, and members should not "steal" or copy software protected by copyright.[22] But at first there had been no such commitment. "It was the same as ham radio," Felsenstein revealingly remarked. And Steve Dompier, a Berkeley electrical engineer and close friend of Draper, made that link clear when he utilized the interference an Altair created to play rudimentary music through a radio receiver. When Felsenstein embarked on a project to design and build a computer to suit this environment, he used off-the-shelf parts so that users would not be dependent on particular corporations or sources.[23]

Felsenstein's project was soon overshadowed by another new device —one that, in bringing the convergence of phreaking and hacking to fruition, would also foster the disintegration of conviviality. A Hewlett-Packard engineer named Allen Baum brought along a former school friend and now fellow HP worker, Stephen Wozniak, to an early Homebrew meeting. Wozniak had been a computer and electronics buff since his schooldays, a booster for the ill-fated Cartrivision video system, and a radio ham to boot—an activity that he later described as "protecting the airwaves from radio pirates." In 1971, he had also collaborated with Steven Jobs on a rather different enterprise. *Esquire*'s article about phreaking had caught Wozniak's attention, and they had found in SLAC's library the *BSTJ* article containing the list of MF tones. They built their own devices to produce the tones, recorded them onto cassette tape, and set about exploring the phone network in the spirit of the phreaks. He and Jobs also sold a few black boxes in Berkeley's student dormitories; they were once robbed of one at gunpoint. Wozniak then resolved to track down the mysterious Cap'n Crunch who had described in *Esquire* the appeal of exploring the network in terms of its being a giant computer. Draper took the initiative and introduced himself first. By the time of the Homebrew Club he, like Wozniak and Jobs, had made the transition in earnest. He ostentatiously refused to engage in phreaking, but had become a regular at the PCC. Draper became a fixture at Homebrew too.[24]

For all that he repudiated phreaking, Draper did help explore the network, not in aid of speech, now, but of data. For example, he helped out an outfit called Call Computer that provided a system allowing people with terminals at home to log into a distant mainframe and communicate with each other. He arranged for the Homebrew Club to have its account on this system. He would also drop more daring hints from time to time about connecting to Arpanet, which had recently been established to provide robust networked communications for the Defense Department. Draper claimed that he could navigate through the telephone system into Arpanet, and thence to MIT's computers, where he could run routines that were too demanding for local machines. Introduced by Wozniak to Sokol, Draper also helped him connect his own computer to the network without contracting enormous phone bills—a moment when the principle of access won out over Draper's reluctance to get involved in something that was sure to get an unsympathetic reception if it were detected. Sokol showed his gratitude by giving Wozniak a boxful of chips and gear suitable to be connected to a Motorola 6800 processor. He took the trove, twinned it with a new MOS 6502 rather than the Motorola chip, and began to build a computer. He would bring the machine to Homebrew to show his progress. He wrote his own version of BASIC for it, which he likewise distributed free at the club; some of its routines were published in *Dr. Dobbs*. As the computer gradually took shape, it became clear that Wozniak's design would be much more powerful than the Altair, and Jobs began to push for selling it commercially. Working frantically, the two of them arrived at a functioning version and put it on the market. They advertised the openness of the design as a distinctive "philosophy," announcing that—unlike Altair—they would continue to "provide software for our machines free or at minimal cost." It was called, of course, the Apple.

Wozniak immediately went to work on a new version, which became the Apple II. Another outcome of extensive Homebrew conversations, the design was immediately recognized as remarkable, and today's cognoscenti still hail it as an archetype of elegant ingenuity. Much of its TV terminal ware originated in a design Wozniak had come up with a year earlier to help Draper hack into Arpanet, however. And some of the video circuitry ultimately derived from his own phreaking box. Not only was the Apple II a cultural emanation of the conjunction of hacking and phreaking, therefore; the machine itself that launched the home computer revolution owed a debt to phreak technologies. Moreover, Draper now became one of Apple's first employees. He was given the task of designing a telephone interface for the hot-selling computer. When he produced something that looked just like a phreak's blue box, however, the young company forthwith scrapped it and dismissed him. Draper went home and continued to experiment, using his own Apple to explore the phone network in search of distant computers. Automating the search, in a few days he logged twenty thousand calls. The telephone company's tracking device sounded the alarm, and the police came to pick him up. Draper thus became the first network hacker ever to be arrested.

As Draper's fate implies, the norms of openness, access, and engagement were coming under intense pressure as microcomputing boomed.

More participants at Homebrew now saw its conventions not as moral principles in their own right, but as means to an end. They treated the club as a proving ground for what would ultimately be commercial ventures, aimed at a mass audience that was envisaged as meekly receptive. The Apple II design was not hostile to interventions by users—Wozniak had been careful to include expansion slots—but neither did it invite them, let alone require them in the way that earlier machines had. It came as a complete system, with BASIC in ROM. Radically opposed ways of proceeding now began to resolve themselves. One was friendlier to nonexperts, and ultimately proprietorial. Apple took this route, and Commodore would take it further with its PET. The other maintained the principled commitment to conviviality—to openness and tweaking. Felsenstein's machine, named the Sol, exemplified this. Its design, a refinement of Felsenstein's earlier public terminals, embodied the convictions of popular radio experiment and the *Whole Earth Catalog*. The success of Apple (and soon of Microsoft) made the second path all the more problematic. A parting of the two ways was imminent. Moore departed in 1975 as entrepreneurial pressures grew, and the Sol became first a niche machine and then an outright failure.[25]

The existence of an alternative had become clear only three months after Homebrew began meeting regularly. The manufacturer of the Altair, MITS, held a publicity show for the machine in Palo Alto. Hobbyists had begun to grumble at the slow pace of improvements to the Altair design, and Homebrew aficionados were increasingly inclined to see MITS as monopolistic and secretive. Some had already paid for a BASIC that had not shipped, and others complained that MITS was tying the program to sales of memory boards that they said did not work, allegedly in a bid to crush Felsenstein's independent effort. Being asked to pay money for bad technology was a cardinal offense, especially when it involved a notoriously monopolistic tying strategy—and all the more when enthusiasts could get a workable BASIC from the PCC for $5. When the MITS crew arrived at a Palo Alto hotel in June 1975, then, several Homebrewers were surprised to find there what seemed to be a working version of BASIC. One enterprising individual—it has never been clear who—noticed a paper-tape copy of the program and "borrowed" it. It found its way into the hands of Sokol, perhaps the staunchest advocate of openness of all, especially when, as he believed was the case here, software had originated in public research. Sokol made more than seventy copies overnight and brought them to the next Homebrew meeting. A feeding frenzy ensued. The code immediately became part of the Homebrew moral economy, in which borrowing one copy was fine as long as one returned two. The problem was that unlike most code that circulated in this way, the BASIC was proprietary. It was the first product from a small company based in Albuquerque, named Micro-Soft.

The BASIC had been a rush job. When William Gates and Paul Allen had brought their raw creation to MITS—by this point desperately in need of a BASIC—they had not even had a chance to make sure it worked. But it had, well enough for MITS to sign up for it and offer a royalty. Gates, twenty, had then more or less dropped out of Harvard to pursue the opportunity. But royalty income had proved far lower than he had anticipated. In fact, MITS seemed to be selling only one copy of Micro-Soft's BASIC for every ten Altairs. It was therefore in a context of crisis that Gates got word that the language had been distributed throughout the very community that ought to have furnished his market. When the editor of a newly formed *Altair Users' Newsletter* asked for his reaction, Gates decided to respond aggressively. He published an open letter to hobbyists that assailed not just the particular perpetrators of the "theft" (as he called it), but, in sweeping terms, the culture that endorsed such actions. Its premise was that a vast potential "market" for microcomputing was being stymied by a lack of good, reliable software, along with the documentation and education that would enable users to make the most of it, and that only a proprietary regime could justify the substantial investments needed to produce those things. Gates claimed that his own BASIC had taken a year and $40,000 of computer time to create, with results the quality of which correspondence from users amply confirmed. But those users had not played their part by actually buying the program. "Most of you steal your software," Gates bluntly accused. What they saw as openness and collaboration was now "theft" pure and simple. Far from being justified by MITS's monopolistic behavior, it was itself a moral offense. It was simply not "fair." Rerecorders of programs gave all hobbyists a bad name, Gates insisted; they should be "kicked out of any club meeting they show up at." The possibility that conviviality might be a principled position was silently trumped by an assertion of this distinct moral community. That a unified authorial body (be it a single writer or a company) and a centralized, industrial system of production were essential to produce "quality" software was implicit and necessary to Gates's case. It was this author that the act of sharing was unfair to, and this system that must be created to allow home computing to thrive.[26]

Gates's letter inaugurated a mini-campaign on Micro-Soft's part, with a successor declaration issued a few months later, and a speech that he gave in March. The effort was never likely to achieve much by itself, however. As Dompier remarked, "complaining about piracy didn't stop anything," because sharing software was "like taping music off the air."[27] Gates himself tacitly conceded as much: he made sure to insulate his company from practices of this kind by signing no more royalty deals. But the publicity served its greater purpose. It made explicit the tensions already present in hobbyists' conventions, and forced recognition of the economic implications of the hobbyists' moral economy. The *Homebrew Computer Club Newsletter* voiced qualified approval of his position, for example, even though it prefaced its own printing of the letter by reminding readers that with the PCC's version "you can homebrew your own BASIC." Yet the more committed still gave Gates a hostile reception. Many were convinced that the BASIC they were sharing was in truth a public good anyway, having been developed on publicly funded machines. It was not just that Gates had called them thieves, therefore, but that an expropriator of common property had called *theirs* a morality of theft. Gates's statement would go down in computer lore as the canonical declaration of a rift over intellectual property and access that would divide the digital world from then on.

FEAR AND LOATHING ON THE NET

Out of the early years of home computing emerged rival approaches to creative property, including those that decreed its outright rejection. Some were aboveboard and would prove themselves as viable modes of creativity. Others were underground, but they too have proved lasting. What made this possible was not the advent of the personal computer, but the later arrival of affordable and reliable digital networking.[28] By the mid-1980s, home computer enthusiasts could buy not only an IBM PC, Apple, or other micro, but also a telephone modem to go with it, and they could connect to the first bulletin boards and networks. Rates of data flow were tortoise-like by today's standards, but they were sufficient for text-only work. Information could be exchanged, and, it was increasingly claimed, communities built. By the mid-1990s, awareness of a single

Internet—descended from the Arpanet that had so fascinated Draper—was becoming widespread. The first browsers were arriving to engage with a graphical World Wide Web. The different approaches to property became more entrenched and the opposition between them, if anything, more emphatic. In the process, a link between credit and property that had been forged in the eighteenth century was finally broken.

Indeed, the situation confronting early Net users was reminiscent of that facing authors and booksellers in the eighteenth century itself. Claims about the sacredness of authorship and a new age of reason had been loud and legion then too. Pirates had been attacked for offenses that ranged beyond literal theft and impugned credit, fidelity, and authenticity. Practices comparable to what are now termed identity theft or phishing (the imitation of institutions) were rampant. Printed communication was hailed as emancipatory, rational, and enlightened in principle, but in practice seemed riddled with problems. Any community claiming to be consti-tuted by print—such as the public sphere—had to tackle such problems if it was itself to be credible. To solve them required not just laws and philosophies, moreover, but street-level nous. As Kant implied, piracy threatened the basic possibility of public reason by perpetrating a kind of ventriloquism. Similarly broad and deep claims were made about the new digital realm of the 1990s. The existence and nature of online col-lectivities became topics of hot debate. The reality, extent, and epistemic implications of piratical practices were held up as not only challenges to intellectual property—though those challenges were widely declared to be fundamental—but as threats to the possibility of a rational online public. The need to articulate the moral economy of digital networks became acute.

The best known of the early networked communities was the Whole Earth 'Lectronic Link, or WELL, a Sausalito group cofounded by Stewart Brand. Before long other online collectives—Usenet, MUDs, MOOs, and the like—were multiplying. The earliest BBS (bulletin board system) was older, having been created by two Chicagoans in the late 1970s as a substitute for swapping cassettes. Some of these groups, like the WELL, were fairly small and localized; others were larger and adopted fictional locations, leading at length to ventures like *Second Life*.[29] It did not take users long to testify that they felt themselves approaching the McLuhanite dream of having the psyche merge into a global electronic net. More in-fluential language for articulating online communities, however, evoked concepts of community and frontier. Their principal exponent, Howard Rheingold, was a WELL veteran who came up with the expression "virtual community" in 1987 in a successor volume to the *Whole Earth Catalog.* Rheingold's representation of an emergent frontier domain—at once a village full of diverse skills, bound together by an "informal, unwritten social contract," and an unsettled landscape of new stakes and homesteads—became probably the most widely adopted model for these pseudo-societies. A prime principle was that members should act like digital versions of barn-raising Amish, sharing information in order to help each other build their online homesteads. But this principle, Rheingold warned, would be sorely pressed by corporations as they took up the rhetoric of online communities to sell themselves. Corporate sites tried to persuade customers that they were engaging in a "community" when all they were really doing was receiving company messages. A true community demanded that its members *work* to cling to the ideal of creativity rather than receptivity—an eminently Miltonic stance, one might say. A "battle for the shape of the Net" was apparently about to ensue.

In that looming struggle another enemy also threatened. If the WELL was one adaptation of the convivial ideals of the seventies, a hacker underground represented another, less respectable adaptation. Its roots lay more with the radical phreaks of Hoffman's ilk—as Bruce Sterling put it, *Steal This Book* had become the "spiritual ancestor of a computer virus."[30] Although much hyped by the press, the black-hat hacker crowd was real and numerous. A BBS to champion it was launched as early as 1980; it went by the name 8BBS and was dedicated at first to phone phreaking. By the mid-1980s, such boards had proliferated, often taking on explicit piratical identities: Pirate-80, Pirate's Harbor, and Pirates of Puget Sound were three among dozens, perhaps hundreds, of BBSs devoted to this scene. They issued pirated code and tips about phone phreaking cheek by jowl. The curious could trawl through these sites for phreak codes, which then became tokens of exchange warranting entry into various groups, much as arcane alchemical recipes had acted as passports to philosophical clubs in the mid-seventeenth century. Contacts could be made through these actual pirate and phreak groups via the BBSs. Some of the sites even acquired public notoriety—none more so than the Legion of Doom, which was named after the old gang led by Superman's foe, Lex Luthor. Originally a gathering of phone phreaks, like many of the online cracker groups, the Legion of Doom moved from phreaking into hacking. Like most of them, it affected the techno-elitist libertarianism and the language of exploration that had been such a feature of phreaking. It even affected the same lexical tics, in particular the ubiquitous *ph*. Above all, Legion of Doom hackers and like-minded digerati appropriated wholesale the phreaks' presumptuous claim—itself descended from interwar radio culture—that as practitioners of the scientific method they should be supported, not restrained. A much-reissued posting of 1986 variously titled "Conscience of a Hacker" or "The Hacker's Manifesto" declared all this explicitly. It was the work of a Legion of Doom hacker named The Mentor. Hackers were firstly explorers of a telephone system, it claimed—a system that ought to be cheap for all, but had been hijacked by "profiteering gluttons." Hence hackers were resistance fighters. But at the same time they were scientists. The Mentor laid claim to the persona of the lone researcher persecuted by an uncomprehending and conformist society. "We explore," he insisted: "We seek after knowledge ... and you call us criminals."[31] And he had a point. When the police moved against the Legion, they found that its members had generally not stolen anything. Even the more serious pirates to whom the Legion did lead them turned out to have circulated copies of commercial software for free.

As more and more phreaks found each other online, so a digital counterpublic came to constitute itself. Hackers developed a number of flamboyantly libertarian periodicals aimed at the knowing. The best known were *Phrack* (a conjunction of *phreak* and *hack*, launched in 1985) and *2600* (named for the fundamental phreaking tone, and proud to claim a pirate identity, as shown in fig. 16.3). The latter was edited by a then-mysterious individual calling himself Emmanuel Goldstein, after the Trotsky figure invoked in the hate rallies of Orwell's *Nineteen Eighty-Four*. His real name was Eric Corley, and he had long been involved in amateur radio. There was even a *Legion of Doom Technical Journal*, parodying the old *Bell System Technical Journal* that had opened the door to the whole phreaking phenomenon. These journals comprised "philes"—independent submissions —more than conventional articles. Today, a generation later, they make fascinating reading. Through the mid-1980s they tracked the convergence of phreaking, coding, and piracy into a single enterprise, captured popularly—but incorrectly, many insisted—by the term "hacking."[32]

By the end of the 1980s the received meaning of the term *hacker* had therefore shifted. It now referred to what digerati distinguished as a *cracker* or "black-hat" hacker—someone who stealthily intruded into online

FIGURE 16.3. Piracy, phreaking, and hacking. *2600* 4, no. 6 (June 1987), cover. Reprinted by permission of *2600*.

computer systems for mischievous ends. When hacking in this demi-monde sense became a focus of serious police and public attention, it was by virtue of its identification with phreaking. In 1989 a probation office in Florida found its calls being rerouted to a phone-sex line in New York. The telephone company investigated, and found that hackers had been not just phreaking its lines, but, in doing so, reprogramming its digital systems. At much the same time, Clifford Stoll's *The Cuckoo's Egg* told the story of a KGB-inspired phreaking/hacking espionage ring. And the first large-scale online virus (technically, a worm) affected some six thousand networked computers. As they proliferated across the media, such episodes galvanized fears about the vulnerability of online information generally. More specifically, they stoked concerns about the amoral character of technically expert groups able to manipulate such systems.[33] Rumors began to fly that the Legion of Doom intended to crash the entire telephone system—that old threat hinted at by Draper long before. When the long-distance network did crash on the following Martin Luther King Day, a hacker attack was immediately suspected, although in fact it turned out to be a fault in the system. New laws and police actions multiplied against a projected threat by criminal or even seditious hackerdom.

This caused considerable soul searching among proponents of online sociability. In the late 1980s and early 1990s repeated debates took place about the implications for digital communities, and about the responsibilities that digital expertise carried with it. They focused on what became the vexed question of the day: whether there was a hacker "ethic." A direct adoption from Merton's portrait of science, the contention that there was such an ethic took its rise from Levy's *Hackers,* which was overtly premised on the idea. But the point of the exchanges that now ensued was to determine whether the norms of such an ethic—assuming it existed—were consequential. Scientists, on a Mertonian account, were not particularly virtuous as individuals, but their work was shaped by moral norms that were upheld and enforced by the scientific community at large. Did something like this hold for hacking? If so, could it be exploited to sustain digital community?

The best-known exchange on these lines was a "conference" held in the WELL in 1989 under the aegis of *Harper's Magazine.*[34] Its immediate trigger was the panic over the first widely distributed worm but the exchange had time to develop broader themes, with participants arguing, changing their minds, and at length diverging irreconcilably. They included a number of veterans, Lee Felsenstein among them. Richard Stallman took part from MIT. Emmanuel Goldstein and two crackers going by the monikers Acid Phreak and Phiber Optik also contributed. The initial subject was the hacker ethic itself, which they variously construed, credited, and disdained. Most accepted that hacking was characterized by contempt for obstacles to technical progress. That was what lay behind its commitment to the free exchange of information, and hence its repudiation of intellectual property. Hackers appeared antiauthoritarian because they claimed the right and ability to "undam the pipes" and allow information to flow freely—a very Wienerian image. "Everything that was once said about 'phone phreaks' can be said about them too," observed one participant. Hacking was reliant on the home, added another, because without privacy it could not exist—a contention suggestive in turn of Kantian ideals of Enlightenment. Nonsense, declared Goldstein: "we're just individuals out exploring." In the end, taking such speculations to an extreme, a few speakers elevated hacking into a supercultural category. It was simply inventive creativity in general, particularly that which involved redeploying existing machines to new uses. Its inventor had been the prehistoric cave dweller who first "hacked" fire. On this basis one participant suggested that the commitment to shared knowledge might represent a primordial human desire for connection. "That's hacking to me," concluded Felsenstein, transfiguring the practice in a different way: "to transcend custom and to engage in creativity for its own sake."

But if hackers were creators, what limits and responsibilities should they acknowledge? This was a major question, with real and substantial political implications. "There's nothing wrong with breaking security," Stallman proposed, "if you're accomplishing something useful." And perhaps crackers *were* doing useful service. The real problem, some suggested, was that institutions and corporations were quietly collecting data on citizens without their awareness or consent, and then treating the data as their own property. In that context, hacking into databases was a moral obligation—it was the only way to reveal a greater problem. Media hysteria notwithstanding, after all, crackers rarely went after private households. "Hackers have become scapegoats," Goldstein charged. "We discover the gaping holes in the system and then get blamed for the flaws." The real expropriation took place long before any hacking was done, and the only way to reveal it was to break rules. "I know I'm doing the right thing," he declared, "on behalf of others who don't have my abilities." In other words, an Internet invasion might be a "manifesto" of public empowerment.

This provoked the disintegration of the colloquy. Clifford Stoll, the exposer of the espionage ring, asked drily whether there had once been a "vandal's ethic." His point was that electronic neighborhoods were "built on trust," as real ones were. Hackers eroded that foundation. No community could survive their "spreading viruses, pirating software, and destroying people's work." A contributor calling himself Homeboy went further still. "Are crackers really working for the free flow of information," he asked, or were they in effect "unpaid tools of the establishment?" At this point, eight days into the conference, John Barlow (author of the *Declaration of the Independence of Cyberspace*) suddenly denied point-blank that a system's flaws could justify hacking into it. A rapid escalation of insults ensued, until Phiber Optik interrupted the flow by posting Barlow's own credit history online. "If you didn't know that they kept such files," he demanded, "who would have found out if it wasn't for a hacker?" Professedly intended to show the civic necessity of piratical hacking, the gesture dramatically refuted itself by bringing the conversation to a grinding halt.

Felsenstein summed up the outcome in a spirit of exasperation. "If you hack, what you do is inherently political," he admonished—but hacking alone, pursued without real political interventions, was futile. The most notable attempt to provide a normative account of digital piracy as a form of scientific citizenship concluded on this dispiritingly realistic note. Without real-world social coordination, a hacker was merely a wannabe "techno-bandit."[35]

FUDDING

The transformation of hackers from anarchic geniuses into criminals and terrorists (language that was leveled even in the WELL) coincided with the rise to dominance of proprietorial approaches in a networked digital economy aspiring to global reach. Issues of trust, access, and security were of central importance to both. As in the eighteenth century, those who could create and sustain trust in a piratical environment stood to win. There were opportunities in this. Hackers could claim to be public agents. The corporate world, meanwhile, could make money by touting "trusted systems" and deploying claims about security. Another part of that world could develop businesses of prevention, detection, and policing. And at the same time, alternatives to proprietorial software proliferated, staking their own moral and economic claims. Richard Stallman at MIT became their best-known and most forthright advocate. Stallman held that the creation and circulation of "free" software—that is, code independent of proprietary restrictions—was a matter of the constitution of communities. He complained that in the digital realm exclusive properties made "pirates" out of what otherwise would be merely good, helpful neighbors. That is, the question of property was, as always, a matter of political philosophy, with the "pirate" label indicating that this was the modern counterpart to debates about perpetual rights and freedom of speech in the Enlightenment. Stallman's was quite a radical position, however, and commercial and would-be commercial allies grew leery of it. In 1998 they came up with the alternative designation "open source." Open-source software was not quite the same thing as free software, because open-source denizens could countenance the integration of code into subsequent products distributed on a proprietary model.[36] But the two did share the ideal of the programmer as citizen and craftsperson, and they would often be paired together under the acronym FOSS (for free and open-source software).

Proprietary software concerns struggled to come up with a strategy to deal with open-source work. Some, IBM being the most prominent, reconciled with open source. Microsoft did not, and as it rose to dominance it struggled to appreciate the nature of the challenge. A remarkable revelation of its strategic perceptions came in the fall of 1998, by which time open source had proved itself a lasting enterprise. That October, an internal memorandum was leaked to the open-source proponent Eric Raymond. It had been written by a Microsoft official named Vinod Valloppillil, and bore the title *Open Source Software: A (New?) Development Methodology?* A second document appeared shortly after, with more following in later months.[37] Together, these "Halloween documents," as they became known, demonstrated that (contrary to Microsoft's public stance at the time) the corporation saw open-source conventions as posing a serious challenge. More significant, however, was what they revealed about Microsoft's efforts to articulate the nature of that challenge and respond to it.

Open source, the initial memorandum conceded, had advantages "not replicable with our current licensing model." It therefore presented "a long term developer mindshare threat." Contrary to what was then Microsoft's public stance, large projects drawing upon communities of expertise extending across continents had already demonstrated the viability of FOSS, and robust legal mechanisms such as the GNU Public License were sufficient to sustain them. "Very dramatic evidence" existed already indicating that the quality of open-source software equaled or exceeded that of proprietary. Not least, the Internet operated largely atop open-source code. In short, open source had the all-important asset: "credibility." Valloppillil reasoned, therefore, that Microsoft was in the difficult position of having to "target" not a specific competitor, but a "process," and one that had earned the trust it enjoyed. He considered buying a solution: Microsoft could simply monitor open-source discussion groups and hire all the outstanding coders (AT&T's old prewar strategy in telecommunications). But that was less a satisfactory response than a backhanded compliment to the virtues of FOSS. His real proposal was more radical.

Valloppillil mooted a strategy of "de-commoditizing" the standards by which commonly used programs interacted with each other. These standards (good examples would be the TCP/IP protocol used in Internet communications, or the various compression algorithms used for audio and video files) were—and remain—basic infrastructure for the digital world. The common perception that digital culture is *intrinsically* universal rests on their being *in practice* shared across manufacturers and nations. The Halloween strategy against FOSS would be for Microsoft to generate its own protocols that could be sold as better than any current standard, and to encourage programmers to write to them. This would inevitably render the standard nugatory, and thus make it very difficult for authors to produce code that would run predictably across different systems. Open source's vital asset of credibility would attenuate quickly in that situation. It was a plausible proposal, and in fact Microsoft adopted a similar strategy to combat the potential of Java to supplant desktop with web computing. When the Halloween documents were revealed, open-source advocates assailed the idea as devious, Machiavellian, and technologically corrosive. The outcry was so fierce that Microsoft found itself forced to disown it.[38]

A more interesting contention about credibility, however, went relatively unnoticed amid this furor. The Halloween memo rested on a distinction between experienced programmers and users. A few experts might feel more secure with access to source code, it conceded. But the laity might well prefer what it called "the trust model + organizational credibility"—and rationally so. That is, the vast mass of lay users would probably vest their trust in not the code itself (which was inaccessible to them whether "open" or not) but the institution that authored and vouched for it. If Microsoft documented that an API (an interchange protocol between programs) acted in a certain way, then few would doubt that it did. Even an expert would reasonably credit a corporate author rather than exert an impractical prerogative to check every subroutine. Writ large, trust in the corporation might well supplant a supposed ability to vet code for oneself. Individual expertise could almost never stand against collective in practice. The point depended, of course, on open source being seen as a mass of individuals rather than an institution in its own right—but that played precisely to its advocates' own libertarian self-image. In effect, the argument confronted the open-source community's championing of democratic access with the contention that trust, as much as individual knowledge, was the more fundamental basis of social and epistemic order, even in technical communities.[39] Raymond suspected that the contention was flawed—only managers relied on "trust," he maintained, while real developers preferred access. But he conceded that this was a strategy by which Microsoft might actually win.

Significantly, however, although Valloppillil's proposal made the competition over credibility into one recognizable in terms of prior computer-industry experience, it acknowledged that Microsoft could *not* win simply by dusting off and reusing tactics familiar from previous generations. The most traditionally insidious strategy in the industry was that known as *fudding.* The acronym FUD ("fear, uncertainty, and doubt") had originally been coined in the sixties a propos of a practice of the old monolith, IBM. It referred to the craft of insinuating suspicions about the longevity, security, and reliability of an opponent's software in order to deter the laity from buying it. The idea was that middle managers would prefer not to take risks in software purchasing, so that if they perceived uncertainties then they would opt for the security of a known program rather than buying a perhaps better alternative. The power of the strategy rested on a link between authorship and credibility that had been forged over centuries of piracy debates. Moreover, it ought to be more effective than ever now, as piracy and cracking encouraged a belief that the Net was a risky, uncertain place. And indeed, fudding was widely recognized to be a pervasive tactic in the Internet's early years. It represented the Net as a viper's nest.

But it turned out that open source was better at resisting snakebites. What the Halloween documents really showed, in the end, was that open source had broken the lockstep between credibility and authorship. Distributed creativity defied an identification that had prevailed since piracy conflicts had forged it in the early Enlightenment. In fact, open-source programs were not only less vulnerable to viruses than Microsoft's, but faster to react to them. If delocalized authorship meant resilience and adaptability, as it now seemed to do, then the very fear that fudding conjured up might work *against* proprietary authors, even those as huge as Microsoft. Strong intellectual property in this realm created uncertainty of its own. Fudding was therefore suddenly futile at best. By the same token, the moment when open source proved itself was the moment when its biggest opponent recognized that the basis of credibility had shifted in this fundamental way. That was why the Halloween document had to consider resorting to an apocalyptic strategy of undermining the very infrastructure of digital networks. Only by challenging technical standards could authorship and credit be secured together again.

Aware of the threat, Raymond urged that open-source proponents respond by developing "trust" protocols of their own. They could not rely on openness itself. Instead, they would have to develop a culture of named authors of credit, or "publishers of good repute" like O'Reilly or Addison-Wesley in the world of print (implicitly, that of scientific print). This culture, he surmised, might "substitute for 'trust' in an API-defining organization." The resemblance of this strategy to criteria of trust that were proposed in earlier, predigital eras was remarkable. A digital world might not be so revolutionary after all: the battlefront would once again be between candidates for credibility in a piratical field.

In sum, the origins of the digital culture we now inhabit—the culture in which piracy is the defining transgression—were shaped by questions of creativity and community, and those questions were cast at the critical moment in terms of an ethos. That this was so was an outcome of the mid-century debates about telecommunications, patent monopolies, and the nature of science. Thanks to the practices from which those debates arose, the domestication of creativity was already valorized and set against a conformist, corporate world of "media" long before digital hacking arose. More specifically, the practices out of which hacking did emerge were those of radio, telephone, and home piracy. Many among the early digerati were committed to libertarian ideals they found originally in pirate or ham radio. Phreaking formed a practical bridge between telephone exploration, on the one hand, and digital exploration, on the other. And the first home computer enthusiasts adopted both the cassette technology and the convivial customs of the home tapers. The effects were manifold, but issues of credit—of trust, authorship, and authenticity—were central to them. For example, expertise no longer went with professional identity. It was once again radically unstable, and peer opinions, abstracted from place and affiliation, were said to be the only guide to its true loca-tion. Where to find authoritative opinions, however, and how to tell them from the spurious, were of course pressing problems.

The corporate world tried to exploit these questions in various ways, of which fudding was one. Fud played on the uncertainties of (business) users to encourage a safety-first reversion to the association between authorship and credibility. It worked for a while, but seemed likely to fail against the distributed form of authorship that had arisen out of those mid-century pirate principles and established itself over the Net. Open source enjoyed "long-term credibility" because publics understood it to carry less likelihood of instability, lower vulnerability to attacks, and less chance of being cast adrift in the future. The ground had shifted—not just because of technological change, but because of deep-rooted cultural con-victions that affected how new technological possibilities were exploited.

One suggested response to this rather radical change was to move to a strategy based on another central element in modern science and tech-nology: standards. The idea was to treat standards not as things to which to conform, but as things to exceed. Had it been pursued, this would have undermined the uniformity of digital networks. That is, it would have endangered the very property that is often taken to be the intrinsic, defining virtue of the Internet, permitting its global reach. It would have done so in order to reassert a tie between authorship and credibility. That tie seemed by now to be the axiom of good order in creativity and com-merce. How to reconcile it with the powers of the Internet remains a central question of our time.

17

Past, Present, and Future

Daniel Defoe created the first classification of intellectual piracy almost exactly three centuries ago. He sorted it into a handful of simple categories like abridgment, epitomizing, and reprinting in smaller fonts.[1] Today any corresponding taxonomy would extend to a vast array of sins—phishing, identity theft, biopiracy, seed piracy, and so on. It would surely baffle even someone as worldly as Defoe. Because more things fall under the aegis of intellectual property today than ever before—including recordings, algorithms, digital creations, genes, and even living organisms—practices that until relatively recently would not have seemed even potentially piratical may now be deemed actually so. Meanwhile, as the information economy has grown, so it seems that piracy has metastasized beyond anyone's ability to understand and master it. Some of its species are industries in their own right. In political and economic rhetoric the accusation of piracy has become the indictment of the age, and a ubiquitous element in the framing of national and international trade politics.[2]

The story of piracy has two major implications in this context. The first derives from the point that intellectual property exists only insofar as it is recognized, defended, and acted upon. That is, it is a practical matter. It takes shape not only through the stipulation of laws and treaties, but also through the actions societies take to put those laws and treaties into effect in homes, offices, factories, and colleges. Challenges demand responses, and the roles of intellectual property in everyday life reflect the history of their interaction. But in recent years the character of that interaction has changed. As piracy has grown and diversified, so a counterindustry has emerged, dedicated to combating it. The coherence and scope of this industry are relatively new and remarkable. In previous centuries, particular groups or industries mounted efforts against piracy; but they did not generally regard them as fronts in one common cause. Now they generally do. The same tools, tactics, and strategies can be seen deployed across what would earlier have been discrete conflicts. So the first implication is that we need to appreciate the historical significance of this industry of antipiracy policing and apprehend its consequences, at every social level. The second implication follows from that. Measures adopted against piracy can sometimes impinge on other, equally valued, aspects of society. Indeed, it is possible that they *must* do so, given the nature of the task. When that happens, however, they can trigger deeply felt reactions. The result is a crisis, with the potential to create a moment of genuine transformation. We have seen that such moments have arisen before. But the change is liable to be all the greater when the scope of antipiracy action has been so enlarged. We may therefore be about to experience a profound shift in the relation between creativity and commerce. It will be the most radical revolution in intellectual property since the mid-eighteenth century. It may even represent the end of intellectual property itself.

THE INTELLECTUAL PROPERTY DEFENSE INDUSTRY

A story has been unfolding quietly between the lines of this book. It is the story of how an industry emerged to confront so-called piracy and uphold what we know as intellectual property. In recent decades this industry has enjoyed rapid growth and consolidation. It has become a coherent, global, high-technology enterprise, standing alongside the better-known sectors of digital media and biotechnology. We may think of it as the intellectual property defense industry.

The intellectual property defense industry began to take its current form in the 1970s. It emerged from what were originally dispersed ventures in particular trades and in-house operations in discrete businesses. As it consolidated, it drew on people, devices, and practices that often originated in police or military circles — ex-officers, surveillance techniques, encryption—to form a distinct enterprise with branches in digital, pharmaceutical, agricultural, and other domains. By the mid-1980s it was multinational. Trade associations had by then established divisions for antipirate policing in Asia, Africa, Europe, and the Americas. The MPAA, for example, maintained what it called "Film Security Offices" not only in Los Angeles, New York, and London, but also in Paris, Hong Kong, and South Africa.[3] Coordinating such offices was a Joint Anti-Piracy Intelligence Group (JAPIG), founded in 1984 as an intellectual property counterpart to Interpol. JAPIG was capable of tracking cargo vessels across the oceans and tapping local customs agents to intercept them when they made landfall. In the 1990s, such bodies became players alongside governments, the United Nations, and Interpol in overseeing globalization. The World Health Organization's International Medical Products Anti-Counterfeiting Taskforce, launched in Rome in 2006, was a late but extremely important addition to their ranks. By this point a huge and multifaceted enterprise, antipiracy policing combines the interests and reach of states, corporations, multinationals, and world bodies.[4] Taken in the round, it effectively shapes intellectual property in countless mundane settings. One could certainly track, and perhaps account for, the increasing consistency of intellectual property in the age of globalization by following this expansion of its practical enforcement across new regions and realms.

Efforts to uphold intellectual property against piracy take place in all areas of today's economy, but they are most prominent in three: media, pharmaceuticals, and agriculture. (Biotechnology is included in the last two.) In each domain, the enterprise of enforcement seeks to discipline what it sees as a world comprising producers and consumers of intellectual property both by intervening preemptively to forestall piracies and by undertaking operations to interdict or respond to those that do occur. But it also coordinates broader efforts to produce changes to national and international laws. At a global level, it surveils the digital world and probes virtual homesteads; at a local, it impinges on physical households, workplaces, and farms. In all, it is an exemplary postindustrial enterprise. Its leading constituents are, fittingly, hybrids, mixing state and private interests and physical and virtual strengths. They are at once technological, administrative, informational, and productive. Moreover, they not only prevent, deter, and detect piracy, but also measure it. What we "know" about piracy—its rates, locations, costs, and profits—is usually what this industry sees and transmits to us. What we do not know about it—principally its cultural bases and implications—is what it does not see.

At the time of writing, the U.S. Congress has just voted to formalize all this. It has passed a law mandating the creation of an "intellectual property enforcement coordinator" to operate out of the president's executive office. This official will be charged with liaising with companies and trade associations to create and pursue a Joint Strategic Plan for worldwide antipiracy policing. The coordinator has inevitably been called a "copyright czar," the implication being that the idea is to mount a "war on piracy" analogous to the war on drugs. The precedent, it must be said, is inauspicious. Even the Bush administration, in its dying days, was leery, both of turning government lawyers into advocates for corporations and of entering into a new and cumbersome war that would surely be open ended. But President Bush signed the measure into law on October 13, 2008. Whatever its future consequences may be, it certainly extends a process that was already well under way.[5]

Exemplary as it is, the historical roots of this enterprise are deep and revealing. Ultimately, its origins lie in the customs for maintaining the orderly reputations of early modern trades that were outlined in chapter 2. In that founding era for literary and mechanical property, what patents and guild registrations had in common was that the holder of a given title had to act to make it real. There was little prospect of state action to uphold such claims. A strong presumption held that members of each specific trade community ought instead to collaborate to maintain them. Tracking down "pirates" of printed books, therefore, was a matter initially for the printers or booksellers concerned. The right to search their co-tradesmen's premises was a critically important privilege in making this practicable. Constables did not enjoy that right; it arose not from citizenship, but from membership of the given trade community. In London it was the responsibility of the Stationers' beadle to organize such searches, and they became routine events. Alleged piracies would be taken to Stationers' Hall, where the grandees of the trade would then decide upon restitution. In other words, the practical delineation and sustaining of literary property (as it later came to be called) was a private matter, both in the sense of being dealt with internally to a trade community, and in the sense that it remained invisible to authors and readers. What kept it honest, in theory at least, was the realization that an officer who authorized the search of a printer's home one year was quite likely to be investigated himself by the same printer during that person's own turn in office. A principle of social circulation—made basic to the political sphere by the civic republicanism of writers like James Harrington—meant that the boundary between acting on behalf of the public and serving a personal interest was often unclear.[6] (The language of "interest," not coincidentally, is one we owe to this period.) It is even plausible that that boundary *had* to be unclear, because success depended on knowledge that came from local acquaintances. An officer had to remain a trusted neighbor to have access to such knowledge. In early modern cities, an interlocking, reticulated array of lay officials—beadles, churchwardens, constables, and so on—permeated and policed society at all levels and in almost all activities. They maintained order by virtue of being categorically indistinct from the people they oversaw. The system made "do as you would be done by" into the basis of order in the arts and trades.[7]

Patents at first glance stood apart from this because they were a matter for courts of law. But in practice their enforcement too was largely a private affair. Pursuing patent infringers relied on the initiative of patentees, and success in the task depended on their access to insider knowledge. Getting a patent in the first place required tactical expertise, patience, constant attendance, and a lot of money; maintaining it required more. Indeed, proposals began to circulate from the late seventeenth century, if not earlier, to *increase* the private character of patent policing, precisely in order to make it fairer. The idea was to take these often highly technical disputes out of ill-informed judges' hands and entrust them to some expert body. The Royal Society in particular repeatedly angled to take on this role. It never did, but its register system pioneered what would become modern scientific norms surrounding discovery and priority. Plans for an autonomous expert tribunal would continue to enjoy support into our own day, and would be partially realized in several countries (including the United States, where the Court of Appeals for the Federal Circuit has this responsibility).

Private as it was, early modern policing led to characteristic forms of engagement with the public authorities. From an early date, those concerned to charge opponents with unsettling good order saw opportunities to extend the scope of that charge, and alleged that they posed a danger to church and state. When they did, transgressors could find themselves before the courts after all—not for piracy, but for unlicensed or seditious printing.[8] At that point, however, other characteristics of early modern enforcement might well come into play. One such was a tendency to turn pirates into policemen. Pirate printers were given patents; one of the most notorious, Henry Hills, was even made master of the Stationers' Company. Another typical response was the recourse to informers. Some pirates, Hills among them, apparently hastened to sell their services to the government, and the conviction took hold early and proved tenacious that making order a reality depended on them. Turncoats and informers were needed because of that basic problem for early modern policing, the inviolability of households. The private enforcement of creative titles thus extended into the public realm, and employed notoriously corrosive agents when it did so.

Private enforcement remained customary to the end of the early modern era. Indeed, there is a sense in which its passing *was* the end of the early modern era. In the eighteenth century several developments cast the principle into doubt and then disrepute. Theories of interest in the idiom of classical republicanism generated skepticism about the principle itself; scandals like that of the Thief-Taker General Jonathan Wild—hanged for colluding with the very criminals he had been charged with capturing—bolstered that skepticism. And when the vast, monopolist East India Company became a target for radicals opposed to monopolist policing in both trade and empire, the controversy they excited swept up domestic corporations too. The policing of literary property duly experienced its own crisis in the same period. Faced by Scottish and Irish reprinters, London's publishing booksellers responded much as the East India oligarchs did in their much wider sphere. They moved to recruit their own corps of "agents" to comb the region for piracies. Their aim was not to secure legal copyright, but to maintain a perpetual literary property grounded in trade custom—a very different, indeed fundamentally incompatible, principle.[9] The effort could perhaps be seen as a bid to extend the old tradition of participant policing beyond London and make it a national reality at the onset of the Industrial Revolution. But in practice it backfired disastrously when the Edinburgh reprinter Alexander Donaldson assumed the mantle of pirate-in-chief and mounted a counterattack. Donaldson maintained that the campaign—which rested on an assumed right of private agents to enter homes—threatened the very existence of a public sphere. In the face of that presumption, he insisted that it was precisely the so-called pirates who were upholders of the public.

Learning and enlightenment depended on them.[10] In 1774 he won his case, in what remains the most definitive copyright verdict in Anglo-American history.

The establishment of copyright was thus a matter of practices of enforcement and their implications for enlightenment, and only secondarily of statute law. Moreover, questions of policing continued to loom large after 1774, taking on international significance as the implicit tension between moral and political economies became increasingly overt in the Industrial Revolution. An Enlightenment ideal of cosmopolitanism could flourish partly because there was no international regime of literary and industrial property to constrain it. The engineer Robert Fulton's peregrinations exemplified the possibilities: he moved from London to Paris, back to London, and finally to America, trying to sell weaponry in support of an ideology of free trade and open seas.[11] With laissez-faire doctrines, ideologies of enlightenment, and the rise of empires and industries, what had previously been broadly consensual measures like registration and patents came to be seen as unnatural and impolitic constraints on behalf of local interests. The French Revolution saw this conviction reach its climax with the outright abolition of literary property. But in the post-revolutionary decades nations reasserted their interests. They competed to establish stricter authorial regimes, which must then be reconciled across borders. Such reconciliation became the project of much of the nineteenth century. What was happening, in effect, was a prolonged process of transformation in the relation between literary and manufacturing privileges and political space. At the height of the industrial age, the Berne and Paris Conventions would signal this by creating the first international rules for what was now called "intellectual property."

The modern intellectual property police originated at that time. But they emerged less by a renunciation of earlier practices than by their recreation. The music industry exemplified this. As private detective agencies in general boomed, its commander in chief, Arthur Preston, recruited his own antipirate force from ex-police officers and dispersed them across the land. Their activities skirted illegality—as they had to in order to have any prospect of success. Constitutional complaints bloomed, with a similar tone to those prompted by the booksellers' conspiracy a century and a half earlier. Against the invasion of homes and the threatening of street vendors, a "People's Music Publishing Company" could readily justify what it was doing in terms of facing down a high-handed monopoly. Legally, the pirate king at its head had no case; but that was not the point. Making the law *work* consistently with liberal society was more at stake than settling what the law *was*. That would remain a principal focus of concern in the new century as the techniques of antipiracy proliferated and allowed electromagnetic surveillance (the detector van) to supplement sharp-eyed men on the doorstep.

Well-funded and enduring antipiracy forces began to appear in the media industries in the 1950s–1960s. They came into their own once again in the era of home taping. The MPAA had a standing office by 1975, staffed by ex-FBI officers, and at the end of the 1970s the RIAA contributed about $100,000 to fund Bureau investigations into record piracy. Dozens of raids, hundreds of arrests, and thousands of seizures took place. By 1982, when the Betamax case was at its height, the MPAA's unit had an annual budget of $10 million to fight video piracy alone.[12] From that point the private policing of intellectual property took off, in concert with the biggest boom in private security, policing, and military companies since the Victorian era. In the United Kingdom, the same year saw the British Videogram Association, the Society of Film Distributors, and the MPAA join forces to establish the Federation Against Copyright Theft (FACT). FACT then vigorously pursued its own actions against pirates, relying on so-called Anton Piller Orders to garner evidence by recruiting informers. These were provisions by which a high court judge gave investigators search and seizure rights, secretly and without representation for their suspects. That is, they recreated the privilege that early modern guild officers had enjoyed, and that Preston's men had assumed to their cost.[13] FACT obtained more than a hundred Piller orders in the second half of 1982 alone. Only when an impertinent Luton pirate chose to contest one was the practice curtailed. At that point, Westminster promptly passed a law making record piracy a criminal offense, and therefore giving the regular police search and seizure powers in its pursuit.

The other pivotal development of this period was the embrace of anti-pirate technologies. One of FACT's earliest initiatives demonstrated the potential. The organization oversaw the insertion of undetectable traces on the 35 millimeter prints of movies distributed to cinemas. When these marks reappeared in pirated copies, they revealed which cinemas had served as sources. A series of police raids followed, which successfully suppressed what had been the country's most successful pirate movie ring.

From successes like this grew a devotion to visionary technologies, some of them preventative, others aimed at revealing (or retaliating for) piracy that had already occurred. Such technologies had long been proposed—the record industry had envisaged them for decades, and arguably printers pioneered the idea in the Renaissance.[14] But now they became the subject of sustained, well-financed, and state-sanctioned researches. By the end of the century they were starting to bear fruit. The satellite broadcaster DirecTV confirmed as much in what remains to this day the most spectacular of all antipirate tech operations. It was targeted at "signal pirates," as the company called them. These hackers used unauthorized decoder cards to receive its satellite's encrypted transmissions gratis. For years they could buy cards relatively freely in Canada, where DirecTV was not a licensed broadcaster. Like Preston, DirecTV pursued the signal pirates not just as copyright violators, but as conspirators, while Canadian entrepreneurs responded by appealing loudly to principles of public interest and open access. In the end the company would win its case in the Canadian courts. But meanwhile, in a feat that became legendary among cognoscenti, it took action of its own. Having quietly prepared the way by transmitting sections of code over a number of months, it broadcast an instruction at the start of the Super Bowl in early 2001 that simultaneously disabled roughly a hundred thousand unauthorized decoders. It reportedly even rewrote the first few bytes of the destroyed cards to read: "Game over." The event became known to traumatized hackers as "Black Sunday."[15]

Spectacular as it was, this action was also unrepresentative. Most antipirate tech has been preventative, aiming to make piracy impracticable. The quest for it took off amid the home taping furor. It did so because of the political unease generated (as always) by the recognition that effective antipiracy actions would require violations of domesticity. If homes were sacrosanct, the thinking went, then the only way to stop home piracy was to forestall it before copying could even be attempted. The most notorious countermeasure to home taping was thus a technology projected by CBS that would have added a high-pitched signal to LPs to prevent their being recorded onto cassettes. The measure aimed to secure intellectual property at the expense of degrading the content itself. It was never deployed in earnest, largely for that reason. In the digital era, however, schemes revived for some such system, because in a digital file a signal can be incorporated without impinging on the recording's quality. The many different digital rights management (DRM) programs of the 1990s and 2000s all exploited that principle. But as such systems proliferated, so they raised two profound—and consequential—difficulties.

In the first place, technological fixes proved notoriously poor at accommodating themselves to the variety of mundane practices (or, put another way, to the moral economies) that existed in their many contexts of use. Being algorithmic, they tended to be inflexible. They could be sophisticated in their handling of encodable rights, yet at the same time crudely imperceptive of fuzzier things like "fair use." By the same token, they were also insensitive to location. In a context of globalizing intellectual property laws, and of expansion by media companies and antipirate bodies into coordinated transnational enterprises, this at first seemed a peripheral concern. But local practices and sensibilities across the world proved stubbornly resistant to subsumption under uniform institutions and doctrines. This was not something that a revision of legal codes could address, because it reflected the impossibility of reducing cultural practices to such codes. Antipiracy technology therefore implied a need for an active commitment to upholding those practices—to the extent that a society wished them to be upheld.

In the second place, technological fixes proved less than dependable. DRM software could be hacked, and was; encryption techniques could be cracked, and were. Such was the ethos of hacker groups that this was likely to happen fast, and the hacks circulated quickly. (It is worth noting that the same may prove true for genetic technology too, thanks to the emerging world of garage biotechnology.) As a result, their de facto robustness in practice reflected less the power of technology than the power of the state to restrain the use of critical skills against that technology.[16] Both points were publicly made as early as 2000, when the Secure Digital Music Initiative, a trade group, challenged hackers to remove its digital watermark from a music file. A Princeton computer scientist named Ed Felten and his group managed to do it in a matter of weeks. That would not necessarily have been fatal to a DRM regime—on the contrary, an antipiracy industry would presumably need such competition in order to remain in business. But it did mean that in practice it would need the buttressing of nontechnological powers—states, norms, and laws—in order to remain effective. So it was that the Digital Millennium Copyright Act outlawed not only the circumvention of copyright-protection software, but the circulation of code facilitating such circumvention. When Felten broke that watermark, the SDMI responded by hinting that he himself might be subject to suit under the Act. Mandated in such ways, an antipiracy technology might just possibly turn copyright into something like a physical law, unbreakable in principle within a certain jurisdiction. But that would inevitably call into question the ideals of a democratic information culture. It would turn hackers into heroes. By trying to translate local practice into universal principle the intellectual property defense industry would have fostered a new age of postmodern social bandits.[17]

What makes this especially ironic—to put it no stronger—is that in some cases antipiracy technologies turned out to create more problems than they professed to solve. The notorious case of Sony-BMG's XCP system is the best-known instance. A piece of code bought from a British company, XCP was circulated on some Sony-BMG music CDs. It would quietly install a root-kit-like process onto the hard drives of customers who played their CDs in their computers. A root kit hides a program from the computer's own operating system; it commonly does so to shield a virus, or "malware," from detection. When its existence was revealed by hackers, the XCP program aroused outrage for this reason. Not only did it resemble a virus, moreover: it also seemed to send information back to the home company, entirely unbeknownst to the user. And it created a secret vulnerability that other Internet viruses might later exploit. It even transpired that if a user tried to delete the code, it might disable the CD drive altogether. Sony rapidly withdrew the program—but with an uninstall routine that generated still more vulnerabilities, potentially leaving computers open to being hijacked from afar. At each stage the initiative had transgressed norms strongly held among the small but vociferous and influential community of computer cognoscenti. More than that, it had highlighted problems implicit in the very idea of an antipirate technology.[18]

The point is that those problems are not problems of intellectual property narrowly construed. They are, in fact, among the core issues of traditional political theory and practice: issues of privacy, accountability, and autonomy. That is why it was worth tracking the history of the enforcement enterprise back all the way to the seventeenth century and the origins of modern political order. Such issues have, it seems, dogged intellectual property policing throughout its history, because of the nature of the enterprise. They continue to do so today in new forms and media. Large-scale, intensive, and internationally coordinated antipirate enforcement is sometimes justified—the effort against counterfeit medicines is a relatively clear example—but in other cases the public good is not so evident. In agribusiness, for example, Monsanto alone—to cite only the usual bête noire—has reported that it "investigates" about five hundred "tips" about seed piracy every year, retaining a unit of seventy-five employees to do so and coordinating its efforts with both private detective companies and public police forces worldwide. For years its agents have been accused of trespassing or acting as agents provocateurs.[19] In the digital realm, similarly, private antipiracy firms have reportedly set up fake bit-torrent sites to lure users into downloading. Moreover, because the industry that raises such concerns remains almost unknown, the vital question of *quis custodiet custodes* currently has no answer. Appropriate divisions of responsibilities, powers, and resources have not been defined. We have heard a lot in recent years about the perils of piracy in all its forms; we have also heard a lot about the perils of excessive intellectual property rights. Yet the questions raised by the antipiracy industry are at once broader and more immediate than these prevailing discussions acknowledge. They are late modern incarnations of the questions foundational to society itself.

THE END OF INTELLECTUAL PROPERTY

The confrontation between piracy and the intellectual property defense industry is perhaps set to trigger a radical transformation in the relation between creativity and commercial life. That idea is not as inconceivable as it may seem. Such turning points have happened before—about once every century, in fact, since the end of the Middle Ages. The last major one occurred at the height of the industrial age, and catalyzed the invention of intellectual property. Before that, another took place in the Enlightenment, when it led to the emergence of the first modern copyright system and the first modern patents regime. And before that, there was the creation of piracy in the 1660s–1680s. By extrapolation, we are already overdue to experience another revolution of the same magnitude. If it does happen in the near future, it may well bring down the curtain on what will then, in retrospect, come to be seen as a coherent epoch of about 150 years: the era of intellectual property.

The relation between creativity and commerce that has characterized the modern age emerged in the mid-eighteenth to mid-nineteenth centuries. It was defined by the establishment of copyright and patents systems and, in the end, by the concept of intellectual property. Received wisdom holds these to be almost axiomatic concepts (and therefore sees no problem in representing history prior to 1700 in terms of them). But ever since their advent they have been dogged by challenges, which have sometimes prospered and have anyway changed the constitution and meaning of creative property. That is by no means a peculiarity of our own, digital age. The critiques of our own time, however, although not the most radical, may prove to be the most effective for centuries. The most evident reason for this is that unlike that of Sir William Armstrong in the Victorian era they can now appeal to practical experience as well as principle. The properties of the Internet, in particular, seem to confirm that there are viable alternatives to proprietary norms. The resulting plausibility matters because while piracy and policing may foment a crisis, they cannot shape a resolution. For the raw materials of such a resolution we will need to look to alternatives of similarly broad ambit. One place to find them is in the sciences.

Claims for a new economics of creativity center overtly on the phenomenon of open-source software, which exploits properties of digital networks for which there is allegedly no precedent.[20] But they also draw support from deeper convictions about how knowledge is properly generated, distributed, and preserved. The mid-century insistence that openness was a guiding norm of true scientific research took on new force in the context of molecular biology and biotechnology. With the boom in biomedical and "life sciences" commerce, concerns grew that property claims could be prejudicial to the common interest in publicly funded science, and even impede research. These were at first distinct from the ethical fears that led the Human Genome Project—the foremost public-science project of its time—to abjure the patenting of genes.[21] But they combined to spark the emergence of an "open-access" movement insisting that state-funded research be made publicly available after a relatively short interval (typically a year or so). Open access has by now won over much of the public medical research establishment in the United States and the United Kingdom, bringing with it the prospect of a profound change in the culture and economics of scientific communication. Although premised on digital publishing, its ideological foundations in fact date back to the mid-twentieth-century patent conflicts, and to the normative view of science as public knowledge that they generated.[22]

The contests about science are fundamental, but one could multiply ad libitum the realms in which strong proprietary models are under challenge in cognate ways. Interestingly, many of the challenges center on transfigured versions of practices that were once decried as piratical. The norms of the open-source movement, for example, align it with the coding customs condemned by what was then Micro-Soft. Mass book-scanning projects foster intimations of a universal library that recall the cosmopolitan piracy of the Enlightenment.[23] Opposition to pharmaceutical patenting revives the compulsory-licensing advocacy of the Victorian antipatentees. Some of the rhetoric of TV pirate viewers descends from that of the pirate listeners of the 1920s. File-sharing acolytes resemble in some respects the home tapers of the 1960s–1970s, and historically their practices did begin with the swapping of cassettes. These recurrences are an indication that more is happening than technological change alone: longer-term commitments and convictions are at stake. Two specific conflicts emerged in the early 2000s as plausible candidates to convert these otherwise disparate trends into occasions for coherent legal and philosophical transformation. The first concerned copyright, the second patents.

In the realm of copyright, the challenge was that of the mass digitization of books. Google announced the largest enterprise dedicated to this task, its so-called Library Project, on December 14, 2004. Four major university libraries (Stanford, Harvard, Oxford, and the University of Michigan) and one public institution (the New York Public Library) would participate in a hugely ambitious project to scan and make accessible digital copies of their printed holdings. The ambition was finally to realize the old dream of a universal library—or at least to provide its online "card catalogue." In succeeding years more libraries would join the project, giving it a reach beyond the anglophone world. But it faced a serious problem—one that had been repeatedly mooted throughout the history of copyright, but now became real and urgent.

Google's proposal was often to make visible only small portions of the digital copies, in response to online searches. In order to do even this, however, it would need to scan and retain its own digital copies of the entire books. That was not controversial for works out of copyright, and in Oxford and New York only works in the public domain were slated to be scanned. But at Michigan—which stood at the vanguard of the venture—no such restriction was envisaged. Google's stance was that such scanning fell under the principle of "fair use." But the publishing industry rose up in protest, objecting to the apparent assumption of a right to copy and, moreover, fearing that at some future point the digital copies themselves might be made accessible. It denounced the venture as a stupendously brazen violation of copyright—one so sweeping as to threaten the very viability of copyright itself.

Google's initial response displayed something of the digital hacker's disdain for an irrational and obsolescent principle left over from the old-media world. It proposed an opt-out protocol, demanding that publishers submit lists of books to be excluded from the program. The suggestion was obviously going to be unacceptable to the publishers, and they duly filed lawsuits in 2005 accusing the company of "massive copyright infringement."[24] If the case had gone to the Supreme Court, it would probably have been the most important in the field since *Donaldson v. Becket* established the copyright principle in 1774. It might well have led to a radical overhaul of the principle.

The stakes for the publishers in particular were fundamental. The prospect of a digital universal library made actual what had for centuries been a complaint in principle: namely, that owners might use copyright to suppress publicly beneficial knowledge. Publishers could do this by invoking copyright against the scanning projects for out-of-print books, even though there was little chance that they themselves would ever re-issue them. As a result, even "orphaned" works—those for which there was no known current copyright owner—might not be made available, for fear of lawsuits springing up in future. The implication was not merely that a given work would not be available online, moreover, but that an inaccurate—or even spurious—version would be, because it happened to be one on which the copyright had expired.[25] Such texts might then become default standards, by virtue of being the ones immediately accessible in the next generation's research tool of first resort. Moreover, by the time the case got to Washington, scanners would inevitably have created a vast digital trove of more authoritative material that would be hidden from public view only because of copyright. It could straightforwardly and instantly be opened up if only copyright were to permit it. In other words, the argument from suppression—which throughout the eighteenth, nineteenth, and twentieth centuries was advanced repeatedly by skeptics, only to fail as hypothetical—would suddenly have real purchase. And this would occur at exactly the moment when the rise of open-access ventures would have made the publishers' contention that copyright encouraged creativity by securing the authenticity and economy of authorship dubious. It might well seem that copyright could remain inviolate only at the expense of its own purpose of enhancing the public good.

The case was never going to be allowed to get that far. After more than two years of negotiations, on October 28, 2008, Google and the publishers announced a settlement. By this point 7 million books had been scanned, 4–5 million of them being in copyright but out of print. The two camps would now cooperate, they announced, not only to resolve the status of those works, but to create a new foundation for creative property in digital books. The import of the deal was widely acknowledged. The technophile magazine *Wired* declared that Google now had a "clear field" for creating a "global digital library."[26] The *New York Times* described it as "a road map for a possible digital future for publishers and authors." The University of California, Stanford University, and the University of Michigan all declared that the result gave greater benefits than would have resulted even if Google had won its case. "It will now be possible, even easy, for anyone to access these great collections from anywhere in the United States," announced Paul N. Courant, University Librarian at Michigan.

The centerpiece of the plan was a new "Book Rights Registry." This would be a nonprofit institution charged with representing the interests of copyright holders —in principle, not just to Google, but to other, similar digital ventures. It would collect 63 percent of the revenues Google obtained from its digital books database and, after skimming off a percentage to fund itself, distribute them to the appropriate recipients, as recorded in its own exhaustive database of copyright owners. Its model was clearly that of the performing rights agencies that had been established at the turn of the twentieth century to deal with the then-new medium of the phonograph, and the Authors' Guild described the BRR as "the writers' equivalent of ASCAP." Google agreed to pay $34.5 million to set up this registry.

The BRR would become the lynchpin of the digital library. The book search program would now be freely accessible from U.S. public libraries or universities. Readers could freely read out-of-print digitized works there, whether or not they were in copyright, and print out pages for a charge. Google's income would come from institutional subscription fees, charges levied on individuals for access to in-print books, and, as ever, advertising. In the future, Google could scan and display online any copyrighted book that was not commercially available (that is, roughly, one not in print) unless the copyright owner explicitly opted out. The company could also scan copyrighted books that *were* in print—but the resulting digital copies would not be displayed openly unless publishers and authors explicitly opted in. Instead an independently hosted "Research Corpus" of these digital works would come into existence, accessible only by "qualified users" for research in computational analysis, informatics, linguistics, and the like. In addition, each participating library would get its own digital copy of every work scanned at that library, for preservation and archiving purposes. Each newly scanned book would earn a sum, hoped to be $200, for being included in the system. And a one-off payment of at least $60 would go to the copyright owner of every work already scanned. From Google's annual subvention, 25 percent would be allocated to these "inclusion fees." The other 75 percent would then be distributed as "usage fees," according to actual consultation of the digital copies. But after ten years the BRR board would appraise the situation and might decide to abandon inclusion fees if revenues did not allow for high enough sums. In the end, therefore, the new world of digital books would come to rest on distinctions of two kinds: between books themselves and between uses of books. Uses could be either display or nondisplay; books could be either in print or not. Copyright per se was declared a secondary issue. But in order for this to carry weight, those distinctions between books and uses would need to be made secure. So the settlement enjoined a common "security standard" for digital books, tying both Google and the BRR into the proliferating intellectual property defense economy.

It therefore looked as though the crisis of digitized books, triggered by Google's scanning project, would be resolved by creatively combining another variant of the old registry concept with the new practices of digital antipiracy. Significantly, however, at the time of the settlement's announcement, responses were not all welcoming. At Harvard, the university library declined to participate in the plan as it applied to in-copyright works. The university librarian was Robert Darnton. Darnton's historical researches into the eighteenth-century book had done more than any other to create awareness of the importance of print and its products in the time of the Enlightenment and French Revolution, when the ideas of copyright and the universal library originated, and in recent years he had been a major proponent of digital scholarship. Now he pointed out that the proposed regime would in fact limit the *uses* of digital books quite severely. Moreover, it would create a single access system—Google's—with no competition. The quality of its copies could vary: "in many cases," Darnton wrote, they would omit "photographs, illustrations and other pictorial works," severely reducing their research and educational value. Others too pointed out that the universal library would apparently be a monoculture, with all that that implied. (Several other projects to digitize and make available old books have in fact existed, and continue to do so, but none is remotely comparable to Google's in scale, nor as closely integrated into the dominant search technology.)[27] All these were good Enlightenment era points, made now in the context of twenty-first-century technologies. Moreover, this settlement—which, with its register system and its focus on one rather paternalist information channel, itself had a distinctly eighteenth-century air—left intact the problems that had led to its formulation. The challenge to copyright was deferred rather than defused.[28]

In the realm of patenting, the potentially transforming predicament had to do with pharmaceuticals. Certain countries—India, Brazil, and South Africa being the best known —had long called for prices on patented medicines to be lowered for life-and-death conditions. In the cases of Brazil and India, domestic industries existed that could produce generic equivalents. Brazil in particular pushed for compulsory licensing to allow them to do so. Compulsory licensing—that old idea of the Victorian antipatent campaigners—was in fact permitted under international trade accords in conditions of emergency. But the pharmaceutical industry remained staunchly opposed to it. The research that led to new drugs was undeniably costly—although exactly how costly is still a matter of much debate—and the industry's position was that an exclusive patents system was the best mechanism to underwrite it. The most plausible alternatives, prizes or Polanyi-style subsidies, seemed politically infeasible, although the former had proved effective in encouraging private ventures in other fields, notably spaceflight. The politics of this position would be complex enough alone, but it arose amid fears for the integrity of science in a realm of proprietorial deals among corporate and academic institutions. At the same time campaigners for indigenous populations continued to level charges of biopiracy against developed-world enterprises. And with the agglomeration of "life sciences" companies in the 1990s (since somewhat reversed), these issues became entwined with conflicts over seed piracy and genetically modified organisms in agriculture. The controversies surrounding the intellectual property defense industry were consequently more violent here than in any other field. Upholding the pharmaceutical patent system became an extraordinarily delicate task, by no means reducible to issues of intellectual property principle alone. Today, the tension between compulsory licensing and patents still seems particularly likely to rise to a climax. If that happens, it will stand to do for the principle of patenting what the mass-digitization projects may still do for the principle of copyright, the Google settlement notwithstanding.

It is therefore appropriate to end on a note of speculation. Intellectual property being a relatively recent concept, it ought to be possible to conceive of an alternative to it that suited the twenty-first century rather than the nineteenth. Suppose, therefore, that the two principal pillars of intellectual property—in effect, intellectual property itself—were to be challenged under these circumstances, and found wanting. What then?

Qualifications and alternatives to copyrights and patents have always existed: compulsory licenses, state subsidies, the provision of "bounties" by civil society, a system of informal courtesies, or even a completely laissez-faire regime. None of them has become consensual or normal, but none has completely vanished either. It is certainly possible that a solution to twenty-first-century problems could be cobbled together by combining them in some way with intellectual property as currently conceived. In principle, such ad hoc measures could be made to work indefinitely. (The war on drugs again comes to mind as unhappy evidence of that.) But it would seem a dauntingly confusing as well as a dispiritingly endless strategy. More promising would be an effort that began by revisiting the system's premises. Those premises should reflect the range of worldly practices at issue. In the eighteenth century, as we have seen, much debate focused on the extent to which they did. We have lost track of this, however, and now tend to infer that copyright in particular arose as an extension of Enlightenment *philosophy*. A process of revision today would have to begin with a similarly informed inquiry into the prevailing practices at stake, and especially into how they change from place to place and develop over time.

Such a process would sit awkwardly with traditional intellectual property assumptions. It is often thought that the great virtue of the fundamental distinction between copyrights and patents is that it captures a simple and natural difference. But in historical perspective it is by no means evident that literary and mechanical invention are natural kinds. On the contrary, the distinction was much debated in the past, and no consensus was really attained. Moreover, the division between literary and mechanical creativity was extrinsic to much of the early modern history of authorship: for centuries people patented books and registered machines. That is not to imply that the division was merely adventitious, however, let alone that it could easily be relinquished. On the contrary, it came about and became entrenched for substantial reasons, the force of which it would be hard to gainsay. Those reasons included the transformed relationship between liberal and mechanical arts in the early modern era, the scientific revolution, the rise of industry, and the advent of a public sphere based in commerce and consumption. Needless to say, these were also the transformations that shaped modernity itself. And it is in that light that one can say that the history of piracy is the history of modernity. The question society has to confront as the crisis of intellectual property reaches a climax is therefore this: should the conjunction of creativity and commerce continue to be defined in terms of a binomial distinction forged (and then controversially) in the Industrial Revolution?

In practice, of course, we already have a more reticulated and flexible system than that. What seem like stable doctrines and concepts in the abstract inevitably fragment into conventional norms and rules of thumb when they are put to use in different areas. The principle of "fair use," for example, is notoriously hard to systematize across domains. Expertise is correspondingly fragmented: populations of specialists exist for software patenting, for example, who work with skills and premises professionally distinct from those devoted to gene patenting. The problem is to frame basic categories of creative commerce in terms of that fact. What is needed, in effect, is a taxonomy rather like Defoe's, fitted for the twenty-first century. For example, algorithms, genes, and cloud-computing applications are as likely to be the bases of progress and prosperity for our descendants as mechanical and poetic works were in Samuel Johnson's day. The distinctions between them are debatable, but we have no reason to expect them to correspond in any straightforward way to those that Johnson's contemporaries struggled to define between orreries and epics. It would make sense to recognize that. In effect, doing so would mean acknowledging that the principles of what is now called "intellectual property" are dynamic—in a word, that they are historical through and through.

In that context it is no coincidence that the problem facing intellectual property coincides with a period of deep unease about the practices that society entrusts with discovering and imparting formal knowledge in general. The foundations and status of the academic disciplines are in question, no less than those of intellectual property. Both the modern disciplinary system and the modern principle of intellectual property are achievements of the era culminating in the late nineteenth century, and the same departure of creative authorship to new projects and identities underlies the anxieties of each. In each case new realms of creative work *can* be accommodated into the existing system, but doing so involves ad hoc compromises and creates increasingly stark inconsistencies. At some point the resulting contraption comes to resemble too clearly for comfort Thomas Kuhn's famous portrayal of a "crisis" state in the sciences. In intellectual property, as in the disciplines at large, a reengagement with history is likely to play a central role in shaping the transformation that such a crisis entails.[29] Indeed, this book has shown how revisions of history have already proved a notable feature of all major transitions in intellectual property thus far, from the invention of piracy through that of intellectual property. New accounts of the digital and biotech revolutions — along with revisionist interpretations of the Gutenberg revolution — herald another. Rather than adducing a discrete "culture" defined by each given technology, they portray a practical, dynamic, and continuous interlacing of technologies and society. They furnish a kind of understanding that could underpin a revision of the proper relation between creativity and commerce.

A reformation of creative rights, responsibilities, and privileges could therefore occur in reaction to a crisis in intellectual property. It could rest on quite different distinctions from that between literary and mechanical fields which has obtained for centuries as fundamental to what we call intellectual property. It might adopt as axiomatic the distinction between digital and analogue, for example, for it is arguable that the act of copying is distinct in the two realms. Or it could embrace a more radical form of reticulation, recognizing multiple categories — genetic, digital, algorithmic, inscribed, and more — rather than a binomial pair. Either way, it would also include the historicity of the distinctions on which it does come to be built. At present we have a system that is conceptually simple, in that it is professedly based on a small number of ideal premises that are impervious to historical change. But it is hopelessly complex in practice, because the everyday life of creativity and commerce *is* historical. A reticulated system would be more complex in theory, because it would require more premises. But in use it might be simpler, because it could hug the contours of creative life more closely. The change, in sum, would be profound. Not everything we attribute to intellectual property would be jettisoned. It might even be said that intellectual property itself had been saved. After all, such property benefits those who create opinions, so the opinions that are created will tend to return the favor—a cynical way to put it, but Henry Carey did so in the nineteenth century, and Arnold Plant agreed in the twentieth. Yet in truth it would have been radically reconceived. Intellectual property in its high-modern form would no longer exist.

All of this is admittedly speculative. But it is not intrinsically implausible. Intellectual property has always been a dynamic compromise between the local and the universal, and between practice and principle. At the time of writing it seems to increasing numbers of people that the balance is set to shift. The long ascendancy of the universal may be coming to an end. Assumptions that had seemed secure and unquestionable are all of a sudden doubtful again. As this happens, many are the possible trajectories on offer, and most are backed by their own zealous adherents. There are not many guides to help us choose the best. It is in our interest to make use of past experience as one tool. We should look again at the variety of convictions that our ancestors held, the arguments they advanced, the actions they took, and the results they experienced. To be sure, history cannot tell us exactly what to do, or what choices to make. The responsibility for those decisions will be ours alone. But the time to take the decisions is surely coming. History can help us prepare for it.

Acknowledgments

This book has taken more than a decade to complete. It deals with themes that extend across the domains of human creativity, over a long timescale, and across a wide geographical area. I have incurred countless intellectual and social debts in writing it. I can signal only a few of them here, but my gratitude to all who have helped is deep and lasting.

In the first place, I must thank the University of Chicago Press, where Alan Thomas shepherded this book into being, showing extraordinary patience and wisdom over a number of years. Mark Reschke did a fine job copyediting the typescript. With any other publisher this project could not have become the book that it is.

Students at the various universities where I have worked have endured courses on piracy and intellectual property from me for several years now. At UCSD, Caltech, and the University of Chicago I have encountered a vast range of views and knowledge on the topic. Many of the young people who took part in these classes were imaginative originators who had already encountered the intellectual property system in their own lives, even before arriving at university. They could speak from experience about the fine structure of its effects on digital, biotechnological, or artistic enterprises. That seems to me a real change — an advance, really — that has taken place in my lifetime and that deserves notice. I benefited in countless ways—probably more than the students themselves—from the conversations we had.

I have also been the beneficiary of many learned responses when I have presented versions of some of the claims published here at academic institutions and societies. Over the years I have been fortunate to have the opportunity to do this many times: at Berkeley, Bucknell University, Harvard, McGill, NYU, the University of Pittsburgh, Princeton, the Society for the History of Authorship, Reading, and Publishing, Stanford, various annual meetings of the History of Science Society, the University of Chicago, UCLA, the University of Illinois at Urbana-Champaign, the University of Michigan, and Yale. Audiences at all these places helped enormously in the refinement of the book's arguments. Even if I did not record the names of those who made particular comments, I always tried to listen to and accommodate the comments themselves. I am grateful for them all.

The story told in this book rests substantially on primary-source evidence, and this could not have been gathered without the aid of many libraries and archives. I am grateful for the opportunity to consult papers at the following institutions—and, no less, for the aid of the staff at these places: the American Antiquarian Society; the American Philosophical Society; the BBC Written Archives Centre; the British Library; the British Telecom Archives; Cambridge University Library; the Historical Society of Pennsylvania; the Houghton Library, Harvard University; the Huntington Library; the University of Glasgow Archives; the London School of Economics Archives; the William L. Clements Library, University of Michigan; the MIT archives; the National Archives (UK); the National Library of Ireland; the Bodleian Library, University of Oxford; the Royal Mail archives; the Royal Society Library; the Regenstein and Crerar Libraries at the University of Chicago; and the Worshipful Company of Stationers and Newspaper Makers.

Financial support for research leave has been vital to the pursuit of this project and to the writing of the book that has resulted. I have received such support from the University of Chicago, the American Philosophical Society (Sabbatical Fellowship, 2002), and the National Science Foundation (2005, grant number 0451472). Any opinions, findings, and conclusions or recommendations expressed in this book are mine and do not necessarily reflect the views of the National Science Foundation or any other of these bodies.

I am no less appreciative of all those individuals I have met over the years who have contributed ideas, criticisms, and suggestions. As I have traveled around the academic and professional worlds I have found that every kind of specialism has its own developed mythology of piracy, often central to its sense of how it itself originated. A multivolume book could have been written from what I learned about them all, and I hope that those who contributed material that I did not in the end use will understand. I can only apologize even more to the many I have doubtless omitted from the following list—please blame my memory, not my manners. But among those whose assistance I particularly remember are Lionel Bently, Mario Biagioli, Geoffrey Bilder (for conjuring up the perfect moment at the Googleplex), Ann Blair, Peter Burke, Graham Burnett, James Chandler, Roger Chartier, Bill Clark, Roger Cooter, Angela Creager, Robert Darnton, Arnold Davidson, Peter Dear, Richard Epstein, James Evans, Paula Findlen, John Forrester, Marina Frasca-Spada, Peter Galison, Anne Goldgar, Jan Golinski, Anthony Grafton, John Guillory, Deborah Harkness, Nicholas Jardine, Daniel Kevles, James Lee, Alan Liu, the late Donald McKenzie, Michael McKeon, Jim Moore, Oliver Morton, Reviel Netz, Shuhei Ogawa, Trevor Pinch, Steven Pincus, Mary Poovey, Wei Ran, Robert Richards, Lissa Roberts, Jonathan Rose, Larry Rothfield, Martin Rudwick, Simon Schaffer, Anne Secord, James Secord, Steven Shapin, Geoffrey Smith, Pamela Smith, Emma Spary, Peter Stallybrass, Stephen Stigler, Kate Stimmler, Fred Swartz, Michael Warner, William Wimsatt, Alison Winter, and Martha Woodmansee

This book focuses on the English-speaking world. But my perspective on that world has been shaped by experiences in Japan, China, and Continental Europe. Investigating practices of digital (and other) piracy in such different settings has helped to cast the peculiarities of my own culture in sharper relief, even though the results of those investigations are not explicit in this volume. My heartfelt thanks go especially to Yoshihisa Ogawa and Naoya Nakanishi of Foursis, Inc., in Japan: my thinking about digital matters and their place in history would not have developed as it has without their extraordinarily generous help. In China my efforts to talk with DVD pirates would have got nowhere but for Wei Ran, and in Hong Kong Stephen Selby, director of Intellectual Property of the SAR, gave of his time very generously.

Those most closely involved with the seemingly endless process of researching, writing, and rewriting this book have been the members of my own family: Alison, David, Elizabeth, Zoe, and Benjamin. It could certainly not have been completed without their help, understanding, and tolerance. But I owe them far more than that implies—far more, indeed, than could ever be put into words.

Although I have always conceived of this book as a single whole, I have benefited from the chance to try out earlier versions of some sections in print. Chapter 3 draws on "The Piratical Enlightenment," in *This Is Englightenment,* ed. C. Siskin and W. Warner (Chicago: University of Chicago Press, forthcoming). Parts of chapter 4 appeared first in "Reading and Experiment in the Early Royal Society," in K. Sharpe and S. Zwicker, eds., *Reading, Society and Politics in Early Modern England* (Cambridge: Cambridge University Press, 2003), 244–71 (© Cambridge University Press; reprinted with permission). "Truth and Malicious Falsehood," *Nature* 451 (February 28, 2008): 1058–60, contains a much-abbreviated version of an argument from chapter 5. Chapter 12 expands on material initially presented in "Pop Music Pirate Hunters," *Daedalus* 131, no. 2 (Spring 2002): 67–77. And a preliminary version of the argument in chapter 14 was published as "Intellectual Property and the Nature of Science," *Cultural Studies* 20 (2006): 145–64.

Notes

I A GENERAL HISTORY OF THE PIRATES

1   See an exposé at http://www.cn.necel.com/en/cprofile/elhk/cprofile_elhk_
    job_disclaimer.html.
2   D. Lague, "Next Step for Counterfeiters: Faking the Whole Company,"
    New York Times, May 1, 2006, C1; D. Lague, "Next Step in Pirating: Faking
    a Company," *International Herald Tribune,* April 28, 2006, 1.
3   S. Vickers, "Confronting the New IP threat," *Asia Law,* April 2006, 37–38.
4   Bruce Sterling, *Distraction* (New York: Bantam, 1998 [1999]), 104; see also
    121.
5   This evocation of the *Communist Manifesto* is not entirely flippant. The
    Manifesto was written to take advantage of the revolutionary moment
    of 1848, when an old order suddenly crumbled amid a technological,
    communications, and industrial revolution. The ferment of that period
    bears comparison with that which prevailed after the implosion of Soviet
    communism amid the advent of digital networked media 150 years later.
    A number of "hacker's manifestoes" attempted to draw the same parallel.
    The most self-important is M. Wark's *Hacker Manifesto* (Cambridge,
    Mass.: Harvard University Press, 2004); the most heartfelt and original,
    The Mentor, "Conscience of a Hacker/Hacker's Manifesto," *Phrack* 1,
    no. 7 (September 25, 1986): 3.
6   Quoted in G. Davies, *Piracy of Phonograms,* 2nd ed. (Oxford: ESC Pub-
    lishing, for European Commission, 1986), 4. To be fair, Davies did then
    advance a more substantive definition.

7   See chapter 10 below, and also B. Sherman and L. Bently, *The Making of Modern Intellectual Property Law: The British Experience, 1760–1911* (Cambridge: Cambridge University Press, 1999).

8   C. Pulling, *They Were Singing: And What They Sang About* (London: G. G. Harrap, 1952), 112–13.

9   D. T. Pottinger, *The French Book Trade in the Ancien Régime, 1500–1791* (Cambridge, Mass.: Harvard University Press, 1958), 151–52.

10 For the issues at stake in framing the subject this way, see A. Grafton, E. L. Eisenstein, and A. Johns, "How Revolutionary Was the Print Revolution?" *American Historical Review* 107, no. 1 (February 2002): 84–128.

11 Miguel de Cervantes, *Don Quixote*, trans. E. Grossman (New York: Ecco, 2003), 270, 423–28, 938.

12 P. O. Long, *Openness, Secrecy, Authorship: Technical Arts and the Culture of Knowledge from Antiquity to the Renaissance* (Baltimore: Johns Hopkins University Press, 2001), 11.

13 R. Chapman, *Selling the Sixties: The Pirates and Pop Music Radio* (London: Routledge, 1992). I mean to explore this further in a future book, to be called *Death of a Pirate*.

14 P.-H. Dopp, *La contrefaçon des livres français en Belgique, 1815–1852* (Louvain: Université de Louvain, 1932).

15 Versions of this hypothesis are articulated explicitly in organs like the *Economist* that believe in a modernization trajectory toward free markets, enforceable contracts, and property rights.

16 N. Anderson, "A War of Attrition," *Ars Technica,* March 18, 2007: http://arstechnica.com/articles/culture/mediadefender.ars; J. A. Halderman and E. W. Felten, "Lessons from the Sony CD DRM episode" (2006), at http://itpolicy.princeton.edu/pub/sonydrm-ext.pdf; Center for Food Safety, "Monsanto vs. American farmers" (2005), at http://www.centerforfood safety.org/pubs/CFSMOnsantovsFarmerReport1.13.05.pdf.

2 THE INVENTION OF PIRACY

1   Liber F (entries of copies March 2, 1656/57 to December 8, 1682). For this and the other register, see R. Myers, *The Stationers' Company Archive: An Account of the Records, 1554–1984* (Winchester: St. Paul's Bibliographies, 1990), 25.

2   Vitruvius, *Ten Books on Architecture,* trans. I. D. Rowland (Cambridge: Cambridge University Press, 1999), 85 (VII:1–3); E. Fantham, *Roman Literary Culture: From Cicero to Apuleius* (Baltimore: Johns Hopkins University Press, 1996), 15; P. O. Long, *Openness, Secrecy, Authorship: Technical Arts and the Culture of Knowledge from Antiquity to the Renaissance* (Baltimore: Johns Hopkins University Press, 2001), 43; H.-J. Martin, *The History and Power of Writing* (Chicago: University of Chicago Press, 1994), 49–50;

L. D. Reynolds and N. G. Wilson, *Scribes and Scholars: A Guide to the Transmission of Greek and Latin Literature*, 3rd ed. (Oxford: Oxford University Press, 1991), 23–29.

3   W. P. McCray, *Glassmaking in Venice: The Fragile Craft* (Aldershot: Ashgate, 1999), esp. 149–63; Long, *Openness*, 89–92.

4   Long, *Openness*, 88–101; M. Biagioli, "From Print to Patents: Living on Instruments in Early Modern Europe," *History of Science* 44 (2006): 1–48.

5   Long, *Openness*, 92–95.

6   Long, *Openness*, 10–11.

7   There are many fine accounts available of these processes, but see especially P. Dear, *Revolutionizing the Sciences: European Knowledge and Its Ambitions, 1500–1700* (Princeton, N.J.: Princeton University Press, 2001), 10–79, 101–30; B. T. Moran, *Distilling Knowledge: Alchemy, Chemistry, and the Scientific Revolution* (Cambridge, Mass.: Harvard University Press, 2005); S. Shapin, *The Scientific Revolution* (Chicago: University of Chicago Press, 1996), 65–96; and W. R. Newman, *Atoms and Alchemy: Chymistry and the Experimental Origins of the Scientific Revolution* (Chicago: University of Chicago Press, 2006). On Paracelsian views of knowledge and the idea of the artisan as a providential agent, see O. Hannaway, *The Chemists and the Word: The Didactic Origins of Chemistry* (Baltimore: Johns Hopkins University Press, 1975), 22–72, esp. 27, 44–53, and P. Smith, *The Body of the Artisan: Art and Experience in the Scientific Revolution* (Chicago: University of Chicago Press, 2004).

8   T. Coryate, *Coryats Crudities* (London: printed by W.S., 1611), sig. D4^r; A. R. Waller, ed., *Samuel Butler: Characters and Passages from Notebooks* (Cambridge: Cambridge University Press, 1908), 247.

9   J. Loewenstein, *The Author's Due: Printing and the Prehistory of Copyright* (Chicago: University of Chicago Press, 2002), 87.

10   J. Buchanan, *Linguae Britannicae vera Pronunciatio* (London: for A. Millar, 1757), "Pirate."

11   P. Kennedy, *A Supplement to Kennedy's Ophthalmographia* (London: printed for T. Cooper, 1739), 37.

12   There is a more detailed treatment of this complex and subtly managed regime in A. Johns, *The Nature of the Book: Print and Knowledge in the Making* (Chicago: University of Chicago Press, 1998).

13   G. Wither, *The Schollers Purgatory* (London: "Imprinted for the Honest Stationers," n.d.), sig. (i)2^v.

14   Wither, *Schollers Purgatory*, 5 and passim.

15   Wither, *Schollers Purgatory*, sig. (i)2^r, 8, 10, 57; S. Wells and G. Taylor, eds., *William Shakespeare: The Complete Works* (Oxford: Clarendon Press, 1986), 45.

16   J. Milton, *Areopagitica* (London: n.p., 1644); G. Winstanley, *The Law of Freedom and Other Writings*, ed. C. Hill (Cambridge: Cambridge University

Press, 1983), 280–81, 291. Compare the republican soldier and printer John Streater, in *A Glympse of that Jewel, Judicial, Just Preserving Libertie* (London: for G. Calvert, 1653), sigs. A2ᵛ–A4ʳ. See also S. Achinstein, *Milton and the Revolutionary Reader* (Princeton, N.J.: Princeton University Press, 1994), 1–70.

17 P. Lake and S. Pincus, "Rethinking the Public Sphere in Early Modern England," *Journal of British Studies* 45 (2006): 270–92.

18 There is an almost infinitely large body of historical work on the civil wars and the politics of this period. For the nexus of literary and political stresses central here, see especially D. Norbrook, *Writing the English Republic: Poetry, Rhetoric, and Politics, 1627–1660* (Cambridge: Cambridge University Press, 1999); N. Smith, *Literature and Revolution in England, 1640–1660* (New Haven, Conn.: Yale University Press, 1994); and Achinstein, *Milton and the Revolutionary Reader.* For the problem of public "reason," see M. Knights, "How Rational Was the Later Stuart Public Sphere?" in *The Politics of the Public Sphere in Early Modern England,* ed. P. Lake and S. Pincus (Manchester: Manchester University Press, 2007), 252–67. The presbyterian booksellers' attempt to recreate licensing took the form of an extended pamphlet war in the 1650s, commencing with Luke Fawne and others' *A beacon set on fire* (London: n.p., 1652): A. Johns, "Coleman Street," *Huntington Library Quarterly* 71, no. 1 (2008): 33–54, esp. 51–52, and J. Collins, "Silencing Thomas Hobbes: The Presbyterians and Their Printers," at http://csb.princeton.edu/index.php?app =download&id=11.

19 For a taste of political argument in these decades, see J. H. Scott, *Commonwealth Principles: Republican Writing of the English Revolution* (Cambridge: Cambridge University Press, 2004).

20 C. Blagden, *The Stationers' Company: A History, 1403–1959* (London: George Allen and Unwin, 1960; repr. Stanford, Calif.: Stanford University Press, 1977), 93, 144.

21 For a fuller account of the Atkyns conflict, see Johns, *Nature of the Book,* 304–20, 338–44.

22 Norbrook, *Writing the English Republic,* 1–22; J. H. Scott, *England's Troubles: Seventeenth-Century English Political Instability in European Context* (Cambridge: Cambridge University Press, 2000), 162–66.

23 Johns, *Nature of the Book,* 313.

24 T. Hobbes, *Behemoth: Or the Long Parliament,* ed. F. Tönnies (Chicago: University of Chicago Press, 1990), 109.

25 See especially A. O. Hirschman, *The Passions and the Interests: Political Arguments for Capitalism before Its Triumph* (Princeton, N.J.: Princeton University Press, 1977).

26 For the printers' objections, see *The London Printers Lamentation, or, the Press opprest, and overprest* ([London]: n.p., 1660); *A Brief Discourse*

Concerning Printing and Printers (London: "Printed for a Society of Printers," 1663); and, in general, C. Blagden, "The 'Company' of Printers," *Studies in Bibliography* 13 (1960): 3–17.

27   R. Atkyns, *The original and growth of printing* (London: by J. Streater for the author, 1664), sig. [B3]ᵛ.

28   P. Seaward, *The Cavalier Parliament and the Reconstruction of the Old Regime* (Cambridge: Cambridge University Press, 1989), 117.

29   Thucydides, *Eight bookes of the Peloponnesian warre,* trans. Thomas Hobbes (London: printed for Henry Seile, 1629), 4; Hobbes, *Leviathan,* ed. R. Tuck (Cambridge: Cambridge University Press, 1991), 67 (Part I, ch. 10); H. A. Ormerod, *Piracy in the Ancient World: An Essay in Mediterranean History* (Liverpool: Liverpool University Press, 1978), 59–70.

30   Cicero, *De Officiis,* II:40, III:107; translation in *On Duties,* ed. M. T. Griffin and E. M. Atkins (Cambridge: Cambridge University Press, 1991), 77–78, 141–42.

31   *Digest* XLIX, 15, 24; Ormerod, *Piracy,* 60. For the cultural importance of speaking truthfully, see S. Shapin, *A Social History of Truth: Civility and Science in Seventeenth-Century England* (Chicago: University of Chicago Press, 1994).

32   Cicero, *De re publica,* III:24a; translation in *On the Commonwealth and On the Laws,* ed. J. E. G. Zetzel (Cambridge: Cambridge University Press, 1999), 67. I am grateful to Reviel Netz at Stanford for identifying the source some years ago.

33   "primo latronicia, deinde valida bella piratarum": Augustine, *De Civitate Dei,* III:xxvi; translation in *Concerning the City of God against the Pagans,* trans. H. Bettenson (Harmondsworth: Penguin, 1984), 127, 142.

34   Augustine, *De Civitate Dei,* IV:iv; *City of God* (1984), 139–42.

35   M. Rediker and P. Linebaugh, *The Many-Headed Hydra: Sailors, Slaves, Commoners, and the Hidden History of the Revolutionary Atlantic* (Boston: Beacon, 2000), 120.

36   J. Dryden, "Heroick Stanza's, on the late Usurper Oliver Cromwell," stanza 30, in E. Waller, J. Dryden, and T. Sprat, *Three poems upon the death of his late Highnesse Oliver Lord Protector of England, Scotland, and Ireland* (London: W. Wilson, 1659), 8.

37   J. Harrington, *The Common-wealth of Oceana* (London: by J. Streater for L. Chapman, 1656), 195.

38   [J. Streater], *Observations Historical, Political, and Philosophical, upon Aristotles first Book of Political Government* (London: for R. Moon; in eleven weekly numbers, April 4 to July 4, 1654), 6–7, 18–20, 37–38; Johns, *Nature of the Book,* 313.

39   J. Milton, "Defence of the People of England," in *Complete Prose Works,* 8 vols. (New Haven, Conn.: Yale University Press, 1953–82), IV, pt. 1, 419; [D. Defoe], "Miscellanea," *Review* VI, no. 104 (December 3, 1709): 415.

Augustine's own seventeenth-century translator used the more generic
"theefe": Augustine, *Of the Citie of God,* trans. I.H., 2nd ed. (London: by
G. Eld and M. Flesher, 1620), 150. Interestingly, Milton remarks that
kings' power is the power of highwaymen rather than poets or painters—
an apposite comparison in the context of Atkyns's case, since the latter
supported his argument by claiming that Charles I had proved his mettle
by his acuity in such aesthetic matters. For the later jurisprudence, see
Ormerod, *Piracy,* 60–61.

40 Johns, *Nature of the Book,* 314–5.

41 J. Vaughn, "The Politics of Empire: Metropolitan Socio-Political Development and the Imperial Transformation of the British East India Company,
1675–1775" (Ph.D. thesis, University of Chicago, 2009), chs. 1–2; S. Pincus,
"Whigs, Political Economy, and the Revolution of 1688–89," in *"Cultures
of Whiggism": New Essays on English Literature and Culture in the Long
Eighteenth Century,* ed. David Womersley (Newark: University of Delaware Press, 2005), 62–81.

42 For the revolutionary character of the post-1688 politics, and political
economy in particular, see S. Pincus, *England's Glorious Revolution, 1688–
1689* (Boston: Bedford/St. Martin's, 2006), 21–26.

3 THE PIRATICAL ENLIGHTENMENT

1 J. Fell to Williamson, August 6, 1674, National Archives, Kew, State Papers
SP 29/361, nos. 188–188(i); T. Brooks, *A string of pearls* (London: for John
Hancock, 1668), final page, "The Stationer to the Reader"; Stationers'
Company, Court Book F, fol. 18^r (1684); Johns, *Nature of the Book,* 344.

2 See, in general, J. P. Kenyon, *Revolution Principles: The Politics of Party,
1689–1720* (Cambridge: Cambridge University Press, 1977), and, more
specifically, S. Pincus, "Neither Machiavellian Moment nor Possessive
Individualism: Commercial Society and the Defenders of the English
Commonwealth," *American Historical Review* 103, no. 3 (1998): 705–36;
also T. Harris, *Revolution: The Great Crisis of the British Monarchy, 1685–1720*
(London: Allen Lane, 2006), 308–63, 491–94.

3 Linebaugh and Rediker, *Many-Headed Hydra,* 148; S. Smith, "Piracy in
Early British America," *History Today* 46, no. 5 (May 1996): 29–37, esp. 30,
33; Vaughn, "Politics of Empire," ch. 2.

4 C. Johnson [D. Defoe?], *A general history of the robberies and murders of
the most notorious pyrates, and also their Policies, discipline and Government*
(Mineola, N.Y.: Dover, 1999; orig. London, 1724), title page, 60–61, 417,
and passim. On "the mock king of Madagascar," see also [Defoe], *The king
of pirates* (London: Hesperus, 2002; orig. London, 1719). For skepticism
about Defoe's involvement, see P. N. Furbank and W. R. Owens, *The
Canonisation of Daneil Defoe* (New Haven, Conn.: Yale University Press,

1988), 100–13. For the recent historiography, see L. Schweikart and B. R. Burg, "Stand by to Repel Historians: Modern Scholarship and Caribbean Pirates, 1650–1725," *The Historian* 46, no. 2 (1984): 219–34; L. Osborne, "A Pirate's Progress: How the Maritime Rogue Became a Multicultural Hero," *Lingua Franca* 8, no. 2 (March 1998): 34–42; Rediker and Linebaugh, *The Many-Headed Hydra,* 157–59; C. Hill, "Radical Pirates?" in *The Origins of Anglo-American Radicalism,* ed. M. Jacob and J. Jacob (London: George Allen and Unwin, 1984), 17–32; C. Hill, *Liberty against the Law: Some Seventeenth-Century Controversies* (London: Allen Lane, 1996), 114–22. All this is controversial work, of course, especially in its portrayal of its subjects not just as a community but specifically as a "proletariat"—a term that for me carries too much nineteenth-century baggage to be useful. But what matters is what readers in London and Philadelphia, say, *thought* pirate life was like. The sources used by Hill, Rediker, and Linebaugh do provide good evidence for that.

5   [D. Defoe], *An essay on the regulation of the press* (London: n.p., 1704), 19–20.
6   [E. Ward], *The Secret History of Clubs* (London: n.p.; sold by the booksellers, 1709), 168; J. Gay, "On a Miscellany of Poems, to Bernard Lintott," in his *Poetical, dramatic, and miscellaneous works,* 6 vols. (London: for E. Jeffery, 1795), VI:77–81; [S. Wesley], *Neck or Nothing: a consolatory letter from Mr. D-nt-n to Mr. C—rll* (London: sold by C. King, 1716), 7; P. McDowell, *The Women of Grub Street: Press, Politics and Gender in the London Literary Marketplace, 1678–1730* (Oxford: Clarendon Press, 1998), 252; S. Johnson, *London: A Poem* (London: for R. Doddesley, 1738), 6.
7   [J. D.] Breval, *The play is the plot* (London: for J. Tonson, 1718), 12–13, 21–22, 35–36, 50. Cibber's rivals were not slow to suggest that the role was fitting. The antimony joke refers to Curll's treatment at the hands of Pope.
8   E. Ward, *A Journey to H— (Part II)* (London: n.p., 1700), Canto VII.
9   M. Rose, *Authors and Owners: The Invention of Copyright* (Cambridge, Mass.: Harvard University Press, 1993), 147; D. Hunter, "Copyright Protection for Engravings and Maps in Eighteenth-Century Britain," *The Library,* ser. 6, 9 (1987): 128–47; F. E. Manuel, *Isaac Newton, Historian* (Cambridge: Cambridge University Press, 1963), 29–36; P. Baines and P. Rogers, *Edmund Curll, Bookseller* (Oxford: Clarendon Press, 2007), 246–76.
10 The origin of modern theories on this subject is, of course, J. Habermas, *The Structural Transformation of the Public Sphere: An Inquiry into a Category of Bourgeois Society,* trans. T. Burger and F. Lawrence (Cambridge: Polity, 1989; orig. 1962). There is now a very large literature on it. Good accounts of the British, French, and German literature are J. Brewer, "This, That and the Other: Public, Social and Private in the Seventeenth and Eighteenth Centuries," in *Shifting the Boundaries: Transformation of the Languages of Public and Private in the Eighteenth Century,* ed. D. Castiglione

and L. Sharpe (Exeter: University of Exeter Press, 1995), 1–21; R. Chartier, *The Cultural Origins of the French Revolution,* trans. L. Cochrane (Durham, N.C.: Duke University Press, 1991); and B. W. Redekop, *Enlightenment and Community: Lessing, Abbt, Herder, and the Quest for a German Public* (Montreal: McGill-Queen's University Press, 2000). For an introduction, see T. C. W. Blanning, *The Culture of Power and the Power of Culture* (Oxford: Oxford University Press, 2002), 103–82; and for theoretical perspectives, extending well beyond the eighteenth century, M. Warner, *Publics and Counterpublics* (New York: Zone, 2002).

11   [D. Defoe], "Miscellanea," *Review* VI, no. 104 (December 3, 1709): 415.

12   J. Girdham, *English Opera in Late Eighteenth-Century London: Stephen Storace at Drury Lane* (Oxford: Oxford University Press, 1997), 83–98; Melvyn New, "Sterne, Laurence (1713–1768)," in *Oxford Dictionary of National Biography* (Oxford: Oxford University Press, 2004); Johns, *Nature of the Book,* 320, 460.

13   R. Darnton, "The Science of Piracy: A Crucial Ingredient in Eighteenth-Century Publishing," *Studies in Voltaire and the Eighteenth Century* 12 (2003): 3–29; J. C. Attig, *The Works of John Locke: A Comprehensive Bibliography from the Seventeenth Century to the Present* (Westport, Conn.: Greenwood Press, 1985); J. S. Yolton, *John Locke: A Descriptive Bibliography* (Bristol: Thoemmes Press, 1998); J.-A. E. McEachern, *Bibliography of the Writings of Jean Jacques Rousseau to 1800,* vol. 1, *Julie, ou la Nouvelle Héloïse* (Oxford: Voltaire Foundation, 1993); Blanning, *The Culture of Power,* 251–52; J. I. Israel, *Radical Enlightenment: Philosophy and the Making of Modernity, 1650–1750* (Oxford: Oxford University Press, 2001), esp. 275–94, 684–703; J. Champion, *Republican Learning: John Toland and the Crisis of Christian Culture, 1696–1722* (Manchester: Manchester University Press, 2003), 45–68; M. C. Jacob, *The Radical Enlightenment: Pantheists, Freemasons and Republicans* (London: George Allen and Unwin, 1981), 182–208. For fireworks, see S. Werrett, "Explosive Affinities: Pyrotechnic Knowledge in Early Modern Europe," in *Making Knowledge in Early Modern Europe: Practices, Objects, and Texts, 1400–1800,* ed. P. Smith and B. Schmidt (Chicago: University of Chicago Press, 2007), 68–69.

14   Marquis de Condorcet, "Fragments concerning Freedom of the Press," extracts trans. A. Goldhammer, in *Daedalus* 131, no. 2 (Spring 2002): 57–59.

15   C. Hesse, *Publishing and Cultural Politics in Revolutionary Paris, 1789–1810* (Berkeley: University of California Press, 1991); C. Hesse, "Economic Upheavals in Publishing," in *Revolution in Print: The Press in France 1775–1800,* ed. R. Darnton and D. Roche (Berkeley: University of California Press, 1989), 69–97; G. S. Brown, "After the Fall: The *chute* of a Play, *droits d'auteur,* and Literary Property in the Old Regime," *French Historical Studies* 22, no. 4 (Fall 1999): 465–91. See also (but with caution) J. Boncompain,

La Révolution des Auteurs: Naissance de la Propriété Intellectuelle (1773–1815) (Paris: Fayard, 2001).

16 The standard discussion of this topic is M. Woodmansee, "Genius and the Copyright," in her *The Author, Art, and the Market: Rereading the History of Aesthetics* (New York: Columbia University Press, 1994), 35–55. Woodmansee is currently writing a book that will give the definitive account of these debates. In the meantime, see also A. Johns, "The Piratical Enlightenment," in *This Is Enlightenment,* ed. C. Siskin and W. Warner (Chicago: University of Chicago Press, forthcoming). The best brief introduction to *Naturphilosophie* in English is N. Jardine, "*Naturphilosophie* and the Kingdoms of Nature," in *Cultures of Natural History,* ed. N. Jardine, J. A. Secord, and E. C. Spary (Cambridge: Cambridge University Press, 1996), 230–45. The best introduction to book piracy in Germany in this period is Reinhard Wittmann, "Highwaymen or Heroes of Enlightenment? Viennese and South German Pirates and the German Market" (paper presented at the conference "The History of Books and Intellectual History," Princeton University, 2004), available at www.princeton.edu/ csb/conferences/december_2004/papers/Wittman_Paper.doc.

17 J. Schmidt, ed., *What Is Enlightenment? Eighteenth-Century Answers and Twentieth-Century Questions* (Berkeley: University of California Press, 1996).

18 I. Kant, "On the wrongfulness of unauthorized publication of books," in his *Practical Philosophy,* ed. M. J. Gregor and A. Wood (Cambridge: Cambridge University Press, 1996), 23–35. E. [*sic*] Kant, *Essays and treatises on moral, political, and various philosophical subjects,* trans. J. Richardson, 2 vols. (London [Altenburg?]: for the translator, 1798), I:225–39. Kant later reiterated the argument in his "Metaphysics of Morals," in *Practical Philosophy,* 437–38.

4 EXPERIMENTING WITH PRINT

1 A. Cowley, "To the Royal Society," in T. Sprat, *The History of the Royal Society of London* (London: J. Martyn and J. Allestrey, 1667), sig. B2^{r}.

2 See, for example, N. Jardine, *The Birth of History and Philosophy of Science: Kepler's "A Defence of Tycho against Ursus" with Essays on Its Provenance and Significance* (Cambridge: Cambridge University Press, 1984), and P. Dear, *Discipline and Experience: The Mathematical Way in the Scientific Revolution* (Chicago: University of Chicago Press, 1995), 93–123.

3 S. Shapin and S. J. Schaffer, *Leviathan and the Air-Pump: Hobbes, Boyle, and the Experimental Life* (Princeton, N.J.: Princeton University Press, 1985), 22–79.

4 A. Blair, "Reading Strategies for Coping with Information Overload, ca. 1550–1700," *Journal of the History of Ideas* 64 (2003): 11–28.

5 R. Hooke, *The Posthumous Works of Robert Hooke,* ed. R. Waller (London: S. Smith and B. Walford, 1705), 18–19, 24, 34–36, 63–65, 139–40; L. Mulligan, "Robert Hooke's 'Memoranda': Memory and Natural History," *Annals of Science* 49 (1992): 47–61, esp. 50–53.

6 There is now an extensive literature on this subject, but see especially S. Shapin, *A Social History of Truth: Civility and Science in Seventeenth-Century England* (Chicago: University of Chicago Press, 1994); S. Shapin, "The House of Experiment in Seventeenth-Century England," *Isis* 79 (1988): 373–404; M. Biagioli, "Etiquette, Interdependence, and Sociability in Seventeenth-Century Science," *Critical Inquiry* 22 (1996): 193–238; M. Biagioli, "Knowledge, Freedom and Brotherly Love: Homosociability and the Accademia dei Lincei," *Configurations* 3 (1995): 139–66; M. Biagioli, *Galileo, Courtier: The Practice of Science in the Culture of Absolutism* (Chicago: University of Chicago Press, 1993).

7 Compare the remarks in D. F. McKenzie, "Speech-Manuscript-Print," in *New Directions in Textual Studies,* ed. D. Oliphant and R. Bradford (Austin, Tex.: Harry Ransom Humanities Research Center, 1990), 87–109, and R. Chartier "Leisure and Sociability: Reading Aloud in Early Modern Europe," trans. C. Mossman, in *Urban Life in the Renaissance,* ed. S. Zimmerman and R. F. E. Wiessman (London and Toronto: Associated University Presses, 1989), 103–20.

8 E.g., H. Longino, *Science as Social Knowledge* (Princeton, N.J.: Princeton University Press, 1990), 62–132; L. Daston, "Baconian Facts, Academic Civility, and the Prehistory of Objectivity," *Annals of Scholarship* 8 (1991): 337–63; L. Daston, "The Ideal and Reality of the Republic of Letters in the Enlightenment," *Science in Context* 4 (1991): 367–86.

9 E. Tyson, *Phocaena, Or the Anatomy of a Porpess, Dissected at Gresham College* (London: B. Tooke, 1680), sig. A2^{r-v}; compare (among many other examples) A. M[ullen], *An Anatomical Account of the Elephant accidentally burnt in Dublin* (London: S. Smith, 1682), 3; W. Petty, *The Discourse made before the Royal Society . . . Concerning the Use of Duplicate Proportion* (London: J. Martyn, 1674), sigs. A3^r–A4^r, A8^{r-v}; and C. Havers, *Osteologia Nova* (London: S. Smith, 1691), sigs. A3^r–A4^v.

10 A. Johns, *The Nature of the Book: Print and Knowledge in the Making* (Chicago: University of Chicago Press, 1998), 475–91.

11 E.g., T. Birch, ed., *The History of the Royal Society of London,* 4 vols. (London: A Millar, 1756–57), 1:487. The pursuit of conversation in weeks following a perusal report was expressly recommended by the Society in 1674, because such reports were becoming technical enough to preclude immediate responses: Birch, *History,* III:153.

12 For remarks on registration and civility see Shapin, *Social History of Truth,* 302–4.

13 Royal Society Cl.P. XX, fol. 92^r.

14 Johns, *Nature of the Book,* ch. 7, 489; A. Johns, "Miscellaneous Methods: Authors, Societies and Journals in Early Modern England," *British Journal for the History of Science* 33 (2000): 159–86.

15 M. Knights, *Representation and Misrepresentation in Later Stuart Britain* (Oxford: Oxford University Press, 2005), 272–334; D. Freist, *Governed by Opinion: Politics, Religion and the Dynamics of Communication in Stuart London, 1637–1645* (London: Tauris, 1997); J. Raymond, *Pamphlets and Pamphleteering in Early Modern Britain* (Cambridge: Cambridge University Press, 2003), 331–55.

16 For Hooke's controversy, see R. C. Iliffe, "'In the Warehouse': Privacy, Property and Priority in the Early Royal Society," *History of Science,* 30 (1992): 29–68; for another example, see G. S[inclair], *The Hydrostaticks* (Edinburgh: printed by G. Swintoun, J. Glen, and T. Brown, 1672), 146, and the separately paginated *Vindication of the Preface* appended to this volume, esp. 4–8.

17 Birch, *History,* II:501; III:1–3.

18 Iliffe, "'In the Warehouse.'"

19 Birch, *History,* III:4, 9, 20.

20 Birch, *History,* III:10–15.

21 Birch, *History,* III:16, 18–19, 52, 63.

22 Birch, *History,* III:318; S. J. Schaffer, "Glass Works: Newton's Prisms and the Uses of Experiment," in *The Uses of Experiment: Studies in the Natural Sciences,* ed. D. Gooding, T. Pinch, and S. J. Schaffer (Cambridge: Cambridge University Press, 1989), 67–104, esp. 85.

23 Birch, *History,* III:269. In fact, Hooke bought Grimaldi's tract only in 1679: H. W. Robison and W. Adams, eds., *The Diary of Robert Hooke . . . 1672–1680* (London: Taylor & Francis, 1935), 417.

24 Birch, *History,* III:278–79.

25 R. S. Westfall, *Never at Rest: A Biography of Isaac Newton* (Cambridge: Cambridge University Press, 1980), 274–80, 310; Schaffer, "Glass Works," 89–91.

26 I. Newton *The Correspondence of Isaac Newton,* ed. H. W. Turnbull, J. F. Scott, A. R. Hall, and L. Tilling, 7 vols. (Cambridge: Cambridge University Press, 1959–77), 1:317–19, 328–29, 358–65.

27 Johns, "Miscellaneous Methods," 182–83; Johns, *Nature of the Book,* 521–31; Birch, *History,* IV:196; R. T. Gunther, *Early Science in Oxford,* 15 vols. (Oxford: for the subscribers, 1923–67), 7:434–36.

28 Birch, *History,* IV:347, 480; I. Newton, *The Principia,* trans. I. B. Cohen and A. Whitman (Berkeley: University of California Press, 1999), 11–13; D. B. Meli, *Equivalence and Priority: Newton versus Leibniz* (Oxford: Clarendon Press, 1993), 95–125; A. R. Hall, *Philosophers at War: The Quarrel bewteen Newton and Leibniz* (Cambridge: Cambridge University Press, 1980); Johns, *Nature of the Book,* ch. 8; R. C. Iliffe, "'Is He like Other Men?'"

The Meaning of the *Principia Mathematica*, and the Author as Idol," in *Culture and Society in the Stuart Restoration: Literature, Drama, History*, ed. G. MacLean (Cambridge: Cambridge University Press, 1995), 159–76.

29 The most famous example is F. E. Manuel, *A Portrait of Isaac Newton* (Cambridge, Mass.: Harvard University Press, 1968), e.g., 141–42, 156, 159; but in less thoroughgoing terms the tendency remains prevalent in many studies of Newton.

30 P. Pellison, *The History of the French Academy* (London: by J. Streater for T. Johnson, 1657), 6–7.

31 The *Mechanick Exercises* was published in 1678–80, and revived in 1683; the *Collection of letters* ran from 1681 to 1684.

32 Birch, *History*, I:116, 391, 397; Royal Society, Journal Book X, 444.

33 H. Oldenburg, *The Correspondence of Henry Oldenburg*, ed. A. R. and M. B. Hall, 13 vols. (Madison: University of Wisconsin Press; London: Mansell; London: Taylor and Francis, 1968–86), IV:525–6 and Birch, *History*, II:306 (for Wallis); Birch, *History*, II:231 (for one Alexander Marshal declining to reveal his craft knowledge of pigments—"they are pretty secrets, but known, they are nothing").

34 Iliffe, "'In the Warehouse'," 41–52.

35 R. E. W. Maddison, "Studies in the Life of Robert Boyle, F.R.S. Part II: Salt Water Freshened," *Notes and Records of the Royal Society* 9 (1952): 196–216, esp. 197.

36 "Tracts consisting of observations about the saltness of the sea," in R. Boyle, *The Works of Robert Boyle*, ed. M. Hunter and E. B. Davis, 14 vols. (London: Pickering and Chatto, 1999–2000), VII:390–412, esp. 400–401; Maddison, "Salt Water Freshened."

37 E.g., "Salt-water sweetned," in Boyle, *Works*, IX:425–37; *The Supplement to a small treatise called Salt-water sweetned* (London: printed by J. Harefinch, n.d.), separately paginated "Conditions."

38 *The case of Mr. Walcot* (n.p., n.d.).

39 H. Walcot, *Sea-water made fresh and wholsome* (London: for R. Parker, 1702), 2, 7.

40 Maddison, "Salt Water Freshened," 206; Boyle, *Works*, III:362.

41 See W. Eamon, *Science and the Secrets of Nature: Books of Secrets in Medieval and Early Modern Culture* (Princeton, N.J.: Princeton University Press, 1994), 234–35.

42 Maddison, "Salt Water Freshened," esp. 206; S. Hales, *Philosophical experiments: containing useful, and necessary instructions for such as undertake long voyages at sea* (London: for W. Innys and R. Manby, and T. Woodward, 1739), xx.

43 Hales, *Philosophical experiments*, xvi.

44 Walcot, *Sea-water made fresh and wholsome*, 14–18.

45 Maddison, "Salt Water Freshened."

46 For the aerial nitre, see R. G. Frank, *Harvey and the Oxford Physiologists: Scientific Ideas and Social Interaction* (Berkeley: University of California Press, 1980), 115–39, 221–74.

47 [N. Grew], *New experiments, and useful observations concerning sea-water made fresh* (n.p., 1683).

48 Hales, *Philosophical experiments,* xi–xii, xix–xx.

49 Birch, *History,* III:456–7, 475, 478, 480, 487, 489, 490–91, 492–93, 497; W. LeFanu, *Nehemiah Grew M.D., F.R.S.: A Study and Bibliography of His Writings* (Winchester: St. Paul's Bibliographies, 1990), 17–18, 20–23, 36, 44–48; T. Guidott, *De Thermis Britannicis tractatus* (London: F. Leach, for the author, 1691), 63–64; B. Allen, *The natural history of the chalybeat and purging waters of England* (London: printed and sold by S. Smith and B. Walford, 1699), 92–94, 122–28; S. Du Clos, *Observations on the mineral waters of France* (London: for H. Faithorne and J. Kersey, 1684).

50 W. R. Newman, *Atoms and Alchemy: Chymistry and the Experimental Origins of the Scientific Revolution* (Chicago: University of Chicago Press, 2006), ix. See, in general, A. M. Roos, *The Salt of the Earth: Natural Philosophy, Medicine, and Chymistry in England, 1650–1750* (Leiden: Brill, 2007).

51 See, canonically, Shapin and Schaffer, *Leviathan and the Air-Pump.*

52 Birch, *History,* III:370–71, 464, 509.

53 Frank, *Harvey and the Oxford Physiologists,* 124–28; B. B. Kaplan, *"Divulging of useful truths in physick": The Medical Agenda of Robert Boyle* (Baltimore: Johns Hopkins University Press, 1993), 86–91.

54 N. Grew, *A Discourse made before the Royal Society, . . . concerning the nature, causes, and power of mixture* (London: printed for J. Martyn, 1675), 21–24, 29–30, 42–43, 48–51, 55–56, 58, 65–67, 69–72, 89–90, 98–100; N. Grew, *Experiments in consort of the luctation arising from the affusion of several menstruums upon all sorts of bodies* (London: printed for J. Martyn, 1678), 114, 116.

55 Grew, *Discourse,* 113–14.

5 PHARMACEUTICAL PIRACY AND
THE ORIGINS OF MEDICAL PATENTING

1 J. P. Ward, *Metropolitan Communities: Trade Guilds, Identity, and Change in Early Modern London* (Stanford, Calif.: Stanford University Press, 1997), 53–55.

2 M. Ford, "Love and Theft," *London Review of Books,* December 2, 2004.

3 For accounts of selling patent medicines through the book-trade network in early national America, see Isaiah Thomas Papers, American Antiquarian Society, 4:1; 4:2.

4 For Grew, see W. LeFanu, *Nehemiah Grew M.D., F.R.S.: A Study and Bibliography of His Writings* (Winchester: St. Paul's Bibliographies, 1990).

5   J. Peter, *Truth in opposition to ignorant and malicious falshood* (London: printed by J.D. for the author, 1701), 24.

6   B. Allen, *The natural history of the chalybeat and purging waters of England* (London: printed and sold by S. Smith and B. Walford, 1699), 7; S. Du Clos, *Observations on the mineral waters of France* (London: for H. Faithorne and J. Kersey, 1684), 3, 106–7; E. Jorden, *A Discourse of naturall bathes, and minerall waters*, 3rd ed. (London: printed by T. Harper, sold by M. Sparke, 1633), 115–25. In general, see L. Daston and K. Park, *Wonders and the Order of Nature, 1150–1750* (New York: Zone, 1998), 137–44.

7   Jorden, *Discourse*, 42; N. G. Coley, "'Cures without Care': 'Chymical Physicians' and Mineral Waters in Seventeenth-Century English Medicine," *Medical History* 23 (1979): 191–214, esp. 198, 205.

8   For Sylvius, see P. Smith, *The Body of the Artisan: Art and Experience in the Scientific Revolution* (Chicago: University of Chicago Press, 2004), 183–236.

9   N. Grew, *A Treatise of the nature and use of the Bitter Purging Salt*, trans. J. Bridges (London: printed by J. Darby, for W. Kettilby, 1697), 1–4, 32–33.

10 N. Grew, *Tractatus de salis cathartici amari in aquis Ebeshamensibus* (London: for S. Smith and B. Walford, 1695). For the tangled bibliographic history of this work, see LeFanu, *Nehemiah Grew*, 49–52, 135–42.

11 Grew, *Treatise*, xiv.

12 M. Hunter, *The Royal Society and Its Fellows*, 2nd ed. (Stanford, UK: BSHS, 1994), 75, 216.

13 Peter, *Truth in opposition to ignorant and malicious falshood*, 58, reprinting advertisement from the *London Gazette*.

14 Grew, *Treatise*, vi–ix.

15 Grew, *Treatise*, v–vi, 85–88.

16 Grew, *Treatise*, 62, 69, 78, 80–81, 83; [D. or T. Coxe], *A Discourse, wherein the interest of the patient in reference to physick and physicians is soberly debated* (London: for C.R., 1669), 18. (It is unclear whether the author of this tract was Thomas or Daniel Coxe.)

17 N. Grew, *The Comparative anatomy of trunks* (London: by J.M. for W. Kettilby, 1675), dedication to Viscount Brouncker (sigs. A5^r–A1^v); Peter, *Truth in opposition to ignorant and malicious falshood*, viii, 2.

18 Peter, *Truth in opposition to ignorant and malicious falshood*, 54–60.

19 A. Johns, "When Authorship Met Authenticity," *Nature* 451 (February 28, 2008): 1058–59.

20 Peter, *Truth in opposition to ignorant and malicious falshood*, 19.

21 Peter, *Truth in opposition to ignorant and malicious falshood*, 24–25, 47–48, 51, 54–55. That death by adulteration was a real possibility is attested by a mid-nineteenth-century tombstone to be found in Eshaness, the Shetland Islands, which reads: "Donald Robertson, born 14th January 1785. Died 14th June aged 63. He was a peaceable, quiet man, and to all appearances a sincere Christian. His death was much regretted which was caused by the

stupidity of Laurence Tulloch of Clothister (Sullom) who sold him nitre instead of Epsom Salts by which he was killed in the space of five hours after taking a dose of it." C. Davies, "Search for Britain's Most Remarkable Epitaph," *Daily Telegraph,* July 24, 2007.

22 Peter, *Truth in opposition to ignorant and malicious falshood,* 26.

23 Peter, *Truth in opposition to ignorant and malicious falshood,* 22–23.

24 Peter, *Truth in opposition to ignorant and malicious falshood,* iv, 2–18.

25 Peter, *Truth in opposition to ignorant and malicious falshood,* 27–29, 32–33.

26 Peter, *Truth in opposition to ignorant and malicious falshood,* 47–48, 51.

27 W. Eamon, *Science and the Secrets of Nature: Books of Secrets in Medieval and Early Modern Culture* (Princeton, N.J.: Princeton University Press, 1994). For Boyle's exchanges, see M. Hunter, "The Reluctant Philanthropist: Robert Boyle and the 'Communication of Secrets and Receits in Physick,'" in *Religio Medici: Medicine and Religion in Seventeenth-Century England,* ed. O. P. Grell and A. Cunningham (Aldershot: Scolar Press, 1996), 247–72.

28 J. W. Estes, "The European Reception of the First Drugs from the New World," *Pharmacy in History* 37, no. 1 (1995): 3–23, esp. 7, 15.

29 R. Palmer, "Pharmacy in the Republic of Venice," in *The Medical Renaissance of the Sixteenth Century,* ed. A. Wear, R. K. French, and I. M. Lonie (Cambridge: Cambridge University Press, 1985), 100–117, esp. 106, 117; also 307.

30 B. Woodcroft, ed., *Abridgments of Specifications Relating to Medicine, Surgery, and Dentistry,* 2nd ed. (London: Office of the Commissioners of Patents for Inventions, 1872), 1–2; B. Woodcroft, ed., *Abridgments of Specifications Relating to Brewing, Wine-Making, and Distilling Alcoholic Liquids* (London: Office of the Commissioners of Patents for Inventions, 1881), 1–5. It is worth noting that these publications were themselves in part contributions to a later debate on the moral, economic, and scientific value of patenting, described in chapter 10 below.

31 P. Vergil, *On Discovery,* ed. and trans. B. P. Copenhaver (Cambridge, Mass.: Harvard University Press, 2002), 159.

32 M. Pelling, *Medical Conflicts in Early Modern London: Patronage, Physicians, and Irregular Practitioners, 1550–1640* (Oxford: Clarendon Press, 2003), 10. See also the marvelous evocation of this culture two generations earlier in D. Harkness, *The Jewel House: Elizabethan London and the Scientific Revolution* (New Haven, Conn.: Yale University Press, 2007), 57–96.

33 Pelling, *Medical Conflicts,* is a brilliant analysis of this situation.

34 [Coxe], *Discourse,* 50–51.

35 [Coxe], *Discourse,* 12, 46.

36 P. Hunting, *A History of the Society of Apothecaries* (London: Society of Apothecaries, 1998), 14, 23, 45–7.

37 Hunting, *History of the Society of Apothecaries,* 48.

38 E. W. Stieb, "Drug Adulteration and Its Detection, in the Writings of Theophrastus, Dioscorides, and Pliny," *Journal mondiale de pharmacie* 2 (1958): 117–34, esp. 121. In general, see E. W. Stieb, *Drug Adulteration: Detection and Control in Nineteenth-Century Britain* (Madison: University of Wisconsin Press, 1966), 3–50.

39 A. P. Favre, *De la sophistication des substances médicamenteuses, et des moyens de la reconnaitre* (Paris: D. Colas and A. P. Favre, 1812), x–xi.

40 R. Porter and D. Porter, "The Rise of the English Drugs Industry: The Role of Thomas Corbyn," *Medical History* 33 (1989): 277–95, esp. 293–94.

41 Peter, *Truth in opposition to ignorant and malicious falshood*, 37.

42 B. B. Kaplan, *"Divulging of useful truths in physick": The Medical Agenda of Robert Boyle* (Baltimore: Johns Hopkins University Press, 1993), 130–31; A. Wear, *Knowledge and Practice in English Medicine, 1550–1680* (Cambridge: Cambridge University Press, 2000), 384–87.

43 G. Sonnedecker, "The Founding Period of the U.S. Pharmacopeia: I," *Pharmacy in History* 35, no. 4 (1993): 151–62, esp. 153.

44 *Pharmacopoeia Londinensis* (London: for J. Marriot, 1618), [216] (note that Marriot took care to have his privilege printed among the introductory materials of the volume too); B. Wolley, *Heal Thyself: Nicholas Culpeper and the Seventeenth-Century Struggle to Bring Medicine to the People* (New York: HarperCollins, 2004).

45 Compare C. Merrett, *A Short view of the frauds, and abuses committed by apothecaries* (London: printed for J. Allestry, Printer to the Royal Society, 1669), 9.

46 See, in general, Stieb, *Drug Adulteration*, 3–34.

47 [Coxe], *Discourse*, 26; Grew, *Treatise*, title page; L. M. Beier, "Experience and Experiment: Robert Hooke, Illness, and Medicine," in *Robert Hooke: New Studies*, ed. M. Hunter and S. J. Schaffer (Woodbridge, UK: Boydell, 1989), 235–51.

48 [Coxe], *Discourse*, 55–56.

49 N. Biggs, *Mataeotechnia Medicinae Praxeos. The vanity of the craft of physick* (London: for G. Calvert, 1650/1651), 97.

50 R. Boyle, *The Works of Robert Boyle*, ed. M. Hunter and E. B. Davis, 14 vols. (London: Pickering and Chatto, 1999–2000), XI, xxxv, 198–280 (esp. 219–29); M. Hunter, "Boyle versus the Galenists: A Suppressed Critique of Seventeenth-Century Medical Practice and Its Significance," *Medical History* 41 (1997): 322–61; Merrett, *Short view*, 9.

51 [Coxe], *Discourse*, 24, 28; Merrett, *Short view*, 13; Grew, *Treatise*, v–vi. For other references to "knacks," see, e.g., [H. Stubbe], *Lex talionis* (London: printed, and are to be sold by M. Pitt, 1670), 3, 6, 10.

52 [Coxe], *Discourse*, "234"–"235." (This work has discontinuous pagination; quotation marks indicate that I have used the printed page numbers even where they were out of sequence.)

53   [Coxe], *Discourse,* sig. A4^r, 14, "271"–"272," "284"–"285"; cf. also 29, on "superannuated Medicines which are fit for the dunghill."

54   [Stubbe], *Lex talionis,* 2, 18–19, 32.

55   Biggs, *Mataeotechnia Medicinae Praxeos,* 23–24, 31.

56   Biggs, *Mataeotechnia Medicinae Praxeos,* 20–21.

57   Biggs, *Mataeotechnia Medicinae Praxeos,* 9.

58   [Coxe], *Discourse,* 80–81, "199," "256"–"261," "272." Compare Stubbe's reply in *Lex talionis,* 11 and passim.

59   Merrett, *Short view,* 34–36; [Coxe], *Discourse,* 62, "218"–"219."

60   For its problems in this effort, and how they led another practitioner into Grub Street practices, see H. J. Cook, *Trials of an Ordinary Doctor: Johannes Groenevelt in Seventeenth-Century London* (Baltimore: Johns Hopkins University Press, 1994), 14–23, 143–57, 202–3.

61   H. J. Cook, *The Decline of the Old Medical Regime in Stuart London* (Ithaca, N.Y.: Cornell University Press, 1986), 246–53.

62   Cook, *Decline,* 250.

63   R. Porter, *Health for Sale: Quackery in England, 1660–1850* (Manchester: Manchester University Press, 1989), 24, 36.

6   OF EPICS AND ORRERIES

1   T. Harris, *Revolution: The Great Crisis of the British Monarchy, 1685–1720* (London: Allen Lane, 2006), 290–302; S. Pincus, *England's Glorious Revolution* (Boston: Bedford/St. Martin's, 2006); J. P. Kenyon, *Revolution Principles: The Politics of Party, 1689–1720* (Cambridge: Cambridge University Press, 1977); *More reasons humbly offer'd . . . for securing property of copies of books to the rightful owners thereof,* (Wing M2714A, c. 1698).

2   J. Boswell, *The decision of the court of session, upon the question of literary property* (Edinburgh: J. Donaldson, for A. Donaldson, 1774), 31.

3   C. Blagden's classic *The Notebook of Thomas Bennet and Henry Clements (1686–1719) with Some Aspects of Book Trade Practice,* Oxford Bibliographical Society, n.s., 6 (Oxford: Oxford Bibliographical Society Publications, 1953 [1956]) contains details on personnel, e.g., in appendixes 12–14.

4   D. Harkness, *The Jewel House: Elizabethan London and the Scientific Revolution* (New Haven, Conn.: Yale University Press, 2007).

5   C. Muldrew, *The Economy of Obligation: The Culture of Credit and Social Relations in Early Modern England* (New York: St. Martin's, 1998), 315–33; J. Hoppit, *A Land of Liberty? England, 1689–1727* (Oxford: Oxford University Press, 2000), 334–38; L. Melville, *The South Sea Bubble* (London: D. O'Connor, 1921), 57; V. Cowles, *The Great Swindle: The Story of the South Sea Bubble* (London: Collins, 1960), 126; J. Carswell, *The South Sea Bubble* (London: Cresset, 1960), 156n.

6   Blagden, *Notebook,* 67–100.

7 R. B. Sher, *The Enlightenment and the Book: Scottish Authors and Their Publishers in Eighteenth-Century Britain, Ireland, and America* (Chicago: University of Chicago Press, 2006), 26; J. Feather, *Publishing, Piracy and Politics: An Historical Study of Copyright in Britain* (London: Mansell, 1994), 65; Blagden, *Notebook,* 97.

8 Blagden, *Notebook,* 76, 86, 91n; T. Belanger, "Booksellers' Trade Sales, 1718–1768," *The Library,* 5th ser., 30 (1975): 281–302; W. St. Clair, *The Reading Nation in the Romantic Period* (Cambridge: Cambridge University Press, 2004), 93–102. St. Clair provides eye-opening quantitative data on the cultural effects of this "high monopoly period."

9 J. How, *Some thoughts on the present state of printing and bookselling* (London: n.p., 1709), 16; [D. Defoe], *An essay on the regulation of the press* (London: n p., 1704), 19–21; [J. Addison], *The thoughts of a Tory author, concerning the press* (London: for A. Baldwin, 1712), 6; *Tatler* 101 (November 29–December 1, 1709); [D. Defoe], "Miscellanea," *A Review of the state of the British nation* 6, no. 91 (November 3, 1709).

10 M. Rose, *Authors and Owners: The Invention of Copyright* (Cambridge, Mass.: Harvard University Press, 1993), 36, 42–47.

11 Feather, *Publishing, Piracy and Politics,* 68–69. For the counterpart strategy among patentees, see C. MacLeod, *Inventing the Industrial Revolution: The English Patent System, 1660–1800* (Cambridge: Cambridge University Press, 1988), 59.

12 A. I. Macinnes, *Union and Empire: The Making of the United Kingdom in 1707* (Cambridge: Cambridge University Press, 2007); K. Bowie, *Scottish Public Opinion and the Anglo-Scottish Union, 1699–1707* (Woodbridge, Suffolk: Boydell/Royal Historical Society, 2007); Hoppit, *Land of Liberty,* 252–57.

13 The "three kingdoms" problem—that of reigning over three distinct realms, England, Scotland, and Ireland, with discrete and often irreconcilable interests—was in the 1990s often identified as the basic cause of the mid-seventeenth-century upheavals. See, for example, C. Russell, *The Fall of the British Monarchies, 1637–1642* (Oxford: Oxford University Press, 1991).

14 R. Foulis to [William Murray], December 20, 1754: D. W. Nichol, *Pope's Literary Legacy: The Book-Trade Correspondence of William Warburton and John Knapton with Other Letters and Documents, 1744–1780* (Oxford: Oxford Bibliographical Society, 1992), 105–6.

15 A. Smith, *An Inquiry into the Nature and Causes of the Wealth of Nations,* ed. R. H. Campbell, A. S. Skinner, and W. B. Todd, 2 vols. (Oxford: Oxford University Press, 1976), 2:630 (IV.vii.c.89).

16 W. McDougall, "Gavin Hamilton, John Balfour and Patrick Neill: A Study of Publishing in Edinburgh in the 18th Century" (Ph.D. thesis, University of Edinburgh, 1974), 117, 120.

17 *The pleadings of the counsel before the House of Lords, in the great cause concern-*

ing literary property (London: for C. Wilkin, S. Axtell, J. Axtell, and J. Browne, [1774]), 3; *A Letter to a Member of Parliament concerning the bill now depending in the House of Commons, for making more effectual an act in the 8th year of the reign of Queen Anne* (broadside, n.p., n.d. [1735]); *Tonson v. Collins* (Trin. 1 Geo. III, KB, and Mich. 2 Geo. III, KB: 1 Black. W. 301, 322), 342.

18   J. M. Vaughn, "The Politics of Empire: Metropolitan Socio-Political Development and the Imperial Transformation of the British East India Company, 1675–1775" (Ph.D. diss., University of Chicago, 2008), ch. 3.

19   [W. Warburton], *A letter from an author, to a member of Parliament, concerning Literary Property* (London: for J. and P. Knapton, 1747), 5; F. Hargrave, *An argument in defence of literary property* (London: for the author, 1774), 28–29; *A letter from an Author to a member of parliament,* (London, April 17, 1735; John Johnson Collection, Oxford).

20   Hargrave, *Argument,* 32.

21   McDougall, "Gavin Hamilton," 124–25.

22   Feather, *Publishing, Piracy and Politics,* 72–74.

23   *Memorial for the booksellers of Edinburgh and Glasgow* (n.p., n.d.) [*Midwinter v. Hamilton,* c. 1748], 3.

24   Sher, *Enlightenment and the Book,* 275–94; W. McDougall, "Copyright Litigation in the Court of Session, 1738–1749, and the Rise of the Scottish Book Trade," *Edinburgh Bibliographical Society Transactions* 5, no. 5 (1985–87): 2–31, esp. 23, 25.

25   McDougall, "Copyright Litigation," 6–8.

26   [J. Maclaurin, Lord Dreghorn], *Considerations on the Nature and Origin of Literary Property* (n.p.: printed for Robert Taylor, 1768 [orig. 1767]), 26.

27   McDougall, "Copyright Litigation," 14–22.

28   Nichol, *Pope's Literary Legacy,* 43–45.

29   [A. Donaldson], *Some thoughts on the state of literary property* (London: for A. Donaldson, 1764), 11–17.

30   Rose, *Authors and Owners,* 74–78; [Dreghorn], *Considerations,* 27; Feather, *Publishing, Piracy and Politics,* 83–84.

31   Sher, *Enlightenment and the Book,* 312–18.

32   [Donaldson], *Some thoughts,* 3–4, 11–17, 19–20.

33   [Donaldson], *Some thoughts,* 9–10, 17–19; [Dreghorn], *Considerations,* 1–2.

34   [Donaldson], *Some thoughts,* 7–8, 24.

35   Feather, *Publishing, Piracy and Politics,* 87–88.

36   *Information for Alexander Donaldson* [et al.] (n.p., 1773), 5; *Speeches or arguments of the judges of the Court of King's Bench . . . in the cause Millar against Taylor* (Leith: for W. Coke, 1771); see esp. appendix, 113–28.

37   *Information for Alexander Donaldson* (1773), 16.

38   The principal modern authority on these debates is Rose, *Authors and Owners,* which is to be preferred to R. Deazley, *On the Origin of the Right to Copy: Charting the Movement of Copyright Law in Eighteenth-Century Britain*

(1695–1775) (London: Hart, 2004). I have a paper in preparation on evidence and history in the literary property debates.

39 L. R. Stewart, *The Rise of Public Science: Rhetoric, Technology, and Natural Philosophy in Newtonian Britain, 1660–1750* (Cambridge: Cambridge University Press, 1992), 260–68. For the origins of this profession in the German lands, see T. Nummedal, *Alchemy and Authority in the Holy Roman Empire* (Chicago: University of Chicago Press, 2007), e.g., 63.

40 [Donaldson], *Some thoughts,* 8 (my italics). Compare earlier Scottish claims that the Act of Anne was intended to create a standardized version of a patents regime, e.g., in *Memorial for the Booksellers of Edinburgh and Glasgow,* 2; cf. [Dreghorn], *Considerations,* 26.

41 *A Vindication of the Exclusive Right of Authors to their own Works: A subject now under consideration before the Twelve Judges of England* (London: printed for R. Griffiths, 1762), 8–9. Blackstone's comment is in *Tonson v. Collins,* 344; compare *Information for Mess. John Hinton* (1773), 10–11.

42 *A Letter to a Member of Parliament.*

43 *Information for Alexander Donaldson* (1773), 12.

44 J. Burrow, *The question concerning literary property, determined by the Court of King's Bench on 20th April, 1769, in the cause between Andrew Millar and Robert Taylor* (London: by W. Strahan and M. Woodfall, for B. Tovey, 1773), 70, 101–2.

45 *Tonson v. Collins,* 307.

46 Boswell, *Decision,* 15, 23–24, 33.

47 "Gentleman," *The cases of the appellants and respondents in the cause of literary property* (London: for J. Bew, W. Clarke, P. Brett. C. Wilkin, 1774), 9.

48 [Warburton], *Letter from an author,* 6–11.

49 P. Dear, *Discipline and Experience: The Mathematical Way in the Scientific Revolution* (Chicago: University of Chicago Press, 1995), 151–79.

50 [Warburton], *Letter from an author,* 12–13.

51 *An enquiry into the nature and origin of literary property* (London: for W. Flexney, 1762), 22–23; *Tonson v. Collins,* 307–8; *Information for Alexander Donaldson* (1773), 23.

52 Burrow, *Question concerning literary property,* 35, 56.

53 *Vindication of the Exclusive Right of Authors,* 8–10.

54 *Enquiry into the nature and origin of literary property,* 22–24.

55 *The Microcosm: Or, The World in Miniature* (n.p., n.d.); E. Davies, *A Succinct Description of that Elaborate and Matchless pile of Art, called, the Microcosm* (Newcastle: by I. Thompson, for E. Davies, n.d.); S. J. Schaffer, "Enlightened Automata," in *The Sciences in Enlightened Europe,* ed. W. Clark, J. Golinski, and S. Schaffer (Chicago: University of Chicago Press, 1999), 126–65, esp. 146–47; A. Chapuis and E. Droz, *Automata* (New York: Central Book Company, 1958), 128–31.

56   *A description of several pieces of mechanism, invented by the Sieur Jacquet Droz* (n.p., n.d.).

57   A. Chapuis and E. Gélis, *Le monde des Automates*, 2 vols. (Paris: E. Gélis, 1928), 2:227–42; Chapuis and Droz, *Automata*, 289–314; D. Brewster, "Androides," in *Edinburgh Encyclopaedia*, 18 vols. (Edinburgh: for W. Blackwood et al., 1830), 2:62–67; Schaffer, "Enlightened Automata."

58   *Enquiry into the nature and origin of literary property*, 25–27; *Information for Alexander Donaldson* (1773), 23. Cf. *Tonson v. Collins*, 307–8, 310, 339–40, 343–44.

59   *Tonson v. Collins*, 343.

60   *Tonson v. Collins*, 344; Boswell, *Decision*, 18–19.

61   [Warburton], *Letter from an author*, 10; *Pleadings of the counsel*, 9, 24–25; *Tonson v. Collins*, 310; Boswell, *Decision*, 20, 23–24; Burrow, *Question concerning literary property*, 56. The booksellers' statement is "The Mode and Manner of Printing Books," appended to *House of Lords. The Case of the Respondents* [in the appeal of *Donaldson v. Becket*] (italics in the original). Among the doubters was Kames, who insisted that copying books was virtuous too.

62   "Gentleman," *Cases of the appellants and respondents*, 6; *Pleadings of the counsel*, 7, 34; Boswell, *Decision*, 18–19.

63   Rose, *Authors and Owners*, 96. I follow Rose's authoritative account closely in what follows.

64   Camden's first supplemental was apparently a 5–5 tie.

65   Rose, *Authors and Owners*, 98–102; W. Zachs, *The First John Murray and the Late Eighteenth-Century London Book Trade* (Oxford: Oxford University Press for the British Academy, 1998), 56–62.

66   W. K. Wimsatt and F. A. Pottle, eds., *Boswell for the Defence, 1769–1774* (New York: McGraw-Hill, 1959), 230.

67   St. Clair, *Reading Nation*, 101.

68   Rose, *Authors and Owners*, 92–97.

69   Blagden, *Notebook*, 219–21; J. Raven, "The Novel Comes of Age," in *The English Novel, 1770–1829: A Bibliographical Survey of Prose Fiction Published in the British Isles*, ed. P. Garside, J. Raven, and R. Schöwerling, 2 vols. (Oxford: Oxford University Press, 1999–2000), 1:15–121, esp. 79–80, 82, 87–88, 90; P. Garside, "The English Novel in the Romantic Era: Consolidation and Dispersal," in *English Novel*, ed. Garside, Raven and Schöwerling, 2:15–103, esp. 47, 63, 74, 88–89; J. Feather, *A History of British Publishing* (London: Routledge, 1988), 82–83; C. Blagden, "Thomas Carnan and the Almanack Monopoly," *Studies in Bibliography* 14 (1961): 23–43; J. Topham, "A Textbook Revolution," in *Books and the Sciences in History*, ed. M. Frasca-Spada and N. Jardine (Cambridge: Cambridge University Press, 2000), 317–37; C. Walsh, *A Bookseller of the Last Century* (London: Griffith et al., 1885), 89–117; A. Fyfe, "Young Readers and the Sciences," in *Books*

and the Sciences in History, ed. Frasca-Spada and Jardine, 276–90; D. Blakey, *The Minerva Press, 1790–1820* (London: Bibliographical Society, 1939), 16–25.

70 St. Clair, *Reading Nation,* 122–39; T. F. Bonnell, "John Bell's *Poets of Great Britain:* The 'Little Trifling Edition' Revisited," *Modern Philology* 85 (1987): 128–52; S. Morison, *John Bell, 1745–1831* (Cambridge: Cambridge University Press for the author, 1930); M. J. M. Ezell, *Social Authorship and the Advent of Print* (Baltimore: Johns Hopkins University Press, 1999), 131.

71 Garside, "English Novel," 80; Feather, *History of British Publishing,* 120; Zachs, *First John Murray,* 250; P. Garside, "Rob's Last Raid: Scott and the Publication of the Waverley Novels," in *Author/Publisher Relations in the Eighteenth and Nineteenth Centuries,* ed. R. Myers and M. Harris (Oxford: Oxford Polytechnic Press, 1983), 88–118.

72 *The Charter and grants of the Company of Stationers* (n.p. [London: J. Ilive], 1762), 15–16, 20; *The Speech of Mr. Jacob Ilive to his brethren the Master-Printers* (London: n.p., n.d. [1750]); D. Foxon, *Pope and the Early Eighteenth-Century book trade,* ed. J. McLaverty (Oxford: Clarendon Press, 1991), 250; C. Blagden, *The Stationers' Company: A History, 1403–1959* (London: George Allen and Unwin, 1960), 229–30; T. C. Hansard, *Typographia* (London: for Baldwin, Cradock, and Joy, 1825), 274–75. For Elinor James, see P. McDowell, ed., *Elinor James,* The Early Modern Englishwoman, B. S. Travitsky and A. L. Prescott, general eds., Series II, vol. 11 (Aldershot, UK: Ashgate, 2005). I have a longer paper on Ilive in preparation, provisionally entitled "God Goes to Grub Street."

73 E. P. Thompson, *The Making of the English Working Class* (London: Vintage, 1966; orig. 1963), e.g., 234–313; G. S. Jones, *Languages of Class: Studies in English Working Class History, 1832–1982* (Cambridge: Cambridge University Press, 1983), 215–16.

74 *Morris v. Bransom* (1776) and *Liardet v. Johnson* (1778), in W. Carpmael, *Law Reports of Patent Cases* (London: by A. Macintosh for the proprietor, 1843), 30–34, 35–37.

75 The literary property debates later came back to haunt Watt: see *Boulton and Watt v. Bull* (1795), in Carpmael, *Law Reports,* 117–55, esp. 126; and in general, MacLeod, *Inventing the Industrial Revolution,* 60–64.

76 W. Kenrick, *An account of the automaton constructed by Orffyreus* (London: n.p., 1770); W. Kenrick, *A lecture on the perpetual motion* (London: for the author, 1771); [W. Kenrick?], "A defence of Dr. Priestley from the cavils of the Monthly Reviewers," *London Review* 2 (1775): 564–67; H. Dircks, *Perpetuum Mobile* (London: E. & F. N. Spon, 1861), 53–59, 178; S. J. Schaffer, "The Show That Never Ends: Perpetual Motion in the Early Eighteenth Century," *British Journal for the History of Science* 28, no. 2 (June 1995): 157–89.

77 "Ontologos" [W. Kendrick], *The grand question debated* (Dublin: for G. Wilson, 1751), v.

78 W. Kenrick, *An address to the artists and manufacturers of Great Britain* (London: for Messrs. Domville, Dilly, Newbery, Williams, Evans, and Riley, 1774), 40, 49–50, 54, 57–60.

79 Kenrick, *Address,* 64–65, 68; Boswell, *Decision,* 10, 12.

7 THE LAND WITHOUT PROPERTY

1 M. Pollard, *A Dictionary of Members of the Dublin Book Trade, 1550–1800* (London: Bibliographical Society, 2000), 618; B. Inglis, *The Freedom of the Press in Ireland, 1784–1841* (London: Faber and Faber, 1954), 21.

2 W. Zachs, "John Murray and the Dublin Book Trade, 1770–93; with Special Reference to the 'Mysterious' Society of Dublin Booksellers," *Long Room* 40 (1995): 26–33, esp. 27.

3 E. Sheridan-Quantz, "The Multi-centered Metropolis: The Social Topography of Eighteenth-Century Dublin," in *Two Capitals: London and Dublin, 1500–1840,* ed. P. Clark and R. Gillespie (Oxford: British Academy, 2001), 265–96, esp. 280–82.

4 R. C. Cole, *Irish Booksellers and English Writers, 1740–1800* (London: Mansell, 1986), 9–10; J. R. R. Adams, *The Printed Word and the Common Man: Popular Culture in Ulster, 1700–1900* (Antrim: Queen's University of Belfast, 1987), 25.

5 S. J. Connolly, *Religion, Law, and Power: The Making of Protestant Ireland, 1660–1760* (Oxford: Clarendon Press, 1992), 68; C. Casey, "Subscription Networks for Irish Architectural Books, 1730–1760," *Long Room* 35 (1990): 41–49, esp. 41–43.

6 T. Barnard, "Print Culture, 1700–1800," in *The Oxford History of the Irish Book, III: The Irish Book in English, 1550–1800,* ed. R. Gillespie and A. Hadfield (Oxford: Oxford University Press, 2006), 34–58, esp. 56; J. Smyth, *The Men of No Property: Irish Radicals and Popular Politics in the Late Eighteenth Century* (New York: St. Martin's, 1998 [1992]), 27–29; M. Pollard, *Dublin's Trade in Books, 1550–1800* (Oxford: Clarendon Press, 1989), 110–64, esp. 132–33; Cole, *Irish Booksellers and English Writers,* 14–17, 22–27, 31–34.

7 National Library of Ireland (NLI) MS 12124, pp. 239–41, 247; R. F. Foster, *Modern Ireland, 1600–1972* (New York: Viking Penguin, 1988), 238–39.

8 Pollard, *Dublin's Trade in Books,* 68–69; Pollard, *Dictionary,* 133; J. W. Phillips, *Printing and Bookselling in Dublin, 1670–1800* (Dublin: Irish Academic Press, 1998), 104.

9 Cole, *Irish Booksellers and English Writers,* 22, 40–42, 46–47.

10 Pollard, *Dublin's Trade in Books,* 83–84.

11 Cole, *Irish Booksellers and English Writers,* 2–3; Pollard, *Dublin's Trade in Books,* 83–84; W. McDougall, "Gavin Hamilton, John Balfour and Patrick Neill: A Study of Publishing in Edinburgh in the 18th Century" (Ph.D. thesis, University of Edinburgh, 1974), 20; National Archives, Kew, Cust 21/71, fol. 166^v. The books' value in this case was estimated at about £4 out

of a total of almost £100, which indicates the small economic role of book smuggling.

12 M. Rose, *Authors and Owners: The Invention of Copyright* (Cambridge, Mass.: Harvard University Press, 1993), 151–53; Pollard, *Dublin's Trade in Books,* 69; T. Maslen, "George Faulkner and William Bowyer: The London Connection," *Long Room* 38 (1993): 20–30, esp. 23; Zachs, "John Murray," 27.

13 S. Richardson, *The case of Samuel Richardson* (London: n.p, September 14, 1753); *Dublin Spy,* October 29, 1753; *Dublin Journal,* November 3–6, 1753; *Pue's Occurrences,* November 13–17, 1753; S. Richardson, "An Address to the Public" (February 1, 1754), in *The history of Sir Charles Grandison,* 3rd ed., I (London: S. Richardson, 1754), 424–42, esp. 441; Phillips, *Printing and Bookselling,* 113; Pollard, *Dictionary,* 393–94; C. C. Ward and R. E. Ward, "Literary Piracy in the Eighteenth Century Book Trade: The Cases of George Faulkner and Alexander Donaldson," *Factotum* 17 (1983): 25–35, esp. 27–28; J. Behrens, "Of What Will Not Men Be Capable? Publishing and Piracy in Eighteenth-Century Dublin and the *Sir Charles Grandison* Episode" (M.A. thesis, University of Chicago, 2008).

14 Zachs, "John Murray," 27–28; H. Forster, "Irish Editions of Edward Young," *Long Room* 18–19 (Spring–Autumn 1979): 14–26, esp. 15–16.

15 *Dublin Gazette,* October 9–12, 1742; R. E. Ward, *Prince of Dublin Publishers: The Letters of George Faulkner* (Lexington: University Press of Kentucky, 1972), 10–11; Cole, *Irish Booksellers and English Writers,* 17–21, 132–33; I. C. Ross and B. L. Fitzpatrick, "David Garrick or Spranger Barry? A Dramatic Substitution in Irish Editions of Smollett's *Sir Launcelot Greaves,*" *Long Room* 30 (1985): 6–10; Pollard, *Dictionary,* 295.

16 Berkeley to Percival, in *The Works of George Berkeley Bishop of Cloyne,* ed. A. A. Luce and T. E. Jessop, 9 vols. (London: Thomas, Nelson and Sons, 1948–57), 8:41–43; Ward, *Prince of Dublin Publishers,* 10; Swift, *Correspondence,* iv, 493.

17 D. Hume to W. Strahan, March 13, 1770; June 5, 1770; June 21, 1770; March 11, 1771, in *The Letters of David Hume,* ed. J. Y. T. Greig, 2 vols. (Oxford: Clarendon Press, 1932), 2:218–19, 225, 227–28, 235–36; Pollard, *Dublin's Trade in Books,* 71; O. Goldsmith, *An history of the Earth, and animated nature,* 8 vols. (Dublin: for J. Williams, 1777), I, sig. b^{r-v}.

18 Cole, *Irish Booksellers and English Writers,* 5, 13, 62–63.

19 *Dublin Journal,* September 2–5, 1758; Cole, *Irish Booksellers and English Writers,* 3, 131.

20 Inglis, *Freedom of the Press in Ireland,* 19.

21 Pollard, *Dublin's Trade,* 102; *Dublin Evening Post,* April 10, 1784.

22 *Dublin Journal,* July 10–13, 1784.

23 *Dublin Mercury,* September 17, 1742; Pollard, *Dublin's Trade,* 170.

24 *Dublin Gazette,* March 28, 1758; Pollard, *Dublin's Trade,* 170–71. It is also possible that booksellers erected actual wooden posts outside their shops:

J. Rauen, *The Business of Books: Booksellers and the English Book Trade* (New Haven, Conn.: Yale University Press, 2007), 276.

25 Pollard, *Dublin's Trade,* 171–72.

26 Richardson, *Case,* 3; *Dublin Evening Post,* March 11–15, 1734; *Public Gazetteer,* February 24–27, 1759, 358; Cole, *Irish Booksellers and English Writers,* 12, 100–101.

27 Zachs, "John Murray," 27.

28 *Advice from fairy-land* (Dublin, 1726); *Dublin Evening Post,* March 11–15, 1734.

29 This is a much abbreviated summary of a history that must be drawn together from many sources. See especially C. Lennon, "The Print Trade, 1550–1700," in *Oxford History of the Irish Book,* ed. Gillespie and Hadfield, 3:61–73; Pollard, *Dublin's Trade in Books,* 2–3; Phillips, *Printing and Bookselling,* 3; R. J. Hunter, "Chester and the Irish Book Trade, 1681," *Irish Economic and Social History* 15 (1988): 89–93; M. Sparke, *Scintilla* (London: n.p., 1641), 2; NLI MS 2511, fol. 24^{r-v}; NLI MS 12121, pp. 43–78; NLI MS 12123, pp. 55–57, 75 (paginated from the end). The guild's charter is in NLI MS 16998. For the guild in general, see especially Pollard, *Dictionary,* ix–xxxiv.

30 NLI MSS 12129, pp. 18–20; 12123, pp. 2, 69, 71, 78; 12121, p. 8 (no. 17); p. 15 (no. 2); Phillips, *Printing and Bookselling,* 307; Pollard, *Dictionary,* 157–58.

31 Phillips, *Printing and Bookselling,* 9; NLI MS 12126, p. 80; NLI MS 12121, no. 2; NLI MS 16998, p. 22; warrants from the reign of Charles II later in the same volume (unpaginated); NLI MS 12121, p. 28; NLI MS 4634; NLI MS 12123, pp. 23, 63, 87 (paginating from the end); and other measures at NLI MS 12123, pp. 36, 144, 146, 220.

32 *Dublin Journal,* April 12–15, 1735; NLI MSS 16998, n.p., n.d.; 12121, p. 24; 12123, pp. 26, 52 (1701); 12125, pp. 6–7, 10.

33 NLI MS 12121, no. 1 (the bylaws, 1671), pp. 5–6 (nos. 6, 8), 7 (no. 14), 9 (no. 19); NLI MS 12123, p. 16; NLI MS 12125, p. 143.

34 NLI MS 12121, p. 30 (from 1683); *A Survey of the Liberties and Franchises of the City of Dublin* (Dublin: J. Exshaw, 1815).

35 NLI MS 12123, p. 132 (1713); NLI MS 16998, unpaginated, summons to the guild from the Lord Mayor on July 31, 1680; NLI MS 12123, p. 58 (1702).

36 *Dublin Journal,* August 4–7, 1764; Phillips, *Printing and Bookselling,* 14; NLI MS 12124, pp. 131–32, 205, 377; NLI MS 12125, pp. 240–41, 243.

37 *A Poem on the Art of Printing* (Dublin, 1761), British Library (BL), classmark 1890.e.5.(58); H. Jones, *The Invention of letters, and the utility of the press* (Dublin: before the Company of Stationers, 1755), BL 1890.e.5.(61); *The Art of Printing* (Dublin, 1764), BL, classmarks 1890.e.5.(60), (61); *A Poem on the art of printing,* BL 1890.e.5.(59).

38 NLI MSS 12121, p. 4 (no. 3); 12124, p. 26.

39 NLI MS 12123, pp. 21, 30, 42; J. Dunton, *The Dublin Scuffle,* ed. A. Carpenter (Dublin: Four Courts Press, 2000), 47, 70–71, 180, 182.

40 E.g., NLI MS 12124, p. 149.

41 Phillips, *Printing and Bookselling,* 139; NLI MS 12123, pp. 101, 108, 126.

42 D. W. Nichol, ed., *Pope's Literary Legacy: The Book-Trade Correspondence of William Warburton and John Knapton* (Oxford: Oxford Bibliographical Society, 1992), lv–lvi; Pollard, *Dublin's Trade,* 173–74.

43 H. R. Plomer, G. H. Bushnell, and E. R. McC. Dix, *A Dictionary of the Printers and Booksellers Who Were at Work in England, Scotland, and Ireland from 1726 to 1775* (London: Bibliographical Society, 1968), 66–67; G. Abbatista, "The Business of Paternoster Row: Towards a Publishing History of the *Universal History* (1736–65)," *Publishing History* 17 (1985): 5–50.

44 *Dublin Journal,* July 23–27, 1745; *Dublin Gazette* April 3–7, 1744.

45 *Dublin Journal,* February 4–7, 1743/44; September 18–22, 1744.

46 *Dublin Spy,* November 5, 1753; Phillips, *Printing and Bookselling,* 111–12.

47 *Dublin Journal,* September 18–22, 1744.

48 *Dublin Journal,* October 20–23, 1744.

49 *Dublin Journal,* October 20–23, 1744; *Dublin Journal,* September 22–25, 1744; July 26–29, 1746; Pollard, *Dictionary,* 23–24, 364–65, 491.

50 A. P. I. Samuels, *The Early Life, Correspondence, and Writings of the Rt. Hon. Edmund Burke LL.D.* (Cambridge: Cambridge University Press, 1923), 246, 269–74.

51 Abbatista, "Business of Paternoster Row," 16–18; *Considerations in behalf of the booksellers of London and Westminster* (n.p., n.d. [1774]); *An account of the expence of correcting and improving sundry books* (n.p., n.d. [1774]).

52 Phillips, *Printing and Bookselling,* 136–47; *Dublin Journal,* July 15–18, 1758; August 5–8, 1758; August 12–15, 1758; [G. Faulkner], *An appeal to the public* (1758), 6.

53 *Dublin Journal,* June 2–6, 1767.

54 Zachs, "John Murray," 32; Pollard, *Dictionary,* 114; NLI MS 12125, p. 87. The initial membership of the company comprised Anne Leathley, W. and W. Smith, G. Faulkner, P. Wilson, J. Exshaw, H. Bradley, W. Watson, S. Watson, and T. Ewing.

55 Pollard, *Dublin's Trade,* 169.

56 *Dublin Mercury,* May 16–19, 1767.

57 Pollard, *Dublin's Trade,* 168; Pollard, *Dictionary,* 7–8.

58 NLI MS 12125, pp. 46–49.

59 Pollard, *Dictionary,* 160–61.

60 Smyth, *The Men of No Property,* 124; their later resurgence in America is described in P. Way, *Common Labour: Workers and the Digging of North American Canals, 1780–1860* (Cambridge: Cambridge University Press, 1993), 92, 195–98, 214–17.

61 *Hibernian Journal,* January 22–24, 1773, 43; February 24–26, 1773, 98; NLI MS 12125, pp. 210, 252.

62 NLI MSS 12125, pp. 309–11; 12126, pp. 52, 96–97. Moody and Vaughan, *New History of Ireland,* 4:295.

63   NLI MS 12126, pp. 124–27.

64   G. Walters, "The Booksellers in 1759 and 1774: The Battle for Literary
     Property," *The Library*, 5th ser., 29 (1974): 287–311; Cole, *Irish Booksellers and
     English Writers*, 4–7.

65   Smyth, *The Men of No Property*, 161.

66   D. Dickson, "Death of a Capital? Dublin and the Consequences of Union,"
     in *Two Capitals*, ed. Clark and Gillespie, 111–32; NLI MS 12126, pp. 204–5.

67   Pollard, *Dictionary*, 383; M. Carey, *Autobiography* (New York: E. L.
     Schwaab, 1942; originally issued in *New-England Magazine*, 1833–34, and
     reprinted for private circulation in 1837), 3; K. W. Rowe, "Mathew Carey:
     A Study in American Economic Development" (Ph.D. thesis, Johns
     Hopkins University, 1933), ch. 1.

68   Carey, *Autobiography*, 4; Connolly, *Religion, Law, and Power*, 68–69.

69   I. R. McBride, *Scripture Politics: Ulster Presbyterians and Irish Radicalism in
     the Late Eighteenth Century* (Oxford: Clarendon Press, 1998), 126–30;
     Pollard, *Dictionary*, 86–87; W. E. H. Lecky, *A History of Ireland in the
     Eighteenth Century*, 5 vols. (London: Longmans, Green, 1913), 2:364, 376–77;
     E. C. Carter, "The Political Activities of Mathew Carey, Nationalist,
     1760–1814" (Ph.D. thesis, Bryn Mawr College, 1962), 21–22, 26, 49–50.

70   Pollard, *Dictionary*, 431–32; Lecky, *Ireland*, 2:382–90; Froude, *English in
     Ireland*, 2:399–400.

71   *Dublin Evening Post*, April 3, 1784; Froude, *English in Ireland*, 2:400–401.

72   *Parliamentary register*, III, 122–44 (April 2, 1784), 147–50 (April 6, 1784);
     Dublin Evening Post, April 6, 1784; Lecky, *Ireland*, II, 392–94; Froude,
     English in Ireland, 2:407–9; J. T. Gilbert, *A History of the City of Dublin*, 3
     vols. (Dublin: J. Duffy, 1861), 3:319–20; Inglis, *Freedom of the Press*, 25–34.

73   *Parliamentary register*, III, 114–16, 151–53; *Dublin Evening Post*, April 8, 1784;
     Inglis, *Freedom of the Press*, 42–45.

74   *Dublin Evening Post*, April 8 and April 10, 1784; McBride, *Scripture Politics*,
     9–10, 152–53; Carey, *Autobiography*, 8–9; Pollard, *Dictionary*, 85–89; Inglis,
     Freedom of the Press, 23–32; T. C. Cochran, *Frontiers of Change: Early
     Industrialism in America* (New York: Oxford University Press, 1981), 53–55;
     Philadelphia [and] Southern Steamship Manufacturers and Mercantile Register
     (Philadelphia: M'Laughlin Brothers, 1866), 9–10, 22–23; W. Clarkin,
     Mathew Carey: A Bibliography of his Publications, 1785–1824 (New York:
     Garland, 1984), xiii; J. Tebbel, *A History of Book Publishing in the United
     States*, 4 vols. (New York: R. R. Bowker, 1972–81), 1:208.

8   MAKING A NATION

1   I. Thomas, *The History of Printing in America*, ed. M. A. McCorison (New
     York: Weathervane, 1970 [1810]), 362–66, 374, 433–34, 604–6.

2   H. Amory and D. Hall, eds., *A History of the Book in America*, vol. 1, *The*

Colonial Book in the Atlantic World (Cambridge: Cambridge University Press, 2000), 33, 142, 156, 168, 270, 321; Thomas, *History*, 147–49, 158, 266, 270–71, 278, 304; S. Botein, "'Meer Mechanics' and an Open Press: The Business and Political Strategies of Colonial American Printers," *Perspectives in American History* 9 (1975): 127–225, esp. 143, 147–48, 192–94; B. W. Levy, *Freedom of the Press from Zenger to Jefferson* (Indianapolis: Bobbs-Merrill, 1966), xxiii.

3   W. Spotswood to J. Belknap, June 19, 1788, in *Collections of the Massachusetts Historical Society*, 6th ser., 4 (1891): 408–12, esp. 410; Botein, "'Meer Mechanics,'" 222; L. A. Peskin, *Manufacturing Revolution: The Intellectual Origins of Early American Industry* (Baltimore: Johns Hopkins University Press, 2003), 13–59; T. H. Breen, *The Marketplace of Revolution: How Consumer Politics Shaped American Independence* (Oxford: Oxford University Press, 2004), 36–41, 48–51, 54–59, 87–89, 222–28; Amory and Hall, *Colonial Book*, 173–75, 177–78; P. L. Ford, *The Journals of Hugh Gaine, Printer*, 2 vols. (New York: Dodd, Mead, and Co., 1902), 1:225–40.

4   D. Hall to W. Strahan, March 21, 1752, D. Hall Letter book, American Philosophical Society, B.H142.1.3 (henceforth DHL), pp. 21–22.

5   D. Hall to W. Strahan, March 24, 1759, DHL; R. Harlan, "A Colonial Printer as Bookseller in Eighteenth-Century Philadelphia: The Case of David Hall," *Studies in Eighteenth-Century Culture* 5 (1976): 355–70, esp. 358–59.

6   D. Hall to W. Strahan, December 18, 1754; Hall to Rivington and Fletcher, November 20, 1758; Hall to J. Rivington, July 22, 1758; Hall to J. Rivington, May 29, 1758; Hall to Strahan, March 24, 1759; Hall to Fletcher and Rivington, December 15, 1759: all in DHL.

7   Amory and Hall, *Colonial Book*, 194, 279–82.

8   Hall to Strahan, December 22, 1760; Hall to Hamilton and Balfour, December 22, 1760: DHL.

9   Amory and Hall, *Colonial Book*, 292; *Oxford Dictionary of National Biography*, s.v. "Rivington family."

10   Thomas, *History*, 103, 120–21, 149–50; Amory and Hall, *Colonial Book*, 33, 89–90, 104, 148, 267–70, 277–79, 320, 326–28; D. D. Hall, *Worlds of Wonder, Days of Judgment: Popular Religious Belief in Early New England* (Cambridge, Mass.: Harvard University Press, 1989), 49–55, 247.

11   Thomas, *History*, 395; for Robertson's copy money, see R. B. Sher, *The Enlightenment and the Book: Scottish Authors and Their Publishers in Eighteenth-Century Britain, Ireland, and America* (Chicago: University of Chicago Press, 2006), 214.

12   R. Bell, "Address to the Subscribers," in W. Robertson, *The history of the reign of Charles V*, 3 vols. (America [Philadelphia]: for the subscribers, 1770–71), III, [24–29]; Harlan, "Colonial Printer," 363; H. Lehmann-Haupt, *The Book in America: A History of the Making, the Selling and the Collecting of Books in the United States* (New York: Bowker, 1939), 94; Amory

and Hall, *Colonial Book,* 283–91, 297–98. See also R. Bell, "A few more
words, on the Freedom of the Press," in J. Tucker, *The True interest of
Britain, set forth in regard to the Colonies* (Philadelphia: printed, and sold,
by Robert Bell, 1776), [67–69].

13 R. G. Silver, "The Costs of Mathew Carey's Printing Equipment," *Studies
in Bibliography* 19 (1966): 85–122, esp. 86–88.

14 M. Carey, *The plagi-scurriliad* (Philadelphia: printed and sold by the author,
1786), viii–x, 16–17, [30].

15 M. Carey, *Autobiography* (New York: E. L. Schwaab, 1942), 13–16.

16 M. Carey to B. Franklin, April 20, 1786, copy in Mathew Carey Papers,
American Antiquarian Society (MCP, AAS), 1:1; *Collections of the Massachusetts Historical Society,* 6th ser., 4 (1891): 390–93, 423.

17 R. C. Cole, *Irish Booksellers and English Writers, 1740–1800* (London:
Mansell, 1986), 48–49; R. Remer, *Printers and Men of Capital: Philadelphia
Book Publishers in the New Republic* (Philadelphia: University of Pennsylvania Press, 1996), 53–54; Rivington to Thomas Bradford, Historical Society
of Philadelphia (HSP) MS Bradford Collection, unbound correspondence, April 26, 1796.

18 Cf. E. L. Bradsher, *Mathew Carey: Editor, Author, and Publisher* (New York:
Columbia University Press, 1912), 6–7. For Washington's concern that
Carey's papers might be intercepted, see Washington to Carey, March 15,
1785, MCP, AAS, 1:1.

19 Peskin, *Manufacturing Revolution,* 49–52.

20 E. G. Carter, "The Political Activities of Mathew Carey, Nationalist,
1760–1814" (Ph.D. thesis, Bryn Mawr, 1962), 88–89.

21 *Columbian Magazine,* 1 (September 1786): 29.

22 W. Spotswood to J. Belknap, October 9, 1788, in *Collections of the Massachusetts Historical Society,* 6th ser., 4 (1891): 420–24; Bradsher, *Mathew Carey,* 6–7.

23 Peskin, *Manufacturing Revolution,* 93–96; T. Coxe, *A brief examination of
Lord Sheffield's Observations on the commerce of the United States of America*
(Philadelphia: Carey, Stewart, and Co., 1791). For a draft by Carey com-
plaining of Coxe's failing to give the *Museum* materials agreed for, see
Carey to Coxe, n.d. (not sent), Mathew Carey Papers, box 1, folder 1, AAS.

24 T. Coxe, "An address to an assembly of the friends of American manufactures," *American Museum* 2 (1787): 248–54.

25 Peskin, *Manufacturing Revolution,* 98, 100–101.

26 *American Museum* 3 (1788), preface, 265; 4 (1788), preface; 5 (1789), preface;
6 (1789), preface; 12 (1792), 225–26, 307–8; Carter, "Political Activities of
Mathew Carey," 108–11; A. Hamilton, *The Papers of Alexander Hamilton,* ed.
H. C. Syrett, 27 vols. (New York: Columbia University Press, 1961–87), X,
9. See also M. Carey, "Thoughts on the policy of encouraging migration,"
in Carey, *Miscellaneous trifles in prose* (Philadelphia: for the author, 1796),
110–24.

27 Coxe's first brief draft is in Hamilton, *Papers,* XXVI, 631–32; the far longer second then follows at 632–47.

28 Hamilton, *Papers,* X, 18.

29 Hamilton, *Papers,* X, 28, 36, 48–49, 230–340nn.

30 [T. Coxe], *A brief examination of Lord Sheffield's Observations on the commerce of the United States* (Philadelphia: orig. issued in *American Museum,* March 1791; reprinted in London, 1792), 8–9, 37–39, 124. For Dobson's *Encyclopaedia Britannica,* see R. D. Arner, *Dobson's* Encyclopaedia: *The Publisher, Text, and Publication of America's First* Britannica, *1789–1803* (Philadelphia: University of Pennsylvania Press, 1991). For Carey's signature opposing a duty on type, see Book Trades Collection, AAS, 2:2 (March 8, 1802).

31 W. Clarkin, *Mathew Carey: A Bibliography of His Publications, 1785–1824* (New York: Garland, 1984), 26–27.

32 See, in general, C. N. Davidson, "The Life and Times of *Charlotte Temple:* The Biography of a Book," in *Reading in America: Literature and Social History,* ed. C. N. Davidson (Baltimore: Johns Hopkins University Press, 1989), 157–79, esp. 161.

33 "To the Members of the American Philosophical Society" (April 1824), in Carey, *Miscellaneous Essays,* 241–46; Bradsher, *Mathew Carey,* 34–35; Carter, "Political Activities of Mathew Carey," 115–17; American Philosophical Society Library, *Report* (1943), 73; Carey, *Autobiography,* 43–44.

34 D. S. Ben-Atar, *Trade Secrets: Intellectual Piracy and the Origins of American Industrial Power* (New Haven, Conn.: Yale University Press, 2004); D. H. Stapleton, *The Transfer of Early Industrial Technologies to America* (Philadelphia: American Philosophical Society, 1987), e.g., 21–22, for the Strickland mission (see below); N. L. York, *Mechanical Metamorphosis: Technological Change in Revolutionary America* (Westport, Conn.: Greenwood Press, 1985), 155–76; J. E. Cooke, *Tench Coxe and the Early Republic* (Chapel Hill: University of North Carolina Press, 1978), 182–200; B. H. Mann, *Republic of Debtors: Bankruptcy in the Age of American Independence* (Cambridge, Mass.: Harvard University Press, 2002), 112–15; Peskin, *Manufacturing Revolution,* 114–18.

35 [M. Carey], *A Short account of Algiers,* 2nd ed. (Philadelphia: printed for Mathew Carey, 1794), 11–13, 16, 33–36; Peskin, *Manufacturing Revolution,* 70.

36 R. Buel, *Securing the Revolution: Ideology in American Politics, 1789–1815* (Ithaca, N.Y.: Cornell University Press, 1972), 54–55, 59–60, 69–70; D. N. Doyle, *Ireland, Irishmen and Revolutionary America, 1760–1820* (Dublin: Mercier, 1981), 194–96; Carter, "Political Activities of Mathew Carey," 135–37, 208–10, 219, 228, 237–38; [M. Carey], *Address to the House of Representatives* (Philadelphia: for M. Carey, 1796); *Treaty of amity, commerce, and navigation . . . to which is annexed a copious appendix,* 2nd ed. (Philadelphia: for M. Carey, 1795).

37 *Evening Star,* October 30, 1810, quoted in C. L. Nichols, "The Literary Fair

in the United States," in V. H. Paltsits et al., *Bibliographical Essays: A Tribute to Wilberforce Eames* (Cambridge, Mass.: Harvard University Press, 1924), 85–92, esp. 85.

38 J. Raven, *London Booksellers and American Customers: Transatlantic Literary Community and the Charleston Library Society, 1748–1811* (Columbia: University of South Carolina Press, 2002), 204–17; for the Philadelphia Society, see Roberts Vaux to Jonah Thompson, August 10, 1805, Vaux Family Papers (Collection 684), HSP.

39 Remer, *Printers and Men of Capital*, 105–8, 116–19; Mann, *Republic of Debtors*, 258–61; Carey, *Autobiography*, 41–43. The seventy-three-year-old Rivington ended up imprisoned for debt after a counterpart whom he had guaranteed defaulted: Rivington to Thomas Bradford, HSP MS Bradford Collection, unbound correspondence, April 20, 1797.

40 M. Carey, *Plumb Pudding*, 2nd ed. (Philadelphia: printed for the author, 1799), 9–12 and passim; M. Carey, *To the public* (Philadelphia, February 5, 1799), 6–8; D. A. Wilson, *United Irishmen, United States: Immigrant Radicals in the Early Republic* (Ithaca, N.Y.: Cornell University Press, 1998), 43–57; Bradsher, *Mathew Carey*, 73; Remer, *Printers and Men of Capital*, 37; Buel, *Securing the Revolution*, 180.

41 M. Carey to J. M. O'Conner, July 10, 1817, MCP, AAS, 1:1; Carter, "Political Activities of Mathew Carey," 112–13; Cole, *Irish Booksellers*, 48–49; Bradsher, *Mathew Carey*, 37n34; W. Charvat, *Literary Publishing in America, 1790–1850* (Amherst: University of Massachusetts Press, 1993 [1959]), 25–26, 30–33; Silver, "Costs of Mathew Carey's Printing Equipment," 100–101; Remer, *Printers and Men of Capital*, 1–4, 50–53, 79–87, 125; R. J. Zboray, *A Fictive People: Antebellum Economic Development and the American Reading Public* (New York: Oxford University Press, 1993), 37–54.

42 Carey, *Autobiography*, 48; Remer, *Printers and Men of Capital*, 5–6, 39–40, 50, 70; Carter, "Political Activities of Mathew Carey," 106, 264–69; J. N. Green, "From Printer to Publisher: Mathew Carey and the Origins of Nineteenth-Century Book Publishing," in *Getting the Books Out: Papers of the Chicago Conference on the Book in Nineteenth-Century America*, ed. M. Hackenberg (Washington, D.C.: Library of Congress, 1987), 26–44.

43 T. Solberg, *Copyright in Congress, 1789–1904* (Washington, D.C.: Library of Congress, 1905), 29–30, 84, 112–26; G. S. Rice, *The Transformation of Authorship in America* (Chicago: University of Chicago Press, 1997), 79–83; Lehmann-Haupt, *The Book in America*, 84–93; Remer, *Printers and Men of Capital*, 55–56; A. D. Schreyer, "Copyright and Books in Nineteenth-Century America," in *Getting the Books Out*, ed. Hackenberg, 121–36, esp. 123–26.

44 Arner, *Dobson's* Encyclopaedia, 14; I. Thomas to [?], March 24, 1797, Isaiah Thomas Papers, AAS, 1:1. For registrations in the archives, see, e.g., the West, Richardson, and Lord papers at the AAS, 1:2.

45   I. Thomas to Hudson and Godwin, March 8, 1790, March 22, 1790, May 28, 1790, August 23, 1790; Thomas to N. Patten, March 11, 1790, Isaiah Thomas Papers, AAS, 1:8.

46   Amory and Hall, *Colonial Book*, 48.

47   Thomas, *History*, 370–71.

48   E. Stewart, "A Documentary History of the Early Organizations of Printers," *Bulletin of the Bureau of Labor* 61 (November 1965): 857–1033, esp. 861–63.

49   Silver, "Costs of Mathew Carey's Printing Equipment," 101–2; cf. E. Andrews to I. Thomas, April 5, 1802, Isaiah Thomas Papers, AAS: 4:2.

50   M. Carey, broadside, quoted in Clarkin, *Mathew Carey*, 43; Remer, *Printers and Men of Capital*, 57–60.

51   Bradsher, *Mathew Carey*, 19–23.

52   Booksellers' Company of Philadelphia, Minutes 1802–3, MS Am. 31175, HSP, February 19, 1802, May 18, 1802; M. Carey, *Address to the Printers and Booksellers throughout the United States* (Philadelphia, 1801: AAS, Bdsds.1801); Stewart, "Documentary History of the Early Organizations of Printers," 861–63; Zboray, *A Fictive People*, 18–24; Nichols, "Literary Fair," 86, 91. The place of educational texts was central in many of these initiatives. An 1803 imprint vouchsafed to reprint all the most valuable European schoolbooks, partly to "add to the common stock of American manufactures," and in 1823 Carey's own firm advocated a law against importing them. See Cole, *Irish Booksellers*, ix–x, 42–44, 50–52, 55–56, 149–55, 168–69; Remer, *Printers and Men of Capital*, 62–65; Bradsher, *Mathew Carey*, 35–37; M. A. Lause, *Some Degree of Power: From Hired Hand to Union Craftsman in the Preindustrial American Printing Trades, 1778–1815* (Fayetteville: University of Arkansas Press, 1991), 92–93.

53   Carey, *Autobiography*, 49–50; Peskin, *Manufacturing Revolution*, 70.

54   [H. Gaine], *An Oration Delivered before the Booksellers Convened in New York, at Their First Literary Fair, June 4th, 1802* (n.p., 1802), HSP, ECGCS, Mathew Carey Papers, Box 83, folder 19; *Constitution of the American Company of Booksellers* (New York, 1804), copy in HSP.

55   *Constitution of the American Company of Booksellers.*

56   Booksellers' Society of Philadelphia, Minutes 1802–3, HSP MS Am. 31175, May 8, 1802, July 1, 1802, November 15, 1804; Carey, *Autobiography*, 50; Nichols, "Literary Fair," 88–89.

57   E. Andrews to I. Thomas, April 5, 1802, Isaiah Thomas Papers, AAS, 4:2.

58   W. McCulloch, "Additions to Thomas's History of Printing," *Proceedings of the American Antiquarian Society*, n.s., 31 (1921): 89–247, esp. 136–7.

59   Remer, *Printers and Men of Capital*, 1, 60–61, 65–67, 118.

60   Carey's *Autobiographical Sketches* was not really an autobiography at all (although it is usually cited as one), but an exasperated narrative of these labors. Carey, *Autobiographical sketches*, 42–43; [M. Carey], *Address of the*

Philadelphia Society for the Promotion of National Industry, No. 2, 2nd ed. (December 1819), 10.

61 *Hansard,* 33: 1099.

62 Philadelphia Society for the Promotion of Domestic Industry [M. Carey], *Addresses,* n.s, 2 (December 24, 1819): 29.

63 Carey, *Autobiographical Sketches,* 52–53, 56, 74; Philadelphia Society for the Promotion of National Industry [M. Carey], *Addresses* (Philadelphia: published by M. Carey and Son, 1819), [ii], [iii], xiv.

64 W. Strickland, *Reports on Canals, Railways, Roads, and Other Subjects* (Philadelphia: H. C. Carey and I. Lea, 1826), "Preface," 35–36; *The First Annual Report of the Acting Committee of the Society for the Promotion of Internal Improvement in the Commonwealth of Pennsylvania* (Philadelphia: printed by J. R. A. Skerrett, 1826), esp. 31.

65 Carey, *Miscellaneous Essays,* 238–40, 469–71; R. H. Thurston, *Robert Fulton: His Life and its Results* (New York: Dodd, Mead and Co., 1897), 135; A. C. Sutcliffe, *Robert Fulton* (New York: MacMillan, 1915), 172–73; A. C. Sutcliffe, *Robert Fulton and the "Clermont"* (New York: Century, 1909), 286–87, 353; W. Hutcheon, Jr., *Robert Fulton: Pioneer of Undersea Warfare* (Annapolis, Md.: Naval Institute Press, 1981), 117, 143; Proposal dated August 23, 1830, MCP, AAS, 1:4. Recent accounts of Fulton's patent struggles are in C. O. Philip, *Robert Fulton: A Biography* (New York: Franklin Watts, 1985), 219–94, 303–9, 314–24, 335–45, and K. Sale, *The Fire of His Genius: Robert Fulton and the American Dream* (New York: Free Press, 2001), 162–69.

66 R. Fulton, *A Treatise on the Improvement of Canal Navigation* (London: by I. and J. Taylor, 1796), 1–7, 11–19, 106, 142; Morgan, *Fulton,* 42, 47, 62; Sutcliffe, *Fulton and the "Clermont,"* 319; A. C. Sutcliffe, *Robert Fulton* (New York: MacMillan, 1915), 102–6, 121; Fulton to Bonaparte, 12 Floreal, Year 6 (May 1, 1798), in *Bulletin of the New York Public Library* 5, no. 8 (August 1901): 348–65; Fulton to Washington, September 12, 1796, and February 5, 1797, in Sutcliffe, *Fulton,* 306–7 and 309–12, respectively; Hutcheon, *Robert Fulton,* 102, 114–15; J. F. Reigart, *Life of Robert Fulton* (Philadelphia: C. G. Henderson, 1856), 90–92, 106–7. For Fulton's lobbying to get an engine exported, see "Letters and Documents by or Relating to Robert Fulton," *Bulletin of the New York Public Library* 13, no. 9 (September 1909): 567–84, esp. 567–70.

67 *American Museum* 12 (1792): 30; *American Museum* 10 (1791): 180; M. Carey to R. E. Robarts, March 11, 1825, MCP, AAS, 1:1.

68 M. Carey, *An Appeal to the Justice and Humanity of the Stockholders of the Chesapeake and Delaware Canal,* 2nd ed. (Philadelphia, 1825), 12; In Re Delaware and Chesapeake Canal, September 28, 1825, MCP, AAS, 1:1; P. Way, *Common Labour: Workers and the Digging of North American Canals, 1780–1860* (Cambridge: Cambridge University Press, 1993), 122–23.

69 R. D. Gray, *The National Waterway: A History of the Chesapeake and Delaware*

Canal, 1769–1985 (Urbana: University of Illinois Press, 1989 [1967]), esp. 30–42, 55–61.

70 For an example, see M. Carey to G. Tibbets, April 13, 1827, MCP, AAS, 1:3.

71 Carey, *Autobiographical Sketches,* 46–48; M. Carey, *A View of the Ruinous Consequences of a Dependence on Foreign Markets* (Philadelphia: M. Carey and Son, 1820), 1; M. Carey to P. R. Tendall, January 30, 1830, September 9, 1830, MCP, AAS, 1:4; M. Carey, Diary, University of Pennsylvania MS Coll. 229; M. Carey, *Addresses of the Philadelphia Society for the Promotion of National Industry* (Philadelphia: M. Carey and Son, 1819), title page verso.

72 Carey, *Autobiographical Sketches,* 153–54; Carey, Diary, April 16, 1823, December 1, 1824, November 10, 1825; R. H. Bayard to M. Carey, June 8, 1824, in Edward Carey Gardiner Collection, Carey Section, Mathew Carey Papers, HSP, Box 83, folder 13; D. W. Howe, *What Hath God Wrought: The Transformation of America, 1815–1848* (Oxford: Oxford University Press, 2007), 428.

73 Carey, *Autobiographical Sketches,* 52–53, 70–71, 88, 92, 109–16, 118–19; Carey, Diary, December 15, 1822, June 11, 1823, January 19, 1825, January 27, 1825, November 17, 1825, January 10, 1826.

74 Carey, *Autobiographical Sketches,* viii–ix, 5, 129–31.

75 Philadelphia Society for the Promotion of National Industry [M. Carey], *Addresses* (Philadelphia: published by M. Carey and Son, 1819), [ii], [iii], xiv.

76 Carey, *Autobiographical Sketches,* 2; "Circular" (May 1830), in Carey, *Miscellaneous Essays,* 401–2; see also the general "Preface," iv–v.

77 Carey, *Autobiographical Sketches,* 12–13n, 144–51; Carey, *Miscellaneous Essays,* iii–v.

78 University of Michigan, William L. Clements Library, Henry Carey Letterbook (hereafter HCL), 33, 49–55, 65–70, 99–102.

79 HCL, 55; for other instances of such moral arithmetic, see T. Augst, *The Clerk's Tale: Young Men and Moral Life in Nineteenth-Century America* (Chicago: University of Chicago Press, 2003), 50–51.

80 HCL, 77–83, 92–93, 99–102, 201–2, 259–62, 287–89.

81 HCL, 51, 482–83, 498–500; Clarkin, *Mathew Carey,* xv–xvi.

82 *Pittsburg Gazette,* July 12, 1828 (repr. as pamphlet, AAS, Dated Pams.); Rowe, "Mathew Carey," 120.

9 THE PRINTING COUNTERREVOLUTION

1 M. Woodmansee, "The Genius and the Copyright: Economic and Legal Considerations of the Emergence of the Author," *Eighteenth-Century Studies* 17 (1984): 425–48.

2 M. Butler, "Antiquarianism (Popular)," in *An Oxford Companion to the Romantic Age: British Culture, 1776–1832,* ed. I. McCalman (Oxford: Oxford University Press, 1999), 328–38, esp. 335. For "novel antiquities," see

J. Chandler, *England in 1819: The Politics of Literary Culture and the Case of Romantic Historicism* (Chicago: University of Chicago Press, 1998), 277–78. For the local history of Kentish antiquarianism prior to Brydges, see S. Bann, *Under the Sign: John Bargrave as Collector, Traveler, and Witness* (Ann Arbor: University of Michigan Press, 1995).

3   J. Britton, *The Rights of Literature* (London: for the author, 1814), vi.

4   A. Grafton, *Codex in Crisis* (New York: Crumpled Press, 2008); R. Chartier, *The Order of Books: Readers, Authors, and Libraries in Europe between the Fourteenth and Eighteenth Centuries* (Cambridge: Polity, 1994), 61–88; P. Keen, *The Crisis of Literature in the 1790s: Print Culture and the Public Sphere* (Cambridge: Cambridge University Press, 1999), 101–8.

5   R. C. Barrington Partridge, *The History of the Legal Deposit of Books throughout the British Empire* (London: Library Association, 1938), 288–90.

6   B. Montagu, *Enquiries and Observations Respecting the University Library* (Cambridge: by F. Hodson; sold by Mawman; and Deighton, 1805), sig. a2ʳ; Partridge, *History of the Legal Deposit of Books*, 30–31.

7   E. Law, *Observations occasioned by the contest about literary property* (Cambridge: by J. Archdeacon; sold by T. and J. Merrill et al., 1770), 3–4; Partridge, *History of the Legal Deposit of Books*, 34–38.

8   Keen, *The Crisis of Literature in the 1790s*, 101–8.

9   B. Montagu, *Enquiries Respecting the Proposed Alteration of the Law of Copyright* (London: for J. Butterworth, by J. M'Creery, 1813), vii–viii.

10   *Beckford v. Hood, Term Reports* VII, 620.

11   Partridge, *History of the Legal Deposit of Books*, 45n3.

12   [J. G. Cochrane], *The Case Stated between the Public Libraries and the Booksellers* (London: by J. Moyes, 1813), 3.

13   *Cambridge University v. Bryer*, 16 East, 317.

14   Haslewood to Brydges, n.d. [1812], British Library (BL) MS Add. 25102, fol. 97ʳ⁻ᵛ; Partridge, *History of the Legal Deposit of Books*, 45–61.

15   Beinecke Library, Yale University, Gen MSS 176, vol. 2, January 7, 1815.

16   E.g., S. E. Brydges, *Modern Aristocracy, or the Bard's Reception* (Geneva: A. L. Vignier, 1831).

17   M. K. Woodworth, *The Literary Career of Sir Samuel Egerton Brydges* (Oxford: Basil Blackwell, 1935), 7–8.

18   S. E. Brydges, *The Autobiography, Times, Opinions, and Contemporaries of Sir Egerton Brydges, Bart. K.J. (per legem terrae) Baron Chandos of Sudeley, etc.*, 2 vols. (London: Cochrane and M'Crone, 1834), 1:2–13, 19–21.

19   Woodworth, *Literary Career*, 33. In the London Library's manuscripts, Brydges numbered his poems by line and work, and dated them; they extend into the thousands in this holding alone.

20   For his biography, see Brydges, *Autobiography*.

21   G. F. Beltz, *A Review of the Chandos Peerage Case* (London: R. Bentley, 1834), vi, viii.

22 See J. Johnson, *Princely Chandos: James Brydges, 1674–1744* (Wolfeboro: Alan Sutton, 1984).

23 S. E. Brydges, *Stemmata Illustria; Praecipue Regia* (Paris: printed by J. Smith, 1825; 100 copies, distributed privately), separately paginated *autobiographical memoir,* 13–14; Brydges, *Autobiography,* 1:105–6.

24 Beltz, *Review of the Chandos Case,* 5–9, 13–15, 38, 83, and passim; Brydges, *Stemmata Illustria,* separately paginated *autobiographical memoir,* 15.

25 S. E. Brydges, ed., *Collins's Peerage of England,* 9 vols. (London: F. C. and J. Rivington et al., 1812), 6:738n.

26 Brydges, *Stemmata Illustria,* 106.

27 S. E. Brydges, *Tabula Genealogia: Descent of Sir Egerton Brydges from the Merovingian Kings,* and *A brief statement of the case of the claim of Mr Brydges of Wotton in Kent, to the Barony of Chandos, 1790–1803,* in BL MS Add. 32375, fols. 127ʳ–129ᵛ.

28 S. E. Brydges, *Lex Terrae* (Geneva: printed by W. Fick, 1831), 42.

29 Brydges, *Autobiography,* 1:181.

30 Brydges, *Stemmata Illustria.*

31 S. E. Brydges, *A Note on the Suppression of Memoirs Announced by the Author in June, 1825; Containing Numerous Strictures on Contemporary Public Characters* (Paris: J. Smith, 1825), 22–27, 44, 46; *Stemmata Illustria,* separately paginated *autobiographical memoir,* 4; M. W. McCahill, "Peerage Creations and the Changing Character of the British Nobility, 1750–1830," *English Historical Review* 96 (1981): 259–84; P. Harling, *The Waning of "Old Corruption": The Politics of Economical Reform in Britain, 1779–1846* (Oxford: Clarendon Press, 1996), 42–55.

32 Brydges, *Collins's Peerage of England,* 6:704–40.

33 Brydges, *Lex Terrae,* 86.

34 Brydges, *Stemmata Illustria,* 104, separately paginated *autobiographical memoir,* 8; Brydges, *Note on the Suppression of Memoirs,* 45–46.

35 S. E. Brydges, *Imaginative Biography,* 2 vols. (London: Saunders and Otley, 1834).

36 Brydges, *Stemmata Illustria,* 108; separately paginated *autobiographical memoir,* 1, 23; Brydges, *Note on the Suppression of Memoirs,* x–xi, 16.

37 E.g., S. E. Brydges to J. Warwick, November 15, 1819, Beinecke Library, Yale, MS Osborn fd 20, pp. 60–64. McCann, *Cultural Politics,* 59–64.

38 Brydges, *Note on the Suppression of Memoirs,* 4, 6–7.

39 Brydges, *Note on the Suppression of Memoirs,* xiii–iv; [S.] E. Brydges, *Gnomica* (Geneva: by W. Fick, 1824), vii.

40 *Stemmata Illustria,* separately paginated *autobiographical memoir,* 24.

41 Brydges, *Stemmata Illustria,* 91.

42 He cited his use of the press as the leading counterexample to prevailing publishing trends: *Stemmata Illustria,* separately paginated *autobiographical memoir,* 23.

43 R. Blum, *Bibliographia: An Inquiry into Its Definition and Designations,* trans. M. V. Rovelstad (Chicago: American Library Association, 1980; orig. 1969); B. H. Breslauer and R. Folter, *Bibliography: Its History and Development* (New York: Grolier Club, 1984).

44 For the development of genealogical methods, see S. Timpanaro, *The Genesis of Lachmann's Method,* trans and ed. G. W. Most (Chicago: University of Chicago Press, 2005), and for the earlier bibliographical tradition, see L. Balsamo, *Bibliography: History of a Tradition,* trans. W. A. Pettas (Berkeley, Calif.: B. M. Rosenthal, 1990).

45 *An account of the rise and progress of the dispute between the masters and journeymen printers* (London: published for the benefit of the men in confinement; sold by J. Ridgway, 1799), iv, 13.

46 H. G. Bohn, *Appendix to the Bibliographer's Manual* [of Lowndes] (London: Bell and Daldy, 1865), 218–25.

47 S. E. Brydges, *Cimelia* (Geneva, 1823), xii–xiii.

48 R. Cave, *The Private Press,* 2nd ed. (New York: R. R. Bowker, 1983).

49 A. Johns, "The Past, Present, and Future of the Scientific Book," in *Books and the Sciences in History,* ed. M. Frasca-Spada and N. Jardine (Cambridge: Cambridge University Press, 2000), 408–26, esp. 415–18.

50 Woodworth, *Literary Career,* 112–18, 128, 134–35; S. E. Brydges, *Res Literariae* (October 1820), 3–4.

51 S. E. Brydges, *Archaica,* 2 vols. (London: Longman et al., 1814–15), 2:vi.

52 S. E. Brydges, *A Summary Statement of the Great Grievance Imposed on Authors and Publishers; and the Injury Done to Literature, by the Late Copyright Act* (London: printed for Longman, Hurst, Rees, Orme and Brown, Paternoster Row, 1818), 18.

53 Brydges, *Summary Statement,* 2.

54 T. Fisher, *The Present Circumstances of Literary Property in England Considered* (London: printed by Nichols, son, and Bentley, 1813); R. Duppa, *An Address to the Parliament of Great Britain, on the Claims of Authors to Their Own Copy-Right,* 2nd ed. (London: sold by Longman, Hurst, Rees, Orme, and Brown, 1813), 34; Brydges, *Summary Statement,* iii–iv.

55 Brydges, *Summary Statement,* 13

56 Brydges, *Summary Statement,* 3n.

57 S. E. Brydges, *Reasons for a Farther Amendment of the Act 54 Geo.III.c.156* (London: Nichols, Son, and Bentley, 1817), 18; S. E. Brydges, *A Vindication of the Pending Bill for the Amendment of the Copyright Act* (London: Longman, Hurst, Rees, Orme, and Brown, 1818), 4, 10. For these units, see J. Johnson, *Typographia,* 2 vols. (London: Longman et al., 1824), 2:576–88, and in general, E. Howe, ed., *The London Compositor: Documents Relating to Wages, Working Conditions and Customs of the London Printing Trade, 1785–1900* (London: Bibliographical Society, 1947).

58 Brydges, *Summary Statement,* 4.

59   Brydges, *Reasons for a Farther Amendment,* 43–44; Brydges, *Summary Statement,* 18–19.

60   Brydges, *Summary Statement,* 10–11.

61   Brydges, *Summary Statement,* 16.

62   Brydges, *Summary Statement,* 14–15.

63   Brydges, *Summary Statement,* 2, 19.

64   Brydges, *Reasons for a Farther Amendment,* 44–48.

65   *Observations on the Copy-Right Bill* (n.p., April 6, 1818); [S. Turner], *Reasons for a Modification of the Act of Anne* (London: Nichols, Son, and Bentley, 1813), 13–15.

66   "Proposed Amendment of Copyright Act. Glasgow Petition—Bodleian Petition," reprinted from *Gentleman's Magazine,* March 1818, in Beinecke Library, Yale, classmark X218.G7.817, no. 6.

67   "Speech of Sir E. Brydges on his motion for leave to Amend the late Copy Right Bill" (June 19, 1817), in Beinecke Library, Yale, classmark X218. G7.817, no. 2.

68   Hansard 1st ser., 36 (1817), 1069 (June 19, 1817): the division was 57:58.

69   For the numbers on Byron, see W. St. Clair, *The Reading Nation in the Romantic Period* (Cambridge: Cambridge University Press, 2004), 327, 585–90, 682–91.

70   S. E. Brydges, *The Lake of Geneva,* 2 vols. (Geneva: by A. L. Vignier, for Bossange and Co., London, and A. Cherbulier, Geneva, 1832), 1:62–5, 113–14; S. J. Schaffer, "Scientific Discoveries and the End of Natural Philosophy," *Social Studies of Science* 16 (1986): 387–420.

71   Fisher, *Present Circumstances,* 8–9.

72   H. W. Lack and D. J. Mabberley, *The* Flora Graeca *Story: Sibthorp, Bauer, and Hawkins in the Levant* (Oxford: Oxford University Press, 1999), 191–225, esp. 215.

73   D. Cadbury, *The Dinosaur Hunters* (London: Fourth Estate, 2000), e.g., 86, 110–11, 243–51, 275–76; M. Rudwick, *Scenes from Deep Time: Early Pictorial Representations of the Prehistoric World* (Chicago: University of Chicago Press, 1992), 74–79; A. Desmond, *Archetypes and Ancestors: Palaeontology in Victorian London, 1850–1875* (London: Blond & Briggs, 1982), 113–46.

74   London Library, Brydges MSS, vol. IV, pp. 21–24 (Memoranda on Beltz, 1835).

75   Brydges, *Cimelia,* iii–iv, ix–x.

76   Woodworth, *Literary Career,* 28–30.

77   B. Hilton, *Corn, Cash, Commerce: The Economic Policies of the Tory Governments, 1815–1830* (Oxford: Oxford University Press, 1977), 270; see also Brydges, *Lex Terrae,* 340–48.

78   S. E. Brydges, *The Population and Riches of Nations* (Paris: J. J. Paschoud, 1819), xvi–xxi; Brydges to J. P. Brooks, April 26, 1820, Houghton Library, Harvard, MS Eng. 1156, folder 7.

79   A. Johns, "The Identity Engine: Printing and Publishing at the Begin-
      ning of the Knowledge Economy," in *The Mindful Hand: Inquiry and
      Invention from the Late Renaissance to Early Industrialisation,* ed. L. Roberts,
      S. Schaffer, and P. Dear (Chicago: Edita/University of Chicago Press,
      2007), 403–28.
80   Beltz, *Review of the Chandos Peerage Case,* vi.

10 INVENTORS, SCHEMERS, AND MEN OF SCIENCE

1   B. Z. Khan, *The Democratization of Invention: Patents and Copyrights in
      American Economic Development, 1790–1920* (Cambridge: Cambridge
      University Press, 2005), 106–27, 182–221, 288–89.
2   For blow-by-blow accounts of these legislative battles, see B. Sherman
      and L. Bently, *The Making of Modern Intellectual Property Law: The British
      Experience, 1760–1911* (Cambridge: Cambridge University Press, 1999), and
      M. Coulter, *Property in Ideas: The Patent Question in Mid-Victorian Britain*
      (Kirksville, Mo.: Thomas Jefferson University Press, 1991).
3   D. Brewster, *A Treatise of the Kaleidoscope* (Edinburgh: for A. Constable and
      Co.; and Longman et al., London, 1819), 113–17, 134–35.
4   J. D. Collier, *An Essay on the Law of Patents for New Inventions* (London: for
      the author, and sold by Longman and Rees, 1803); Sherman and Bently,
      Making of Modern Intellectual Property Law, 107.
5   Coulter, *Property in Ideas,* 16–18.
6   W. R. Grove, "Suggestions for Improvements in the Administration of
      the Patent Law," *The Jurist,* n.s., 6 (January 28, 1860): 19–25, esp. 22.
7   Brewster, *Treatise,* 7; *Description and Method of Using the Patent Kaleidoscope
      Invented by Dr. Brewster* (n.p., 1818); D. Brewster, *The Kaleidoscope: Its
      History, Theory, and Construction* (London: J. Murray, 1858), 6–7 and n1,
      185–89; M. M. Gordon, *The Home Life of Sir David Brewster* (Edinburgh:
      Edmonston and Douglas, 1869), 95–99; M. Kemp, "'Philosophy in Sport'
      and the 'Sacred Precincts': Sir David Brewster on the Kaleidoscope and
      Stereoscope," in *Muse and Reason: The Relation of Arts and Sciences, 1650–
      1850,* ed. B. Castel, J. A. Leith, and A. W. Riley (Kingston, Ontario: Royal
      Society of Canada, 1994), 203–32; A. D. Morrison-Low, "Brewster and
      Scientific Instruments," in *"Martyr of Science": Sir David Brewster, 1781–
      1868,* ed. A. D. Morrison-Low and J. R. R. Christie (Edinburgh: Royal
      Scottish Museum, 1984), 59–65, esp. 60–61; B. M. Stafford, *Artful Science:
      Enlightenment Entertainment and the Eclipse of Visual Education* (Cambridge,
      Mass.: MIT Press, 1994), 67, 107.
8   S. Shapin, "Brewster and the Edinburgh Career in Science," in *"Martyr of
      Science,"* ed. Morrison-Low and Christie, 17–23.
9   Brewster to Babbage, February 12, 1830, in *Gentlemen of Science: Early
      Correspondence of the British Association for the Advancement of Science,* ed.

J. Morrell and A. Thackray (London: Royal Historical Society, 1984), 24–25 (Brewster's emphasis).

10   [D. Brewster], "[Review of] *Reflexions on the Decline of Science in England*," *Quarterly Review* 43 (1830): 305–42; [D. Brewster], "The Paris Exposition and the Patent Laws," *North British Review* 24 [American edition, vol. 19] (November 1855–February 1856), 122–42, esp. 131.

11   Brewster to Whewell, November 4, 1830, in *Gentlemen of Science: Early Correspondence,* ed. Morrell and Thackray, 29–30.

12   J. Morrell and A. Thackray, *Gentlemen of Science: Early Years of the British Association for the Advancement of Science* (Oxford: Clarendon Press, 1981), 41–44.

13   Morrell and Thackray, eds., *Gentlemen of Science: Early Correspondence,* 144; Morrell and Thackray, *Gentlemen of Science: Early Years,* 259–60; J. B. Morrell, "Brewster and the Early British Association for the Advancement of Science," in *"Martyr of Science,"* ed. Morrison-Low and Christie, 25–29. "Banditti" was one of Charles Johnson's (or Defoe's) words for pirates: see C. Johnson [i.e., D. Defoe?], *A General History of the Robberies and Murders of the Most Notorious Pyrates* (Mineola, N.Y.: Dover, 1999 [orig. London, 1724]), 30.

14   W. Whewell, review of Somerville, *Quarterly Review* 51 (March 1834): 58–60; W. Whewell, *Philosophy of the Inductive Sciences* (London: J. W. Parker, 1840), 1:cxiii; S. Ross, "*Scientist:* The Story of a Word," *Annals of Science* 18 (1962): 65–85.

15   A. Desmond, *The Politics of Evolution: Morphology, Medicine, and Reform in Radical London* (Chicago: University of Chicago Press, 1989), 15, 229–35; A. Johns, "The Ambivalence of Authorship in Early Modern Natural Philosophy," in *Scientific Authorship: Credit and Intellectual Property in Science,* ed. M. Biagioli and P. Galison (New York: Routledge, 2003), 67–90, esp. 84–88. For the rise of scientific engineering, see C. Smith and M. N. Wise, *Energy and Empire: A Biographical Study of Lord Kelvin* (Cambridge: Cambridge University Press, 1989), 30, 653–54.

16   J. Watt, "Thoughts upon Patents, or Exclusive Privileges for New Inventions," in E. Robinson and A. E. Musson, *James Watt and the Steam Revolution* (New York: A. M. Kelley, 1969), 213–28.

17   Sherman and Bently, *Making of Modern Intellectual Property Law,* 131. In the end, these debates led into general considerations of the role of scientific "expert testimony" in the courts at large.

18   *Report of the Select Committee on the Law Relative to Patents for Inventions* (London, 1829), e.g., 38, 40; Coulter, *Property in Ideas,* 30–36.

19   Coulter, *Property in Ideas,* 49–50. For manufacturers' hostility to exhibitions, see Morrell and Thackray, *Gentlemen of Science: Early Years,* 264.

20   "An Act to Extend the Provisions of the Designs Act, 1850, and to Give Protection from Piracy to Persons Exhibiting New Inventions at the

Exhibition of the Works of Industry of All Nations in 1851," 14 & 15 Vict., c. 8.

21 Gordon, *Home Life of Sir David Brewster,* 207–9; Coulter, *Property in Ideas,* 42.

22 15 & 16 Vict., c. 83; Coulter, *Property in Ideas,* 53–55, 82.

23 Coulter, *Property in Ideas,* 60–61.

24 Sherman and Bently, *Making of Modern Intellectual Property Law,* 111–28.

25 *An Act for Amending the Law for Granting Patents for Inventions,* 15 & 16 Vict. c. 83, §xviii, in J. Coryton, *A Treatise on the Law of Letters-Patent* (London: H. Sweet, 1855), 440–66, esp. 446–47.

26 G. Heuman, "The British West Indies," in *The Oxford History of the British Empire, III: The Nineteenth Century,* ed. A. Porter (Oxford: Oxford University Press, 1999), 470–93, esp. 477–78, 482; M. Havinden and D. Meredith, *Colonialism and Development: Britain and Its Tropical Colonies, 1850–1960* (London: Routledge, 1993), 27–37.

27 Some of MacFie's work on the patents question is traceable in his family's papers at the University of Glasgow archives, which include his common-place books; for the early complaint of a multiplicity of patents on manufacturers, see MS DC120/5/20/5 (April 15, 1851).

28 Grove, "Suggestions," 23, 25; Coulter, *Property in Ideas,* 154.

29 M. J. Bastable, *Arms and the State: Sir William Armstrong and the Remaking of British Naval Power, 1854–1914* (Aldershot: Ashgate, 2004), 19–20, 23–24, 28–31, 34, 36–37; P. McKenzie, *W. G. Armstrong* (Newcastle: Longhirst Press, 1983), 16–19; see also 19–29 for early hydrostatic experiments preceding his hydraulics.

30 Coulter, *Property in Ideas,* 104, 111–15.

31 [Brewster], "Patent Laws," 337; Morrell and Thackray, *Gentlemen of Science: Early Years,* 345; Coulter, *Property in Ideas,* 106–10. For Kant's arguments see above, 54–56, and the sources cited in A. Johns, "The Piratical Enlightenment," in *This Is Enlightenment,* ed. C. Siskin and W. Warner (Chicago: University of Chicago Press, forthcoming).

32 R. A. MacFie, ed., *Recent Discussions on the Abolition of Patents for Inventions* (London: Longmans, Green, Reader, and Dyer, 1869); R. A. MacFie, ed., *Copyright and Patents for Inventions,* 2 vols. (Edinburgh: T. and T. Clark, 1879–83).

33 MacFie, *Copyright and Patents for Inventions,* 1:155–56, 229–72; 2:565–66, 580–86. H. C. Baird returned the compliment by reprinting MacFie's two volumes in Philadelphia.

34 MacFie, *Copyright and Patents for Inventions,* vols. 1 and 2, notes before title pages. MacFie's *Patent Question under Free Trade* was extracted and translated into French: see University of Glasgow Archives, MS DC120/5/24/20.

35 Coulter, *Property in Ideas,* 64–65.

36 Grove, "Suggestions," 19–25, esp. 21–22; Sherman and Bently, *Making of Modern Intellectual Property Law,* 50–56.

37 H. Dircks, *Inventors and Inventions* (London: E. and F. N. Spon, 1867), v, 109, 114.

38 *Report from the Select Committee* (1871), 23; Bastable, *Arms and the State,* 37–38, 60, 181.

39 Coulter, *Property in Ideas,* 77.

40 *Scientific Review* 1, no. 1 (March 1865): 9; *Scientific Review* 1, no. 3 (May 1865): 42, 44; Sir David Brewster, "On the Claims of Science, Literature, and the Arts to National Recognition and Support," part 2, *Scientific Review,* 2, no. 7 (October 1866): 117–18; *Scientific Review* 2, no. 9 (December 1866): 149–50; *Scientific Review* 2, no. 11 (February 1867): 193–94; Smith and Wise, *Energy and Empire,* 653; I. R. Morus, *When Physics Became King* (Chicago: University of Chicago Press, 2005), 232–33; Feather vs. The Queen, 6 Best & Smith 257 (February 3, 1865).

41 [Brewster], "Paris Exposition," 130, 134, 136; Gordon, *Home Life of Sir David Brewster,* 211–12.

42 [Brewster], "Paris Exposition," 139; *Scientific Review* 2, no. 8 (November 1866): 134–35. Cf. *Scientific Review* 1, no. 7 (September 1863): 106.

43 *Scientific Review* 1, no. 3 (May 1865): 44; *Scientific Review* 1, no. 7 (September 1865): 106; "Sir David Brewster, K.H., Ll.D., F.R.S., etc., on the Patent Laws," *Scientific Review,* January 1866, 169; *Scientific Review,* February 1866, 185; *Scientific Review* 7, no. 3 (March 1872): 35; [Sir David Brewster], "The Patent Laws," *Westminster Review,* n.s., 26 (July–October 1864), 322–57, esp. 332.

44 *Scientific Review* 1, no. 8 (October 1865): 121; W. Fairbairn, "The Rights of Inventors," *Scientific Review* 2, no. 1 (April 1866): 1–2; T. Richardson, "A Review of the Arguments For and Against the Patent Laws," *Scientific Review* 2, no. 13 (April 1867): 223; T. Richardson, "A Review of the Arguments For and Against the Patent Laws" (cont.), *Scientific Review* 2, no. 15 (June 1867): 257–58; *Scientific Review* 4, no. 6 (June 1869); *Scientific Review* 4, no. 9 (September 1869): 183–85; *Scientific Review* 7, no. 2 (February 1872): 19. For Armstrong's role in industrial conflict at this time, see E. Allen, J. F. Clarke, N. McCord, and D. J. Rowse, *The North-East Engineers' Strikes of 1871: The Nine Hours' League* (Newcastle: F. Graham, 1971), 79–85, 108–10, 125, 148.

45 *The Engineer,* August 28, 1861, 106; "The Patent Question," *The Engineer,* September 13, 1861, 162; "Sir William Armstrong and Patents" (repr. from *London Journal of Arts and Sciences*), *The Engineer,* October 18, 1861, 231; "Inventions and Patents," *The Engineer,* August 23, 1861, 107; *Scientific American,* n.s., 5, no. 11 (September 14, 1861): 167; *Scientific American,* 5, no. 15 (October 12, 1861): 236. See also succeeding weeks of the *Scientific*

American for repeated attacks on Armstrong, and, for an earlier one, see 14, no. 33 (April 23, 1859): 277.

46 Sir William Armstong, "On the Patent Laws," *The Engineer,* September 13, 1861, 154.

47 A. T. Blakely, *A Letter from Captain Blakely, H.P., Royal Artillery, to the Secretary of State for War, Claiming the Original Invention of an Indispensable Feature of the Armstrong Gun* (London: J. Ridgway, 1859), esp. 13. For his invention, see also A. T. Blakely, *A Cheap and Simple Method of Manufacturing Strong Cannon* (London: J. Ridgway, 1858).

48 P. Barry, *Shoeburyness and the Guns: A Philosophical Discourse* (London: Sampson, Low, son, and Marston, 1865), 49, 52–53, 55–57, 60.

49 D. Treadwell, "Rifled Cannon," in Treadwell, *Papers and Memoirs concerning the Improvement of Cannon* (Cambridge, Mass.: University Press, 1865), 3–4, 6; D. Treadwell, *On the Construction of Improved Ordnance* (Cambridge, Mass.: Welch, Bigelow, and Company, 1862), 7–8; A. L. Holley, *A Treatise on Ordnance and Armor* (New York: D. Van Nostrand; London: Trübner and Co., 1865), 1, 855–70; Armstong, "On the Patent Laws," 154. For the charge of using inferior materials solely to avoid dealing with Blakely, see Blakely, *Letter,* 13.

50 Coulter, *Property in Ideas,* 151–53.

51 E.g., *Scientific Review* 6, no. 6 (June 1871): 105; *Scientific Review* 6, no. 10 (October 1871), 183 (on Grove's testimony in 1871).

52 *Report from the Select Committee* (1871), 139–40; *Report from the Select Committee* (1872), 22–23.

53 Sherman and Bently, *Making of Modern Intellectual Property Law,* 133, 138–40. On Woodcroft, see J. Hewish, *The Indefatigable Mr. Woodcroft* (London: British Library, 1980).

54 MacFie, *Copyright and Patents for Inventions,* 2:51.

55 R. Hyam, *Britain's Imperial Century, 1815–1914: A Study of Empire and Expansion* (New York: Harper, 1976), 33–35, 109–10. In general, see D. Bell, *The Idea of Greater Britain: Empire and the Future of World Order, 1860–1900* (Princeton: Princeton University Press, 2007).

56 J. E. Tyler, *The Struggle for Imperial Unity (1868–1895)* (London: Longmans, Green and Co., 1938), 6n1, 99; T. R. Reese, *The History of the Royal Commonwealth Society, 1868–1968* (London: Oxford University Press, 1968), 11, 29, 62, 65.

57 MacFie, *Copyright and Patents for Inventions,* 2:592.

58 R. A. MacFie, *Cries, in a Crisis, for Statesmanship Popular and Patriotic to Test and Contest Free-Trade in Manufactures,* 2nd ed. (London: E. Stanford, 1881), 51, 53, 58.

59 MacFie, *Cries, in a Crisis,* v, 32–33, 226, 167; see also 153–55.

60 R. A. MacFie, *Colonial Questions* (London: Longmans, Green, Reader, and Dyer, 1871), ix, 16–17, 25; MacFie, *Cries, in a Crisis,* 48–49.

61 Tyler, *Struggle for Imperial Unity*, 10–11.
62 J. A. Froude, *Oceana: Or England and Her Colonies* (New York: Charles
    Scribner's Sons, 1888), 1–17, 153, 215–21, 383–96.
63 *Hansard*, 353: 438.
64 G. E. Folk, *Patents and Industrial Progress* (New York: Harper, 1942), 118–19;
    E. Schiff, *Industrialization without National Patents: The Netherlands, 1869–
    1912; Switzerland, 1850–1907* (Princeton, N.J.: Princeton University Press,
    1971), 124–26. For the Berne process, see S. Ricketson and J. C. Ginsburg,
    *International Copyright and Neighbouring Rights: The Berne Convention and
    Beyond*, 2nd ed. (Oxford: Oxford University Press, 2006), and, especially,
    C. Seville, *The Internationalisation of Copyright Law: Books, Buccaneers and
    the Black Flag in the Nineteenth Century* (Cambridge: Cambridge University
    Press, 2006).

11 INTERNATIONAL COPYRIGHT AND
THE SCIENCE OF CIVILIZATION

1 J. Fiske, *Edward Livingston Youmans: Interpreter of Science for the People*
   (New York: D. Appleton and Co., 1894); R. M. MacLeod, "Evolutionism,
   Internationalism and Commercial Enterprise in Science: The Interna-
   tional Scientific Series, 1871–1910," in *Development of Science Publishing in
   Europe*, ed. A. J. Meadows (Amsterdam: Elsevier, 1980), 63–93; L. Howsam,
   "An Experiment with Science for the Nineteenth-Century Book Trade:
   The International Scientific Series," *British Journal for the History of Science*
   33 (2000): 187–207, esp. 193–202; *Times* (London), October 20, 1871, 10.
2 The American editions of Darwin's *Origin* furnish another good example.
   At Gray's urging, based partly on a mistaken belief that new content could
   guarantee the U.S. copyright to Darwin, these editions, produced by
   Appleton, included significant new material that was not included in
   the English text for another ten years: see the appendix to the *Darwin
   Correspondence* on this subject.
3 *Addresses of the Philadelphia Society for the Promotion of National Industry*
   (Philadelphia: M. Carey and Son, 1819), title page; J. A. McGraw, *Most
   Wonderful Machine: Mechanization and Social Change in Berkshire Paper
   Making, 1801–1885* (Princeton, N.J.: Princeton University Press, 1987),
   95–116, 118–25.
4 J. Tebbel, *A History of Book Publishing in the United States*, 4 vols. (New York:
   R. R. Bowker, 1972–81), 1:270–71; M. Winship, "Printing with Plates in
   the Nineteenth-Century United States," *Printing History* 5 (1983), 15–26;
   R. Remer, *Printers and Men of Capital: Philadelphia Book Publishers in the
   New Republic* (Philadelphia: University of Pennsylvania Press, 1996),
   95–98; R. J. Zboray, *A Fictive People: Antebellum Economic Development and
   the American Reading Public* (New York: Oxford University Press, 1993),

5–11; M. Carey, *Address to the Booksellers of the United States* (Philadelphia: T. S. Manning, 1813). On stereotyping, see also A. Johns, "The Identity Engine: Science, Stereotyping, and Skill in Print," in *The Mindful Hand,* ed. P. Dear, L. Roberts, and S. Schaffer (Chicago: Edita/University of Chicago Press, 2007).

5   A. J. Clark, *The Movement for International Copyright in Nineteenth-Century America* (Washington, D.C.: Catholic University of America Press, 1960), 34–35.

6   D. Kaser, *Messrs. Carey & Lea of Philadelphia: A Study in the History of the Booktrade* (Philadelphia: University of Pennsylvania Press, 1957), 119–23.

7   Kaser, *Carey & Lea,* 108–10.

8   Kaser, *Carey & Lea,* 25–28, 93–98.

9   E. L. Bradsher, *Mathew Carey: Editor, Author, and Publisher* (New York: Columbia University Press, 1912), 79, 84; Kaser, *Carey & Lea,* 98–107.

10   W. Collins, *Considerations on the Copyright Question Addressed to an American Friend* (London: Trubner and Co., 1880), 5, 11–12.

11   Kaser, *Carey & Lea,* 69–70, 81 (Kaser's figures for the Cooper contract seem to differ, however, between $4,000 and $5,000); Clark, *Movement for International Copyright,* 34–35. One satisfied recipient of a Carey honorarium was the phrenologist George Combe: see Combe to Carey and Hart, May 7, 1841, Edward Carey Gardiner Collection (ECG), Carey Misc., Carey Section, Historical Society of Pennsylvania (HSP), Box 82, folder 8.

12   Kaser, *Carey & Lea,* 98–107; M. Carey to H. C. Carey, July 18, 19, 22, and 23, 1822, Lea and Febiger Papers, 1822, HSP, Nos. 22302–6.

13   E. Exman, *The Brothers Harper* (New York: Harper and Row, 1965), 57–58; J. J. Barnes, *Authors, Publishers, and Politicians: The Quest for an Anglo-American Copyright Agreement, 1815–1854* (London: Routledge and Kegan Paul, 1974), 57.

14   A. Chase to E. Norton, November 5, 1828, Book Trades Collection, American Antiquarian Society (AAS), 1:8; McCarty and Davis Papers, AAS, 1:3, No. 101; M. Winship, "Getting the Books Out: Trade Sales, Parcel Sales, and Book Fairs in the Nineteenth-Century United States," in *Getting the Books Out: Papers of the Chicago Conference on the Book in Nineteenth-Century America,* ed. M. Hackenberg (Washington, D.C.: Library of Congress, 1987), 4–25, esp. 9, 12–20; Zboray, *A Fictive People,* 24–29; Kaser, *Carey & Lea,* 127–32.

15   R. G. Silver, "The Convivial Printer: Dining, Wining, and Marching, 1825–1860," *Printing History* 4 (1982): 16–25; M. A. Lause, *Some Degree of Power: From Hired Hand to Union Craftsman in the Preindustrial American Printing Trades, 1778–1815,* (Fayetteville: University of Arkansas Press, 1991), 26.

16   J. Parton, "International Copyright," *Atlantic Monthly,* October 1867, 430–53, esp. 441.

17   Exman, *The Brothers Harper,* 53–55, 393–96.

18   McCarty and Davis Papers, AAS, 1:5, nos. 319, 320, 321; 1:7, nos. 500, 510.

19   Bradsher, *Mathew Carey,* 86–87; M. Carey to H. Carey, July 13, 1821, in Lea and Febiger Papers, HSP, no. 18649; MacLeod, "Evolutionism, Internationalism, and Commercial Enterprise," 66; Fiske, *Youmans,* 149–50; Parton, "International Copyright," 441, 443.

20   Clark, *Movement for International Copyright,* 37; Zboray, *A Fictive People,* 11–12, 74; M. McGill, *American Literature and the Culture of Reprinting, 1834–1853* (Philadelphia: University of Pennsylvania Press, 2003), 21–23.

21   McGill, *American Literature and the Culture of Reprinting;* I. Lehuu, *Carnival on the Page: Popular Print Media in Antebellum America* (Chapel Hill: University of North Carolina Press, 2000), 59–75; Barnes, *Authors, Publishers, and Politicians,* 6–29; J. L. Sibley to J. Wood, March 3, 1938, Book Trades Collection, AAS, 1:11.

22   Barnes, *Authors, Publishers, and Politicians,* 13–15.

23   *The New World,* 2 (January–July 1841): 94; Clark, *Movement for International Copyright,* 42, 48, 51–52.

24   N. M. Ashby, *Charles Sealsfield* (Duarte, Calif.: N. M. Ashby; Stuttgart, Germany: Sealsfield-Gesellschaft, 1980), 1–50; C. Sealsfield, *Gesammelte Werke,* 18 vols. (Stuttgart: J. B. Melzer, 1846 [1842–46]); for the lunar hoax, see D. Schiller, *Objectivity and the News: The Public and the Rise of Commercial Journalism* (Philadelphia: University of Pennsylvania Press, 1981), 76–95.

25   *Corsair* 1, no. 1 (March 16, 1839): 9; 1, no. 2 (March 23, 1839): 26; 1, no. 4 (April 6, 1839), 54–56; 1, no. 5 (April 13, 1839), 69–70. On Willis, see T. N. Baker, *Sentiment and Celebrity: Nathaniel Parker Willis and the Trials of Literary Fame* (Oxford: Oxford University Press, 1999). The *Corsair* merits comparison with the British *Pirate* of 1833.

26   AAS, classmark Bdsds. 1837; Barnes, *Authors, Publishers, and Politicians,* 61–65; Clark, *Movement for International Copyright,* 39–45, 51–55, 58–63.

27   G. S. Rice, *The Transformation of Authorship in America* (Chicago: University of Chicago Press, 1997), 90.

28   "An American," *A Plea for Authors, and the Rights of Literary Property* (New York: Adlard and Saunders, 1838), 5–6.

29   P. H. Nicklin, *Remarks on Literary Property* (Philadelphia: P. H. Nicklin and T. Johnson, 1838). For Carey's concurrence, see, e.g., H. C. Carey, *Letters on International Copyright* (Philadelphia: A. Hart, 1853), 58–59.

30   Nicklin, *Remarks,* 24–25, 33, 50, 58–63, 83; cf. J. Sklansky, *The Soul's Economy: Market Society and Selfhood in American Thought, 1820–1920* (Chapel Hill: University of North Carolina Press, 2002), 80.

31   HSP, Lea and Febiger Papers, 1821; University of Michigan, Clements Library, Henry Carey Letterbook, p. 5; W. Elder, *A Memoir of Henry C. Carey* (Philadelphia: Henry Carey Baird & Co., 1880), 24; J. L. Huston, *The Panic of 1857 and the Coming of the Civil War* (Baton Rouge: Louisiana State

University Press, 1987), 134–35; K. Marx, *Grundrisse*, trans. M. Nicolaus (London: Penguin, 1993 [1973]), 754, 883–93. W. E. Gienapp, *The Origins of the Republican Party, 1852–1856* (New York: Oxford University Press, 1987), 397, 403; Huston, *Panic of 1857,* 241–42, 249–50. For Carey's position with respect to early sociology, see Sklansky, *Soul's Economy,* 171–204. Smith's correspondence with Carey is in the HSP: see, e.g., Smith to Carey, October 31, 1869, HSP, Carey Section (CS), ECG, H. C. Carey Papers (HCC), Box 78, folder 4; April 14, 1850, January 15, 1854, February 22, 1854, March 2, 1854, March 4, 1854, and February 22, 1855, Box 77, folder 16.

32 Carey, *Letters on International Copyright* (1853), 58.

33 E. P. Smith to Carey, January 22, 1854, February 22, 1854, HSP CS, HCC Papers, Box 77, folder 19; H. C. Carey, *The Unity of Law; As Exhibited in the Relations of Physical, Social, Mental, and Moral Science* (Philadelphia: H. C. Baird, 1872), 16–17, 71–75; K. McKean, *Manual of Social Science* (Philadelphia: H. C. Baird, 1864), title page, iv–v.

34 H. C. Carey, *Essay on the Rate of Wages* (Philadelphia: Carey, Lea and Blanchard, 1835), esp. 232–45; Carey, *Unity of Law,* 16–17; Sklansky, *Soul's Economy,* 83–85; McKean, *Manual of Social Science,* ix; Elder, *Memoir of Henry C. Carey,* 15; Carey, *Unity of Law,* x–xi, 382–92. For Ricardo's theory, see D. Ricardo, *On the Principles of Political Economy,* 3rd ed. (London: John Murray, 1821), ch. 2.

35 Carey, *Principles of Social Science,* 1:41–43; Carey, *Unity of Law,* 80–82.

36 H. C. Carey, *Review of the Decade, 1857–1867* (Philadelphia: Collins, 1867), 5; Carey, *Unity of Law,* v–x, xi. In general, see C. Smith, *The Science of Energy: A Cultural History of Energy Physics in Victorian Britain* (Chicago: University of Chicago Press, 1998).

37 H. C. Carey, *Contraction or Expansion? Repudiation or Resumption? Letters to the Hon. Hugh M'Culloch, Secretary to the Treasury* (Philadelphia: H. C. Baird, 1866), 20–25, esp. 21; A. Desmond, *Huxley: The Devil's Disciple* (London: Michael Joseph, 1994), 192–93. For electro-biology, see also I. Morus, *Frankenstein's Children: Electricity, Exhibition and Experiment in Early Nineteenth-Century London* (Princeton, N.J.: Princeton University Press, 1998), 147–52. See also M. Schabas, *The Natural Origins of Economics* (Chicago: University of Chicago Press, 2005), 70–74, and M. Poovey, *Genres of the Credit Economy: Mediating Value in Eighteenth- and Nineteenth-Century Britain* (Chicago: University of Chicago Press, 2008).

38 Carey, *Unity of Law,* 206; Carey, *Principles of Social Science,* 2:175; T. A. Freyer, *Producers versus Capitalists: Constitutional Conflict in Antebellum America* (Charlottesville: University Press of Virginia, 1994), 3, 7–8, 49–51; Sklansky, *Soul's Economy,* 88, 90; E. P. Thompson, "The Moral Economy of the English Crowd in the Eighteenth Century," in Thompson, *Customs in Common* (New York: New Press, 1993), 185–258, e.g., 193, 205–6.

39 Carey, *Unity of Law,* 190–91, 219–23.

40   H. C. Carey, *The Prospect* (Philadelphia: J. S. Skinner, 1851), 13; H. C. Carey, *Commerce, Christianity, and Civilization, versus British Free Trade* (Philadelphia: Collins, 1876), 5, 36; Carey, *Unity of Law*, 198–99; H. C. Carey, *The Way to Outdo England without Fighting Her* (Philadelphia: H. C. Baird, 1865), 7–8, 31–32.

41   Carey, *Unity of Law*, 7; Carey, *Letters on International Copyright* (1853), 29–31.

42   Carey, *Unity of Law*, xvii–xix, 27–28, 92–93, 270–80, 325–27; Carey, *Principles of Social Science*, 1:40; F. Engels, *The Condition of the Working Class in England* (London: Penguin, 1987 [1845]), 139–49; Sklansky, *Soul's Economy*, 75–76; E. P. Smith to Carey, October 21, 1854, HSP CS, ECG, HCC Papers, Box 77, folder 16.

43   K. Marx, *Capital*, 3 vols. (London: Penguin, 1990–91), 1:705–6. For commonplacing, see A. Blair, "Reading Strategies for Coping with Information Overload, ca. 1550–1700," *Journal of the History of Ideas* 64 (2003): 11–28; A. Moss, *Printed Commonplace-Books and the Structuring of Renaissance Thought* (New York: Oxford University Press, 1996).

44   E. L. Youmans, ed., *The Correlation and Conservation of Forces* (New York: D. Appleton and Co., 1865). For Carey's use of this, see, e.g., *Unity of Law*, xi–xii.

45   Youmans, *Correlation and Conservation of Forces*, xxxvi.

46   Fiske, *Youmans*, 184–85.

47   H. Greeley, *Essays Designed to Elucidate the Science of Political Economy* (Boston: Fields, Osgood, and Co., 1870), 49–51.

48   Carey, *Letters on International Copyright* (1853), 8; Carey, *The Way to Outdo England*, 31; H. C. Carey, *The Resources of the Union* (Philadelphia: H. C. Baird, 1866), 22; Carey, *Unity of Law*, 206–9; Carey, *Commerce, Christianity, and Civilization*, 5–6, 18–20, 24.

49   Carey, *Principles of Social Science*, 2: 123, 251.

50   Carey, *Unity of Law*, 101–2, 111.

51   Carey, *Resources of the Union*, 24; Carey, *The Way to Outdo England*, 31.

52   Carey, *Principles of Social Science*, 1:322–25; Carey, *Unity of Law*, 99, 172, 182; Carey, *The Prospect*, 83.

53   Carey, *Letters on International Copyright* (1853), 37–48, 54, 65, 70–71; Carey, *International Copyright Question Considered*, 23.

54   Carey, *Letters on International Copyright* (1853), 28; H. C. Carey, *Letters on International Copyright*, 2nd ed. (New York: Hurd and Houghton, 1868), 11.

55   Carey, *Letters on International Copyright* (1853), 11–12, 61–63; Carey, *International Copyright Question Considered*, 7–8, 25–26; Freyer, *Producers versus Capitalists*, 125–27.

56   Carey, *Letters on International Copyright* (1853), 10–13, 15–17, 21–23, 25, 44; H. C. Carey, *The International Copyright Question Considered* (Philadelphia: H. C. Baird, 1872), 3.

57   Carey, *The Way to Outdo England*, 3, 17–18; Carey, *International Copyright*

Question Considered, 8–9, 12, 29–30; Carey, *Letters on International Copyright* (1868), 87–88.

58 Carey, *The Way to Outdo England,* 3, 15, 34; Carey, *Letters on International Copyright* (1853), 67, 70–71; Carey, *International Copyright Question Considered,* 13, 24.

59 D. A. Redmond, *Sherlock Holmes among the Pirates: Copyright and Conan Doyle in America, 1890–1930* (New York: Greenwood Press, 1990).

12 THE FIRST PIRATE HUNTERS

1 D. W. Krummel, "Music Publishing," in *Music in Britain: the Romantic Age, 1800–1914,* ed. N. Temperley (London: Athlone, 1981), 46–59, 49.

2 For those unfamiliar with pre-decimal British money, a pound = 20s (shillings) = 240d (pence). A shilling was 12d. A guinea was 21s.

3 N. A. Mace, "Litigating the *Musical Magazine:* The Definition of British Music Copyright in the 1780s," *Book History* 2 (1999): 122–45; D. Hunter, "The Publishing of Opera and Song Books in England, 1703–1726," *Notes,* March 1991, 647–85, esp. 651–55, 657–66. For another detailed example, see N. A. Mace, "Haydn and the London Music Sellers: Forster v. Longman & Broderip," *Music & Letters* 77 (November, 1996): 527–41, esp. 533 and n24.

4 H. Berlioz, *Evenings with the Orchestra,* trans. J. Barzun (Chicago: University of Chicago Press, 1999 [1956]), 67; H. Berlioz, *Les Soirées de l'Orchestre* (Paris: Grund, 1968 [1852]), 84–86; D. Hunter, "Music Copyright in Britain to 1800," *Music & Letters* 67 (1986): 269–82; J. Girdham, *English Opera in Late Eighteenth-Century London: Stephen Storace at Drury Lane* (Oxford: Oxford University Press, 1997).

5 J. M. Picker, *Victorian Soundscapes* (Oxford: Oxford University Press, 2003), 41–81; P. Bailey, *Popular Culture and Performance in the Victorian City* (Cambridge: Cambridge University Press, 1998), 207.

6 Berlioz, *Evenings with the Orchestra,* 57–59. For Gilbert and Sullivan, see M. Aingier, *Gilbert and Sullivan* (Oxford: Oxford University Press, 2002), 94, 174–82.

7 In the parliamentary committee of 1904, members disagreed on whether a piracy produced in the room was photographed or not; they eventually concurred that it was a photographic but nonidentical copy. See *Report of the Departmental Committee . . . to Inquire into the Piracy of Musical Publications* (Cd. 1860. London: HMSO, 1904), 14. Henceforth this is cited as *Report* (1904). Note that the report proper, and the minority report by Caldwell, are separately paginated from the records of the interviews.

8 See C. Ehrlich, *The Piano: A History,* rev. ed. (Oxford: Clarendon Press, 1990), 88–107.

9 David Day saw his first action in 1897, against a pirate reprinting *The*

Soldiers of the Queen (using movable type, in this early instance, not photography): *Report* (1904), 27, 28.

10 *Report* (1904), 8–9, 33.

11 *Report* (1904), 33; J. Coover, *Music Publishing, Copyright and Piracy in Victorian England* (London: Mansell, 1985), 84–85. Coover's collection of snippets from primary sources is the essential starting point for this story.

12 For "commandoes," see also the letter by "Anti-Pirate" quoted in Coover, *Music Publishing,* 85.

13 *Report* (1904), 33; J. Abbott, *The Story of Francis, Day and Hunter* (London: Francis, Day and Hunter, 1952), 31.

14 British Library (BL), Music Library (ML), MS. M. 55, henceforth cited as Preston, scrapbook, fragment from Leeds, n.d.; Coover, *Music Publishing,* 88.

15 Coover, *Music Publishing,* 108–9.

16 St. Helens, January 8, 1904; Preston, n.d.: both in Preston, scrapbook.

17 *Report* (1904), 17.

18 *Report* (1904), 67.

19 *Report* (1904), 33–35.

20 *Report* (1904), 15, 29.

21 *Report* (1904), 32.

22 A. Lamb, *Leslie Stuart: Composer of Floradora* (New York: Routledge, 2002), 166.

23 *Report* (1904), 19–20, 31–32.

24 *Report* (1904), 45.

25 The obvious inference is a background in minstrelsy, or else in the less formal world of late Victorian street musicians, who sometimes adopted blackface. But I have found no firm evidence either way.

26 Preston, scrapbook. Preston also amassed a collection of 268 piracies on his travels, presumably to help with prosecutions; these are now bound in several large volumes under the title "Pirated music" as BL ML H.1848. The items are direct copies of originals, sometimes including publishers' names and warnings (although these are occasionally blacked out). The print quality is variable, and often poor; but almost all would be usable. Most of the pieces are light fare like Sousa marches and operetta and music-hall songs.

27 *Report* (1904), 49.

28 *Report* (1904), 16, 50.

29 *Liverpool Express,* October 15, 1903; fragment in Preston, scrapbook. For the O'Neile raid, see also *Report* (1904), 48.

30 *Report* (1904), 17.

31 J. Coover, "Victorian Periodicals for the Music Trade," *Notes,* March 1990, 609–21, esp. 616 n23.

32 *Report* (1904), 49. Many of the middlemen in the pirate trade were portrayed in the press in terms that implied Irish or Continental Jewish descent.

33   Preston, scrapbook, fragment from Cardiff, n.d. Cf. P. Stallybrass and
A. White, *The Politics and Poetics of Transgression* (Ithaca, N.Y.: Cornell
University Press, 1986), 27–31.

34   *Report* (1904), 52. For Cohen, see various fragments in Preston's scrapbook, e.g., *Manchester Evening News,* October 7, 1903.

35   Preston, scrapbook, July 28, 1904; cf. also another fragment, also from
Sheffield, dated February 24, 1902, when Preston actually gave up the
prosecution rather than go through this ordeal.

36   *Report* (1904), 9, 15, 16.

37   *Report* (1904), 29.

38   *Sheffield Telegraph,* December 1, 1903, in Preston, scrapbook.

39   On the raid, see *Report* (1904), 18. On his embezzlement, see *Report*
(1904), 85.

40   *Report* (1904), 12, 16, 35, 51–52, 77.

41   See Preston, scrapbook, for all these actions (and many more).

42   *Report* (1904), 76–83.

43   *Report* (1904), 32.

44   *Report* (1904), 77. For a 1901 denunciation of this "ring," see Coover, *Music
Publishing,* 77.

45   *Report* (1904), 79.

46   *Report* (1904), 78.

47   *Report* (1904), 48. For the precedent in Russell's proposal, see above, 274–75.

48   L. Harding, "You've Heard of the Flights, but Would You Buy a No-Frills
CD?" *Guardian,* July 5, 2004.

49   *Report* (1904), 35–36, 45–46, 64, 70, 74–75.

50   *Report* (1904), 79–80.

51   *Report* (1904), 31.

52   *Report* (1904), separately paginated reports, 11–19.

53   Lamb, *Leslie Stuart,* 167; L. Kriegel, "Culture and the Copy: Calico,
Capitalism, and Design Copyright in Early Victorian Britain," *Journal of
British Studies* 43 (2004): 233–65.

54   *Report* (1904), 23–24.

55   *Report* (1904), 70.

56   *Report* (1904), 52.

57   *Report* (1904), 40, 52, 68–69.

58   *Report* (1904), 66.

59   *Report* (1904), 26, 47, 64.

60   Coover, *Music Publishing,* 116.

61   Coover, *Music Publishing,* 114, 118; *Musical Times,* August 1, 1904, 534–35.

62   *Report* (1904), 59–60. In point of fact reference had been made to pirates'
conspiracies in the music publishing trade since the 1890s (Coover, *Music
Publishing,* 68), but I believe that Poland's remarks were independent of
those previous claims.

63 *Report* (1904), separately paginated reports, 6.

64 Coover, *Music Publishing,* 125–27.

65 Copyright Act, 1911, 1 and 2 Geo. V, c. 46. The history of early gramophone recordings and piano rolls in this context is fascinating but too
complex to address here; for the American story, see L. Gitelman, *Scripts,
Grooves, and Writing Machines: Representing Technology in the Edison Era*
(Stanford, Calif.: Stanford University Press, 1999), 97–147.

66 V. Guest, *So You Want to Be in Pictures* (London: Reynolds and Hearn,
2001), 26–27, 73.

13 THE GREAT OSCILLATION WAR

1   A. Briggs, *The History of Broadcasting in the United Kingdom,* 5 vols. (London: Oxford University Press, 1995 [orig. 1961–95]), 1:18; *Experimental
Wireless Radio Call Book* (London: Percivall Marshall and Co., n.d. [1924]);
Hansard, *The Parliamentary Debates, House of Commons* (London: HMSO),
5th ser., 150, p. 638 (February 13, 1922).

2   Briggs, *History,* 1:95–6.

3   BBC Written Archives Centre, Caversham (henceforth BBC WAC),
CO 58/1.

4   Royal Mail Archives, Mount Pleasant, London (henceforth RMA),
POST 33/703, March 31, 1922.

5   Hansard, *Commons,* 151, pp. 1077–79 (March 7, 1922); 153, pp. 1600–1601
(May 4, 1922); Briggs, *History,* 1:66–7.

6   Briggs, *History,* 1:85.

7   RMA, POST 33/703, April 21, 1922, May 10, 1922.

8   RMA, POST 33/703, May 10, 1922.

9   BBC WAC, CO 2; Hansard, *Commons,* 153, pp. 1600–1601 (May 4, 1922); Sir
Frederick Sykes (chair), *The Broadcasting Committee Report* (Cmd. 1051)
(London: HMSO, 1923), 7; Briggs, *History,* 1:107–14.

10 BBC WAC, CO 1/1.

11 RMA, POST 33/703, June 16, 1922. Note that I refer to both the British
Broadcasting *Company* and the later British Broadcasting *Corporation* as
"the BBC," in accord with contemporary usage; they were, however,
distinct entities.

12 BBC WAC CO 1/1.

13 F. J. Brown evidence, Sykes committee, RMA, POST 89/18, I, unpaginated.

14 Sykes, *Report,* 8–9; RMA, POST 33/703, June 28, 1922; Earl of Crawford
(chair), *Report of the Broadcasting Committee* (Cmd. 2599) (London: HMSO,
1926), 19. In fact some six to eight thousand U.S. crystal sets reached the
UK before the embargo began. They were admitted provided they
furnished a royalty, met technical standards, and were given a special
mark: BBC WAC, CO 1/2, p. 13.

15 Briggs, *History,* 109.

16 RMA, POST 33/703.

17 Sykes, *Report,* 22.

18 Sykes minutes, evidence by Noble and McKinstry, May 8–10, 1923, RMA,
    POST 89/18, I, §§254–61, 504–28; Hansard, *Commons,* 150, p. 638 (Febru-
    ary 13, 1922); 153, pp. 1600–1601 (May 4, 1922); 156, p. 184 (July 4, 1922);
    Briggs, *History,* 1:128–9.

19 Hansard, *Commons,* 157, pp. 50 (July 24, 1922), 463 (July 26, 1922).

20 Hansard, *Commons,* 157, pp. 1951–64 (August 4, 1922).

21 Hansard, *Commons,* 153, pp. 1600–1602 (May 4, 1922); RMA, POST 33/704;
    BBC WAC, CO 2; BBC WAC, CO 58/1.

22 BBC WAC, CO 1/1.

23 *Daily Mail,* April 9, 1923.

24 Noble, in Sykes evidence, RMA, POST 89/18, I, §251 (May 8, 1923).

25 BBC WAC, CO 1/2, October 9, 1922.

26 RMA, POST 33/704, September 28, 1922, October 2, 1922.

27 RMA, POST 33/703, June 16, 1922.

28 Marconi memo on experimental licenses, September 27, 1922, BBC WAC,
    CO 58/1, CO 1/2, p. 10 and September 12, 1922; Hansard, *Commons,* 164,
    p. 2192 (June 6, 1923); Briggs, *History,* 1:53; RMA, POST 33/704, Septem-
    ber 20, 1922.

29 Sykes evidence, RMA POST 89/18, III, §2340.

30 Hansard, *Commons,* 157, pp. 706–7 (July 27, 1922); RMA, POST 33/704,
    March 23–April 3, 1923; "Wireless Handicaps," *Observer,* December 31,
    1922; Marconi memo, September 27, 1922: BBC WAC, CO 58/1. For the
    Danubian case, see also Sykes evidence, RMA POST 89/18, I, §1736.

31 RMA, POST 33/703, May 18, 1922; Hansard, *Commons,* 157, pp. 1951–64
    (August 4, 1922).

32 *Daily Mail,* March 26, 1923; F. W. Challis and A. H. Rose, Sykes evidence,
    RMA POST 89/18, II, §1232 (May 29, 1923); *Daily Express,* April 5, 1923.

33 BBC WAC, CO 1/2, p. 10 and September 12, 1922.

34 Marconi memo, September 27, 1922, BBC WAC, CO 58/1; Report on
    meeting with N. Chamberlain, February 15, 1923, BBC WAC, CO 7/1.

35 F. J. Brown, Sykes evidence, RMA POST 89/18, I, unpaginated; *Daily
    Mail* April 11, 1923.

36 RMA, POST 33/704, September 16, 1922.

37 Briggs, *History,* 147, 150–51.

38 Briggs, *History,* 146; Hansard, *Commons,* 160, pp. 661–62 (February 19,
    1923), 1794 (February 27, 1923); 162, p. 2241 (April 19, 1923).

39 F. Ruffini, *Report on Scientific Property* (Geneva, Switzerland: Kundig, 1923).

40 On the distinction of expertise, see P. White, *Thomas Huxley: Making the
    "Man of Science"* (Cambridge: Cambridge University Press, 2003); I. R.
    Morus, *When Physics Became King* (Chicago: University of Chicago Press,

2005); R. Yeo, *Defining Science: William Whewell, Natural Knowledge and Public Debate in Early Victorian Britain* (Cambridge: Cambridge University Press, 1993); and G. J. N. Gooday, *The Morals of Measurement: Accuracy, Irony, and Trust in Late Victorian Electrical Practice* (Cambridge: Cambridge University Press, 2004).

41 Sykes, *Report,* 21–22.

42 Marconi memo, September 27, 1922, BBC WAC, CO 58/1.

43 Swinton testimony, in Sykes evidence, RMA POST 89/18, III, §§2307–45. On the importance of teamwork in American scientific identity at this point, see S. Shapin, *The Scientific Life: A Moral History of a Late Modern Vocation* (Chicago: University of Chicago Press, 2008), 190–97.

44 Minutes, April 12, 1923, BBC WAC, CO 7/1.

45 RMA, POST 33/1080 (Sykes evidence), Chappell and Co. testimony; Gramophone Company testimony, papers 58, 75. The persistent copyright disputes between these forces and the BBC can be traced through fairly extensive records at the British Telecom Archive, Holborn, London.

46 RMA, POST 89/18, I, pp. 4–8; §504.

47 F. J. Brown, in Sykes evidence, RMA, POST 89/18, I, unpaginated.

48 Hansard, *Commons,* 163, pp. 277–78 (April 24, 1923).

49 BBC WAC, CO 1/2, p. 12.

50 Sykes evidence, RMA POST 89/19, I, §261.

51 BBC WAC, CO 1/2, September 27, 1922.

52 Crawford, *Report,* 20.

53 J. M. Keynes, *The End of Laissez-Faire* (London: L. & V. Woolf, 1926).

54 L. Lessig, *The Future of Ideas: The Fate of the Commons in a Connected World* (New York: Random House, 2001); T. Streeter, *Selling the Air: A Critique of the Policy of Commercial Broadcasting in the United States* (Chicago: University of Chicago Press, 1996), 59–110.

55 BBC WAC, CO 1/1; Hansard, *Commons,* 162, pp. 2440–46 (April 19, 1923).

56 Sykes evidence, RMA POST 89/18, I, §§530–42.

57 BBC WAC, CO 58/1.

58 RMA, POST 89/18, I, pp. 4–8.

59 RMA, POST 33/963B, March 28, 1923, April 18, 1923.

60 R. M. Ford, *The Wireless "License" Ramp: "A Lesson in Bureaucracy"* (London: St. Giles Press, 1929), 161.

61 Ford, *Wireless "License" Ramp.*

62 RMA, POST 33/963B; "New Wireless Move," *Daily Express,* April 11, 1923.

63 Ford, *Wireless "License" Ramp,* 126–28, 135.

64 S. Landman and J. H. Beaumont, Sykes evidence, RMA POST 89/18, III, §2974.

65 M. Hilmes, *Radio Voices: American Broadcasting, 1922–1952* (Minneapolis: University of Minnesota Press, 1997), 39.

66 Ford, *Wireless "License" Ramp,* 113.

67 RMA, POST 33/1559, July 15, 1927.
68 *Daily Express,* March 22, 1923.
69 BBC WAC, CO 52/1, pp. 13–14, March 22, 1923.
70 Hansard, *Commons,* 162, pp. 2440–46 (April 19, 1923).
71 RMA, POST 33/1559, February 18, 1932 and passim.
72 BBC WAC, T16/90/1, June 1, 1953; RMA, POST 110, e.g., PRD Nos. 0116, 0159, 0430, 0510, 0536, 0547, 0558, 0583, 0597, 0618, 0645, 0646, 0671, 0795, 1005.
73 BBC WAC, T16/90/1, February 27, 1952, May 7, 1953; BBC WAC, R78/1, 127/1, September 3, 1976.
74 Compare, on the American context, J. Sterne, *The Audible Past: Cultural Origins of Sound Reproduction* (Durham, N.C.: Duke University Press, 2003), 87–36. For writing and reading clubs, see C. Hilliard, *To Exercise Our Talents: The Democratization of Writing in Britain* (Cambridge, Mass.: Harvard University Press, 2006), 34–69 and J. Rose, *The Intellectual Life of the British Working Classes* (New Haven, Conn.: Yale University Press, 2001), 73–91.
75 R. H. Coase, *British Broadcasting: A Study in Monopoly* (London: Longmans, Green, and Co., 1950). For Eckersley's plan, see P. P. Eckersley, *The Power behind the Microphone* (London: Cape, 1941), 195–236, M. Eckersley, *Prospero's Wireless: A Biography of Peter Pendleton Eckersley* (Romsey, Hants, UK: Myles Books, 1998), 187–88, 234, and W. J. West, *Truth Betrayed* (London: Duckworth, 1987), 120–25.
76 C. Ginzburg, *The Cheese and the Worms: The Cosmos of a Sixteenth-Century Miller* (Baltimore: Johns Hopkins University Press, 1980).

14 INTELLECTUAL PROPERTY AND THE NATURE OF SCIENCE

1 A. K. Rai and R. S. Eisenberg, "Bayh-Dole Reform and the Progress of Biomedicine," *Law and Contemporary Problems* 66 (2003): 289–314.
2 F. L. Vaughan, "Suppression and Non-working of Patents, with Special Reference to the Dye and Chemical Industries," *American Economic Review* 9 (1919): 693–700; F. L. Vaughan, *Economics of Our Patent System* (New York: Macmillan, 1925), 225; F. I. Schechter, "Would Compulsory Licensing of Patents Be Unconstitutional?" *Virginia Law Review* 22 (1936): 287–314; G. E. Folk, *Patents and Industrial Progress* (New York: Harper, 1942) 257–78.
3 A. D. Chandler, *The Visible Hand: The Managerial Revolution in American Business* (Cambridge, Mass.: Harvard University Press, 1977), 88–89, 188–89, 200–203, 464–76; J. Yates, *Control through Communication: The Rise of System in American Management* (Baltimore: Johns Hopkins University Press, 1989), 21–64; J. Guillory, "The Memo and Modernity," *Critical Inquiry* 31 (2004): 108–33, esp. 114–22. See also J. R. Beniger, *The Control*

Revolution: Technological and Economic Origins of the Information Society (Cambridge, Mass.: Harvard University Press, 1986), e.g., 221–87.

4   The origin of this story is slightly obscure. Merton cited Stamp as having given his speech at the BAAS's Aberdeen meeting in 1934, but he in fact spoke rather innocuously on "The Need for a Technique of Economic Change" (BAAS, *Report,* 1934, 341–42). However, Stamp did speak at the previous year's meeting on the more controversial question, "Must Science Ruin Economic Progress?" Here he called attention to the prevalent claim that the rapidity of scientific change caused mass unemployment. This being so, he claimed, "the world might be better served in the end if scientific innovation were retarded to the maximum rate of social and economic change." Among the principal problems Stamp identified was the fact that new technologies might render existing ones outmoded before their real utility were exhausted, and see them scrapped for marginal benefits. "A responsible socialist community would see each time that the gain was worth while," he observed. But it would take "a *tour de force* of assumptions" to construct such a system. In short, Stamp steered clear of a call for the scientific planning of society or the social planning of science, but he did advocate that "all classes" should become "economically and socially minded, [by] large infusions of social direction and internationalism, carefully introduced" (BAAS, *Report,* 1933, 578–83). It seems that Stamp revisited some of these arguments a year later, so he may also have made remarks about scientific research that were not reported in the published abridgment. In 1936, as president, Stamp again addressed "The Impact of Science upon Society," and repeated some of the same cautious gestures (BAAS, *Report,* 1936, 1–26). For his denial of the call for a moratorium, see the revised version of "The Impact of Science upon Society," in Sir J. Stamp, *The Science of Social Adjustment* (London: MacMillan and Co., 1937), 59. And for evidence that he had been mulling over the details of these topics for some time, see Stamp, "Invention," in Sir J. Stamp, *Some Economic Factors in Modern Life* (London: P. S. King and Son, 1929), 89–121, esp. 96–101. Otherwise, the call for a moratorium can be traced to an earlier speech to the BAAS by the Bishop of Ripon in 1927; and in the United States similar calls were associated with Southern conservatives: B. J. Stern, "Restraints upon the Utilization of Inventions," *Annals of the American Academy of Political and Social Science* 200 (1938): 13–31, esp. 31.

5   R. Bain, "Scientist as Citizen," *Social Forces* 11 (1933): 412–15.

6   J. Hettinger, "The Problem of Scientific Property and Its Solution," *Science Progress* 26 (1931–32): 449–61; F. Ruffini, *Report on Scientific Property* (Geneva, Switzerland: Kundig, 1923); S. B. Ladas, "The Efforts for International Protection of Scientific Property," *American Journal of International Law* 23 (1929): 552–69, esp. 555–59.

7   R. Seidel, "The Origins of the Lawrence Berkeley Laboratory," in *Big Science: The Growth of Large-Scale Research,* ed. P. Galison and B. Hevly (Stanford, Calif.: Stanford University Press, 1992), 21–45, esp. 26–27; P. Galison, B. Hevly, and R. Lowen, "Controlling the Monster: Stanford and the Growth of Physics Research, 1935–62," in *Big Science,* ed. Galison and Hevly, 46–77, esp. 50; D. J. Kevles, *The Physicists: The History of a Scientific Community in Modern America* (Cambridge, Mass.: Harvard University Press, 1995 [1971]), 268; M. Fishbein, "Medical Patents," *JAMA* 109 (1937): 1539–43; R. H. Shryock, "Freedom and Interference in Medicine," *Annals of the American Academy of Political and Social Science* 200 (November 1938), 32–59, esp. 45–46; W. H. Whyte, *The Organization Man* (New York: Simon and Schuster, 1956), 225–53.

8   Kevles, *Physicists,* 252–53, 264, 266; N. R. Danielian, *A.T.&T.: The Story of Industrial Conquest* (New York: Vanguard, 1939), preface (unpaginated), 1–7.

9   Danielian, *A.T.&T.,* 92–172; P. Latzke, *A Fight with an Octopus* (Chicago: Telephony Publishing Co., 1906), 42, 52, 55, 59, 73; Federal Communications Commission, *Report on Telephone Investigation* (76th Congress, 1st Session, House Document No. 340) (1939), 214, 216, 222–23; FCC, *Proposed Report: Telephone Investigation* (Washington, D.C.: U.S. Government Printing Office, 1938) 96–97, 145, 150, 240–42, 254–63.

10   Danielian, *A.T.&T.,* 92, 100; Kevles, *Physicists,* 188–89.

11   Latzke, *A Fight with an Octopus,* 109; AT&T, *Brief of Bell System Companies on Commissioner Walker's Proposed Report on the Telephone Investigation* (1938), 56; Danielian, *A.T.&T.,* introduction (unpaginated); FCC, *Proposed Report,* ix–x, 2–3, 5, 243, 248–53, 279–88. This *Proposed Report* was a very controversial document, yet the full *Report* that appeared a year later, while couched in less confrontational terms, adopted most of its perspectives and recommendations.

12   AT&T, *Brief,* 41, 44–45; AT&T, *Telephone Investigation, 1935–1937: Comments Submitted to Federal Communications Commission . . . on Commission Exhibit 2110* (October 29, 1937), 1–4, 8–10, 14–15.

13   D. M. Kennedy, *Freedom from Fear: The American People in Depression and War, 1929–1945* (Oxford: Oxford University Press, 1999), 358–59; D. M. Hart, *Forged Consensus: Science, Technology, and Economic Policy in the United States, 1921–1953* (Princeton, N.J.: Princeton University Press, 1998), 135–36; W. Hamilton, *Patents and Free Enterprise,* TNEC monograph 31 (Washington, D.C.: Government Printing Office, 1941), 43–44, 87–93, 104–5. George Folk, long-time patent attorney for AT&T, subjected Hamilton to withering attack: Folk, *Patents and Industrial Progress,* 3–4, 23–61, 63, 77–106, 257.

14   Folk, *Patents and Industrial Progress,* 112–13, 144–48, 153, 170, 188, 206, 229; Hamilton, *Patents and Free Enterprise,* 153–55; Kevles, *Physicists,* 294.

15   Hart, *Forged Consensus,* 148–49.

16   Folk, *Patents and Industrial Progress,* 315; D. J. Kevles, "The National Science
      Foundation and the Debate over Postwar Research Policy, 1942–1945:
      A Political Interpretation of *Science—The Endless Frontier,*" *Isis* 68 (1977):
      4–26; Kevles, *Physicists,* 341–66.
17   Kevles, "National Science Foundation," 13–14 n34.
18   Hart, *Forged Consensus,* 158 ff; Zachary, *Endless Frontier,* 232–34, 252–60,
      327–34.
19   Vaughan, "Suppression and Non-working of Patents," 699–700; Hart,
      Forged Consensus, 140–43, 186.
20   See G. P. Zachary, *Endless Frontier: Vannevar Bush, Engineer of the American
      Century* (New York: Free Press, 1997), 158.
21   R. K. Merton, "The Normative Structure of Science," in *The Sociology of
      Science: Theoretical and Empirical Investigations,* ed. N. Storer (Chicago:
      University of Chicago Press, 1973), 267–78, esp. 275; R. K. Merton,
      "Priorities in Scientific Discovery" (1957), repr. in *The Sociology of Science:
      Theoretical and Empirical Investigations* (Chicago: University of Chicago
      Press, 1973), 286–324; R. K. Merton, "Fluctuations in the Rate of Indus-
      trial Invention," *Quarterly Journal of Economics* 49 (1935): 454–70, esp. 454;
      R. K. Merton, *Mass Persuasion: The Social Psychology of a War Bond Drive*
      (New York: Harper, 1946); R. K. Merton, "The Matthew Effect in Science,
      II: Cumulative Advantage and the Symbolism of Intellectual Property,"
      Isis 79 (1988): 606–23, esp. 619–23; R. K. Merton, *Social Theory and Social
      Structure: Toward the Codification of Theory and Research* (Glencoe, Ill.: Free
      Press, 1949), 292; P. Lazarsfeld, "An Episode in the History of Social
      Research," in *The Varied Sociology of Paul F. Lazarsfeld,* ed. P. L. Kendall
      (New York: Columbia University Press, 1982), 52; S. Heims, *The Cybernetics
      Group* (Cambridge, Mass.: MIT Press, 1991), 183, 187–93; I. B. Cohen,
      "The Publication of *Science, Technology and Society:* Circumstances and
      Consequences," *Isis* 79 (1988): 571–82.
22   Plant's papers at the LSE provide ample evidence of the extent and detail
      of his researches in these matters: e.g., Plant folders 32, 453–57 (on
      patents), Plant folders 36–37, 41–42, 130, 210 (on copyright). His notes on
      the term *pirate* are in Plant folder 37. There is not space here to delve more
      deeply into them, but I hope to publish a study in due course.
23   Sir A. Plant, "The Economic Aspects of Copyright in Books" (1934) and
      "The Economic Theory concerning Patents for Invention" (1934), repr.
      in Plant, *Selected Economic Essays and Addresses* (London: RKP for the
      Institute of Economic Affairs, 1974), 57–86 and 35–55.
24   Sir A. Plant, "The New Commerce in Ideas and Intellectual Property," in
      Plant, *Selected Economic Essays and Addresses,* 87–116.
25   W. T. Scott and M. X. Moleski, *Michael Polanyi: Scientist and Philosopher*
      (Oxford: Oxford University Press, 2005). For the context, see D. Edger-

ton, *Warfare State: Britain, 1920–1970* (Cambridge: Cambridge University Press, 2006).

26   J. D. Bernal, *The Social Function of Science* (Cambridge, Mass.: MIT Press, 1967 [orig. 1939]), 144–47.

27   M. Polanyi, "The Republic of Science," *Minerva* 1 (1962): 54–73; M. Polanyi, "Cultural Significance of Science," *Nature* 3717 (January 25, 1941): 119; M. Polanyi, "Rights and Duties of Science," *Manchester School of Economic and Social Studies* 10 (October 1939): 175–93; M. Polanyi, "The Planning of Science," *Political Quarterly* 16 (1945): 316–28, esp. 323; M. Polanyi, "The Autonomy of Science," *Memoirs and Proceedings of the Manchester Literary and Philosophical Society* 85 (1941–43), 19–38, esp. 30–36; M. Polanyi, "The Growth of Thought in Society," *Economica,* November 1941, 428–56, esp. 448; M. Polanyi, *Personal Knowledge: Towards a Post-critical Philosophy* (1958; repr. Chicago: University of Chicago Press, 1974), 237.

28   M. Polanyi, "Patent Reform," *Review of Economic Studies* 11 (1944): 61–76; Scott and Moleski, *Polanyi,* 182–209.

29   Cf. Polanyi papers, University of Chicago Library, box 29, folder 9, pp. 209–26 (1944).

30   Polanyi papers, box 29, folders 1, 5–8, and 11–12; M. Polanyi, *Full Employment and Free Trade* (Cambridge: Cambridge University Press, 1945). The Plant review copy of Polanyi's paper is in the LSE archives, Plant folder 32.

31   Polanyi papers, box 29, folder 5, unpaginated (Polanyi's emphases).

32   For an argument that modern military secrecy traces its genealogy to corporate trade secrets, see P. Galison, "Removing Knowledge," *Critical Inquiry* 31 (Autumn 2004), 229–43.

33   Polanyi papers, box 29, folder 10, no. 8, p. 1.

34   D. A. Mindell, *Between Human and Machine: Feedback, Control, and Computing before Cybernetics* (Baltimore: Johns Hopkins University Press, 2002), esp. 4–5, 11–12.

35   F. Conway and J. Seigelman, *Dark Hero of the Information Age: In Search of Norbert Wiener, the Father of Cybernetics* (New York: Basic Books, 2005), 52–59, 63–65, 73; Jackson to Compton, June 13, 1931; September 12, 1930; "Memorandum on American Telephone and Telegraph Company's Contributions" (n.d.); "Memorandum of discussion" (n.d.): all in MIT AC4/15/8.

36   U.S. Patents 2,024,900, 2,124,599, and 2,128,257; Conway and Seigelman, *Dark Hero,* 76.

37   Lee to Wiener (telegram), July 3, 1930, MIT Norbert Wiener Papers (NWP), MC22/2/32; FCC, *Report* (1939), 223–24; Bush to Lee, May 14, 1931, MIT NWP, MC22/2/33; Bush to Lee, October 19, 1931, MIT NWP MC22/2/34.

38   L. K. Clark to Y. W. Lee, February 12, 1932, MIT NWP, MC22/2/35; N. Wiener, *I Am a Mathematician: The Later Life of a Prodigy* (New York:

Doubleday, 1956), 152–53; Lee to Wiener, September 7, 1931, MIT NWP MC22/2/34; Lee to Wiener, June 14, 1932, MIT NWP, MC22/2/34; Clark to Wiener, February 12, 1932, MIT NWP, MC22/2/35.

39   J. G. Roberts to N. Wiener, September 26, 1935, MIT NWP, MC22/3/43; Wiener to L. K. Clark, February 14, 1936, MIT NWP, MC22/3/44; Y. W. Lee to V. Bush, July 25, 1941, MIT MC22/4/60; MIT AC4/133; Conway and Seigelman, *Dark Hero,* 86, 88; Wiener, *I Am a Mathematician,* 133–35, 273–75; E. Lee, *A Letter to My Aunt* (New York: Carlton Press, 1981), 508.

40   Mindell, *Between Human and Machine,* 42–43, 50, 53–54, 60–66, 82, 87, 277–88; Wiener, *I Am a Mathematician,* 190, 195, 244–54; N. Wiener, *Cybernetics: Or Control and Communication in the Animal and the Machine* (Paris: Hermann et Cie; New York: Technology Press, 1948), 12–20.

41   Heims, *Cybernetics Group;* K. Hayles, *How We Became Posthuman: Virtual Bodies in Cybernetics, Literature, and Informatics* (Chicago: University of Chicago Press, 1999), 50–57.

42   Wiener, *Cybernetics* (1948), 36–39.

43   October 26, 1944, MIT AC4/238/3; Conway and Seigelman, *Dark Hero,* 126–27, 146–47.

44   N. Wiener, *Invention: The Care and Feeding of Ideas* (Cambridge, Mass.: MIT Press, 1993); Conway and Seigelman, *Dark Hero,* 172–77.

45   Wiener, *Invention,* 5, 14–15, 22, 25–36, 55–65, 67, 77–114.

46   N. Wiener, *The Human Use of Human Beings: Cybernetics and Society* (Boston: Houghton Mifflin, 1954), 128, 131.

47   Wiener, *Invention,* 127–39, 150–54.

48   Wiener, *Invention,* 67.

49   N. Wiener, *Ex-Prodigy: My Childhood and Youth* (New York: Simon and Schuster, 1953), 281.

50   O. Heaviside, *Electrical Papers,* 2 vols. (London: MacMillan, 1892), 1:vi–vii, ix–x; 2:119–24, 147; O. Heaviside, *Electromagnetic Theory,* 3 vols. (London: "The electrician," 1893–1912), 1:3–4, 443–45; B. A. Behrend, "The Work of Oliver Heaviside," in Heaviside, *Electromagnetic Theory,* 3 vols. (New York: Chelsea Publishing, 1971), 1:469–504, esp. 485.

51   M. I. Pupin, "Wave Transmission over Non-uniform Cables and Long-Distance Air-Lines," American Institute of Electrical Engineers *Transactions* 17 (1900): 445–512; U.S. Patents 652,230 (esp. p. 4), 652,231, and 761,995; Behrend, "Work of Oliver Heaviside," 487–88; FCC, *Report* (1939), 246. For the negative feedback amplifier, see Mindell, *Between Human and Machine,* 105–12, 114–15, 119–22.

52   M. Pupin, *From Immigrant to Inventor* (New York: Charles Scribner's Sons, 1960 [1922]), 332–43; M. Pupin, *Romance of the Machine* (New York: Charles Scribner's Sons, 1930), 72–77, 86–87.

53   B. A. Behrend to Wiener, September 6, 1931; Rollo Appleyard to Wiener, September 23, 1931: both in MIT NWP MC22/2/34; Behrend to Wiener,

November 6, 1931, MIT MC22/2/34; Lee to Wiener, November 4, 1931, MIT NWP MC22/2/34; Jackson to Wiener, March 4, 1930, and March 15, 1930, MIT NWP, MC22/2/32; also MIT, NWP, 27C/524. It is possible that "plagiator" was an homage to Heaviside's own fondness for cod-Latin tags of this kind.

54 Wiener to O. Welles, June 28, 1941, MIT NWP, MC22/4/60. Wiener was probably using the word "pirated" loosely here. His assertions were not usually made without some basis, and Heaviside's publishing history was indeed fraught, as he himself ruefully remarked more than once. But I have not been able to find instances of piracy, let alone a Chinese printing. Tsing Hua University does not seem to possess one.

55 N. Wiener, *The Tempter* (New York: Random House, 1959).

56 Wiener to Killian, December 2, 1951, MIT AC4/238/3.

57 Conway and Seigelman, *Dark Hero*, 125–26, 203–5, 217–34, 273–75; Hayles, *How We Became Posthuman*, 75.

58 D. Livingstone, *Putting Science in Its Place: Geographies of Scientific Knowledge* (Chicago: University of Chicago Press, 2003), 1–16, gives an analysis of this ideal.

59 S. Shapin, *The Scientific Life: A Moral History of a Late Modern Vocation* (Chicago: University of Chicago Press, 2008), esp. chs. 4–5.

60 Compare J. Hughes, *The Manhattan Project: Big Science and the Atom Bomb* (Duxford, UK: Icon, 2002) on "big science."

15 THE PIRATE AT HOME AND AT LARGE

1 A. Millard, *America on Record: A History of Recorded Sound* (Cambridge: Cambridge University Press, 2005), 202–8.

2 A. Johns, *The Nature of the Book: Print and Knowledge in the Making* (Chicago: University of Chicago Press, 1998), e.g., 129, 114–36.

3 E.g., R. S. Cowan, *More Work for Mother: The Ironies of Household Technology from the Open Hearth to the Microwave* (London: Free Association Books, 1989), 69–101; S. Lebergott, *Pursuing Happiness: American Consumers in the Twentieth Century* (Princeton, N.J.: Princeton University Press, 1993), 110–21; J. C. Williams, "Getting Housewives the Electric Message: Gender and Energy Marketing in the Early Twentieth Century," in *His and Hers: Gender, Consumption, and Technology,* ed. R. Horowitz and A. Mohun (Charlottesville: University Press of Virginia, 1998), 95–113; L. Carlat, "'A Cleanser for the Mind': Marketing Radio Receivers for the American Home, 1922–1932," in *His and Hers,* ed. Horowitz and Mohun, 115–37.

4 R. R. Wile, "Record Piracy: The Attempts of the Sound Recording Industry to Protect Itself against Unauthorized Copying, 1890–1978," *ARSC Journal* 17, no. 1 (1985): 18–40, esp. 19.

5 For the roots of this issue see L. Gitelman, *Scripts, Grooves, and Writing*

Machines: Representing Technology in the Edison Era (Stanford, Calif.: Stanford University Press, 1999), 131–33, 139–47.

6   N. Cohodas, *Spinning Blues into Gold: The Chess Brothers and the Legendary Chess Records* (New York: St. Martin's, 2000), 77–79; C. Heylin, *Bootleg: The Secret History of the Other Recording Industry* (New York: St. Martin's Press, 1995), 28–36; J. Fenby, *Piracy and the Public: Forgery, Theft, and Exploitation* (London: F. Muller, 1983), 70–71; W. Livingstone, "Piracy in the Record Industry," *Stereo Review* 24, no. 3 (February 1970): 60–69.

7   Millard, *America on Record,* 226–35.

8   D. Morton, *Off the Record: The Technology and Culture of Sound Recording in America* (New Brunswick, N.J.: Rutgers University Press, 2000), 136–43.

9   C. E. Smith, "Background to Bootlegging," *Record Changer* 11, no. 1 (January 1952): 3–4, 16.

10 Smith, "Background to Bootlegging"; D. Mahony et al., "The Labels of Dante Bolletino," *Matrix* 58 (April 1965): 3–29.

11 "Art and the Dollar," *Record Changer* 10, no. 11 (November 1951): 7.

12 The controversy continued in *Record Changer,* vol. 10 (1951), with contributions in virtually every issue. For the RCA revelation, see especially "Victor Presses Bootlegs!" *Record Changer* 10, no. 11 (November 1951): 1, 6–7.

13 "Bootlegging: The Battle Rages," *Record Changer* 10, no. 12 (December 1951): 3–5; *New York Herald Tribune,* January 31, 1952, 27.

14 I. K[olodin], "Masked '*Masked Ball,*'" *Saturday Review* October 27, 1951, 57.

15 "Striking the Jolly Roger," *Time,* February 11, 1952.

16 Livingstone, "Piracy," 66, 68–69.

17 E. Cushing, "The 'Ring' Stolen Again," *Saturday Review,* April 10, 1954, 42; G. W. Waldrop, "Piracy of the Airways?" *Musical Courier* April 15, 1954, 2; E. A. Lumpe, "Pseudonymous Performers on Early LP Records: Rumours, Facts and Finds," *ARSC Journal* 21, no. 2 (Fall 1990): 226–31; E. A. Lumpe, "Pseudonymous Performers on Early LP Records: An Update," *ARSC Journal* 27, no. 1 (Spring 1996): 15–40.

18 "Attacking the Record Pirates," *Christian Science Monitor,* April 20–25, 1974.

19 Livingstone, "Piracy," 63, 69.

20 Morton, *Off the Record,* 136–43, 154–70.

21 C. Stark, "The Great Tape Robbery: Weighing the Ethical Issues Involved in Home Tape Copying," *Stereo Review* 28, no. 3 (March 1972): 60–64.

22 It was also, of course, the target of Adorno's critique of mass culture—a critique that I think the history of piracy does much to undermine.

23 M. Schrage, "The War against Home Taping," *Rolling Stone* 378 (September 16, 1982): 59–67.

24 Pub.L. 92–140, 85 Stat. 391.

25 Morton, *Off the Record,* 154–70; T. Gillespie, *Wired Shut: Copyright and the Shape of Digital Culture* (Cambridge, Mass.: MIT Press, 2007).

26   J. Lardner, *Fast Forward: Hollywood, the Japanese, and the Onslaught of the VCR* (New York: W. W. Norton, 1987), 49–51, 57–70; *Genryu: Sony Challenge, 1946–1968* (Tokyo: Sony Corporation, 1986), 76–77.

27   R. Lindsey, "Monumental Battle Shaping Up in Bid to Bar Color TV Recorders," *New York Times,* March 25, 1977, D1, D8; A. Morita, *Made in Japan: Akio Morita and Sony* (New York: E. P. Dutton, 1986), 168.

28   Universal City Studios, Inc. vs. Sony Corporation of America, 659 F.2d 963; Lardner, *Fast Forward,* 107. A full archive of documents relating to the Betamax case is available online at http://www.eff.org/legal/cases/betamax/.

29   C. M. Mathias, "Stealing from the Screen," *Washington Post,* February 11, 1983, A23; "Tube Thieves," *New York Times,* October 28, 1981, A26; *Chicago Tribune,* October 23, 1981, 18; P. Shenon, "Copyright v. 'Reprography' Revolution," *New York Times,* October 25, 1981, E7; H. Fantel, "Home Taping: The Legal Issue Comes to a Boil," *New York Times,* August 29, 1982, B17; "The Tube Tomorrow," *Washington Post,* October 22, 1981, C1; W. Patry, "In Praise of the Betamax Decision," *South Texas Law Journal* 22 (1982): 211–48, esp. 213; H. Kurtz, "Chariots for Hire," *Washington Post,* July 4, 1982, B1, B5.

30   J. Greenfield, "Revenge of the Video Recorders," *Chicago Tribune,* October 31, 1984, 9; Lardner, *Fast Forward,* 303; M. Preston, "Eeek!" *Chicago Tribune,* October 27, 1981, sec. 2, 5; H. Fantel, "Sound," *New York Times,* June 31, 1982, B25; H.R. 4808, 97th Congress, 1st Session; S. 1758, 97th Congress, 2nd Session; Kurtz, "Chariots for Hire."

31   F. Barbash, "Betamax Uproar Is Channeled into Supreme Court Arguments," *Washington Post,* January 19, 1983, A4; Lardner, *Fast Forward,* 102.

32   17 USC §107. My narrative here is based on the Thurgood Marshall Papers (TMP) at the Library of Congress (335-81-1687); for a slightly different reading, see J. Band and A. J. McLaughlin, "The Marshall Papers: A peek behind the Scenes at the Making of *Sony v. Universal,*" *Columbia-VLA Journal of Law and the Arts* 17 (1993): 427–51.

33   *Folsom v. Marsh,* 9 F.Cas. 342 (C.C.D. Mass. 1841), No. 4,901.

34   J. P. Stevens, Memorandum to the file, January 20, 1983, TMP; Stevens to Blackmun, January 24, 1983, TMP.

35   Marshall, memorandum to the conference, October 4, 1983, TMP; O'Connor to Chief Justice W. Burger, June 28, 1983, TMP.

36   E. Goodman, "The Right to Zap," *Washington Post,* January 24, 1984, A13; "But Is It Piracy?" *Washington Post,* January 23, 1983, C6; M. Brown, "Video-Tape Ruling Sets Stage for Battle on Hill," *Washington Post,* January 18, 1984, A16.

37   "What Price Home Taping?" *New York Times,* March 30, 1984, A30; Kurtz, "Chariots for Hire" ; M. Isikoff, "Hollywood Lobby Blitzes Hill," *Washington Post,* February 22, 1984, D8; Lardner, *Fast Forward,* 220.

38   D. Edwards, "It's Time for a Truce in the Betamax Battle," *Washington Post,*

August 19, 1983, A23; Lardner, *Fast Forward,* 233–34; J. Lardner, "Video Wars," *Washington Post,* May 2, 1982, F1; Lardner, "Tales of a VCR User," *Washington Post,* June 16, 1982, D1.

39   P. F. Drucker, "Japan's Choices," *Foreign Affairs* 65, no. 5 (Summer 1987): 923–24; C. Johnson, *MITI and the Japanese Miracle: The Growth of Industrial Policy, 1925–1975* (Stanford, Calif.: Stanford University Press, 1982), 313–14.; M. Crichton, *Rising Sun* (New York: Knopf, 1992); G. Friedman and M. Lebard, *The Coming War with Japan* (New York: St. Martin's Press, 1991); P. Choate, *Agents of Influence* (New York: Alfred A. Knopf, 1990); R. Kearns, *Zaibatsu America: How Japanese Firms Are Colonizing Vital U.S. Industries* (New York: Free Press, 1992). The definitive rebuttal of the whole genre is *Economist* editor Bill Emmott's *Japanophobia: The Myth of the Invincible Japanese* (New York: Times Books, 1993).

40   C. Sims, "Wounded by Patent Piracy," *New York Times,* May 13, 1987, D1.

41   Kearns, *Zaibatsu America,* 15–23; Y. Miwa and J. M. Ramseyer, *The Fable of the Keiretsu: Urban Legends of the Japanese Economy* (Chicago: University of Chicago Press, 2006), 54–58.

42   C. V. Prestowitz, *Trading Places: How We Allowed Japan to Take the Lead* (New York: Basic, 1988), 206–7, 214; Lardner, *Fast Forward,* 238, 260.

43   "Sony's Morita Bashes Back," *Business Week,* October 16, 1989, 58; S. Wagstyl, "Chief of Sony Tells Why It Bought a Part of America's Soul," *Financial Times* October 4, 1989, 4.

44   *Congressional Record,* H8486-7; E3783-98 (November 13–14, 1989); E3952-2 (November 17, 1989); *New York Times,* August 4, 1989, A7; F. Lewis, "Japan's Looking glass," *New York Times,* November 8, 1989, A31; "Shintaro Gephardt," *Wall Street Journal,* November 14, 1989, A22. For the Japanese context, see M. F. Low, "The Japan That Can Say No: The Rise of Techno-Nationalism and Its Impact on Technological Change," in *Technological Change: Methods and Themes in the History of Technology,* ed. R. Fox (Amsterdam: OPA/Harwood, 1996), 210–24.

45   N. Wade, "America's Japan Problem," *New York Times,* October 5, 1989, A30; L. Summers, "Tough Talk from Tokyo: What to Do When Japan Says No," *New York Times,* December 3, 1989, A2; C. H. Farnsworth, "Japanese Author Brushes Up His Image with Journey to U.S. Enemy's Lair," *New York Times,* January 29, 1990, A16.

46   S. Ishihara, *The Japan That Can Say No,* trans. F. Baldwin (New York: Simon and Schuster, 1991), 8–12, 141, 145; *New York Times,* January 18, 1990, D8.

47   H. S. Becker, *Art Worlds* (Berkeley: University of California Press, 1982).

48   G. Davies, *Piracy of Phonograms,* 2nd ed. (Oxford: ESC Publishing, for European Commission, 1986), 7–8, 12–13, 16, 33–35; R. Wallace, "Crisis? What Crisis?" *Rolling Stone* 318 (May 29, 1980): 17, 28, 30–31; G. Davies (for IFPI), *The Private Copying of Phonograms and Videograms* (Strasbourg: Council of Europe, 1984), 17–18, 22–23, 34.

49 P. Manuel, *Cassette Culture: Popular Music and Technology in Northern India* (Chicago: University of Chicago Press, 1993), 65, 67–69, 79, 83, 85–88, 148–49. I am grateful to Ravi Sundaram of the Sarai project in Delhi for a presentation entitled "The Copy Itself" that he gave at the University of Chicago in early 2007. In print, see his "Uncanny Networks: Pirate and Urban in the New Globalisation in India," *Economic and Political Weekly,* January 6, 2004.

50 M. Foucault, "The Revolt in Iran Spreads on Cassette Tapes," in J. Afary and K. B. Anderson, *Foucault and the Iranian Revolution* (Chicago: University of Chicago Press, 2005), 216–20, esp. 219; A. Stille, *The Future of the Past* (New York: Farrar, Straus and Giroux, 2002), 182–99.

16 FROM PHREAKING TO FUDDING

1 D. Campbell, "Are Telephones Addictive?" *New Scientist* 60, no. 876 (December 13, 1973): 756–60, esp. 758; B. Sterling, *The Hacker Crackdown: Law and Disorder on the Electronic Frontier* (New York: Bantam, 1992), 12–14.

2 C. Breen and C. A. Dahlbom, "Signaling Systems for Control of Telephone Switching," *Bell System Technical Journal,* 39, no. 6 (November 1960): 1381–1444.

3 S. Wozniak and G. Smith, *iWoz* (New York: W. W. Norton, 2006), 107; http://www.webcrunchers.com/crunch/.

4 B. Levin, *The Pirates and the Mouse: Disney's War against the Counterculture* (Seattle: Fantagraphics, 2003).

5 A. Hoffman, *Steal This Book* (New York: Pirate Editions, 1971), 119, 144.

6 *Radical Software* 1 (1970), 1: www.radicalsoftware.org.

7 *Youth International Party Line* 1 (June 1971); 8 (February 1972); editor's page at http://cheshirecatalyst.com/tap.html.

8 C. M. Kelty, *Two Bits: The Cultural Significance of Free Software* (Durham, N.C.: Duke University Press, 2008), 28–29.

9 Campbell, "Are Telephones Addictive?"

10 R. Rosenbaum, "Secrets of the Little Blue Box," *Esquire,* October 1971, 117–25, 222–26.

11 S. Levy, *Hackers: Heroes of the Computer Revolution* (New York: Penguin, 2001 [1984]), 50–52, 94–95.

12 J. Markoff, *What the Dormouse Said: How the Sixties Counterculture Shaped the Personal Computer Industry* (New York: Viking, 2005), 85–87; Levy, *Hackers,* 23, 39–49, 60, 88, 124–36.

13 T. J. Sturgeon, "How Silicon Valley Came to Be," in *Understanding Silicon Valley: The Anatomy of an Entrepreneurial Region,* ed. M. Kenney (Stanford, Calif.: Stanford University Press, 2000), 15–47, esp. 44.

14 Markoff, *What the Dormouse Said,* 94–97, 103–4.

15 Markoff, *What the Dormouse Said,* 28, 116; Turner, *From Counterculture to Cyberculture,* 70; T. Roszak, *From Satori to Silicon Valley* (San Francisco: Don't Call It Frisco Press, 1986), 8–9.

16 T. Nelson, *Computer Lib/Dream Machines* (Chicago: T. Nelson, 1974), DMX; M. Orth, "Whole Earth $$$ Demise Continues," *Rolling Stone,* March 16, 1972; Turner, *From Counterculture to Cyberculture,* 69–73, 78–97, 113–14; Levy, *Hackers,* 159.

17 T. Albright and C. Perry, "The Last Twelve Hours of the Whole Earth," *Rolling Stone,* July 8, 1971; Levy, *Hackers,* 197–98; Markoff, *What the Dormouse Said,* 197–99, 261–62.

18 Markoff, *What the Dormouse Said,* 275–87.

19 I. Illich, *Deschooling Society* (New York: Harper & Row, 1971), 77; I. Illich, *Tools for Conviviality* (New York: Harper & Row, 1973), 18–21.

20 Illich, *Tools for Conviviality,* 11–12, 16, 43, 109; *Deschooling Society,* 19–20, 72–104. Giap was the South Vietnamese General Vo Nguyen Giap; ITT was International Telephone and Telegraph, a conglomerate originating in telephony patents and associated with conservative causes, including the anti-Allende conspiracy in Chile.

21 Nelson, *Computer Lib/Dream Machines,* CL59, DM3, DM58; T. Nelson, *Literary Machines,* 5th ed. (Swarthmore, Pa.: T. Nelson, 1983), 2/35, 2/37–38, 2/54, 4/4–6. For the relation between classical (J. S. Mill) liberalism and hacker ideologies, see E. G. Coleman, "The Social Construction of Freedom in Free and Open-Source Software: Hackers, Ethics, and the Liberal Tradition" (Ph.D. diss., University of Chicago, 2005), 196–200.

22 *Homebrew Computer Club Newsletter* 2, no. 13 (January 19, 1977), 3. For Felsenstein's debt to Illich, see "Convivial Cybernetic Devices: From Vacuum Tube Flip-Flops to the Singing Altair," *Analytical Engine* 3, no. 1 (November 1995), at http://opencollector.org/history/homebrew.

23 Levy, *Hackers,* 186.

24 Wozniak and Smith, *iWoz,* 28–29, 93–111; Markoff, *What the Dormouse Said,* 271–73; Levy, *Hackers,* 244–46. See also Wozniak's own reminiscences at www.woz.org.

25 Levy, *Hackers,* 251–54, 271–74; Turner, *From Counterculture to Cyberculture,* 115; Markoff, *What the Dormouse Said,* 275–87.

26 B. Gates, "An Open Letter to Hobbyists," *Homebrew Computer Club Newsletter* 2, no. 1 (January 31, 1976). See also S. Manes and P. Andrews, *Gates: How Microsoft's Mogul Reinvented an Industry and Made Himself the Richest Man in America* (New York: Doubleday, 1993), 91–96, and (for a more slanted reading) J. Wiley and J. Erickson, *Hard Drive: Bill Gates and the Making of the Microsoft Empire* (New York: Wiley, 1992), 101–7.

27 Levy, *Hackers,* 230.

28 The most thoroughgoing argument for the transformative economic effect of networks is Y. Benkler, *The Wealth of Networks: How Social*

Production Transforms Markets and Freedom (New Haven, Conn.: Yale University Press, 2006).

29   For the elaborate synthetic realities that these have developed into, see E. Castronova, *Synthetic Worlds: The Business and Culture of Online Games* (Chicago: University of Chicago Press, 2005).

30   H. Rheingold, *The Virtual Community: Homesteading on the Electronic Frontier* (Reading, Pa.: Addison-Wesley, 1993), 56–59, 133–34, 310; Turner, *From Counterculture to Cyberculture*, 156–62; Sterling, *Hacker Crackdown*, 45–47, 50.

31   *Phrack* 1, no. 7 (September 25, 1986), 3; Sterling, *Hacker Crackdown*, 67, 73–77, 83, 85–87.

32   Sterling, *Hacker Crackdown*, 63–67, 88–95; http://www.2600.com/. Old issues of many of these organs, including *Phrack* and the *Legion of Doom Technical Journal*, are sometimes accessible at http://www.textfiles.com/ magazines/.

33   Sterling, *Hacker Crackdown*, 55–57, 100–101; Turner, *From Counterculture to Cyberculture*, 167.

34   "Is Computer Hacking a Crime?" *Harper's Monthly* 280, no. 1678 (March 1990): 45–57; Rheingold, *Virtual Community*, 44; Turner, *From Counterculture to Cyberculture*, 167–70.

35   "Is Computer Hacking a Crime," 53. For Barlow's *Declaration*, see P. Ludlow, ed., *Crypto Anarchy, Cyberstates, and Pirate Utopias* (Cambridge, Mass.: MIT Press, 2001), 27–30.

36   S. Weber, *The Success of Open Source* (Cambridge, Mass.: Harvard University Press, 2004), 47, 114; R. M. Stallman, *Free Software, Free Society: Selected Essays* (Boston: GNU Press, 2002), 16.

37   http://www.catb.org/%7Eesr/halloween/index.html.

38   At the time of writing, however, rumors are flying that Microsoft may be trying the strategy again with its Silverlight program, this time targeting Adobe's Flash standard for online video. The importance of uniform standards for science and technology has been a leitmotif of much recent work: see, for example, B. Marsden and C. Smith, *Engineering Empires: A Cultural History of Technology in Nineteenth-Century Britain* (New York: Palgrave MacMillan, 2005).

39   S. Shapin, *A Social History of Truth: Civility and Science in Seventeenth-Century England* (Chicago: University of Chicago Press, 1994), 410, 415–16.

17 PAST, PRESENT, AND FUTURE

1   D. Defoe, *An essay on the regulation of the press* (London: n.p., 1704), 19–21.

2   See especially A. C. Mertha, *The Politics of Piracy: Intellectual Property in Contemporary China* (Ithaca, N.Y.: Cornell University Press, 2005), 35–76.

3   B. Norris, "Video Report," *Sight and Sound* 52 (1983): 106–8; R. Murphy,

"Off the Back of a Van," *Sight and Sound* 54 (1985): 78; V. C. Gatzimos, "Unauthorized Duplication of Sound Recordings: Transnational Problem in Search of a Solution," *Vanderbilt Journal of Transnational Law* 14 (1981): 399–443, esp. 419–20.

4 See the record of a recent Interpol congress, at http://www.interpol.org/ Public/FinancialCrime/IntellectualProperty/Meeting/ 2ndGlobalCongress20051114/Default.asp (June 23, 2006).

5 The "Enforcement of Intellectual Property Rights Act of 2008": http:// www.opencongress.org/bill/110-s3325/show.

6 J. Harrington, *Oceana*, ed. J. G. A. Pocock (Cambridge: Cambridge University Press, 1992 [orig. 1656]); J. Scott, *Commonwealth Principles: Republican Writing of the English Revolution* (Cambridge: Cambridge University Press, 2004), 164–65.

7 C. B. Herrup, *The Common Peace: Participation and the Criminal Law in Seventeenth-Century England* (Cambridge: Cambridge University Press, 1987), 59–61, 69–70; A. Johns, *The Nature of the Book: Print and Knowledge in the Making* (Chicago: University of Chicago Press, 1998), 187–265; S. Hindle, *The State and Social Change in Early Modern England, c. 1550–1640* (New York: Palgrave, 2000), e.g., 27.

8 On the interrelation of literary property and the regulation of the press in this period, see L. Maruca, *The Work of Print: Authorship and the English Text Trades, 1660–1760* (Seattle: University of Washington Press, 2007), J. Greene, *The Trouble with Ownership: Literary Property and Authorial Liability in England, 1660–1730* (Philadelphia: University of Pennsylvania Press, 2005), and J. Loewenstein, *The Author's Due: Printing and the Prehistory of Copyright* (Chicago: University of Chicago Press, 2002).

9 [A. Donaldson], *Some thoughts on the state of literary property* (London: printed for A. Donaldson, 1764), 11–17.

10 [Donaldson], *Some thoughts on the state of literary property*, 3–4, 7–19, 24.

11 J. F. Reigart, *Life of Robert Fulton* (Philadelphia: C. G. Henderson, 1856), 90–92, 106–7; and, in general, J. R. Harris, *Industrial Espionage and Technology Transfer: Britain and France in the Eighteenth Century* (Aldershot: Ashgate, 1998), 453–77.

12 "Video Bootleggers," *New York Times,* October 23, 1982, 41.

13 Gatzimos, "Unauthorized Duplication," 416–17.

14 R. R. Wile, "Record Piracy," *ARSC Journal* 17:1 (1985), 18–40, esp. 27–30.

15 http://www.directv.com/DTVAPP/aboutus/mediacenter/NewsDetails. jsp?id=06_24_2002A. There are countless accounts of Black Sunday accessible online. The "game over" line comes from the account at http:// slashdot.org/articles/01/01/25/1343218.shtml.

16 For technological copyright enforcement technologies in the digital era, see T. Gillespie, *Wired Shut: Copyright and the Shape of Digital Culture* (Cambridge, Mass.: MIT Press, 2007), esp. 137–91 on SDMI and its offshoots.

17   The potential impact was dramatically demonstrated in 2000, when
      Dmitri Sklyarov, a Russian graduate student, was briefly held in the
      United States for promulgating a program capable of penetrating copy-
      protection software in Adobe's e-books. Sklyarov immediately became
      the focus of large public demonstrations in several U.S. cities; he was
      released, and in the end the prosecution lost its case against his employer.
      Full documentation is online at http://www.eff.org/IP/DMCA/US_v_
      Elcomsoft/. For open-source biotech, see J. Hope, *Biobazaar: The Open
      Source Revolution and Biotechnology* (Cambridge, Mass.: Harvard University
      Press, 2008).

18   J. A. Halderman and E. W. Felten, "Lessons from the Sony CD DRM
      episode" (2006), at http://itpolicy.princeton.edu/pub/sonydrm-ext.pdf;
      see also the discussion by Finnish hacker Matti Nikki: http://hack.fi/
      -muzzy/sony-drm/.

19   The report on these practices by the Center for Food Safety (http://www.
      centerforfoodsafety.org/pubs/CFSMOnsantovsFarmerReport1.13.05.pdf,
      2006/06/23), interested as it undoubtedly is, provides plentiful empirical
      citations and buttressing for its claims.

20   Y. Benkler, *The Wealth of Networks: How Social Production Transforms
      Markets and Freedom* (New Haven, Conn.: Yale University Press, 2006).

21   For a provocative general statement, see M. Heller, *The Gridlock Economy:
      How Too Much Ownership Wrecks Markets, Stops Innovation, and Costs Lives*
      (New York: Basic Books, 2008), 49–78.

22   J. Willinsky, *The Access Principle: The Case for Open Access to Research and
      Scholarship* (Cambridge, Mass.: MIT Press, 2005).

23   J.-N. Jeanneney, *Google and the Myth of Universal Knowledge* (Chicago:
      University of Chicago Press, 2007).

24   *The Authors Guild, Inc., et al. v. Google Inc.,* Case No. 05 CV 8136 (S.D.N.Y.).

25   For examples of the consequences of neglecting editorial intervention
      in digitizing books, see P. Duguid, "Limits of Self-Organization: Peer
      Production and 'Laws of Quality,'" *First Monday* 11 (2006): http://
      firstmonday.org/issues/issue11_10/duguid/index.html.

26   C. Snyder, "Google Settles Book-Scan Lawsuit, Everybody Wins," http://
      blog.wired.com/business/2008/10/google-settles.html.

27   L. G. Mirviss, "Harvard-Google Online Book Deal at Risk," *Harvard
      Crimson,* October 30, 2008; R. Darnton, "The Library in the New Age,"
      New York Review of Books 55, no. 10 (June 12, 2008).

28   M. Helft and M. Rich, "Google Strikes Deal to Allow Book Scans," *New
      York Times,* October 29, 2008, B1, B8.

29   "The Fate of Disciplines," *Critical Inquiry,* special issue, 35, no. 4 (Summer
      2009); T. S. Kuhn, *The Structure of Scientific Revolutions,* 3rd ed. (Chicago:
      University of Chicago Press, 1996 [1962]), 66–91.

Index

Coxe, Tench, 188–93
crackers, 486–91
craft communities and state, cooperation between, 20. *See also* artisans, intellectual authority and
craft custom, primacy of, 153
craft identity, 162
craft vs. prerogative, 161
craft(s), 8, 11, 26, 27, 32, 34, 125, 140
Cragside, 265, 266f, 267, 268f
Crawford, Earl of, 381
creative rights, 124–25, 425, 517
creativity, 21, 248, 277; commerce and, 15, 498, 508–9; patents and, 419; sociology of, 412
credit, financial, 111, 112, 194
Crichton, Michael, 455
Crokatt, James, 165
Cromwell, Oliver, 31, 37
Croune, William, 80
Crown, 56, 78, 251; patenting power, 28–29, 39, 71; press licensers, 104; printing and the, 28–30, 33, 41
Crown messengers, 26
Cubitt, William, 269
Cullen, William, 184
Culpeper, Nicholas, 101
Cumming, Thomas, 161
Curll, Edmund, 5, 44, 46, 47, 151
"customary rights," 302
customs. *See* book trade, moral and cultural constitution of; "courtesies"
cybernetics, 424–25, 427–29
Cybernetics (Wiener), 424–25
Cyclopaedia (Chambers), 118, 119, 180

D. Appleton & Co., 291, 293, 294, 302, 312, 319–20. *See also* Appleton, D.
Daily Express, 365
Daily Mail, 350, 358, 368
d'Alembert, Jean Le Rond, 53, 118, 165
Dalrymple, John, 135

Dampier, William, 43
Dante Alighieri, 45
Darnton, Robert, 53, 513
Darwin, Charles, 230, 291, 293, 294, 296
d'Aubigné, Jean-Henri Merle, 304
Day, David, 332, 333, 337, 346
De Forest, Lee, 405, 407, 418, 474
de Tocqueville, Alexis. *See* Tocqueville, Alexis de
de Vaux, Theodore, 80
decentralization, 317, 318, 322–23, 325
"Declaration of the Rights of Genius," 53
Defense Advanced Research Projects Agency (DARPA), 459–60
Defense Department, 473, 480
Defoe, Daniel, 38, 43–44, 48, 112–14, 497, 516
Dekker, Thomas, 23
deposit, legal, 215, 234–41, 323; copyright and, 215, 219, 222, 234, 236, 307; protection and, 234; Samuel Brydges on, 235–37; Samuel Brydges's campaign against, 215, 234, 245, 307–8; struggle to revive, 219–20. *See also* universal library/libraries, and the ends of enlightenment
deposit tax, 234–37
Der Ring des Nibelungen (Wagner), 442–43
Derry, Bishop of, 149
Desaguliers, Jean Theophilus, 125
desalination, 73–74, 135
desalination machines, 74–80, 87, 94
Descartes, René, 52, 67
detector vans, 394–96, 504
detectors, scientific pirate, 391, 393f
di Romani, Paolo, 98
Dibdin, Thomas, 232, 235
Dickens, Charles, 5, 295, 297, 298, 302, 304, 306, 307, 322, 325
Dickson, Richard, 165, 168